ESSAYS REVIEWS AND REPORTS

Also in Reprints of Economic Classics

By Joseph Dorfman

THORSTEIN VEBLEN AND HIS AMERICA (1934). With New Appendices and Additions to the Bibliography *(1966).*

THE ECONOMIC MIND IN AMERICAN CIVILIZATION, 5 volumes (1946-1959).

By Thorstein Veblen

THE THEORY OF THE LEISURE CLASS. *An Economic Study of Institutions* (1899). With a review by William Dean Howells from *Literature An International Gazette of Criticism.*

THE THEORY OF BUSINESS ENTERPRISE (1904). With a review by James H. Tufts from *The Psychological Bulletin.* And an Introductory Note by Joseph Dorfman *(1964)*

THE INSTINCT OF WORKMANSHIP AND THE STATE OF THE INDUSTRIAL ARTS (1914). With an Introduction by Joseph Dorfman *(1964).*

IMPERIAL GERMANY AND THE INDUSTRIAL REVOLUTION (1915). With an Introduction by Joseph Dorfman *(1939).*

AN INQUIRY INTO THE NATURE OF PEACE *and the Terms of Its Perpetuation* (1917).

THE HIGHER LEARNING IN AMERICA. *A Memorandum on the Conduct of Universities by Business Men* (1918).

THE VESTED INTERESTS AND THE COMMON MAN. *"The Modern Point of View and the New Order"* (1919).

THE ENGINEERS AND THE PRICE SYSTEM (1921).

ABSENTEE OWNERSHIP AND BUSINESS ENTERPRISE IN RECENT TIMES. *The Case of America* (1923).

ESSAYS IN OUR CHANGING ORDER. *Edited by Leon Ardzrooni* (1934). With the Addition of a Recently Discovered Memorandum "Wire Barrage" supplied by Joseph Dorfman *(1964).*

WHAT VEBLEN TAUGHT. *Selected Writings of Thorstein Veblen. Edited with an Introduction by Wesley C. Mitchell* (1936).

About Veblen

VEBLEN *by John A. Hobson* (1936).

THE INNOCENTS AT CEDRO *by Robert L. Duffus* (1944).

THORSTEIN VEBLEN
Bust Executed 1920 by Blanca Will.
Photograph by Joel W. Spingarn.

THORSTEIN VEBLEN

ESSAYS REVIEWS AND REPORTS

PREVIOUSLY UNCOLLECTED WRITINGS

EDITED AND

WITH AN INTRODUCTION

NEW LIGHT ON VEBLEN

BY JOSEPH DORFMAN

AUGUSTUS M. KELLEY • PUBLISHERS

CLIFTON 1973

First published in the United States 1973

Published 1973 by

AUGUSTUS M. KELLEY PUBLISHERS

Reprints of Economic Classics

Clifton New Jersey 07012

LIBRARY OF CONGRESS

CATALOGUING IN PUBLICATION DATA

Veblen, Thorstein Bunde, 1857-1929.

Essays, Reviews and Reports.

Most of the writings originally published in *The Journal of Political Economy.*

1. Economics--Addresses, essays, lectures.
I. Dorfman, Joseph, 1905- *New Light on Veblen.* 1973.

HB119.A2V42 1973 330 72-13590

ISBN 0 678 00960 0

PRINTED IN THE UNITED STATES OF AMERICA
by SENTRY PRESS, NEW YORK, N. Y. 10013

TABLE OF CONTENTS

New Light on Veblen by Joseph Dorfman 5

Essays Reviews and Reports
Writings in *The Journal of Political Economy*

I. Essays

The Price of Wheat Since 1867 331
The Food Supply and the Price of Wheat 381
Adolph Wagner's New Treatise 399
Levasseur on Hand and Machine Labor 409
The Later Railroad Combinations 413

II. Reviews

A History of Socialism by Thomas Kirkup 417
Geschichte des Socialismus und Communismus im 19 Jahrhundert by Dr. Otto Warschauer 420
The Land Systems of British India by B. H. Baden-Powell 421
Der Parlamentarismus, die Volksgesetzgebung und die Socialdemokratie by Karl Kautsky 426
A Study of Small Holdings by William E. Bear 429
Bibliographie des Socialismus und Communismus by Joseph Stammhammer 430
History of the English Landed Interest (Modern Period) by Russell M. Garnier 432
L'Agriculture aux Etats-Unis by Emile Levasseur 434
Socialism by Robert Flint 440
Misère de la Philosophie by Karl Marx 447
Socialisme et Science Positive by Enrico Ferri 449
Einfuhrung in den Socialismus by Richard Calwer 455
La Viriculture. Ralentissement de la Population – Dégénerescence – Causes et Remèdes by G. de Molinari 459
Essais sur la Conception Materialiste de l'Histoire by Antonio Labriola 461

Sozialismus und soziale Bewegung im 19 Jahrhundert by Werner Sombart . . . 463
Esquisses de Littérature politico-economique by N. Ch. Bunge . . . 465
Social Facts and Forces by Washington Gladden . . . 470
Inequality and Progress by George Harris . . . 470
Uber einige Grundfragen der Socialpolitik und der Volkswirtschaftslehre by Gustav Schmoller . . . 471
Aristocracy and Evolution: A Study of the Rights, the Origin and the Social Functions of the Wealthier Classes by W. H. Mallock . . . 476
Reflections on the Formation and the Distribution of Riches by A. R. J. Turgot . . . 484
Die Entstehung des socialen Problems by Arnold Fisher . . . 487
Pamphlets Socialistes: Le Droit á la Paresse; La Religion du Capital; L'Appetit Vendu; Pie IX au Paradis by Paul Lafargue . . . 489
Social Laws. An Outline of Sociology by G. Tarde . . . 490
The Impending Crisis; Conditions resulting from the Concentration of Wealth in the United States by Basil A. Bouroff . . . 491
Associations industrielles et commerciales: Fédérations – Ententes partielles – Syndicats – Cartels Comptoirs – Affiliations – Trusts by Jules Gernaert and Vicomte de Herbais de Thun . . . 493
Psychologie Economique by G. Tarde . . . 495
Der moderne Kapitalismus by Werner Sombart . . . 498
Vaerdi – og Prislaerens Historie by T. H. Aschehoug . . . 506
L'Imperialisme allemand by Maurice Lair . . . 507
Imperialism: A Study by J. A. Hobson . . . 508
The New Empire by Brooks Adams . . . 511
Financial Crises and Periods of Industrial and Commercial Depression by Theodore E. Burton . . . 514
Pure Sociology: A Treatise concerning the Origin and Spontaneous Development of Society by Lester F. Ward . . .
Bevolkerungsbewegung, Kapitalbildung and periodische Wirtschaftskrisen by Ludwig Pohle . . . 518

Kartell und Trust: Vergleichende Untersuchungen über dem Wesen und Bedeutung by S. Tschievsky 520
An Inquiry into the Nature and Causes of the Wealth of Nations by Adam Smith 521
Adam Smith by Francis W. Hirst 522
Zur Genesis des modernen Kapitalismus: Forschungen zur Entstehung der grossen burgerlichen Kapitalvermogen am Ausgang des Mittelalters und zu Beginn der Neuzeit, zunachst in Augsburg by Jacob Strieder 523
The Code of Hammurabi, King of Babylon about 2250 B. C. by Robert Francis Harper 525
L'Individualisme économique et social: ses origines – son évolution – ses formes contemporains by Albert Schatz 527
Der Bourgeois: zur Geistesgeschichte des modernen Wirtschaftsmenschen by Werner Sombart 529
The Ruling Caste and Frenzied Trade in Germany by Maurice Millioud 533

Other Essay Reviews and Reports

I. ESSAYS

On the General Principles of a Policy of Reconstruction 535
Introduction to the Translation of *The Laxdaela Saga* 541

II. REVIEWS

The Development of English Thought: A Study in the Economic Interpretation of History by Simon N. Patten 553
The Cost of Competition. An Effort at the Understanding of Familiar Facts by Sidney A. Reeve 563
England: Its Political Organizations and Development and the War against Germany by Eduard Meyer 568

III. REPORTS

As To a Proposed Inquiry into Baltic and Cretan Antiquities 575
Expense and Time Required for Executing Project 580
Interim Report on the I. W. W. and the Food Supply 583

A Poem: The Following Lines are Respectfully Dedicated to the Class of '82 by One who Sympathizes with Them in Their Recent Bereavement ... 587

APPENDIX

Selected Obituaries

Thorstein Bunde Veblen 1857-1929 by John Maurice Clark ... 595
Thorstein Veblen: 1857-1929 by Wesley C. Mitchell ... 601
Thorstein Veblen 1857-1929 by Wesley C. Mitchell ... 606

Selected Reviews

Reviews of *The Theory of the Leisure Class*

The Luxury of Lazihead by Stephen MacKenna ... 615
The Theory of the Leisure Class by Lester Frank Ward ... 619
An Opportunity for American Fiction by William D. Howells ... 630
The Dullest Book of the Month. *The Theory of the Leisure Class*. Dr. Veblen Gets the Crown of Deadly Nightshade by Robert Benchley ... 637

Other Reviews

The Theory of Business Enterprise by J. H. Tufts ... 643
An Inquiry into the Nature of Peace by Francis Hackett ... 651
The Higher Learning in America in *The North American Review* ... 659

Reports, etc.

Veblen's Record at Carleton College ... 665
Signers of Petition Asking for Nomination of Thorstein Veblen as President of the American Economic Association ... 667
Mitchell's Translations of Extracts from Simiand ... 675
Addendum 683

NEW LIGHT ON VEBLEN

NEW LIGHT ON VEBLEN

After the publication in 1934 of *Thorstein Veblen and His America*, I kept collecting material on this most creative of American economists of our age. As his fame grew there occurred from time to time opportunities to make some of the new material available to the republic of learning. One way was through additions and corrections in the sixth (1961) and subsequent editions of my Veblen book, which have been issued by Augustus M. Kelley Publishers. Thus when some valuable letters from his graduate school days in the early 1880's turned up in the papers of the eminent American historian, J. Franklin Jameson, I included them along with related materials as an appendix in these later editions.[1] An-

[1] All references to *Thorstein Veblen and His America* are to the seventh edition (1967) issued by Augustus M. Kelley Publishers through arrangement with The Viking Press. Hereafter it will be referred to as the "Veblen book."

Jameson and Veblen entered the graduate school of Johns Hopkins at the same time in 1881. "Proud of his New England birth and scornful of anything 'westernish,' he [Jameson] was yet able to recognize the unusual powers of Thorstein Veblen." Veblen left at the end of the first semester to enter Yale, but "the acquaintance . . . . was never dropped though communication between the two was infrequent." [*An Historian's World: Selections from the Correspondence of John Franklin Jameson,* edited by Elizabeth Donnan and L. F. Stock (Philadelphia: American Philosophical Society, 1956) pp. 2, 219]. In 1910 in a private letter Jameson wrote that Veblen "is an extraordinary man, indeed in many respects his attainments may fairly be called marvelous. I have known of him chiefly as a most ingenious student of economic phenomena." (Jameson to R. S. Woodward, president of the Carnegie Institution of Washington, Jameson Papers, Library of Congress).

other channel was through papers for conferences dealing with his contributions; notably the celebration of the centenary of his birth by the American Economic Association in 1957[2]; and the year long seminar on Veblen at Carleton College in connection with the celebration of the centennial of his *alma mater* (1966-1967).[3]

Still another mode of dissemination was by means of introductions and additions to new printings of Veblen's books. I supplied introductions for reprints of *The Theory of Business Enterprise* (1904),[4] *The Instinct of Workmanship and the State of the Industrial Arts* (1914),[5] *Imperial Germany and the Industrial Revolution* (1915),[6] and the first collection of his published essays, *The Place of Science in Modern Civilisation and Other Essays* (1919).[7] For the 1964 printing of *Essays in Our Changing Order*,[8] I included the memorandum, "Wire Barrage," which had been sought in vain at the time of the preparation of the original edition. The document, which is in the Andrew Veblen Papers in the Minnesota Historical Society, describes Veblen's invention

---

[2] "The Source and Impact of Veblen's Thought," *The American Economic Review*, May 1958. This was reprinted with some additions as Appendix II in the sixth and subsequent editions of the Veblen book.

[3] "The Background of Veblen's Thought," in *Thorstein Veblen: The Carleton College Veblen Seminar Essays*, edited by C. C. Qualey (New York: Columbia University Press, 1968) pp. 106-130, 154-157.

[4] Augustus M. Kelley Publishers, 1965.

[5] Augustus M. Kelley Publishers, 1964.
Having discovered a copy of *The Instinct of Workmanship* in which Veblen had made corrections, I contributed these as well for the 1964 printing.

[6] Viking, 1939; Augustus M. Kelley Publishers, 1964. The reprint includes Veblen's corrections, which were supplied by his heirs.

[7] Russell and Russell, 1961.

[8] Augustus M. Kelley Publishers, 1964.

of a submarine catcher, which he submitted to the United States Navy during World War I.

The addresses, introductions, etc., by no means exhausted my fund of accumulated information. Furthermore the fund was being constantly augmented, especially by the availability in whole or in part of papers of Veblen himself, of his oldest brother Andrew, of his teachers, colleagues and students, such as Richard T. Ely, Herbert J. Davenport, Jacques Loeb and Wesley C. Mitchell; of his first publishers — Macmillan and Scribner's; and not least, the papers bearing on his federal government service in World War I, which were deposited in the National Archives in 1934. I also had accumulated a considerable amount of significant published materials on Veblen. Thanks to the publisher who has done so much to keep Veblen in print, I now have the opportunity to make available practically all of my holdings. Mr. Augustus Kelley proposed that I prepare a volume of Veblen's hitherto uncollected but important essays, reviews, reports, etc. He accepted the suggestion that the introduction be largely devoted to bringing together the additional information.

I shall first discuss Veblen's books and then the other writings and materials.

I

BOOKS

The Theory of the Leisure Class

Of course, we open with the first book, his perdurable classic, *The Theory of the Leisure Class* (1899), that powerful interpretation of American civilization. We now know many additional details surrounding its publication. As I noted in the Veblen book, he definitely had begun writing it in November 1895. On September 22, 1896, the head of the New York branch of the British publishing house of Macmillan wrote Veblen that he would like to see the manuscript, which one of the firm's authors had praised without giving any particulars.[9] The informant was his former student and later colleague at Chicago and Missouri and always steadfast friend, Herbert Joseph Davenport, who was then well on his way to becoming one of the leading advanced orthodox economists.[10] Veblen promptly replied that "the draft which Mr. Davenport has seen will require revision and will scarcely be ready in less than six weeks time. I shall feel at liberty to forward it as soon as it is completed. The title (provisional) is 'The Theory of the Leisure Class: A Study in the Evolution of Economic Institutions.' The ms. will contain some 90,000 words."

The revision took approximately eight months and in the process the ms. increased by 35,000 words, of which 10,000 were on pages "prefixed to the regular rotation of the sheets

[9] The New York branch later became an independent house.

Unless otherwise noted the correspondence between Veblen and Macmillan is in the Macmillan Papers, New York Public Library.

[10] The intimacy of their relations was such that Veblen declined to review Davenport's *Value and Distribution* (1908), on the ground that "I am bound by too close relations of friendship with the author to admit of my writing with all the freedom which a reviewer should use."

in the body of the ms." (June 7, 1897). On the basis of the opinion of two readers, the publisher wrote Veblen that he did not think that the book would have a sufficient sale to warrant the expenses of production. The publisher added, however, that feeling that it might have more of a market in England, he wished to express a willingness to send the manuscript to "one of our English readers." Veblen, however, was tenacious, and in a letter which has been described as "a masterpiece of self-control,"[11] he wrote that while he wished to thank the firm "for the suggestion which you make with regard to its possible availability for an English audience, . . . my extreme reluctance to forego the advantage of having the book published by your company must serve as apology for troubling you further with the matter. I beg leave also, on the same ground, to suggest that I should be glad to enter into some arrangement whereby your company would be insured against loss on the production of the book." He also asked for specific criticisms from the readers "that would help me toward an effective revision of the ms." (July 14, 1897).

The house replied that the readers' major criticism was with the language but that this fault of style would probably disappear in the course of revision. Should Veblen desire to resubmit the ms. the firm would be glad to inform the English reader of "our own standpoint in relation to the work." In sending the revision in September 1898, Veblen wrote, "I am still quite sensible of the shortcomings of the language used, but I believe that it is now in appreciably more readable shape than it was in the first draft. In revising the ms. the introductory portion has been abridged somewhat, and some

---

[11] "Macmillan's Author Files, 1892-1960, Go to the N[ew] Y[ork] P[ublic] L[ibrary]," *Publishers' Weekly*, December 24, 1966, pp. 22-23.

considerable changes have also been made in the later portions." He pointedly expressed the hope that the ms. would be resubmitted to the firm's American readers "before forwarding it to England," because he thought that they might find it acceptable in its present shape.

The publisher granted his wish and wrote that the two readers recommended publication of the ms. because of its interesting matter, while warning "that the book might not have any very considerable sale." In fact one doubted that the sale would be enough to cover the initial expense. Nevertheless the house would print the work if it could make Veblen what he would consider a reasonable offer.

The publisher suggested a plan that in his estimation would recoup for Veblen in any event his outlay and prevent the house from suffering too great a loss. Accordingly, it proposed to pay "all expenses of manufacture and issue," and pay Veblen, in the event of its financial success, a half of the net profits yearly resulting from its publication, and if not successful Veblen would pay the firm at the end of the first year after issue a half of "the net loss at that time standing against the book on our manufacturing account. This method of publication implies that we keep an account with the book, charging it with all the expenses of its issue and crediting it with the sales of all copies sold at the average trade price, that the balance of the account at the end of the first year, if a loss, be divided into two parts, one of which shall be remitted to us by you within thirty days thereafter, or in the event of there being a profit, that we shall remit to you one half of such profits. After the first year's accounting, in case the book meets with a loss, we charge off to our own account the losses that we ourselves have sustained and credit you with one half of the future earnings less the expenses, and of course in the event of there being a profit in the first year, each succeeding year we credit you and pay one half the profit as agreed."

Veblen in reply asked for an estimate of the cost. He found the offer "eminently fair," and went on to say, "but the chance of my having to pay one-half the net expenditure outstanding at the end of the first year makes it necessary for me to know something of the probable cost before entering into an agreement. If the cost should be considerable and the sales small, such an obligation would become very inconvenient to me. I am, therefore, constrained to beg you to let me know (1) the size of the edition contemplated, and (2) the price at which the volume would probably be sold, as well as (3) an estimate of the probable cost. Will you also kindly let me know in what relation, if any, I should stand to the expenses of advertising, and to any other expenses incident to marketing the book." The publisher promptly answered Veblen's questions (October 19): The first edition would probably be 900 or 1000 copies and "would probably sell at from $1.50 to $2.00 retail, as it would make 475 pages in the style in which we propose to bring it out, i.e., ordinary crown octavo form."

The estimate of cost was as follows:

Cost of plates, exclusive of corrections	$450[12]
Cost of paper	$100
Cost of printing	$40
Cost of binding 500 copies	$60

There would also be the costs of advertising and other

[12] The printer's estimate was broken down as follows: 475 pages at 92¢ a page, or $437.00, plus 10 boxes at 75¢ each, or $7.50, for a total of $444.50, author's corrections to be charged at 60¢ per hour. The actual cost of the plates turned out to be close to the estimate. It was $452.85. But the number of pages was 400 instead of 475. "Boxes" refers to extra fonts of type kept at the press to replace letters broken and damaged in the course of printing. The retail price was $2.

business expenses but "as these are only calculated on the sales they do not affect our present figures."[13]

Thus the total manufacturing cost of 1000 copies (500 bound) and exclusive of corrections would be about $650.00 and the sale of 500 copies at the "ordinary trade price" would leave only a very small balance against the book at the end of the first year of publication. "If the book had any success at all it would be quite safe to expect the sale of 500 copies, between the sales here and the sales abroad."[14]

Veblen found the terms equitable but apparently his awareness of the pitfalls of translation and his thriftiness led him to ask as a favor for the translation rights. He informed the publisher (October 22) "There is one point probably of very slight importance to you. . . . I should like, if I may, to reserve the right of translation to myself. At the same time if this request does not meet with your approval, I should by no means wish it to stand in the way of an agreement." The publisher naturally enough consented, after Veblen's courteous but persistent reminders.

Veblen closely watched every detail of the printing, so as to avoid undue elegance and added cost. He gave suggestions on the type, number of lines on the page, the paper, etc. As in almost everything else, Veblen's dealings with the publisher were courteous but tenacious, as the following letters

[13] The view of selling expenses taken by the house found acceptance in dominant economic theory thirty years later.

According to a later letter of the firm (December 22, 1917), it seems that the Veblen account was originally charged 20% of proceeds for general "publishing expenses" which "covers all our so-called overhead expenses." The firm claimed at a later date that twenty per cent was now too low and that "the actual figure for all our publications in recent years has risen to from 23 to 25%."

[14] The upshot was that Veblen's account was charged with one half the actual cost of plates, or $226.42. Later in 1918 he obtained complete possession of the plates by paying the other half, or another $226.42.

so well illustrate. The first dated November 15, 1898, reads

> . . . Enclosed is the specimen page of the "Leisure Class" which you were kind enough to forward to me, with a suggestion or two entered in the margin. The page submitted is, I see, identical with the one employed in [J. Mark] Baldwin's *Mental Development* [*in the Child and the Race*], and after looking it over and getting an impression from Baldwin's book – I venture to make this suggestion:
>
> The result would be a more pleasing page if the width were reduced by about one em and if its height increased by about one line, leaving the heading and the running title as they are. But if such a change involves serious inconvenience, I should by no means wish to press the suggestion.
>
> I have taken the liberty to suggest a slightly smaller type for the title at the head of the text, as it stands it seems too heavy. I have also struck out the ornamental rule under the heading, and suggest that everything of an ostensibly decorative character be omitted.
>
> Baldwin's book above referred to also suggests to me that it would be a mistake to use a highly finished paper in printing the book. A smooth-finished wove paper and cut edges do not seem to go well with old-style type and an Italic running title.
>
> I believe it is not very necessary for me to see the specimen page again if the above suggested alterations are made.

Ten weeks later, on receipt of the first proofs – page not galley – Veblen wrote:

> The proofs mailed herewith under separate cover (pp. i-viii and 1-61) of the "Leisure Class" have come to hand from the Norwood Press, but they are returned to

> you rather than direct to the printer because of a suggestion to which I beg your attention. In returning the specimen pages which you were kind enough to submit to me, I ventured to suggest that the page be reduced in width by one em and increased in length by one line. In the proofs now submitted I find that this suggestion has been followed in part, and in part not. The present page is one em narrower, but it is also one line *shorter*, instead of one line *longer* as suggested. My desire was to make the page 33 lines, instead of 31 as at present. It has occurred to me that the shortening of the page may have been due to my not having made myself sufficiently clear on the point. You will therefore pardon my calling your attention to the matter in this way.
>
> If it seems preferable to use the shorter page, I do not wish my preference for a larger page to decide the matter contrary to your judgment; but if there is nothing to hinder it, it would be a pleasure to have the printer use a page of 33 lines instead of 31.
>
> It will be unnecessary for you [to] communicate your decision of this matter to me, or to delay the printer, as whatever decision you think best to make will be satisfactory to me.

Macmillan, however, countered Veblen on the matter of the size of the page. Using his own grounds of aesthetics and cost, the house contended that the present page was more pleasing and that the cost would be increased substantially (especially since the book was in page proofs) if Veblen's proposal was accepted. The publisher on December 3, wrote: "We are extremely sorry that we misunderstood your instructions in regard to the size of the page desired for your forthcoming volume, but we should prefer not to change the page now as it will make us much extra cost and we may perhaps be permitted to say that in the printed book the page as it now is will be perhaps somewhat more artistic and satisfactory than if the change which you suggested had been carried out." Veblen, being cost conscious, apparently wisely decided not to reply. His meticulousness and knowledge of the manufacturing process is easily understandable, for not only was he at the time managing editor of *The Journal of Political Economy,* but it appears also that he had been a printer.[15]

At first the book did so badly that when a fellow boarder in Chicago said that he had just finished it, Veblen quipped, "I am glad that a second copy of that book has been sold. I had thought I am the only purchaser."[16]

---

[15] One of Veblen's Missouri students wrote me while I was working on the Veblen book, that "one little item about his early life might be of some interest. I have seen no reference to it in any printed material. Apparently he was at one time of his life a printer. He told me that one day when I expressed surprise at the very careful proofreading he did on a paper which I was preparing under his supervision." (J. Ray Cable to Joseph Dorfman, December 22, 1932).

Veblen may have worked in a print shop while in the country town of Stacyville, Iowa, after his marriage. He was also a brick mason, a trade which he claimed to have learned while attending the "Academy," which doubtless was Carleton College's preparatory school.

[16] Dora Wells to Joseph Dorfman, August 29, 1936.

Mrs. Wells also supplied a characteristic Veblen story of an "experience on an Illinois Central suburban train. It occurred during the days when the conductors would pass through the train punching commutation tickets. Dr. Veblen was riding with another university [of Chicago] instructor on a local train. They were deep in conversation. At 57th street, the conductor punched the tickets of both men. As he passed through the train at 53rd street, Dr. Veblen's companion absent-mindedly held out his ticket and the conductor punched it again. The same thing happened at 51st street, at 47th street, at 43rd street and at 39th street. The companion was so interested in the conversation that he did not know what he was doing.

"At this point I interrupted and said, 'And you let him waste his money that way!' Dr. Veblen replied, 'Well, it wasn't my ticket. Besides, I wanted to see how many times he would let the conductor punch it.'"

The sales shortly began to pick up under the impact of such powerful, positive reviews as those by William Dean Howells and Lester Frank Ward,[17] already noted in the Veblen book, and the outrage expressed by most of the critics. An example of the latter is the five page review in the July 1899 issue of the high level, quasi-popular journal, *The Sewanee Review*.[18] The reviewer, after asserting that this was "one of the most curious books" of the season, devoted most of the remaining space to quotations which characterize "the leisure classes of today with a good deal of exaggeration and much amusing paradox." He concluded with: "It is hardly worthwhile to extend this already long review. The reader will get from the extracts we have given a sufficient idea of the

---

[17] Reprinted in the Appendix below.

A well received book meant much to Veblen. He was forty-two and still an instructor. He had the previous year vainly written President Harper for a promotion. "Your repeated expression of good will and appreciation have encouraged me to look with more confidence for an advance, and in this connection I beg to remind you, perhaps unnecessarily, that I am now at work for the third year with the grade and pay of an instructor." (Veblen to William Rainey Harper, November 1898, given in Abram L. Harris, review of Bernard Rosenberg, *The Values of Veblen: A Critical Appraisal,* in *The Journal of Political Economy,* April 1959, p. 422). This episode may be the one to which reference is made in the Veblen book, p. 174. He was promoted to assistant professor in 1900 when the book was a success.

[18] The advertisement in the journal stated that "it will be directed to reviews of leading books and papers on such topics of general literature as require fuller treatment than they receive in specialist publications. In other words, the *Review* will conform more nearly to the type of English reviews than is usual with American periodicals."

The *Review* was published under the auspices of the faculty of the University of the South at Sewanee, Tennessee, which, the journal stated, was "under the joint control of fifteen dioceses of the Protestant Episcopal Church."

The reviewer of *The Theory of the Leisure Class* was Benjamin W. Wells, a man who wrote generally on literary topics.

book, much of which is excellent fooling, much of it just irony, and much of it a vicious attack on Christian ideals. It is not worth reading for instruction, in spite of its assumption of economic terminology; but there is an element of truth in its satire, and there is a taking incisiveness in some of its epigrammatic statements. It is to be read for amusement, and in that spirit we have reviewed it here at a length that its serious value is far from justifying." This interpretation of the book as merely satire took a long time to be dispelled and it still lingers on for many readers.

There were two revealing anonymous reviews, which have heretofore been overlooked. One was the first clearly favorable review.[19] It appeared in the March 1899 issue of the short-lived New York *Criterion* under the signature "M. K." The reviewer was the philosophic Irishman Stephen MacKenna, who would become one of the most eminent of Ireland's men of letters, but who was then struggling in New York City to make a bare living by reviewing and odd jobs at *The Criterion*. The review noted: "[It is] a book, too, which is immensely educative: no one could take it up and even dip into it, casually here and there, without feeling a distinct freshening of interest in the deeper signification of the most commonplace principles, habits, venerations, and dislikes of everyday existence. At every step one is flung back from the present, as by a catapult, into the most distant past. One gets a new sense of the depth of the daily things; a new feeling for the mystery of the ways of men; a keener percep-

[19] "I enclose a review of the *Leisure Class* which the publisher sent me. I have seen some six or eight notices of it, some favorable – one in the *Criterion* particularly so – and some unfavorable, but on the whole it has not been much noticed. I don't know yet how it is selling." Thorstein Veblen to Andrew Veblen, April 27, 1899, Andrew Veblen Papers, Minnesota Historical Society.

There is a legend that MacKenna swept a restaurant for meals and found shelter from the cold in a Turkish bath.

tion of the oneness of mankind through all the variations of all the centuries."[20]

The other doubtless impressed Veblen more than most for its appreciation of the book as a work of science. This appeared in *Appleton's Popular Science Monthly*, which commanded as writers leaders in the sciences, material and social.[21] To the book it accorded the honor in the September 1899 issue of occupying the position of the one full-scale review of the month—"Special Books"—in the department of "Scientific Literature." The review was in the form of a summary that clearly indicated its scientific character. It began with: "*The Theory of the Leisure Class* is primarily an inquiry into the place and value of the leisure class as an economic factor in modern life. Hardly less attention, however, is given to the origin and line of derivation of the institutions and the features of social life not commonly classed as economic, into the heart of some of which the study goes. The institution of the leisure class, which is defined generally as that class whose occupation is not industrial, is found in feudal Europe or feudal Japan. Which ever way we go from this point it is modified."

Veblen could write to brother Andrew in October: "Reviews of the *Leisure Class* are coming in, for the most part quite severe. Opinion seems to be divided as to whether I am a knave or a fool, though there are some who make out that the book is a work of a genius – I don't know just how. It is said to sell fairly well." In a little more than a year since publication [March 1900], the sales were so improved that

---

20 The review is printed in full in the Appendix below.

21 The journal was founded originally to expound the views of Herbert Spencer and continued to do so at least in the editorial columns.

the publisher was asking for a photograph.[22] Veblen characteristically replied (March 3, 1900): "I greatly regret that it is impossible for me at present to comply with your very courteous request for a photograph. I feel it a great honor, and it would be a great pleasure to me to send you what you ask, but I have at present no photograph so recent, as to be worthwhile sending. I shall assume that I have your consent to send such a photograph, however, when I have one, and shall keep it in mind."

As the years went on, the book became so popular that in 1912 the publisher issued a cheap edition at 50¢. The book now acquired the distinction of being the only one of Veblen's works to have an index. This addition was made after Veblen informed the publisher that there was one available and the publisher accepted it.[23]

As the nation moved into the Great Depression that began in 1929, the sale of the book began to mount. This accompanied an increasing realization that the book was more

[22] At this point Veblen made strenuous efforts to persuade Macmillan to take his first wife's ms. of a book for children, "The Goosenbury Pilgrims." He informed the publisher that "it contains some 35,000 words, and is to be fully illustrated. . . . The characters are taken from the 'Mother Goose's Melodies,' and the book is a narrative of the adventures that befell them on going out to see the world. It has been tested by reading to children, and appears to be successful under that test." The firm agreed to examine it, but much to Veblen's dismay it proved not acceptable. It was later published in 1902 by Lothrop.

On Ellen Rolfe Veblen's book, see Robert Duffus, *The Innocents at Cedro* (New York: Macmillan, 1944) pp. 146-147. "Cedro" was the anglicized version of the name of Veblen's home, *Ysidro,* in the Stanford University period (1906-1909). W. C. Mitchell used to refer to it as "Veblen's rancho."

[23] Up to the transfer to B. W. Huebsch of publication rights in 1918 Macmillan sold 3,326 copies of the original edition and 3,651 of the cheap edition.

The firm used in advertisements the statement from the Minneapolis *Journal:* "The study is a thoughtful and interesting one and is couched in clear and straightforward English."

than an amusing essay on upper class mannerisms. Thus in the introduction to a selection from Veblen in a book of readings, *Science and the Scientific Method* (1931), the compilers wrote:

> Veblen was distinguished by his contributions to economic theory, especially as that theory is modified by modern business practices. His mood was essentially that of a satirist, and when his first important book, *The Theory of the Leisure Class*, appeared, he was received as such by the critics and not as a new thinker in the field of economics. At first they regarded the anthropological and historical evidence that he gave for an explanation of social foibles as being merely an effective literary device and not as a method of approach to the study of social problems. The true aspect of the work was soon realized, and gradually it did much to turn the attention of economists from the purely abstract and hypothetical method of reasoning, which for generations had characterized their thinking, to the results of modern psychology and biology. In all of his writings Veblen had interpreted society historically and philosophically in connection with an analysis of the instincts, interests and activities of men, which go to make up the total life of a race of people; and as a result of this procedure, he has provided the way for a more comprehensive interrelation of the sciences in building the new civilization.[24]

As the depression deepened some of the harshest critics began to have second thoughts. Henry L. Mencken, for example, complained in a private letter in 1934 that he had

[24] Leo E. Saidla and Warren E. Gibbs, *Science and the Scientific Method* (New York: McGraw-Hill, 1931) pp. 416-417. Their selection from Veblen was the essay, "The Place of Science in Modern Civilisation."

never intended that his elaborate castigation of 1919[25] should be taken seriously. "On gloomy afternoons my conscience has pricked me about that article I wrote so many years ago. It was planned as buffoonery, but it turned out to be rather serious."[26]

A sardonic aspect of the book was portrayed in a photograph[27] (and the description of it) of a session of the famous hearings in 1939 before the Senate Munitions Committee headed by Senator Nye. The picture was titled "As One Member of the Leisure Class to Another." The subscription read "Senator Nye (left) and J. P. Morgan were snapped in a moment of animated discussion at a meeting of the Munitions Committee at which Mr. Morgan described members of the Leisure Class of America as 'those having at least one servant.' "

As the New Deal went on, there was much evidence that the book had become a classic. The Princeton *Alumni Weekly* (on January 25, 1935) under the section "Princeton's Recreational Reading" referred to Veblen as "one of the most in-

---

[25] "Professor Veblen," originally appeared in *The Smart Set;* and was reprinted in Mencken's *Prejudices, First Series* (New York: Knopf, 1919) pp. 59-82; see also p. 154.

Incidentally the characteristic Mencken mood is to be found in the publisher's note in a 50¢ edition issued in 1926 by Vanguard Press under license from The Viking Press: "American capitalism has established a larger number of boors of actual or potential leisure than can be found anywhere else on the face of the habitable globe. *The Theory of the Leisure Class* is a thoroughly readable inquiry into their mode of life, their views and their habits of expenditure, enlivened by an undercurrent of polite sarcasm that forms the main characteristic of Veblen's writings. . . . [I]ts pertinent, concise criticisms of the mentality of the average run of well-to-do people is as fresh and as vital now as at the time of first publication."

[26] Mencken to Huebsch, November 18, 1934. Huebsch supplied a copy to Joseph Dorfman.

[27] New York *World-Telegram,* February 5, 1936.

fluential thinkers," and added that his "*Theory of the Leisure Class* has lasted thus far through the twentieth century and will remain a masterpiece." Three years later (in 1938), *The New Republic* canvassed outstanding "educators, historians, critics, lecturers or publicists,"— that is, "men . . . engaged in the business of moulding the public mind"— to ascertain what books had "affected their own ideas." It found that one of the two titles that "recurred most frequently" was *The Theory of the Leisure Class.*[28]

Though but slowly acknowledged, the impact of the book on the economics profession and related disciplines has been as great as on the minds of the community. Thus, the eminent heterodox British economist, John A. Hobson, who described Veblen as "one of the few original thinkers of his age in the field of sociology and economics," noted in 1935 that *The Theory of the Leisure Class* "found its way into a wider reading public [than his other books] even in England, though its exploratory wisdom lost some of its appeal because of the protective colouring of a certain linguistic humour."[29]

---

[28] The other was *The Economic Interpretation of the Constitution* by Veblen's admirer, Charles A. Beard. [*Books that Changed Our Minds,* edited by Malcolm Cowley and Bernard Smith (1939; New York: Doubleday, Doran, 1940) pp. 19, 21. "Counting authors instead of titles, Thorstein Veblen came first." (p. 20)].

[29] "A Great American Thinker," *The New Statesman and Nation,* October 18, 1935; "The Economics of Thorstein Veblen," *Political Science Quarterly,* March 1937, p. 139.

In explanation of the style of the book, Veblen once told his artist friend, B. K. Nordfeld, that "until he was nine or ten his speech was Norwegian and that Latin came next, on which English was built." (Nordfeld to Joseph Dorfman, June 1, 1930).

Jameson's recollection of a conversation with Veblen at Hopkins helps bear out Veblen's first wife's memory that Veblen knew practically no English when he entered the preparatory school of Carleton

By 1923, however, the book's language, though perhaps not all of its substance, had invaded one of the strongest bastions of orthodox economics. That able student of Alfred Marshall, Sir Alfred Flux, in discussing "demand and value," noted that "Apart, too, from the desire for distinction, as the result of conspicuous consumption of highly valuable goods, superior qualities of goods afford higher gratification than inferior qualities, and expenditure on food and clothing is capable of expansion, far beyond the limits provided by the

---

College in 1874. In a letter to Lord Bryce in 1917, he wrote: "Your foot-note on page 18 [of Lord Bryce's presidential address before the British Academy] about forms of the Norwegian language brings to mind what I was told thirty years ago by a young Minnesota Norwegian, who was one of my companions at the Johns Hopkins University. He said that nearly all the people of his township in Minnesota had come from one valley in Norway, and that late comers from that valley told him, on visiting the village, that they were preserving old dialectic forms which in the valley itself had become extinct by reason of the constant influence of the Danish newspapers from Copenhagen and Christiania [now Oslo] – the same fossilizing colonial dialect that is so familiar in the case of the Canadian French, South African Dutch, and in a way the English of Ireland and America." [Jameson to Bryce, October 31, 1917, in *An Historian's World: Selections from the Correspondence of John Franklin Jameson*, p. 219].

A student of English literature has discovered that "Veblen's vocabulary is overwhelmingly Latinate; a review of the origins of words in a sample list of favorites reveals that about 85 per cent of them are of Latin origin, although many of them came into English through French. Two of Veblen's favorite words, barbarian and strategem, are of Greek origin; the majority of his favorites (conspicuous, vicarious, consumption, instinct, etc.) come from the Latin." (Stephen S. Conroy, "Thorstein Veblen's Prose," *American Quarterly*, Fall 1968, p. 60).

In going over some old notes, I found that a close friend of Veblen in his New York period (1918-1926) recalled that Veblen told her also that his English was quite limited when he entered Carleton, and that his mother never spoke English except when displeased because the other party could not speak Norwegian. (Conversation with Mrs. Mildred Bennett, March 17, 1930).

sheer needs of existence, in procuring the satisfactions afforded by the consumption of superior qualities of food and clothing."[30]

Recently in more neutral fashion, Veblen's discussion of consumption patterns has been developed to serve as a foundation for analysis in dominant economic theory. As I have noted elsewhere,

> Veblen's "pecuniary emulation" and "conspicuous consumption," especially when given a less colorful name, such as the "demonstration effect"—the increase in consumption expenditures through contact with superior goods — helped to bring about a revision of the conventional demand theory, including a special aspect of this theory, the "consumption function," as analyzed, for example, by James S. Duesenberry, in *Income Saving and the Theory of Consumer Behavior.* Falling into the same category and given increasing attention, especially by those interested in geometric presentation, was the case that has acquired his name, the "Veblen Case." This has been well described by Sidney Weintraub in *Price Theory* as consisting of goods that "appeal to the snob as a vehicle for 'conspicuous consumption'. . . only when the price goes sufficiently high to prevent these items from being widely bought."[31]

[30] *Economic Principles* (1904; 2nd edition, London: Methuen, 1923) pp. 24-25.

[31] "The Source and Impact of Veblen's Thought," 1958; reprinted in *Thorstein Veblen and His America* (1934; 7th edition, New York: Augustus M. Kelley Publishers, 1972) p. 554.

"He [Duesenberry] introduced the Veblen-like hypothesis that the fraction of income a man saved depended much upon his percentile rank in the income pyramid of his peer group (whether he be a Negro in Columbus, Ohio, at the top of the income pyramid with a $3,000 income in 1935-36, or an executive in Scarsdale, New York, with a $12,000 income)." [Paul A. Samuelson, "A Brief Survey of Post-

Professor P. Sargant Florence, dean of British specialists in industrial organization, has broadened one aspect for research in industrial development. He wrote: "Veblen with his conception of conspicuous consumption had already stressed the importance of emulation of families with higher by families with lower incomes, and 'keeping up with the Jones's' in affluent, highly developed countries, has its counterpart in the peoples of the underdeveloped countries wanting to keep up with people in the developed countries – in the 'demonstration effect.' "[32]

The Theory of the Leisure Class also has been used in a slightly different manner by other specialists in economic development. Thus Thomas (now Baron) Balogh, of Oxford University, used the book to attack the doctrine of consumer sovereignty, a backbone of neo-classical economics. "Consumption was not . . . the expression of the needs and tastes of the individual. There was a conspicuous competitive element in it which . . . could be stimulated and played upon to make a profit for others. This was clearly recognized by Thorstein Veblen, by the only wholly American sociological economist, in his theory of the leisured class."[33] Professor Gunnar Myrdal has recently expanded a Veblen concept by urging that among the major factors impeding rapid economic development in underdeveloped nations "is the disinclination of most of those who are wealthy to risk their funds

[32] *Economics and Sociology of Industry: A Realistic Analysis of Development* (Baltimore: The Johns Hopkins University Press, 1969) pp. 235-236.

[33] "The Consumer and Economic Development," 1958; reprinted in his *The Economics of Poverty* (New York: Macmillan, 1966) p. 48.

Keynesian Developments" (1963), in *Keynes' General Theory: Reports of Three Decades*, edited by Robert Lekachman (New York: St. Martin's Press, 1964) p. 337].

in productive investment and their preference for speculation, quick profits and conspicuous consumption and investment."[34]

Davenport in his interpretation gave a slightly different twist, especially of rational calculation of consumer expectations in his critique of Alfred Marshall's neo-classical economics. Take for example, he asked, the conventional necessaries that parents give their children. "[W]hy do you do it at all – or even send them to college? You might look at *The Theory of the Leisure Class,* if you are seriously thinking that these outlays are not mainly – or surely partly – your own certification, or your own defense against ranking as a *piker.* The saving of faces is not exclusively a Chinese game. And if some economist other than Veblen interprets you as, with most of these outlays, busily investing in the present worth of your offspring's putative salary increments, you will prefer to believe it, but unless you are pretty much a fool, you will not."[35]

In his favorite public lecture to non-academic groups, "The Economics of Feminism," Davenport stressed another famous institutional aspect of the book. Thus, he said that "To

---

[34] *The Asian Drama,* 3 volumes (New York: Harper, 1968) II, pp. 717-718.

In his methodological critiques of "conventional economics" Myrdal increasingly echoes Veblen's views, particularly as expressed in the essays "Why is Economics not an Evolutionary Science?" and "The Preconceptions of Economic Science" (1898-1900). Thus, for example, Myrdal wrote in 1969 that "conventional economic theory remains . . . largely in the moulds provided long ago by psychological hedonism and the moral philosophies of natural law and utilitarianism"; in short, "the old discredited rationalistic, psychological and utilitarian classical line." [*Objectivity in Social Research* (New York: Pantheon, 1969) pp. 59, 88]. He has recently publicly saluted Veblen as "one of the great American economists." ("Response to Introduction," *The American Economic Review,* June 1972, p. 457).

[35] *The Economics of Alfred Marshall* (1935; New York: Augustus M. Kelley Publishers, 1965) pp. 307-308.

the women, as helpless victims of the competition for display, the function of spending has been delegated. Institutionally the wife is a mere agent of the process."[36]

Another of Veblen's outstanding students, Robert F. Hoxie, in an uncorrected draft of a "History of Political Economy," viewed the book as an illustration of a valid methodology for scientific economics:

> Ideal Method: take situation as [it] appears to exist specifically systematized and try in [the] case of each specific element of the organic situation to explain *how* the present came to be by probing back into the past of actuality and opinion, with this definite end in view; e.g., elements would be private ownership [,] the entrepreneur and wages system, monopolistic production[,] valuation, the various elements of income, the

[36] Unpublished address entitled "The Economics of Femininity," in Walton H. Hamilton, *Current Economic Problems; A Series of Readings in the Control of Industrial Development* (Chicago: University of Chicago Press, 1914; 3rd edition, 1925) p. 149. Hamilton titled the adaptation "The New Domestic System."

It seems the address was originally given early in 1914, at a meeting of the Kansas City (Missouri) Credit Men's Association. It was widely quoted in the newspapers of the day.

An amusing sort of summary appeared in a Lincoln, Nebraska, newspaper edited by an old acquaintance. It read: "Prof. H. J. Davenport of Missouri State University, universally remembered in Nebraska as one-time principal of the Lincoln High School, has been making shocking attacks on what he calls 'the parasitic woman.' He defined her thus at a meeting of the Kansas City Credit Men's Association: 'The woman of the wealthy home who bears no children and does no work except to demonstrate to the world the financial success of her husband.' Professor Davenport pronounces this woman 'the center of all modern evils.' " (Clipping in letter from Will Owen Jones, managing editor of the *Nebraska State Journal* and *Lincoln Daily News*, April 3, 1914, Davenport Papers, in possession of Joseph Dorfman).

The editor wrote Davenport: "Since publishing the enclosed paragraph concerning your Kansas City address, we have had requests from readers for the text of your entire address. If you have a copy we would be glad to receive it."

various forms of taxes, etc. This sort of definite research in[to] the past would avoid stilted chronology and would solve automatically the problem of selection of material. Nothing would be done or considered apart from a perfectly definite, conscious end. Ideal results would be achieved from the standpoint of practical possibilities. Example of this sort of study is Veblen's *Theory of the Leisure Class*. Unfortunately this method is not yet practicable and the explanation of [its] impracticability can only be given in historical terms. Education in the past has had culture, erudition, as its end, rather than the fitting for the practical solution of the social problems. Consequently we have not the investigations, literature and training for this sort of work. But this is the ideal and holding it before us as such will help fully modify the method which we actually adopt.[37]

The concept of conspicuous consumption has been used by an expert on the Physiocrats to elucidate their theory of luxury. He states: "[N]ot all expenditure on luxury goods constitutes luxury. It is necessary to make a clear distinction between conspicuous consumption . . . and luxury. . . . Conspicuous consumption . . . is not luxury when it does not detrimentally affect the capitalization of land; [i.e., capital expenditure on land]. . . . But some kinds of conspicuous consumption are preferable to others, so that a further distinction has to be made between conspicuous consumption in the way of consumption . . . and conspicuous consumption in the way of ornamentation. . . . Generally speaking, the former is to be preferred to the latter. . . . [T]he conspicuous consumption of primary produce is healthy in so far as it helps to secure the 'proper price'. . . . [T]he conspicuous consumption of

[37] "History of Political Economy," ms., 1915; copy in possession of Joseph Dorfman.

manufactured products is less healthy, since, although the expenditure ultimately finds its way back to the productive class, it does so burdened with all sorts of commercial costs."[38]

Another and more generic meaning of conspicuous consumption recently has been made explicit. This view states that among the leading motives of "economic man" is "the desire to gain the esteem of friends, acceptance in whatever circle is of importance to him. For instance, an individual rents a fine house to impress other people although his income does not favor such an expenditure. In this case the individual has to do with 'conspicuous consumption' in the terminology of Veblen."[39]

So too, David Friday, the American pioneer in the study of capital formation, made use of the book in describing the increase of capital equipment through the corporate surplus rather than through the presumed pains of individual saving. He explained in his humorous manner in the influential *Profits, Wages and Prices* (1921), "that it involved hardly any consciousness of painful abstinence on the part of the stockholder. It is vicarious saving in which the directorate takes upon itself all the groaning and backache involved in the decision to postpone consumption to the future."

From time to time, a writer, having discovered that Veblen had predecessors in the use of the concept "conspicuous consumption," questioned that Veblen really made any contribution. Thus one wrote in 1950 that while Veblen made the concept famous and the designation of "Veblen effects"

---

[38] Ronald L. Meek, *The Economics of Physiocracy* (London: Allen and Unwin, 1963) p. 317; see also *Quesnay's Tableau Économique*, edited by Marguerite Kuczynski and Meek (New York: Augustus M. Kelley Publishers, 1972) p. 12.

[39] Boris Ischboldin, *Economic Synthesis* (New Delhi: New Book Society of India, 1958) p. 37.

was convenient, he "was neither the discoverer nor the first to elaborate upon the theory of conspicuous consumption. John Rae, writing before 1834, [in his *Statement of Some New Principles of Political Economy*], has quite an extensive treatment of conspicuous consumption, fashions, and related matters pretty much along Veblenian lines."[40] One answer had been given fourteen years earlier: Rae had expressed the idea, but Veblen "took Rae's sketchy appended chapter and developed it into a classic essay which bears the mark of genius."[41]

---

[40] Harvey Leibenstein, "Bandwagon, Snob, and Veblen Effects in the Theory of Consumers' Demand," *The Quarterly Journal of Economics*, May 1950, p. 184.

[41] Read Bain, review of Joseph Dorfman, *Thorstein Veblen and His America* and *What Veblen Taught* (selected writings edited with an introduction by Wesley C. Mitchell) in *The American Sociological Review*, June 1936, pp. 485-486.

Bain, after noting "the high batting average of his predictions," suggested that "In a sense, he is the Darwin of economics. While the details of his theories are as unsound as Darwin's, the general pattern is correct, and his influence on more detailed and scientific research has been tremendous. . . . One might say he made a Darwinian analysis of culture more radical (fundamental) than any ever achieved by the so-called 'social Darwinists.' They proceeded by specious analogy; he by intensive analysis. . . . [H]is teaching and writing is an excellent example of the cross-fertilization of science and philosophy, of the reciprocal relations between empirical and theoretical science." The Indian economist, Radhakamal Mukerjee, drawing explicitly in large part on *The Theory of the Leisure Class*, later pointed out that "with Veblen are introduced for the first time into economics Darwinian ideas of the selection and survival of institutions and patterns of behavior." [*The Institutional Theory of Economics* (London: Macmillan, 1940) p. 142].

An Indian historian of economic thought has noted that "as a system of thought institutionalism developed in the first quarter of the present century only with the spread of the ideas of Veblen" and that "it influenced . . . European and Indian economists." He also argues that for the last half century Indian economists in their researches "have adopted . . . the institutional approach; and laid emphasis on the development and refinement of institutions which greatly effect the eco-

There is an amusing story on Veblen's handling of the Rae issue, which was told to Professor J. M. Clark around 1924 by a student. The student had attended a party at the home of a colleague of Clark, and Veblen had been present. The colleague "steered the talk around to John Rae. Veblen and the others could feel something coming. . . . [T]he fellow who told me the story described it as . . . [the colleague's] way of maneuvering quietly in position to stick something into somebody, or to corner them without their knowing it. Then . . . [the colleague] asked Veblen 'Are you familiar with the work of John Rae?' 'Yes,' Veblen drawled in his deliberate way, and then: 'Some people have accused me of stealing my ideas from him.' "[42]

The shift in the attitude of professional economists toward Veblen's work in general and *The Theory of the Leisure Class* in particular kept growing. So much so, that in the 60's a number of able theorists with the best of accepted credentials reversed themselves even more clearly than Mencken had. For example, Eric (now Sir Eric) Roll had described the book in 1954 as "audacious charlatanism," with "such glib phrases as 'instinct of workmanship.' "[43] In 1968,

---

[42] J. M. Clark to J. B. Clark, January 11, 1924, in Joseph Dorfman's possession.

As early as 1908 Veblen referred to Rae's work in a review article on Irving Fisher's *Rate of Interest.* He characterized the author as being in the line of "so good and authentic a utilitarian theorist as John Rae." ["Fisher's *Rate of Interest,*" *Political Science Quarterly,* June 1909, reprinted in *Essays in Our Changing Order,* edited by Leon Ardzrooni (1934; Augustus M. Kelley Publishers, 1964) p. 138].

[43] *A History of Economic Thought* (London: Faber and Faber, 1938; 3rd edition, 1954) pp. 446, 447.

---

nomic development of the country." [S. K. Srivastava, *History of Economic Thought* (Delhi, India: Atma Ram, 2nd edition, 1965) pp. 470, 488, 646].

he wrote of man's "capacity for enjoyment . . . from the exercise of the 'instinct of workmanship'" and of the far-reaching character and "seminal influence" of the book.[44] Kenneth E. Boulding, in his presidential address before the American Economic Association that same year, also forthrightly revised his estimate of Veblen and in effect called attention to the basic role of the book in the development of dynamic economics. "It was Veblen's . . . contribution to formal economic theory, to point out that we cannot assume that tastes are given in any dynamic theory, in the sense that in dynamics we cannot afford to neglect the processes by which cultures are created and by which preferences are learned."[45]

The Theory of the Leisure Class continues to have an impact on a host of other disciplines, especially in areas related to economics and economic sociology.[46]

In France, as early as 1905, the book attracted the "keen

---

[44] *The World After Keynes* (New York: Praeger, 1968) pp. 10-11, 44, 46.

[45] "Economics as a Moral Science," *The American Economic Review*, March 1969, p. 2.

Seventeen years earlier, Boulding maintained in a public address that Veblen had substantially retarded the progress of economics. He then contended that "the ultimate impact of . . . Veblen on the main stream of economic thought may have been to make economists draw in upon themselves in the logical and mathematical refinement of their own theories rather than to encourage them to reach out for a broader conceptual base." ["Economics as a Social Science," in *The Social Sciences at Mid-Century;* papers delivered at the dedication of Ford Hall, April 19-21, 1951 (Minneapolis, Minn.: University of Minnesota Press, 1952) p. 71].

[46] From sociology has come the first comprehensive book on *The Theory of the Leisure Class* – Peter von Haselberg, *Funktionalismus und Irrationalität: Studien über Thorstein Veblens "Theory of the Leisure Class,"* in the series, Frankfurter Beiträge zur Soziologie (Frankfurt am Main: Europäische Verlagsanstalt, 1962).

The Theory of the Leisure Class was translated into German in 1959 under the title, *Theorie der feinen Leute,* which a German friend of the translator has told me was a stroke of inspiration.

interest" of the internationally known sociologist, economist and statistician, Maurice Halbwachs, who found Veblen's works "so profound and so rich in original insights and yet difficult to comprehend because of their complex and 'abstract' character."[47] He acknowledged the influence of *The Theory of the Leisure Class* in his 1913 classic, *La Classe ouvrière et les niveaux de vie. Recherche sur la hierarchie des besoins dans les societés industrielles contemporains* ("The Working Class and the Standard of Living. Research into the Hierarchy of Wants in Modern Industrial Society"). He informed Veblen in 1919 that he had also referred to it in a preliminary article on the subject of his treatise, "an article of which my former professor, M. Bergson, told me how suggestive he found your ideas."[48] France too was the first foreign country that showed a decided interest in a translation of the book. Professor Raymond Chalmel of St. Omer, Pas de Calais, with Veblen's assent, had undertaken early in 1914 a French translation of *The Theory of the Leisure Class*, and had secured a leading publisher for it – Alcan.[49] On the outbreak of World War I, however, the translator's area was overrun by the German armies and Veblen heard no more from him.

[47] Halbwachs to William Jaffé, September 20, 1924; copy through the courtesy of Professor Jaffé.

[48] Halbwachs to Veblen, July 16, 1919, Thorstein Veblen Papers, State Historical Society of Wisconsin.

The essay is "Remarques sur la position du probleme sociologique des classes" ("Remarks on the Present Position of the Problem of Sociology of Classes") in *Revue de Metaphysique et de Morale*, November 1905. For comments on Veblen's "very suggestive" *Theory of the Leisure Class*, see pp. 897 ff.

In a letter in 1924, Halbwachs declared that Veblen's views found support not only in the investigations of "Franz Boas and the ethnographers of the Indians of the American Northwest, about the 'potlach' and the secret societies," but also in "Max Weber's studies of Capitalism and Protestantism [1906]." (Halbwachs to Jaffé, September 20, 1924).

[49] Chalmel to Veblen, June 22, 1914, in Thorstein Veblen Papers.

In the realm of political theory, most of Veblen's works, including *The Theory of the Leisure Class,* had been viewed as "far reaching studies on the border line between economics and politics."[50] Professor George H. Sabine of Cornell, in his standard *A History of Political Theory,* brought out something of the starkness that lurks in some of Veblen's phrases that seem at first sight to be merely humorous. Thus, in examining the argument of Rousseau and Hegel that "coercion is not really coercion because when a man individually wants something different from what the social order gives him, he is merely capricious and does not rightly know his own good or his own desires," Sabine contended: "This kind of argument . . . was a dangerous experiment in juggling with ambiguities. Liberty had become what Thorstein Veblen called an 'honorific' word, the name for a sentiment with which even attacks on liberty wish to be baptised." In discussing the race theories of the Hitlerites, Sabine noted that "the national socialists used prejudice quite cynically for ulterior purposes; they practised what Thorstein Veblen called 'applied psychology.' "[51]

---

[50] Charles E. Merriam, *American Political Ideas* (1920; New York: Augustus M. Kelley Publishers, 1969) p. 415.

[51] *A History of Political Theory* (New York: Holt, Rinehart and Winston, 3rd edition, 1961) pp. 591, 909.

Arthur F. Bentley, whose *Process of Government* (1908) is one of the foremost American contributions to political theory since the *Federalist Papers,* was at the University of Chicago while Veblen was there. While working on the Veblen book, I inquired of him in 1933 whether they had ever met at the university. He replied: "Extremely sorry: but I never knew Veblen. I am not good at remembering people: but if I had ever known *him* I am sure I would not have lost track of it. While I was around the University of Chicago for a year, my contact was sketchy, as I was engaged with a set of problems that had no place there. I had even forgotten that Veblen had ever been there. Best wishes for your work. Sincerely yours. (The italics are Bentley's).

Historians and especially economic historians concerned with economic growth have also found insights in *The Theory of the Leisure Class.* Take the mediaeval period, for example. A specialist on town gilds has used "conspicuous consumption" as an argument for their economic and social justification. She writes that: "In most lines of consumer goods the mere existence of gild society went far to stimulate demand. Participating in the political and religious ceremonial of the towns, leading gildsmen had double opportunity and incentive to demonstrate social importance, through expenditure of the collective funds of their gilds in symbolic display and in feasting and through expenditure on their personal clothing, on the dress of members of their family, and in their household furnishing. Sumptuary legislation sought in vain to hold this game of conspicuous consumption in check . . . [G]ilds . . . contributed much to the zest with which it spread downward in the social scale, obliterating outward signs of rank."[52] An authority on mediaeval agrarian society in Russia notes that "the land deals of the lords . . . seem in the main not aimed at directly raising the consumption level of the lord, but at raising vicarious consumption to increase his status and power."[53]

As we turn to the modern period, we find a British economic historian discoursing on "The Development of London as a Centre of Conspicuous Consumption in the Sixteenth

---

[52] Sylvia Thrupp, "The Gilds," in *The Cambridge Economic History of Europe,* volume III, *Economic Organization and Policies in the Middle Ages,* edited by M. M. Postan, E. E. Rich and Edward Miller (Cambridge, England: Cambridge University Press, 1961) p. 280.

[53] Robert E. F. Smith, "Russia," in *The Cambridge Economic History of Europe,* Volume I, *The Agrarian Life of the Middle Ages,* edited by M. M. Postan (Cambridge, England: Cambridge University Press, 1966) p. 546.

and Seventeenth Centuries."[54] So again an English economic historian of the age of mercantilism comments that Daniel Defoe's "observations of the habits of workmen might be thought to point to the dangers of conspicuous consumption by the poor. He describes how he saw workmen take their wages to the alehouses – lie there till Monday, spend it every penny and run in debt to boot and not give a farthing of it to their families, tho' all of them had wives and children."[55]

The concept has begun to play a key role in the controversy over the source of capital for the industrialization of Great Britain that became so marked after 1750. Some have used it against the traditional view that the capital came from the profits of successful merchants. They have contended that "the first goal of many a merchant was the acquisition of a landed estate with a stately home, and an unknown proportion of all mercantile profits in the eighteenth century was poured into this form of conspicuous consumption."[56]

Similarly concepts of *The Theory of the Leisure Class* have played a role in such recent lively historical topics as the economics of southern slavery. Thus a writer points out that, in determining whether southern slavery retarded the

---

[54] Title of article by F. J. Fisher, in *Transactions of the Royal Historical Society*, 4th series, volume 30 (1948), pp. 37-50.

See also Gordon Vichert, a Canadian English teacher, "The Theory of Conspicuous Consumption in the 18th Century" in *The Varied Pattern: Studies in the 18th Century*, ed. by Peter Hughes & David Williams (1971).

[55] Charles Wilson, "Mercantilism: Some Vicissitudes of an Idea," 1957; reprinted in his *Economic History and the Historian* (New York: Praeger, 1969) p. 78.

[56] M. W. Finn, *The Origins of the Industrial Revolution* (1966), pp. 44-45, quoted in R. G. Wilson, *Gentlemen Merchants, The Merchant Community in Leeds 1700-1830* (Manchester: Manchester University Press, 1971) p. 222.

growth of the South as against the North, such questions as the following must be answered: "To what extent did conspicuous consumption cause the South to lag behind the North in economic growth? Was such conspicuous consumption any more characteristic of the South than of the North, of planters than of business and professional men of similar incomes?"[57] An anthropologically minded economist had paradoxically commented that "since Veblen's day the leisure class in the United States has almost died out, while conspicuous consumption is evident in every rank of society."[58]

Philosophers too have been impressed with the book. The pragmatist, J. H. Tufts, characterized it as combining a "wealth of concrete materials with psychological analysis and philosophical method."[59] The eminent philosopher of science, Karl (now Sir Karl) Popper, wrote "that the idea that nomads or even hunters constituted the original upper class is corroborated by the age-old and still surviving upper class traditions according to which war, hunting and horses, are the symbols of the leisured classes, a tradition which is

---

[57] Jane H. Pease, "A Note on Patterns of Consumption Among Seaboard Planters, 1820-1860," *The Journal of Southern History,* August 1969, p. 351.

[58] Elizabeth E. Hoyt, *Choice and the Destiny of Nations* (New York: Philosophical Society, 1969) p. 56.

Thinking of William Graham Sumner's classic *Folkways*, a Chicago anthropologist placed Veblen and Sumner among those "economists [who] from time to time become so discontented with the limitations of formal theoretical economics [of their day] that they push past its limitations. They fall to investigating and describing the actual motives and conduct of men." (Robert Redfield, "Social Science among the Humanities," *Measure,* Winter 1950, p. 65).

[59] In a review of *The Theory of Business Enterprise,* in *Psychological Bulletin,* June 15, 1904, p. 398. The entire review is reprinted below in the Appendix. Tufts was co-author with John Dewey of the famous *Ethics.* See also the salute to the book's "brilliant analysis" in Edward L. Thorndike's "Psychological Notes on the Motives for Thrift," *The Annals,* January 1920, p. 213.

still alive, as Veblen . . . [has] shown."[60] So, too, an authority on the philosophy of art has written that Veblen is essentially correct in diagnosing many of the costly and useless complications of life, as an assertion of the intense craving for display of economic power through the exercise of conspicuous waste."[61]

---

[60] Popper, *The Open Society and Its Enemies* (Princeton, New Jersey: Princeton University Press, revised edition, 1950) p. 504.

[61] Helen Huss Parkhurst, *Beauty: An Interpretation of Art and the Imaginative Life* (New York: Harcourt Brace, 1930) p. 38.

To the criticism that Veblen's work was that of a philistine mind, the philosopher-turned-economist, Clarence E. Ayres, made a spirited reply in 1935: "I have heard economists urge it against Veblen as a criticism that he has none but a biological standard of value, as though this were a dreadful defect. If it is, I am prepared to throw in my lot with the biologists and the other scientists who are subject to similar defects and abandon economics, along with philosophy, to the shamans and medicine men for whom facts are not enough. What disturbs many people when the biological theme is sounded is the sincere conviction under which they labor that the application of biological standards to man necessarily means confining man's activities to those of the pig or dog —'mere eating and drinking'— and so forth, and so forth. Of course, it means nothing of the sort. Not even the activities of pigs are confined to eating and drinking. Such a notion is a gross libel on a pig and an even grosser one on man. Human activity is not limited to breathing because breathing is an essential human activity. Neither China nor the United States is reduced to mere 'animality' by the mention of the number of live organisms residing in each country." Drawing on Veblen's "antithesis between his celebrated 'instinct of workmanship' and 'the instinct of sportsmanship' of which *The Theory of the Leisure Class* is the fullest exposition" and identifying the former as "technological and related to work," Ayres argued that it is "to this [technological aspect of civilization] we owe all the material comforts, all the intellectual and artistic achievements, and all the progress we have attained." ["The Gospel of Technology," in *American Philosophy Today and Tomorrow,* edited by Horace M. Kallen and Sidney Hook (New York: Lee Furman, 1935) pp. 29, 35, 36].

Of course Veblen did not go so far in applauding technology for to him technology was an institution and subject like all institutions to deficiencies. Ayres has his own system but his approach stems from

Another type of interest was manifested in *The Theory of the Leisure Class* in the late 1920's, as Americans became increasingly concerned over the problem of leisure. *The Saturday Review* asked Veblen to review *The Threat of Leisure* (1926) by George Barton Cutten, president of Colgate University. The fact that the book included *The Theory of the Leisure Class* in the bibliography led the prestigious Playground and Recreation Association of America to invite Veblen to attend its five day conference in Atlantic City, on "the problems involved in America's use of leisure."[62] The editor wrote Veblen that the book "might offer opportunities for interesting comment."[63]

The book has had some other amusing uses. Thus a wealthy acquaintance, Joseph Halle Schaffner, with evident relish wrote Veblen in 1919:

> Dear Dr. Veblen,
>
> As I told you in New York, last month, I don't suppose that Lydia Pinkhamwise you collect testimonials to the efficacy of *The Leisure Class*, whether in small

[62] T. E. Rivers to Veblen, August 9, 1926, Thorstein Veblen Papers.

[63] Amy Loveman to Veblen, June 10, 1926, Thorstein Veblen Papers. A review not by Veblen appeared in the issue of September 25, 1926, under the title, "A Time-Killing Generation."

Veblen. As he puts it, "Institutionalism has always seemed to me to derive its distinctive pattern from Thorstein Veblen, to whose earlier works Walton Hamilton had introduced me when I was first associated with him in 1915. Others shared Veblen's tough-minded realism and his impatience with the phantasms of price theory. But insofar as institutionalism is characterized by a distinctive conception of the industrial economy—and of human behavior and organized society generally—it is Veblen's conception.... In attempting to clarify the 'Institutionalist conception' of economic process and economic policy I have followed his lead." [From Ayres's introduction to the forthcoming reprint of his earlier works, *Science the False Messiah* and *Holier than Thou* (New York: Augustus M. Kelley Publishers, 1972)].

doses or in large, but I thought the following from a letter from an eminently properly reared girl to whom I gave the book might interest you:

"You say I have failed in my bargain to tell you in detail what I think of Veblen's *Theory of the Leisure Class*. I can't tell you in detail now because all my energies, at present, are directed to hardening myself against the details of leisure class existence.

"Perhaps if I am able to tell you what has happened in this last week and what my future plans are, that will tell you more plainly than anything else what I think of Veblen's theory. When I read it in Washington I thought it was true, but as I was not leading a leisure class life at that time the poignancy of its truth did not strike me. But now the whole tremendous extent of its truth has struck me with such force that the light has almost blinded me.

"Of the utterly false circumstances under which I gave up everything that was fine and decent I need not enlarge. . . . They are as clear an example of the effects of the pecuniary standard of living on a sentimental, hysterical woman as could be given. I cannot accuse my mother of having lied because she has never had any consciousness that there was any truth, and I should have remembered that when I made my decision. At any rate, the veil I have always kept before my eyes has been lifted for me in this past week.

"Because she was my mother I suppose I had fancied her rather better than the women of her class. I see now that she is rather worse. We never have been able to get along but now we hardly speak. I keep silent for fear of saying what I think – and after all she is not well – she because she considers me very selfish because I don't babble with filial affection on my return from Washington and because for the good of both of us I stay with her as little as possible.

"I had never lived in the house more than two weeks at a time before, and because my stays were always so temporary and because it was my custom to ignore the unpleasant, I was never conscious of its tawdriness. If ever there was an example of outdoing one's neighbor, of hideous costliness for the sake of the expense, this house – all but my room, the nursery, and part of the library – is it. I feel every minute that I am in it that I shall vomit up my soul the next. My little cubbyhole in the Widener stacks and ———'s plain little house are my only refuge.

"I suppose when one sees the truth in a unified manner, applied not only to oneself and one's own past and future, but that of a whole class of society and through that class of the world – when one has even a glimpse for the first time, I suppose it is natural to be blinded. In a way I am entirely. I can't express myself at all. It is only with the greatest difficulty that I can write even this sketchy impression of what I am undergoing. For once in my feeble life even my garrulousness has ceased. If I could talk there would be no one to talk to and much as I want to write, I can't.

"The two thoughts that are continually in my mind are, 'How could any person who even thought she had a mind have lived as blindly, as stupidly, as self-deceivingly, and as cheaply as I have?' and 'There can no longer be any compromise.'

"Dad comes home from Europe next week. I shall give him a week in which to boast of his exploits and then he's got to know the truth. I think he ought to have a chance to help me. The only thing that mother and I have in common is our sex and a tendency to self-pity and sentimentality, so there wouldn't even be any point in trying to tell her the truth.

"I shall try to tell Dad as clearly as I can why I think it is wrong to live this way, and I shall ask him to give me a small income, one large enough on which to live decently, but not at all in the way I have lived. If he will do this I want to study for the next year beginning in July. If he won't do this, I shall have to do remunerative work and with the very small income I have acquired from gifts, will, etc., I could live quite decently. Of course, in the end he'll give in to me because mother would be afraid of what people would say.

"Elizabeth and I are going to live together in New York next winter and since her mother also lives there that will be an added bone of contention. However, we've both made up our minds to fight to the bitter end since we agree in thinking that and there can be no compromise. We do not believe that we can live this way and keep our intellectual integrity.

"It isn't that I am afraid of the scrap. After all, four months' pettiness and misery are a small price to pay for work and freedom and companionship. It's the dirty way they have of scrapping that nauseates me so. Politeness and civility and kindness are as much a part of the conspicuous display as the red satin furniture, and the only people to whom one can be rude and uncivil are those whom one doesn't have to impress; i.e., one's family. When I think of the days we shall sit at table with neither Mother or Dad speaking to me, the days when I shall have to ignore Mother's injured air – well, everything just looks black and miserable, and it does keep one from concentrating on one's work. It's all so infinitely complicated and it takes so much diplomacy and tact in which I am entirely lacking. Yet I am sure there can be no compromise. One can't wear $200 dresses knowing why one wears them and keep one's self-respect, and as long as I live with my mother or even away from her and allowing her to support me in the way she chooses, I can't help myself.

"Of course, I know I am feeling very violently now. Perhaps people can live in a house like this – I once thought it very beautiful – and still be working people, but I am sure they couldn't have the kind of companionship they craved, because the people one wants to know wouldn't want to come into a house like this. . . ."

I hope that you are going to have a very fine and satisfying summer and that when you go through Chicago you'll look me up.

With my kindest regards,
Sincerely yours,
Joseph Halle Schaffner[64]

Equally humorous from the other side was the note on "What is Waste?" on the editorial page of the New York *Times* in 1936 as the nation was slowly getting out of the depression that followed the crash of 1929, and about to enter another severe depression in 1937. The columnist argued that while many of the things we eat, for example, were "not designed for nutrition but for social status," such things "emphatically do not come under the head of the

[64] Schaffner to Veblen, July 13, 1919, Thorstein Veblen Papers.

Schaffner was an eminent industrialist. His father was the founder of the clothing manufacturing firm of Hart, Schaffner and Marx, a firm notable for its encouragement of economic research and a pioneer in unemployment insurance and collective bargaining.

late Thorstein Veblen's Conspicuous Waste. . . . The money that goes for display in food, display in housing, display in dress and other human activities is designed to preserve our self-respect. . . . The other day a dancer in a raided cabaret applied for relief and the authorities hastened to say that her rather advanced style of dancing excluded her from relief. But if professional cabaret dancing is a legitimate occupation in normal times there can be no question that it is legitimate in times of unemployment."[65]

On the other hand, one aspect of the far reaching grim implication of the book was revealed recently in a discussion of the trade in arms by government. "For the developing countries such purchases are pure conspicuous consumption – important prestige projects that always accompany newly-won independence, at the expense of education, medical services and housing."[66]

That this grim view of *The Theory of the Leisure Class* implied in the above has been inadequately probed in economic analysis was put sharply by the eminent Canadian economic historian, Harold A. Innis. He went as far as to exclaim that it had been unfortunate that the book had "proved his most popular work. . . . Its style was unfortunate, not because of its difficulty, but because of the manner in which the phrases stuck. From that work Veblen's reputation never recovered. He was regarded as the satirist with

---

[65] January 6, 1936. A Polish sociologist has recently noted: " 'Conspicuous consumption', which was discussed by Veblen in his classic work *The Theory of the Leisure Class,* is . . . concerned with the struggle of life as a criterion of class affiliation." [Stanislaw Ossowski, *Class Structure in the Social Consciousness* (New York: Free Press of Glencoe, 1963) p. 48].

[66] Anthony Hartley, "The War Business," review of George Thayer, *The International Trade in Armaments,* New York *Times,* September 21, 1969, p. 12.

barbed phrases. Conspicuous consumption, pecuniary emulation, became 'Veblenian' terms."[67]

It should be noted that the book or at least its language relatively early made its appearance on the stage and in novels. For its impact on playwrights a good example is the well received *Why Not?*, which was described in its billing as a "Comedy of Conventions," and in its printed version as a "Comedy of Human Nature versus Human Institutions." It was written by the Pulitzer prize winning playwright, Jesse Lynch Williams, and was presented by Equity Players in New York City in December 1922. The play is about two couples. One team (Mary and Leonard) is forced to become butler and maid because the husband while successful in love has proved to be unsuccessful as a writer. It turns out that their new master (Bill) was the first and presumably only true love of the maid, and the mistress (Evadne) a woman of wealth in her own right was in the same position as regards the butler. So plans are made for amicable divorces and remarriages. In the course of the discussions the butler and the maid present the advantages of the prospective change.

> Mary (sweetly). The nicest thing about Evadne is her husband.
>
> Leonard. Oh! Yes, indeed. Fine fellow. Just the man for you, Mary. At last, you will have the useful, well-ordered life you are fitted for – church work, charity, a beautiful home adorned with butlers and the orthodox forms of "conspicuous waste and honorific display," the nicest people believe in. You'll love it, and be happy, Mary.

[67] Innis, "The Work of Thorstein Veblen," 1929; reprinted in *Essays in Canadian Economic History,* edited by Mary O. Innis (Toronto: University of Toronto Press, 1956) p. 22.

> Mary. And you – now you can write, dear – with Evadne to inspire and pay for you.[68]

For the novel there is *The Ladies of Lyndon* (1923) by one of England's finest, enduring writers, Margaret Kennedy. Not far from the beginning of this book, there appear four striking pages of good Veblen. The characters are all from the leisure class, with one exception, Gerald Blair, who is a physician anxious to give up catering to the idle wealthy and serve the "proletariat." The following discussion takes place:

> [Gerald]: "All art is founded upon economics. . . . Every opinion you express betrays your social status. Your tastes are all acquired tastes; and acquired tastes are the mark of the man of *leisure*. . . . And what's an acquired taste but a piece of conspicuous waste? Waste of time. Proof that the acquirer has time to waste. Proof that he needn't work. Why do Chinese grandees let their fingernails grow? Why do they crush their wives feet? Same reason. . . ."
>
> [Lois]: "We are perfect monuments of conspicuous waste, I suppose."
>
> [Gerald]: "Of course you are. The ideal of beauty set up before the women of a leisured class is almost always incompatible with usefulness. They must look incapable of hard work; their dress must hamper them; their health is often injured; their duties as mothers are set aside. They are to be decorative luxuries, unfitted for any uses save one, and they must look it. Simply because that's a standard of appearance which can't be attained by the working classes. . . . Such women . . . women of the odalisque type, are symbols of an assured, un-

---

[68] Williams, *Why Not?* (Boston: Walter H. Baker, 1924) p. 67.

earned income. A piece of blatant waste like a scratch handicap."

[Lois]: "I know that in theory beauty and utility should go together. But practically I have never found that they do. You don't see anything to admire in those wretched, squalid women one sees in slums and places, surely? You don't call them beautiful?"

[Gerald]: "An overworked woman is a shocking sight. . . . Though not as bad as one who does no work at all. Our society is made up of extremes. We have lost all standards of how a woman should look."

[Hubert]: "A beautiful woman is a work of art in herself. But then we have learned that Blair has no use for works of art."

[Gerald]: "I never said that. . . . Works of art are all right. So are artists. But I don't include them in the leisured class. The man of leisure is an amateur. When he leaves off being that, he leaves off being a man of leisure. His art isn't an exploit, it's a profession."

[Hubert]: "I agree. But the amateur forms the cream of the artist's public."

[Gerald]: "I doubt it. He's a drone, and inclined to demand work which only drones can appreciate."

The discussion breaks off at this point. Toward the end of the book there occurs a powerful Veblenese scene. The young recently married wife of a baronet informs her mother that she is going to get a divorce and marry her first and true love, Gerald, and is willing to endure a precarious existence both economically and socially in America where he will work in a clinic. The mother tells her bluntly that she will never be able to face such a life. "You are the sort of woman who takes, who accepts sacrifice; the prize and privilege of successful men, not the helpmate of the failures. You were expensive to produce and you are even more expensive . . . to keep. Don't wince like that! It's a very useful type and stimulates nine tenths of the culture and civilization of the world."[69]

In the fine arts we have two British admirers of *The Theory of the Leisure Class:* Roger Fry (1866-1934), professor of fine art at Cambridge University, and his student, Quentin Bell, now professor of the history and theory of art at Sussex University. Both were identified with the famed Bloomsbury circle of *avant garde* artists and scholars that included John Maynard Keynes. Fry was a patriarch of the group, and Quentin Bell, the son of two charter members, was its historian.[69a]

We shall first take up Fry who was already a celebrity in the world of art at the turn of the century and dominated aesthetic thinking for a generation. In his most famous work, *Vision and Design* (1920), Veblen's concepts are easily recognized. For example, in discussing the so-called art objects in a railway refreshment room, Fry wrote: "Display is indeed the end and explanation of it all. Not one of those things has been made because the maker enjoyed the making; not one has been bought because its contemplation would give any one any pleasure, but solely because each of these things is accepted as a symbol of a particular social status. I say their contemplation can give no one pleasure; they are there because their absence would be resented by the average

[69] *The Ladies of Lyndon* (London: Heinemann, 1923) pp. 80-84, 287.

[69a] Bell has recalled in the history how Keynes gave him when a child the argument of what became *The Economic Consequences of the Peace*. "Keynes told me that he was going to Versailles to tell the allies that the Germans could not pay what they had not got." [*Bloomsbury* (London: Weidenfeld and Nicholson, 1968) p. 87].

man who regards a large amount of futile display as in some way inseparable from the conditions of that well-to-do life to which he belongs or aspires to belong. If everything were merely clean and serviceable he would proclaim the place bare and uncomfortable."

In an essay in 1931 on painting and sculpture, Fry described another and closely related social function of art as "the luxury value of the work. This is ultimately one of the ways in which the individual proclaims his social superiority over his fellow men. Professor Veblen, in his *Theory of the Leisure Class*, has developed and explained this phenomenon. People desire to proclaim that they belong to the dominant caste in society, the caste which directs and controls the working classes and enjoys the fruits of their labour. The most effective way to do this is to show that they possess the spoils of victory in the social struggle – objects which are rare and generally coveted, such as gold and precious stones, are the most obvious means of such display of social superiority. But objects which are the result of prolonged and skilled labour are equally, if not more, effective, since here also the supply is limited, and they are even more striking evidence that the efforts of the best of the workers are exercised for the owner's benefit. Works of art in which this particular demonstration of social superiority is envisaged we may call objects of luxury."[69b]

[69b] Fry, "The Arts of Painting and Sculpture," in *An Outline of Modern Knowledge*, edited by William Rose (London: Gollancz, 1931) pp. 913-914.

Bell, in calling attention to Veblen's influence on Fry, wrote that Fry "saw that the horrors of modern art and architecture are produced not by a hatred of beauty but by an injudicious love of it; that the trimmings and refinements added for social reasons, the polite suppression of sensibility, the falsifications of fashion, are more fatal to art than any crudity or ineptitude." [*Roger Fry* (Leeds, England: Leeds University Press, 1964) p. 15].

In discussing domestic architecture in *Vision and Design,* Fry made use in slightly different form of Veblen's concepts. "Homes are either builders' houses or architects' houses." Of course, "speculative builders" employed architects but they are the kind that "generally efface themselves behind the deadly conventionality and the bewildering fantasy of their facades. Architects' houses are generally built to the order of a gentleman who wishes his house to have some distinctive character, to stand out from the common herd of houses, either by its greater splendour or its greater discretion. The builder's house, like the dresses of the lower middle class, is generally an imitation of the gentleman's, only of a fashion that has just gone out of date and imitated badly in cheaper materials. . . . No one enjoys it, no one admires it, it is accepted as part of the use and wont of ordinary life. The gentleman's and architect's house is different. Here time and thought and perhaps great ingenuity and taste are employed in giving to the house an individual character. Unfortunately this individual character is generally terribly conscious of its social aspect, of how the house will look, not to those who live in it so much as to those who come to visit. We have no doubt outlived the more vulgar forms of this social consciousness, those which led to the gross display of merely expensive massiveness and profusion. . . . But its subtler forms are still apparent. They generally make them-

---

Sir Kenneth Clark interpreted the idea in the following words: "since the possession of an art object was a proof of power, the rich man wished to show what a superfluity of labour has gone to the making of his possession." After noting Fry's acknowledgment of the concept to Veblen, he wrote, Fry "might have argued the exact opposite: that the rich man wanted all signs of labour to be expunged from his possessions because any evidence of honest toil gave him a bad conscience." [Clark, "Introduction," in Fry, *Last Lectures* (New York: Macmillan, 1939) p. xxi].

selves felt in the desire to be romantic. As it requires much too much imagination to find romance in the present, one looks for it in the past, and so a dive is made into some period of history, and its monuments studied and copied, and finally 'adapted' to the more elaborate exigencies of modern life. But, alas, these divers into the past seem never to have been able to find the pearl of romance, for, ever since the craze began in the eighteenth century, they have been diving now here, now there, now into Romanesque, now into Gothic, now into Jacobean, now into Queen Anne. They have brought up innumerable architectural 'features' . . . , and still the owners and the architects, to do them justice, feel restless, and are in search of some new 'old style' to try. . . . Now style is an admirable thing, it is the result of ease and coherence of feeling, but unfortunately a borrowed style is an even stronger proof of muddled and befogged emotions than the total absence of style. The desire for a style at all costs, even a borrowed style, is part of that exaggerated social conscience which in other respects manifests itself in snobbery."

Fry's line of thinking was put sharply in a lecture at Oxford, *Art and Commerce* (1926). After mentioning Veblen's "remarkable book on *The Theory of the Leisure Class*," he declared: "According to him, the warrior caste in any primitive society had a right to the biggest spoils of successful warfare. A man was known as a member of that caste by the trophies he was able to display on his own person and the persons of his womenkind and dependents. Modern societies have not altogether forgotten these facts, and, consequently, the gentleman is known by the hints – sometimes blatant, sometimes subtle – which he throws out to all the world that he possesses spoils and is one of our conquering class. [Art objects] . . . of all kinds, from the gold bangles on the negro chieftain's wife to the splendid liveries of a lord's footmen, are the readiest means to make the situation plain. And the rarer and more expensive they are the better they answer their purpose. . . . Societies of all kinds . . . behave, . . . indeed, almost exactly like individuals in this respect. Big banking firms encase their offices in marble, and load their doors with chased bronze; town councils expand the façades of their town-halls, and have frescoes advertising the glory of the town's history painted on their walls; nations flaunt their Law Courts and pile up expensive national memorials in their capitals; and when kings stood for the nation, they advertised in innumerable ways the pre-eminence of their persons and the splendor of their reigns."[69c]

Turning to Bell, we find that his first book, *On Human Finery* (1947), was devoted to championing *The Theory of the Leisure Class* and its forerunner, the essay "The Eco-

[69c] *Art and Commerce* (London: published by Leonard and Virginia Woolf at the Hogarth Press, 1926) p. 8.

In his *Last Lectures,* Fry exclaimed: "Works of art have always had a great prestige value. Invading conquerors of a country do not only carry off gold and silver, they transport even at great cost large works of sculpture and painting. The possession of these works confers national prestige. And similarly the conquering millionaire carries off great works of art. He may of course desire to indulge in a purely spiritual pleasure in contemplating them, but he cannot be unaware that the knowledge he possesses them causes him to be envied and sought after, even by a great many people who are themselves but little moved by works of art. They give him personal prestige in the society to which he belongs." (*Last Lectures,* p. 38).

Something of Fry's spirit was expressed by a British economist in the following: "It is an easy matter to point to the many feudal survivals in a country like England, for example; but it is not quite so easy to trace their many variations in the customs and habits of the leisure class which modern capitalism has produced. *The Theory of the Leisure Class* was one of the first real essays in this branch of economic inquiry. And it is this which makes the book so important, and, one may add, so fascinating." (Joseph Wild, "Thorstein Veblen, Interpreter of the Leisure Class," *The Millgate,* October 1935, p. 28). The journal was a leading voice of the National Cooperative movement. It was published by the Cooperative Press.

nomic Theory of Woman's Dress" (1894), as providing "the most valuable contribution . . . to the philosophy of clothes." He chided the "historians of fashion" for having "strangely neglected" Veblen's work. More significant for our purposes was his comment that "the economists, who have perhaps realized something of the greatness of Veblen, tend, I think, to neglect his theory of dress, and perhaps to see in the subject little save a vain peering into bonnet shops and haberdasheries, a vent for the interminable vaporings of Teufelsdröckh." He emphasized that "no student of costume can possibly afford not to read and master *The Theory of the Leisure Class* and the posthumously published essay on dress in *Essays in Our Changing Order*." The basic question, he maintained, was one of expenditure. According to Bell:

> Conspicuous consumption is but the putting of wealth upon the person, conspicuous leisure the demonstration of a wealthy ease, and conspicuous waste of wealthy activity. Our feelings concerning the right spending of money on dress are, however, so blended with other emotions, our sense of beauty, martial glamour, sexual desirability, etc., that it is not easy to disentangle one factor from the other. It is difficult for us to tell to what extent these standards which Veblen calls the "pecuniary canons of taste" affect our judgment. And yet it is surely just that nice perception of financial worth which makes the difference between the civilized man, and the barbarians. On the face of it, it may seem that the bejewelled lady of Europe differs little from the savage with her necklace of beads. But although a diamond cross upon the bosom of a young beauty serves all the purposes of a Moroccan charm, leading us, in the one case, as in the other, to think well of the person, the principles, and the aspect of the wearer, the effect will be totally

> marred in *our* eyes if the ornament be a tawdry and vulgar thing of glass in "atrociously vulgar taste." Our sense of value cannot ever be quite divorced from our sense of cost or class.

Bell went on to examples of vicarious consumption:

> The dressing of very small children gives us an example of vicarious consumption in a very pure form. The "long clothes" of silk, satin, and lace, adorned with ribbons and bibbons on every side, which the children of the very rich may be seen wearing at christenings, etc., are presumably a matter of indifference, or perhaps even of vexation, to those who wear them. Indeed, the pretty clothes of small children generally would seem to be a matter of more pleasure and concern to the parents than to the instruments of display. . . .
>
> Servants, no less than children, are instruments of vicarious consumption, especially where their duties consist mainly of an exhibition of decorative idleness.

Bell concluded that "The value of Veblen as a philosopher of clothes lies in his economic approach to his subject, an approach which leads him directly to the formulation of those illuminating theories of social behavior which he calls the Laws of Conspicuous Consumption, Vicarious Consumption, and Conspicuous Leisure. He fails, so it seems to me, to explain the history of dress, when he relies upon notions which are not derived from economics, and when his attention has been too closely engaged by the conditions of his own time and country."

Despite the gradual, growing approval of *The Theory of The Leisure Class,* it should not be implied that there never have been further influential dissents after the attacks at the time of its original publication. One of the most interesting was the dissent of the Associate Justice of the United States Supreme Court, Oliver Wendell Holmes. Holmes has a deservedly great reputation for his role in the adaptation of the constitution to the social requirements of a modern industrial state, especially through his famous dissents in support of protective labor legislation. His views of Veblen are rather clearly stated in his published correspondence of 1917-1921 with a young teacher who admired both Veblen and the Justice. This was Harold Laski, then at Harvard and later at the London School of Economics and Politics.[70]

The first reference to Veblen in the exchange is in a letter from Laski. He asked the Justice: "Did you ever read Veblen on the Leisure Class? If you did what did you make of it?" Apparently Holmes's reply was lost; somewhat later it does appear that the Justice had read nothing of Veblen, but he had decided opinions about Veblen and his work based on ideas reported to be in *The Theory of the Leisure Class.* Thus in the Justice's first reference to Veblen in the correspondence, he wrote: "I won't attempt to continue the argument over Veblen now. He is remarkable and stimulating but I incline [blank] that you . . . overrate him – which may mean only that I am an old fogey." In the spring of 1919 he added: "I think that the ideals of men like Veblen besides cherishing illusions are ugly. No doubt I, like every-

---

[70] Laski was also prominent in the British Labor Party. Innis noted in 1929 that "the intelligentsia of the British Labor Party have each in turn paid tribute to Veblen's influence." (Innis, "The Work of Thorstein Veblen," p. 25).

In recent years it has been noted that Veblen's work, especially *The Theory of the Leisure Class,* exercised considerable influence on one of the most powerful leaders of the party, Aneurin Bevan. It seems he was even in the habit of giving copies of *The Theory of the Leisure Class* to socialist friends and fellow workers. (Michael Foot, *Aneurin Bevan, A Biography* (London: MacGibbon and Kee, 1962) pp. 36-37.

one, am influenced in my aesthetic preferences by my environment past and present – but I have intended to be detached. However, as the question at bottom is what kind of a world do you want, I, for whatever reason, do so far sympathize with the strug-for *lifeurs,* as the French put it, that in the ultimate necessary self-preference, I desire a world in which art and philosophy in their *useless* aspect may have a place. I say useless, to mark the point that they are ends in themselves. Of course I think them useful even in Veblen's world."

As might have been expected, he was enthusiastic over Mencken's attack. He wrote in January 1920: "Do you know H. L. Mencken's *Prejudices?* He I suspect would prove more or less a Philistine at bottom, but Lord with what malevolent joy do I see him smash round in the China shop – a pretty sound sense of real values as far as I have heard. (F. reads to me during solitaire.) I am happy to note that he has a smash at Veblen which I haven't read and at Amy Lowell which I have." The following month he continued in the same vein: Veblen "takes an ungodly time to say the few things that he has to say, that in my opinion amount to anything. I took malevolent pleasure in Mencken's *Prejudices,* which devotes a chapter to speaking ill of him. . . . With various foibles he [Mencken] has a sense of reality and most of his prejudices I share."[71]

The jurist's last reference to Veblen in the exchange is in Holmes's discussion of William Bayard Hale's *The Story of a Style* (1920), an influential book that attacked President Wilson's efforts to secure senate approval for the peace

---

[71] Laski to Holmes, April 25, 1917; Holmes to Laski, August 10, 1918, May 24, 1919, January 28, February 10, 1920. *Holmes-Laski Letters,* ed. by Mark DeWolfe Howe, 2 vols. (Cambridge, Mass.: Harvard University Press, 1953) I, 81, 162, 208, 236, 240.

treaty that included the League of Nations. The author used Veblenian literary techniques, with phrases at various points drawn from *The Theory of the Leisure Class*.[72] The Justice wrote that "I have read *The Story of a Style* – a scalding criticism of Wilson for the style of his writing – which so far gratified me. But having drawn and tasted blood, Mr. Hale went in to kill generally and I cared less the further I read. Also he worked on rather a crude acceptance of Veblen and Freud."[73]

So much have Veblen and the leisure class become synonymous that a popular historian has protested that "the role of the leisure class [in history] existed independently of Veblen."[74]

---

[72] "The learned prologue is significant of leisure and of aristocracy. This is not only because it wastes time at each repetition but also because it demonstrates to the audience that the speaker has all his life wasted time in acquiring the habit of circumlocution and in familiarizing himself with recondite and elegant modes of expression. . . . The sentence preface, like all affectations of polite letters, belongs in the category of conspicuous consumption, and is of quite special honorific value in the scheme of predatory life. It is in this little book assumed that it is unnecessary to argue what Mr. Veblen twenty years ago made clear in *The Theory of the Leisure Class* – that the leisure class culture, which maintains even to-day in human society, ranks of warriors, priests, sporting-men, parasites and delinquents, practices battle, religion and games, and believes in prowess, prayer and luck, is a survival of the savage or infantile mind, and is not motivated by reason. At every point, where we may pursue to their basis the peculiar phenomena of Mr. Wilson's style we shall be, it seems, in danger of coming upon irrationality." [Hale, *The Story of a Style* (New York: Huebsch, 1920) pp. 105-106].

[73] Holmes to Laski, August 22, 1921, *Holmes-Laski Letters*, I, p. 360. Interestingly four other Justices of the Supreme Court all of whom are roughly in the Holmes tradition, had a high opinion of Veblen's work. They are Hugo Black, Louis Brandeis and Felix Frankfurter, and a member of the present court, William O. Douglas.

[74] Barbara Tuchman, "Can History be Served up Hot?" New York *Times*, March 8, 1969.

We can appropriately close this section of supplementary notes on *The Theory of the Leisure Class* with the amusing experience of a New York bookstore in trying to sell Veblen a copy. The time was in the immediate post World War I period. The lady bookseller in her reminiscences recalled "A man used to appear every six or eight weeks quite regularly, an ascetic, mysterious person with keys to unlock things, I took him to be, and with a gentle air. He wore his hair long and looked Scandinavian. I do not know just why or when I made him a Swedenborgian minister. He always bought interesting things – Greek texts, the less read work of William Morris; and when we did not have what he wanted, he asked us to order it, and a long-legged rosy young girl with long straight braids came for it. His niece I thought. I decided he lived with his sister – a spare Swedish woman with a cool bright face, serious not cold, and eyes like clear glass, very erect and with a small hat like a Zorn portrait of a lady I had once seen at a Swedish exhibition. I used to try to interest him in economics. The clergy should be informed

---

She grants that if a book's analysis exercises substantial influence on the course of development, then the writer becomes a maker of history. That *The Theory of the Leisure Class* helped to give Veblen that role is most strikingly shown in an advertisement by the University of Chicago Press, New York *Times*, December 15, 1963. It was headed "Great Moments at Chicago." Then came a picture of a stick of dynamite encased in candy wrappers. The accompanying note read: "In 1899 a Stick of Dynamite Went off in a Rented Room." Then came an explanatory note: "By day he taught economics at the University of Chicago. By night he labored alone in a small room rented from a friend. His first book was to shatter the foundations of economic classicism, with reverberations that still shake the world today. The book was *The Theory of the Leisure Class,* its author – called by Lewis Mumford 'a stick of dynamite wrapped up . . . to look like a stick of candy' – Thorstein Veblen. Once again, the quietly pondered pages of a book had released a vast and revolutionary power."

on these things, I thought, and he was an especially remote clergyman. I plied him from time to time with important importations. I even once tried to get him to begin with *The Theory of the Leisure Class.* I explained to him what a brilliant port of entry it is to social consciousness. But it became clear that if he was ever to be interested in sociology and economics, he would not be interested in them by me. He listened attentively to all I said and melted like a snow drop through the door. One day he ordered a volume of Latin hymns.

" 'I shall have to take your name because we will order this expressly for you,' I told him. 'We shall not have an audience for such a book as this again in a long time, I am afraid.'

" 'My name is Thorstein Veblen,' he breathed rather than said."[75]

The Theory of Business Enterprise

Veblen's second book owes its origin in good part to another economist in the main tradition, the highly respected Professor F. W. Taussig of Harvard. In January 1900, Taussig suggested to the president of the American Economic Association, Richard T. Ely, that he invite Veblen to give a paper at the annual meeting of the Association in December on a "theoretic subject" that was characteristic of Veblen's major works.[76] Taussig declared that Veblen "has done some writing of late on what he calls the difference between 'productive' and 'pecuniary' activity. The distinction is a novel one, although following the same direction as the writings

[75] Madge Jenison, *Sunwise Turn: A Human Comedy of Bookselling* (New York: Dutton, 1923) pp. 125-126.

[76] The Taussig-Ely and Veblen-Ely correspondence are in the Ely Papers, State Historical Society of Wisconsin.

of Marx and his associates.[77] I think a paper by Veblen, setting forth his conclusions, would be a fresh contribution and would stimulate interesting discussion . . . I think well of Veblen's work and believe it would be worth while to interest him in the active work of the Association."

Taussig's suggestion was strongly backed by the eminent economist and historian, Charles H. Hull of Cornell, who as Secretary-Treasurer of the Association had charge of publications.[78] Hull informed Ely: "I believe that Veblen would give us a good paper, and that it would be likely to lead to a discussion, as Taussig thinks. If you write him to read, please make it clear that the Association now *expects to have the right of the first publication* of the papers presented before it. This has not always been the case, as you know, and on account of Veblen's connection with *The Journal of Political Economy*, it seems desirable to avoid misunderstanding."[79] Ely then sent an invitation to his one-time Johns Hopkins graduate student.

Veblen in reply expressed willingness to present a paper on "a theoretical topic like the one in question. . . . I beg to make the suggestion that the caption of the paper should read: 'The Distinction between Industrial and Pecuniary Activity,' rather than as formulated by Professor Taussig." Veblen, it should be noted, had deftly changed the title so as to accord more closely with the heart of his own thinking, and shortly afterwards he made it even closer by substituting "employments" for "activity." As meeting time approached, he found that the manuscript's length far exceeded

[77] Later Taussig spoke of Veblen's work as being "semi-socialistic" like that of Werner Sombart. (Taussig to Roswell C. McCrea, November 25, 1908, McCrea Papers, in possession of Joseph Dorfman).

[78] Hull is especially notable for his classic edition of Sir William Petty's economic writings (1899; Augustus M. Kelley Publishers, 1964).

[79] Hull to Ely, January 27, 1900, Ely Papers.

the customary limit. In the middle of November he wrote Ely, "You were good enough to honor me with a request that I prepare a paper on the distinction between industrial and pecuniary employments. I have written out such a paper but in my endeavor to present the matter, I regret very much to say, I have greatly exceeded the limits which the occasion would impose. At the same time I find myself unable to abridge the paper to the requite extent, without crippling the argument to such an extent as to leave it of little or no effect. I shall accordingly have to forego the honor intended for me, and beg you to leave my name off the program." Ely proposed a compromise which can be gathered from Veblen's reply. "I shall act on the suggestion that you are kind enough to make: submit the paper in full for printing [in the *Proceedings*] and present the subject in the form of an abstract, not to take more than some twenty to thirty minutes." Veblen never did present an abstract, for pleading illness, he did not appear, but the fifty-two page typed ms., which would take more than an hour to read, was published under the abbreviated title of "Industrial and Pecuniary Employments."[80] The paper exercised no little influence. Thus Mitchell recalled that it "had a good deal to do with opening my eyes . . .," to see the problem "in a much larger way"; that is, in the context of a study of the money economy. Even his famous book, *Business Cycles* (1913), which Mitchell viewed as a section of the larger investigation, owes much to the Veblen paper.[81]

[80] *Publications of the American Economic Association*, Series 3, volume II (1901) pp. 190-235, reprinted in Veblen's *The Place of Science in Modern Civilisation and Other Essays*, selected by Leon Ardzrooni, W. C. Mitchell and W. W. Stewart (1919; New York: Russell & Russell, 1961) pp. 279-323.

[81] Mitchell to J. M. Clark, August 9, 1928, in *Methods in Social Science*, edited by Stuart A. Rice (Chicago: University of Chicago Press, 1931) p. 679.

The paper directly provided the backbone for Veblen's second book. On July 10, 1901, six months after the session, he informed his publisher that he had prepared a "revised and amplified form of the paper" for a proposed book of 36,000 to 37,000 words, which would be titled "The Captain of Industry and His Work." Taking no chances on being outwitted in the matter of the manufacture of the book, Veblen added "I beg to suggest that in case the manuscript is accepted, I should like to have it appear in a form resembling the limp-cloth covered form of the *Temple Classics* published by J. M. Dent & Co. of London [and distributed in the United States by Macmillan], but without vignette or illuminated title page. It should probably also be printed in larger type than what is usual in the *Temple Classics* (perhaps 10 point) and should be a trifle more freely leaded, so that the page would contain some 210-230 words." The publisher rejected the ms., even though Veblen offered a guarantee. It is interesting to note that one of the publisher's readers, who had accepted *The Theory of the Leisure Class*, now rejected *The Theory of Business Enterprise*. He was a man of reputation in both economics and sociology.

Veblen then proceeded to prepare a much larger study of over 100,000 words. Two years later, J. Laurence Laughlin, head of the University of Chicago department of political economy, performed the same role for this ms. that Davenport had done for that of *The Theory of the Leisure Class*. Laughlin was one of the most conservative of economists but he had a high respect for his colleague's abilities and his judgment of people.[82] He informed his publisher, Charles Scribner's Sons, in March 1903 that the house should con-

[82] Laughlin wrote Veblen in 1908 that "your advice as to Hoxie has worked well." (Laughlin to Veblen, August 27, 1908, Mitchell Papers, Columbia University Libraries).

tact Veblen for the ms. Thereupon Scribner's wrote Veblen that when he had completed the "new and important book," of which Laughlin had written, the firm would like to see it.[83]

In the summer, Veblen sent a manuscript with a slightly revised title: "The Theory of Modern Business"; in the winter he recalled it for revision, and, after dropping the last chapter and a number of passages and paragraphs in other chapters, returned the ms. in February 1904. It was now reduced to 100,000 words and bore its present title, "The Theory of Business Enterprise." The house accepted it. The matter of the guarantee, however, took a little time to settle. Veblen complained in January 1904 that the firm's proposal seemed "somewhat onerous, so much so indeed that I may find myself obliged to resort to a less advantageously placed publishing house merely to avoid the initial expense." It was finally agreed in March 1904 that Veblen would pay initially the cost of the plates.[84] As in the case of *The Theory of the Leisure Class,* he carefully scrutinized all the details of the manufacture of the book, including the selection of type, the number of lines on a page, the type size of the chapter titles, the binding, etc. He found, however, as before that the publishers had their own ideas on most of these matters. On receiving the first galleys in March, he wrote: "The proof looks well, though there are an unnecessary number of printer's errors. I regret that you should have found it necessary to change from the type and page first agreed on,

---

[83] The papers of Scribner's are in the Princeton University Library.

[84] The cost of the plates turned out to be $552.95. Veblen was forced to postpone full payment for a few months because as he informed the firm in January 1905 "a sale of property from which I expected to pay the entire amount last November was delayed by circumstances and finally fell through."

particularly as the cost of the plates should have been appreciably smaller for that type and page. The present type seems to me one point larger than necessary, and the page smaller than necessary. With the type as it stands, however, I beg to suggest that the type of the running title should be one point smaller than it is, and my preference would be for a page not less than two lines longer than the sample. Indeed, I think 30 lines, making a full 8vo. page, would be preferable to the present form."

As he had requested, Veblen received from the printer galley proofs as well as page proofs. He said there would be several insertions by way of footnotes, especially "a few additional mathematical footnotes to go in Chapter VI and VII, and I find that your proof readers are particularly unreliable on the mathematical footnotes." Such insertions would disarrange the paging, if that was to be the only proof that he would receive. The publisher explained when presenting the bill for the plates that their actual cost of $552.95 had considerably exceeded the estimate in great part because of the corrections; in particular "the recasting of the formulae in the footnotes required more time than we anticipated."

Veblen had an amusing discussion with the publisher over the likely character of the market. The publisher, in presenting the advantages of a more elegant (and thus more costly) volume, thought that considerable quantities would be sold to "the business man of scholarly and refined tastes." The firm concluded this letter with regrets that the cost of the plates was so much larger than the original estimate, "but we think that the greatly improved appearance of the book as compared with the model which we first selected will prove to be worth more than the difference and will be reflected in the reception which will be accorded to the volume both by the press and the public."[85] Veblen, on the other hand, held that "you overestimate the probable sales of the volume to the 'man in the street.' I anticipate that the sales will be practically confined to university circles and to the readers of . . . *The Theory of the Leisure Class.*" In this letter of May 21, he went on to say that "to this class of purchasers the date of publication will be a small hindrance. For university readers, I believe, the publication in June would be rather fortunate than otherwise, as the book would in that case be fully brought to their knowledge before the opening of the school year in the fall."[86] This of course suggested, as the publisher interpreted the letter, that Veblen believed that the book's market would be as a textbook. Actually, however, as Veblen informed the sociologist and economist, E. A. Ross, an admirer, "the book was published with some misgivings – chiefly that it would pass unnoticed by the gild of economists to whom it was addressed."[87]

---

[85] Veblen discussed the question of the desirability of an index with the publisher. He wrote the firm in March 1904, "will you kindly let me have your advice as to whether the book should have an index. I am inclined to omit it." Scribner's agreed with him.

[86] The book was published on September 11, 1904.

[87] Veblen to Ross, October 20, 1904, Ross Papers, State Historical Society of Wisconsin.

Ross, shortly afterwards, was considering finding a haven for Veblen at the University of Nebraska, where he was then stationed. Among those whose opinions he sought on the matter was Albion Small, the sociologist and a power at the University of Chicago, where Veblen's position was precarious. He agreed with Ross that Veblen was a genius, but went on to say that Veblen "has, however, his share of the peculiarities of genius, and . . . the wisdom of adding him to another faculty would of course depend on careful measure of the personal equation." (Small to Ross, February 3, 1905, Ross Papers).

Ross in his reminiscences stated: "Delving into bushels of dull economic books I have sometimes wondered what a *man of genius* would do in the field. Thorstein Veblen whom I first met in 1905, gives the

In accordance with this attitude, Veblen urged the publisher to send review copies to fifteen leading professional journals – including a few high level socialist ones – in continental Europe."[88] The publisher, however, replied that "it is not customary for us to send review copies to continental journals and periodicals, experience having shown that such reviews as are published are of little assistance to the sale of a book in this country."

Veblen had hopes of a relatively large British market. He sent the publisher a letter from Hobson, suggesting the desirability of placing *The Theory of Business Enterprise* on sale in England and doing something toward its circulation there. Scribner's replied that it had tried to secure a British house for the book, but with no success. If Hobson could possibly find one, the firm "would make the very lowest possible terms for sheets." Perhaps Veblen might have had the

[88] Veblen supplied the publisher with their names, addresses and editors. The following is the list of the journals with their place of publication: *Archiv für Sozialwissenschaft und Sozialpolitik,* Leipzig; *Annales des Sciences Sociales,* Brussels; *Zeitschrift für Sozialwissenschaft,* Berlin; *Statsvetenskaplig Tidskrift,* Lund; *Statsökønømisk Tidskrift,* Christiania (now Oslo); *Die Neue Zeit,* Berlin; *Annales de l'Ecole libre des sciences politiques,* Paris; *La Revue Socialiste,* Paris; *L'Humanité Nouvelle,* Neuilly-sur-Seine; *Rivista Italiana di Sociologia,* Rome; *La Riforma Sociale,* Turin; *Giornale degli Economisti,* Rome; *Sozialistische Monatshefte,* Berlin; *Nationalökønømisk Tidskrift,* Copenhagen; *Ekonomisk Tidskrift,* Uppsala.

answer. A genius is just what this slow-spoken ironic Veblen was. He was so original that he could stroll up and pick gold nuggets out of a ledge I had looked at dully a hundred times. No one in a social science can afford to dispense with the Canon of Conspicuous Waste he developed in *The Theory of the Leisure Class.* And then his *Theory of Business Enterprise* – what insight, originality, and wit!" [*Seventy Years of It: An Autobiography* (New York: Appleton-Century, 1936) p. 248].

Ross included *The Theory of the Leisure Class* and "Industrial and Pecuniary Employments" in his select bibliography in *Foundations of Sociology* (1905).

dubious satisfaction of feeling vindicated as to the probable readership had he seen the following letter from the venerable British house of John Murray: "We fear it is too theoretical and the style somewhat too heavy to succeed – in our hands at least." The letter noted that the judgment referred "to the commercial aspect only – in other respects we like it and consider that it contains most valuable information."[89] Some American economists equated "too theoretical" with trash, in the case of Veblen. Thus one of these, on seeing the announcement of Veblen's forthcoming treatise on the jacket of another Scribner's book, informed the house that he was distressed that the cover of a book by a man of "high scientific reputation" should carry the notice of the work of a man of "low scientific reputation like Professor Veblen."[90]

The Theory of Business Enterprise had a steady but small market; until it achieved paperback status in 1958, the total sales for the fifty-four years was in round numbers 10,000 (5,000 after 1934). The publisher reported on December 17, 1917, that the year's sale of 153 copies was the largest since its first year of publication. The slight rise during the first severe post World War I depression led Veblen to make a characteristic remark. As recorded in Mitchell's Diary of April 1921, Veblen said the book "was out of date through development of the business situation and hence the sales were twice as large as in any previous year."[91]

[89] A. H. Hallam Murray to L. W. Bangs, July 16, 1904, in Scribner's Papers.

[90] Arthur Twining Hadley to Scribner's, March 26, 1904, Scribner's Papers.

[91] The Diary is in the W. C. Mitchell Papers.

Up to May 28, 1934, the sales were 4,840. The yearly sales from 1908 to December 18, 1917, were as follows: 1908 – 49; 1909 – 42; 1910 – 133; 1911 – 142; 1912 – 22; 1913 – 81; 1914 – 113; 1915 – 71; 1916 – 95; 1917 – 153.

We have some information on one of the book's most explosive and controversial discussions, that of credit, or as Veblen called it, "loan credit." Professor Mitchell once suggested to the editor that the closest forerunner to Veblen was *A Few Doubts as to the Correctness of Some Opinions Generally Entertained on the Subjects of Population and Political Economy* (1821). I shall quote the opening paragraph and closing sentence of Mitchell's extract from that work, which he titled "Theory of Loan Credit."

> Commercial paper I consider to be nothing more than a register of commercial transactions. Its amount will depend not so much on the real exchanges, on those which are necessary for the supply of the consumer, (the only legitimate object of commerce), as on the imaginary exchanges, the purchases which are made with a view to sell again. These are the only transactions which require credit, the only dealings which are obliged to produce their vouchers. . . . Commercial paper, we have seen, is quite useless; it is only a register of all the exchanges which take place in property; its effects are absolutely null; it neither adds to the amount of property to be exchanged, nor to its value; it does not facilitate real exchanges, it only tends to increase imaginary transactions.[92]

Veblen's formulation is perhaps more sophisticated. To quote Mitchell's description of Veblen's theory of credit:

> [An] impressive point . . . is that the whole modern

---

[92] The name of the author on the title page is "Piercy Ravenstone," but it is generally accepted now that this is a pseudonym. The editor has advanced the hypothesis that he was the British economist, the Reverend Edward Edwards. See Joseph Dorfman, "Piercy Ravenstone and His Radical Tory Treatise," introductory essay to reprint of *A Few Doubts* (New York: Augustus M. Kelley Publishers, 1966) pp. 1-23. The Mitchell extracts are given in the introductory essay.

structure of credit, which is so strictly a feature of modern business enterprise, does not add to the country's equipment for production. That . . . seems at first blush a most extraordinary statement. It is a view which . . . runs counter to a common implication, if not to a common explicit contention of modern theory. We take it for granted that credit is a necessary and serviceable part of the arrangements for producing goods. Veblen does not argue that credit is not necessary to modern business. On the contrary, he argues that it is precisely necessary to modern business, not to modern industry as such. The business man in his effort to make profits is compelled practically to use borrowed funds, because thereby he can enhance his profits, and any opportunity applied to business enterprise for increasing the amount of business, and thereby increasing the amount of profits he can make, is something which every business man under competitive conditions must take advantage of. That is to say, if a business man borrows and thereby increases the amount of business that he can do and thus the amount of profits he can make, he must enter into competition with all the other people who are trying to sell the same kind of goods in the same market. Veblen points out, however, that the heaping up of credits by itself does not increase either our knowledge of technical processes or stock of machinery. It is a fact of an altogether different order from the material facts and the knowledge which relate to productive efficiency.

Only one concession does he make to the claim that credit increases production. That admission, however, is, I am inclined to think, very important. He admits that in so far as credit transfers control over material factors of production from people who are not in a posi-

> tion to utilize them to advantage to people who can do so, just that far does credit increase productive resources but here again it involves productive resources not in a material sense, but as preventing certain uncomfortable consequences which would result from the institution of ownership. [A person] . . . may be an orphan quite destitute of any power to use property which has come into . . . [his] hands by inheritance. In that case, under the institution of private property, this item of resource for production must remain unused unless some means can be found for transferring it to some person who does have the capacity for utilizing it. Credit does admit of such transfers, so that it prevents a restriction upon production which could result from the institution of property, of property getting into the hands of people who could not utilize it. That far credit is productive, but only that far, on Veblen's showing.

Another point on credit was its major role in making possible that in "the typical case, the large corporation is really run to make money primarily for the people who happen to be in control"—to use Mitchell's description of Veblen's argument.[93]

---

[93] *Types of Economic Theory: From Mercantilism to Institutionalism,* edited by Joseph Dorfman, 2 volumes (New York: Augustus M. Kelley Publishers, 1967, 1969) II, 665-667.

Another writer has formulated Veblen's theory of credit in more conventional terms. After declaring that Veblen introduced the "inflationary" approach, he goes on to say "Veblen made a lasting contribution to the theory of credit by emphasizing that in the actual financial phase of capitalism the creation of an artificial investing power tends to cause not only a swelling of money substitutes and thus a certain credit inflation but also an abnormal rise of the market value of securities which vest formal capital. . . . Veblen's theory of credit has practically the entire dynamic theory of credit in its background. Yet, it is especially congenial to the actual financial phase of capitalism, in which the vendible securities, that vest formal capital, represent an impor-

Another of Veblen's basic contentions — that the traditional distinction between capital and credit could hardly be maintained in discussing the dynamics of business enterprise — has been echoed recently by a leading British monetary theorist. He declared that "a distinction between 'credit' and 'capital' is no more helpful in monetary analysis than the distinction between banks and other creators of credit."[94]

An economic statistician suggested in a private letter that Veblen may have acquired the unusual term "loan credit" from his and Veblen's Yale graduate teacher in economics, William Graham Sumner.[95] "Veblen uses the term loan

[94] R. S. Sayers, "Monetary Thought and Monetary Policy in England," *The Economic Journal,* December 1967, p. 713.

[95] As I noted in the Veblen book, Veblen and Sumner had high respect for each other. The Veblen-Jameson correspondence reveals that Veblen admired Sumner not only as an economist but also as an historian. He wrote Jameson May 16, 1883, that "Professor Sumner's two-year course of lectures on United States political and financial history will be completed at the close of this year. He is now at Hayes's election [to the presidency]. I have liked the lectures very much and think they have grown more interesting the farther they have gone on."

Other letters in the correspondence further reveal that Sumner was a major factor in making Yale attractive to Veblen. In his first letter from Yale to Jameson (April 2, 1882) he wrote "I am taking political economy with Prof. Sumner, two classes in philosophy under Pres. [Noah] Porter, and am very well pleased with both, particularly with Prof. Sumner." In a later letter (May 16, 1883), after mentioning that he had reluctantly applied for a fellowship in philosophy at Johns Hopkins at President Porter's urging, he said "I am still of the opinion that on the whole Yale is preferable to J. H. U. so far as Political Economy goes, but as you know in the event of getting a fellowship there would be other circumstances to be taken into consideration."

---

tant merchandise. Furthermore, very modern is his idea that price inflation can be deepened by an inflation of formal capital." [Boris Ischboldin, *Economic Synthesis* pp. 373, 386-387]. He referred to *The Theory of Business Enterprise* and *Absentee Ownership* as the basis for his discussion of Veblen.

credit rather than simply credit and this usage may well have come from Sumner, who used it extensively in his lectures. Sumner had a genius for picking concepts from earlier writers and phrasing them in a striking way."[96]

Though the sales were never spectacular, it continued to intrigue some of the most eminent economists and to influence promising minds. Taussig, for example, remained greatly interested in it. While Mitchell was lecturing at Harvard in 1909, he wrote Mrs. Gregory that

> Taussig wants me to take over Economics 2 for three weeks. This is his pet course. The men read the standard theorists and he carries on a Socratic discussion in class. He wants me to go through Veblen's *Business Enterprise* with them. If it were any other writer I should decline the invitation and spend the time on my own reading. But I am rather anxious to see how a capable body of students, familiar with such men as [John Stuart] Mill, [Alfred] Marshall, [Eugen von] Böhm-Bawerk and [J. B.] Clark, will take Veblen: and I am much more anxious to see that Veblen is presented in a sympathetic fashion. So I will do as Taussig wants me to and hand back a class which will be restive under the type of economic theory dispensed here. That would be fine, tho' it might not make me friends. [Thomas Nixon] Carver, I know, would not approve [his colleague] Taussig's plan and still less would he approve my scheme of improving the opportunity.[97]

---

[96] John P. Norton to Joseph Dorfman, December 12, 1933.

[97] Mitchell to Mrs. Warren Gregory, March 24, 1909, from transcript of extracts of letters from Mitchell to Mrs. Gregory, made by Mrs. Lucy Sprague Mitchell in 1949; a copy is in Joseph Dorfman's possession.

Carver had written a scathing review of *The Theory of Business Enterprise*, but at least in class he seems to have thought *The Theory of the Leisure Class* of some importance. For "Economics 3, Factors

A week later, he regretfully wrote to Mrs. Gregory that Taussig dropped the proposal, because he "had gone off upon another line with Economics 2. You know that he is engaged in writing a general treatise. He seems to have developed some views regarding the unintelligibility of Marshall's theory of production, which he is anxious to exploit— perhaps merely to try out in class. If he holds to that course, I shall . . . miss the chance to inoculate the class with Veblen."

Mitchell, while working on his landmark book, *Business Cycles* (1913), reported to the same correspondent that *The Theory of Business Enterprise* was playing a vital role even in the most technical aspects of his study, "particularly the crucial . . . [chapter] on the breeding of crises. The theory propounded is fairly close to Veblen's on the most important point – a decline in prospective net earnings leads to a shrinkage of business credit and thus brings on a liquidation of

---

in Social Progress," he included it in the reading list – *Printed Reading and Collateral References 1904-1905* – though his use of it was somewhat unusual. A student in recording Carver's explanations of why people did not read the Bible (session of January 16, 1905) wrote: "A second reason, . . . besides the one of reaction, is the craze for distinction, which leads people to throw over the Bible as 'middle class morality' and to distinguish themselves by being wicked. Also we say 'Drunk as a Lord.' Also we call particularly artistic those books and plays which tamper with the seventh commandment. The intellectual elite want to 'be so wicked.' It has come to be a sort of fashion to ignore our religion, first by those who wish to be distinguished, and second by those who want to be like them." [In the margin in the middle of the paragraph the note taker wrote: "(Veblen's Theory of the Leisure Class)." The note taker was Nicholas Kelley, who became Assistant United States Secretary of the Treasury under President Wilson and later general counsel of the Chrysler Corporation. He was the son of the famous social reformer Florence Kelley. The notes are in the possession of his son Augustus M. Kelley.

outstanding accounts. . . . The real wonder is, however, how Veblen divined the facts without ascertaining them."[98]

Further, *The Theory of Business Enterprise* influenced Mitchell's presentation of the leading features or "conspectus of the economic order," both in the first edition and in the first part of the revision, *Business Cycles: The Problem and Its Setting* (1927). In short, both editions, as J. M. Clark put it, betrayed "symptoms of Veblenian influence: particularly in the distinction between technical and pecuniary occupations, in the subordination of technical to profit-making considerations, in the emphasis on the motive of profit-making and the planlessness of production without corresponding emphasis on the checks and ordering influences of the 'natural economic laws' of the traditional economics. Competition is mentioned but not normal competitive price, and the 'law of supply and demand' is conspicuously absent." Clark commented that "One may conjecture that Mitchell's natural leanings received aid and comfort from Veblen's

---

[98] Mitchell to Mrs. Gregory, May 2, 1911, in Lucy Sprague Mitchell, *Two Lives* (New York: Simon and Schuster, 1953) p. 178.

In the first edition of *Business Cycles,* Mitchell noted that "Professor E. R. A. Seligman has worked out a theory of crises which resembles Veblen's in the run of ideas and in phraseology. See his introduction to *The Currency Problem and the Present Financial Situation,* a series of addresses delivered at Columbia University, 1907-1908." [*Business Cycles* (Berkeley: University of California Press, 1913) p. 15].

Professor Mitchell found that Irving Fisher much later developed a somewhat similar theory of crises which he called the debt-deflation theory of depression. As I wrote elsewhere, "[In] *Booms and Depressions* (1932) he [Fisher] explained that the critical factor in determining the swing of the cycle was the expansion or liquidation of debts. . . . After Wesley C. Mitchell called Fisher's attention to Veblen's view in *The Theory of Business Enterprise,* Fisher generously acknowledged that Veblen came nearest to his position." [*The Economic Mind in American Civilization,* 5 volumes (1946-1959; Augustus M. Kelley Publishers, 1967-1969) V, 685].

doctrine of replacing assumed harmonies by an observed sequence of matter-of-fact cause and effect."[99]

Mitchell continued to have deep respect for Veblen's opinions on business cycles. In his Diary under December 23, 1922, he recorded, "To see Veblen with whom I discussed [Hudson] Hastings's theory of crises [as presented in his *Cost and Profits*]." In his lectures on business cycles at Columbia in the 1920's, he noted the technical importance of Veblen's profits theory of recession: "Recession flows from the guidance of industrial activity by profits," or, "to use a shorthand form, from a discrepancy between current and future capitalization." In other words, "Veblen's is a significant variant or type of the profits theory. Each of the types explains how some class or classes of business enterprise may suffer such losses as to embarrass them, alarm creditors, produce a cautious policy regarding future commitments or start liquidation. . . . Veblen's theory [is] of special value as showing the mechanism through which any of the changes analyzed by other theorists produces its effects."[100]

---

[99] "Wesley C. Mitchell's Contribution to the Theory of Business Cycles," in *Methods in Social Science*, pp. 666, 669.

Mitchell in an outline in 1937 for his course on Current Types of Economic Theory at Columbia contended that Veblen contributed to the advance of the theory of competition: "Veblen's point, expressed especially in *The Theory of Business Enterprise* . . . and *Absentee Ownership* . . . [is] that competition may develop salesmanship where expenditures do not add to the national dividend." (*Types of Economic Theory*, I, 584).

[100] Outlines, "Business Cycles," October 30, 1923, April 5, 1927, Mitchell Papers.

Mitchell noted in his Diary under October 31, 1923: "Attended business cycle dinner of American Statistical Association. Sat between Veblen and Davenport."

So little aware are the present generation of economists of the relationship between Veblen and Mitchell that one of the most prominent could write in 1960 that "the lasting achievements of . . . Mitchell [in

Another expert on business cycle theory, Alvin H. Hansen, beginning with his Ph. D. dissertation, *Cycles of Prosperity and Depression*, found useful leads in *The Theory of Business Enterprise*. In *A Guide to Keynes* (1953), he suggested that J. M. Keynes, in contending that the "expectation of a lower interest in the future may have some 'depressing effect' upon

---

business cycles] . . . would not seem to reside in anything that [he] had particularly in common with Veblen." [Paul A. Samuelson, "American Economics," in *Postwar Economic Trends in the United States*, edited by Ralph E. Freeman (New York: Harper, 1960) p. 38].

A similar comment of Professor Samuelson as to the relationship between Veblen and John R. Commons seems also questionable. A leading student of Commons's type of institutional theory has pointed out, for example, that a fundamental basis of Commons's economics is essentially similar to one propounded by Veblen a quarter of a century earlier. As Professor Kenneth H. Parsons put it, "[Commons] has traced out what appears to him to be the many fallacies in economic thought which have been involved in the failure to distinguish things from ownership, producing from withholding, in short, what Commons calls efficiency from scarcity." Then Parsons added in a footnote "This is evidently Veblen's distinction between industry and business." ["John R. Commons's Point of View," 1942; reprinted in Commons's posthumous *The Economics of Collective Action*, edited by Parsons (New York: The Macmillan Company, 1950) p. 369.

A more recent episode indicates that Veblen's distinction is periodically being discovered by able minds. Thus a writer noted in 1966 that "the I.L.O. [International Labor Organization] studies make the point that low productivity is frequently caused by top management's concern with the commercial and financial affairs of the firm rather than with the running of the factory. The latter was frequently treated as a very subordinate task." (Harvey Leibenstein, "Allocative Efficiency vs. 'X-Efficiency'," *The American Economic Review*, June 1966, p. 406). In a subsequent issue a commentator pointed out that the distinction was "reminiscent of Veblen's distinction between making goods and making money." (Paul J. McNulty, "Allocative Efficiency vs. 'X-Efficiency': Comment," *The American Economic Review*, December 1967, p. 1250).

current investment, might well at this point have cited Veblen's *Theory of Business Enterprise*."[101]

The British reviewer of *The Theory of Business Enterprise* in 1908 clarified Veblen's view of "cycles of trade and depression" by comparing it with that of John A. Hobson. "In *The Evolution of Modern Capitalism*, Mr. Hobson declares that overproduction is the cause of trade depression. We have, he says, so much capital that new concerns are continually being started which compete with former ones, and go on producing until the market is overstocked. Professor Veblen replies that 'the supply of consumable goods is practically never greater than the community's capacity for consuming them.' Depression, he insists, has been too often looked at from the side of production and consumption, instead of from the side of business enterprise. The tendency in every modern enterprise is to overcapitalize at the start.

[101] *A Guide to Keynes* (New York: McGraw-Hill, 1953) pp. 121, 125. In his earlier book, *Economic Stabilization in an Unbalanced World* (1932), which was written during the Great Depression, Hansen called attention to other important aspects of Veblen's theory of business cycles as expressed in *The Theory of Business Enterprise*. Thus he pointed out that "business men . . . will not, as a class, lower prices, merely because costs are lower, until they have passed through the disillusionment and bitter experience of a depression." In a footnote he wrote "The best analysis of the psychological aspect of this forced readjustment to the new facts requiring a new equilibrium of prices is found in Veblen's *The Theory of Business Enterprise*, pp. 237-238. Veblen describes this aspect of depression as a 'malady of the affections'!" Again in discussing measures for moderating depressions, he takes up the view that "If monetary control is not within the realm of possibility we can at least control production all around by extending the organization of trusts, combines, cartels and trade organizations." Then he continued: "This point of view is most effectively advanced by Thorstein Veblen." [*Economic Stabilization in an Unbalanced World* (1932; Augustus M. Kelley Publishers, 1971) pp. 289, 316-317]. The latter proposal, Hansen also describes more accurately as follows: "To ward off depressions the business community resorts to a 'salutary use of sabotage,' as Veblen puts it," in *The Engineers and the Price System*, 1921.

This does not mean what Mr. Hobson means by overcapitalization. The tendency is not to introduce too much machinery, but to capitalize its future earnings on too high a basis." The reviewer noted that Veblen meant by modern business enterprise, "corporation finance," the rule of the great financiers or group of financiers. In the old order, according to Veblen, he continued, "The producer, so long as he had complete control over the processes of production, made it his aim to turn out a steady stream of goods which he would sell at a price sufficient to pay him interest on the capital invested. But the producer is no longer master in his own household. There has arrived upon the scene a new and strange phenomenon, the 'business man' proper, who controls the financial part of the business and leaves the productive process to the paid manager. . . . The aim of these 'business men' is not to turn out the greatest number of goods which will sell at a profit. Their attention is mainly concentrated on the 'vendibility of corporate capital.' " The reviewer concluded that the book "handles in a bold and vigorous manner, the new economic problems which have sprung up during the last thirty years, and the book should be carefully studied by all who are interested in the economic developments of the future."[102]

[102] J. St. G. Heath, review of *The Theory of Business Enterprise* (second American printing), in *Economic Review*, October 1906, pp. 493, 495, 497. The journal was published by the Oxford branch of the Christian Social Union.

Earlier in 1905, a reviewer declared that Veblen maintains that modern business is no longer based so much upon mere commerce and trade as upon the processes of industry. "We deal now in capital, in stocks and bonds, as well as in goods themselves. Industry is no longer so much a quest for livelihood as it is a seeking of profits." The reviewer added that "A commendable feature [of the book] is the formulation of his statements in symbols of mathematics, which are not incorporated in the text but in footnotes." (J. C. Duncan, review in *The Annals of Political and Social Science*, May 1905, p. 612).

Hardly any major provocative work dealing with the "managerial revolution," and regulation of corporations and security markets, has failed to show the influence of *The Theory of Business Enterprise* and its sequel *Absentee Ownership.* When the influence was not explicitly acknowledged it was often quickly pointed out by critics. Thus the daily reviewer of the New York *Times,* after commenting that "Veblen is more than Veblen," went on to say "When Messrs. Berle and Means write on *The Modern Corporation and Private Property* (1932), they are developing aspects of Veblen's thought as elaborated in *Absentee Ownership* and *The Theory of Business Enterprise.*[103] When John T. Flynn traces the com-

[103] This was most incisively explained by a reviewer of the book in the *Columbia Law Review.* As he puts the book's argument, "in the large corporations which dominate our economic life, ownership has abdicated control to a small group. Control is reducing ownership to the mere function of supplying capital and is entrenching itself through a dozen and one modern corporate devices, such as management stock, non-voting common stock, power over dividends and publicity regarding profits and losses, the issuance of prior preference stock, stock option warrants, bonuses, the waiver of preemptive rights, parasitic stock, and many more. To this point the reviewer is in complete accord with the observations of the trend of things made by the authors, and although discovery of such trends has excited the surprise of other reviewers, they have been the subject of more or less similar observation by other economics students – Thorstein Veblen, for example." The reviewer referred in particular to *Absentee Ownership* and *The Engineers and the Price System,* and noted Veblen's accurate comprehension of the legal principles of modern property. (Joseph V. Kline, review of A. A. Berle and Gardiner Means, *The Modern Corporation and Private Property,* in *Columbia Law Review,* March 1933, p. 559).

J. M. Clark in 1927 pointed out the importance of the matter. It was a case of Veblen making fruitful, "finer distinctions than the orthodox." Clark began by declaring that among Veblen's contributions to the advance of economic theory was his "distinction between industrial and pecuniary employments, and industrial and pecuniary capital. This is . . . a vehicle for much keen descriptive analysis of facts. They are distinctions which naturally tend to disappear or to be of no importance in static economics, but under dynamic conditions it becomes essential

plex of evils flowing from periodic overcapitalization, he is corroborating an insight that was old to Veblen in 1912. I could go on and on with these 'whens.' But there is no use turning a column into a doctoral dissertation that will some day be a profitable task for some graduate student."[104]

More recently writers of different political outlooks have noted that J. K. Galbraith's extremely popular *The New Industrial State* (1967) builds upon *The Theory of Business Enterprise* and other works of Veblen. This was clearly shown by a specialist in the field of industrial organization, Myron W. Watkins.[105]

---

[104] John Chamberlain, in New York *Times*, November 27, 1934. Chamberlain was rather acute in his interpretation of the distinction between business and industry. "Veblen's greatest antithesis is the one between 'business' and 'industry,' the first relating to the mechanics of money-making and the second relating to technological ability to deliver the goods. At times these coincide; at other times they don't. (When investment bankers are busy over-capitalizing an industry, and thickly sowing the seeds of depression, it is obvious that the functions of the engineer and of the man who benefits by pecuniary manipulation do not coincide)."

[105] Watkins, who studied with Veblen at the University of Missouri in the academic year 1914-1915, has left a personal portrait of him. "Within the range of my experience, no other social scientist is so difficult to comprehend simply from his writing. Personality counts in teaching and Veblen was a most lovable teacher. Not only did the ladies love him! Earnest students found him fascinating. He was not didactic. His humor was distinctive. To an inquiring mind he was generously helpful, and he enjoyed 'catching up' either a pretentious

---

to distinguish capital as funds saved by ultimate investors, as loan funds furnished by credit institutions, resulting in purchasing power in the hands of business enterprises, as supply of tangible productive instruments, as ultimate supply of means to produce more such instruments, and as capitalized income. It is important because these do not move in harmony over limited periods, and their discrepancies are the roots of much disturbance." [Clark, "Developments in Economics," in *Recent Developments in the Social Sciences,* edited by E. Hayes (Philadelphia: Lippincott, 1927) pp. 246-247].

Watkins emphasized in his review that Galbraith's arguments applied "in some degree to the modern economic system entire, but apply more particularly to its most distinctive components, the industries comprised chiefly of mature corporations, the part which Galbraith designates as did Veblen, the modern industrial system. For half a century, . . . no economist has been properly introduced to the subject matter of the profession without being made aware of the complementary elements of the machine technique: specialization and coordination. Veblen and his followers, like Walton Hale Hamilton, made the whole profession recognize that under the aegis of the machine technique there had inevitably developed an ubiquitous enlargement of the scale

---

novice or a *jejune* mistake. I recall once offering what I thought was an extraordinary insight on the Physiocratic doctrine of *L'impot unique* as illustrated by the *Tableau économique*. Exactly how I interpreted that baffling formula I do not recall. But when I had finished expounding my 'find,' Veblen remarked in this vein, not haughtily but with humble patience and a gentle smile: 'Watkins, truth is often difficult to come by. Your speculation appears to resolve an enigma which hitherto for a century and a half has puzzled not only economists but everyone else.' That set me down solidly. I made no further attempt to explain the inexplicable. If Adam Smith, James Mill, Stanley Jevons and the senior Keynes could find neither head nor tail to the *Tableau*, what chance had I?"

Watkins noted "the disdain and incredulity so commonly found . . . [in Veblen's eyes] in discussion with or concerning, snobbish savants," and recalled that Veblen's "facial expression as a whole" was "that of a Norwegian one generation removed from the Norse farms and fjords, hardly less proud of his artisan skill than of his intellectual eminence." (Review of *Thorstein Veblen: The Carleton College Veblen Seminar Essays*, in *The Anti-Trust Bulletin*, 1969, pp. 523-524).

To this might be added Hobson's characterization: "He brought certain Viking qualities of fearless adventure and of playfulness into the treatment of the world in which he found himself." ("The Economics of Thorstein Veblen," *Political Science Quarterly*, March 1937, p. 139).

of operation of the modern industrial system, an intricate interdependence of its parts and a tendency toward incessant change. . . . While Galbraith's argument starts with and is primarily founded on, the machine technique and its implications for industrial scale, for planning, for innovation, for automation, for managerial expertise, for group-decision making and for much else, he nowhere acknowledges that it was Thorstein Veblen who pioneered this field of inquiry. His *Theory of Business Enterprise* and his *Engineers and the Price System* contain the gist of all that Galbraith sets out as the distinctive features of the modern industrial system."[106]

An aspect of Watkins's positive point was presented earlier in *The New Republic* in 1939, in a discussion of *The Theory of Business Enterprise*, by a leading member of President Roosevelt's original "brain trust." R. G. Tugwell noted that "the opening statement of *The [Theory of] Business Enterprise*, describing the discipline of the machine and how it differed from the old enterpriser's rule of thumb, seems commonplace now; but that is because it has been so thoroughly accepted. It is only with something of an effort that it is recalled how little he had to go on in making this

---

[106] Watkins, review of J. K. Galbraith, *The New Industrial State*, in *The Anti-Trust Bulletin*, April 1968, pp. 273-274.

Until recently Galbraith primarily noted *The Theory of the Leisure Class* in his writings; and on this work his opinion accords with the overwhelmingly dominant view. Thus in his discussion at the Carleton College Seminar, "comparing 'Veblen's Methodology' with his own" he declared: "It's been sixty-seven years since *The Theory of the Leisure Class* was published and only eight and a half years since *The Affluent Society* was published and I have no very high hope that *The Affluent Society* will survive to be the subject of a seminar sixty-eight years eight months from now." (Quoted in C. C. Qualey, "Centennial Seminar in American Studies," *The Voice of Carleton Alumni*, March 1967, p. 4). Unfortunately unlike all the other speakers at this seminar, Galbraith did not provide a manuscript of his 1966 discussion for inclusion in *Thorstein Veblen: The Carleton College Seminar Essays*.

generalization. Taylor and scientific management were known then to a small circle of engineers, but probably no economist had heard of either – the name was not yet invented – and certainly none had seen that any modification of common sense was necessary. All that is not so strange or remarkable as the intellectual effort was, leading to the further generalization that concatenation was of the essence of the entire standardized industrial process. Taylor was still working at his simple time-and-motion studies; he had not yet written even *Shop Management;* not until a few years before the war would he approach such an apprehension as Veblen had of the significance of series-operations." With this as a "bearing foundation of his structure," Veblen "went on to show how the system at large was taking on the character of 'a comprehensive, balanced mechanical process' and to conclude that 'any degree of maladjustment in the interstitial coordinations' was dangerous. But it was, he said, by 'business transactions that the balance of working relations . . . is maintained or restored, adjusted and readjusted.' And business men had not knowledge of a duty to coordinate."[107]

---

[107] "Veblen and 'Business Enterprise.' Seventh of the 'Books that Changed Our Minds.'" *The New Republic,* March 29, 1939; reprinted in *Books That Changed Our Minds,* pp. 102-103.

Tugwell who served successively as Assistant Secretary and Under Secretary of Agriculture from 1933 to 1937, was at the time chairman of the New York City Planning Commission and was soon to become governor of Puerto Rico.

We now know that Henry L. Gantt, another pioneer in scientific management, was influenced by Veblen. According to his biographer, "during the middle months of 1916 Gantt had been reading the writings of Thorstein Veblen." He told friends that while Veblen was "entirely outside of industry" and "had no connection with its operation," he hardly had a peer in being "able to diagnose accurately the primary causes of industrial ills." [L. P. Alford, *Henry Laurence Gantt, Leader in Industry* (New York: Harper, 1934) p. 264].

Specialists in the growing field of legal economics have found the book's discussion of the legal foundations of capitalism a stimulus for intelligently adjusting economic theory and the law to the ever changing requirements of the modern machine technology. Thus a pioneer in the study

---

It is indicative of the fact that Veblen early enjoyed the acquaintance of forward looking socially minded engineers that he requested Scribner's at the time of publication to send a copy to Calvin Winsor Rice of New York, who was prominent in a number of influential engineering organizations. He graduated from the Massachusetts Institute of Technology in 1890, and then held high executive posts first in the Westinghouse Company and later in the General Electric Company. In 1905, he was elected the first full time secretary of the powerful American Society of Mechanical Engineers, while serving as engineer in the New York office of the General Electric Company. In the immediate post World War I period, he turned up in conferences on the social function of the engineer, where Veblen was also prominent (see Veblen book, p. 414). Rice also served on the General Council of a broadly related organization promoted by their mutual friend, Guido Marx, professor of mechanical engineering at Stanford. The aims were described on the letterhead in good part in Veblenian language, which is not surprising: "The Inter-Professional Conference. A National Organization formed November 1919. To discover How to Liberate the Professions from the Domination of Selfish Interests. Both Within and Without the Professions, to Devise Ways and Means of Better Utilizing the Professional Heritage of Knowledge and Skills for the Benefit of Society, and to Create Relations between the Professions Leading to This End." (See letter of Guido Marx *et al* to Professor Underhill Moore of the Columbia University Law School, April 6, 1920, Moore Papers, Columbia University Libraries). The letter read: "Dear Professor Moore, You are invited to attend a meeting at the New School for Social Research . . . on Thursday evening, April 15, to discuss the possibility of forming a local conference group in New York City of the Inter-Professional Conference. Twenty to thirty members of various professions are expected to be present." The executive treasurer of the organization was the well known architect, Robert D. Kohn of New York, who was also active at the time in the Technical Alliance and later in its temporary rebirth as Technocracy. Felix Adler, a founder of the Ethical Culture Movement, was also listed as a member of the General Council.

of legal economics stated that "Veblen pointed out in 1904 in Chapter VIII, . . . that when, in accordance with the theory of 'natural rights,' conventional restrictions on individual liberty were abolished, 'natural liberty' did not include liberty to transgress 'prescriptive rights' of ownership; and that, as a consequence of this remaining restriction, combined with the development of the machine process of industry, sufficient pecuniary pressure could be exerted by some to force others to abandon any *de facto* freedom of action."[108]

The Theory of Business Enterprise is notable for at least one uncanny forecast. This was referred to in 1929 by the Canadian economist, Harold A. Innis. This admirer wrote: "The following prediction is worth quoting. 'Barring accidents and untoward cultural agencies from outside of politics, business or religion, there is nothing in the logic of the modern situation that should stop the cumulative war expenditures short of industrial collapse and consequent national bankruptcy such as terminated the carnival of war and politics that ran its course on the [European] continent in the sixteenth and seventeenth centuries' – a prophecy amply fulfilled ten years later."[109]

---

[108] Robert L. Hale, "Economic Theory and the Statesman," in *The Trend of Economics*, edited by R. G. Tugwell (New York: Crofts, 1924; reprint 1935) p. 193. On Hale, see *The Economic Mind in American Civilization*, IV, 160-163, 588.

[109] Innis, "The Work of Thorstein Veblen," 1929; reprinted in his *Essays in Canadian Economic History*, p. 23.

There is much to be said for Innis's view that Veblen's "position in the industrial revolution, is, to a large extent, similar to that of Adam Smith at the beginning of the revolution. He has been the first to attempt a general stock taking of general tendencies in a dynamic society saddled with machine industry, just as Adam Smith was the first to present a general stock taking before machine industry came in." (p. 25).

Some of Veblen's predictions did not turn out so well or at least are controversial. As Mitchell put it: "How uncannily right he was in his

Like *The Theory of the Leisure Class, The Theory of Business Enterprise* exercised an influence on forward looking sociologists; for example, the famous Edinburgh team of Victor V. Branford and Patrick (later Sir Patrick) Geddes.[110]

[110] Both had a long and deep interest in economic theory. See Geddes, *An Analysis of the Principles of Economics* (1885); and Branford, "Accountancy in its Relation to the Economic Theory of Value," in *The Encyclopedia of Accounting* (1903) and *On the Correlation of Economics and Accountancy,* a paper delivered at the meeting of the London Economic Club, May 14, 1901 (London: Gee, 1901). As for Geddes's general view on economics, this was aptly put by his friend, H. Stanley Jevons, the economist son of W. Stanley Jevons. "He [Geddes] realized that an economist who could be weaned from figures and abstractions like the 'economic man' and be given the biological sense would have a useful and rather unusual combination of qualities." (Jevons, "An Economist's View," obituary note on Geddes, *The Sociological Review,* October 1932, supplement, p. 383). Branford in a private letter to Professor E. R. A. Seligman of Columbia in 1901 wrote: "For half a generation I have been a close student of the development of the theory of value from the classicists to the Austrians and Marshall." (Branford to Seligman, June 21, 1901, Seligman Papers, Columbia University Libraries).

---

forecasts in some cases may be judged by reading H. T. Oshima, 'Veblen on Japan,' *Social Research,* November 1934. How wrong he could be in other cases may be judged from his forecast in 1904 in *The Theory of Business Enterprise* that business cycles would degenerate into a dragging depression from which only now and then would some extraneous happening produce a spurt of activity." (*Types of Economic Theory,* II, 696). Heath in his review of the book in 1906 similarly observed that Veblen's argument if taken "as an *a priori* piece of reasoning . . . is very convincing." (*Economic Review,* 1906, p. 496).

J. M. Clark in his copy of the Veblen book commented that "[Veblen's] law of chronic depression in a mature economy includes underspending and underinvestment rather parenthetically but focuses on overcapitalization relative to obsolescence of industrial processes, but→ reduced margin of product over consumption." (Clark's note was based on pp. 343-344 of the Veblen book. His copy is in the possession of Joseph Dorfman).

We shall take up Geddes first. He held chairs in the biological sciences, sociology and civics in the universities of Scotland and India, and did pioneering work on the development of urban and regional planning. Besides their mutual interest in the social sciences, Veblen and Geddes had in common an intense interest in botany. They met on Geddes's lecture tour in the United States in early 1900. "Veblen, whose *Theory of the Leisure Class* had just appeared, was a kindred spirit who at once became his friend."[111] A biographer of Geddes in referring to the meeting stated that "as P. G.'s Edinburgh artist friend, John Duncan,[112] once remarked, 'to meet Veblen in the University of Chicago in those days was like coming upon an oasis in the Sahara.' And on visiting Scotland in 1902, Veblen must have looked on his sojourn in the Geddes home with a similar pleasure, for it was always a haven for men of advanced ideas and to academic thorns in particular."[113]

In the classic *Cities in Evolution: An Introduction to the Town Planning Movement and to the Study of Civics* (1915), Geddes, after paying tribute to *The Theory of the Leisure Class,* which was "at length becoming a classic," went on to salute *The Theory of Business Enterprise,* as likewise by "the most penetrating, and hence, 'till lately least read, of

---

[111] Philip Mairet, *Pioneer of Sociology: The Life and Letters of Patrick Geddes* (London: Humphries, 1957) p. 100.

[112] A leader in the renaissance of Celtic art.

[113] Philip Boardman, *Patrick Geddes: Maker of the Future* (Chapel Hill: University of North Carolina Press, 1941) p. 218.

Veblen may have visited Geddes (and perhaps also Branford) again in 1914. On the Certificate of Registration of American Citizenship which Veblen prepared in Christiania (now Oslo) in August, the American Consul General wrote that "he intends returning to the United States *via* Scotland, leaving Norway within the present month."

American economists, though in his new and seeming abstruse way the first of American humorists also."[114]

In *The Theory of Business Enterprise* "there are for the first time keenly analysed out and contrasted the diverse tendencies of the machine process, and of the commercial process, which traditional economists have hitherto treated as in the main a harmonious whole, but of which he brings out the mutual disorganization they at present involve. His idea once mastered, the student of cities will find that it applies to the places he knows in detail; and, to begin with, that it throws no little light upon the contrasted commercial wealth of the City [the financial district of London] and the comparative industrial poverty of East London. Similarly in New York, upon the strange juxtaposition of Wall Street and the Bowery. Yet through all Veblen's apparent pessimism (as through the descriptions and arguments of this volume, we trust, also) there runs an unbroken clue – that of observed and reasoned science – not without threads of life, and faith in it, woven through its tough cord. With direct physicist-like argument, he works out the inevitable, however difficult and gradual, victory of the machine process over the commercial process: for the linking up of the chain of physical efficiencies all the way from Nature to life must needs overpower and eliminate all present and possible parasitisms in transit. Thus in his own

[114] Veblen always loved to tease. Henry W. Stuart tells of how he and a fellow graduate student, H. Parker Willis, on a long walk with Veblen on the outskirts of Chicago tried to discover what his middle initial "B" stood for. "We suggested Biorne, Bodvar, Bruse, Bjornstierne, Bruno, Bolivar and even Bonaparte, but could not break his stony silence." (Not until the Veblen book appeared did Stuart learn that the "B" stood for "Bunde"). Stuart also recalls how "Veblen used to enjoy telling me of the confidential manner of the printer of *The Journal* [*of Political Economy*] who found the many interpolations and corrections of my mss. confusing if not undecipherable. 'Is this man really quite all there?' he seriously inquired." (Stuart to Joseph Dorfman, May 19, 1949).

way he practically expresses and explains that birth of the neotechnic age from the paleotechnic, which is a central thesis of the present volume."[115]

As for Branford, he had connections with the academic world through his membership on the Board of Sociological Studies of the University of London, and as the editor of *The Sociological Review.* He had a more intimate knowledge of economic affairs than Geddes, for he was a financial and banking expert, as a member of the London-Edinburgh accounting firm of Ross, Branford and Company, and then as a "banker's agent in the City" – London's financial center. He was especially interested in the economic development of Latin America, and achieved quite a business reputation as managing director of the Paraguay Central Railroad and as the builder of the Cuban telephone system.

Branford, who first met Veblen in England,[116] likewise expressed a deep respect for his works. In *Interpretations and Forecasts* (1914), the companion volume to Geddes's *Cities in Evolution,* he began with "There are two recent treatises of remarkable insight and originality. . . . The latest sociological study of 'Leisure' [is] the only one as yet which treats it in the truly detached and monographic way of science." The "critical and analytical" study was provoked by "the ostentatious misuse of Leisure in America." Branford continued: "It is not an accident that the same author has

[115] A similar view of Veblen is presented by one of Geddes's American disciples, Lewis Mumford in *The Culture of Cities* (1938).

[116] Hobson wrote me that on their first meeting in England Veblen was in the company of Branford. Hobson in an obituary of Branford wrote that "it was an amazing experience to me to find a busy City man, with heavy financial engagements, who was willing to give himself heart and soul to the drudgery of secretarial and editorial work for a cause that would have no meaning for his work-a-day associates." ("In the Small Band of Prophetic Thinkers," *The Sociological Review,* October 1931, p. 195).

traced the evolution of 'Business Enterprise,' and worked out with unique clearness the tendencies of industrial development. Seeing human life as an oscillation between the poles of Labour and Leisure, and following this thread through the complex warp and woof of civilization, he finds, in the tendencies that make for the divorce of Labour and Leisure, a main, indeed a sufficient cause of those periodic reversions to barbarism and savagery in the most advanced and progressive of contemporary societies, which it has puzzled the students of [Auguste] Comte and [Herbert] Spencer to account for. Mr. Veblen closes his investigations as he began them, in the indicative mood, and with punctilious scientific correctitude, he leaves his generalizations there. Yet there is not much left either of the 'leisure class' or of 'business enterprise,' as either is commonly understood when Mr. Veblen has done with them, and the reader, yielding to ethical impulse, will probably rise from perusal of these two volumes of masterly analysis with a conclusion remarkably like the old theological pronouncement, discredited for his country and time though it may be, that 'the love of money is the root of all evil.' "[117] As another writer put it, in Veblen's view "the only certainty in the decade before World War I was the end of business domination in its present form."[118]

Branford's later description (in *Our Social Inheritance*, 1919) of the domination of the economy by finance and financiers followed the line of the book. "[D]espite the fact

[117] *Interpretations and Forecasts* (New York: Mitchell Kennerley, 1914) pp. 240-241, 364. The book was largely composed of Branford's lectures in American universities. It has been noted that Branford "had much in common with Thorstein Veblen, whose genius he was one of the first in Europe to recognize and hail." (Lewis Mumford, "Victor Branford," *The New Republic,* August 27, 1930, p. 467).

[118] Sandra R. Herman, *Eleven Against War: Studies in American International Thought 1898-1921* (Stanford: Hoover Institute Press, 1969) p. 161.

that inventors and pioneers generally ruined themselves in their enthusiasm of construction, and that this constructive ecstasy pervaded the most successful cotton-spinning or railway-making, it is in finance that these culminate. It nowadays has come to be only too clearly realized by all concerned, that people are in manufacturing, or business, or the carrying trade, not simply to create, collect, distribute and 'deliver the goods,' but for money gains, for dividends. In fact it requires some acquaintance with the classical literature of political economy, some definite recalling of the Great Exhibition of 1851, to realize nowadays the old joys of manufacturing for its own sake. And if you recall to a modern captain of industry this old lyricism of his fathers, he is either incredulous, contemptuous, or both; and he assures you that he at any rate is not in business 'for the sake of his health.'

Branford continued: "A corresponding change has taken place in the meaning of the word 'Business,' as used in metropolitan cities of finance. The term has, for many, shed its technical content, and come to mean the 'making' of money almost in the direct and literal sense of the coiner and banknote printer. Success in this sort of business depends upon skill and boldness in initiating and carrying through a certain sequence of 'Operations' – still another of the many terms, transferred from the realities of the workshop to the phantoms of the city 'office.' These operations begin with the acquisition of what is called 'Control.' And again 'control' carries at best a second- or third-hand reference to the facts of productive industry. 'Control' in the financial sense means a majority of voting interest; and is thus an idea and method imported from politics into business. The next stage of Finance is in the manufacture of paper claims on the 'controlled' property, which may be a gold mine or a 'concession'; a brewery or a casino; a steel plant or a shipbuilding yard; a cotton factory or a railway; or various combinations of these; or, again, the 'controlled' property may be itself some mere fractional or paper interest in an actual or prospective 'business.' In this stage of creation, division, multiplication and compounding of legalized claims, the Financier offers magnificent rewards to barristers and solicitors, and so engages the best heads in that able profession for specialized manipulation of the 'Company Laws.' "

As Branford traced the rise of the dominion of the "financier," he contended that "the final and culminating stage in the sequence of the Financier's 'operations' is the transformation of his paper claims into legal tender currency. It is here that the business of Finance blossoms into the high refinements of artistry. Just as it was in the preliminary stages the politician and the lawyer who were first the exemplars, then the allies, and finally the servants of the Financier, so now a similar transition from colleague to satellite overtakes and masters the Banker and the Journalist.

"For the Financier as artist, it may be said that he, long before poet or painter, was a 'Futurist.' His 'Prospectus' may indeed be regarded as a classic document of the somewhat uncritical 'Futurism,' which believes that the achievements of tomorrow must inevitably surpass those of yesterday. The fortune of the Financier comes in the last resort to be measured by his success in converting the public to adopt his rosy views of the future. For that feat of persuasion he invokes the prestige of the Banker and the ardour of the Journalist for 'news.' . . . Thus with Lawyer and Politician on his left, and supported on his right by Banker and Journalist, the Financier advances to the pinnacle of greatness and authority, his turn as Chief of the New Social Order. . . . The public has been correspondingly 'educated' into an acceptance of this social order, so thorough-going as to be not only habitually willing, but eager to exchange their coin of the realm for the Financier's paper 'claims' upon the land of promise, so enticingly pegged out in his prospectus. In short, this type of personage has in effect accomplished in rare degree that union of temporal and spiritual powers which Caesars and Tudors have adorned before his day, and so he becomes High Priest of the Golden Calf he has set up in the market place of each metropolitan and even secondary city. His practising worshippers constitute (or hope through his merits to attain to) that vast and ever-growing 'Leisure Class,' whose habits and mode of life are admirably described in the work thus named by Professor Thorstein Veblen, that rare bird, a naturalistic observer and interpreter amongst the economists."[119]

Branford in collaboration with Geddes and the economic historian Sir Gilbert Slater brought out a relatively more prosaic aspect of *The Theory of Business Enterprise* in *Ideas at War* (1917). They stated: "[The] real triumph of the financial age was made possible in England by the legaliza-

---

[119] Branford and Geddes, *Our Social Inheritance* (London: Williams and Norgate, 1919) pp. 41-45. The above discussion is taken from Branford's part. (See Branford to Veblen, May 27, 1919, Thorstein Veblen Papers).

Branford also followed Veblen in saying that "The 'Science of Advertisement' (as its expert practitioners call it) is the inevitable and characteristic spiritual institution created by and . . . for the Financial Age. The present vogue of advertisement marks the historic climax of the Financiering System. In establishing the prevalence of this vogue, that system has fulfilled itself, by creating its own appropriate and accepted Spiritual Power." (pp. 56-57).

For Veblen's discussion of advertising in *The Theory of Business Enterprise,* see pp. 51-66. This analysis probably makes Veblen the pioneer in the systematic formulation of the role and character of what is now called selling costs in price theory.

A popular presentation of *The Theory of Business Enterprise* along the lines of Branford's "financier" is David T. Bazelon's *The Paper Economy* (1963). He declared that he "relied substantially on Veblen's . . . thinking about credit and capitalization in America" which he described as "an original, non-Marxist and uniquely American contribution."

tion of limited liability in 1862 [General Incorporation Act]; and it can scarcely be said to have been consummated till the time of the great rage for the conversion of private businesses to Limited Liability Companies [Corporations] towards the end of the nineteenth century; some of the most striking incidents of which were the Kaffir boom, the cycle boom, the Westralian boom, the brewery boom, and the rubber boom . . . [T]he process of contriving the representation of the assets of all sorts of businesses by bonds and shares has been pushed forward to a degree which is brought home to the mind immediately in glancing over the financial column of a daily paper.

"This process is such a constant part of our daily experience that its significance escapes examination. It involves new conditions both numerous and important to our lives. In the first place, the object which is increasingly sought after by responsible heads of business is to make their assets fluid and realizable, so that they can, if necessary, borrow on the strength of every asset they possess, whether it be land, buildings, unexpired leases, stock, machinery, debts due to them, or the anticipation of expected profits. As business is conducted at the present time, the power of seizing opportunities for expansion on old lines of enterprise, or of initiation of new lines, depends very largely upon the facilities which are provided for the treatment of all these assets as securities on which to borrow. . . .

"Next we have to note that the new system involves the use of the shares and debentures of the businesses, as counters to be gambled in, and as income-producing entities to be bought and sold on a valuation based upon the current expectation of the amount of income likely to be yielded. . . . [In the modern developed corporation] the real owners are a completely heterogeneous body of men, women, and trustees for minors, scattered over this and possibly other countries, knowing nothing of one another except by accident, and utterly unfitted to bear any of the responsibilities which naturally appertain to the ownership of the business. . . . The . . . owners are people who are not called upon as owners to do more than buy stocks when they are likely to appreciate, and sell them when they are likely to depreciate: The art of business success is thus seductively simplified—'Getting to know of a good thing' and 'Being let in on the ground floor.' "[120]

The work of the Italian economist, Achille Loria, revealed that the book early had some influence on the continent. In discussing the distribution of wealth, he cited the treatise in support of the view that in the modern corporation, "the capital represented by the ordinary shares (when preference shares are issued), or by the shares (when debentures are issued), is simply *water,* that is to say, it is merely fictitious and supposititious wealth, serving solely to receive a conspicuous share of income as the entrepreneur's reward at the expense of the capital." He concluded again with acknowledgement to *The Theory of Business Enterprise* that in consequence of this and various other practices in modern business "a conscientious observer does not hesitate to affirm that it is doubtful whether, throughout the whole field of modern industry, there exists a single successful undertaking into whose success there enters no element of monopoly."[121] On this point Veblen's passage reads as follows: "The broad principle which guides producers and merchants, large and

[120] Geddes and Slater, *Ideas at War* (London: Williams and Norgate, 1917) pp. 117-122. A biographer of Geddes noted the "almost Veblen-like character of the book." (Boardman, p. 371). The volume was the outgrowth of lectures given by each at Kings' College London in 1915. They left to Branford who served as editor the task of completing the book.

[121] *The Economic Synthesis; A Study of the Laws of Income,* translated by M. Eden Paul (London: George Allen, 1914) pp. 259, 274.

small, in fixing the prices at which they offer their wares and services is what is known in the language of the railroads as 'charging what the traffic will bear.' Where a given enterprise has a strict monopoly of the supply of a given article or of a given class of services this principle applies in the unqualified form in which it has been understood among those who discuss railway charges. But where the monopoly is less strict, where there are competitors, there the competition that has to be met is one of the factors to be taken account of in determining what the traffic will bear. Competition may even become the most serious factor in the case if the enterprise in question has little or none of the character of a monopoly. But it is very doubtful if there are any successful business ventures within the range of the modern industries from which the monopoly element is wholly absent. They are, at any rate, few and not of great magnitude."[122]

It has been gradually recognized that Veblen should be ranked as a pioneer in the formulation of what is now called in dominant economic theory "imperfect competition" or "monopolistic competition."

The realm of letters too has felt the impact of *The Theory of Business Enterprise*. For example, one of Sinclair Lewis's recent biographers has declared that "in some ways the major contribution of Lewis's novels was their continuation (or, at least, popularization) of certain leading ideas of Veblen, especially as to the leisure class and business enterprise . . . Looking . . . at *Babbitt* from this point of view, we can see it as a dramatization of the divorce between industry and business, of the disappearance in a transitional America of inter-

[122] *The Theory of Business Enterprise* (1904; New York: Augustus M. Kelley Publishers, 1965) pp. 53-54.

dependence and individuality in the machinelike processes of a mass culture."[123]

The last item on *The Theory of Business Enterprise* bears on the readership and romance. A copy of the first edition has turned up which is inscribed to a female admirer of beauty and intelligence. The inscription reads: "To Mrs. Laura McAdoo Triggs, With all my heart. Thorstein Veblen." The woman, who was the sister of the future Secretary of the Treasury in President Wilson's cabinet, William Gibbs McAdoo, was at the time married to a Chicago colleague in the English department. Later, in 1911 she played an important role in the development of one of Europe's finest writers, Anatole France, who had much in common with Veblen. According to France's most recent biographer, "his liaison with '*la belle Floridianne*,' as France called her, was one of his most serious affairs. She had literary taste and some talent. France helped her with some articles and she was his audience for much of *Les Dieux ont soif*." This novel of the French Revolution and the Terror is considered his greatest.[124]

---

[123] Mark Schorer, *Sinclair Lewis, An American Life* (New York: McGraw-Hill, 1961) p. 472. The distinction is clear in the sentence in which Veblen is mentioned in Lewis's first great novel, *Main Street* (1920): "He [Miles Bjornstam] had but one room . . . and a row of books incredibly assorted; Byron and Tennyson and Stevenson, a manual of gas-engines, a book by Thorstein Veblen, and a spotty treatise on The Care, Feeding, Diseases and Breeding of Poultry and Cattle!" [*Main Street. The Story of Carol Kinnicott* (New York: Harcourt, Brace and Howe, 1920) p. 117].

Another professor of English literature declared that "Sinclair Lewis often seems to be nothing but dramatized Veblen." [Edgar Johnson, "Thorstein Veblen; The Man from Mars," *The New Republic*, July 28, 1951, p. 122].

[124] David Tilden-Wright, *Anatole France* (New York: Walker, 1967) pp. 266-267.

The Instinct of Workmanship and the State of the Industrial Arts

Veblen, as I noted, had originally planned as his second treatise *The Instinct of Workmanship and the State of the Industrial Arts.* It appeared much later than he had envisaged – fifteen years after *The Theory of the Leisure Class.* Among the major factors that prevented its completion were the vicissitudes of involuntary changes of position. Mitchell, about nine months after Veblen came to Stanford in the fall of 1906, reported to Mrs. Gregory that, "Veblen is looking well indeed but says he is not doing any work. . . . He was his old humorous self – not embittered in the least. His headaches have stopped, and I felt much encouraged about him in every way. . . . He is thinking somewhat of going to Chicago for a month, but is not certain that he shall not remain quietly at Cedro Cottage all summer. If he does I fancy he will be writing the 'Economic Psychology' before September [1907]."[121] Three years later, however, in the midst of seeking another post, Veblen wrote Mitchell of the delay: "The explanation of all that is very simple. You may remember my expressing a hope that I might write something about the Instinct. I arranged to go to work, and directly, just as has happened before, the hoodoo which rests on that topic became operative. Domestic circumstances, interesting enough in their own way but unprofitable, are all there is time for."[122]

An economist who was anxious that Veblen finish the study

---

[121] Part of what follows on *The Instinct of Workmanship* is from the editor's "Preface" to the 1964 edition which was issued by Augustus M. Kelley Publishers by arrangement with The Viking Press.

[122] Veblen to Mitchell, August 3, 1910, Mitchell Papers.

was Taussig.[123] In November 1910, with support of the Harvard department of economics, he was prepared to invite Veblen to give a series of lectures at Harvard on the instinct of workmanship. Before extending the invitation, Taussig wrote Mitchell: "Do you happen to know just how much Veblen has done on his inquiry as to the instinct of workmanship? I have had some correspondence with him about it and we have a provisional arrangement by which he is to send an article on to *The* [*Quarterly*] *Journal* [*of Economics*], when ready. Do you know whether his inquiries have yielded enough in the way of specific information to make a short course of lectures? The suggestion has been made that he be invited to come and give a set of, say, three lectures upon this subject, printing the substance of them later as an article or articles in the *Journal.* As you know, I think well of Veblen and have learned from [Allyn A.] Young[124] of his difficulties for the present year. Tho' we should not for a moment think

---

[123] Taussig's interest in Veblen's "instinct of workmanship" seems to have begun with Veblen's original essay "The Instinct of Workmanship and the Irksomeness of Labor," September 1898 (reprinted in *Essays in Our Changing Order*). Thus, Taussig, according to a student's notes of 1904, after stating in class that "the change in psychological speculation has begun to affect economic speculation," continued with "Veblen says that in mankind is an instinct for workmanship, a desire for doing things for the pleasure of doing them. This kind of speculation has not yet issued in anything." (Notes of Nicholas Kelley, Economics 2, lecture of November 12, 1904).

[124] Young, an old friend of Mitchell's and an admirer of Veblen, was then on a year's leave from Stanford as a visiting professor at Harvard. On the Stanford affair, Young declared at the time "I am inclined to *think* that Veblen has been the victim of a gross piece of injustice." (Young to Davenport, November 14, 1909, Davenport Papers).

While differing, especially in the post World War I years, with Veblen on formal methods, Young conceded "that neither Veblen nor any of his followers who need to be reckoned with in economic science ever held that the genetic method is the 'only really scientific mode.'" (Young to Mitchell, March 1927, Mitchell Papers).

of asking him to lecture here for the mere purpose of helping him out, I for one should be glad to do him a good turn if he has enough to say."[125]

Unfortunately Mitchell's reply has not been located. Shortly afterwards Veblen received an appointment at the University of Missouri through the strenuous efforts of Davenport, who was then head of the department of economics.[126] There he wrote the book, while living in the home of his colleague and former student, Walter W. Stewart. Stewart recalled with considerable awe, that Veblen had such a systematic command of his material that he sat down and wrote steadily without consulting any literature or notes.[127]

---

[125] Taussig to Mitchell, November 16, 1910, Mitchell Papers.

[126] DR Scott, who was a student and colleague of Veblen at Missouri and later achieved prominence as a philosopher of accounting, has written of Veblen's arrival at the institution: "One day in January 1911 I was alone in the economics office. . . . When Professor Davenport returned to the office, I reported 'There was a seedy looking man with a gray-brown beard and a brown suit looking for you, but he left without giving his name or telling his business.' That was Veblen's arrival at the University of Missouri. He was the mildest mannered, most self-effacing individual imaginable." Scott went on to describe other characteristics of Veblen, "His strange vocabulary was sometimes an expression of his humor. Sometimes his vocabulary was a parody upon the jargon of orthodox economics which he was fond of ridiculing. But mostly, I think, he took a kind of artistic delight in expressing his ideas in such language." Scott also recalled some Veblen stories: Asked what he thought of a session of a discussion group of eminent faculty in the social sciences, "he commented that 'they seemed to be flailing around in the dark, hitting a foul once in a while.'" Scott also noted that "correspondence irked him as much as the clerical work connected with teaching. One day Veblen remarked that 'there never was a letter which wouldn't answer itself if you left it in your desk for six months.'" ("A Recollection of Veblen at Missouri," *The Missouri Alumnus*, February 1953, pp. 6, 12).

[127] Stewart returned to the University in 1912 as a full faculty member, because he wanted to study with Veblen. He became among other things the first economic adviser to the Bank of England.

By February 1913, Veblen had completed the draft. He wrote Jacques Loeb that he "had on hand a manuscript for a small volume of theoretical speculations waiting for final revision and a possible publisher."[128] He informed Mitchell at the same time that: "The Instinct of Workmanship – I don't like this title but have found nothing to take its place – is as nearly written as it is likely to be for some time, the text being complete except for passages that have to be rewritten and others that have to be filled in, but there are references and other apparatus of erudition to be included, and the publication, if any, is in the indefinite future. As it lies it is something of a disappointment, it seems neither clear nor convincing, nor is the discussion (some 90,000 words) adequate as an outline of systematic treatment."[129]

At least one economist of distinction was not disappointed with the book. Taussig praised it highly. Readers, however, may sympathize with his annoyance at Veblen's "failure to help guide his readers at all, – no index, no contents, and the most general chapter headings. He has been equally negligent of the convenience of his readers in all his books. I wrote him on this topic myself."[130]

---

[128] Veblen to Loeb, February 20, 1913, Loeb Papers, Library of Congress.

[129] Veblen to Mitchell, February 20, 1913, in possession of Joseph Dorfman.

[130] Taussig to Mitchell, September 11, 1914, Mitchell Papers. Taussig had Mitchell review the book in *The Quarterly Journal of Economics*. Taussig apparently was unaware of the exception: the 1912 edition

---

He has summed up in a letter the view of Veblen as a theorist that was entertained by his students: "While Veblen was not a system-builder, he had one of the most systematic minds and was always consciously aware of the fundamentals underlying his thought." (Stewart to Myron Watkins, October 29, 1957). Watkins kindly sent me a copy.

Davenport recounts how one far reaching concept of the book could be fitted into the main tradition as formulated in his *The Economics of Alfred Marshall.* "The stress of living grows as new needs are maturing along with the ways of serving them, if only the response of effort be neither over-niggardly nor over-generous. Just here is the significance of Veblen's pithy comment: 'You know, necessity isn't the mother of invention.' 'No?' 'Invention is the mother of necessity.' 'Yes, but –' 'You see, if we don't know how to do these things, we can't do them, can we?' " Then Davenport added "It must then be clear that the more things Crusoe had to do, the less he could do each of them."[131]

An early specialist on the role of psychology in economics noted the influence of the original Veblen article of 1898. As Z. Clark Dickinson read the essay, it presented "the view that common labor is ordinarily distasteful, less by reason of its fatigues and pains (which are also encountered in many sports), than because of the social disesteem in which it is held." Among those influenced by this idea was Hobson, especially in a major study – *Work and Wealth* (1914) – where he holds "the view that much work is not intrinsically unattractive to the workers."[132] Another writer has pointed out that Vilfredo Pareto's "Instinct of Combination" in the

[131] Davenport, *The Economics of Alfred Marshall,* p. 221. In the footnote Davenport gave the source of the Veblen story as follows: "no reference; it was in a chat before the fire."

[132] Dickinson, "The Psychological Approach in Economics Represented by the Work of J. A. Hobson," in *Methods in Social Science,* p. 494.

of *The Theory of the Leisure Class* does have an index. He was not the only reader of Veblen who was annoyed. A Dutch admirer, who was translating his books into Dutch, wrote him in 1925, "My heartfelt thanks for the copy of the *Leisure Class* (with an index such as I miss in most of your publications)." J. A. Sandfort to Veblen, December 12, 1925, Thorstein Veblen Papers.

Trattato di sociologia generale (1916) "has striking similarity to Veblen's instinct of workmanship and Taussig's instinct of contrivance."[133]

Of the character of the instinct, perhaps Professor J. M. Clark has presented a clear statement of the most widely held position. In his view, "Veblen's *Instinct of Workmanship* is the outstanding economic elaboration of . . . [the] theme that instrumental activities can become ends." He declared:

> Man has one illogical but very useful trait whereby, when an activity is undertaken as a means to some ulterior end – as work is – it can come to command our interest in its own right and become an end in itself. The difference . . . rests on the distinction drawn by William James between voluntary and spontaneous attention.[134] When we do something merely as a means to something else, we must make ourselves pay attention to it; and this kind of attention soon flags and has to be renewed, and fatigue comes quickly. But if our interest is spontaneous, it is sustained with a minimum of fatigue, we can accomplish more, and we want to do

---

[133] Max S. Handman, "The Sociological Methods of Vilfredo Pareto," *Methods in Social Science*, p. 148.

Handman was a student of Veblen at the University of Missouri. Later he was Professor of Economics at the University of Michigan.

[134] A philosopher friend who was with Veblen at Chicago at the time of the writing of the original essay, cast light on Veblen's derivation of the instinct from James. In a letter Warner Fite wrote: "at that time James's instinct-theory was still new – instinct as the explanation of human character as against the association of ideas initiated by the environment; and Veblen's 'instinct of workmanship' was in line with James and against [Herbert] Spencer." (Fite to Dorfman, March 1, 1933). Fite could have added Jeremy Bentham. On this see Mitchell, "Bentham's Felicific Calculus," 1918, reprinted in his *The Backward Art of Spending Money and Other Essays*, edited and compiled by Joseph Dorfman (1937; New York: Augustus M. Kelley Publishers, 1951) p. 195.

the job well for its own sake, or for our own sakes, and not merely well enough to "get by."

This seems to happen normally if the activity is not one that goes positively contrary to our natures. It is one of the chief secrets of making the most of our powers. But it also leads to lavishing effort beyond what the occasion calls for, or going through ritual technicalities that may actually obstruct the original end in view. And it can reinforce efficiency about as well where the end is parasitic, or even criminal, as where it is serviceable. A man takes pride in being a good workman, but not necessarily in giving his industry, or the consumer, the benefit. He may get interested in the parasitic maneuvers of bargaining as a game, or an economist's theory may become an end in itself to him, to be refined at the expense of realism, rather than as a means to the understanding of his world.[135]

---

[135] *Alternative to Serfdom* (New York: Knopf, 1947; revised ed., 1960) pp. 56-57.

A somewhat too condensed though suggestive version of the Clark view was presented by Ischboldin as follows: "Desire for activity or an 'instinctive desire for workmanship,' in Veblen's terminology. Such an instinct sometimes hurts the principle of economizing, especially when it is connected with extreme idle curiosity. All of these instincts usually are influenced by environment and thus are no longer pure 'instincts.'" (*Economic Synthesis*, p. 37).

The last sentence might seem to explain why Ayres a consistent admirer of Veblen could write in an amusing personal letter that Veblen was no believer in the instinct psychology. He recalled in 1935 that "He [Veblen] once asked me if I had ever noticed his definition of 'instinct' and when I replied with a grin that I never had, he matched my grin and remarked that no such definition appeared because if you define instinct exactly 'there ain't no such animal.'" (Ayres to Dorfman, March 15, 1935).

Perhaps the confusion is cleared up by Handman's recollection that Veblen said to him "I mean by instinct a direction – *anlage*." (Handman in conversation with editor, December 1931).

Perhaps it might be added that the excesses were described by Veblen as largely institutionally created perversions of the instinct of workmanship.[136]

On the other hand, an economic historian has used the concept to argue that the instinct in its primordial, beneficent form is in good part institutionally created. Thus the craft gilds of the medieval cities "through their regulations and practice instilled into their members some incipient instinct of workmanship and at the same time tended to establish some basic precepts of commercial honesty."[137]

In recent years the concept in the book that seems to have attracted most attention, especially from economists with a broad social approach, is one that falls under the category of perverted forms of the instinct of workmanship. The discoverer was not an economist or a practitioner of the social sciences but a specialist in linguistic philosophy. R. A. Hall Jr. of Cornell in "Thorstein Veblen and Linguistic Theory," in the May 1960 issue of *American Speech,* declared that the work of the economist Veblen was important for linguistic theory, because he had developed in his works

---

[136] The process of perversion was also described by Veblen as "self-contamination of the instinct of workmanship." The philosopher, William Ernest Hocking of Harvard, defended the underlying philosophy of "self-contamination." He wrote: "In making this plea for the encouragement of an anthropomorphic imagination, I am shamelessly favoring what Professor Thorstein Veblen has called the 'self-contamination of the instinct of workmanship' (*The Instinct of Workmanship,* pp. 52 ff.), a deliberate mixing of the personal and impersonal phases of the world which it may prove difficult later on to resolve into a wholly naturalistic deadness of attitude toward the physical. I do so with my eyes open." [*Human Nature and Its Remaking* (New Haven: Yale University Press, 1918) p. 241]. A reader of the same library copy of the book that the editor used wrote in the margin of this passage "Influence of Nature."

[137] Alexander Gerschenkron, *Europe in the Russian Mirror* (Cambridge, England: Cambridge University Press, 1970) p. 57.

"several concepts which are of considerable usefulness in understanding not only social conditioning factors, but some of the mechanism underlying the use of language and linguistic change." The concepts that he discussed came with one exception from *The Theory of the Leisure Class*. The exception, which was from *The Instinct of Workmanship*, is "trained incapacity." He asserted that Veblen explicitly uses it or its slightly altered form "trained inability" only in passing when discussing the lack of understanding that pecuniarily oriented managers show with regard to manufacturing processes.[138] He felt that Veblen "might have used it much more extensively in his own discussions, particularly in connection with conspicuous waste: a trained incapacity to deal with mundane matters is often a carefully cultivated mark of presumed superiority, especially on the part of some European intellectuals." Hall argued that "in language, the concept of trained incapacity is very fruitful in explaining certain aspects of language learning and attitudes, and of the way linguistic topics are treated in our schools."

At the end of that very same year, an economist who was shortly afterwards appointed by President Eisenhower as Assistant Secretary of Defense (Comptroller) used the concept "trained incapacity" in an address at the Brookings Institution on "The Uses of Economics." After noting the usefulness of economists on many public policy problems, Charles J. Hitch pointed out that "[economists] also have some negatively useful characteristics in tackling such problems, a considerable dose of what Veblen so aptly termed 'trained incapacity.'" He elaborated in a manner that recalled Veblen's criticisms of the traditional methodology. "First, and most frustrating, is the passion of the economic

[138] Hall pointed out that Veblen presented both "trained incapacity" and "trained inability" on the same page (p. 347).

theorist for unequivocality and perfection. The typical welfare theorist [in the main tradition as expressed by Pareto], for example, wants to wash his hands of a problem if he cannot prove, with certainty, that the lot of every single individual in a society will be either bettered or not worsened. Let me suggest that a part of his intellectual difficulty may stem from his tradition of considering each decision in isolation. I think that *distributive* effects and *spillover* effects, as well as uncertainties, become much less inhibiting if we think instead, and much more realistically, of the appropriate criteria for a large set of decisions. . . .

"Another trained incapacity stems from our past emphasis on static models. We became so bemused by static theory that we usually forgot that profit maximization is an ambiguous or multidimensional criterion. . . . Thirdly, we have fallen into the lazy habit of making convenient but naive assumptions about some of the critical inputs of economic analysis – notably naive assumptions about individual, business, and government behavior. . . . And, finally, like the practitioners of nearly every science, we have a marked tendency to go it alone." He warned that the economists "must unlearn the phrase 'as an economist' ('as an economist there is nothing I can say about the problem,' or 'as an economist, all that I can say is . . .'). Promoting economic growth is an economic problem, but much more than an economic problem. Choosing good transportation systems is an economic problem, but can't be solved without sociologists and engineers. . . . And those problems of acceptability and implementation, which we can't ignore without being irresponsible, require sophistication in politics and psychology. Allocating frequencies is an economic problem, but the economist who tackles it without knowing a great deal of electronic technology, or getting help from someone who does, is asking for trouble and frustration." Hitch concluded: "in the future, . . . as I see the future, economists, if they are to remain useful, will have to tackle a lot of impure problems for which their special tools, while useful, are not enough."[139]

The pervasive appeal of the book doubtless lies in the elaborate outlining of the growth of western civilization, especially in setting forth the conditions of economic development; or as a teacher of American history put it: Veblen

[139] "The Uses of Economics," in *Research for Public Policy*, Brookings Dedication Lectures (Washington, D.C.: Brookings Institution, 1961) pp. 105-108.

Hitch has become president of the University of California. He was the editor of the American edition of James (now Sir James) Meade's Keynesian *An Introduction to Economic Analysis and Policy* (1938). At the time the address was delivered, Hitch was chairman, Research Council, Rand Corporation, "a non-profit, organization engaged in research on problems related to national security and the public interest." It took a full page ad in the September 1958 issue of *The Scientific American* to salute Veblen. Three quarters of the space was occupied by a portrait of Veblen and the remainder, under the title "Veblen . . . on place of science," was devoted largely to quotations from Veblen's famous essay, "The Place of Science in Modern Civilisation" (1906).

An extreme form of Hitch's interpretation was presented by staff members of another influential research organization devoted to problems of national security. They stated that "more and more decisions may be made by relatively narrow minded technocrats, who, intelligent, responsible and well trained as they may be, still may have what Veblen called a 'trained incapacity' to consider problems which are outside their special point of view or sphere of interest." [Herman Kahn and Anthony J. Wilner, "Faustian Powers and Human Choices: Some Twenty-First Century Technological and Economic Issues," in *Environment and Change: The Next Fifty Years,* edited by William R. Ewald (Bloomington, Indiana: Indiana University Press, 1968) p. 119].

Kenneth Boulding recently has made use of the concept to attack the studied neglect of the history of economic thought and institutional theory in the universities. He declared that as a consequence "Our graduate schools may easily be producing a good deal of the 'trained incapacity' which Veblen saw being produced in his day, and this is a negative commodity unfortunately with a very high price." [*Economics as a Science* (New York: McGraw-Hill, 1970) p. 156].

thought of the instinct of workmanship as "a broadly conceived term for growth."[140] Along this line was the interpretation of the book presented by Maurice Halbwachs. In his posthumous *The Psychology of Social Class* (1955), he attributed to Veblen the view that Britain and the United States led in the adoption of modern industrialism, the capitalist system, "because most of the people, or at any rate the leading manufacturers in these countries, are of the Anglo-Saxon race, and . . . this is a breed more energetic and positive than others. Its members have more inclination for the business of industry and trade, are without magical and religious beliefs, and apply their practical and scientific minds to the analysis of reality. According to this theory the capitalist would have distinguished himself from other men and outstripped them simply by perceiving more lucidly what was necessary to the running of an efficient enterprise. Efficiency engineers and what is called scientific organization of factories are all in the line of such positive and tenacious activity."[141]

Doubtless Halbwachs heard of the book from the stress upon it in the account of Veblen's work in the study of Maurice Roche-Agussol of the University of Montpelier, *Étude bibliographique des sources de la psychologie économique chez les Anglo-Américains* (1919) and in his earlier doctoral dissertation, *Psychologie économique chez les Anglo-Américains* (1918). By these works he seems to have

[140] C. C. Qualey, "The Thought of Thorstein Veblen," Boston *Herald,* August 21, 1966.

[141] *The Psychology of Social Class,* translated from the French by Claire Delavenay (London: Heinemann, 1958) p. 52. The above was substantially a summary of his review article of *The Instinct of Workmanship,* "Le Facteur instinctif dans l'art industriel," *Revue philosophique de la France et de l'Étranger,* March-April 1921, pp. 214-233.
As *Imperial Germany* makes clear, Veblen attaches relatively little importance to the factor of race.

established Veblen's position in France as a major "critic of the hedonist, equilibrium" approach of the classical and neo-classical schools.[142]

Perhaps we might note at this point that a number of economists have pointed out the influence of Veblen upon Joseph A. Schumpeter, especially in his most famous work, *Theorie der Wirtschaftlichen Entwicklung (The Theory of Economic Development),* which originally appeared in 1912. Thus a reviewer declared that the "psychology of Schumpeter's entrepreneur includes such elements as love of activity for its own sake, love of distinction, love of victory over others, love of the game and other traits which the newer psychology has been emphasizing, and with which such writings as those of Veblen . . . have made American students familiar. . . ." Anderson closed the review with: "The economist had too long been content with static theory and work like Schumpeter's and Veblen's is full of significance for the better understanding of economic life."[143] Relatively recently

---

[142] While working on the dissertation he wrote to Veblen for biographical and bibliographical information, saying that he was encouraged to do it at the suggestion of the supervisor of his thesis, Professor Germain Martin, Correspondent of the Institut de France. Professor Martin "has devoted a large part of his scientific activity to develop in our country an interest in American economic ideas." (Roche-Agussol to Veblen, August 3, 1917, Thorstein Veblen Papers).

Professor Martin's field was the economic history of France and in particular large industry, credit and public finance.

[143] B. M. Anderson, Jr., "Schumpeter's Dynamic Economics," *Political Science Quarterly,* December 1915, pp. 653, 660.

Another reviewer, after noting Schumpeter's extraordinary familiarity with American economic literature, declared in terminology reminiscent of Veblen that "Schumpeter's thought has advanced beyond the mechanistic interpretation of the physicist-economist. He has made a significant contribution in carrying us over to the newer evolutionary methods and evolutionary point of view." (R. C. McCrea, "Schumpeter's Economic System," *The Quarterly Journal of Economics,* May 1913, p. 529).

a Swedish economist concretely phrased the relationship between Veblen and Schumpeter in the following manner: "Schumpeter's theory of economic development is to a large extent founded on Austrian theory of capital and money – inclusively [Knut] Wicksell's . . . and Veblen's . . . more sociological approach."[144]

One of the most intriguing discussions of the instinct of workmanship was Sir Gilbert Slater's attempt to make it a major part of economic theory. He wrote in "The Psychological Basis of Economic Theory" in 1923 that "Veblen's *Theory of the Leisure Class*, an analysis of the working of the principles of conspicuous waste, conspicuous leisure and pecuniary repute illustrates throughout the insatiability, on the one hand, of desires springing from positive and negative self-feeling, and on the other, from the instinct of workmanship." As the starting point of his analysis he took the orthodox base as described by the current neo-classical economist, Philip H. Wicksteed in *The Common Sense of Political Economy*. As Slater put Wicksteed's position economic theory is concerned "with people's dealings with one another in one sort of relation, the Economic Relation, the characteristic feature of which is that normally in that relation each party is concerned only with his own side of the

[144] Johan Åkerman, *Theory of Industrialism: Causal Analysis and Economic Plans* (Lund, Sweden: Gleerup, 1960) p. 63.

Veblen has recently again been recognized as a pioneer in the recognition of so-called "non-economic motivation" in economic theory: "The past 20 years have seen a strong reaffirmation of the importance of non-economic as against economic motivation, for employees as well as managers and entrepreneurs. This is one of the control points – certainly one of the most widely quoted of [Chester I.] Barnard's *The Functions of the Executive* (1936). It was earlier emphasized by Veblen . . ." [Herbert A. Simon and Andrew C. Stedry, "Psychology and Economics," in *The Handbook of Social Psychology*, 5 volumes, edited by Gardner Lindzey and Elliot Aronson (Reading, Mass.: Addison-Wesley, 1954; 2nd edition, 1969) V, 285].

transaction." Slater in his summary declared "(1) That the economic relation is seldom, if ever, purely economic. (2) That all economic contacts, like other social contacts between individuals, stir in those individuals in greater or less degree some of the primary instinctive emotions, and that the economic relations established are coloured accordingly. (3) That the economic relation may in consequence be poisoned, by the excitation of anger, disgust, the mortification of self-esteem; or (4) It may be sweetened and consolidated by the excitation of the generalised parental instinct, of the instinct of comradeship, of the complex of instincts which generate the sentiment of loyalty, and by a common sharing of the gratification of the constructive instinct (Veblen's 'Instinct of Workmanship')."[144a]

Perhaps the deepest impress of the book, especially of the instinct of workmanship, was in the area of industrial relations, including what is now called industrial psychology and industrial sociology. This was brought out by a British admirer in 1926. R. M. Fox, a product of Ruskin College, Oxford, prefaced his comments by chastising his countrymen for their neglect of Veblen's work. "Amid the flood of superficial writing on industrial problems," he wrote in the prestigious *Nineteenth Century and After*, "it is perhaps not surprising that the work of Thorstein Veblen, well known in America, should have been neglected in this country. But more and more the Veblen point of view and even the characteristic Veblen phrases are creeping into the work of English social thinkers such as Professor Patrick Geddes and others of the LePlay House group, whose quarterly journal, *The Sociological Review*, treats economic problems in a comprehensive way." Fox noted Veblen's emphasis on what is

[144a] "The Psychological Basis of Economic Theory," *The Sociological Review*, October 1923, pp. 279, 284.

today called raising "the quality of life." He wrote: "The ramifications of factory influence faces us as one of the gravest problems of our industrial age. Whatever affects the workshop is bound to affect society. It is the center of life for those masses who are moulded by machine production. Yet our industrial psychologists ignore the need for industrial adjustment. Where investigators such as Veblen differ from them is in the possession of a deeper, wider, social outlook. This gives value to the work of the industrial philosophers, whether their immediate conclusions are tenable or not. The general view of the Veblen school is that industry, as conducted today, allows no place for the varied instinctive needs of men."

Striking was Fox's contrast between Veblen and Jeremy Bentham. "Veblen often appears like a high-powered Bentham, driven, as it were, by a dynamo instead of by a treadle. He applies a similar utilitarian view to life.... Bentham, in the early days of machinery, expressed the idea that society could be geared up in a mechanistic 'reasonable' way and made to run on strictly rational lines.... Where Veblen differs is that, with all his perception of the momentum and force of industry, he combines a knowledge of psychology and so of human instincts. He sees that industry may run counter to fundamental needs of personality. In allowing for the human recoil against machinification he stands head and shoulders above those who are merely blind instruments of the machine era. He voices the human criticism of the mechanical order. – 'The limit of tolerance native to the race, physically and spiritually, is short of that unmitigated materialism and unremitting mechanical routine to which the machine technology incontinently drives.' (*The Instinct of Workmanship*, p. 320)." Previously Fox quoted from the book (p. 318), "In all the various peoples of Christendom there is a visible straining against the drift of the machine's teaching, rising at times and in given classes of the population to the pitch of revulsion."

In a summary, he wrote, "Veblen advances the scientific abstraction of a perfectly adjusted industrial mechanism which is logical but fortunately not practicable. It is necessary to push these ideas to their logical end, because only so can we get people to see that there must be a compromise between those who would sacrifice humanity for the sake of machinery and those who would scrap machinery and hurl us back to savagery, in their zeal for personality. The little efficiency engineer with his scrappy, distorted view of life is too limited and purblind to realize that his perfect universal machine would be a monstrosity. Running through all Veblen's work is a hint of the human recoil, but he does not claim to be a prophet: He is an investigator, and a very dispassionate one. He deals with tendencies, conflicts, impulses that go towards making a rounded complete, fully-regulated industrial order that will interpenetrate our whole life, even more thoroughly than it does today."

Four years later in his obituary of Veblen in *The New Statesman* he presented the view in more clear cut fashion: "Veblen is not only a prophet; he is also a critic of the new time, for he recognizes that a completely mechanistic view of life is far too rigid for humanity. 'The instinct of workmanship,' he says in his book of that name, 'brought the life of mankind from the brute to the human, and in all the later growth of culture it has never ceased to pervade the works of man.' To preserve and use that instinct is one of the key problems of mass production today." Fox's opening and closing sentences were prophetic. "Professor Thorstein Veblen was a redoubtable intellectual champion of the 'common man.' Like most original thinkers, he will probably be known far more widely after his death than during his life time. . . .

Long after the names of presidents of august and venerable associations have been forgotten Veblen will be remembered as a man who laboured honestly to dig the foundations of thought upon which the new social order will be built."[144a]

[144a] "Towards a Philosophy of Industry" and "Thorstein Veblen," in *The Nineteenth Century and After,* August, November 1926, pp. 204, 684, 691, 696; "Thorstein Veblen," in *The New Statesman,* September 13, 1930, p. 707.

In *The Triumphant Machine* [(London: Published by Virginia and Leonard Woolf at the Hogarth Press, 1928) pp. 58-59], Fox declared that "America is fortunate in possessing a painstaking social thinker such as Professor Thorstein Veblen who has examined machine influence from a psychological standpoint and has produced a whole new fascinating literature on the subject."

In his autobiography Fox recalls that economics professors at the University of California and at the University of Minnesota requested permission to reproduce his writings on industrial relations. [*Smoky Crusade* (1937; London: Published by Virginia and Leonard Woolf at the Hogarth Press, cheap edition, 1938) pp. 54-55]. This was doubtless one of the ways Americans learned of Veblen's work.

An extreme version of Fox's position was the comment on *The Instinct of Workmanship* which The Viking Press quoted on the jacket of *The Engineers and the Price System,* (7th printing, 1940): "A profound and masterly analysis of the impulse for achievement which is man's highest gift. . . . He traces the instinct from its purity in the savage to its contaminated state in the present-day machine man; and the picture is the living truth behind the veil of modern business methods." The writer was Temple Scott, a critic and essayist, well known in England and the United States. His edition of Swift was long the standard one; like Veblen he was an admirer of William Morris. His book *The Use of Leisure* (1913) was published by Huebsch.

There is much to be said for Macmillan's statement in the original blurb: "At every point the author endeavors to throw new light on economic theory."

It should be noted that in 1959 a British industrial sociologist was so overwhelmed by the many important insights in Veblen's works he warned that "it would, however, be an error to think that all the industrial sociologists need do to redress the balance of the naive empiricism of the past 20 years is to reread their Thorstein Veblen." [J. A. Banks, "Veblen and Industrial Sociology," *The British Journal of Sociology,* September 1959, p. 241]. He included among Veblen's concepts: "The corporate revolution which Berle and Means first documented in 1933." (p. 238).

Imperial Germany and the Industrial Revolution

We now turn to the most prophetic of Veblen's books, *Imperial Germany and the Industrial Revolution* (which was originally published on June 23, 1915). As Hitler seized power in Germany in 1933, the publisher was urged to reprint the book as "the best picture of the residual barbarisms in German civilization; the soil out of which Nazism grew."[145] The publisher then felt, however, that the book did not fit, because whatever else the Germany of Hitler was it was not the old Imperial Germany. But when Hitler seized Czechoslovakia in 1939, the book was put in stock. The enthusiastic reception of the reprint was in striking contrast to the reviews of the original edition.[146] Those had been lukewarm at best; now the general keynote was that the book was as applicable to Hitler's Germany as to Kaiser Wilhelm's. Walton H. Hamilton in *The New Republic* wrote: "As an interpreter of the Munich pact Veblen is somewhat at a disadvantage. The last of his scribbles dates from the first year of the World War, and the great event to which his

---

[145] Mumford, *Men Must Act* (New York: Harcourt, Brace, 1939) p. 176.

[146] The ardor of some admirers of Veblen in the pre-Hitler period was cooled by the appearance of the first edition of *Imperial Germany*, for as one then said: "I was quite opposed to [President] Wilson's policy of intervention at that time and could not believe in the peculiar traits of the German people which Veblen stressed, until the second World War revealed the unusual degree to which the Teutonic myths and dynastic inheritance had dehumanized so many Germans." (Charles McKinley to Joseph Dorfman, January 31, 1963). McKinley was professor of political science at Reed College and had served as president of the American Political Science Association. He was a highly respected expert on public administration to the Federal government during the New Deal era. He had become interested in Veblen through the influence of his undergraduate teacher of economics at the University of Washington. This was Theresa McMahon, a student of Commons and a specialist in industrial relations.

comment moves lies a quarter of a century ahead. But if he had to write without knowledge of later acts, his was the gift of sensing the currents which move beneath the stream of things; and a larger sweep and a deeper insight have more than atoned for years of history his essay never knew. . . . An estimate is likely to fade as it comes across the years. But only in superficials is Veblen dated . . . [T]rappings of style and current concretion aside, the book does not reveal its age. . . . Read Fascist for Imperial Germany, write the Führer for the Emperor, remember that the state is still *über alles* – and it all goes for today. . . . If one would probe the failure of the late [Weimar] republic to fit Germany, the push into Austria, the rape of Czecho-Slovakia, the decadence of English diplomacy, the formal act of fealty by [Britain's prime minister] Mr. Neville Chamberlain to the Führer, the abdication of Great Britain as a continental power, the irony of the accord at Munich, the frantic locking of the British stable after title to the stolen horse has passed, he need seek no further. Not one of these things is named in the book – yet the why of them is all here."[147]

Henry A. Wallace, then United States Secretary of Agriculture (and later Vice President) took time off to write a ten page review article in the December 1940 issue of the *Political Science Quarterly*. This long time admirer of Veblen's insight, especially into the underlying forces behind

---

[147] "Veblen on the Munich Pact," *The New Republic*, August 30, 1939, pp. 107-108.

Another writer added in 1958 that "not only has Veblen proven an uncanny prophet relative to the outcome of the first World War, he also foretold the coming of the cold war." (Harry Elmer Barnes, "A New Assessment of Veblenian Economics," *The Southern Economic Journal*, July 1958, p. 92).

the various economic systems, declared the book to be "the most acute analysis of modern Germany which has ever been written, yet strangely enough the Solicitor of the Post Office Department of the United States denied to the book . . . mailing privileges while the United States was in the Great [World] War [I]. The Post Office Department in that day apparently was unable to appreciate that Veblen's book was a harder blow to Germany for the very reason that it was fair, objective and did not say a single word against Germany."

Incidentally, Wallace, who was a distinguished geneticist as well as economist and statesman, strongly supported Veblen's line of argument against the myth of German racial superiority, which was used by proponents to explain Germany's rapid technological advance. As Wallace put Veblen's argument, "The hybrid people of Germany by heredity in any given degree of latitude are about the same as the people in a corresponding degree of latitude in any of the adjoining countries. From England to St. Petersburg [now Leningrad], the people at birth have about the same characteristics. Those of us who are well acquainted with the Germans of the third and fourth generation in the United States know that Veblen is substantially right. As a geneticist I am convinced that he is right. Most, though perhaps not all, of the anthropologists will agree with him. There is no basis whatever for the myth that the Germans by heredity are a superior race." The editor of the journal commented in a footnote: "This review article, except for minor typographical changes, is printed exactly as Secretary Wallace wrote it in early March. The Secretary believes it is a rather remarkable confirmation of the soundness of Veblen's fundamental analysis that the striking events since March of this year should not have made it necessary to alter any part of the review."[148]

[148] "Veblen's *Imperial Germany and the Industrial Revolution*," *Political Science Quarterly*, December 1940, pp. 435-436.

Secretary Wallace, however, made one change in the final version, which illustrates some of the complexities of Veblen (as well as the Secretary's willingness to give serious attention to criticism). Tugwell sent me a note dated March 25, 1940, along with a copy of the original draft. The note read "Secretary Wallace has just written this, and gave it to me today. I know you would be interested, so I send it on." In my letter to Wallace two days later I took exception to the sentence: "Apparently he [Veblen] believes in returning our business and our way of life to the village." I commented as follows: "Yet his *Theory of Business Enterprise* was devoted to a considerable extent to showing the unworkability of small scale business enterprise under the modern technology. I think he thought that a good deal of the trustification had little technological justification, only a financial justification, but one of his great points was that modern machine technology had rendered obsolete the ancient small order of things." In the printed version of the review Secretary Wallace made a modification that reconciled our differences to a certain extent. The sentence now read: "Some of his writings would lead us to think that he believed in returning our business and our way of life to the village." Then he added the following gracious footnote: "Friends, who have read Veblen's works more extensively than I, tell me that he had a strong appreciation, as exemplified in his *Theory of Business Enterprise*, of the unworkability of small-scale competitive business enterprises under modern technology. While he had no patience with the building up of great trusts purely on a financial basis, he did realize that modern machine technology had rendered obsolete the ancient small order of things. It may be, therefore, that my emphasis on Veblen's homesickness for the village and farm economy is not completely warranted. His researches in anthropology led him in that direction but his appreciation of modern technology led him to understand the need for bringing rapidly and continuously up to date the customs and institutions based on a small-scale economy, in order that modern civilization might not destroy itself."

It should be noted, however, that *Imperial Germany*, especially the anthropology, was used by at least one federal justice department official in support of anti-trust philosophy. He declared: "On the demonstrable premise that the greatest single factor in the economic potential of a country is the resourcefulness and enterprise of its people,

At about the same time as the Wallace review, the influential newspaper columnist, Dorothy Thompson, drew on Veblen as "an American who knew all about it," in her "Thoughts on the Fall of Paris." She warned that "Hitler is winning the war because he has been fighting it with an industrial and engineering economy, while the democracies have been fighting it with a money or financial economy."[149]

Among the book's basic contributions to the theory of industrial development is the concept of the "penalty of taking the lead" for the advanced industrial countries in the struggle to maintain industrial supremacy; or to put it in another form, "the merits of borrowing" for vigorous underdeveloped countries. As Hamilton expressed it, "as the creator [of modern technology] England is held in leash, staggered by the dead hand of past performance; as the borrower Germany experiences none of the drawbacks of innovation. It

[149] New York *Herald Tribune,* June 17, 1940.

Judge [Learned] Hand's system of small producers is, at once again, to be preferred to a system of monopolistic combines. The promotion of managerial incentive is still, I think, in line with the Latin maxim: 'Better first man in a little Iberian village, than second in Rome.' The wellsprings of economic democracy and advance are better maintained in an economic society where Thorstein Veblen's political sentiments of local autonomy and insubordination [as expressed in *Imperial Germany*] prevail – those sentiments which distinguished the Anglo-American democratic system from the German and Japanese feudalistic one. Feudalism and authoritarianism in the body politic and in the body economic are closely allied, for those two bodies have become increasingly one." (Sigmund Timberg, "Some Justifications for Divestiture," *The George Washington Law Review,* December 1950, p. 144. Timberg was then Chief, Judgment and Judgment Enforcement Section, Anti-Trust Division).

I would like to suggest here that Veblen may be using the "anthropology" to point out that dominant thinking has its rationale in the context of the "obsolete . . . ancient, small order of things."

has been able to select, to improve, to be up to date."[150] Secretary Wallace formulated the matter thus: "[Germany by 1870] . . . found ready to her hands a system which England . . . had already worked out. But in taking over the technological system, she had all the advantages which are enjoyed by a manufacturer who is constructing a new plant. The Germans, therefore, promptly became more efficient than the British in many fields of endeavor."[151]

Thus a nation lately entering upon the process of industrialization has the opportunity of being able to take over the accumulated technological advances achieved by the early entrants without suffering the institutional restraints to further rapid advance that accompanied its development by the leaders.[152] Veblen's doctrine is now recognized in domi-

---

[150] "Veblen on the Munich Pact," p. 107.

Hamilton led in emphasizing Veblen's contribution through his adaptation of the section under the title "The Penalty of Taking the Lead" in his *Current Economic Problems: A Series of Readings in the Control of Industrial Development*, pp. 154-156.

[151] "Veblen's *Imperial Germany and the Industrial Revolution,*" p. 435.

[152] "All this does not mean that the British have sinned against the canons of technology. It is only that they are paying the penalty of having been thrown into the lead and having shown the way. At the same time it is not to be imagined that this lead has brought nothing but pains and penalties. The shortcomings of this British industrial situation are visible chiefly by contrast with what the British might be doing if it were not for the restraining dead hand of their past achievement, and by further contrast, latterly, with what the new-come German people are doing by use of the British technological lore. As it stands, the accumulated equipment, both material and immaterial, both in the way of mechanical equipment, appliances in hand and in the way of technological knowledge ingrained in the population and available for use, is after all of very appreciable value, though the case of Germany should make it plain that it is the latter, the immaterial equipment, that is altogether of first consequence, rather than the accumulation of 'productive goods' in hand. These 'productive goods' cost nothing but labor; the immaterial equipment

nant international trade theory as among the major determinants of industrial specialization.[153]

The concept of "the penalty of taking the lead" and the correlative "the merits of borrowing" has had considerable influence on a current school of anthropology, a school which has revived in a modified form the old view of definite stages in the evolutionary progress of man. A prominent exponent

[153] It is amusing to note that recently a controversy broke out between two claimants for the title of discoverer of the concept: Professor E. H. Carr of Oxford and Professor Alexander Gerschenkron of Harvard, both experts on the economic development of Russia. Gerschenkron noted that Carr "proceeds to argue that Russian industrialization was not backward because in the process much more advanced methods were used than had been the case in more advanced countries." He then complained that "the trouble with this argument is that [it] . . . is not Professor Carr's, but very much my own, and I must protest against infringement of my property rights. In my studies of industrialization in conditions of backwardness, I went to considerable length to stress what I called the advantages of backwardness, that is to say, the advantages of the latecomers. The most important of these advantages was precisely the possibility of application of more efficient modern technology." (*Europe in the Russian Mirror*, pp. 109-110).

A Columbia historian in 1958, after pointing out the "great contribution" of the book to comparative economic history went on to say that the concept of the penalty of taking the lead "perhaps more than others in Veblen's comparison has come into the common parlance and common thought of economists." [Carter Goodrich, "The Case of New Countries" in *Thorstein Veblen: A Critical Reappraisal* edited by Douglas F. Dowd (Ithaca: Cornell University Press, 1958) pp. 265, 266]. Goodrich was a student of Hamilton at Amherst.

of technological proficiency costs age-long experience." *Imperial Germany* (1915; New York: Augustus M. Kelley Publishers, 1964) pp. 132-133. Thus to Veblen the immaterial equipment included the skill to apply the store of knowledge.

Professor Paul Samuelson follows somewhat Hamilton's version: "As in Veblen's thesis, the U. K. came early to its industrial revolution and became frozen and fossilized too early." [Samuelson, as reported by D. C. Hague in *Backward Areas in Advanced Countries*, Proceedings of a Conference held by the International Economic Association, edited by E. A. G. Robinson (London: Macmillan, 1969) p. 378].

of the school, E. R. Service, in 1960 raised Veblen's concepts to a 'law of anthropology." Veblen, he stated, advanced in *Imperial Germany* two fruitful ideas: "One is that Germany became more efficient industrially than her predecessor, England, because of the 'merits of borrowing'; the other is that England conversely was finally less efficient than Germany because of 'the penalty of taking the lead. . . .' " These ideas Service developed into the "Law of Evolutionary Potential. . . . The more specialized and adapted a form in a given evolutionary stage, the smaller is its potential for passing to the next stage"; more concisely, "Specific evolutionary progress is inversely related to general evolutionary potential."[154]

Veblen's notion that the great destruction of material equipment in modern warfare need not prove disastrous for post war reconstruction received an important development at the hands of Geddes and Slater in 1917. They said in *Ideas at War:* "But, as a matter of fact, war tends to create a vastly quickened appreciation of the value of mechanical knowledge and invention, and the material value of the effect thus attained may be stupendous. For example, a banker estimated that the introduction of the eucalyptus tree into Mexico by the French under Napoleon III in a dozen years counterbalanced the loss caused by the terrible civil war that followed upon that disastrous expedition. Or, again, we may note that, while the armies have been making deserts, Professor Bottomley in King's College has been pushing forward his researches into the conditions of plant-growth with results which promise a new and wonderful era for intensive culture, and this largely through utilization of the

[154] Service, "The Law of Evolutionary Potential," in *Evolution and Culture,* edited by Marshall D. Sahlins and E. R. Service (Ann Arbor, Michigan: University of Michigan Press, 1960) pp. 97, 99.

peat mosses which have been hitherto such comparatively unproductive assets of all the northern Powers. In many ways, then, war acts as a stimulus to inventors, and the best of their results substantially help to pay for it. The increased respect for German efficiency in scientific and technical knowledge is plainly reacting upon all other countries; arousing Russia, for instance, from her backwardness, and us from our too-easy self-satisfaction and habitual reliance upon our former leadership."[154a]

A student of American intellectual history has also found suggestive ideas in *Imperial Germany and the Industrial Revolution.* Thus the authority on the Puritan mind of colonial New England, Perry Miller, called attention to a little known insight in the treatise; namely, how changes in the national "frame of mind" are brought about. He introduced his *Jonathan Edwards* (1949) with the following passage from the book.[155]

> The changes that alter the face of national life have small beginnings; the traceable initial process having commonly set in with some overt act on the part of a small and distinctive group of persons, who will then presently be credited with insight and initiative in case the move proves itself by success. Should the movement fail of acceptance and consequent effect, these spokesmen of its propaganda would then prove to have been fanciful project-makers, perhaps of unsound mind. To describe the course of such a matter by analogy, the symptoms of the new frame of mind will first come in evidence in the attitude of some one individual, who, by congenital proclivity and through an exceptional

---

154a *Ideas at War,* pp. 156-157.

155 Professor W. H. Cowley of Stanford University called my attention to the reference in Miller's book. The passage from *Imperial Germany* is on pp. 58-59.

> degree of exposure, is peculiarly liable to its infection. In so far as the like susceptibility is prevalent among the rest of the population, and so far as circumstances of habituation favor the new conceit, it will then presently find lodgement in the habits of thought of an increasing number of persons, – particularly among those whom the excursive play of hybrid heredity has thrown up as temperamental variants peculiarly apt for its reception, or whom the discipline of life bends with exceptional rigor in the direction of its bias. Should the new idea also come to have the countenance of those in authority or in a position to claim popular deference, its vogue will be greatly helped out by imitation, and perhaps by compulsory observance, and so it may in a relatively short time become a matter of course and of common sense. But the reservation always stands over, that in such a hybrid population the same prevalent variability of temperament that so favors the infiltration and establishment of new ideas will at the same time render their tenure correspondingly precarious.

It is not surprising that the passage has suggested to readers a fruitful explanation of the rise of Hitler and his kind.

Veblen did not engage in combat with the publisher of the last two books over printing details, as he did over *The Theory of the Leisure Class* and *The Theory of Business Enterprise*. The explanation is very simple. He completely controlled their manufacture by having them produced at his own expense at a local printshop in Columbia, Missouri. Macmillan became the publisher again, but acted essentially as a distributor and charged for its services a commission of fifteen per cent of the proceeds. Veblen, however, complained of the failure of the firm to advertise the books adequately. The firm explained to him on March 29, 1917, with not a little humor, that "Your complaint in regards the matter of the pushing of your books which we publish on commission, is perhaps well founded, at any rate so far as spending money on advertising these books is concerned, but as you will find by turning to your agreements, there is no obligation on us to advertise these books or give advertising publicity except in a very limited way."

We now come to the last of the three books which were published during his University of Missouri period.

An Inquiry into the Nature of Peace and the Terms of its Perpetuation

Meanwhile Veblen had completed the manuscript of the book that would appear under the title *An Inquiry into the Nature of Peace and the Terms of Its Perpetuation,*[156] and was having it manufactured also at a local print shop.[157] At the same time he sent a copy of the ms. to Francis Hackett, "the Irish born critic and liberal," who had built up a reputation by his "brilliant editorship of the Chicago *Evening-Post Literary Review,*" and then added to his laurels and power in the world of books as an editor of the recently established *New Republic.*[158] He took the ms. to Macmillan with his high commendation. On March 27, 1917, Veblen wrote Macmillan "Mr. Hackett tells me that you have taken an interest in a manuscript of mine, lately submitted by him, and suggests that I write you further concerning the book

[156] This was not the original title, which seems to have been simply "The Nature of Peace."

[157] E. W. Stephens Publishing Co., Columbia, Missouri.

[158] F. L. Mott, *A History of American Magazines*, 5 volumes (Cambridge, Mass.: Harvard University Press, 1930-1968) V, 196. Hackett later became a writer of historical novels.

and its manufacture with a view to your undertaking its publication." The letter amply bears out the idea that Veblen must have been at one time a printer. After giving the full title of the book, he went on to say that "the lettering of the back will presumably read, 'The Nature of Peace.' The proposed running title would be the same as the lettering on the back. The volume will be put up as nearly as may be in the same form as *The Instinct of Workmanship*, which you published for me some time ago. I expect this earlier volume in this case to be duplicated very closely in all respects."

After informing the publisher of his arrangements for the local manufacture of the book, he went on to state that the print shop would produce an edition of 1250 copies, "at the same time having matrices made for plates for future use in case further copies are wanted – the present impression to be taken from the type." As he figured it, "the cost of the present edition, after allowing for review and presentation copies, will be about 75¢ f.o.b. here. This cost will necessitate the listing of the book at $2.00. After allowing the usual 35% discount to dealers, there will therefore be left over rather less than 50¢ per copy for royalty and commission, and it seems to me that this margin might fairly be divided about evenly between royalty and commission."[159] In concluding Veblen even set the date of publication. It "should presumably be fixed for about the middle of April, as the printer has engaged to deliver the finished volumes before that time."

Meanwhile the firm's anonymous reader, after stating that

[159] Veblen reached the conclusion that there would be less than fifty cents to divide doubtless by presumably including but not stating such matters as the transportation expense. Interestingly, Veblen used such terms as "royalty and commission" and "margin" but not "surplus" or "profits."

his synopsis gave a scant notion of Veblen's argument, went on to say: "This manuscript is really a sort of sequel to his other books and needs to be considered in connection with them. Further, as is usual with Veblen, his argument is not put in direct form, but always with a large amount of irony. Further, his book is valuable not so much because it is convincing as because it is extremely suggestive.

"There is, apparently, a considerable number of men in this country who read whatever Veblen writes, and these readers are by no means confined to men of one group or one opinion. I think this manuscript is likely to have lasting sale, since it is based on very broad considerations and far-reaching arguments. It will have special interest at the present event, because . . . he argues for the absolute destruction of the German imperial state."

The publisher replied on March 29 to Veblen that "I am glad to learn that Mr. Hackett has told you of my interest in your new book, and we shall be very glad to publish it for you if we can make arrangements with you to issue it under some equitable plan that will be likely to give you satisfaction." After commenting on Veblen's complaint about the inadequate advertising of his books, he declared "When I suggested to Mr. Hackett a method for the publishing of your book which might perhaps be satisfactory to you I had in mind this matter of advertising and publicity which would be necessary in the case of the new volume." He then turned to point out that Veblen's calculations left hardly any profit to the firm. "When I analyze the figures of costs of the book as given in your letter and the price at which you wish the book sold to the public, I cannot, I am sorry to say, see that there is any margin left either for exploiting the book or even for the bare costs of its distribution. What most people outside of the book business do not understand is that it costs 25¢ for every dollar's worth of books sold for the expenses of selling them, the costs included in this 25¢ being rent, travelling expenses, clerk hire, etc., etc.

"So that if we take your costs of 75¢ a copy as stated in your letter for the bound book in Columbia, we get a profit and loss account for the volume somewhat as follows:

Cost of book per copy	$0.75
Freight & cartage to publisher	.05
Expenses of sale	.32
Making a total cost of	$1.12

against an average return of $1.30 under the proposed price at retail of $2.00, i.e., with an average discount of 35% up to 40%, and as of course the largest buyers get the largest discount it is probable that the average return would be a little less than is here stated. This leaves a net profit per copy of 18¢ per book sold, which might perhaps be divided evenly between author and publisher if both are to make a profit out of the sale of the first edition, and would give each of them 9¢ per copy for each book sold.[160]

"I may say frankly that we don't consider this profit adequate, and figure here that we must make at least ten per cent upon our turnover, so that our profit on the book, as we figure it, ought to be 13¢ per copy.

---

[160] On the margin of Veblen's letter was written in pencil another and slightly different estimate by someone at Macmillan. This calculation yields a profit of half the amount detailed in the letter sent to Veblen.

Cost	$0.75	$1.30
Freight	.04	
Expense to sell	.32	
Advertising matter, Edi[torial] exp[en]se	.10	
	1.21	
Profit		0.09

As I stated in the Veblen book, he paid, according to Isador Lubin, $700 for its manufacture. For this as well as for his previous works the actual contracts are not available.

"My suggestion to Mr. Hackett was that you should decide upon a price at which we should account to you for the books as sold, this price to include whatever profit you desired on the transaction, we then to be free to fix a retail price for the volume which would allow us our usual margin of 25% for business expenses and 10% for profit after the deduction of the average trade discount, and if the volume is to be handled by us I think that some such arrangement as this one ought to be made.

"Of course we can handle the book for you on the usual commission arrangement which allows us, as you will remember, 15% upon what we receive from the sale of the volume, but as it costs us 25% to sell the book you will readily see that we could not afford to push a book published on commission to any considerable extent. We shall, as I say, be very glad to publish your book as it seems to be one well worth while and of immediate importance. . . ."

A contract was relatively quickly signed and the book was published on April 25.[161] It had such an immediate impact, thanks in good part to Hackett's powerful review in *The New Republic*, that it led to a considerable revival of public interest in Veblen and his works. There was, of course, a continuous interest in Veblen but it did not approach the amount of attention that he received for a period after the publication of *The Theory of the Leisure Class*.[162] This is illustrated by a story told by Robert Duffus. Around 1911, Ida Tarbell, famed journalist of the progressive era, had suggested to Duffus that he do "a personality piece" on Veblen for the reform minded *The American Magazine*, of which she was a star editor. He prepared the article with the aid of Veblen's first wife (Ellen Rolfe Veblen), but the

[161] Hackett's review is reprinted in the Appendix.

[162] *The Theory of the Leisure Class* continued to enjoy considerable sales.

journal rejected it on the ground that "I hadn't made Veblen exciting enough." Duffus added, "and anyhow his vogue had not yet begun as it did a few years later."[163]

But after Hackett's efforts to push Veblen and the book, his importance began to be acknowledged at home and abroad. The influential London based *Asiatic Review* noted that "of the critics of a searching calibre the war has discovered not a few and some even antedated the war, as Mr. Belloc and Mr. G. K. Chesterton here and Mr. Thorstein Veblen in America."[164]

Branford, who had just resumed the editorship of *The Sociological Review,* wrote Veblen in 1919, "There is nothing I should like better than to have an article from you sometime. Why, for instance, should the *Sociological Review* not publish simultaneously anything you care to have published in Europe at the same time that it appeared in America? I should so much like also if sometime, when you can spare time, you would do us one or two or more articles setting out for European readers a sort of summary of your whole

---

[163] Duffus, *The Innocents at Cedro,* p. 148.

On the basis of evidence in the Veblen book (p. 496), Duffus states that the marital relations between Veblen and his first wife "could not have been satisfactory." (*The Innocents at Cedro,* p. 146). Since some writers on Veblen have not been as perceptive as Duffus in reading my account, I would like to clarify the matter by quoting from a letter from one of the wife's closest friends. After reading the Veblen book, Mrs. Harry A. Millis wrote me on August 4, 1936: "She [Ellen] would have given her life, I should almost say her soul, to bear a child." Mrs. Millis in the same letter left a vivid description of her. "She was very, very thin and helpless, her skirts dragged down at the waist for we all wore the shirtwaist style at that time; her hats were askew on her head, her hair was always in disorder. Even when I went shopping with her, I could not induce her to buy suitable clothes. But she was so delightful that none thought of her appearance, i.e., none who loved her and many did."

[164] Quoted from "A Great Game," in inside of front cover of Branford, *The Drift to Revolution* (London: Headley, 1919).

doctrine. People here know something of your theory of the leisured classes, but hardly anything of the rest of your writings.[165]

The problem of enduring peace has always played a large part in Veblen's works but doubtless his attention was directed toward a book on the subject at least as early as 1911 by the activities of two of his British friends, Sir Patrick Geddes and Victor Branford. According to Mumford, it seems that the team had then "come to the conclusion that the great war was inevitable, unless there was a decisive reorientation in the economic and political policies, and indeed in the fundamental life philosophies of the contending nations. They privately circulated a memorandum that year . . . which conditionally predicted the war not later than 1915, and outlined a series of books on The Making of the Future, which would enable the English speaking peoples to understand the nature of the war itself and the defects and evils of the civilization that engendered it." Mumford continued, "Veblen, incidentally, was named as one of the possible American contributors."[166] Branford wrote Veblen that "the new book on Peace should be brought out in a 50¢ edition."[167]

---

[165] Branford to Veblen, May 27, 1919, Thorstein Veblen Papers.

Since Veblen did not do so, Branford undertook the task in part on the occasion of the first British publication of some of Veblen's books in 1924, in a review article. See "Thorstein Veblen," *The Sociological Review,* January 1925.

[166] Mumford, "Introduction," to Boardman, *Patrick Geddes,* pp. xi-xii.

[167] Ann B. Veblen [step-daughter of Veblen] to Isador Lubin, June 29, 1917, copy. Original is in possession of Lubin.

A review signed S[ybella] B[ranford] (Mrs. Victor Branford) appeared in *The Sociological Review,* autumn 1917. It read: "Mr. Veblen uses his remarkable analytic powers to describe with pitiless realism the 'Victorian peace' from which we have emerged and which presumably the 'League of Nations' is to reestablish. . . . Mr. Veblen's book is one of those pieces of masterly analysis of a complicated social situ-

Another admirer of the book was his former Stanford chief, Chancellor David Starr Jordan. He wrote Veblen, "I am just reading your book on *The Nature of Peace.* I agree practically with all its statements, except those regarding prehistoric man, none of whom I have ever met, at least not under that guise (and so I know nothing about him). I also feel an unholy joy at the subtle and inimitable satire with which you describe the enthusiasm of that group of men which Gelett Burgess recognized as 'Bromides.' It is a real pleasure once in a while to find a Sulphite – a man who can go around 'without any mark or brand on him,' as Lincoln put it, and occasionally break out in a new spot."[168]

The Nature of Peace, as I noted in the Veblen book, was bitterly attacked as pro-German and unpatriotic in the influential New York *Tribune* by Henry A. Wise Wood early in 1918.[169] We now know that Veblen was able, with the help of his publisher and also of Professor E. R. A. Seligman and President Nicholas Murray Butler of Columbia, to obtain

[168] Jordan to Veblen, August 22, 1917, Thorstein Veblen Papers.

[169] Wood was chairman of the Conference Committee on National Preparedness. He also filed a complaint with the United States Department of Justice.

---

ation which he has accustomed us to expect from his pen. But Mr. Veblen does not stop at an analysis of the Victorian peace, he deals also in the chapter 'On the Conditions of a Lasting Peace' with the conditions of mind of the German people. Here he points out that a special evil of the German state system is, that it has succeeded in suppressing all independence of mind among the Intellectuals. 'It plainly appears' (p. 116) 'that the Intellectuals are to be counted as supernumeraries, except so far as they serve as an instrument of publicity and indoctrination in the hands of the discretionary authorities.' An intellectual of Mr. Veblen's type cannot avoid feeling that such a state of things makes even the Victorian peace desirable by contrast. . . . The book should be read and re-read, and it should be taken into careful consideration by all those who are preparing to deal with the problems of reconstruction." (pp. 184-185).

a retraction from the *Tribune*. In its March 1, 1918, issue in a lengthy editorial the editors expressed regret that they had read the "difficult book" only after they had printed Wood's condemnation. With the aid of extensive quotations, the editorial concluded that *The Nature of Peace* was "one of the most anti-German books in English print."[170]

The attack on Veblen was blunted, but Wood kept attacking. On March 27, he wrote to the publisher for a spare copy. "I have exhausted my supply of copies and need another to work from." The firm replied the next day that it had no copies in stock and negotiations were under way for transfer of the book to another publisher.

The attack on the book came not only from super patriots but also from at least one prominent radical journal, *The Radical Review*, the organ of the most militant of the Socialist parties, – the Socialist Labor Party.[171] The gist of the review was effectively presented in the complaint to the reviewer by Isador Lubin, then a student and assistant of Veblen at the University of Missouri. He wrote that "your review of his

170 "Veblen's Book," New York *Tribune*, March 1, 1918.

See also Veblen, "Another German Apologist," *The Dial*, April 19, 1917, pp. 344-345. This is reprinted below.

At about the same time, B. M. Anderson, Jr., who came from a prominent Missouri family, wrote to Seligman that: "Trouble is being made by some stupid fools for Veblen at the University of Missouri on the charge of writing in behalf of Germany. I think I shall be able, through my father and others, to choke it off. [I] have written a letter, for local publication, defending him. The poor fellow has had academic trouble enough! I regard him as one of the greatest thinkers – if not always a well balanced thinker – of our time. Don't you? I should be glad to be able to quote your estimate of him, if things go further."

171 The journal took over from Veblen his rhetoric, at least to the extent of borrowing his phrase, the "industrial republic." It proclaimed that in the interest of the socialist movement it "sought to cement and improve the social position of the working class in its struggle against the capitalist class for the abolition of the Wage System and the inauguration of the Industrial Republic."

[Veblen's] book, and the implication that he is trying to hold on to his job by making radical statements in roundabout ways belittles the man. I hold Mr. Veblen in too high regard to see such implication go unanswered."[172]

Twenty-two years later, like *Imperial Germany, The Nature of Peace* began again to attract considerable attention as the United States prepared to help defend civilization against the onslaught of Hitler and to plan for enduring peace. The United States Department of Agriculture appears to have been a leader in promoting interest in the book.

Secretary Wallace had closed his review of the 1939 edition of *Imperial Germany* with: "After I finished this review, I became possessed of a great desire to take a fresh look at Veblen's work, *The Nature of Peace,* which I had read twenty years ago but had forgotten. This book which was published in early 1917 before the United States entered the war is just as remarkable in its prophetic insight as the volume on Germany. In no sense is Veblen pro-British. But he is convinced that the British gentleman is at the end of his rope and that the ruthlessness of the Germans and Japanese in utilizing modern technology in a factual instead of a gentlemanly wasteful manner will force the whole world to face certain eventualities.

"If Veblen were alive today, he would doubtless make a number of changes in his analysis. And yet in the main his understanding of the trend of economic and political events is so profound that his two books *Imperial Germany* and *The Nature of Peace* should be required reading for the statesmen of all the democratic countries of the world. They

---

[172] Lubin to David S. Reisz, November 11, 1917; copy supplied by Lubin to Joseph Dorfman.

The review appeared in the October 1917 issue, pp. 192-196. The reviewer's lectures on Marxian doctrine before Section Cleveland, Socialist Labor Party, appeared in the journal.

cannot afford to make at the time the next peace comes the same errors that were made in 1919 and the early 1920's."

Then Lazar Volin, of the Office of Foreign Agricultural Relations, prepared a "summary" in 1940 in mimeographed form for internal circulation.[173] "A Review of Thorstein Veblen's *The Nature of Peace and the Terms of Its Perpetuation*" began with "This book ought to be made required reading for isolationists and apostles of 'appeasement.'" It closed with "The book . . . is valuable for its interpretation of international strife in psychological and institutional terms. While by no means ignoring economic factors and motives, Veblen does not exaggerate their influence . . . and does not make a fetish out of them, as is the modern fashion in writing on the subject. He performed a service, too, by the distinction he draws between the pacific and dynastic states – the latter being the relatively gentle prototypes of the modern totalitarian state. This distinction is of capital importance, especially today when there is much loose talk about power politics and imperialism without differentiation between the various historic types of imperialism. The book, moreover, is full of brilliant and often prophetic insight . . . such as the clear vision of the grave danger arising from the alliance of modern technology and science with a militaristic state bent on aggrandisement; and the impossibility of 'appeasement' of such a power save by the peace of submission."

There still remains the question "as to the reason why one modern nation is warlike and another relatively pacific. Veblen finds the cause of such variation in the course of national historical development. In the case of Germany 'the move into modern economic conditions has been made so precipitately compared with that of Great Britain as to have

[173] Volin received a Ph. D. from the University of Michigan and was an authority on Russian agriculture.

carried the medieval frame of mind over virtually intact into the era of large business and machine development.' "

The conditions for the maintenance of peace are along "the familiar lines of what he calls 'neutralization,' and of what we would call internationalization, 'of all those human relations out of which international grievances are wont to arise.' Foremost among these is the abrogation of all discrimination in international trade. . . . Veblen also proposes 'neutralization in merchant shipping,' 'neutralization of citizenship,' and, finally, as it would be termed in the parlance of today, a system of collective security, called, when he wrote this book, a League to Enforce Peace. The United States . . . must join such a League. For the American 'position is no longer defensible in isolation under the later state of the industrial arts.' "[173a]

[173a] As a historian explained, on the outbreak of World War I "Various projects for international cooperation [for the maintenance of peace] were formulated and discussed. One of these was that of the economist Thorstein Veblen. . . . In 1795 during the French revolutionary wars, the German philosopher Immanuel Kant had proposed the formation of a league consisting of republican states to secure the peace. In 1917, in an *Inquiry into the Nature of Peace,* Veblen suggested a modern version of such a league. The principal members would be North Atlantic countries, including not only the United States and the English speaking dominions, and France, but the Scandinavian countries and the Netherlands as well. By and large these people have come to the tolerant attitude that finds expression in the maxim 'Live and let live.' Veblen considered them mature enough 'to have abjured dynastic ambitions of dominion.'

"Around this nucleus of democratic nations, Veblen explained, later would be ranged the peoples of Central and East Europe – freed from dynastic rule – and then the still less developed colonial peoples overseas. While the degrees of influence would differ, the relations among the three groups would be no longer exploitative and imperial. The league was to follow the pattern of the United States, in which states, territories and outlying possessions exercise different degrees of autonomy and sovereignty. There were to be no economic discriminations and privilges, the resources of every part of the globe would be accessible to all peoples on an equal basis, trade was to be free, and diplo-

Meanwhile back in early 1918, Hackett had rendered another important service to Veblen. Veblen as I noted in the Veblen book was dissatisfied with his publishers. Hackett arranged for the four Macmillan books to be transferred to Ben W. Huebsch, then a struggling publisher who was beginning to achieve a reputation as an outstanding pioneer in the advance of American publishing.[174] Huebsch informed

[174] Of Ben W. Huebsch's creative role in helping to make Veblen an enduring figure more will be said later in the text. Here I should like to give additional examples of his role as a midwife to the advancement of American publishing as an instrument for the development of American culture. He shaped and titled Sherwood Anderson's greatest book, *Winesberg, Ohio.* He published Elizabeth Madox Robert's first book of poems, *Under the Tree,* and then her novels beginning with *The Time of Man,* those classics in American literature. Harold Laski was only one of "the many men of strong opinions for whom Ben made a cause – even if he did not always agree with them." He found an audience in the United States for a host of continental writers from the biographies of the Austrian Stefan Zweig to the twelve volume, *The Thibauts,* by the Nobel Prize winner Roger Martin du Gard. Not least was his role in nourishing the genius of James Joyce. According to Joyce's latest biographer, when in 1916 "about twenty-five English printers and almost as many publishers refused to handle. . . . [*A Portrait of the Artist as a Young Man*], and when other American publishers were either frightened or disinterested," Huebsch brought out the first edition. Their relationship was such that in the contract for *Finnegans Wake,* "Joyce insisted on the insertion of the famous clause that, if Ben should leave The Viking Press to go into another firm, the author and his book might follow him. In spite of this written tribute, Joyce was not always so transigent, and Ben once or twice mentioned to me that Joyce sometimes behaved like a boyar." Perhaps the best way to sum up Huebsch's influence is to recount the story he once told me of how he managed to survive in his early struggling years. Some of his promising authors, themselves not flush with cash, would temporarily desert him, obtain advances from other publishers and turn over the money to him. [Quotations are from addresses of Marshall A. Best and Richard Ellmann in *1876 B. W. Huebsch 1964* (New York: privately printed, 1964) pp. 8, 16].

macy was to become 'open' and public." Solomon F. Bloom, *Europe and America; The Western World in Modern Times* (New York: Harcourt, Brace & World, 1961) pp. 512-513.

me that "I cannot easily ascertain the date on which Hackett brought Veblen and me together, but I find a letter from Veblen, written from the Faculty Club, Columbia, on February 4, 1918, in which he alludes to an interview 'the other day' and states that [Leon] Ardzrooni [Veblen's *fides Achates*] is empowered to make arrangements with respect to the details of my becoming his publisher.[175] Evidently we went ahead on the oral agreement, for I find that plates of two Veblen books were received by me in May 1918. In June 1918 the business transaction was consummated in writing."[176]

[175] Ardzrooni had arranged for Veblen to live temporarily at the club. Ardzrooni, who had studied with Veblen at Stanford and Missouri, was then pursuing graduate studies and teaching at Columbia, while a younger brother managed their prosperous fruit growing business in Fresno, California, during the academic year. A quip went the rounds at the time that Ardzrooni practised peonage in California in order to preach socialism at Columbia.

A fellow Missouri student has written the following account of the discussions between Veblen and Ardzrooni at the Davenport home where Veblen lived at first in the Missouri period: "Veblen sawed a little now and then, or chopped some brush and things, just as the spirit moved him. Ardzrooni was good with the head axe and would chop and argue with Veblen now and then when he came to smoke Thors out on some line of discussion or other. But I guess the Herr Professor wasn't so easy to smoke out, as Leon no doubt realized. He'd shout louder and louder, till the axe helve gave way or his lungs gave out. He could outshout anybody, but Thors wasn't a shouter. He'd just politely chuckle or laugh at Leon with sly gibes on the side." (Stuart Updegraff to Joseph Dorfman, September 26, 1935).

A Stanford college mate described Ardzrooni as "short, burly, dark-skinned, dark-haired and [he] could look extremely ferocious." (Duffus, *The Innocents at Cedro,* p. 154).

[176] Huebsch to Dorfman, April 9, 1934. The rights to all the four books published by Macmillan were transferred to Huebsch as of April 2, 1918. Because Veblen owned the plates, Huebsch agreed to pay a royalty rate of forty per cent of the sales price less the cost of printing new editions of the four books transferred. At Veblen's request Huebsch wanted to take over *The Theory of Business Enterprise* from Scribner's, but Scribner's was unwilling.

As I noted in an addition in the seventh edition of the Veblen book (p. 381), after the transfer was arranged, "Hackett received $250 from Judge Learned Hand, Elsie Clews Parsons and others to advertise *The Nature of Peace.*" Veblen now had a publisher of whom he never seems to have complained. The paths of Veblen, Huebsch and Hackett were to cross again a few years later. In 1922 Hackett wrote Huebsch: "I think I have earned your friendship. I sought your interest not my own, when I urged Veblen to go to you." Two years later he asked: "How is Veblen doing? The man, and his work?" In 1925 when Huebsch joined the newly formed Viking Press (with the colophon a Viking ship) he wrote Hackett about it. And that ardent, witty Irishman replied: "I wish the name of the press were not so aquatic and so unlike their [the organizers'] names, but if anyone wants to pin his name to such disgraceful, bloodthirsty, and disreputable cutthroat savages as the Vikings, I make no kick. It will suit you anyway, since you see Sweden tenderly. And Veblen will smile to be under this imprint."[177]

The Higher Learning in America: A Memorandum on the Conduct of Universities by Business Men

Meanwhile towards the close of World War I in 1918, appeared the first of Veblen's books under the imprint of B. W. Huebsch, his third publisher. Actually as we have dis-

[177] Hackett to Huebsch, April 5, 1922, January 20, 1924, September 28, 1925, Huebsch Papers, Library of Congress. Huebsch's wife was Swedish and they spent much time in Sweden.

Macmillan sales of Veblen's books were as follows: *The Theory of the Leisure Class* (1899-1919) – 6,977; *The Nature of Peace* (1917-1919) – 1739. Macmillan informed me in 1932 that the record cards on sales of the other two titles "seem to have been lost." It has been estimated, however, that Macmillan sold (in round numbers) 800 copies of *The Instinct of Workmanship* and 850 of *Imperial Germany*.

covered, Veblen had it ready in 1904 while at Chicago. As I noted above in the discussion of *The Theory of Business Enterprise,* he had dropped the last chapter of the original ms. of that book. That "left over" section, which paralleled the closing chapter of *The Theory of the Leisure Class* – "The Higher Learning as an Expression of Pecuniary Culture" – was elaborated into another book. As he explained to his friend Jacques Loeb, it was "a somewhat long chapter which offered an analysis of the working of business enterprise in the administration of the university." He added, "The argument was, of course, of an entirely impersonal character."[178]

In less than four months after the completion of *The Theory of Business Enterprise,* Veblen had ready for the publisher the ms. for a small book with the title "Business Principles in American University Policy," and since, as he said, it was in some respects "supplementary" to *The Theory of Business Enterprise,* he proposed accordingly that Scribner's publish both of them at the same time.[179] The publisher, according to Veblen, had received an adverse reader's report from a leading college president.[179a] Scribner's informed him that "We have decided that the work is too highly specialized and would appeal to too narrow an audience to justify us

[178] Veblen to Loeb, February 10, 1905, Loeb Papers.

Loeb was largely responsible for Veblen's appointment to Stanford in 1906. As his involuntary departure from Stanford approached, Veblen wrote Loeb on October 29, 1909, "it is like you to stand by your friends, but your assurance of sympathy and confidence under the circumstances is doubly welcome to me. I seem to have few friends here." (Veblen to Loeb, October 29, 1909, Loeb Papers).

[179] Veblen to Scribner's, June 26, 1904, Scribner's Papers.

[179a] The reader in question, Veblen declared, was President Harper. "In the search for a publisher the manuscript came into the hands of the president . . . , but the president was apparently not pleased with it and seems to have seen in it some reflexion on the regime here." (Veblen to Loeb, February 10, 1905, Loeb Papers).

in placing it on our list." Fourteen years later it was published by Huebsch as *The Higher Learning in America: A Memorandum of the Conduct of Universities by Business Men.*

There were some additions and changes since Veblen prepared the first ms. He even revised the preface of the last version at Huebsch's suggestion. Before it was set up in type Huebsch wrote him in August 1918. After informing Veblen that the ms. was at the printers, he said: "I have, however, held the preface because of the suggestions made by readers both friendly and sympathetic to you and I enclose the manuscript for your reconsideration. It is their opinion and I agree with it that you do not help the book by stressing the personal note in the preface. The book itself is free from the color that the preface possesses and its impersonal tone gives it an effectiveness which the preface weakens. Of course the book is yours and it will be printed just as you wish but I urge that you give due consideration to the criticism." Veblen in his reply showed appreciation: "I thank you very much for calling my attention to the shortcomings of the preface, a revised ms. of which is enclosed herewith. I trust that this version will pass inspection, so far as regards the question of personalities. It is perhaps unnecessary for me to add that I think you were quite right in your opinion of the earlier version of the preface."[180]

---

[180] Huebsch to Veblen, August 16, 1918, copy; Veblen to Huebsch, August 24, 1918, Huebsch Papers.

Huebsch was always on the lookout for writing opportunities for Veblen. When he undertook to serve as publisher of the newly established forward looking *Freeman,* in 1920, he promptly asked Veblen to have lunch with him and the editor, Albert Jay Nock. Though Veblen was unable to accept the first invitation, he expressed a desire to meet with them "as soon as practicable and find out something about *The Freeman,* even apart from your flattering remarks about its possible use of things which I may write." (Veblen to Huebsch, March 3, 1920, Huebsch Papers).

The Jameson correspondence reveals that his old friend from Johns Hopkins days suggested to him the basic idea of the substantial addition to the introductory chapter. In this addition Veblen skillfully portrayed the opportunity and responsibility of the United States to take the leadership in the safeguarding and advancement of scholarship in the face of the disastrous impact of the war on the European academic community, and the need for reconstruction in the realm of learning. As Jameson wrote November 20, 1918, to the president of the Carnegie Institution, Washington, of which he was then head of the Bureau of Historical Research, "Some time ago Professor Thorstein Veblen told me he was preparing to publish a book on the higher education in the United States which he had written before the war. I urged him to take account in it of the new situation in which the United States would be put at the end of the war in respect to the sustainment of learned and scientific researches and laid before him much the same thoughts in that regard that I have at times expressed to you. . . . Lately I received from him for criticism, some pages of text which he resolved to include in his book on account of my representations. He has, with his usual cleverness, expressed the thing much better than I could and therefore I send his pages to you herewith. . . . The remedy or devices which he suggests for meeting the situation are distinctly . . . his own. . . . But whatever method may be best for achieving profitable results I feel no doubt of the main doctrine of Mr. Veblen's memorandum, nor of the cogency and intelligence with which he has stated it."

The editors of Jameson's letters (*An Historian's World: Selections from the Correspondence of John Franklin Jameson*) then stated: "The work to which Jameson referred was Veblen's *The Higher Learning in America*, N. Y., B. W. Huebsch, 1918, of which pages 48-58 were those prompted by Jameson's suggestions. The section begins: 'The progress and the further promise of the war hold in prospect new and untried responsibilities, as well as an unexampled opportunity. . . . The fortunes of war promise to leave the American men of learning in a strategic position, in the position of a strategic reserve, of a force to be held in readiness, equipped, and organized to meet the emergency that so arises, and to retrieve so much as may be of those assets of scholarly equipment and personnel that make the substantial code of Western civilization' (52). His proposal is for a great central university where teachers and students of all nationalities may meet as guests of the American people."

In his reply to Jameson's request for permission to show the pages to President Woodward, Veblen said "I shall of course be glad to have my ms. turned to any account, and shall be particularly glad if it can be made to contribute to some action at the hands of the Carnegie Institute. . . . It is also true as you say, that the passage is designed to call attention to the state of things, rather than to suggest a specific method of remedying them."[180a]

Veblen's thinking about this addition was revealed most clearly in a young admirer's report of a conversation with Veblen at the time: Veblen said that "one of the things that should be jealously guarded is the preservation of university education standards. He said that Russian universities are bankrupt, that Germany cannot be counted on for great university work, and that the hope of the world lies in France, England and the United States. . . . I enjoyed the old boy very much."[181]

180a Veblen to Jameson, December 9, 1918, Jameson Papers.

181 Harold G. Moulton to Walton Hale Hamilton, May 31, 1918, Papers of War Labor Policies Board, National Archives. Moulton was then at the University of Chicago; later he was president of The Brookings Institution.

The text has inspired a variety of suggestions and controversies. A writer has noted that Veblen was "one of the first observers to describe an educator as a production manager,"[182]; but perhaps the appropriate Veblenian term should be "business manager." She quotes the following passage from *The Higher Learning* (pp. 87-89): "[The university administrator] must be able to show by itemized accounts that the volume of output is such as to warrant the investment. So the equipment and personnel must be organized into a facile and orderly working force, held under the directive control of the captain of erudition at every point, and so articulated and standardized that its rate of speed and the volume of its current output can be exhibited to full statistical effect as it runs. . . . [T]he various universities are competitors for the traffic in merchantable instruction. . . ."

The discussion of *The Higher Learning* might appropriately close with comments that J. M. Clark scribbled on his copy of an article by one of Veblen's Freudian critics. In "Veblen and the Higher Learning," the sociologist, David Riesman, wrote that "it is Veblen's insistent assumption that an autonomous faculty, free of any bureaucracy, would return to a primal state of disinterested, generous, and collective pursuit of idle curiosity." Clark wrote at the top of p. 15, "I don't think Veblen said that. He assumed that was *the* purpose of a university. Maybe the one ought to imply the other with a mind more responsible [in the sense of offering solutions] than Veblen's." Clark also put question marks after "generous" and "collective" and underlined "pursuit of idle curiosity." Where Riesman said that "Veblen

---

[182] Marcia K. Freedman, "Business and Education," in *The Business of America,* edited by Ivar Berg (New York: Harcourt, Brace and World, 1968) p. 378.

thought the universities could run themselves, once outside interference were removed, precisely as he thought the economy could run itself, as a technical engineering problem, once the vested interests were liquidated," Clark wrote "Comment on this similar to that at top of p. 15; if he *thought* that, why should he avoid *saying* it (and I *think* he did avoid saying it)."[183]

Clark's position had been elaborated much earlier by a European philosopher and sociologist in a review of the first edition. He pointed out that Veblen's criticism of American universities was directed especially at "executive power and excessive centralization." His concluding sentence read "The pessimistic insight of the author is an indication of the possibility of a new orientation."[184]

By the 1950's, Professor Duprat's view, it seems, had become the dominant attitude toward the book. In 1957, two Stanford professors in a Stanford publication began a review of the paperback edition with the statement: "The present edition testifies to the book's rank as a classic and probably to the persistence of Veblen's educational ideas." They pointed out that Simon Flexner, the highly respected adviser to foundations on higher education, "echoed some of . . .

---

[183] Riesman's article appeared in *The University of Chicago Magazine,* January 1953. Clark's copy is in the possession of Joseph Dorfman.

The journal credited Veblen with being the originator of the concepts "conspicuous consumption," "vested interest," "idle curiosity" and "instinct of workmanship."

[184] G. L. Duprat, review of *The Higher Learning in America,* in *Revue international de sociologie,* June 1919, p. 312. The review was notable for being about the only one in a leading professional journal that was relatively sympathetic. In sending the review to Huebsch, Veblen wrote that he did so because Huebsch possibly may not have seen it.

Huebsch called Veblen's attention to the lengthy review in the March 1919 issue of the eminently respectable *The North American Review.* The review is reprinted in the Appendix.

[Veblen's ideas] in his 1930 volume, *Universities, American and German* and . . . in 1936 [Robert M.] Hutchins appropriated the title [*The Higher Learning in America*] and much of the point of view of Veblen's book. Thus his conceptions of the functioning, structuring, government, and administration of American colleges and universities have continued to live on and, further, in some academic circles to be highly influential." They concluded that Veblen's criticisms "have powerfully contributed to the success of efforts that have been made to mitigate some of the evils he exposed."[185]

By way of a footnote I should like to point out that there was a curious, futile attempt in 1937 to found near Hightstown, New Jersey, an institution to be called Veblen College. The chairman of the organizing committee informed readers of *The New Republic* that the school "is to be experimental in its technique, but it is to be carried on within a general frame of reference, namely the fuller development of American democracy." He further stated that Veblen "was a realistic thinker in economic and social areas, and a rebel against all forms of exploitation and shams. His thinking is indigenously American. It appeals to all liberal men, yet bears no party label."[186]

We now turn to Veblen's post World War I books.

---

[185] W. H. Cowley and JB Lon Hefferlin, "Thorstein Veblen, *The Higher Learning in America*," *Epitome*, May 28, 1957, pp. 1-4.

In this spirit, the acting president of a leading eastern liberal arts college informed the editor, in September 1967, that college presidents should read the book every five or ten years.

[186] "A New College," letter from Joseph K. Hart, *The New Republic*, October 6, 1937, pp. 245-246.

Veblen seems to have had some impact on the secondary schools. Thus in an article on social studies in the official journal of the California Teachers Association, the author gives the progressive program of what seems to be a hypothetical high school – "Thorstein Veblen High School" in "Wampumsville, Minnesota." (Dorothy Ann Cum-

The Vested Interests and the Common Man[187]

In this treatise composed of essays originally published in *The Dial* from October 1918 to January 25, 1919, Veblen in part continued the the theme that ran through *Imperial Germany* and *The Nature of Peace*: he was critical of the British socio-economic structure, but he believed that it was preferable to that of imperial Germany. This was well evidenced by a letter he received from Professor Thomas C. Hall of Göttingen University, who wrote, "I would like to take exception to a statement in the interesting study of *The Vested Interests*. On page 127 you say 'Chicanery is a more humane art than corporal punishment. Imperial England is, after all, a milder-mannered stepmother than Imperial Germany.' Now I very much doubt that. Even laying aside my prejudices as far as possible as an Irishman . . . I would say that Imperial Germany was before the war giving the individual a liberty for self-expression nowhere found in either America or England, and I know both lands well."[188] Bearing somewhat on what one of his Missouri students has humorously called Veblen's Norwegian chauvinism,[189] was a criticism of a passage in the book by a learned admirer, who wrote him that on page 150 "I note that you remark

[187] This is the title of the second (1920) and subsequent printings. The title of the first printing was *The Vested Interests and the State of the Industrial Arts*. In some respects the original subtitle was closer to Veblen's general view.

[188] Hall to Veblen, April 6, 1925, Thorstein Veblen Papers.

[189] Isador Lubin.

mings, Stanford University, "The Social Studies in the High School, A Student Teacher's Prophecy," *Sierra Educational News*, November 1934, p. 327).

See also a program for a mythical "Veblen College" in Francis Ballein, Theodore Brameld, Wendell Thomas, "Design for a Curriculum," *Educational Forum*, July 1939, pp. 205-211.

about living conditions being much more favorable in Norway than Denmark and Sweden. I think you are incorrect in this, and I should put Denmark first."[190]

The book, or more accurately, the original essay of the same title played a role in a hilarious situation that might well have been included in *The Higher Learning in America.* The episode is revealed in two dispatches in the New York *Times,* February 17 and 18, 1919.[191] The first, which was

---

[190] Charles E. Haugland to Veblen, August 16, 1919, Thorstein Veblen Papers.

[191] My attention was called to the first by Irving S. Michelman, executive vice-president, Budget Finance Plan, Los Angeles, California. He has a sprightly chapter on Veblen in his *Business At Bay* (1969).

The Michelman book brought a letter to him that may be of interest to those who wish to know something of the history of the Veblen book. It was from an old acquaintance that I had not seen since 1929, S. G. Rubinow. He wrote Michelman: "I agree with your statement . . . that 'no research into the life of Veblen can proceed without gratefully encountering Joseph Dorfman's definitive biography *Thorstein Veblen and His America.*' Back in the early 20's Joe Dorfman was one of a group of four of us who were employed by the National Industrial Conference Board as researchers into various phases of national and international economic subjects.

"In 1929, three of our group moved to California. I had been in San Francisco only one week when Joe Dorfman came . . . [from New York] and informed us at a dinner . . . that he had collected for five years material for the Veblen study, and that the . . . documents, much of Veblen's correspondence, together with an extra pair of pants, two shirts, some socks, etc., comprising all of Joe's belongings, were in the old and battered suitcase he was lugging around.

"I suggested to Joe that it would be safe to lock the suitcase in our car while we [were] dining; he did so. When we escorted Joe to the car to bid him farewell, lo and behold, the suitcase was gone. Apparently we had a crime wave in those days, too. We thought poor Joe would lose his mind. I ran an advertisement in San Francisco's dailies for two weeks, offering a reward for the return of the suitcase.

"Fortunately, Joe . . . was able to [do] . . . a phenomenal job [of replacement of material]. . . . Loss of the original documents, the letters, etc., was a tragedy."

headed "Society League Starts a Revolt," told how "Members of the Junior League, a social organization comprised of young women from families prominent in society," were protesting against a movement of a faction in the society to compel all members to attend the lectures of three "radical" professors at the recently opened New School for Social Research; namely, Charles Beard, James Harvey Robinson and Veblen.[192] And Veblen was especially assailed for having written in a recent article, "The Vested Interests and the Common Man," that "a vested interest is a legitimate right to get something for nothing."[193] The following day the *Times* informed the country that "Junior League Official Denies Arranging Courses at New School."[193a]

---

[192] Beard and Robinson were strong admirers of Veblen.

[193] *The Dial,* January 25, 1919.

A selection from the book was published in one of the series of volumes edited by a committee of the Association of the American Law Schools, a committee which included leading scholars and philosophers of the law. The title of the selection was a sentence from the book: "A Vested Interest is the Prescriptive Right to get Something for Nothing" and it appeared in *Rational Basis of Legal Institutions,* edited by John H. Wigmore and Albert Kocourek, with an introduction by Oliver Wendell Holmes. [(1923; Augustus M. Kelley Publishers and Rothman Reprints, 1969) pp. 275-283]. The editors described the Veblen piece as "an ironic castigation of the modern industrial system." (p. xxiv).

[193a] The incident served as the occasion for the humorist Robert C. Benchley to review a supposed reissue of *The Theory of the Leisure Class* as "the dullest book of the month," in *Vanity Fair* (April 1919), a journal noted for its stable of sophisticated writers and "snob appeal" advertisements. He said that the book had been chosen for the first review "for two reasons, both of them being that Dr. Veblen has recently been the storm-center of a soviet uprising among the young

---

I would like to add that perhaps the irreplaceable item that I miss most was Veblen's response to my request for information. As I recall the letter, he courteously informed me that he was taking the liberty to suggest that I discontinue the study on the ground that there was little worth while in his life to write about.

A number of interesting additional reviews have turned up. One said: "Professor Veblen is not a socialist, perhaps, nor yet a social reformer of any familiar type, but rather a sort of Diogenes going about with a lantern in hand looking for an honest man and finding none." The anonymous reviewer pointed out that "Professor Veblen's chief attack is launched against the highway robbery so frequently practised under the guise of corporation finance." The critic believed that "probably the chief evils connected with corporation finance will be removed by the gradual education of the small investors, by the growth of higher standards of business ethics and by legislation, and the residue of incurable badness will be no more than would necessarily attach to any form of business activity."[194] Another, which appeared in the Chicago *Daily News*, September 24, 1919, under the title "A Philosophic Economist," was by Babette Deutsch, who achieved fame as a poet. She wrote: "It is typical of Veblen's work that he emphasizes his difference from the socialists who divide the haves from the have-nots. For him the division is rather between those who own wealth enough to make it count and those who do not." She continued "The argument is sometimes brought against Veblen that his

[194] "A Modern Diogenes," *The Review: A Weekly Journal of Political and General Literature*, August 16, 1919, pp. 301, 302. The publisher was the economist Fabian Franklin, whose major field originally had been mathematics.

---

ladies in New York who compose the Junior League. From recent press reports, it appears that a revolutionary element among the members of New York's exclusive *demoiselles* refused to attend lectures at the New School for Social Research (a training table for *The New Republic* squad) because of the presence on the faculty of Dr. Veblen and several other savants who were suspected of having radical leanings and therefore of being unsuited to act as docents for our social register debutantes."

The entire review is printed in the Appendix below.

writing is repetitious and less novel than his involved sentence structure might lead the untutored to believe. But if he is repetitious it is as blameworthy in him as it would be in any workmanlike hammerer. And it is a significant truism that science is only organized common sense, and philosophy itself platitudinous as it sounds. Veblen deals in both, bringing to philosophy the scrupulous concern of the scientist, to science the unbiased lucidity of the philosopher, interesting both alike with the touchstone of his fine irony."

A most whimsical review was written by a man with the unusual name of Lockie Parker in *Reedy's Mirror,* a sort of *New Yorker* of its day which was published in St. Louis, Missouri. The journal took its name from its famous flamboyant editor and publisher, William Masson Reedy. It was one of the most influential and prestigious weeklies for the three decades of its existence and especially notable for the many contributors who later achieved fame. I have not been able to discover who "Lockie Parker" was; indeed it may be one of the many pen names of Reedy himself, who often wrote most of an issue of the journal.

The reviewer, after pointing out that "all its fundamental ideas have been previously stated in *The Instinct of Workmanship* and *The Theory of Business Enterprise,*" said "The attention which this last book of Mr. Veblen's has received from the critics and reviewers of even the most conservative dailies and periodicals is rather interesting. To a reader of Veblen's earlier works, this is obviously not due to the book itself, which is probably the least important of his publications. Therefore we must take this interest as another recognition of the power and influence that Veblen's ideas are gaining in the economic thought of the country.

"Perhaps the best testimony is that of the New York *Times.* I can remember when Veblen was never mentioned in the *Times* – perhaps buried under their rule of only 'the news that is fit to print' – and a later period when they handled him with such arm's length phrases as, 'we have heard that Mr. Veblen says –' or, 'someone has told us that Mr. Veblen in one of his books –.' In comparison with that, a two column review is quite a tribute, even . . . [though] they disagree with Veblen in general and in particular." The reviewer finally noted the usual criticism of Veblen's works, including *The Vested Interests.* "His materialism is rather too rigorous for most of us, who, without discounting the iniquity of the destruction of useful goods, might find very serious harm in less tangible evils. Then to the novice in what is being called the Veblenite cult his language seems to sound like something other than English. I take this latter criticism from hearsay, as having been initiated some years ago, I cannot remember that I ever found Veblen's language weird. In fact I have always thought him particularly careful in defining his terms and using no word whose meaning might be doubtful. Naturally one cannot repeat definitions – that sometimes extend over pages – in each succeeding volume; which probably accounts for this later criticism of his style. Possibly an habitual reader cannot fully realize to what extent he has built up a language of his own."[195]

From Mencken's bailiwick, *The Baltimore Sun,* August 16, 1919, came the lament: "Mr. Veblen will be remembered as the man who does not understand 'national honor' and considers the refinements of the 'leisure class' merely an attempt at 'conspicuous consumption.' One thing at least can be said of this latest book – it is not as turgid in style as the earlier lucubrations. *The Dial* is improving Mr. Veblen's style."

The critic Roger Fry found use for the book. He had held

[195] "Veblen on the Vested Interests," *Reedy's Mirror,* December 11, 1919, pp. 872-873.

an exhibition at the Grafton Galleries of the works of pioneers of what he called the "post impressionist" movement, Cézanne, Gauguin, Van Gogh, etc. The "cultured Public" had charged him with "revolutionary Anarchism." He gave his reply in *Vision and Design* that "my crime had been to strike at the vested emotional interests." Bell recently added "here again we see how alert Fry was to questions of social motivations, how close in his thinking to Thorstein Veblen."[196a]

We now turn to the sequel volume which appeared in 1921.

The Engineers and the Price System

On this most controversial of Veblen's books there is some relevant information on two of its most important concepts – sabotage and the engineer. The first essay "On the Nature and Uses of Sabotage" attracted, it appears, considerable attention both at home and in England, when it first appeared in *The Dial*, April 5, 1919. Such was the demand, that it was quickly reprinted as a booklet bearing the title "Sabotage." In England it seems that it stimulated Branford to publish an anonymous pamphlet, *The Drift to Revolution*, which was in the series of Papers of the Present issued for the Cities Committee of the Sociological Society.[196]

Branford brought out some of the far reaching implications of Veblen's use of the concept. He declared that "Big business is the organization of the small supply at the high price. . . . For it is the natural and inevitable tendency under our

[196a] Bell, "Roger Fry" in *Vision and Design. The Life, Work and Influence of Roger Fry 1866-1934*, an exhibition arranged by the Arts Council and the University of Nottingham (London: Council of Great Britain, 1966) p. 8.

[196] "I send you accompanying this a recent paper I published anonymously for our Cities Committee [of the Sociological Society], *The Drift to Revolution*, which was largely suggested by an article of yours I read in *The Dial*." (Branford to Veblen, May 27, 1919, Thorstein Veblen Papers).

system of production for profit rather than for use. Success in business under this system turns upon the skill in limiting the supply to the point where competition of the buyer is keenest. In other words success depends on steady and continuous application of what Mr. Thorstein Veblen calls 'judicious sabotage.' And 'big business' is the art of combining manufacturers and merchants for the better practise of judicious sabotage. Increasingly is recognized, in this regime, the value of an apprenticeship to the bank and the stock exchange. These being – the generalized markets that touch all others, it is through them that the Combine becomes the monopolist Trust. Big business is, therefore, in effect, a form of finance. Now the financier is a skilled psychologist. He studies the working of the human mind. It is his business to play upon human weakness. Simultaneously with the limitation of supply he organizes the stimulation of demand and so creates a public mind attuned to his blandishments. Hence appear all those modern developments, which its cultivators call the Science of Advertisement. . . . Sabotage and Advertisement are the twin stars of the financial firmament. But the millionaire is merely their most manifest emanation. Their subtle influence has penetrated the structure of contemporary civilization; it pervades our habits of thought and deflects our outlook often when we are least aware of its insidious bias."[197]

---

[197] *The Drift to Revolution,* pp. 31, 35, 44.

Branford in the same pamphlet echoed Veblen also in declaring that "assuredly in the matter of sabotage, latent or patent, judicious or aggressive, the business man and the working man are in the same galley." The difference was that while it was practised "covertly by men of business," it was "advocated openly by the extremists of labor." (pp. 34, 35). It should be noted that the program of Branford's "Party of the Third Alternative" differed, in the words of Mumford, from the "historic aims and programs of the 'party of order' and the 'party of revolution' . . . in that its emphasis was . . . upon definite, concrete, real-

Branford also plays a role in the clarification of the character and importance of Veblen's "engineer." This occurred in two war-time pamphlets (May 1918) *The Banker's Part in Reconstruction* and *The Modern Midas; Man-Power and Money-Power: Bankers, Financiers, Profiteers.* In these he was concerned with a scheme of managed money and credit that would as elsewhere avoid "the Scylla of Individualism and the Charybdis of Socialism." As a model he suggested in the first pamphlet consideration of the war created Coal Control Sub-Department of the Board of Trade. "Here quite a definite problem was put to a group of railway engineers, assisted by their natural allies the chartered accountants [for costing analysis]. Given – (a) the geographical situation of the collieries and of the towns and villages supplied therefrom by railway, (b) the normal coal consumption of such towns and villages, (c) the truck and engine capacity of the railways available – find the most economical distribution. The department has recently given the answer in an official plan estimated to effect a saving of 700,000,000 ton-miles during the ensuing twelve months. The solution, it will be noticed, is in terms of a compound unit called

izable aims: reforestation, better houses, more adequately designed towns, cooperative agriculture, socialized credit, regenerated schools." Mumford went on to describe Branford's "socialized credit," based on loans at insurance rates as follows: "An expert on finance, he proposed to substitute insurance, plus a definite charge for actual service, for the haphazard and often extortionate incidence of interest." (Lewis Mumford, "Victor Branford," *The New Republic*, August 27, 1930, p. 467).

Another admirer using the pen name *Confrère* described his social finance in two lines of poetry:

Social Finance your aim, your guide; thus free
From gamblings, profiteerings. . . .

("Memorial Poem for Victor Branford," *The Sociological Review*, January-April 1931, p. 5).

ton-miles. This concept was the creation of engineers concerned by occupational training and consequent habits of mind not to achieve maximum profits but to deliver the goods as quickly and cheaply as possible. This engineering unit was slow to get accepted on English Railways for two reasons. First, because the idea of ton-miles was somewhat unfamiliar to the many directors who are gentlemen of classical education. And secondly because Boards of Directors inherit the tradition of emulative trading and so are mentally oriented otherwise. Now it is possible promptly to carry out the scheme of railway economy worked out by the Coal Control Department, because the railways were at the outset of the war put in charge of a committee of their own several managers, who are usually engineers or accountants or something of both. . . . The urgencies of mobilization compelled the Government in the interests of national economy to supersede the Boards of Directors."

Similarly in the area of money and banking Branford brought the concept of the "engineer" into play for the war effort. He proposed for banking the supersession of the many boards of directors by "a single committee of bank managers" who would be joined by a picked group of accountants. The problem for that committee would be the preparation of "a scheme of economizing credit methods and sources in such a wise as to effect the least interference with the legitimate demands of industry and trade and most to facilitate national finance." He looked toward the scheme as including at least a reduction of the rate of interest. It included a number of devices that have since been described as Keynesian. For example he proposed a scheme of "automatic rationing" of consumer spending power, which was a forerunner of Keynes's proposal in World War II of withholding a portion of incomes until the return to peace.

In the companion pamphlet, in discussing the workings of the reconstruction scheme, he declared: "Picture the situation in detail. The problem is to transform an ordinary pottery-making business into a leadless glaze one. Engineers and perhaps architects make plans. Laborers and artisans working under skilled supervision execute the plans. The material for reconstruction is taken from stock or manufactured afresh. Pardon me for mentioning these commonplaces. I do so, in the hope that you will grant me the generalization that reconstruction is done not with money but with life and labor."[198]

In a later work *Science and Sanctity* (1923), Branford emphasized in effect one of Veblen's qualifications of the leadership role of the engineer. In the section headed "Technological Economy; Its Qualities and Defects," Branford noted that "The Pecuniary Culture is split by a rift that runs between the technological and the more purely financial interest," between the habit of mind of "financial directors" and "technical managers" – the "engineers." He went on to warn that "engineers, . . . like museum curators and most of 'us others,' are moral chameleons – too ready to take the hue of their mental texture from the dominant colors of their social

[198] Branford's passing reference to Veblen's "new book," *The Nature of Peace,* in the first pamphlet may recall to the reader Veblen's emphasis on the engineer in the last chapter of that book, Peace and the Price System. In it Veblen wrote that modern industry "is carried on by technological processes subject to surveillance and direction by mechanical engineers, or perhaps rather experts in engineering of the mechanistic kind." [*An Inquiry into the Nature of Peace* (1917; New York: Augustus M. Kelley Publishers, 1964) p. 303].

Fox cited a passage in *The Instinct of Workmanship* (p. 306) which calls attention to the role of the engineer. It begins "The designing engineer takes his measures on the basis of ascertained quantitative fact . . ." (Quoted in *The Triumphant Machine,* p. 69).

milieu. . . . It is not to the engineers we can look for a new purging of its money-changers from the temple. Already we see leading engineers, in response to financial custom, well fixed in the habits of setting up their own stalls in the Market of magic tokens . . ." And then bringing in the work for which Geddes achieved his enduring fame, Branford closed the section with, "the Market of magic tokens . . . having usurped the temple's focal place on the town-plan, has naturally identified itself with 'the city.' The Pecuniary Culture has achieved its own apotheosis by submitting its rival, the City (a name consecrated by immemorial tradition), to the supreme historic degradation of an alternative title for the Money Market. A society which continues to tolerate the desecration presumably does not wait to be broken from without; it rots from within. It follows a natural course of decay, that runs from mild turpitudes practised in the marketplace to predatory wars hatched in its forum."

In an essay "The Engineer in Sociology" in 1921, which bears all the earmarks of being Branford's, it was stated that "The technique of the engineer as practitioner in the economy of physical energies should be capable of definite relation to the technique of the banker as a practitioner of the economy of credit, since credit is manifestly a mode of directing these energies to their industrial, mercantile and social uses. But again in point, there is a serious gap in the scientific literature of the subject; for where in the writings of economists and sociologists is to be found any systematic effort to relate credit and the processes of banking and finance, to physical energies on the one side, and social uses on the other? The writings of Mr. Thorstein Veblen touch on these matters with illuminating flashes, but even these have by no means been incorporated into descriptive and theoretic economics."[198a]

A posthumous work by an American, which was rejected by several publishers in 1920 but finally appeared in 1969, also helps to clarify Veblen's concepts of "sabotage" and the "engineer." This was *Makers, Users and Masters* by Arthur F. Bentley, who first won renown as a political theorist and later also as a philosopher. He wrote: "Sabotage is the trouble with manufacturing, and sabotage not merely as the war-weapon of the more reckless workers' organizations, but as the settled 'financial function' of profiteering industrial control. Sabotage may be described as the destruction or hampering or decreasing of production undertaken by any party to the manufacturing process for purposes of private gain. Veblen has broadened the term from the misdeeds of labor to those of capital, and the Supreme Court of the United States has written down some of the facts authoritatively for the benefit of future generations in the Standard Oil and Tobacco Trust decisions." He contended that today sabotage from the employers' side "settled down into the systematic control and limitation of output with respect to price and profit, exercised through chairmen of the boards of directors, as distinct from presidents and managers, and gradually centered for all the greatest industries in one close financial harmony of management. Permanently, deliberately, tribute is levied by it on the comforts, conveniences and necessities of the entire population: — tribute that benefits the recipients only in small fraction of the injury it inflicts on the tribute-payer." He quoted with approval from the original *Dial* essay, "The Captains of Finance and the Engineers," that "the owners now repre-

[198a] "The Engineer in Sociology," *The Sociological Review*, January 1921, p. 26.

sented in effect by the syndicated investment bankers, continue to control the industrial experts, and limit their discretion arbitrarily, for their own commercial gain, regardless of the needs of the community."[199]

At the time, too, it seems, that Veblen's original series in *The Dial*, especially "The Captains of Finance and the Engineers" (June 1919), caught the discontent of a number of highly respected leaders in the field of scientific management. For example, there was the case of Harlow S. Person, who had gone from the directorship of the Amos Tuck School of Administration and Finance, Dartmouth College, to the managing directorship of The Taylor Society, "a Society to Promote the Science of Management." Shortly after "The Captains of Finance and the Engineers" appeared, Person gave a summary of it as an editorial in the August issue of the society's organ, the *Bulletin of the Taylor Society*. He began by calling attention of members to *The Theory of Business Enterprise*. He said that he had read the book on publication fifteen years ago, and had found it "a most searching analysis of the nature and interrelations of the governing motives and the developing mechanisms in American industrial life." Then he attempted to explain why it had not attracted any particular attention. "Possibly the American business man was too absorbed in the enterprise there analyzed to care about any analysis; possibly he was not ready for such strong medi-

---

[199] Bentley, *Makers, Users and Masters*, edited by Sidney Ratner and Peter Asch (Syracuse, N. Y.: Syracuse University Press, 1969) pp. 84-85, 135-136.

Bentley described the quoted essay and the series of *Dial* essays that made up *The Vested Interests and the Common Man* as "brilliant." He was trained in economics at Johns Hopkins by Richard T. Ely, Simon N. Patten and J. B. Clark. He also had the benefit of study abroad with Gustav Schmoller, the leader of the younger German historical school, and Georg Simmel, the sociologist and author of the notable *Philosophie des Geldes* ("Philosophy of Money").

cine, for his *industrial constitutional troubles* were not as apparent to him as they have become since his *system* has been weakened by the exposures of war; probably the obscure style of the author made the medicine seem impossible. Such expressions as 'the concatenation of industrial processes' do not go down easily." He then gave a summary of the book.

He noted that "the organization of natural resources and mechanical processes . . . was made more complex and delicate by the development of a vast credit mechanism which was embarrassed by an archaic banking system. The corporate form of organization led gradually to the separation of management and ownership. The system became a body of diverse and interlocking processes, the due working of one part of which depended on the due working of the rest, and lent itself to systematic control under the direction of captains of industry [corporation financiers]. Systematic control led to systematic manipulation. The captains of industry of the eighties and nineties dominated industry and accumulated fortunes, not primarily by promoting technical productivity, but by disarranging and manipulating values, by securing 'rakeoffs' made possible by substituting in the public mind artificial and varying values of corporate properties and enterprises for their real values." He continued, Veblen has in *The Dial* series presented "the same general thesis, this time simpler in style and much more readable, and enhanced in effectiveness by references to developments of recent years which are well known to every business man."

Person emphasized that the essay whose title he used for the caption of the editorial was "especially noteworthy." He noted that "Veblen uses the terms 'business men' and 'commercial' in a sense more restrictive than that in which they are ordinarily used. The shop superintendent, the production manager, the sales manager and the general manager are not 'business men,' they are technologists; the 'business man' is he who is outside of and above the operating personnel; he is engaged in the field of the larger industrial – political, financial – commercial strategy, studying and manipulating values on behalf of 'vested interests,' and concerned with production only as its advancement or repression will contribute to his larger purposes. The term 'commercial' refers to these industrial – political – financial operations and not to the buying and selling of the technologist." He then sketched the developments "Veblen says, brought the regime of the captains of industry to a close and has shifted control to the syndicated investment bankers to whom has passed the function of 'regulating the rate and volume of output in those industrial enterprises' which have passed into their hands."

As he read Veblen's message, "The engineers are the technological general staff of the industrial system. . . . With a reasonably free hand 'the production experts would today readily increase the output of industry by several fold' . . . Yet they are restricted by the owners through the syndicated investment bankers and by business as usual."

Person most clearly discussed Veblen's policy conclusions in a short editorial at the beginning of the issue. There he attributes to Veblen the view of the role of the engineer that has risen to prominence in our own day. He informed the readers that they would "undoubtedly be stimulated by Professor Veblen's keen analysis of the industrial system of the United States and of the dominant characteristics given our industrial life by the captains of industry. . . . They will be startled by the concluding suggestions. To the statement that the dominant influence of the captains of finance is now held on sufferance of the engineers, they may give a reserved assent; but the suggestion that the engineers permit a nascent class-conciousness to develop into an organized guild for the purpose of exercising a balance of power in the struggle of industrial classes and of compelling a return to the motive of livelihood and of productive efficiency — we wonder if *that* suggestion may not provoke a few letters which will make interesting reading in the *Bulletin.* Is it more startling to imagine a guild of engineers registering a demand to participate in the settlement of policies on the higher plane of industrial-political policy determination, than it would have been five years ago to imagine the workers making a demand to participate in the settlement of policies on the plane of shop-policy determination?"[199a]

Another prominent figure in the scientific management movement, Morris L. Cooke, who was a lifelong friend and associate of Person and an admirer of Veblen, displayed similar sentiments. Thus in 1923 he complained to another acquaintance of Veblen, Calvin W. Rice, Secretary of the American Society of Mechanical Engineers, about a committee chosen to represent A.S.M.E. at a World Power Conference that year. "The members . . . represent practically the business as contrasted with the professional mind and outlook of the industry. . . . I am protesting against the conception that business — big or little — is engineering."[199b]

[199a] Both editorials are unsigned, as editorials generally are. They were obviously Person's because he was the editor. The constitution of the society stated that the managing director among other things "shall edit and publish its bulletins." ("Reorganization of the Society," *Bulletin of the Taylor Society,* April 1919, p. 4).

It should be noted that in the essay Veblen placed class-consciousness in quotation marks.

[199b] Cooke to Calvin W. Rice, December 17, 1923, quoted in Jean Christie, "Morris Llewellyn Cooke: Progressive Engineer," Ph.D. dissertation, 1963, Columbia University, p. 48. The letter is in Cooke Papers, Franklin D. Roosevelt Library.

As early as 1917 at least, Cooke had shown the influence of Veb-

There is still considerable controversy over just what precisely is Veblen's concept of the appropriate role of the engineer in society, especially as sketched in *The Engineers and the Price System.* Probaby the most balanced statement on the matter is Mitchell's comment in the introduction to his volume of readings, *What Veblen Taught* (1936). "Veblen has no definite specifications for the new structure of institutions that will grow up in place of the present one, beyond the expectation that technically qualified engineers will have a larger share in the managing of industry. His evolutionary theory forbids him to anticipate a cataclysm, or to forecast a millenium. What will happen in the inscrutable future is what has been happening since the origin of man. As ways of working shift, they will engender new habits of thinking, which will crystallize into new institutions, which will form the cultural setting for further cumulative changes in ways of working, world without end."

A continuing, intriguing question about the book is the nature of his relations with Howard Scott, the chief promoter

---

lenian concepts in the very title of one of his pamphlets – *How About It? Comment on the 'Absentee Management' of the American Society of Mechanical Engineers and the Virtual Control Exercised by Big Business – Notably by the Private Utility Interests.*

Lubin has just informed me that another pioneer figure in scientific management, Frank B. Gilbreth, was a Veblen admirer. Lubin recalled that he was in Veblen's home in 1917 when the consulting engineer stopped off at Columbia, Missouri, just to meet Veblen.

It has been asserted that Veblen's proposals for the administration of the economy were relatively closely paralleled by a contemporary, Walter Rathenau, a leading German industrialist, statesman and theorist on industrial organization. [Carl Dreher, *The Coming Showdown* (Boston: Little, Brown, 1942) pp. 124-125]. This refers to Rathenau's *Die Neue Gesellschaft* (1919) which in the English translation bears the title *The New Society* (1921).

of the short-lived Technical Alliance in the immediate post World War I era and of its revival under the name of Technocracy in 1932. Some light is thrown on the matter by a letter that has turned up. The letter, dated October 5, 1919, was addressed to Leo Wolman, who was then Veblen's colleague at the New School for Social Research. It reveals that Veblen was originally impressed with Scott (although soon after, as I noted in the Veblen book, he would have grave doubts of the man's technical competence). The letter reads:

Dear Wolman,

I believe you would do well to look up Howard Scott, Civil Engineer, 143 West 4th Street (telephone, Spring 1262) and have some talk with him about industrial conditions and statistics of production and resources as stated in terms intelligible to the engineers. I believe it should be to his advantage as well as yours. He has a mass of materials on this line, gathered by himself and a large number of associates during the past two years, and as near as I know his notions of the meaning of this information and the situation which it reflects are very much in line with your own.

I made Mr. Scott's acquaintance last year, and he looked me up again a couple days ago, and the more I see of him and hear what he has to say the more I believe he is one of the men who can deliver the goods. He has also, tentatively, a scheme for a statistically workable unit of industrial values, which might interest you.

I have spoken to him of my wishing to have you make

his acquaintance, and you will find him glad to meet you half way.[200]

There is something to be said for the assertion of a writer that "the managerial revolution has brought the engineers nearer to the control [of industry], which Veblen imagined as a possibility [*The Engineers and the Price System*, Chapters IV and V], but did not expect."[201]

In a sense a most significant comment on the book came from Lockie Parker at the close of his review of *The Vested Interests*. He said "if there is any conspicuous change in his later work, it is toward concrete application and propaganda, and away from the abstraction, detachment and greater impartiality of his early work." Pointing to the new series running in *The Dial*, that would become *The Engineers and the Price System*, he continued that in these Veblen "has made a still further departure and has undertaken to be constructive, a role which seems rather odd and is certainly new for Veblen."

At various times the book has enjoyed more popularity than any other Veblen book, with the exception, of course, of *The Theory of the Leisure Class*. In the publisher's statement for the six months from April 30, 1921, to October 31, 1921, the period in which the book appeared, the sale was 590 copies,[202] but for the period from November 1, 1925

---

[200] Wolman gave me the letter in the 1940's.

A recent interpretation holds that "Veblen would have retained the price system and a modified form of private property." E. Jay Howenstine, "The Least Means Principle: A Synthesis of A Priori and Institutional Methodologies," *The Indian Economic Journal*, July-September 1966, p. 34.

[201] Florence, *Economics and Sociology of Industry*, p. 33.

[202] The published price was $1.50 and the royalty rate was 15%. For the same period there were eight Canadian sales, for which the royalty was one half, or 7½%.

to April 30, 1926, the sale had fallen to thirty-one. The total sale to February 1, 1930, was approximately 1300; but the actual sale from February 1, 1930, to September 30, 1934, was 3025; the substantial rise was doubtless caused in large part by the widespread interest in Technocracy in the fall and winter of 1932-1933.[203]

Technocracy as a social movement shortly passed away, but *The Engineers and the Price System* would soon acquire the status of being the fountainhead and point of departure for studies of the ever expanding role of the engineer and in particular the "master engineer," in the economic order and society.[203a]

---

[203] The book was generally viewed as the "germ from which the whole movement sprang." It was said that "one of the valuable things that Veblen and the Technocrats have done is to emphasize the importance of the engineers – something that traditional Marxism had largely neglected." (Edmund Wilson, "The Great Revelation," *The New Republic,* February 22, 1933, pp. 50, 51).

Wilson viewed Veblen as "the Technocrats' master," and declared that the book was a much more responsible and coherent performance than most of the literature of the Technocrats. He contended that Veblen had not disregarded the prime engineering problem involved in bringing "a government of engineers into existence and enabling it to endure: 'the engineering of human consent.'" Veblen "made it plain that his proposed soviet of technicians would have to have worked out 'a common understanding and a solidarity of sentiment' with 'the working force engaged in transportation and in the greater underlying industries of the system: to which is to be added as being nearly indispensable from the outset, an active adherence to the plan on the part of the trained workmen in the great generality of the mechanical industries.'" Wilson, however, complained of Veblen's largely "literary sinuosity" in dealing with the issue. "His irony . . . enabled him to slip around and in and out of this problem."

[203a] Another movement that was somewhat related to Technocracy but emphasized much more a monetary panacea, also drew heavily on Veblen. This was Major C. H. Douglas's Social Credit proposal, which aroused interest not only in Britain, but also in the United States and especially in Canada. One of the chief expositors and fervent disciples declared that after [the writings of the major] "I am

The other Veblenian concept developed in the book, "Sabotage" in connection with conspicuous waste, has even invaded the field of psychiatry. Adolf Meyer, an American pioneer in the field, in discussing the effects of alcohol, noted:

---

most deeply indebted to Mr. Thorstein Veblen, who is much the most enlightening – and sometimes the most entertaining – of American writers on economics and sociology. His work has been almost wholly analytical and critical but is none the less valuable for that." [Hilderic Cousens, *A New Policy for Labour: An Essay on the Relevance of Credit Control* (London: Palmer, 1921) preface]. It should be noted, however, that while Cousens used a good number of Veblen's concepts, such as "sabotage," "vested interest," the only study of Veblen's to which he referred was *The Theory of the Leisure Class.* He stated: "We live under a culture of Conspicuous and Competitive Waste, which is deeply rooted (see Veblen, *Theory of the Leisure Class*), and can only be threatened if prosperity is secured. The availability of a high standard, not sermons on asceticism, is the only likely cure for vulgar luxury. That given, we may well have a reaction to civilized, not primitive simplicity of life." (p. 88).

The major referred to *The Engineers and the Price System* (without chapter or page designation) in showing the central and overriding importance of "technology" in "wealth production." He declared: "There is now a fourth factor in wealth production, the multiplying power of which far exceeds that of the other three [land, labor and capital], which may be expressed in the words of Mr. Thorstein Veblen (although he does not appear to have grasped its full implication) as the 'progress of the industrial arts.'" [*Social Credit* (1924; revised ed., New York: Norton, 1933) p. 49].

Shortly after the Veblen book appeared in November 1934, I received a letter from an American leader of the movement. He said that because of the condition of his eyes he had made only a hasty examination of the book, and concluded "I am still inclined to the view that Veblen was largely instrumental in putting Major Douglas on the right track but that Veblen did not quite reach to the point now presented by Major Douglas and his followers." (R. S. Gray to Joseph Dorfman, April 21, 1935). That point apparently was the major's specific program which he described in an attached printed *Memorandum* of March 1935. "Social Credit proposed, primarily, government control of credit on a purely scientific, non-political and statistical basis. Secondarily, adjustment of the retail price system with a national dividend system so as to afford ample purchasing power to the consuming class as ultimate consumers."

"It is quite likely that a civilization living less on what Th. Veblen called 'conspicuous waste' as the mark of social status, and more on output of work and contributive performance will do much to reduce the lure and sanction of alcohol as an element of social pride and glory, and habitual cult. One cannot help feeling that the alcohol industry and the alcohol traffic are practically bound to favor what one might properly designate as a *sabotage of human health*, ranking with the exploitation of other appetites capable of overstimulation."[203b]

Absentee Ownership and Business Enterprise in Recent Times: The Case of America

The last of Veblen's books on economics turned out to be larger than he had expected. On seeing the page proofs (July 25, 1923), he informed Huebsch "the number of pages (445) is more than I would have preferred, but I see no way around it." He gave a more elaborate explanation than previously for not supplying a photograph for publicity.

My dear Mr. Huebsch:

In belated reply to your very courteous suggestion of using a photograph of my person as an item of sales-publicity, I can only say that in my opinion such a portrait, would have no value for the purpose whatever; indeed I believe quite simply that it would have less than no value. On this account, as well as on grounds of a sentimental revulsion, I would rather not. I trust this will not disappoint you nor in any degree incommode you.

Sincerely yours,
Thorstein Veblen

[203b] Meyer, "Alcohol as a Psychiatric Problem," in *Alcohol and Man; the Effect of Alcohol on Man in Health and Disease* edited by Haven Emerson (New York: Macmillan, 1932) p. 300. Meyer was then Psychiatrist in Chief, Johns Hopkins Hospital, Baltimore, Maryland.

Narrowly speaking *Absentee Ownership* is a sequel of *The Theory of Business Enterprise.* It has the distinction of being the first of his works to be cited in the highest court of the nation. Justice Brandeis, in one of his famous minority opinions, *Liggett Co.* v. *Lee,* 218 U.S. 565 (1933), referred to it in his concern over the encroachment of mammoth corporations and financial power.

I have written elsewhere that in this case "Justice Brandeis used *Absente Ownership* to support his contention that 'able, discerning, scholars . . . compare the evolving "corporate system" with the feudal system.' There is no basis in anything that Veblen specifically said to demonstrate that this was exactly Veblen's position. But Brandeis's statement nevertheless indicates that though Veblen did not enjoy a wide popular audience he did have among his readers forward-looking thinkers. This was later borne out by a statement of Justice Felix Frankfurter, in *Mr. Justice Holmes and the Supreme Court* (1938), linking the writings of Veblen and Brandeis as giving substantially similar views of the tendency of the large financial interests to dominate industry."[203c]

Another United States Supreme Court Justice, William O. Douglas, has stated that he was introduced to *Absentee Ownership* by his Columbia Law School teacher, Underhill Moore. Douglas's successor as chairman of the S.E.C., Jerome Frank, was likewise deeply impressed with *Absentee Ownership.*[204] Mitchell noted in a private letter in 1936, more concretely, that "perhaps Veblen himself did not exaggerate greatly in *Absentee Ownership* in developing his old theme of the importance of the increasing separation of ownership of property from management of property. . . .

203c *The Economic Mind in American Civilization,* IV, 358.

204 Ralph F. De Bedts, *The New Deal's S. E. C.: The Formative Years* (New York: Columbia University Press, 1964) p. 158.

Certainly his recognition of this separation calls at the very least for a restatement of some fundamental parts of classical economics and I doubt whether any competent person who undertook the statement could stop without altering some of the conclusions rather profoundly."[205] Another writer has elaborated on one aspect: "Shareholders as a whole cannot be expected to govern their company. As an extension of the sleeping partnership device they may be called sleeping shareholders and are the prime example of Veblen's 'absentee ownership.' "[206]

That *Absentee Ownership* was the culmination of Veblen's economic studies was amply illustrated by the description of

---

[205] Mitchell to W. Z. Ripley, December 1936, Mitchell Papers.

In speaking of the role of branch plant managers in the modern corporation, a professor of political science has asserted that "The phenomenon of absentee ownership, on which Veblen lavished his irony, has developed into the practise of absentee management by non-owners." (Norton E. Laing, "The Corporation, Its Satellites and the Local Community," in *The Corporation and Modern Society*, edited by Edward S. Mason (Cambridge, Mass.: Harvard University Press, 1959; paperback edition, 1961) p. 204.

The point has been clarified in the following discussion of conflicts of interest in the large corporation: "The actual or potential conflict of interest between owner and hired manager has been considered at length in the economic literature . . . and has in fact, supplied the impetus for much of the development of accounting practice . . . designed to 'protect' the absentee owner from mismanagement of funds by his employees, at both managerial and lower levels in the hierarchy." (Simon and Stedry, "Psychology and Economics," in *The Handbook of Social Psychology*, V, 289).

[206] Florence, *Economics and Sociology of Industry*, p. 148.

A student of the field of accounting and finance called attention recently to the importance of "absentee ownership" in the development of business accountancy. "Thus while corporations, with their absentee ownership, stimulated the growth of business, they created many problems of recording and of preparing financial statements, and in this way again challenged accountancy and stimulated its growth and development." (Adolf J. H. Enthoven, "The Changing Role of Accountancy," *Finance and Development*, June 1969, p. 19).

his work by two of his British friends, Victor Branford and John A. Hobson. Branford in a review article suggested a striking connection between *Absentee Ownership* and the first of Veblen's books, *The Theory of the Leisure Class,*[207] as he sketched what happens to leisure class occupations "when the industrial system reaches the stage of development where it bases itself on a money economy. A change from the system of payment in kind to payment in money means a revolution in the operative conventions of the industrial system. It involves great possibilities of wealth acquisition by audacious manipulation of the symbols and tokens of industrial values. Here, in fact, are new and abundant opportunities for achievements of exploit and prowess (cunning increasingly aiding force); and their gains consequently admit of the creation and multiplication of new occupations, honorific, and other. These later refinements in the progress of civilization are broadly spoken of as Financiering."[207a]

---

[207] The occasion was the first British publication in 1924 of any of Veblen's books. George Allen and Unwin, one of England's most forward looking publishers, brought out *The Theory of the Leisure Class, The Vested Interests* and *Absentee Ownership.* The books were printed in Leipzig.

The firm has generously supplied me with the following printing history as of July 1971:

Absentee Ownership – 1300 printed, of which 482 were destroyed by enemy action in 1940.

The Vested Interests and the Common Man – 1500 printed of which 888 were destroyed by enemy action in 1940.

The Theory of the Leisure Class – 1500 printed of which 613 were destroyed by enemy action in 1940; 1949, 1500 printed; 1957, 1500 printed. Paper edition published in 1971, of which approximately 895 copies sold to date.

[207a] In a section entitled "The Leisure Class Ideal," in a subsequent essay, Branford presented with a "slight change" his abstract of *The Theory of the Leisure Class:* And the tale of how "Western Civilization is pushed back by the exigencies of the Price System, into the barbarism of a hunting society.... With the elaboration of a money economy

In turning to *Absentee Ownership* and building on Heath's review of *The Theory of Business Enterprise*, Branford took up a familiar criticism of Veblen. An anonymous reviewer in the London *Daily Herald* (December 3, 1924), which supported the British Labour party, began with "so good a judge as Mr. J. A. Hobson describes . . . [*Absentee Ownership*] as 'the most formidable attack upon Capitalism ever delivered.' One pauses before dissenting from such a downright opinion from such an established judge; but the truth is that the force of . . . [its] attack is all but nullified by . . . [its] abominably tortuous, affected and repetitive style." He then proceeded to give what Branford called "the main thesis of *Absentee Ownership* in summary." Branford after referring to the *Daily Herald* review by its subhead "A Famous American Writer's Warning," opened his discussion by quoting the entire main thesis of the review.

> The established codes of law and morals, and with them the habitual assumptions of current political prac-

---

go increasing possibilities of wealth acquisition by audacious handling of the monetary tokens which express economic values. First, coin, then, far more effectively, 'instruments of credit,' become active pieces on the chessboard of life. And the point is, that cunning replaces exploit in achievements of prowess at this order of game. The financier's success is estimated not by deeds of bravery, but by manipulation of symbols. What tells is sustained passion and mental agility in invention, refinement, elaboration, sharpening, of abstract tools to serve the ends of emulative desire and acquisitive impulse. Reward of legalized loot and authentic prestige go therefore far more to cunning of age than to daring of youth. In other words, the conditions of survival and success that hold in the wild life of primitive hunters are inverted in the civilized life of urban financiers. Hence, to all the tendencies that make for reversion of modern youth in an age of commercial competition and social emulation, there are added under our system of money economy and its pecuniary culture, others of like kind that double their net social 'efficiency'." ("Economic Roots of Evils and Ideals," in *The Sociological Review*, July 1925, pp. 213-214).

tice, are increasingly in conflict with the real facts of the developing industrial system; and . . . this conflict between the forces and methods of production and the legal restraining *conditions* of production, will in time intensify to such a pitch that either the institutions must change or production (and with it human existence) will become impossible.

The essence of the accepted code in law and morals is the Right of Property in the means of production and the Freedom of all to "pursue happiness" on the basis of this right without State interference or public constraint. The Individual, his Rights, his Liberties, and his Responsibilities — these are the entities around which the whole of our accepted institutions were built.

In England in 1688 and in America in 1776 these assumptions corresponded closely with the state of social existence. There were few men then absolutely without property in land or in the means of production. These last might only be the slender kit of an independent craftsman, but as the bulk of production was in the hands of him and his like the law and morality that secured him had a valid claim to secure the greatest good of the greatest number.

But while the code has remained and gathered sanctity from age and force from habituation, the industrial facts have been transformed beyond recognition. Not only has the independent craftsman gone — and his kit of tools with him — the small manufacturer into which he grew (if he were fortunate) has gone too. And the limited liability company, owning the big factory into which the small workshop ultimately grew, that, too, has grown into the Big Business which has lost its independence in a "merger" or "combine," and become subjected in turn to the control of the financiering interests. [207b] . . . The owner has ceased to be a worker in the productive sense, and the worker has become something for which the law has no provision and morality no category.

These facts carry with them consequences. Even in the days of small manufacture it occasionally arose that it was advantageous for the craftsman to limit his output. More usually he went wider afield and sought a new market. The theory of the accepted code is that the free play of competition will establish an equitable equilibrium between competing egoisms – and on the basis of small production there was truth in the supposition. Now that free competition has worked itself out into its logical opposite – a whole hierarchy of monopolies and combinations for the suppression of competition – the theory of the law and the accepted code becomes a grim and mocking barrier to defend monopoly against every consideration based upon equity.

Nothing shows this better than the conflict (as Veblen expresses it) between the needs of production and the interests of salesmanship. Originally the capital of a business meant the cash-value of the plant or stock; nowadays it means a sum calculated from the annual earning power of the business in terms of the current average rate of interest. And as the earning power of each successful business grows more and more to depend upon a monopoly either of materials, of the market, or of salesmanship, and expensive modern advertising, earning power depends in increasing measure less upon the production of goods than upon systematic curtailment of production.

[207b] "Financiering interests" was substituted for "the banks" which was in the *Herald* review.

Branford then commented: "The above epitome of Mr. Veblen's latest book by a *Herald* reviewer would seem to be a fair statement of the author's central thesis in *Absentee Ownership;* but how much it loses when Veblen's irony is translated into pedestrian prose!" Branford followed his comment with: "a word, however, should be said about the financial aspect of the thesis," and then gave his discussion of what a member of the Geddes-Branford group called "leisure class finance."

Giving a new twist to an old theme, he wrote: "The current system of financiering, Mr. Veblen sees as a means 'to get rich quick,' which increasingly draws into the snare of a masked predation the cleverer and more forceful men from well-nigh all classes. Financiering in this analysis is to be understood as the art of acquiring expertise in a complex process. The purposes of financiering, as practised by its greater masters, may be broadly viewed as: (a) to inflate the money-earning capacity of a business, a concession, a right, or other marketable entity; (b) to capitalize in paper securities, this earning power, at the top of its curve; (c) to 'unload on the public,' which means converting these paper securities into legal tender, actual or potential, by ingenious combinations of the Banking System, the Stock Exchanges, the Press; (d) to 'invest' the proceeds in securities calculated to yield an ample and steady income to 'absentee owners.' "[208]

Hobson in an obituary declared: "More and more in his later works Veblen comes to concentrate upon the distinction

---

[208] "Thorstein Veblen," *The Sociological Review,* January 1925, pp. 66, 68.

"*Absentee Ownership and The Theory of Business Enterprise* is a continuation of the analysis begun in *The Theory of the Leisure Class.*" (Wild, "Thorstein Veblen, Interpreter of the Leisure Class," *The Millgate,* October 1935, p. 29).

between the business man and the financier, or, as he expresses it, in the title of one of his later and most brilliantly written little volumes, *The Engineers and the Price System.* The most complete statement, however, of his later doctrine is found in his *Absentee Ownership.* . . . Here the happenings of the Great War caused him to consider the relations between modern business enterprise and the politics of States, including war. As usual, his method is historical, and the early story of the national State is exhibited as 'a competitive enterprise of war and politics, in which the rival princely and dynastic establishments, all and several, each sought its own advantage at the cost of any whom it might concern.' "[209]

Shortly afterward a controversy over the book occurred in the London *Times Literary Supplement* similar to that over the review in the *Daily Herald.* The anonymous reviewer (April 2, 1925) claimed that *Absentee Ownership* was merely "a restatement of Marxism." A reply (May 28) came from a British trained barrister, R. M. Estcourt, who had taken time out from his profession to obtain a Ph.D. in economics from the University of California in 1916. He declared that "While not lacking the ability, your reviewer appears to have lacked the needful energy to probe the meaning of Veblen. Veblen has much to say that was never contemplated by Marx. His 'Absentee Owner' is by no means the medieval investor contemplated by [St. Thomas] Aquinas. For the origin of the 'Absentee Owner' one must go back to Greco-Roman times. The absentee owner in Veblen's mind is obviously the lineal descendant of the Greco-Roman exploiter of franchises, an individual who never saved or invested, but merely,

[209] "Thorstein Veblen," *The Sociological Review,* December 1929, p. 344. The quotation is from *Absentee Ownership,* p. 22.

Hobson in a letter of October 7, 1932, wrote me: "I am an admirer of his economic work, especially his development of 'the money power' and the conflict between the entrepreneur and 'the engineer.' "

through chicanery or favor obtained some grant of a share in the collection of revenue which was originally nothing else than the State appropriation of economic rent of all sorts, whether accruing from land or monopoly.[209a]

"Again, Veblen's 'underlying population' differs in concept from the proletariat of Marx. It is more inclusive. Professor Veblen's theory is built on conditions that are becoming peculiar to this country alone, although originally applicable to all post-Reformation foundations of States. This country [U.S.], and the British Self-Governing Colonies as well as many of the Latin American Colonies, took over the Greco-Roman institutions *en bloc.* Except in this country there have been modifications. There is a prevalent belief that the legal institutions of the United States of America are based on those of England. This is the theory. But examination will reveal that most of the English law which obtains in practice is the obsolete procedure swept away by the Judicature Act of 1883. With few exceptions the property laws of this country are pure Greco-Roman. In Europe, as you are aware, those laws have been considerably modified by Chaldean economics which became a holdover of the Church in the Middle Ages.

"An intelligent and patient reading of *Absentee Ownership* would make evident that it commences with the American 'Small Town,' a very different thing from a European village; in fact, economically almost a peculiarly American institution. For its counterpart in economic history one must

---

[209a] Later another admirer of Veblen, after describing such appropriation as "toll-taking," declared "Toll-taking in its generic form is plunder – predation in the terminology of Veblen." He cited *The Theory of the Leisure Class,* p. 20. [Niles Carpenter, "An Examination of Certain Influences Inimical to an Economy of Competition," in *Explorations in Economics: Notes and Essays Contributed in Honor of F. W. Taussig* (1936; New York: Augustus M. Kelley, 1967) p. 446.

go back to the Roman *Gens.* On that has been superimposed a favoured class of franchise holders, some of whom, admittedly, were originally members of the derived *Gens.* Veblen traces the natural evolution of the superimposed class from the 'small town,' a process that can only be paralleled by reference to Greco-Roman economic history. It is a condition of affairs that never came under the purview of Marx, who was almost wholly occupied with the conditions of English industrialism, which in its turn was evolved from the European medieval walled city. Comparable results may have accrued, but if we jump at conclusions we lose the opportunity of enlightenment on the extremely subtle and novel problems of the present day, almost of the present century, because the conditions giving rise to these things really only accelerated sufficiently to become obvious in 1896.

"In economics as in chemistry a few grains of an unfamiliar element, out of an apparently similar solution, will make something entirely different. By noting such variations the unprejudiced mind can acquire invaluable knowledge. The humility of Sir Isaac Newton is as applicable to economic as to physical science."

About the same time, a Dutch admirer was having considerable difficulty in obtaining a publisher for a Dutch translation of *Absentee Ownership.* J. A. Sandfort wrote Veblen in 1925 that the translation "is by this time landed with publisher no. 5,"[210] De Wereldbibliotheck of Amsterdam, a prominent, enterprising firm. He informed Veblen that the house had a long list of well selected translations. It included writ-

---

[210] J. A. Sandfort to Veblen, December 12, 1925, Thorstein Veblen Papers.

A year later he received Veblen's consent to issue *The Nature of Peace* in abridged form, "if possible." Sandfort over the years published a number of translations but it does not seem that they included any of Veblen's works.

ers like Bergson, Freud, Eisler, Darwin and H. G. Wells. The executive with whom he dealt, N. van Suchtelden, "is a widely read and often inspired novelist who started as a doctor in the political sciences and who did much to make Sigmund Freud well known to a great number of my countrymen." This executive, he continued, has informed him that the firm had lately a "good commercial success" with the Dutch translation of Henry Ford (in collaboration with Samuel Crowther) *My Life and Work.* [It appeared under the title *Productie en Welvaart*]. Once terms had been arranged with Viking, Sandfort wrote, the Dutch house was prepared to publish an edition of 6,000 copies to sell at the relatively low price of two gulden and a half ($1.00). The job he said had taken seven months of industrious work.

Apparently translating was not a very lucrative employment, for he was to receive 500 gulden ($200) less whatever had to be paid to the American publisher. At the date of writing Veblen (December 12), he had already waited over six weeks for an answer from his prospective publisher. He went on to say that "I today finished a translation of *The Engineers and the Price System.* I cancelled some few lines that should require so much tedious explanation (for non-American readers), that the quantity of it would blunt the edge of the argument. I did nothing of the sort in *Absentee Ownership* and only added three (marked) footnotes." But his efforts to get this book into print depended upon a favorable answer from De Wereldbibliotheck. He said he had taken up the matter of a translation of *The Theory of the Leisure Class* with the house and had decided to go ahead with it. "I have now burned all my bridges to go ashore where there will not grow much to consume conspicuously. Yet the work will be a real pleasure and a good thing to do."

Of equal if not more interest was Sandfort's complaint of

the slow progress of appreciation of Veblen in Europe. "It makes me sometimes impatient to see your concepts permeate European thought so slowly. When I see Franz Oppenheimer (an honest and diligent worker, although a little blinded by his own little discovery about the state as an instrument of predation, which you formulated so much clearer in [*The Instinct of*] *Workmanship*)[211] – when I see that same Oppenheimer in his *System der Sociologie* making a mess of his classification of human instincts; when I think of Sidney Webb writing his *The Decay of Capitalist Civilization*[211a] without the necessary insight in financial matters, which your work would have given him; when I admire [? *sic*] Henri Bergson spending his attention on [Baron Ernest] de Seillière's 'imperialism' [*La Philosophie de l'imperialisme*], and fighting Einstein instead of fighting you as his most able opponent, to give all the world the benefit of that clash of ideas; when Eden and Cedar Paul write their *Creative Revolution* [*: A Study of Communist Ergatocracy*] without at the same time assigning the people who alone could make the thing happen; – when I hear that gifted journalist, Maximilian Harden, fulminating against chauvinism by mere instinct, unaided by the lantern kindled in your *The Nature of Peace;* when George Bernard Shaw relies upon the *élan vital* creating the human race more long-lived, and not upon the engineers creating [for] society a sound circulation – when all those things happen around me it makes [me] feel strongly for how great a part scientific discourse is a product of pure chance. Perhaps you will have no room for my confidence

[211] Oppenheimer's book is a classic; Huebsch issued a translation under the title *The State.*

[211a] The book extensively discussed and highly commended *The Theory of the Leisure Class* and *The Theory of Business Enterprise.* [Sidney and Beatrice Webb, *The Decay of Capitalist Civilization* (New York: Harcourt, Brace, 1923) pp. 38, 44, 131, 139, 200-201].

in your work, but from here I see your work in a more isolated position than wherein it will stand in reality."

There was, however, one area of Europe where there was little question of appreciation of Veblen in influential academic circles. That was Scandinavia. In fact he was offered a newly established professorship in political economy in 1920 at the University of Kristiania (now the University of Oslo), then Norway's only university. This would have been the first and only time that he would have been a full professor in a university. How this came about is itself a fascinating story. The man who started the chain of events that led to the offer was an American admirer who knew him "only through your writings and mutual acquaintances." This was Charles E. Haugland, who seems to have had a doctorate in engineering and at the time was in the higher echelons of the National Non-Partisan League and the North Dakota state administration, especially in educational matters. He wrote Veblen that he had heard that a new professorship exclusively of economics was to be established at the University of Kristiania and that Veblen ought to apply for the post. The teaching load was five hours of lectures a week. There was a salary of at least 12,000 kroner,[212] and a decent state pension on retirement. The incumbent is "free in a REAL sense," since once in the position he can practically not be removed.[213] As he informed Veblen, he proceeded to communicate with his old friend, Professor Halvdan Koht, the historian, who was a dominating figure in the university. Koht wrote Haugland in October 1919 that there was under consideration, subject to the approval of parliament (the Storting), the creation of a professorship of political economy in the faculty of law. For this professor-

[212] The exchange rate for a krone at the time was 24¢.

[213] Haugland to Veblen, August 6, 1919, Thorstein Veblen Papers.

ship he had been able to convince the authorities that candidates should not be restricted to Norwegians, as with other professorships in the faculty of law, and under the circumstances "a name like Thorstein Veblen would be hard to disregard."

Koht went on to say that "I know him personally. I met him ten years ago [on his American trip in 1908-1909] at Leland Stanford University" and what is more important, "I know his reputation as a most prominent person in political economy." Koht stated that the salary might not be attractive; it would be the highest allowed but would be only half of his present stipend. Yet the situation might otherwise prove to be attractive for an intelligent person like Veblen. There would be compensations because the economists that we "have had and have are all mediocrities without originality. A progressive man like him would be able to lift up the whole faculty and we need a man like him."[214] Haugland sent Koht's letter to Veblen with his covering note: "I believe it would be a great thing for Norway, and particularly at this juncture in human affairs, to secure your services; and the conditions that would surround you there, I believe, would be in essentials more favorable than you could find in the United States; and therefore tend to make your future even more useful than your past has been to social progress and thinking." Veblen could supplement his salary by making "a connection with the Nobel Institute and Parliamentary committees to the extent that you desired and that your time allowed."[215]

Koht wrote directly to Veblen on July 1, 1920 on the matter

---

[214] Koht to Haugland, October 11, 1919, Thorstein Veblen Papers. Koht was not only a broad gauged historian but also a diplomat and at one time foreign minister. He also acquired a reputation as a student of Ibsen.

[215] Haugland to Veblen, October 31, 1919, Thorstein Veblen Papers.

of a chair in political economy. "The University proposed last year the founding of a new chair in this field, and the government supported the proposal. It was rejected by the Storting but with the express remark, however, that if it had been suggested to invite an eminent foreigner as professor, the Storting would certainly have taken a different position. This remark seemed aimed at you. . . . The situation consequently is that if there is a proposition to invite you to be Norwegian Professor of Political Economy this proposition will in all probability be passed in the Storting. . . . We would now like to know if there is any possibility of you accepting an invitation. . . . We badly need a political economist who could stir up our ways of thinking. . . . We work here as everywhere with extremely important social matters but there is little understanding of this science here and our own economists have not understood the need to get into thorough contact with the general public, so there is enough work here for an energetic researcher."[216]

On November 11, Mitchell recorded in his Diary that "Veblen has just received an offer of professorship in Norway." Veblen, however, did not go to Norway, because, as I recorded in the Veblen book, "every time terms were agreed upon, the changes in exchange rates required new terms. . . ."

This, however, was by no means the last of the interest of Scandinavian scholars in Veblen. Five years later there occurred an episode that carried the faint suggestion of a possibility of a Nobel Prize for Veblen. On April 8, 1925, Mitchell wrote Veblen at a Chicago address: "Yesterday I had a call from Professor Jacob S. Worm-Muller, an historian from the University of Stockholm and a member of the Nobel Prize Commission. . . . The one man Dr. Worm-Muller seems most eager to see in this country is yourself.

[216] Koht to Veblen, July 9, 1920, Thorstein Veblen Papers.

I have told him what I believe to be your present whereabouts, and encouraged him to think that you would be willing to receive him. I found him a most agreeable person, probably not yet forty years of age, much interested in the economic side of institutional history, and modern-minded."[217] We know that Worm-Muller went to Chicago two weeks later to try to see Veblen but apparently and unfortunately they never met. Veblen was not then at the Chicago address. Worm-Muller's postcard from a Chicago hotel requesting a meeting turned up in Veblen's correspondence in his summer camp at the isolated Icelandic settlement, Washington Island, Door County, Wisconsin.

This leads to Veblen's last book, the translation of one of the greatest sagas, which appeared in 1925.

The Laxdaela Saga[218]

On this book, two letters from authorities to the publisher have become available. One was written by the philologist in the department of English of the University of Wisconsin, William Ellery Leonard. He wrote:

> [T]he very problem of *how* it could be done into English has interested me for several years while I've been going over it with little groups of graduate students. Of course my comments take for granted that I've tested out Veblen's *scholarship* – the version had of course this lower accuracy of linguistic knowledge of the old Norse. But he has solved the higher problem with a more re-

[217] Mitchell to Veblen, April 8, 1926, Thorstein Veblen Papers.

Similarly N. S. B. Gras, then at Minnesota, later of Harvard, expressed in 1926 a wish to meet Veblen, as part of his endeavor "to take every opportunity in America and abroad to converse with those who have been prominent in economic fields. I am putting together some of the chief facts and developments in the history of economic history." (Gras to Veblen, July 6, 1926, Thorstein Veblen Papers).

[218] The "Introduction" is reprinted below.

markable success, a problem (aside from the linguistic difficulties in the most difficult of all mediaeval or modern languages of Western Europe) mainly of idiom and tone of idiom. His English in the flavor of the words, in the homely raciness of sturdy intimate turns of our folk speech, and in the dry grimness and pathos of its laconic sentence structure is as imaginatively vital a transfer from language to language as can well be. He has instinctively avoided both "literary elegance" and commonplace slang. And he gets the organic tempo and rhythm of the narrative. Is Veblen by any chance himself an Icelander – else, as an economist, how comes it he can read this speech of the twilight of the Gods? If I'd seen the manuscript, I'd have suggested jarl for earl [earle] – a monocled gent, with his mouth half open.[219]

Another authority on Scandinavian literature, Francis P. Magoun Jr. of Harvard, informed the publisher that Veblen's edition was "an enormous improvement" over the older translations. "Early Germanic literature is, by the way, extraordinarily quaint in a Romance language garb . . . I have been struck and delighted by Veblen's taste in rendering Old Icelandic prose into everyday English."[220]

The book attests to Veblen's long sustained interest in anthropology. As I noted in the Veblen book the Laxdaela

[219] Leonard to Ben W. Huebsch, May 16, 1925, Thorstein Veblen Papers.

[220] Magoun to Huebsch, July 7, 1925, Thorstein Veblen Papers.

Veblen reported to the publisher on a translation by Robert Proctor that "the translator's rendering of the Laxdaela Saga is a very close translation almost word for word, and in extremely archaic diction. . . . It is good work of its kind. Published in a limited edition (of 250 copies) and in a special font of type. A copy is to be found in the New York Public Library." (Veblen to Huebsch, July 14, 1924, Huebsch Papers).

Saga was first translated by Veblen in the 1880's at a time when he was unable to obtain a post. But he continued to have a deep interest in anthropology, especially the Scandinavian field. It furnished much of the foundation of his economic thinking. Some light is thrown upon his pervading interest in this area by several letters to his oldest brother Andrew in 1899, shortly after the publication of *The Theory of the Leisure Class*. Andrew had become deeply interested in tracing the family genealogy back to its roots in Valders, Norway. Veblen, however, was not so much interested in genealogy as he was in archeological and etymological matters for his work.[221] In the first, April 22, 1899, he wrote:

> I thank you for the clippings from *Skandinavin* and the *Republican* as also for the information contained in the last and a previous letter.
>
> I am not much impressed with *Skandinavin's* etymology of Veblen; nor with their review of the book, which seems to be mostly talk. The etymologist seems

---

[221] In a letter of January 22, 1925, to Andrew he gave genealogical data on his wives as follows:

"The information which you ask for, so far as I can give it, runs like this: married, 1888, Ellen M. Rolfe, daughter of Charles G. Rolfe and Ellen (Strong) Rolfe, born 1859; married, 1914, Ann Fessenden Bradley, daughter of Alex. S. Bradley and Harriet (Towle) Bradley, born (Chicago) 1877, died 1920, no children. Mr. and Mrs. Rolfe were born – or at least grew up – in Chelsea, Vermont; Mr. and Mrs. Bradley, born in Fryeburg, Maine. This is all I know, and I don't see the sense of that much."

He reported the death of his second wife in an equally laconic manner on October 8, 1920. "Ann died yesterday in the hospital at Waverley, [Mass.], where she has been for something over a year past, from the effects of an abcess in the lung, complicated with symptoms of pneumonia. I have been here [Worcester, Mass.], with her sister's folks, going back and forth between Waverley and here. Next week I am to return to New York, where work begins at the New School on the fifteenth." (The sister was the wife of Wallace Attwood, president of Clark University).

not to have known of the *o* in the name, which makes it practically impossible to derive the word from *vifl*. Unless there has been something peculiar in the past handling of it, it should come from a word whose main vowel in the nominative is *a* (possibly *e* or *u*). *Vafl* (English wabble) might do, so far as regards the phonetics of the thing. There is always the chance, I believe, that place names in the out-of-the-way parts of Norway may be of Finnish derivation, and there is no particular reason why this one should not be. I don't know enough about Finnish to guess, but I believe it comes easily within the scope of Finnish phonetics. Probably a knowledge of Icelandic and an intimate knowledge of the topography of the place would settle the matter, and probably nothing else would.

I hope you will make up your mind to go to Valders this summer, and we will then dispose of the whole matter. I am not quite sure of going, but the chances are that I shall. If so, I shall leave here about 23d June.[222]

---

[222] A close friend claimed that Veblen's primary reason for spending his summers in Washington Island, Wisconsin, was "to get a first hand knowledge of the Icelandic language from the colony of Icelanders that live here." She added: "he saw and fell in love with a plot of land which lay between Green Bay and a small inland lake on our property where he could see the sunrise over the small lake and the sunset over Green Bay." (Mrs. K. Bjornasson to Joseph Dorfman, September 16, 1934). Veblen chose well; Washington Island has been made into a nature conservancy principally on account of its unusual flora.

I have been given the following anecdote on the matter by a present-day inhabitant of the island: "Veblen came to Washington Island at first in search of a place to board for the summer. He went to John Gislason (the leader of the original four to emigrate from Iceland) to ask his wife if he could stay there, but only on his own terms: At no time could any English be spoken. They must all – children included – speak Icelandic in the house. It was agreed upon and Veblen stayed for the summer. Mrs. Gislason was curious and wanted to know of Veblen's marital status and though she asked him many times 'Are you

Veblen went alone but kept his brother informed of his adventures. On August 16, he wrote Andrew:

> I came here [Valders] something over two weeks ago, and go on to Christiania today. I came here over Bergen and Laerdal. So far there is nothing to tell in the way of adventures. I have seen some relatives and some of the places connected with the ancient history of the tribe, but there is not a great deal to say for either. I believe I have got no photographs that are worthwhile, as I have the impression that my camera is out of order, besides which I am also of no account in the photographing way.
>
> The people here view me with alarm because I talk

---

married, Mr. Veblen?' he always gave a one word answer in Icelandic meaning *'Much!'* " (Mrs. Esther V. Gunnerson to Joseph Dorfman, June 23, 1963).

I had in the Veblen book noted his linguistic facility. An admirer, who knew him well in California in the 1920's and who will be discussed later, has supplied some interesting additional details. Hans Otto Storm wrote me in 1932 that Veblen "enjoyed also experimenting with minor and outlandish tongues. Living in our house for a short time, he moved into a room recently vacated by another tenant, and found a letter in one of the drawers. 'The man who lived there was a Filipino,' he said. 'How did you know?' 'Because part of the letter was written in Tagalog.' He went on to analyze the letter as an example in the diffusion of words. The word *dinero,* he pointed out, appeared in Spanish because it was not used in the remoter provinces; for a parallel reason the word *laundry* appeared in English."

Incidentally in discussing Veblen's facility with languages, Storm filled in some details of Veblen's recollection of his acquisition of English. "He told me that he was twelve years old before he learned to speak English. He further said that although his mother could speak quite acceptable English, he himself was thirty years old before he found this out, and then quite by accident, to her considerable confusion. She had spoken till then only Norwegian in his presence. But a woman had come into the house who did not speak Norwegian, and to whom she very much wanted to communicate something, so she forgot herself." (Storm to Dorfman, November 6, 1932).

Valders, and look like an Englishman – which is held to be fundamentally wrong. I shall spend a couple of weeks in Christiania and in Sweden and then go to Copenhagen. What I want there is mostly northern antiquities and ethnographic material.

On his return he sent his brother some family heirlooms which he described in the manner of the anthropology in *The Theory of the Leisure Class* and *Imperial Germany*. He wrote in a letter of October 17: "I am sending two books and a 'Aölkniv' (?) that once belonged to grandfather. The catechism is said (by John Jome) to be the one by which grandfather learned to read; the other with the title page gone which is known as 'Assenatti's Bog,' is the one with which he habitually amused himself during the latter part of his life. Don't take offense at the knife! The sheath and handle are grandfather's workmanship, the blade is the work of Tömmös Tumblöigarn ('Kvekörn'). I am told that grandfather carried it habitually at the time of his death."

Veblen was always encouraging able students to read anthropological works. In sending such literature in 1896 to a former student who was recuperating from an illness at her home in California and about to be married, he wrote: "My dear friend,[223] this line of reading is particularly interesting to me. My own knowledge of the anthropological and ethnological lore is very meager and fragmentary, and it is somewhat presumptive in me to offer advice, but it goes without saying that I shall want to try my hand at all questions that may occur to you, if you will give me a chance.

"I have mailed to your address two parcels of books. xxx

[223] The "xxx" signified omissions by the recipient. This was Sarah McLean Hardy (later Mrs. Warren Gregory).

I would begin with Topinard, follow that with [G. and A. de] Mortillet *(Le Prehistorique)*, follow that with Brinton and Keane. Of the two last Keane is the most to be relied upon where they differ.xxx Make no effort to remember any of it. The salient points of classification will fix themselves sufficiently by iteration and the details are not worth remembering.xxx The book on art, by the way, is put in to break the monotony; I think you will find it curious and interesting. xxx."

This particular letter also reveals Veblen's interest in anthropological research of the Pacific coast and more of the islands of the Pacific area, where so much anthropological research had been going on. "I wish, and always have wished, to see the coast, even if I cannot find a chance to stay there, and the same is true of the Islands, perhaps even more so. The chance of my achieving it seems very small at present, and as the next best thing to seeing it all xxx I will recklessly ask you to tell me all about it xxx your life down there in that strange world which I may never see.xxx

"Please let me know what is to be your address. I wish, having undertaken your education, to send a couple more books."[224]

We know that a decade later Veblen got the opportunity to be on the Pacific coast as a teacher at Stanford University, and that this episode ended with his involuntary resignation at the end of 1909. The resignation incidentally provided

---

[224] Veblen to Hardy, February 6, 1896, from extracts of Veblen's letters to her.

Mrs. Gregory made the extracts for me at the urging of Mitchell. She later wrote Mitchell that one thing that lightened the task of making the extracts was "the enthusiasm of seeing our Veblen emerge once more." Going through the letters gave her great satisfaction, she added, "because it has given me once more the image of the whimsical, charming, unique genius whom we all loved and I adored – but not

one benefit to the researcher into his life and work.[225] Not knowing where he was going to be,[226] he left a substantial portion of his books with a graduate student, William R. Camp. He provided me with the following list of them,[227] a list which includes a goodly number of anthropological works:

List of Books Left With William Camp

1. Dunbar, Charles F., *Chapters on Theory of Banking*, second edition edited by O. M. W. Sprague.
2. Dorsey, James Owen, *Omaha and Ponka Letters.*
3. Fite, Warner, "Contiguity and Similarity," offprint from *Philosophical Review*, Vol. IX, no. 6, 1900.
4. Ghent, W. G., *Mass and Class*, 1904.
5. Kidd, Benjamin, *Social Evolution.*
6. *Fabian Essays in Socialism.*
7. Fite, Warner, "Art, Industry and Science. A Suggestion towards a Psychological Theory of Art," offprint from *Psychological Review*, March 1901, pp. 128-144.
8. Letourneau, Charles J. M., *Property: Its Origin and Development.*

---

[225] The resignation was dated December 19, 1909; he was paid for the rest of the academic year.

[226] "He is packing his books, and does not know where to send them, is sad and troubled, and sick. He has a numbness of one side and heart very, very, slow." (Ellen Rolfe Veblen to Mrs. H. A. Millis, December 15, 1909. Letter in Joseph Dorfman's possession).

[227] Camp reported that the list was incomplete because at the time he was occupied with making arrangements for a trip east from California. (Camp to Dorfman, June 3, 1933).

---

enough to do for him in these later years what I might have." (Mrs. Gregory to Mitchell, March 1934, Mitchell Papers). Mrs. Gregory was referring to the fact that she might have helped more when he seemed financially distressed.

9. Leroy-Beaulieu, Paul, *Traité De La Science Des Finances*, 2 vols.
10. Marx, Karl, *Capital*, English translation, 1 vol.
11. Jones, Lloyd, *The Life, Times and Labours of Robert Owen*, edited by William Cairns Jones.
12. Peixotto, Jessica, *The French Revolution and Modern French Socialism.*
13. Rogers, Thorold, *Six Centuries of Work and Wages: The History of English Labor;* also the abridgement, *Work and Wages.*
14. Schäffle, A., *Quintessence of Socialism.*
15. Scott, Wm. A., *Money and Banking.*
16. Smart, Wm., *Studies in Economics.*
17. Smart, Wm., *The Distribution of Income.*
18. Spencer, Herbert, *Works.*
19. Stuart, Henry W., "The Logic of Self-Realisation," University of California Publications, *Philosophy*, vol. I (1904), no. 9, pp. 175-205.
20. Thomas, Cyrus, *Catalogue of Pre-historic Works East of the Rocky Mountains.*
21. Thomas, W. I., "Psychology of Race-Prejudice," offprint from *The American Journal of Sociology*, vol. 9, no. 5, March 1904, pp. 593-611.
22. Wilson, Sir Daniel, *Anthropology;* Appendix on Archaeology by E. B. Tylor.
23. *Sociological Papers* (1904), with an introductory address by James Bryce, President of the Society. Published for the Sociological Society: London, Macmillan, 1905: Westermarck, E.; Galton, Francis; Geddes, Patrick; Durkheim, E.; Mann, Harold H.; Branford, Victor.
24. Tarde, G., *Psychologie Économique*, 2 vols.
25. Industrial Commission of U.S., Reports, 19 vols.

26. Several volumes of accumulated numbers of *The Journal of Political Economy* and miscellaneous numbers of other economic journals.
27. Wallace, Alfred R., *The Distribution of Life*.
28. Reports of the Smithsonian Institution, 1888; 1891; 1892.
29. Ward, Lester F., "Contemporary Sociology," offprint from *The American Journal of Sociology*, vol. 7, January-May 1902, pp. 475-500, 629-658, 749-762.
30. Boehm-Bawerk, Eugen von, *Capital and Interest*.

A Missouri student informed me that Veblen had there "besides a collection of sagas, copies of Hakluyt's *Voyages* and some copies of Herman Melville's novels on his shelves, anthropologists' reports of the Smithsonian Institution, and such lore. He [also] had a second hand copy of the elementary text in Greek used at M.U."[227a]

II

PROJECTS

We now turn to various projects; for some Veblen sought research grants; others arose from government service (as during World War I). The projects throw light on his interests and in most cases provided material for books, memoranda and articles. Some of them were discussed in the Veblen book, but on all these we have a good deal of additional information, and besides several new projects have come to light.

The first was a pre World War I anthropological project (1909-1913). Then comes his war time activities for the House Inquiry and the Food Administration (1917-1918) and finally four somewhat interrelated projects in the immediate post war period (1919-1925).

[227a] Stuart Updegraff to Dorfman, September 30, 1935.

Investigation of Baltic and Cretan Antiquities

For the first Veblen sought funds from the Carnegie Institution for the Advancement of Science, Washington, for a field study of the ancient Aryan culture, specifically an "Inquiry into Baltic and Cretan Antiquities," along the lines of his famous course "Economic Factors of Modern Civilization." As he explained to his old friend Jameson: "At the suggestion of my friends here I am applying for support from the Carnegie Institution for an inquiry into European – Scandinavian and Cretan – prehistoric antiquities, with a view to an early relationship between these two cultural regions. The inquiry is designed to approach its problem from the economic – industrial and pecuniary – side, and so to look into the derivation and growth of popular institutions in the two regions. I may add it has largely been prompted by the generalizations made or made possible by the Pumpelly explorations in Turkestan, carried out under the auspices of the Institution, and is proposed to be conducted in the light of the results these arrived at. . . . I am aware that this outline may suffer serious modification in any attempt to work it out; in particular it may prove necessary to review and make use of the results of the Pumpelly explorations in a larger degree than appears from the outline [enclosed], and it may also prove desirable to go somewhat afield into Homeric and early Greek civilization."[228]

Veblen began seeking funds for the project in early 1909, a search that was intensified by his resignation from Stanford. With the backing of Chancellor Jordan, he formally sought

---

[228] Veblen to Jameson, May 23, 1910, Jameson Papers.

The original application with an editorial note by Joseph Dorfman was printed in *The American Journal of Sociology,* September 1933. This is reprinted below without the note but with the addition of the "Statement of Expense and Time Required for Executing the Project."

a three year grant in 1910 from the Carnegie Institution. To support the application, Mitchell sent a mimeographed letter to "a few scholars whose word will carry weight with the director of the Institution." He stated: "Mr. Veblen is desirous of making a study of the early stages in Aryan culture by means of a close examination of the Baltic and Cretan antiquities now available. So far these remains have been studied mainly by archeologists. Veblen thinks that much of great value to students of culture can be added to the results already reached if the evidence is carefully reviewed by one familiar with the earlier stages of industrial development and interested in the growth of economic technique."[229]

Mitchell was especially anxious that Veblen obtain the grant in order to turn him away "from the kind of work represented in his recent critical activities in which he has indulged in speculation rather freely," and towards his more constructive bent.[230] Veblen's application was turned down. Mitchell urged him in 1911 "to push his second application to the Carnegie Institution but he exhibited his characteristic reluctance to take energetic measures." Two years later Veblen reported to Mitchell in February 1913 that "The Carnegie negotiations closed the other day with a final rejection of my proposal, not greatly to my surprise, the reason given by President Woodward being the adoption of a policy on the part of the Institution not to employ or subsidize men associated with universities but on the other hand to keep the work of the institution distinct and under a set

[229] This copy, dated May 15, 1910, was sent to Laughlin. It is in the Laughlin Papers, Library of Congress. Laughlin wrote an enthusiastic letter in support of the project.

[230] Interestingly in planning as President of the American Economic Association the program for the annual meetings in December 1924, he recorded in his Diary, May 5: "To see Veblen about reading a paper on method."

organization. He writes cordially enough as might be expected and professes a continued interest in the line of investigation proposed but the refusal is quite definitive." What Veblen went on to give as the true explanation may not be the full story, but it does indicate a characteristic of Veblen's work: that exclusively "economic" facts hardly explain the actions of men and organizations. Veblen went on to say "I get the impression that he was piqued at my not writing him a year ago at the time the whole matter was waiting on the decision of a Central American expedition; he says there was nothing in all that and intimates that the matter would have been decided in my favor if I had kept in direct correspondence with him all the time." Veblen by no means gave up the project or ethnological inquiry. As he continued in the same letter, "all of which I am writing with a view to troubling you further. Do you happen to know whether President Vincent, of Minnesota – our old friend, George Vincent [formerly of Chicago], as you no doubt know – is inclined to regard me with suspicion or any degree of ill will? This question is not prompted by sentiment, and an answer to it would stir no emotions but would afford valuable information.

"He is, as you are aware, in a community in which, as he is apparently just beginning to appreciate, the Scandinavian element is to be catered to by anyone who seeks popularity, as he is doing. So he is now proposing that the university should make some special effort to serve the scholarly interest of this Scandinavian constituency, by providing for a larger attention to Scandinavian topics and by cultivating especially intimate relations with the Scandinavian universities and scholars. So it occurs to me that this antiquarian proposition of mine might well appeal to him as the right sort of thing to encourage, in case I am not *persona non grata* to such an extent as to make me impossible. I may add that

I stand well with the Norwegians in Minnesota, largely on the ground of the very extensive popularity of an older brother of mine."[231] What he would propose to Vincent was what Davenport vainly sought for him, "a free professorship"; that is, "that he give me an appointment on his faculty (in economics, sociology, ethnology or at large) with sufficient freedom and support to pursue this inquiry that I have proposed and with a view to making use of any results, both in class room and through publication under the auspices of the university. As you are probably aware, the point of departure for the inquiry would be the Scandinavian antiquities, and the greater part of the inquiry would be within the Scandinavian field. And Minnesota has plenty of funds.

"Please let me know what you think of it. The whole thing is too close to my interest to allow me to see it in perspective and judge of its practicability, besides which I have no means of knowing the state of Mr. Vincent's sentiments."[232] This too did not materialize.

With the outbreak of World War I and American participation, Veblen had hopes of finding a suitable place in the administration. We shall here present supplementary information bearing on his work for the House Peace Inquiry, the United States Food Administration, and the abortive attempts to secure Veblen's services for the War Labor Policies Board.

Government Service

In the fall of 1917, President Wilson set up the United States Government Inquiry into the Terms of Peace. The House Inquiry, as it was popularly called, was organized by

---

[231] Andrew A. Veblen, professor of physics at Luther College, and father of the famous mathematician, Oswald Veblen.

[232] Veblen to Mitchell, February 20, 1913, in possession of Joseph Dorfman.

president Wilson's intimate friend, Colonel Edward M. House, for the purpose of aiding the president to prepare for the eventual peace conference. Headquarters were in New York City. The director was Colonel House's brother-in-law, Sidney E. Mezes, president of the College of the City of New York, but its actual operating head was the secretary, Walter Lippmann, who had achieved prominence as an editor of *The New Republic.* At a meeting in October, it seems Veblen who was then at Missouri, had discussed with Lippmann the possibility of his employment by the Inquiry.[233] In a letter to the secretary shortly afterwards, Veblen indicated not only that he was interested in a post but also suggested that his policy proposals in *The Nature of Peace* were along the lines that the president was taking. He wrote Lippmann "that the progressively more and more definite position taken by the administration as touches the peace terms for which it is willing to stand have hitherto somewhat consistently run a close parallel with the analysis offered in *The Nature of Peace*. . . . Kindly note that this is not an expression of conceit running to the effect that the Administration has been in any degree indebted to my lucubrations; it is only that I flatter myself that I too have arrived at a sane and sound apprehension of the logic of facts involved in the case."[234] Lippmann in his reply expressed interest in having Veblen's cooperation but held out no definite offer of employment. "The kind of work I have in mind for you to do is meditative and analytical. . . . I should like especially to

[233] Lippmann was familiar with Veblen's writings. Thus while his influential *Drift and Mastery* does not mention Veblen by name, it makes considerable use of his concept of "the instinct of workmanship." (Lippmann called it "the instincts of workmanship").

[234] Veblen to Lippmann, October 10, 1917. All the House Inquiry correspondence that is mentioned here is in the National Archives.

feel free to submit plans and proposals to you for your criticism and to receive from you any suggestions as to topics for research and methods of approach."[235]

The next move seems to have come at the end of the month through Manley O. Hudson, a colleague in the law school of the University of Missouri (later of the Harvard Law School). He was a broad gauged specialist in international law. At the time Lippmann was urging him to join the Inquiry as his deputy; and in the course of the negotiations Hudson wrote the secretary: "I wish very much that Veblen could be used in your undertaking. As you know his grasp of the whole international situation is very thorough and far reaching. I think he would be very glad to be used in some way."[236]

Hardly had he himself joined the Inquiry, when Hudson drafted a letter for Lippmann to request Veblen to undertake an assignment. The letter read: "Would you be willing to undertake the preparation of a memorandum dealing with the economic penetration of undeveloped countries by foreign interests, for use in connection with the Inquiry? The collation and elaboration of some of the suggestions in your recent book on *The Nature of Peace* might be the large part of such a memorandum. If it is possible for you to undertake this, would you address yourself particularly to an outline of the general policies which you think should be adopted with reference to both the nationalization and the internationalization of protection to foreign investors and of administration of spheres of investment, if an attempt should be made to effect a more cohesive political organization of the international community for the attainment so far as practicable, of these objects (a) protecting backward or semi-backward peoples from unjust exploitation; (b) reducing to a minimum

[235] Lippmann to Veblen, October 19, 1917.
[236] Hudson to Lippmann, October 29, 1917.

the economic and political advantage of concession holders as against nationals of other allegiance. Do you have facilities in Missouri for doing such work there, at least for the present? And will your engagements admit of your sending some report of it before the first of January?"[237] Veblen in his affirmative response said: "As you indicate, the time which you are in a position to allow me, as well as the facilities for inquiry in this place, are such as will limit the proposed memorandum to somewhat general terms and leave it at the best in a sketchy shape. I shall endeavor to indicate what is, in my apprehension, the line of argument that must necessarily be taken by negotiations looking to settlement of these questions, and to call attention to the salient limitations under which the work of making suitable arrangements of the kind must be carried on."[238]

Hardly had Veblen despatched to New York the memorandum, "Outline of a Policy for the Control of the 'Economic Penetration' of Backward Countries and of Foreign Investments,"[239] when he was queried on the same matter by his old Stanford colleague and friend, Allyn A. Young, who was about to leave his Washington post with the United States War Trade Board and become chief economist for the Inquiry. Young, who wanted Veblen to be a regular member of the Inquiry, wrote him on January 2, 1918: "It is pos-

---

[237] Hudson's draft has the date December 7, 1917. Lippmann's letter is dated December 11.

[238] December 17, 1917.

[239] This memorandum, along with the second, "Suggestions Touching the Working Program of An Inquiry into the Prospective Terms of Peace," were originally published by Joseph Dorfman in the *Political Science Quarterly*, were reprinted in *Essays in Our Changing Order*, and also in 1967 as an appendix in *The Historian and the Diplomat*, edited by Francis L. Loewenheim (New York: Harper and Row, 1967) Appendix 6.

sible that you have already heard from certain parties at 3755 Broadway, New York, asking you to co-operate in some work now in hand. If not, this will serve as an introduction to the matter, and if so, this may be regarded as supplementary to any previous communications. Your writings and particularly your book on Peace, suggest that your point of view and your knowledge ought in some way be available for those who will represent this country at the Peace Conference. It happens that I am trying to help in this work and it goes without saying that personally I should greatly appreciate your advice and suggestions. A reasonable honorarium could, I think, be paid to you.

"Two general subjects suggest themselves to me as worthy of your attention. In the first place, there is the whole problem of economic penetration in its different forms and phases. Detailed studies will be made with respect to economic penetration in different countries, but you might be able to give an illuminating survey of the whole process with special reference to its roots and to the international agreements that will be necessary to deal with it effectively. In the second place, a study might be profitably made of the relation of business interests to national economic policies. I mean by this a study of the extent to which national economic policies, though supposedly based on national interests, are really but the expression of private economic interests. The world is full of a neo-mercantilism."

Veblen in his reply after informing Young (January 6) of his memorandum and expressing his willingness to co-operate further with the Inquiry, went on to discuss how it could most effectively proceed with its research. "The suggestion conveyed in your letter falls in very closely with my own speculations in the same connection. There can be little doubt but that the neo-mercantilism which you speak of is likely to prove the most delicate and still the most stubborn complication of difficulties with which the peace negotiations will have to deal." Characteristic of his "loner" attitude in investigation was his suggestion in connection with that matter that "several phases of this confusion or complication of national and private interests should be taken up in a detached way for deliberate argument and exposition in the shape of a series of briefs or bulletins, preferably issued under the name of some member of the Inquiry rather than under the corporate name of the Inquiry as such. The reason for this last suggestion is what seems to me the desirability of avoiding premature commitment to any too definite program on the part of the Inquiry as a corporate body; at the same time that the semi-official irresponsibility attaching to the signature of any one man connected with the Inquiry would admit of freer publicity and an outspoken advocacy of far-reaching reforms."[240]

Veblen went on to explain to Young that "The memorandum is drawn in too general terms to apply to any concrete situation that may arise; partly for the reason that the prospective situation to which any argument would have to apply has not taken on a concrete form. At least not so far as one can see from this distance. You will easily appreciate that, at this distance, one has a chance to know much less and to believe much more than would seem at all reasonable to a man who is engaged in the middle of things. So, e.g., the information that comes through the newspapers and on which we habitually depend has all the appearance of being well censored or else a product of collusive journalistic optimism, designed to leave a very sanguine state of mind in the

---

240 A more concise discussion of individually signed bulletins is in the second memorandum.

reader; on the other hand, what reaches us through personal channels, fitfully and in fragmentary shape, argues a state of confusion and infirmity in the Administration and in the counsels of the Entente such as to leave one doubtful of any sort of a tolerable outcome. I am speaking of this matter in extenuation of the short-comings of the memorandum enclosed. With your more intimate knowledge of the present state of things and the prospect of the calculable future, you will be able to make the allowances needed in the case. . . .

"It would seem to me that in order to know in detail what to inquire into in the matter of economic policy one would need, as an indispensable preliminary, to be in possession of the fullest possible information with regard to what may be the basis on which a settlement will be made. I may overstate the matter or it may overstate itself in my mind, but as I see it the economic policy which is possible or necessary to be pursued is conditioned very closely at almost every point by the degree of freedom with which the representatives of the Entente will be able to shape things in the prospective settlement; and I feel that I know next to nothing – and much of that may be misleading – as to what is known, aimed at or expected by those who know most about that matter or who will have most to say in the shaping of it. . . .

"At this distance I unavoidably feel that I do not know what I am talking about in speaking to any point that can be characterized as 'detailed' or 'concrete.'" Veblen went on to say: "I am expecting to be in New York for a few days around the 18th of this month, at which time I am expected to read a paper before the National Institute of Social Sciences ['On the General Principles of a Policy of Reconstruction']. . . . At that time I shall probably have a chance to hear what one and another of the men in the east know or think about the situation; and I should like more than anything else to have a chance at that time to talk things over with you."[241]

Young sent the correspondence to Mezes with the following note: "To make Veblen really useful, he ought to be brought in closer touch with the specific problems of the Inquiry. . . . I have so much confidence in his originality and fertility of suggestion that I recommend using him in whatever way seems best." Mezes, however, while willing to have Veblen's cooperation claimed that the financial situation of the Inquiry precluded any honorarium.[242]

Meanwhile the United States Food Administration became interested in Veblen. In the Veblen book, I noted that an employee, Alice Boughton, a friend of Veblen, had brought his name to the attention of the chief of the Statistical Division, who was Raymond Pearl, the noted biometrician.[243] The records of the Food Administration in the Na-

[241] The address, which was originally published in the journal of the Institute, deals with both the domestic and the international situation. The part on domestic affairs was promptly reprinted in *The New Republic,* and subsequently in the second collection, *Essays in Our Changing Order.* The first part, on "international frictions," is reprinted below.

The essay is in effect a sequel of *The Nature of Peace.* A specialist on the history of American foreign policy thus summarized both the second memorandum and the address: "[Veblen] quite sensibly insisted that if the administration was really serious about a people's rather than a victor's peace, the Inquiry would have to campaign for it in the United States. . . . Moreover, in striking out for such a peace, the Inquiry would have to opt for the spokesmen of any necessary 'revision or adjustment' within the established order over the spokesmen of the vested interests and of the unqualified maintenance of the established order. With revolutionary Russia as a backdrop, Veblen warned of the hazards of returning to the *status quo ante;* the war to make the world safe for democracy would also have to make America 'safe for the common man.'" (Arno J. Mayer, "Historical Thought and American Foreign Policy in the Era of the First World War," in *The Historian and the Diplomat,* edited by Francis L. Loewenheim, p. 82).

[242] Mezes to Young, January 14, February 8, 1918.

[243] Miss Boughton had studied with Mitchell at Columbia University and had visited Veblen at the University of Missouri.

tional Archives reveal that Lubin, then too on the staff of the division, was also instrumental in the matter. Hearing from Lubin that Veblen would be in New York on January 18, Pearl wired Veblen there (on the 14th) to stop over in Washington on his return to Missouri, so that they could discuss certain problems with which the Statistical Division was confronted, especially in dealing with the control of prices. A few days later he again wired Veblen and this time for his opinion as to whether the statistical information bulletin of the division should be eliminated because of the expense. Veblen replied: "To me statistical information bulletins on crops and weekly retail prices are of highest value. Continue them by all means, especially retail prices. Bulletins necessary both for administrative control of prices and correct public information."[244] After some discussions with Pearl early in February in Washington, Veblen sent both a wire and a letter on the 14th from New York accepting the position of "special investigator." He wrote Pearl: "The formalities and the considerations involved having been disposed of I am free to accept the invitation which you so kindly extended to me the other day, and to take my place on your staff. So, doubting the expedition of the mail service, I have just wired you to that effect. Kindly advise me as to anything which I need to know or to do in this connection.

"I am going on the presumption made necessary by my lack of a livelihood and by my definitely going on leave from the University for the rest of the academic year, that my relations with your office will not be interrupted during that

[244] The Veblen-Pearl correspondence is in the National Archives. Veblen always had a high appreciation of statistical work. Thus he wrote in *The Instinct of Workmanship* that "modern science at large looks to the use of statistical methods and precise mechanical measurements." (p. 322).

period. I shall be glad of some assurance to that effect, if it can be given without embarrassing you." Then he turned to his plans for preparing to carry out Pearl's suggestion that he first make a study of labor conditions in the grain producing states of the Northwest. He added in his letter to Pearl: "Meantime I am intending to stay here the rest of the week, to see several men from whom I hope to get help and light, and also to see a meeting of socialists and radicals about to be held here. So that my present expectation is to return to Washington next week to consult with you, and probably as I see it, presently after to make a short visit to some parts of the grain states in the Northwest." After being assured of continuation of work, except for an unforseen sudden end of the war, Veblen proceeded west on his first mission.[245]

[245] Officially he was employed from February 19, 1918, to June 30, 1918.

Lubin reports that "soon after he [Veblen] arrived a sign was put on Veblen's door: Dr. Thorstein B. Veblen. His comment to me when he saw the sign was: 'Get that goddam sign off of there. The only reason I came here was to get rid of the title Doctor.'" (Lubin, "Recollections of Veblen," in *Thorstein Veblen: The Carleton College Veblen Seminar Essays,* pp. 137-138). There is an earlier "Dr." story: "On one of his ocean voyages some one who knew him had put his name on the ship's register as 'Dr. Veblen.' He never used his doctoral title himself. An inquisitive fellow passenger having looked him up on the register asked what kind of doctor he was. 'Well,' he replied gravely, 'I am a horse doctor but I would rather you wouldn't mention it as I don't want it known.'" (Florence Veblen, "Thorstein Veblen: Reminiscences of his Brother Orson," *Social Forces,* December 1931, p. 193).

At the Food Administration, he was no more an observer of administrative procedures than in the academic world. For example, he was scheduled to give a series of lectures at Amherst late in May 1918, which became the basis of *The Vested Interests and the Common Man.* On May 8 he wrote Pearl from Amherst the following note: "I ran away from Washington yesterday afternoon on a hurried notice, and did not find time to tell you of my going. The folks here have been moving the dates up for my lectures, as they found that the students are showing symptoms of scattering when the month is out, to go into various industrial occupations. I expect to be back within a week."

Several pointed memoranda resulted, of which the most important is "Using the I. W. W. to Harvest Grain."[246] Lubin, who served as Veblen's assistant in the Food Administration, has recently presented a lucid summary of the report:

> [T]he report was in no way radical or revolutionary, Veblen simply said that the I. W. W. membership were being harassed by the government. He suggested that the harassment be stopped and that the I. W. W. be given a chance to prove their loyalty to the government. His second suggestion was that since the I. W. W. was suspicious of Mr. Burleson, the Secretary of Agriculture, who opposed the organization of agricultural labor, the task of producing food during the war be taken away from the Department of Agriculture and like food conservation, be made the responsibility of the Food Administration. He suggested that the Food Administration make an agreement with the I. W. W., giving it the job of harvesting the crop of the area, instead of having every farmer hire his own workers and worry whether there would be enough of them to harvest the grain. I

[246] This was published originally with an introduction by Joseph Dorfman in *The Journal of Political Economy,* December 1932; reprinted in *Essays in Our Changing Order.*

In the Food Administration as elsewhere Veblen admired efficient activity. Lubin recalls: "We were located in one of those 'temporary' buildings that had been erected in a hurry in Washington after the United States entered the war. It was newly built and was a whole block long. We had all kinds of messenger boys running around on rubber-wheeled roller skates. Veblen was fascinated by them. The messenger would rush by the door at twenty miles an hour. Veblen was very much impressed with it all and commented that his feeling that the government was inefficient had to be changed." (Lubin, "Recollections of Veblen," in *Thorstein Veblen: The Carleton College Veblen Seminar Essays,* p. 138).

> might add, incidentally, that in 1950, when my fitness to hold the job of United States representative to the Economic and Social Council of the United Nations was being looked into – this was at the height of the McCarthy days – it was interesting to find that this report on the I. W. W. was one of the charges that was made against me. All that Veblen did was to suggest a simple way to solve the farm manpower problem in the Northwest. To him the answer was obvious. He was thinking of the ultimate goal – getting more food to help win the war.[247]

It is interesting to note that one organ of the I. W. W. later considered Veblen an exception to their distrust of non-worker writers and leaders, a distrust which was almost as great as their dislike of the state. The editor of the Canadian *One Big Union Bulletin* wrote to him as follows: "I have forwarded to you under separate cover an article we have recently published in our paper entitled 'Veblenesque' or the 'Psychology of Labor.' The author of this article has been

---

247 "Recollections of Veblen," in *Thorstein Veblen: The Carleton College Veblen Seminar Essays*, pp. 140-141.

One reviewer of the book has said on this point: "Lubin makes Veblen's proposals for getting in the wartime crops make better sense than has been supposed hitherto." (C. E. Ayres, *The Journal of Economic History,* June 1969, p. 386).

Ayres also asserted in the review, "Worth noting, too, is Lubin's insistence, not only in his essay but also in seminar discussion as reprinted by the editor [of the book] that the widely held supposition of Veblen's 'animus toward capitalistic society' is not true."

In the Carleton seminar discussion Lubin declared: "Now in all our [Veblen: Lubin] discussion I think I can honestly say I never saw any evidence of animus or any dislike of the economic system as a whole or the people who run the system. In other words, he wasn't a reformer. The system to him was a system and he was trying to analyze it . . ." (Quoted in C. C. Qualey, "Centennial Seminar in American Studies," *The Voice of the Carleton Alumni,* March 1967, p. 3. The brackets are Qualey's).

all his life and still is in overalls, consequently his brief story of the History of Labor is unique. Others have written Labor's History who have been otherwise connected with Labor. Kerrigan's idea is that Labor is competent not only to run industry but also to write about it. Nevertheless, Kerrigan, myself and others feel indebted to you, one of the modern intellectuals for your many contributions."[248]

For the "Memorandum on a Schedule of Prices for the Staple Foodstuffs,"[249] Veblen provided an illuminating preliminary statement, which is addressed to Pearl:

> Mr. Lubin will hand you statistical tables and charts covering certain information about prices of farm products, which he has collected and tabulated during the past six weeks, accompanied by a memorandum drawn by Mr. Lubin to describe and explain these tables and charts. I am also enclosing herewith a brief memorandum intended as an introduction to Mr. Lubin's work and as a general description of the purposes for which these data were collected and tabulated. The tables and charts are for use as a preliminary survey of the present price situation, so far as it bears on the production of the main staple grains and meats, with a view to controlling the prices of these farm products and thereby their production. It is, of course, not intended to submit this memorandum and its statistical tables and charts as in any sense an exhaustive or sufficient survey of the situation for the purpose so indicated. It is rather to be taken as a preliminary survey and a point of departure for a more exhaustive statistical study in case the Food

[248] T. E. Moore to Veblen, September 19, 1925, Thorstein Veblen Papers.

[249] This was originally published with an introduction by Joseph Dorfman in *The Southwestern Social Science Quarterly*, March 1933; reprinted in *Essays in Our Changing Order*.

Administration should decide to undertake anything in the way of a comprehensive and systematic regulation of the production of staple foodstuffs by a systematic control of their prices.

At an early date I propose also to submit a report on an enquiry recently undertaken into the retail establishments in country towns, with a view to the supply of farm labor possibly to be drawn from among their employees."[250]

The last paragraph calls attention to another memorandum, "Farm Labor for the Period of the War," which was published in elaborated form shortly after Veblen left the administration in June and reprinted in *Essays in Our Changing Order.*

As Veblen's employment with the Food Administration drew to an involuntary close at the end of June, Manley O.

[250] Veblen to Pearl, June 27, 1918.

At the time, Professor Mitchell, who was working on price controls for the federal government, would have Veblen attend staff conferences on the appropriate presentation of the statistics, both to affected business men and for administrative purposes.

The records of the Statistical Division seem to indicate that Veblen was most anxious to obtain a quantitative determination of the production of grain. The details are not too clear. All we have on the matter is a copy of a letter from the assistant chief of the Statistical Division, Frank A. Surface, a biologist by training. He wrote Veblen, May 17, 1918: "I found the accompanying report by Mr. Stearns on my desk. It seems to me it would be a very excellent thing to have undertaken the collection of certain of these data." Surface thought, however, that the procedure was subject to serious limitation, especially in the use of a "threshing machine measure." Furthermore, he thought that he had heard that another division of the Food Administration, the Grain Corporation, was "planning on attempting something of this kind."

Hudson again sought a post for Veblen, this time with the War Labor Policies Board, which was headed by his friend and another Veblen admirer, Felix Frankfurter, on leave from the Harvard Law School (and later associate justice of the United States Supreme Court). Hudson wrote to Frankfurter (June 14) that "such men as Veblen ought to be at work" with Frankfurter's Board on the matter of "reconstruction after the War." Frankfurter replied that for the Board's Reconstruction program "I have had my eyes on Veblen and have assigned a definite task to him." (June 19). What that task was we learn from a letter of Mitchell to his wife: "Veblen has been offered a fascinating job by Felix Frankfurter. He is asked to sketch a reconstruction policy for labor." (June 14, 1918). Veblen, it seems, eventually turned it down for a post with *The Dial*, and the expectation of a position with the New School for Social Research, which was in the planning stage.[251]

Survey for the Full Utilization of Productive Capacity

Let us turn to his post World War I projects. The first, which was discussed in the Veblen book, was hatched at a

---

251 In 1951, in response to a query from Joseph Dorfman, Justice Frankfurter wrote: "It was while I was chairman of the War Labor Policies Board that I got Veblen to do some piece-work for that Board on some phases of post-war reconstruction. This was in 1918 and perhaps the [National] Archives, which has the records of my old Board, can locate Veblen's memo for you." (Frankfurter to Dorfman, July 11, 1951). There is, however, no such memorandum in the surviving records of the War Labor Policies Board.

Helen Marot, a stockholder in *The Dial*, with Mitchell's encouragement, had as early as January sought to persuade Veblen to join *The Dial*.

The historian James Harvey Robinson was largely responsible for the New School inviting Veblen. On this episode Mitchell has written: "One trait of Robinson's that especially endeared him to me was his warm admiration of Thorstein Veblen. Not many men of Robinson's

conference on a July 1919 weekend at Amherst, for an investigation of the economic order, especially the credit system. I mentioned that among the participants besides Veblen were Hamilton, Walter W. Stewart[252], Leo Wolman and Lubin. It now appears that Robert L. Duffus, who helped to take care of Veblen's "rancho" in return for room and board in the Stanford period, was also there. Duffus, who was at the time a New York City newspaperman, has written that "I was there to listen with a view of doing some writing

[252] Stewart, who became an international authority on monetary theory and policy, had been a protegé and colleague of Davenport at Missouri, but Veblen had been and continued to be the dominant influence. Early in 1915, he told another of Veblen's students at Missouri that he had received a call to the University of Chicago because he was supposed to put in action Veblen's economics in the field of money and banking. Davenport, he added, thought that the appointment was in expectation that he would teach Davenport's economics and he never had the heart to disillusion Davenport. (From notes of R. C. Journey's conversation with Dorfman, February 5, 1933). Stewart instead decided not to go to Chicago at all, but arranged to join Hamilton at Amherst.

---

antecedents had the openmindedness to understand Veblen's quizzical critique of modern culture. But though he came from that genteel tradition which Veblen had studied from the outside looking in, Robinson had emancipated himself by sheer dint of straight thinking from the conventional fetters upon free thought that bound most sons of New England in his generation, and bound none more tightly than the New Englanders [like Robinson] born in the Middle West. No doubt Robinson learned much from Veblen, but he had made discoveries of his own about cultural change before he read *The Theory of the Leisure Class*, and he could appreciate as few colleagues could both the ironical humor and the devastating import of Veblen's analysis. The authorities of most universities were afraid of Veblen, as well they might be. James Harvey Robinson welcomed him to the New School." (Mitchell, "James Harvey Robinson," Memorial Meeting, New School, April 16, 1936, Mitchell Papers).

later on."[253] Efforts, however, to raise $25,000 from a foundation to start the project proved fruitless.

The second, which was planned early in 1920, was an offshoot of the first, according to Lubin. It was discussed in the Veblen book in a sentence, as one for which Veblen's supporters tried to raise $40,000 to help him develop his ideas on the engineer. We now have more information on the subject thanks to the Underhill Moore Papers in the Columbia University Library and in the Yale University Library. The campaign for the project was started just as Veblen began preparing *Absentee Ownership* in late 1919. The prime movers were Ardzrooni, who was teaching at Columbia, and working closely with him Underhill Moore, a law professor at Columbia who was an authority particularly on bills and notes or more broadly the law of commercial paper,[254] and Harold Kellock, Moore's old friend and college mate (Columbia College class of 1900). Kellock was a novelist and journalist and at the time in public relations as secretary of the American Commercial Association to Promote Trade with Russia.[255] It appears that in the early spring of 1920 Ardzrooni and Moore met at the Columbia University Faculty Club to draw up a prospectus and budget of a project for Veblen for submission to philanthropists.[256]

---

253 *The Innocents at Cedro*, p. 151.

Duffus was for a long period until his retirement a member of the editorial board of the New York *Times*.

254 Moore in his previous post at the University of Wisconsin played a vital and little known role in the preparation of social security bills for John R. Commons to submit to the state legislature.

255 The officers of the association were leading American industrialists.

256 The document, which is in the handwriting of Ardzrooni and on Faculty Club stationery, is undated and anonymous. Ardzrooni, in a letter of July 4 to Moore, in regard to Moore's request for a tentative budget for the project, stated: "I think I left one with you. If I

The opening paragraph which is heavily crossed out reads in outline form:

"1. Bureau of Production Studies.

2. [Cannot be read].

3. Division of Production and Resource Investigation."

It then states "The paramount need of current times is greater production. To meet this need effectively it is necessary to inquire into the condition and character of the country's resources; to study the management and control of those resources; to investigate the control and management of the technological equipment used or to be used in processes of production and distribution; to inquire into the financial and business machinery with a view to bringing into fullest productive use all the available economic resources and industrial equipment of the nation.

Basic Resources and Industries

Coal
Iron and Steel
Oil
Electric Power
Lumber and Cotton
Transportation and Communication
Production and Distribution of Foodstuffs
Advertising
Mail Order Merchandising
Wholesale and Retail Trades

---

remember correctly it was in some detail." The budget is the document in question. Ardzrooni added "You can make use of that of course with any modifications that may be dictated by the circumstances of which you will be better informed than I." Ardzrooni had left New York some time in May to return to Fresno, California, to take care of his extensive raisin vineyards.

"To carry on this work of investigation a staff of men trained in research is required. There must also be available on occasion, engineers and technicians—all of which involves an outlay of $25,000-$40,000 annually depending on the extent of investigations. As a matter of practical necessity the members of the research staff must be secured in their employment for a reasonable number of years. Aside from this, investigations of this nature to bear best results cannot be undertaken on the basis of a limited time such as one year. It seems that five years is a reasonable number of years to insure best results. On the basis of the following budget this would involve a guaranteed fund of from $125,000 to $200,000, to cover the five year period." At different places in the document there were presented the two budgets on a per annum basis.[257]

[Original Budget of $25,000 and $40,000 per annum]

Veblen	$ 7,500	per annum
Tryon	4,000	
Schuyler	3,000	
Rosenberg	3,000	
G. Robinson	3,000	
Office help, etc.	4,500	
		$25,000
Levine	$ 4,000	
DR Scott	4,000	
Lubin	2,500	
Deutsch	2,500	
Additional office help, etc.	2,000	
		15,000
		$40,000

[257] Both are lightly crossed out. The first one immediately followed the above. The second came at the end of the document.

[Alternative or later budget of $25,000 per annum]

Veblen	$ 7,500	
Tryon	4,000	
DR Scott	4,000	
Robinson	2,000	
Schuyler	3,000	
	20,500	
Clerical help	4,500	
		$25,000

Kravitz
Pogue

The identified members of the proposed staff were admirers of Veblen and the special interests of some indicate that the project was concerned with the economic development not only of the United States but also of the Soviet Union. Veblen doubtless expected the investigation to furnish the factual base for the book he was just beginning to write, *Absentee Ownership.*[258]

[258] Tryon is F. G. Tryon who achieved an outstanding reputation as a mining economist, especially in the coal industry. Robinson is Geroid Tanquary Robinson who had worked with Veblen at *The Dial.* Later he was professor of Russian history at Columbia and made his reputation with a study of the history of the Russian peasantry under the old regime. Pogue is Joseph E. Pogue, eminent resources engineer and later also vice president of the Chase National Bank.

Lubin is Isador Lubin then a specialist in industrial relations. Scott was also Veblen's student at Missouri where, as noted before, he became professor of statistics and accounting. Deutsch is Babette Deutsch who was then writing on industrial Russia.

Schuyler was Montgomery Schuyler. According to a member he had some connections with the group that sponsored the Technical Alliance. (Frederick L. Ackerman to Joseph Dorfman, August 6, 1932). Lubin has recently said that Schuyler was also at the Amherst Conference. He turned up in the 1930's as an associate of people sympathetic to the Technocracy movement. [See *The Chart of Plenty; A Study of America's Productive Capacity Based on the Findings of*

The concluding paragraph reflects more Ardzrooni's interest in trade unions and Kellock's interest in dissemination channels than it did Veblen. It reads: "The studies are to be published under the auspices of the New School for Social Research in the form of occasional bulletins. These publications are to be distributed at the cost of printing and publication through American News Service agency and trade union channels."[259]

Attached to the document in the Moore papers is another undated, anonymous "application," but this is in the handwriting of Veblen and is characteristically written in pencil on yellow unruled paper.[260] It seems to have been a recasting by Veblen of the previous document and when compared with it, clearly evidences Veblen's professional skill as a writer of applications.

[259] Both documents are in the Moore Papers, Columbia University Library. Mitchell, Diary, December 11, 1919, records: "Ardzrooni dined with me, and discussed plans for contacts with trade unions." Recording the proceedings of a faculty meeting at the New School in the Diary, Mitchell wrote, January 7, 1922, "Called on Veblen to discuss Charles Beard's proposition that we close the New School and hand over the remains to Workers' Education Movement. Veblen heartily opposed."

The suggestion of "bulletins," however, seems to have been Veblen's, for as noted above he had proposed this for the House Inquiry in 1918.

[260] Lubin has described Veblen's writing habits. "Veblen did most of his writing in bed, sitting up with a couple of pillows behind him

the National Survey of Potential Capacity by Harold Loeb, Director and Associates, Felix Frazer, Graham Montgomery, Walter Polakov, William D. Smith, Montgomery Schuyler, with a foreword by Stuart Chase (New York: The Viking Press, 1935). This was a project set up in 1934 by the Civilian Works Administration. Schuyler in association with Frazer was listed as making a survey of printing]. In 1931 while serving as assistant editor of *Collier's* he referred to Veblen as "that grand old fellow." (Schuyler to Dorfman, May 23, 1931). Rosenberg is Edwin G. Rosenberg who was a student of Veblen at Missouri and specialized in accounting; he later became the accountant of Sears, Roebuck.

I cannot identify Kravits and Levine.

> *An Inquiry Into Business and Production*
>
> It is proposed, under the auspices of the New School, to undertake a detailed inquiry into several lines of productive industry and business enterprise, with a view to the publication of the findings arrived at in the form of bulletins to be issued by the New School from time to time. The aim is to present the facts of the case in documentary form, uncolored, as near as may be. The several lines of inquiry provisionally selected, as indicated below, have been chosen partly because of their peculiar importance in the present industrial situation, partly because men trained for inquiry in these particular lines are available. It is believed that an inquiry of this character can not profitably be undertaken without the assurance of funds to support it for several years. Nearly all the persons to be employed are dependent for their livelihood on their own work from year to year. The work will require something in the way of clerical help, and it will also be necessary to consult with specialists and technical men elsewhere; which will involve some expense for travel and incidentals.

Then began the search for well disposed philanthropists. Kellock interested in the project Edgar Salinger, of the New York firm of E. Heller and Brother, Inc., manufacturers of handkerchieves with plants in Jersey City, Passaic and Belfast, Ireland. The importance of Salinger was that he had a very wealthy, philanthropically inclined uncle, Mr. Erdman.

---

and a small bed table in front of him. He always wrote on yellow unruled paper and always with a pencil. This was true even when he was on *The Dial* editorial staff and had a secretary. As he once said to me: 'I think through my fingers.' " (Lubin, "Recollections of Veblen," in *Thorstein Veblen: The Carleton College Veblen Seminar Essays*, p. 135). As regards letter paper, he would when connected with an institution use its stationery.

On May 4, Kellock informed Moore of Salinger's conversation with Erdman on the project.

> He talked the matter over with Mr. Erdman Sunday. Erdman will be away all summer and does not want to do anything until fall. He is also away for this month but will see us and talk over plans about June 1.
>
> He is not particularly impressed with the pamphlet idea. Thinks less emphasis should be laid on that. Says real studies of industries must inevitably be intricate and detailed, and the rank and file would not read them. The great point is to get your information to the working-class leaders – union leaders, etc. Let the studies be made and give the information to leaders direct – possibly in a sort of extension lectures from Veblen's school. Salinger believes Erdman will contribute $15,000 or $20,000 a year toward the research and this work.
>
> This at any rate gives us an entering wedge and lets Erdman in for something. Salinger thinks once he gets in he will follow through with a great enthusiasm, and the educational part of the work can follow the most practical plan that can be worked out.
>
> I suppose, under the circumstances, Ardzrooni can leave for the Coast [to his vineyards] and you and I can handle Erdman when he returns.
>
> We'll talk this over more throughly when I see you.

On June 20, Kellock reported to Moore that "I got in touch with Salinger about June 1 – before our party at Englewood, though I forgot to speak to you about it.

"He said his uncle would not arrive until June 10, and was going right up to Maine, but Salinger would see him on the Veblen matter and if possible arrange an appointment for us. When uncle arrived, he had only a day in town, and that on Sunday, but Salinger had a long talk with him. He wants to go through with the Veblen matter, showed no diminution in interest, and arranged to have Salinger go to his country place to see him about August 1, and arrange details. Salinger wants to go over the whole plan thoroughly with us before he goes to uncle, and it might be well, I fancy, to have something on paper in the way of a budget. There will be plenty of time."

At this point Moore wrote for a budget to Ardzrooni, who was still in California. In his reply of July 4, Ardzrooni reminded Moore that he had left a budget with him.[261]

On the 22nd Kellock informed Moore that "Salinger will be in town until August 15. He is available to discuss the Veblen plan at any time." Six days later Kellock wrote Moore, "Salinger is planning to go up to see his uncle about August 15. If you are not coming to town, don't you think you had best send in some sort of outline or schedule of the proposed plan, so that he can take it with him?" On August 6, he reported to Moore: "Saw Salinger today. He says he has two invitations to uncle's, one mid-August, another beginning about a week after Labor Day. If you contemplate being in town by the latter date, he will wait over and accept the second invitation instead of the first. Will you let me know so I can pass the word to him?"

A month later (September 24) Moore wrote to Ardzrooni: "Please let me know as soon as you return [to New York], so that we can take up at once the Veblen-Salinger matter. The matter ought to be presented before October 1, when I believe the principal sails for Europe." Ardzrooni replied,

---

[261] He added that Veblen had been with him. "Veblen has been pretty well, but it got too warm for him here. He left last week for his shack in Detroit Harbor [later named Washington Island, Wisconsin]."

the 30th, "I wish it were possible to be there by the first of October to take up the Salinger matter, although I am pessimistic of the outcome."[262]

A month after the election of Warren G. Harding to the presidency under the banner of a "return to normalcy," Salinger wrote Moore that Ardzrooni had prophesied the bad news. "Pending the return of Mr. Erdman from abroad I took no further steps with reference to our conversation this spring about Veblen. Mr. E. has just come back from England and is I regret to say in no mood to entertain any suggestion along the lines discussed by us. I am afraid that under the ministrations of well trained British butlers and valets his desire for social change has undergone a cooling process and he shows no enthusiasm for anything remotely calculated to disturb the (at present) even tenor of his way. I have communicated with Kellock on the subject and thought the information was due you as well. Moral: Keep our 'prospects' away from the 'best people' in England.[263]

Moore wrote Ardzrooni on the 16th, "Day before yesterday I received from Mr. Salinger a letter stating that his uncle has just returned from Europe, but that he has grown cold toward the Veblen project. This is too bad, but is perhaps not unexpected. I shall keep in touch with Salinger, and perhaps

[262] He added that because of a recent illness requiring an operation from which he had not fully recovered, he doubted he would be able to return for the first term of school, but he hoped to be able to return for the second. He continued: "I think that Veblen will be in the city and you will probably call him up, and it may be just as well to take up the matter directly with him."

Up to this point all documents and letters are in the Underhill Moore Papers, Columbia University Libraries. After discovering and identifying these scattered materials, I suggested that they be assembled and recorded in the manuscript catalogue under Veblen's name. This was done.

[263] Salinger to Moore, December 13, 1920, Moore Papers, Yale University Library.

after a few years of the Harding Administration, the uncle's mind may be prepared for change."[264]

The next phase in Veblen's search for financing for a project is also briefly sketched in the Veblen book. This was the attempt begun in late 1924 to raise a modest fund to enable him to conduct in England a two year inquiry into British imperialism. We now have more details, especially the financial details. He obtained a passport in August to visit the "British Isles, France, Italy, Norway, Denmark, Sweden, Germany." He wrote on the application that he would sail "as soon as the passport arranged." But adequate funds were not forthcoming, even with Mitchell and Alvin Johnson of the New School of Social Research as the chief money raisers. At first Veblen was hopeful. He informed Lubin on December 13, "There seems to be a chance of my going to Europe late in the winter or early in the spring to stay for some time. Alvin Johnson is hopefully managing a campaign for funds for my use."[265]

He wrote his brother Andrew in January 1925 from the New School that "I am here [at the New School] as a transient, having quit lecturing, at least for the time, not having the necessary energy to do the work but otherwise as well as usual. Meantime there is some talk, which may or may not come to anything, of a fund to be made up among my Jewish friends to pay my expenses in Europe for a couple of years, more or less, in the course of which I would be expected to write something or other about conditions in Europe, particularly in England. Something like one-half of the necessary funds has been subscribed, and if the rest comes

[264] Moore to Ardzrooni, December 16, 1920, copy, Moore Papers, Columbia University Library.

Moore wrote to Salinger to the same effect. (Moore to Salinger, December 16, 1920, copy, Moore Papers, Yale University Library).

[265] Letter supplied by Lubin.

through in time I should be going away some time this spring. Otherwise I may go west, perhaps to California, and go into cold storage."[266]

Meanwhile in December 1924, Mitchell in a private letter to Ardzrooni, said that he was once more writing him about the Veblen fund.[267]

"You may have heard that Veblen became very tired of teaching last year and is at present taking a sabbatical. He is eager to go to England for two years to study British imperlialism. To do so he needs a subvention. A Mr. Kaplan about whom I know nothing has promised to contribute $1,000 per annum toward such a trip.

"I can maintain my annual contribution of $500. Do you feel disposed towards joining in the scheme? This plan has nothing to do with the New School beyond the fact that those of us who are interested in it have in the past been interested in that institution. . . . All his [Veblen's] thoughts seem to be centering nowadays around the problem which he feels he can study to advantage only in England. For his happiness

---

[266] Thorstein Veblen to Andrew Veblen, January 22, 1925, in Andrew Veblen Papers.

[267] Ardzrooni was no longer doing any teaching.

The fund was composed of the contributions by admirers to Veblen's support from almost the beginning of the New School in 1919 until his death. The fund was handled through the New School. The "former Chicago student," to whom I referred in the Veblen book as contributing $8,000 from 1919 to 1929, was Mitchell.

Mitchell, at least as early as 1922, was the main money raiser for the fund. In May of that year he wrote Moore about joining himself and Ardzrooni in making pledges for the fund, and at the same time asked Moore about getting in touch with Erdman. Moore replied: "I am sending your letter to Mr. Harold Kellock of *The Freeman* [which was published by Huebsch], a friend of mine through whom Ardzrooni and I got in touch with Mr. Erdman a couple of years ago. I do not know Mr. Erdman myself. If you do not hear from Mr. Kellock in a reasonable time, I suggest that you write to him." Moore added that he could not afford to pledge anything at the time since he was shortly sailing for Europe. (Moore to Mitchell, May 20, 1922,

as well as for the benefit of the world, I think we should help him to get there if we can."[268]

Three months later in February 1925, Ardzrooni wrote Moore. He said: "Some time ago I wrote to Mitchell to get in touch with you in connection with a travel fund he is trying to raise for Veblen. When Mitchell wrote me, I thought of your connection with Salinger and Erdman. Veblen is

[268] Mitchell to Ardzrooni, December 9, 1924, Mitchell Papers.

Abram I. Kaplan was an entrepreneur heavily involved in the sugar and molasses business in the Caribbean, especially Cuba, and in lumber in New Mexico. (See Anthony Ripley, "How an Heir Escaped Jail by Air," The New York *Times*, September 5, 1971).

Kaplan also provided monthly payments for another New School faculty member, the anthropologist Alexander Goldenweiser.

Earlier in the year Mitchell noted in his Diary, March 21, 1924: "To see Alvin Johnson . . . about Veblen's position in the New School. He said the one thing certain was $2600 plus the Veblen fund of perhaps $1200."

---

copy, Moore Papers, Yale University Library). Kellock wrote Moore that "I have forwarded the Veblen letter to Salinger and asked him to get in touch with Mitchell." (Kellock to Moore, May 27, [1922]). Mitchell noted in his Diary, March 11, 1923, "call from Miss Boughton who will contribute $500 and canvas for other gifts."

Jacob Billikopf, a prominent figure in industrial relations and at the time director of the Labor Standards Association of Philadelphia, also contributed to the fund, it seems, at various times. Ardzrooni in a letter of August 8, 1929, informing Billikopf of Veblen's death, wrote: "I had told him of your efforts and your anxiety to make his life as comfortable as possible, which he said he appreciated very much. . . . He was perceptibly depressed and dejected [the last few years] because he no longer possessed the strength or opportunity to lead an active life." Billikopf sent me in April 21, 1944, a copy of the following letter which his secretary sent to Johnson on August 1, 1929, "Perhaps you already know that Mr. Billikopf is sailing for Europe tomorrow to attend several important conferences in Zurich.

"Mr. Billikopf has asked me to write you and I know you will be delighted with the news – that the School will be in a position to supplement the amount that Prof. Veblen is now receiving. Mr. Billikopf will have $350 a year for a period of three years and will see that the allowance is forwarded to you when he returns from Europe in September."

very anxious to go over to England and study the British at first hand but of course he lacks the wherewithal. I wonder if you can approach Salinger and through him Erdman in the hope that they may still be interested in Veblen and give them an opportunity to be of some use to him in this connection."[269] Moore in his reply a month later informed Ardzrooni as he had Mitchell that he "had to act through Harold Kellock as an intermediary"; consequently there was considerable delay.[270] "The upshot was a letter from Salinger dated March 6 of which I enclose a copy." The copy has not been located,[271] but the substance of the gloomy response is in a letter of Ardzrooni to Veblen at the time. He wrote: "I received a letter from Underhill Moore in reply to my letter some time ago. It appears that Erdman is undergoing a change of mind in regard to liberal or radical ideas, which he once entertained, but Salinger seems to be quite willing to do something himself. I am writing to Mitchell conveying this information. Salinger should be good for a few hundred dollars. In any case I hope there have been enough contributions to the fund by this time so that you can start on the trip."[272]

Just about that time, Johnson was reporting difficulties in completing the fund. He informed Veblen that he had written to Mr. Edward Filene, the Boston philanthropist, "as you suggested and have received from him as his contribution to your fund $100. As of that date the fund consisted of Kaplan's contribution of $1200 a year for the two years,

---

[269] Ardzrooni to Moore, February 3, 1925, Moore Papers, Yale University Library. Ardzrooni added that he could not do his bit because of heavy losses in the last three years.

[270] *The Freeman* had ceased publication in 1924 and Kellock obtained employment with The Russian Information Service, Washington, D.C.

[271] Moore to Ardzrooni, March 7, 1925, copy, Moore Papers, Yale University Library.

[272] Ardzrooni to Veblen [March 19, 1925], Thorstein Veblen Papers.

$1000 from the Garland fund, $500 from Mitchell and from Joseph H. Schaffner, and the $100 from Filene," which Johnson said should be calculated on for only one year.[273] Johnson added: "Of these sums the contributions of Mr. Kaplan and Mr. Mitchell are not contingent upon your going to England. The contributions from the Garland fund, Mr. Schaffner, and Mr. Filene have been pledged on the assumption that you are going to make this trip and try to put through the study you contemplated. . . . In your letter you say that in any case you will make a visit to England this year, possibly this spring. Could you tell me definitely whether with the fund as it now stands you would undertake to spend the two years and make the study? Of course I should continue my efforts to increase the fund but the process is a slow one and I am afraid that the interest of the donors will lapse if nothing is done about it soon."[274]

Veblen apparently replied that he could not go through with the project, giving a familiar conventional excuse, namely ill health. Johnson wrote in April "I am very sorry your health will not permit you to work on the study you outlined.[275] I hope you may be able to do it another year, and if you will permit me, I will do my best then to raise an adequate fund. In the meantime I am afraid that I will have to release the Garland fund, Schaffner and Filene from their pledges to contribute.[276] So far as Kaplan is concerned I have a specific agreement with him that his contribution is entirely independent of your going abroad or doing any specific piece

[273] It would seem that the total would be for the two years: $2400 from Kaplan, $1000 from the Garland fund, $1000 from Mitchell, $500 from Schaffner and $100 from Filene, or a total of $5000.

[274] Johnson to Veblen, March 19, 1925, Thorstein Veblen Papers.

[275] Veblen's ill health had become something of a joke. Mitchell, for example, recorded in his Diary, March 22, 1923, "Veblen came back from his vacation admitting that he felt well."

[276] Johnson to Veblen, April 2, 1925, Thorstein Veblen Papers.

of work. Therefore, I shall forward the sums to you as they come in. They amount to $100 a month, but I cannot yet say with what regularity they will come in." Apparently Mitchell attempted to mollify Veblen for he wrote him in June.

"Johnson tells me that . . . the contribution . . . made by Mr. Kaplan . . . is expected will run on at a rate which will enable Johnson to send you regularly $100 a month. . . . I may also report that a contribution of $500 has come into the fund pure and simple which the New School will transmit to your account in the . . . Corn Exchange Bank. Johnson also tells me that there is an excellent prospect that the Garland fund would be willing to contribute at least $1000 per annum to the Veblen fund if you desired to undertake any investigations while you were abroad. My own guess is that they might go a little higher than this but I am not sure."[277]

The reference to "any investigations while you are abroad," and not exclusively to British imperialism, may well have

[277] Mitchell to Veblen, June 1, 1925, Thorstein Veblen Papers.

In the same letter, Mitchell transmitted to Veblen an invitation to spend the summer at Kaplan's estate. Mitchell wrote: "Mr. Kaplan has an enormous estate in Westchester county [New York] somewhere above Katonah, which troubles him because it is unoccupied. He has asked Johnson whether there is not some scholar or artist who would like to make use of the place and its facilities, which include a staff of servants and all appurtenances. For you Mr. Kaplan entertains great admiration, and Johnson is sure that if you cared to spend the summer in this pleasant spot he would be delighted to have you." A month earlier, Kaplan in acknowledging receipt of a copy of *The Laxdaela Saga* from the publisher had invited Veblen to his estate. "If you are in the city – and if you are free – I would be highly honored to have you as a guest on my farm which is . . . about ninety minutes ride from New York – at your pleasure – for a day or better still – for days." (Kaplan to Veblen, May 7, 1925, Thorstein Veblen Papers).

Veblen doubtless never accepted the invitation, for he was then at his own summer place, the place he loved so much, isolated Washington Island, Wisconsin, where both letters were found.

referred to a related episode that also has only recently come to light. Almost at the beginning of the drive for the British imperialism project, there appears to have arisen the possibility that Veblen would receive an invitation to visit the Soviet Union. At Veblen's request Mitchell made inquiries on the matter; he reported: "Regarding the Soviet invitation, I got in touch with Underhill Moore, who is my only source of information concerning it, and after talking with him, wrote a letter to Mr. Harold Kellock, in which I suggested that if he is free to do so he communicate directly with you at your Chicago address. I hope you may have heard from him ere this."[278] Unfortunately this is all we have been able to discover of this "intriguing" project which never materialized. Veblen as I noted in the Veblen book was very early interested in the Soviet experiment and always seeking information upon it. Thus he accepted Moore's dinner invitation in 1921 to hear the journalist Henry Alsberg tell of his two years in Russia.[279]

Moore played a leading role in a tribute that Yale paid to Veblen. I referred in the Veblen book (p. 517) to the successful drive in 1933-1934 of members of the law faculty to raise funds for a portrait of "one of Yale's most distinguished alumni," which hangs in the Sterling Hall of Graduate Studies. Moore, who had transferred to the Yale Law School

[278] Mitchell to Veblen, May 28, 1925, Thorstein Veblen Papers. The letter was addressed to the home of a niece, Mrs. Ralph Sims.

Kellock saw Veblen twice. These are recorded in the Veblen book. In the first (p. 426), he was described as "the gentleman" who late in 1919 arranged a meeting between Veblen and the Soviet engineer C. A. K. Martens. In the second (p. 485), he was described as "one of Huebsch's men, working on *The Freeman*" at the time that Veblen brought *Absentee Ownership* to the publisher.

[279] "It is very good of you to ask me to your dinner Monday night [December 12] and I shall be glad to come. Sincerely yours, Thorstein Veblen." (Veblen to Moore, December 7, 1921, Moore Papers, Yale University Library). This is the only Veblen letter in the Moore papers.

in 1929, was in charge of the drive with Walton H. Hamilton, who seems to have been the instigator and the chief aide along with Thurman Arnold.[280] The portrait was painted from the original of the photograph which appears opposite p. 239 of the Veblen book.[281]

There is a story about the present location of the portrait which was told me in 1966 by the then dean of the graduate school, the economist John Perry Miller. He wrote: "You may be amused by my first act as dean. I took over for administrative purposes a classroom in which for some years I had taught the History of Economic Thought underneath a portrait of Veblen. It was, therefore, necessary to find a place to 'hang' Veblen. In the Faculty Lounge of the Hall of Graduate Studies there are three panels at the front of the room, one of which was empty. In the center panel hangs a portrait of Edgar Furniss, and on the right facing inward is a portrait of Arthur Twining Hadley, sitting in his usual forbidding manner and dressed in white pants and a dark coat. I finally decided to hang Veblen on the empty panel so that he faces inward toward Furniss, sitting in a 'dandi-

---

[280] Moore, it is interesting to note, attempted to push the institutional approach in law while at Yale. See, for example, Moore and Theodore S. Hope, "An Institutional Approach to the Law of Commercial Banking," *Yale Law Journal*, April 1929.

[281] The original had been given to me by the photographer, Eva N. Schütze. She and her husband, Professor Martin Schütze of the German department of the University of Chicago, were old friends of Veblen.

When the drive got under way the New York *Times* of January 25, 1934, stated that "A committee of scholars and writers plan to honor the late Thorstein Veblen, author of *The Theory of the Leisure Class*, by hanging his portrait in the Sterling Hall of Graduate Studies, Yale University, from which Veblen received his degree of Doctor of Philosophy, and are asking for small contributions to pay for such a portrait. . . . On the committee are Jerome Frank, Harold J. Laski, Edgar S. Furniss [dean of the graduate school and later provost], Wesley C. Mitchell, Walton H. Hamilton and Underhill Moore of 127 Wall Street, New Haven, who is Treasurer."

fied' fashion dressed in white pants. Of course, I did not dare to do so without the permission of the senior Professor of the Faculty [Alfred Raymond Bellinger] for fear he would charge me with having dressed the whole Graduate School in symbols of the dismal science."[282]

III

ARTICLES, REVIEWS, ETC.

A considerable amount of significant information has become available on Veblen's contributions to professional journals. First we shall deal with the essays in the two published collections.

Writings for the *Political Science Quarterly*[283]

A new source of material is Veblen's correspondence with the *Political Science Quarterly*. This centered on his review articles of Irving Fisher's *The Nature of Capital and Income* and *The Rate of Interest*, and J.M. Keynes's *The Economic Consequences of the Peace*. It began in the summer of 1906, when Professor Seligman, the managing editor of the journal, asked Veblen for a short review of Fisher's *The Nature of Capital and Income*. Veblen replied: "I should not like to write a brief review of his book, because it belongs in a fairly large group of current theoretical writings which need attention — critical attention — as a whole and as marking a tendency in theoretical speculation." He would like to attempt "such a comprehensive review of Fisher *et al.* . . . during the year. But this would mean an indefinite delay, and might in any case not suit your purposes. What I have in mind, somewhat vaguely, would be an extended paper — perhaps six or eight thousand words — and would not be

[282] Miller to Dorfman, February 15, 1966.

[283] Unless otherwise specified all correspondence with the *Political Science Quarterly* is in the possession of Joseph Dorfman.

ready until late winter or spring, as I have other work on hand just now."

At the end of 1907, Veblen sent in a review of *The Nature of Capital and Income* which was over thirty pages, but the editor returned it with comments reminiscent of Macmillan's criticism of the first ms. of *The Theory of the Leisure Class*: the language and size. Since Fisher meanwhile had also published *The Rate of Interest,* Seligman suggested that Veblen treat both works in the review. In his reply, Veblen proposed that the second work have a "brief review" of its own in a subsequent issue. "It will take me a little time to get acquainted with it, and I have the impression that it merits separate insertion." As for revisions of the review of *The Nature of Capital and Income,* Veblen continued: "I do not see my way clear to reduce the length of the paper materially, but will do what I can. I recognize that it is longer than it should be. . . . As to language used, the reading of the paper gives me the same impression as is conveyed by your friendly suggestion. I hope to reduce its asperities somewhat, but an adequate allowance for the really meritorious work of the school of economists, for which Mr. Fisher stands would involve qualifications that consume space."[284]

In sending the revised manuscript, he wrote: "I regret to say that I have succeeded in doing very little to carry out your kindly suggestions. Any attempt on my part to shorten the paper seems to cripple it, and any attempt to

[284] Veblen doubtless had in mind Frank A. Fetter, among others. He wrote Fetter in 1902 "to congratulate you, as well as your readers, on the excellent papers which *The Quarterly Journal* [*of Economics*] has been printing for you." (Veblen to Fetter, November 26, 1902, Papers of the American Economic Association, in Northwestern University Library). He and Fetter had held fellowships together at Cornell in 1891-1892, one as the protegé of Laughlin, the other of Jeremiah Jenks.

rewrite it seems to lengthen it. So I am returning it very much as it was. I have marked two passages (A and B—pp. 22-24 and pp. 28-31) which may be omitted if you think best. My own preference is to let them stand." He had something to say to the printer too: "I would only add the caution that the printer's attention should be called to the reference at the bottom of p. 25, which refers to an earlier page of the manuscript and would have to be altered accordingly in the type." The review occupied fifteen pages in the March 1908 issue.

The review of *The Rate of Interest* was relatively brief—only seven pages in the June 1909 number. The latter attracted the attention of William Warrand Carlile, British expert on monetary theory and critic of orthodox methodology. In a review of the fourth edition (1911) of W. Stanley Jevons's *Theory of Political Economy,* he included a passage from it: "'The phenomena of modern business, including the rate of interest,' remarks Professor Veblen, the most brilliant of the younger American economists, 'can no more be handled in non-pecuniary terms than human physiology can be handled in terms of the amphioxus. . . . There is (probably) no science except economics in which such an endeavor to explain the phenomena of an institution in terms of one class of the rudiments, which have afforded the point of departure for the growth of the institution, would be listened to with any degree of civility. The philologists, for example, have various infirmities of their own, but they would have little patience with a textual critic who should endeavor to reduce the Homeric hymns to terms of those onomatopoetic sounds out of which it is presumed that human speech has grown.'"[285]

---

[285] Carlile's review appeared in *The Economic Review,* April 1912. The quotation from Veblen is on p. 211. He was attacking the ortho-

Veblen doubtless used the discarded material from the original ms. review of *The Nature of Capital and Income* for the essay which he had suggested as a future possibility to the editor; namely, a paper covering the dominant type of theory, the marginal utility school as a whole. " 'The Limitations of Marginal Utility,' " he wrote Seligman (April 19, 1909), was "in great part suggested or at least provoked by Mr. Fisher's books, which you have let me review, and by other writings of the same school published during the last two or three years." Seligman rejected it on the ground that "we try to avoid technical articles and pure theory as much as possible." Veblen in asking for the return of the ms. commented that he had not appreciated that "the *Quarterly* confined itself so strictly to practical topics." Of course, Veblen was not opposed to the inclusion of practical topics in professional journals. In fact, in 1902, while managing editor of *The Journal of Political Economy,* he suggested that the American Economic Association instead of starting its own journal "take over or make working arrangements" with his journal and *The Quarterly Journal of Economics,* to serve as the official journals of the Association,

dox view that money was a matter of mere convenience, and consequently economic phenomena can be better explained without it.

Carlile elaborated on Veblen's position in *Monetary Economics* (1912). There he also expressed agreement with Veblen's definition of capital in *The Theory of Business Enterprise.* As he put it, "Capital has been appropriately enough defined as being in modern business usage 'capitalized earning capacity.' " He also referred to *The Theory of the Leisure Class* in his discussion of fallacious ideas on the monetary standard. "Even with ornaments in the modern world, the more we search into the grounds of the subjective motive we attach to them, the more we find it interpenetrated with the associations of their pecuniary efficiency." Then he stated in a footnote: "For some very suggestive observations on this point see the chapter headed 'Pecuniary Canons of Taste' in *The Theory of the Leisure Class* by Professor Thorstein Veblen." [*Economic Method and Economic Fallacies* (London, 1904) pp. 155-156].

with the *Quarterly* "taking the field of general theoretical discussion, the other, the detailed discussion of practical questions."[286]

The essay was published in the University of Chicago's *Journal of Political Economy* in 1909 and reprinted in the first collection of Veblen's essays, *The Place of Science in Modern Civilisation and Other Essays.* A passage in the essay was cited in 1949 by a writer sympathetic to a quantitative-statistical-institutional approach to economic theory. That lengthy quotation concludes with: "The wants and desires, the end and aims, the ways and means, the amplitude and drift, of the individual's conduct are functions of an institutional variable that is of a highly complex and wholly unstable character."[287]

Along this line, Professor Mitchell earlier suggested a

---

[286] Veblen to Fetter, November 26, 1902, Papers of the American Economic Association.

[287] Quoted by Rutledge Vining in "Koopmans on the Choice of Variables to be Studied and of Methods of Measurement," *Review of Economics and Statistics,* May 1949, pp. 82-83.

Another of Veblen's articles, first rejected by *The Hibbert Journal,* was published in another Chicago based periodical, *The International Journal of Ethics,* in 1910; (it was reprinted in the second collection of essays, *Essays in Our Changing Order*). This was "Christian Morals and the Competitive System," which in its appeal to "the impulsive bias of brotherly love" is suggestive of his "instinct of workmanship" in the generic unsophisticated sense. He wrote Davenport in 1909: "You may remember my writing a paper for *The Hibbert Journal.* . . . [T]he editor returned [it] because the style was too obscure and difficult for the *Hibbert* readers, which makes me think that I had better not write another paper on a religious topic for a pious magazine."

He wrote to Mitchell later in the year. "I have some notion of sending the Christian paper to the *Journal of Ethics,* on a chance. So the ms. should be returned to me some day soon. And if it should not tax you unduly I would be very glad of an expression of opinion as to the propriety or expediency of so doing and to whether it is fit to print anyway." (Veblen to Mitchell, September 30, 1909, Mitchell Papers).

striking similarity between Veblen's essay and the much later critique of orthodox economics by the historical and statistical minded economist, François Simiand, in his *La Méthode positive en science économique* (1912). On the margin of his translation of a passage from Simiand which he headed "Criticism of the Theory of Exchange Value," Mitchell wrote "cf. Veblen's article 'The Limitations of Marginal Utility.' " The passage in question reads as follows:

> All this analysis starts from the initial hypothesis that the sellers and buyers of a thing arrive at market with an estimate of this thing. In this very hypothesis itself it must be perceived that there is implied the previous existence of a market price for this thing. Let us consider the facts: Individual estimates are derived from a price already realized and known. They are constituted in the mind of the individual by the difference above or below the value which he knows has been already commonly recognized; and the proof of this is that in the case of a new article or of a thing for which no established price is known to those effecting the exchange, the estimate of the latter will be entirely indeterminate and arbitrary, or even cannot be fixed; will not exist as a definite quantitative idea. The radical defect of this theory is then, finally, that it seeks to explain a phenomenon of a social nature by individual phenomena which are derived precisely from this very social phenomenon, and exist only through it. And this defect will be found in every theory which takes the same course. Others, then, must be adopted. The phenomenon must be taken in its very reality; and since in this reality it is found to be social, it must be studied and explained as such. The psychology of introspection and ideological analysis cannot fail to miscarry here;

the only method, on the contrary, that can succeed, is an experimental objective method."[288]

Veblen's last review for the *Political Science Quarterly* is a good example of the independence of his mind; he wrote a sharp critique of J. M. Keynes's *The Economic Consequences of the Peace,* a book generally enthusiastically praised at the time,[289] and even by some of Veblen's own constant admirers. One of the few dissenters was then the managing editor of the *Quarterly,* the Columbia historian, Robert Livingston Schuyler. In sending galleys (August 1920), he wrote: "I cannot refrain from telling you how admirable your review seems to me to be. It strikes a note different from that in any of the reviews that I have seen of Keynes, and your view that the treaty [of Versailles] is merely a starting point for further diplomatic maneuvers seems to me to be entirely supported by what is happening."[290]

---

[288] *La Méthode positive en science économique* (Paris: Alcan, 1912) pp. 201-209. The translation is in the Mitchell Papers, Columbia University Libraries. Mitchell's other translations from the book are printed below. The translations were done by Mitchell in December 1912. (See Mitchell, Diary, December 12, 1912). Later, Roche-Agussol also noted the similarity of the critiques of Veblen and Simiand.

[289] The review was written on unruled yellow sheets and in pencil. He wrote the managing editor, June 21, 1920: "Enclosed is copy for a review of Keynes's book. I trust this lead pencil ms. will prove legible. Kindly let me see the proof if any."

[290] Schuyler wrote to Joseph Dorfman, May 14, 1935, that "It may interest you to know that it was through the good offices of Leon Ardzrooni that I was able to secure for the *Political Science Quarterly* . . . Veblen's remarkable article on 'The Intellectual Preeminence of Jews in Modern Europe' and his review of Keynes's *Economic Consequences of the Peace.*"

Schuyler asked Alvin Johnson to review Veblen's first collection of essays, *The Place of Science in Modern Civilisation.* Johnson made two attempts. On September 28, 1920, he wrote Schuyler: "I have been trying in the last few days to do the review of Veblen, but it doesn't come out right, for want of the time to make up my mind just what is unitary in it, as well as what is tenable." Six months later

Today there seems to be more acceptance of Veblen's minority view, especially of Keynes's treatment of President Wilson. As one scholar wrote in 1967:

> Not that he [Veblen] approved of the President's course. Just the same, he could not accept Keynes's widely acclaimed interpretation in which personal factors counted for so much and that hinged so heavily on a misreading of the President. Was Wilson (as Keynes wrote) really the "Non-conformist Minister . . . [whose] thought and . . . temperament were essentially theological and not intellectual, with all the strength and the weakness of that manner of thought, feeling and expression?" Was it really true that it "was harder to de-bamboozle this old Presbyterian than . . . to bamboozle him"?
>
> In his retort . . . Veblen looked behind the "smoke-screen" of the Covenant: ". . . [The] difficult but imperative task of suppressing Bolshevism . . . has no part in Mr. Keynes's analysis. . . . Yet it is sufficiently evident now that the exigencies of the Conclave's campaign against Russian Bolshevism have shaped the working out of the Treaty hitherto. . . . Mr. Keynes has much that is uncomplimentary to say of the many concessions and the comprehensive defeat in which the President and his avowed purposes became involved. . . . Due appreciation of the gravity of this anti-Bolshevik issue, and of its ubiquitous and paramount force in the deliberations of the Conclave, should have saved Mr. Keynes from those expressions of scant courtesy which mar his characterization of the President and the Presi-

(March 14, 1921) he gave up the attempt and wrote: "I can't say anything about it that I can say in the limit of a thousand word review. If you care to devote the space of 3000 to 3500 words to it, I shall be glad to write about this book." (Files of the *Political Science Quarterly*).

> dent's work as peacemaker[291]. . . so that a well-considered view of the President's share in the deliberations of the Conclave will credit him with insight, courage, facility, and tenacity of purpose rather than with that pusillanimity, vacillation and ineptitude which is ascribed to him in Mr. Keynes's too superficial view of the case."
>
> For Veblen, then, the tragedy of Versailles was rooted not in Wilson's betrayal but in the nascent civil war; and Wilson, whatever the limitations of his mid-Victorian liberalism, had known how to fight it. Veblen did not like the outcome either abroad or at home, but he had to give grudging credit where credit was due.[292]

Veblen's last written views on the future of socialism are revealed in 1922 in a letter declining to review several books for the journal. The managing editor of the journal, then Professor Parker T. Moon, had asked him to review together "two new and important books. One is entitled *Socialism in Theory and Practice* by Heinrich Strobel, Minister of Finance in the Prussian Revolutionary Government of 1918, the translation being by H. J. Stenning. It is a study of the communistic experiments by the Russian Bolshevists, by the Hungarian Communists and by the Revolutionary German Government.

"The other volume, about 270 pages in length, is *Le Bilan de l'etatisme* by Adolphe Delemer, with a preface by

---

291 That ardent Irishman Francis Hackett then in England reported to Huebsch at about the same time: "I've met many of my conquerors, but the most stuck up is J. M. Keynes." (The message is on a postcard, the date of which is indistinct, but seems to be June 19, 1920. It is in the Huebsch Papers).

292 Arno J. Mayer, "Historical Thought and American Foreign Policy in the Era of the First World War," in *The Historian and the Diplomat*, edited by Francis L. Loewenheim, p. 89. The brackets are Mayer's, the parentheses are Joseph Dorfman's.

Jacques Bardoux, Professeur a l'École des Sciences Politiques, President de la Societé d'Étude et d'Information Économiques. This seems to be a scholarly study of the problems of State Socialism and of the impetus given by the war to socialistic innovations." In a postscript the editor added: "Perhaps to these two volumes might be added the comparatively brief monograph by the Hon. Charles Whiting Baker on *Government Control and Operation of Industry in Great Britain and the United States during the World War,* published under the auspices of the Carnegie Endowment for International Peace." Veblen replied: "I can only thank you for your very courteous invitation to review certain books on Socialism for the *Quarterly*. The fact is that the books do not interest me. I take the liberty to add, although it may be of slight interest to you, that in my opinion Socialism is a dead issue. Too dead to be a live topic, and too lately dead for objective, historical treatment." The editor retorted: "I am sorry that you feel that the growth of socialistic omnicompetence on the part of the modern state is a dead issue, but I hope that at some time in the future we may have the good fortune to elicit a contribution from your pen anent some other topic."[293]

---

[293] Moon to Veblen, August 11, September 1, 1922; Veblen to Moon, August 26, 1922.

In the recent attempts to revive a socialist movement in the United States, Veblen's works have played a major role. Thus in 1967, an editor of *Studies on the Left* made use of his concept of the penalty of taking the lead to predict a promising future: "Precisely because the American Socialist movement is one of the most backward and feeble in all the world, it possesses what Veblen called 'the advantage of the borrower,' the possibility of utilizing the most advanced concepts of the European Left without also inheriting the dead weight of the past under which European socialism must labor." (John Cowley, "Crisis of the European Left," *Studies on the Left,* March-April 1967, p. 12). Four participants in a recent conference of socialist writers on methods of reviving socialism mentioned Veblen, and one in the most

One of the lighter aspects of his dealings with the *Political Science Quarterly* was his courteous but persistent request for payment for his reviews, or more properly review articles. After finishing the second Fisher review, he wrote Professor Seligman in 1909 that "About a year ago you were kind enough to publish a review article for me of Fisher's *Capital and Income*. I had, perhaps mistakenly, got the impression at the time it was spoken for that some payment would be made for it after publication, as would be reasonable since such a paper entails a certain cash expense to the writer.

---

comprehensive treatment asserted that in effect *The Engineers and the Price System,* interpreted along Bentley's line, must be the starting point of discussion. "In his *Engineers and the Price System* Thorstein Veblen anticipated the debate which rages in all advanced industrial countries, both capitalist and 'state socialist.' Nearly fifty years ago Veblen argued that the technicians as the bearers of technical and scientific knowledge were the crucial element in modern production. . . . Veblen was clearly speaking about the managers of capitalist enterprise who were neither owners nor ordinary wage earners. The critical importance of the group derived from their actual control over the production and distribution process. . . . The beginning of the separation of ownership from management initiated by corporate capital at the turn of the century was reaching maturity as the corporation became the characteristic form of capitalistic enterprise. Veblen acutely recognized that the corporations were centralizing control over production in the hands of a new manager who combined organizational and scientific knowledge." [Stanley Aronowitz, "Does the United States have a New Working Class?" in *Revival of American Socialism,* Selected Papers of the Socialist Scholars Conference, edited by George Fischer *et al* (New York: Oxford University Press, 1971) pp. 194-195].

Veblen, it seems, debated socialism in his Carleton College days. The grandson of one of his classmates recalled from his grandfather's diaries and letters that the question of one public debate between the two was "'Resolved: That the progress of Socialism is an Evil' – a debate on which my grandfather, who was an uncompromising Republican, took the negative and won the Plymouth Prize." [From an address by Thomas L. Hughes (now president of the Carnegie Endowment for International Peace) at Carleton College, in *Voice of the Carleton College Alumni,* March 1967, p. 6].

I have, however, received nothing and beg of you to let me know if the omission is due to oversight or if I have been mistaken in expecting anything." The editor replied: "With reference to your inquiry as to payment, I would say that while it is our custom to pay the moderate compensation of $2 a page for articles, we have never yet paid either for reviews or leading reviews [review articles], it being considered that the receipt of the book was a fair compensation. As, however, you seem to think that in some way you were led to expect compensation for your previous review, we are very glad indeed to meet your expectations in this matter, and to send you herewith a check of $30, which is compensation at the rate of $2 a page for the fifteen pages. I sincerely regret the misunderstanding in this matter and hope that this may be satisfactory to you. I wish that we were sufficiently well endowed to be able to pay contributors what they are really worth." Veblen got paid for the second review article at the same rate of $2, or $15 for the seven pages minus $8 [sic] for prepayment at 75¢ a copy for twelve issues requested by Veblen. By the end of World War I the journal ceased paying for any contributions but Veblen managed to secure payment on the ground of "expenses" incurred in its preparation and he obtained a flat $25 for "Intellectual Preeminence of Jews in Modern Europe."[294]

[294] Veblen took the same position as regards payment to contributors to the official organ of the American Economic Association, *The American Economic Review,* from its beginning. The editor said he agreed with Veblen (and Davenport) that payments should be made to contributors but added "it is impossible, however, to do this at the outset; therefore, for the present, I must ask for some charity." (D. R. Dewey to Veblen, December 9, 1910, Papers of the American Economic Association).

Later, to no avail, the editor wrote Veblen for a contribution: "As I understand it you do not write or publish until the spirit moves and are impregnable to all appeals. I write to inquire, however, if the spirit is not moving you at about this time; and if it is, if you can not

Essays in *The Quarterly Journal of Economics*

There are also some bits of information on Veblen's contributions to the journal that he regarded as the professional organ of "students whose interest is prevailingly theoretical." To *The Quarterly Journal of Economics*, Veblen contributed his basic critical and methodological essays. These occupied more than half the space in the first of Veblen's volumes of collected essays, *The Place of Science in Modern Civilisation and Other Essays.*

The most widely quoted passage of the most famous of the essays, "Why is Economics not an Evolutionary Science?" (1898), has recently been used even as the basis for a castigation of the dominant neo-classical model of modern economic theory for its neglect of the active role of the entrepreneur. The writer states "The management group becomes a passive calculator that reacts mechanically to changes imposed on it by fortuitous, external developments, over which it does not exert, and does not even attempt to exert, any influence."[295] The passage as quoted in the article reads: "Veblen . . . described the economic man as 'a lightning calculator of pleasures and pains, who oscillates like a homogeneous globule of desire of happiness under the impulse of stimuli that shift him about the area, but leave him intact. He has neither antecedent nor consequent. He is an isolated, definitive human datum, in stable equilibrium except for the buffets of the impinging forces that displace him in one direction or another. Self-imposed in elemental

[295] W. J. Baumol, "Entrepreneurship in Economic Theory," *The American Economic Review*, May 1968, p. 67.

let it quicken the pages of *The American Economic Review*. It seems to me that it is a long time since I have seen any article by you. You ought therefore to be loaded by this time." (D. R. Dewey to Veblen, March 18, 1915, Papers of the American Economic Association).

The *Review* now pays for contributions.

space, he spins symmetrically about his own spiritual axis until the parallelogram of forces bears down upon him, whereupon he follows the line of the resultant. When the force of the impact is spent, he comes to rest, a self-contained globule of desire as before. . . . [He] is not a prime mover. He is not the seat of a process of living, except in the sense that he is subject to a series of permutations enforced upon him by circumstances external and alien to him.' "[296]

---

[296] A somewhat different view of the entrepreneur is derived from Veblen's conception by the Swedish economist Johan Åkerman. In discussing the prosperity phase of business cycles he declared: "Meanwhile 'the instinct of the herd among entrepreneurs' (Veblen) . . . causes an increasing number of weak and ill-assorted firms to be established." The "scientific and technical urge" which is basic to industrialization "is mainly the result of 'idle curiosity' (Veblen). Anyway it is much less influenced by the profit motive than was assumed a hundred years ago." [*Theory of Industrialism*, pp. 143, 213]. In an earlier work he gave Veblen as an example of synthesizing equilibrium and institutional analysis by the use of his theory of cumulative causation. [*Das Problem der sozialökonomischen Synthese* (Lund: Ohlsson, 1938) pp. 232-236]. In this book he used *The Place of Science in Modern Civilisation, Essays in Our Changing Order, The Theory of Business Enterprise,* and Mitchell's volume of selections, *What Veblen Taught.*

More generally speaking, the passage in the text has been described by another Swedish economist as one of the sharpest attacks on the rationality assumption of dominant economic theory, especially of the "idea of the well-ordered system of preferences, within which a decision-maker can rank his alternatives and select the best. The forcible wording of Th. Veblen's frontal attack on the 'economic man' has made it perhaps the best known." He concludes on this point that Veblen's "criticism, made in 1898, may or may not be justified. It is worth emphasizing, however, that it has at least not become antiquated as the result of any subsequent alteration to the basic assumptions of economic theory." [S. B. Linder, *The Harried Leisure Class* (New York: Columbia University Press, 1970) p. 62].

Gerhard Colm of the National Planning Association contended in 1959 that another passage was "still true: 'There is the economic life process still in great measure awaiting theoretical formulation.' " ["Eco-

Illustrative of some of the difficulties of understanding Veblen is the brave attempt of J. M. Clark to decipher another famous passage in the essay, which deals with the theories of wages and interest in dominant economic theory. It reads: "If we are getting restless under the taxonomy of a monocotyledonous wage doctrine and a cryptogamic theory of interest, with involute, loculicidal, tomentous and moniliform variants, what is the cytoplasm, centrosome, or karyokinetic process to which we may turn, and in which we may find surcease from the metaphysics of normality and controlling principles?" On a slip of paper Clark jotted down his interpretation: "Cairnes's type of economics, postulates few and simple, afford standard of normalcy. Taxonomic science is a theory of normal case: a discussion of concrete facts of life in respect of the degree of approximation to normal case.

"Monocotyledonous: seed-plants' first leaves may come in pairs or singly. This [monocotyledonous] defines the single type, to which grasses, lilies, belong.

"Cryptogam: plant that does not produce flowers or seeds. What is its method of reproduction?

"Involute; with whorls closely coiled.

"Loculicidal:

"Tomentous: Tomentose? covered with densely matted hairs.

"Moniliform: Jointed or constricted at regular intervals, so as to resemble a string of beads."[297] My publisher, Augustus M. Kelley, has looked up in a dictionary the one

[297] Clark placed the note in his copy of *The Place of Science in Modern Civilisation and Other Essays*, which is in Joseph Dorfman's possession.

nomic Stabilization Policy" in *Economics and the Policy Maker*, Brookings Lectures 1958-1959 (Washington: Brookings Institution, 1959) p. 44].

word that Clark left blank: "Loculicidal." He found that in botany it is defined as "cutting into or through the loculus." Under 'loculus" we find two definitions: (1) "specifically, any small cavity, cell or chamber in plant or animal tissue"; (2) "in ancient tombs, a recess or small chamber for the reception of an urn or body."[298] Some further light on this sentence is shed by Professor Mitchell's comment in class in 1925 that most of the sentence was a parody on the dominant type of the theory of interest, the most controversial issue among orthodox economists at the time. Unfortunately he did not elaborate this suggestion.

On Veblen's survey of the history and method of economic doctrine in the sequel essays, "The Preconceptions of Economic Science" (1899-1900), we have a related comment by another student. In his uncorrected ms. "History of Political Economy" (1915), Robert F. Hoxie wrote: "Under the modern scientific influence the ideal of the historians of political economy is to characterize the various schools in general terms and to interpret their doctrines as reflections of the general industrial and general thought-content of their times. Only man I know of who seems to have made progress in this interpreting in the nineteenth century is Veblen.[299] Dr. Davenport thinks Veblen's work in this line represented

[298] Webster's *New Twentieth Century Dictionary of the English Language* (Cleveland: World, 1966) p. 1062.

Veblen, as previously noted, always had a deep interest in botany and horticulture. It was certainly strong in the 1890's. For example, he wrote Sarah McLean Hardy, November 30, 1895, "The chrysanthemums are out now, and I have to put in some time with them to see how they get along." Another of his students at the time recalled that "he came to my father's home one afternoon when he had been wandering around the vacant lots in that neighborhood on a botanizing tour and told my father he had found two new varieties of pigweed." (A. P. Winston to Joseph Dorfman, October 15, 1932). I have not checked the accuracy of Veblen's "discoveries."

[299] Hoxie is apparently referring to Veblen's essays of 1898-1900.

more of an aspiration than a reality. Veblen, however, was always telling us that classical economics as represented in Ricardo and [J. S.] Mill, etc., was [a] product of the development of the individualist[,] large business enterprise on the one hand[,] and of the associational psychology and utilitarian philosophy on the other. And he characterized the classical economic theory as altogether individualistic, hedonistic, optimistic and taxonomic—a pre-Darwinian pain economy, based on the conception of man as an economic globule."

Halbwachs was deeply impressed with these methodological-historical essays. In a private letter in 1924 he noted that Veblen "will live as the most penetrating critic of economic hedonism. . . . His sociological view of the origin of natural law seems to me to be the very truth itself. Furthermore, . . . he has had the merit of having been interested in the dynamic aspects of social facts—the statics and mere taxonomy ("La classification pure et simple") are not yet science. He has a very original conception of the role of causality."[300]

---

[300] Halbwachs to William Jaffé, September 20, 1934; Professor Jaffé kindly supplied a copy. Halbwachs was also an admirer of Simiand.

Interestingly when Laughlin asked Veblen in 1908 to persuade Mitchell to leave the University of California, he wrote as a sort of postscript: "By the way, I should like to see Mitchell develop his 'Taxonomic vs. Evolutionary Theory.' " (Laughlin to Veblen, August 27, 1908, Mitchell Papers).

Veblen wrote Mitchell at the time, "I trust I am violating neither your feelings nor the dues of courtesy in forwarding the enclosed note from Laughlin. It is semi-official at least.

"I have told him in reply that for all I know you are all right as a teacher; that you are fond of Berkeley; and that you have assurances of a substantial advance in pay when you return to work [from a visiting lectureship at Harvard]. I hope, again, that I have been violating no confidences; and, by the way, I told him that you have talked the matter over with me somewhat freely." (Veblen to Mitchell, September 6, 1908, Mitchell Papers).

Mitchell called attention in 1937 to the fact that Veblen's methodology as expressed in these essays provided for effective analysis of the role of custom in economic behavior. He said "progress in treating problems of custom has been slow in economics but progress there has been, particularly at the hands of institutional economists. To Veblen, e.g., the central problem of economics is the cumulative growth of those widely prevalent habits of thinking, feeling and acting that he calls institutions. He shows how a theoretical explanation can be developed of the way in which 'custom' in [John Stuart] Mill's language grows out of the effects they produce."[301]

These essays have also been viewed as making Veblen a pioneer in what is called the sociology of knowledge, for in this "series of brilliant and penetrating essays he explored the intricate relationships between cultural values and intellectual activities."[302]

In the *Quarterly* in 1906-1907 also appeared the substance of his lectures and discussion on Marx, delivered at Harvard in 1906. Hobson in his *Veblen* quoted *in extenso* from the printed version passages that supported his comment: "When it is borne in mind that these lectures were delivered in 1906, the interpretative genius of Veblen will be realized."

This applied particularly to a famous "prediction that accorded with the Darwinian norm." It read: "It may be [as Marx argued] that the working classes will go forward,[303]

[301] Mitchell, Supplementary Outline, May 27, 1937, in *Types of Economic Theory*, I, 584.

[302] Louis Wirth, "Preface," to Karl Mannheim, *Ideology and Utopia: An Introduction to the Sociology of Knowledge*, translated from the German by Louis Wirth and Edward Shils (New York: Harcourt, Brace, 1936) p. xvii.

[303] *Veblen* (London: Chapman and Hall, 1936) p. 62.

Of the lecture given in the General Seminar of the department – "Seminary of Economics, Harvard University," a brief note by the

along the line of the socialistic ideals and enforce a new deal, in which there shall be no class discrepancies, no international animosity, no dynastic politics. But then it may also, so far as can be foreseen, equally well happen that the working class, with the rest of the community in Germany, England, or America, may be led by the habit of loyalty and by their sportsmanlike propensities to lend themselves enthusiastically to the game of dynastic politics which alone their sportsmanlike rulers consider worth while."[304]

Drawing on Veblen's essays "On the Nature of Capital" (1908), Hobson stated in his obituary of Veblen that "Veblen's close analysis of current economic teaching gives a far more convincing exposure of capitalist theory than is contained in any of the Marxist or other avowedly socialist treatises. For it shows that the main source of economic inequality and oppression is not to be found in the monopoly of land or material capital but in the control and utilization for personal gain of the new technical knowledge, and the new environmental and social opportunities."[305]

[304] Quoted from "The Socialist Economics of Karl Marx and his Followers," II (1907), reprinted in *The Place of Science in Modern Civilisation and Other Essays*, p. 442.

[305] This was the main point of "The Nature of Capital," 1908, which originally appeared in *The Quarterly Journal of Economics;* reprinted in *The Place of Science in Modern Civilisation*, pp. 324-385.

Mitchell recorded in his Diary, March 31, 1908: "Veblen read me his paper on Capital as a means of cornering technological knowledge of the race . . . In evening read Veblen's paper again."

secretary states: "April 9, 1906. At a meeting of the Seminary on April 9 Prof. Thorstein B. Veblen of the University of Chicago spoke on 'The Distribution of Socialist Sentiment.' Prof. Veblen alluded to the central source of socialism in the region about the North Sea and to its radiation from that point. He mentioned the different kinds of socialism, including the Marxian and the Latin, and discussed the relation of these kinds to races and religious sects. General discussion followed." "Economics Seminary Records, 1903-1908," p. 103, Harvard University Libraries. Stuart Daggett was the secretary at the time.

Contributions to *The American Journal of Sociology*

In this University of Chicago journal, Veblen published four major essays: "The Instinct of Workmanship and the Irksomeness of Labor" (September 1898), "The Beginnings of Ownership" (November 1898), "The Barbarian Status of Women" (January 1899) and "The Place of Science in Modern Civilisation" (March 1906).[306] "The Instinct of Workmanship and the Irksomeness of Labor" and "The Place of Science in Modern Civilisation," he held to be his most important essays.

The first three, it seems, thanks in good part to information from the Macmillan papers, were involved in the preparation of *The Theory of the Leisure Class.* The reader may recall that in the discussion above of the revision of the ms. of his first book, he informed the publisher on June 7, 1897, that he had "prefixed some 52 pages to the regular rotation of the sheets in the body of the ms. . . . The sheets, I believe, will be found to average about 190 words each—perhaps rather over than under; that is, approximately 10,000 words." In the letter of September 2, 1898, he wrote, that in revising the ms. "the introductory part has been abridged somewhat." Now a lead to what was in the "prefixed" part and the "abridged" part is supplied by a paragraph in a letter to Sarah McLean Hardy of December 15,

[306] The first three have been reprinted in the second and posthumous collection of essays, *Essays in Our Changing Order,* and the last is reprinted in and gave the title to the first collection, *The Place of Science in Modern Civilisation and Other Essays.*

While Mitchell was at the University of California and Veblen at Stanford they often spent week ends together to discuss not only their manuscripts but also recent developments in economic theory. Thus Veblen wrote Mitchell on December 1, 1909: "Unless I am warned not to, I am coming to Berkeley Friday this week to stay until Monday morning. . . . I hope to see quite a deal of you and get all the latest on economic theory." (Mitchell Papers).

1895. He then wrote: "I have quite forgotten what scheme of subdivision I may have had in mind when I talked with you about the three chapters. The scheme actually in operation is to write what will at a guess make some thirty pages (12mo), and then write in a new caption and actually make a new start. Also I should scarcely be able to revise and complete the three chapters, until the whole stands forth in its symmetrical entirety; partly because it would be impossible, and partly because it would be too much bother."

The "three chapters" seem likely to have been the "prefixed" part of the ms. originally sent to the publisher and in the final draft they were removed from the ms. and arrangements made for their publication in the form of three successive essays just prior to the appearance of the book. As he states in the preface of *The Theory of the Leisure Class*, "At some points the discussion proceeds on grounds of economic theory or ethnological generalization that may in some degree be unfamiliar. The introductory chapter indicates the nature of these theoretical premises sufficiently it is hoped to avoid obscurity. A more explicit statement of the theoretical position involved is made in the series of papers published in Volume IV of *The American Journal of Sociology* on 'The Instinct of Workmanship and the Irksomeness of Labor,' 'The Beginnings of Ownership' and 'The Barbarian Status of Women.' "[307]

[307] As Veblen informed the publisher in the letter of September 2, 1898, that accompanied the final draft: "The papers referred to in the preface are not yet in print, but they are in type and will appear in successive numbers of *The American Journal of Sociology*, beginning with the issue for this month."

The second, "The Beginnings of Ownership," attracted the attention of John R. Commons "as an original and discerning discussion." Commons was then presenting his general theory of institutionalism. ["A Sociological View of Sovereignty," Number 1, 1899; reprinted in his *A Sociological View of Sovereignty*, edited by Joseph Dorfman (New York: Augustus M. Kelley Publishers, 1963) p. 63].

Perhaps the article which gives the title to the volume of methodological essays has the greatest current vogue. As mankind faces the promise and problems that the tremendous advance of science and technology has involved, this sixty-six year old paper, "The Place of Science in Modern Civilisation," commands increasing interest. As an editorial in the New York *Times* put it in 1957, "One of the most provocative thinkers this country has ever produced, Thorstein Veblen, would probably derive great satisfaction from the current national discussion about science were he alive today. As long ago as 1906 in his famous essay . . . he called attention to the problems which arise because of men's slowness to adjust their cultural attitudes to the rapid changes proposed by scientific and technical advance. Since Veblen's time the pace of that scientific advance has speeded up far beyond anything ever known before, posing correspondingly greater problems of adjustment in attitudes and actions."[308]

For Veblen this was doubtless to be complemented with a concern over science, which after all is also an institution. As a reviewer put it in 1936, paraphrasing Veblen, "The quest of science is . . . the most dominant note in our culture. Veblen thinks we should keep a close eye on it."[309] Doubtless the reviewer had in mind the passage: "The ideal man, and the ideal of human life, even in the apprehension of those who most rejoice in the advances of science, is neither the finikin skeptic in the laboratory nor the animated slide-rule."[310]

Some additional light is shed on the essay by some cor-

---

308 "Science and Civilization," New York *Times,* February 2, 1957.

309 Review of *What Veblen Taught,* edited with an introduction by Wesley C. Mitchell, in Minneapolis *Tribune,* May 22, 1936.

310 "The Place of Science in Modern Civilisation," 1906, reprinted in *The Place of Science in Modern Civilisation,* p. 30.

respondence and recent discussions. In a letter to his friend, Jacques Loeb, he declared: "my endeavor is to make economics a science in the same sense of the term as the material sciences."[311] Popper, who treats the essay with respect as a defence of "pure research," has helped to clarify a major point; namely, the supremacy of "a purely theoretical or 'idle' curiosity[,] . . . of the rights of 'pure' or 'fundamental' research [as] against the narrow view, unfortunately again fashionable, that scientific research is justified only if it proves to be a sound investment." Veblen would have doubtless subscribed to Popper's quotation from Kant, whom he viewed as the greatest philosopher, that "To yield to every whim of curiosity, and to allow our passion for inquiry to be restrained by nothing but the limits of our ability, this shows an eagerness of mind not unbecoming to *scholarship*. But it is wisdom that has the merit of selecting, from among the innumerable problems which present themselves, those whose solution is important to mankind."[312] Reenforcing this

[311] Veblen to Loeb, March 29, 1905, Loeb Papers.

[312] *The Poverty of Historicism* (London: Routledge and Kegan Paul, 1957; revised edition, paperback, 1961) pp. 55, 56.

Mitchell, in a review of John R. Commons's *Institutional Economics*, clarified Veblen's conception of scientific procedure on this point. As Mitchell puts it, Commons "proceeds to argue that institutional economics is concerned precisely with human purposes as summed up in 'worldly wisdom' – a mental attitude which Veblen regards as 'at cross purposes with the disinterested scientific spirit.'

"Of course, Veblen did not conceive human beings as devoid of purpose. Commons himself presently recognizes that the 'instinct of workmanship' brings purpose into the foreground of behavior (p. 661). That was not the only instinct with which Veblen endowed mankind, and all instincts are purposive. His chief criticism of hedonism is that it pictures men as passive creatures, controlled by the pleasure-pain forces which impinge upon them.

"What Veblen was driving at is that science assumes no purpose in 'nature,' or in 'the course of events' outside of man. In dealing with human behavior, he tries to give an account of human purposes in terms of an evolutionary process of natural selection. For these purview is the suggestion that from Kant's *Der Streit der Facultäten*, Veblen may have gotten his primary idea of the university; "namely, that the faculty of philosophy (concerned with esoteric knowledge) must be ranked superior to the faculties of law, medicine, and theology, whose concern must be with utilitarian knowledge."[313]

There is an interesting article by Roger Fry, "Art and Science," which is quite revealing about this essay. It originally appeared in the prestigious *The Athenaeum* (June 6, 1919), in response to two essays in the same journal by a writer who used as a signature the initial "S." ("The Place of Science," April 11, 1919, and "The Justification of the Scientific Method," May 2, 1919). Fry said of the first that

[313] W. H. Cowley and JB Lon Hefferlin, review of paperback edition of *The Higher Learning in America*, in *Epitome*, May 28, 1957, p. 4.

poses are an evolutionary product and so can be explained in the same fashion as man's opposable thumb. The scientist should refrain, so far as is possible for such a purposeful creature as man, from mixing his own purposes into his explanations of cumulative changes in the purposes of others. That rule of intellectual honesty Commons accepts in principle and practices with indifferent success, like Veblen and the rest of us." ("Commons on Institutional Economics," 1935; reprinted in *The Backward Art of Spending Money*, p. 333).

This position has been amplified by Morris A. Copeland who speaks as "one in the Veblenian tradition." ["Social Evolution and Economic Planning," condensed version of a 1936 review of Commons's *Institutional Economics*, reprinted in his *Fact and Theory in Economics: The Testament of an Institutionalist*, edited by Chandler Morse (Ithaca, N. Y.: Cornell University Press, 1958) p. 4]. He declared for example in 1931 that "in place of a static, quasi-psychological, tautological theory of the factors behind demand, the natural science view would substitute specific socio-historical theories. Veblen's *Theory of the Leisure Class* offers some interesting explanations of changes in consumers' demand. We can state the problem statistically in terms of changing family budgets. Sales campaigns, public education in hygiene and home economics, changes in household technology, the rise of feminism, are sample historical factors to be reckoned with." ["Economic Theory and the Natural Science Point of View" (1931); reprinted in *Fact and Theory in Economics*, p. 41].

the author "distinguishes between two aspects of intellectual activity in scientific work. Of these two aspects one derives its motive power from curiosity, and this deals with particular facts. It is only when, through curiosity, man has accumulated a mass of particulars, that the second intellectual activity manifests itself, and in this the motive is the satisfaction which the mind gets from the contemplation of inevitable relations. To secure this end the utmost possible generalization is necessary.

"In a later article S. says boldly that this satisfaction is an aesthetic satisfaction: 'It is in its aesthetic value that the justification of the scientific theory is to be found, and with it the justification of the scientific method.' I should like to pose to S. at this point the question whether a theory that disregarded facts would have equal value for science with one which agreed with facts. I suppose he would say No; and yet, so far as I can see, there would be no purely aesthetic reason why it should not. The aesthetic value of a theory would surely depend solely on the perfection and complexity of the unity attained, and I imagine that many systems of scholastic theology, and even some more recent systems of metaphysic, have only this aesthetic value. I suspect that the aesthetic value of a theory is not really sufficient to justify the intellectual effort entailed unless, as a true scientific theory – by which I mean a theory which embraces all the known relevant facts – the aesthetic value is reinforced by the curiosity value which comes in when we believe it to be true."

"Kant's Critique of Judgment"

This brings us to Veblen's one known publication in philosophy, "Kant's Critique of Judgment," which he wrote as a Yale graduate student in philosophy in 1884. His contemporaries in philosophy accurately recalled that "it reveals much of the same type of intellectual peculiarity that became characteristic of his later economic work."[314]

We have known that Veblen was interested in Charles Pierce's course in logic at Johns Hopkins, and that he had a lifelong admiration for Kant, at least since his Yale days, especially for the greatest of the critiques, *The Critique of Pure Reason.*[315] We now know that in his graduate school days he had been deeply interested in other philosophers. Maurice Roche-Agussol pointed out, presumably on the basis of information supplied him by Veblen, that he had originally specialized in German philosophy of the eighteenth and nineteenth centuries, and then gone on to study particularly Auguste Comte, as well as Herbert Spencer and Darwin.[316]

We now learn too from the Veblen-Jameson correspondence that in his first term of graduate study at Johns Hopkins in the fall of 1881, he had been primarily interested in George S. Morris, who might best be classified as something of a Hegelian.[317] Then at Yale, he became quite intrigued with Hegel's work in 1883. He wrote Jameson on February 12 "Just now Hegel is all the rage, that is, with me, and, by consequence with Pres. Porter. Hegel is 'tough'; very much

---

[314] Mitchell, *Types of Economic Theory,* II, 621.

[315] To the evidence presented in the Veblen book, let me add another item: One of his Missouri students who was interested in Kant wrote in a private letter "Veblen remarked that I would eventually learn the German language in order to read Kant's *Critique of Pure Reason* in the original." (J. S. Urie to Joseph Dorfman, June 1, 1934). Urie prepared the table of contents for *The Nature of Peace.* (Urie to Dorfman, May 20, 1934).

[316] *Étude bibliographique des sources de la psychologie économique chez les Anglo-Américains* (Montpelier: Darsac, 1919) p. 90.

[317] Veblen wrote Jameson on April 2, 1882, "I miss Professor Morris." Morris was the teacher of John Dewey.

so in fact, but I like him more the more I see of him." He said that his chief teacher in philosophy, President Noah Porter, "does not agree with Hegel, but so far I have not let myself be disturbed by that." This phase passed,[318] but as Hegelianism and pragmatism became the dominant and contending philosophies, the Kantian Veblen became suspect for his philosophy as well as his economics.

This was revealed in curious fashion in a letter of 1909 that came to light in the Davenport correspondence. Davenport had just gone to the University of Missouri and was desperately trying to get Veblen an appointment in his department. He wrote Veblen in April 1909 that he was trying to arrange a deal between the department of economics and the department of sociology whereby they would agree to "the appointment of a free professor to wobble more or less between economics and sociology with occasional modest advances upon history and philosophy." But he found that the president was opposed for the time being to Veblen. "During the summer he has struck something in the East that has perplexed him and has decidedly cooled him. . . . And he is not impressed by what the philosophy people generally

[318] Hegelian concepts are by no means absent from Veblen's bag of tools. Thus he contended in 1894 that "as near as the bizarre characters in which it is written can yet be deciphered, the message of the Army of the Commonweal [Coxey's Army movement] says that . . . the concept of 'property' or of ownership is in process of acquiring a flexibility and a limitation that would have puzzled the good American citizen of a generation ago. By what amounts to a subconscious acceptance of Hegelian dialectic it has come about that an increase of a person's wealth, beyond a certain ill-defined point, should not, according to the new canon of equity, be permitted to increase his command over the means of production or the processes which these means serve. Beyond an uncertain point of aggregation the inviolability of private property in the new popular conception declines. In Hegelian phrase, a change in quantity if it is considerable enough amounts to a change in kind." ("The Army of the Commonweal," 1894; reprinted in *Essays in Our Changing Order*, p. 99).

have said to him with regard to your insurgency in philosophical questions."[319]

His last published article, "Economic Theory in the Calculable Future" (1925), fittingly was based on that distinction between employments that ran through all his major economic works, as Innes exemplified in drawing from the article the point: "The adaptability of the monetary system with its mathematical bias to the calculating machine has done much to validate the predictions of Veblen in his emphasis on the pecuniary and industrial bifurcation of western civilization."[319a]

Having finished my notes on Veblen's books and volumes of collected essays, memorials, etc., the time has come to discuss the uncollected published writings that are reprinted below.

IV

UNCOLLECTED WRITINGS

By far the largest number of his uncollected publications appeared in *The Journal of Political Economy.*[320] "The Price of Wheat Since 1867" and "The Food Supply and the Price

---

[319] Davenport to Veblen, April 8, October 4, 1909, Davenport Papers. It should be added that thanks to Davenport's tenacity and President Hill's willingness to set aside his doubts Veblen received an appointment a year later.

In a conversation I had with ex-president Hill in Kansas City, Missouri, after the appearance of the Veblen book, he expressed great pride in having secured Veblen. He also told me that leading economists like Alvin Johnson had congratulated him on the appointment, for with Veblen and Davenport Missouri had the most forward looking, productive economists.

[319a] *Political Economy in the Modern State* (Toronto: Ryerson, 1946) p. 125.

[320] Veblen was in fact if not always in name the managing editor of the journal from its inception in 1892 almost to the time of his departure from Chicago in 1906. Formally he was managing editor

of Wheat," which he had begun as a fellow at Cornell in 1891-1892, have long been held not only as a major contribution to the history of American agriculture, but also as models of analysis of economic facts. He presented a "strictly price analysis, with great emphasis on the state of the industrial arts, on the introduction of railroads and the ocean steamship, and agricultural machinery. He predicted that the price of wheat would remain below 91 cents for the next decade and with the exception of 1898, when it was 93 cents, his prediction was fulfilled."[321] In 1962, the first essay

[321] Innis, "The Work of Thorstein Veblen," 1929; reprinted in his *Essays in Canadian Economic History,* pp. 19-20. See also, Leslie Fishman, review of Joseph Dorfman *et al, Institutional Economics, Veblen, Commons and Mitchell Reconsidered,* in *The Economic Journal,* December 1963, p. 760.

Lubin recalls a story that resulted from a class discussion on agricultural matters at Missouri. "One day I had difficulty in following his discussion, being from a middle-sized city in Massachusetts, with virtually no knowledge of agriculture or the economics of agriculture. I took issue with something he said about agricultural economics. He looked at me and said 'Lubin, it's very evident that you were brought up on the pavement.' That closed the argument." (Lubin, "Recollections of Veblen," in *Thorstein Veblen: The Carleton College Veblen Seminar Essays,* pp. 131-132).

One of his associates on the editorial board of *The Dial* wrote me in 1934 that "He looked and at times talked something like a Yankee farmer, except, of course he was even more quick-witted. But in fact

1895-1904, and for the remaining two years at the University of Chicago he was a member of the board of editors.

Robert Morss Lovett of the English department of the university in describing Veblen in his early years as managing editor or, as he called it, "the working editor," wrote that "As I used to meet him on his way to his chief's [Laughlin's] sanctum, a long, lean, cadaverous figure, with smoldering eyes in a pallid, usually unshaven face, I thought of the description of William Langland, the 'Long-Will,' reputed author of *The Vision of Piers Plowman.* A few years later, in the series of books beginning with *The Theory of the Leisure Class,* Veblen unveiled a vision of society in the twentieth century as devastating as was Langland's in the fourteenth." [*All Our Years* (New York: The Viking Press, 1948) p. 69].

(without the tables) served as the opening article of the two-volume *Landmarks of Political Economy,* which comprised the "masterpieces" of the journal's seventy volumes.

As for his reviews in that journal, some of them seem to be what editors supply as "fillers," but for the most part they supplement and clarify the books and articles of this many-faceted man. They fall largely into the following categories: history of economic theory, agriculture, business cycles and corporation finance, socialism and imperialism and economic psychology. Thus the reviews of three of Werner Sombart's works (including *Der moderne Kapitalismus*),[322] and of a volume of Schmoller's essays on methodology, supplement Veblen's treatment of the German historical school in the review article, "Gustav Schmoller's Economics."[323] Veblen's

[322] Hoxie early noted that Veblen's "distinction between pecuniary and industrial is brought out also by Dr. Werner Sombart in *Der moderne Kapitalismus* (Leipzig, 1902)." (Hoxie, "The Demand and Supply Concepts: An Introduction to the Study of Market Price," *The Journal of Political Economy,* June 1906, p. 1).

[323] It appeared originally in *The Quarterly Journal of Economics* and was reprinted in *The Place of Science in Modern Civilisation.* The essay contains all the criticisms of the German Historical School which have since become the standard ones.

Veblen's last review of Sombart, that of *Der Bourgeois: zur Geistesgeschichte der modernen Wirtschaftsmenschen* (1915), takes the author to task for accepting "quite uncritically, linguistic and national frontiers . . . as marking racial distinctions, and therefore as marking distinct lines of inheritance." None of the peoples "cited by Sombart as illustrative instances, are racial groups, but only social groups made

he appeared rather reticent and retiring, and never advanced his opinions with the merciless finality that I have often heard on other editorial boards. He dressed somewhat like a farmer too – a sort of careless farmer that had come to the city, and was not averse to letting the city 'folk' know just where they got off, to use the old phrase. There was none of his complexity of style in his speech; as I say, he was – or appeared to be – almost shy. But at times he would make one or two penetrating remarks that were devastating, when you finally caught the full implications." (Harold E. Stearns to Dorfman, October 15, 1934).

critique of Gabriel Tarde's *Social Laws* and *Psychologie économique,* Lester Frank Ward's *Pure Sociology,* and W. H. Mallock's *Aristocracy and Evolution,* supplement the "Preconceptions of Economic Science," and other methodological essays reprinted in *The Place of Science in Modern Civilisation.* Running through the relatively large number of reviews of works on business cycles and on industrial combinations is Veblen's conception of business cycles as a phenomenon intimately associated with the pervasive modern corporate organization. Thus when Mitchell informed him in 1913 that the landmark *Business Cycles* was to appear shortly, he wrote "I have been lately shifted back into work in that neighborhod this year, having to give a course on trusts and corporations, ostensibly, and I am finding it hard work."[323a]

The reviews of books on socialism amplify his highly sophisticated concept of the materialistic conception of

[323a] Veblen's deep interest in the area of money and banking as well as corporations is attested by his term examination in the undergraduate course "Introduction to Economics" on June 13, 1906, at the University of Chicago:

"1. Explain the effect of the increase of the gold supply on prices and interest?

2. How does Gresham's law work out in relation to silver in the U.S.?

3. (a) Compare the English banking system with that of the U.S.
(b) Show what changes, if any, should be made in American banking.

4. What legal regulation of labor should be made, if any, as to trade unions, as to factory regulation, mode and hours of employment?

5. What is the effect of trusts on prices and wages?

6. What should be done to regulate Trusts? State reasons.

7. Does credit raise or lower prices? State reasons for your conclusion."

Mary Bostwick Day, who sent me these examination questions, said that she had written them in the textbook, *Introduction to Economics,* by Henry Rogers Seager.

up out of the same range of social elements combined in approximately the same proportions."

history, his sharp criticisms of the Marxian doctrine of surplus value and class struggle. A note on the third volume of *Das Kapital* (1894), which has the earmarks of being Veblen's, contains what is now a basic standard criticism of the doctrine of surplus value. It reads:

> Among the surprises of economic literature is the fate that has overtaken Karl Marx's theory of surplus-value in the third volume of his *Kapital,* lately published. Advocates, expositors and critics of the Marxian economics have exercised their ingenuity in futile attempts to reconcile that theory with obvious facts, while its author has put them off with the assurance that the whole mystery would be explained and made right in the Third Book of his work. In the mean time the Marxian dogma of surplus-value has served the present generation of "scientific" socialists as their fundamental "scientific" principle and the keynote of their criticism of existing industrial relations, and its acceptance (on faith) by the body of socialists, avowed and unavowed, has contributed not a little to the viciousness of their attack on the existing order of things. And now, after the theory, accepted literally and with full naiveté, has done service for a generation as the most redoubted engine of socialist propaganda, the "Third Book" comes along and explains with great elaboration, in the course of some 200 pages, that the whole of that jaunty structure is to be understood in a Pickwickian sense. It appears now that the need which has been felt for some reconciliation of this theory of the rate of surplus-value with the everyday facts of the rate of profits is due simply to a crude and gratuitous misapplication of the Marxian doctrine of surplus-value to a question with which it has nothing

> to do. That theory has none but the most remote and intangible relation to any concrete facts. The full extent of the relation between "surplus-value" and "profits" is this (and even this suffers material qualification in the course of the discussion), that the aggregate profits in any industrial community at any given time may also be styled "aggregate surplus-value." The rate of surplus-value bears no tangible relation to the rate of profits. The two vary quite independently of one another. Nor does the aggregate profits in any concrete case, in any given industry or enterprise, depend on or coincide in magnitude with the aggregate surplus-value produced in that industry or enterprise. For all useful purposes the entire surplus-value theory is virtually avowed to be meaningless lumber.[324]

As for Veblen's opinion of Marx, there is much to be said of the view expressed by the most recent comprehensive historian of socialism. "Marxism, he [Veblen] disliked, as exaggerating the purely economic at the expense of psychological factors in social evolution."[325]

It should be noted, however, that decades before it became fashionable as today for Anglo-American economists generally to acknowledge that Marx was a great economist – in fact a landmark thinker – Veblen had done so in the two part essay on Marx while subjecting the Marxian system to one of the most drastic critiques.[326]

---

[324] *The Journal of Political Economy,* March 1895, pp. 218-219.

[325] G. D. H. Cole, *History of Socialist Thought,* Volume 3, Part 2, *The Second International 1889-1914* (London: Macmillan, 1956) p. 816. Cole added: "Little read in his own day beyond a circle of devoted admirers, he has exerted a growing influence in recent years but not mainly among socialists."

[326] "The fact that the theoretical structures of Marx collapse when their elements are converted into terms of modern science should of itself be sufficient proof that those structures were not built by their

In his last review in *The Journal of Political Economy,* that of Maurice Millioud, *The Ruling Caste and Frenzied Trade in Germany* (1916), Veblen asserted that the German case of imperialism is "the consummate type-form of its species. What the facts cited [by the author] entitle us to say is that Germany has been affected with an aggravated case of imperialism, accentuated in all its symptoms, but not specifically divergent from the common run of imperialism that affects modern nations."

The other items in the collection for the most part, like the reviews in *The Journal of Political Economy,* serve to amplify and clarify his views. We conclude the main body of the volume with his amusing Carleton College poem "The Following Lines are Respectfully Dedicated to the Class of '82 by One Who Sympathizes With Them in Their Recent Bereavement." This was a parody on the traditional New England college sophomore custom of burying Caesar or Euclid. It will doubtless be most appreciated by those interested in the evolution of his style as a satirist. The traits that these effusions manifested of course by no means remained dormant between his Carleton and Chicago days. They were exhibited at the Winona academy where he taught for a year after his B.A. in 1880. As a colleague recalled, he was very jovial and a master of repartee, which caused hilarity at gatherings. He gave two anecdotes as illustrations: "I heard a student (not his own) say to him:

---

maker out of such elements as modern science habitually makes use of. Marx was neither ignorant, imbecile, nor disingenuous, and his work must be construed from such a point of view and in terms of such elements as will enable him to stand substantially sound and convincing." ["The Socialist Economics of Karl Marx and his Followers," (1906) II, reprinted in *The Place of Science in Modern Civilisation,* p. 437].

'What do you take me for anyway?' T. V. answered at once: 'Who says I take you for anything at all?' I heard another say to him at a party: 'Well, you are cracked, Veblen.' V. answered quickly: 'That is all right, but you are too soft to crack.' "[327]

His humor began to take a more droll form when he was in the Yale graduate school. He wrote his former Johns Hopkins companion, Jameson, June 2, 1882: "The Base Ball game between Yale and Harvard took place the other day – Yale was beaten, as you may have heard – and Jumbo was here [in New Haven] yesterday. It has been some surprise to me to see how kindly the puritan of today takes to Baseball and circuses. I noticed a Prof. from the Theological Seminary at the Baseball game. Athletics and c. is decidedly the most characteristic virtue of Yale, and perhaps of New Haven, and I am afraid it covers a multitude of sins." On May 16, 1883, he informed Jameson, "Forepaugh's circus and the anniversary exercises of the [Yale] Theological Seminary, together with the national anniversary of Norway, come tomorrow, so that you see I am on the eve of a great holiday."

Now let me briefly refer to some missing writings of Veblen. We know that while he was a graduate student at Johns Hopkins, the first semester of the academic year 1881-1882, he wrote two papers on rent theory. Of the first, "[J. S.] Mill's Theory of the Taxation of Land," reference was made in the Veblen book to a short abstract which was published in 1882. Since no copy of the paper has been found, it seems desirable to reproduce here the abstract:

With the advance of society the rent of land increases.

---

[327] Reverend H. B. Thorgrimsen to Joseph Dorfman, April 8, 1930. The writer also commented that "I have the impression that he had at that time not found himself nor knew what was to follow."

> This increase is independent of any effort on the part of the landlord, being the product of the activity of the community. The State should therefore by a peculiar tax, appropriate this "unearned increment" and not permit it to go to the owner of the land. To obviate all injustice to owners who have bought land with the expectation of being permitted to enjoy the future increase of its rent, the State is to offer to buy the land of the owners at its market price as an alternative to their keeping it and paying to the State the increase of rent. As a consequence of such an alternative, land having a speculative value would be sold to the State in order to avoid loss to the owners. The measure would act as a fine on the holding of land, to the amount of the speculative value, and lead to an almost universal nationalization of land; differing, however, from generally entertained schemes for the State's getting possession of land, in that the expense of the change would be more equitably distributed on all classes of the community. No immediate redistribution of wealth would take place, but, neglecting all probable undesirable secondary effects of the change on the people, an advantage would accrue from an increased compactness of population, making possible a saving of labor.[328]

We have known from the Veblen book that Veblen planned a sequel, "Relation of Rent to the Advance of Population." Thanks to the Jameson correspondence we now have some information on what happened to it. On February 12, 1883, while at Yale, he wrote his friend, who had remained at Hopkins: "I have not written disquisitions on

[328] Johns Hopkins University, *University Circulars*, February 1882, p. 176.

vexed points of political economy this year, neither have I been encouraged to do so. You may perhaps not know that I got up a certain essay last year, while at the J. H.U., which Dr. Ely [the instructor in economics] advised me to send to a periodical to have printed. Well, I sent it and, as might have been expected, the 'periodical' died of it. That discouraged me a little, though it increased my admiration of the Dr., who, as I understand, had a grudge against the 'periodical.' "

Still missing too is his John Addison Porter Prize essay of 1884 with the title, "The Distribution of Surplus Revenue in 1837." The prize was established in 1872 by the Kingsley Trust Association(Scroll and Key Society of Yale College) and named in honor of John Addison Porter, Yale 1844, one of the founders of the award. The contest was (and is) open to all students of the university and carried a substantial stipend for those days, $250 (it is now $1000). According to the terms of the award each competitor must sign his essay with an assumed name and send with it an envelope with the name on the outside, and the real name within. In 1930 a member of the society informed me that "the following notation appears in the Society's file of John Addison Porter Prize Essays: 'The original essay for 1884 having been lost and not procurable from Mr. Veblen the following essay on the same subject by "O. D. Warner" is here preserved.' This notation is in the handwriting of Mr. Samuel R. Betts [class of '75] a member of the Committee on the prize [in that year]."[329]

[329] Albert B. Crawford to Joseph Dorfman, March 25, 1930.

It seems that the essay although catalogued in the Scroll and Key Society Library in 1899 disappeared afterwards when the essays were being bound.

My informant suggested that I send him a specimen of Veblen's handwriting for comparison with the handwriting of the substituted essay. Mitchell kindly let me have a letter from Veblen, but the handwriting turned out to be quite different.

No trace has been found of the most important of the missing items, his Ph.D. dissertation, "Ethical Grounds of a Doctrine of Retribution." So much for Veblen's writings. I might add, however, that we have a *little* more information but precious little on that most obscure but highly important period of his life: the years between his acquisition of a Ph.D. at Yale in 1884 and his return to academic life as a graduate student at Cornell in 1891. As Sarah McLean Hardy lay ill and despondent in a Wellesley hospital in 1895, he wrote her, "I believe I have been at pains to inform you that I once 'lay low' for several years, and I have to say that part of the years which I spent to no purpose was some of the most enjoyable time I have had. And the years were not wholly lost either. If it should appear as the people at the hospital have predicted, that you will have to lie low for two or three years, I venture that you will scarcely regret it in the end. 'There's night and day, brother, both sweet things; there's likewise a wind on the heath. Life is very sweet, brother; who would wish to die?' "

The bright lady was naturally curious about those missing years. Shortly after, Veblen wrote her again: After concluding a recital of various matters with " 'Ther nyr no more to tel,' " he said "you ask what I did during my years off. That is precisely the point. I did nothing and as I like that sort of thing I enjoyed it; and enjoyment and profit are pretty nearly synonymous with me. I wish you a Merry Christmas, and I wish you had a sufficiently indolent temperament to let go as cordially as you ought to. May I add that I wish I could help you do it! For I can do that sort of thing well."[329a]

[329a] Veblen to Sarah McLean Hardy, October 28, December 15, 1895.

Veblen was equally skilled in writing recommendations for students. The following written while he was at Chicago is a sample:

V

ON THE APPENDIX MATERIAL

In the Appendix below will be found some striking obituaries and reviews of his books. Also, there is included the list of 214 of the most distinguished names in the economics profession that were on the petition to the nominating committee of the American Economic Association in the fall of 1925 requesting that Veblen be given the nomination to the office of the presidency.[330] We now have information which supplements that given in the Veblen book on this dramatic episode. The chief promoter of the petition, as I had noted, was Paul H. Douglas, then at the University of Chicago (later United States Senator from Illinois).

Earlier in the summer Douglas had asked Veblen to become a candidate. Veblen replied: "I still find myself constrained to avoid it. . . . I still find that neither is the office

[330] Veblen had heretofore held one office in the association – membership (1894-1906) on the Council (now defunct) during his Chicago period.

May 23, 1899

George A. McFarland,
Principal, North Dakota State Normal School

Dear Sir,–

Mr. A. B. Maynard, who is an applicant for work in your school, has done a very satisfactory year's work as student in the classes conducted by me – in History of Political Economy, Scope and Method of Political Economy, and Economic Factors in Civilization.

He shows excellent capacity as a student, good scholarship and a broad preliminary training.

Through my acquaintance with Mr. Maynard outside of his work as a student, I can say that he is a man of unexceptionable character and habits of life, and that, he is painstaking and hard-headed. He should make an excellent disciplinarian and I am confident that he would be a very fortunate choice for the class of work that you require.

Yours very truly,
Th. B. Veblen

to my task nor am I possessed of the qualifications which the office should require. To my mind, the office should be filled by the younger men, who are in touch with what is doing and are looking to get something done in the common interest. Whereas I have neither the requisite interest nor the requisite familiarity with the Association's aims and affairs."[331] Douglas, however, doggedly persisted in collecting signatures to the petition.

The list included exponents of practically every type of economic theory: Henry L. Moore and his disciple, Henry Schultz, in the fields of mathematical economics and econometrics; the monetary expert and student of Vilfredo Pareto, James Harvey Rogers[332]; John R. Commons and his disciple, Selig Perlman, another major figure in the development of labor theory and history. There was also John Cummings, then at the Federal Reserve Board, who had changed his mind about Veblen since his thirty page drastic attack on *The Theory of the Leisure Class* in 1900. Also on the list was the name of the reader for Macmillan who had rejected the preliminary version of *The Theory of Business Enterprise.* The names of eleven future presidents were among the signatories: Morris A. Copeland, Paul H. Douglas, Edwin F. Gay, E. A. Goldenweiser, Alvin H. Hansen, Frank H. Knight, Frederick C. Mills, E. G. Nourse, Sumner H. Slichter, Jacob Viner and A. B. Wolfe. Some leading economists, who approved of nominating Veblen but for various reasons preferred not to sign the petition, wrote letters instead to members of the committee.

---

[331] Veblen to Douglas, July 27, 1925; copy in possession of Joseph Dorfman.

[332] As indicated in the Veblen book, Rogers and Douglas had been the minority of two of the nominating committee of the previous year which had supported Veblen for the nomination. The nomination went to Allyn A. Young, who was elected.

Among these was H. G. Brown of the University of Missouri, who had collaborated with Irving Fisher on the famous *Purchasing Power of Money*. Addressing his letter to J. M. Clark, he declared: "So far as I am aware, no academic American economist of equal years and distinction, has ever failed of election to that office and a considerable number have been chosen whose distinction is far less. But there is another aspect of the problem, to which I believe attention should be directed; viz., the growth of the feeling, in the minds of many members, that the system of election throws control into the hands of an 'Old Guard' and that, under the circumstances, there is no chance of ever electing as president a person, no matter how distinguished for scholarship, of such radical proclivities as Veblen. It seems to me that the election of Veblen should do something to hearten those members who believe that scholarly contributions of importance should bring no less honor to radicals than to conservatives."[333]

Douglas, in presenting the petition to the chairman of the nominating committee, Professor E. R. A. Seligman, wrote: "Our desire that the Association should honor itself by the nomination of Mr. Veblen springs from the belief that Veblen had after all been one of the small handful of American economists who have made substantial contributions to economic thought. I am sure that it would not be a happy situation for Mr. Veblen to die, and for the Economic Association to have to face the question as to why he had not been recognized by it during his lifetime."[334]

There was opposition, to be sure, to offering the nomination to Veblen; Mitchell, after reading over the comments

[333] Brown to J. M. Clark, September 24, 1925; copy in possession of Joseph Dorfman.

[334] Douglas to E. R. A. Seligman, October 3, 1925; in the possession of Joseph Dorfman.

of opponents, informed Seligman that "of course a number of people will oppose his candidacy, and that for reasons which are as much mixed and as little realized in consciousness as most human motives. The petition should at least help you and your committee to find out whether there is a strong feeling among our members that Veblen should be elected."[335]

The committee was duly impressed by the quality of the signatories, especially, as one put it, by the fact that there were at least a dozen who in the ordinary course of events could be expected to occupy that office. Seligman then on behalf of the committee offered the nomination to Veblen, which was tantamount to the election. At the same time, (December 5) Douglas made a deeply emotional appeal to Veblen to accept the nomination.

> Members of the Nominating Committee have told me of their desire that you serve as President during the ensuing year and I am taking the liberty of writing to add my own personal word of hope that you will serve. There are quite literally hundreds of members of the Association who would be grievously disappointed and hurt were you to refuse. The general desire on the part of so many diverse groups within the Association that you serve became clearly manifest to me this spring and summer. From all parts of the country men wrote of how they wanted you to be the next President of the Association and of their desire to help. Seeing this as I did,

---

[335] Mitchell to Seligman, June 15, 1925; in possession of Joseph Dorfman.

An amusing objection was that Veblen was not a member of the Association. President Young, however, reported that "I am advised by Mr. Harriman, our counsel, that there is nothing in our form of organization that prevents us from electing an outsider as president if we so desire." (Young to Seligman, December 10, 1925; letter in possession of Joseph Dorfman).

I am sure of what I say, when I write that a refusal would grievously chill and disappoint many. Your acceptance, on the other hand, would make the vast majority of the Association very happy and that I hope will appeal to you, even though acceptance might mean some physical discomfort and rearrangement of plans.

It is our earnest hope that you will accept the presidency.

Faithfully yours,
Paul H. Douglas[336]

As I noted in the Veblen book, Veblen declined in his usual, courteous manner, but we now have some additional information largely that goes beyond his attribution of his

---

[336] Douglas to Veblen, December 5, 1925, Thorstein Veblen Papers.

Douglas's recollections of his own meeting with Veblen adumbrate the views of others. "I was struck with the extraordinary difference between his speech and his writing. His writing, as you know, was highly complicated and polysyllabic, while his speech was simple and lucid. I came to the conclusion after an evening's conversation with him that his style was, as many of us suspected, something of an affectation and therefore a more or less conscious effort at artistry. I have a number of amusing stories about Veblen which illustrate his ironic impersonality. Thus one day he met a friend of mine, Professor Martin Schütze, on the street after not having seen him for over twenty years. They had formerly been close and intimate friends but Veblen's only remark was after looking at Schütze to say, 'Your thatch is getting frosted too.' He then passed on without another word. There was almost an inhuman element of impersonality and aloofness to what he did which was probably in part the result of the great personal unhappiness which he had had in life and which led him to adopt this attitude as a protection against the buffets of the world. There was something, however, natively aloof in his whole attitude towards life." (Douglas to Dorfman, October 3, 1931).

Professor Schütze had written me a slightly different version of his encounter story while I was working on the Veblen book. Veblen and Schütze had not seen each other for a few years when they met in Chicago in 1926. "What Veblen did and said was this: He looked under the brim of my hat and drawled: 'Well, they have bleached you a bit, too!'"

action to ill health.[337] For one thing, the offer seemed to provide no solution for his problems, including what he conceived to be financial insecurity. He was hoping against hope that his projects for a study in Britain on her imperialism and/or a visit to the Soviet Union would materialize. In desperation he even expressed the desire to return to teaching in October 1925, but at his age of 68 there proved to be little prospect.[338] Hobson recalled that he met Veblen for the last time that year in Washington – "a beaten man." He began to realize that there was no longer much interest in him and his work. This was evidenced in the course of a sister-in-law's attempt in 1928 to obtain information for a projected biography from other members of the family. He wrote brother Andrew: "There is no probability of her getting anything printed. Possibly she might have got into print about me a few years ago; but that is all past now, and I have gone off the program of news."[339]

---

[337] His health was not of the best, or so it seemed. A former Chicago student, H. Parker Willis, a major architect of the Federal Reserve System, recalled that at about that time he met Veblen on the New York subway "and thinking that he looked very pale and feeble I urged him to come to my home and spend a little vacation there, letting Mrs. Willis make things a little more comfortable for him than perhaps they were in New York at the time. This I might not have suggested had it not been that in former years he had made visits to my home in this way and had always expressed the thought that they did him good and were helpful to him. . . . I always thought highly of his workmanship and his unusual traits of character." (Willis to Joseph Dorfman, February 25, 1935).

[338] From the Mitchell Diary: October 1, 1925, "Miss Mildred Bennett tells of V's desire to return to teaching"; October 4, 1925, "see Alvin Johnson about V. returning to New School. Wrote to Miss Bennett"; February 10, 1926, "[William] Camp has reported that Veblen has gone to Chicago [and then he went to California]."

[339] Thorstein Veblen to Andrew Veblen in the fall of 1928, quoted by Andrew Veblen in letter to "Dear Sisters" – Emily, Mary and Hannah, April 9, 1931, in Andrew Veblen Papers.

VI

ON THE INFLUENCE OF VEBLEN SINCE THE VEBLEN BOOK

Let me conclude with a brief running account of Veblen's influence since I published the Veblen book in 1934. As I noted there, with the outbreak of the Great Depression

---

Characteristically Veblen went on to say "and by the way it is not quite true that I consented to her asking or getting any material you may have, unless 'silence gives consent.' She asked me and I neglected to answer the question, though I did not refuse leave to write about me. She had a sort of claim on my good will just then, in that she (or her sister) had just paid up the mortgage which I held on her house in full, and it would make no difference anyway. Also I don't see there is anything to write about."

A step-daughter declared in 1932: "He told me that it was impossible for biography to be true – psychologically speaking, I presume – and only exceptionally could autobiography as such be of more account." (Becky Veblen to B. W. Huebsch, July 1932, quoted in letter from Marshall A. Best of The Viking Press to Joseph Dorfman, July 18, 1932).

I might add that I had begun collecting materials for the Veblen book. Professor Mitchell was helping me to get to knowledgeable members of the family. He sent the following letters to Veblen's sister Emily and to his nephew:

New York City
December 22, 1926

My Dear Mrs. Olsen,

I believe that you have already had some correspondence with Mr. Joe Dorfman, who is seeking to collect materials for a biography of Dr. Thorstein Veblen. The purpose of this note is merely to say that I think Mr. Dorfman is a man whom you can safely trust. His purpose in writing about Dr. Veblen is, I believe, to give as fair and accurate a picture of a most remarkable man as he can. I think Dorfman is remarkably free from distorting prejudices. I do not think that he will lean towards sensationalism; but of course his success will depend upon the accuracy of the materials he collects.

To my way of thinking, Dr. Veblen is the most significant figure of his generation in the whole round of the social sciences. As we come to see more clearly that the most important thing in human history is what happens in the realm of mind, we shall appreciate more and

shortly after his death in August 1929,[340] the splash of Technocracy in 1932 and the coming of the New Deal, Veblen's star began to rise once more. As a lawyer-economist commented in 1933, "If Technocracy did nothing else in its short life, it dramatized the persistent recurrence and vitality of the social and economic analyses of Thorstein Veblen. Twelve years ago [in *The Engineers and the Price System*] Veblen pointed out the dominant factor of a developing

---

more the significance of his scientific labors. There is, therefore, strong reason why a clear and honest picture of the man should be drawn for the general public.

Yours faithfully,
Wesley C. Mitchell

New York
January 6, 1926

Dear Veblen,

Mr. Joe Dorfman tells me that he has had some talk with you about his efforts to secure materials concerning the life of Thorstein Veblen and that you would like to know something about him.

I have known Dorfman for some two years. He came to Columbia from one of the Oregon colleges and made his mark at once as an uncommonly original student. Later I found that he was deeply interested in the development of your uncle's ideas. Of course that is a subject which has interested me ever since our Chicago days. Some competent person ought to give us an objective account of his life.

Dorfman seems to me well qualified for the task, not only by his keen interest and his industry in collecting materials, but also by his intelligence. I am confident that he is candid and scientific in his attitude toward the subject. He will, I think, respect any confidences that are reposed in him.

If you can help him in any way, directly or indirectly, you will, I think, feel yourself justified by what he produces.

With kind regards

Yours faithfully,
Wesley C. Mitchell

Professor Oswald Veblen
Princeton University
Princeton, New Jersey

340 Obituaries by Mitchell and J. M. Clark are reprinted below in the Appendix.

technology in modern life; and even the somewhat hasty exploitation of that analysis applied to the current depression seemingly does not prevent its constant recurrence in sounder economic discussion."[341]

The reviewer, Norman L. Meyers went on to say: "And it is not mere coincidence that at this time in *The Modern Corporation and Private Property,* his [Veblen's] theory of *Absentee Ownership and Business Enterprise in Recent Times* (1923) is elaborated by a statistical but scholarly, and nevertheless practical study of the two hundred largest non-banking corporations in the United States. . . . It demonstrates in detail, and as a matter of cold fact, Veblen's theories concerning the separation and degradation of the investors' stake in an enterprise, historically dubbed 'ownership,' from the 'control' of the business enterprise; and presents a lucid analysis of the legal devices whereby 'control' has been shifted to minority groups or to the 'management.' The first half of the title of this book amply deals with the first half of the title of Veblen's; the book proves concretely what has been obvious for a decade to the hitherto submerged economists familiar with Veblen." He went on to add another Supreme Court Judge to the list of four who reflected the climate of opinion that Veblen had done so much to create.

"In a recent dissenting opinion, Mr. Justice [later Chief Justice] Stone has begun the process of creating a majority recognition of the legal significance of this part of the [Berle and Means] book." Meyers in a footnote quoted from the opinion which cited the book: " 'Extension of corporate activities, distribution of corporate personnel, stockholders and

[341] Norman L. Meyers, review of A. A. Berle and Gardiner Means, *The Modern Corporation and Private Property,* in *Yale Law Journal,* April 1933, p. 997. Meyers had been editor of the *Yale Law Journal* 1930-1931, and was then associate attorney of the Federal Power Commission.

directors through many states, and the diffusion of corporate ownership, separated from the corporate management, make the integrity of the conduct of large business corporations increasingly a matter of national rather than local concern to which the Federal courts should be quick to respond when their jurisdiction is rightly invoked.' *Rogers v. Guaranty Trust Co.*, October term, 1932, decision handed down on January 23, 1933 (involving protest against over allotment of securities to management and employees of American Tobacco Co.)." Then Meyers began to point out some deficiencies of the study: "However, regarding 'Private Property' in the large scale 'Business Enterprise' there are many generalizations in the [Berle and Means] book which challenge attention, in the light either of Veblen's analysis or of the experience of the past few years." In the light of the difficulties of the giant corporations in the depression, he questioned, for example, the authors' prediction as of January 1, 1930, of constantly ever growing size, of "even super-giant corporations the size of the combined two hundred under observation."

On this point, Meyers commented: "the prediction is strongly reminiscent of the sanguine but comparatively inept Marxian prophecy of the concentration of wealth into a few hands before *Der Tag*. . . . The explanation of the weakness of these giant corporations – and others not so gigantic – must include consideration of the nature of business enterprise. Veblen's dichotomy of business and industry, of the pecuniary institution and the industrial appliance should not have been overlooked when predictions of the future were made. After the zoom of the recent stock jobbing to enlarge the pecuniary institution, we are now made sadly aware of the resulting problems of industrial management, of the mastering of irrepressible new technological advances, of the domestication of the exuberant and troublesome machine. Events since January 1, 1930, indicate the existence of centrifugal as well as centripetal forces affecting the aggregations of wealth."

Meyers went on to question the omission of banking institutions from the study. He contended that "a casual reading of Veblen or an eye on the passing scene, even that of 1929, would have gained recognition for the part the larger use of credit plays in the Modern Corporation. A tardy revival of interest in the Pujo Committee findings and in Brandeis' *Other People's Money* indicates that the authors were not alone lulled by the glow of the era of Banking Statesmanship. However, it would seem that the rigor of the logic of their thesis would compel a further isolation of 'control' by tracing the dictates of the credit institutions on to the boards of directors. Even a 'minority' on a board of directors may 'control.' Senator Norris' recent attack indicated the intricacy of the mesh of directors of banking institutions and the directorates of these large corporations. The demand for consideration of the part the banks play in the 'control' of corporations, along with the 'minority control,' and the 'management,' is not unwarranted. . . ."

Meyers then raised grave doubts whether the so-called controlling group in a large corporation actually controls from the standpoint of industrial efficiency. "The authors define 'control' as the power to elect the majority of a board of directors. But what actual control does a board of directors exercise in a modern corporation? It would be a matter of superhuman intelligence and ability for the small number of men who served as interlocking directorates of these two hundred corporations to control them according to the theory of the functions of directorship. At best they now juggle with balance sheets and financial reports; technical problems, labor policy and industrial detail are given but summary concern. The recent revelations in the more pathological cases – the Krueger and Toll kingdom, the Insull empire, the Bank of the United States bailiwick, and the less notorious principalities such as the Gillette merger – give ample evidence of the lack of full control, even knowledge, by directors; not as a matter of legal theory perhaps, but certainly as an actuality. The same and other cases of common report likewise absolve 'management' from full control, and even knowledge. A literal acceptance of the authors' concept of control would compel the conclusion that the Modern Corporation was anarchic even before 1929. . . . Above all, an analysis of 'control' must recognize the concomitant power of organized society with that of the board of directors. . . . The State has not yet surrendered supremacy to the Corporations."

Drawing on *The Engineers and the Price System* again, he wrote "technological advances attack the price system and threaten to raise the Engineer to a position of power equal to that of the financial status of the directors of credit or the politico-social status of the State." Drawing on "The Place of Science in Modern Civilisation," he concluded that "Science has become a matter of major business concern." (pp. 997-999, 1000).

I have pointed out in the Veblen book the claims that his writings exercised a key influence on the New Deal.[341a] Here let me add that occasionally he was referred to with approval even in conservative quarters which sharply opposed the New Deal. A writer in the *New Outlook* in early 1934 com-

[341a] It might be noted that a good number of recruits were from the University of California, where "Veblen was still being read with attention." [John Kenneth Galbraith, "Berkeley in the Thirties," 1969; reprinted in his *Economics, Peace and Laughter* (Houghton Mifflin, 1971) p. 378].

plained that various measures restricted production and consumption and he attributed them to the misapplication of "economic talent with its gift for formula-making"; that is, to "the neo-economists"; to use his terminology, "Thorstein Veblen pointed out some time ago how business sabotages industry. Examining the ruling economic formulas, it is easy to see how they sabotage society."[342]

The appearance in 1934 of the posthumous collection of published articles, *Essays in Our Changing Order,* brought forth an overwhelming preponderance of reviews that carried the note that Veblen was "a thinker whose thoughts echo and react all around us today."[342a]

The respectable *Review of Reviews* (October 1934) under the title "Veblen's Joke," commented that "it is one of the prize ironies of existence that the ideas of Thorstein Veblen, which reaped for him a harvest of abuse in his own day, should now exercise so much influence upon current economic thought. Veblen would have appreciated the joke. It is unfortunate that he did not live beyond August, 1929." *The Science Newsletter* (October 20, 1934) added that "Veblen is recognized as one of the pioneer minds in our present day analysis of the impact of science and engineering upon civilization." Under the title "Veblen Speaks Again,"

---

[342] Cedric Fowler, "Twilight of the Economists," *New Outlook,* March 1934, p. 16. The editor-in-chief was former New York Governor Alfred E. Smith.

[342a] The quotation is from Ray Redman's department of book notes, "Old Wine in New Bottles," in the New York *Herald Tribune,* October 25, 1934. The occasion was the appearance of the inexpensive (95¢) Random House Modern Library edition of *The Theory of the Leisure Class,* under license from The Viking Press. This edition up to 1971 sold 134,000 copies. Redman urbanely called attention to the previous relative obscurity of Veblen by casually commenting that the book "was noticed in this department back in 1926." This was when Vanguard Press issued under license from Viking a 50¢ edition.

The Christian Century (January 2, 1935, p. 17) wrote "When Thorstein Veblen died in August 1929, there passed from the American scene one of the best informed of our economists, and one of the most profound thinkers of the immediate past generation. . . . Veblen wrote numerous books, articles and editorials, and taught at several universities under varying degrees of tolerance. He was, despite these activities, a lonesome and obscure man. Driven from pillar to post . . . he was accorded scant recognition by the academic world . . . and was forced to carry on his activities with but little benefit of institutional sponsorship. His philosophy was forged in the crucible of social and intellectual conflict, and he paid the penalty of being a prophet. Had he lived but a few months longer he would have witnessed the first definite fulfillment of his predictions; and were he alive today, he would undoubtedly find himself reinstated in the academic world and acclaimed as a great leader by many of those who shunned him years ago.

"Since 1929 Veblen's influence has grown steadily. Many able critics . . . , and even members of the President's brain trust, have acknowledged their debt to him. It is therefore not only fitting, but highly important that his writings be made accessible to every student of contemporary affairs. They have value, not only as a background against which present day radicalism can be understood, but as an analysis valid and applicable in its own right. . . ." His major weakness was: "he could analyze but could not prescribe. . . ."[342b]

[342b] A Chicago student in Veblen's course on Trust Finance informed me: "I frequently asked this question, 'What do you recommend that we shall do about it?' Mr. Veblen's whimsical answer was along this line, 'Mr. Fleming is not satisfied with the question implied in the philosopher's statement "I want to know," Mr. Fleming wants to do something about it.' Then with the laugh evoked by this comment, he would let it go at that." (Fleming to Dorfman, October 3, 1932).

The New York *Herald-Tribune* reviewer cited as evidence of Veblen's current role as a living voice that "his translation [in a *Dial* essay] of *panem et circenses* as 'the breadlines and the movies' carries more force in the present year of our disgrace than when he coined it fifteen years ago." There were of course some attacks reminiscent of the first reception of *The Theory of the Leisure Class.* As is generally known by now, the essay, "The Economic Theory of Woman's Dress," is an important forerunner of *The Theory of the Leisure Class.* One horrified reviewer of the *Essays in our Changing Order* (*The American Spectator,* November 1934) commented that "the prize of this collection is the theory of why women dress as they do, which succeeds in omitting entirely the element of sexual ornament and attraction!"

The reviewer in *The Review of Reviews* also used the essay but saw it as an illustration of the fact that it shows that for Veblen, "Nothing is beyond investigation. For example, ladies might well squirm when he noted many similarities in the dress of modern women and the regalia of tribal wives in the Congo."

Reviews of *Thorstein Veblen and His America* the following year indicated some of the sources of his enduring quality. The first that I shall discuss is an unpublished one by Hans Otto Storm, an engineer and a writer of novels and prose about Spanish America.[343] "He had been a close neighbor and reader of Thorstein Veblen. The engineer whose ways projected into writing had read not only *The Theory of the Leisure Class* and *The Engineers and the Price System* but practically everything else by the writer whose mind

---

[343] Storm wrote Joseph Dorfman, January 30, 1935 that the review "died a natural death for want of any publication connection." Storm's executor, David Greenhood, kindly gave me the ms. in 1948.

reached over into engineering."[344] Storm wrote in the ms. of the romance of "the man who invented a special style of writing, faintly suggestive of the great geographers in its impressive unornateness and stolidity in front of new discoveries, but refined and yet again refined and pared until it lay hard against the bare rock and resisted by virtue of the hardness of the rock itself. And how that style, forged in intense sincerity to call attention to ironic facts, grew to be famous as amusing satire, and how the facts year by year became more ironic and were still accepted, while his description of them, labelled irony, was stored in the literary archives. . . . The hammer in Veblen's bag of tools . . . was the bringing into economic writing of the rules of good poetics – the deep seated art of prose scansion together with a wide vocabulary in which every word is understood not only in its immediately purposeful meaning, but with all its nimba of picturesqueness, background and suggestion: Compare, for instance, the long argument about university architecture in [Upton] Sinclair's *Goose Step* with Veblen's single phrase [in *The Theory of the Leisure Class*] –'better adapted to the mustering of a company of unruly men-at-arms.' . . . [M]any important thinkers in the field have been bad writers, and there have been those who thought an unpoetic cast of writing necessary to sincerity. The trick of the business, which they did not understand, was to clean poetics of its parasites, unconscious emotion, sentiment, naiveté. 'Silent

---

[344] David Greenhood, "Introduction," to Storm, *Of Good Family, Stories and Observations of Spanish America,* collected and edited by David Greenhood (New York: Swallow Press and William Morrow, 1948) p. vii. In "Biographical Note and Writings," at the close of the above volume, Greenhood writes that Storm was "killed, December 11, 1941, by electrical shock while rushing to completion a large radio transmitter for the Army, in laboratory of Globe Wireless, San Francisco, where he was chief engineer." (p. 307).

upon a peak in Darien' is good poetics, but one must remember that it was Balboa. . . .

"[Veblen's] circumlocutions are like those of a rabbit who, fleeing a dog, suddenly runs under a barbed wire fence. . . . [T]he structure of most of the now-quoted Veblenisms . . . consists of the use of words and phrases in their exact dictionary meaning but with their connotations – those situations under which it is felt appropriate to use them – deliberately perverted from the usual. Thus: force and fraud (illegal connotation to legal), idle curiosity (derogatory to commending), businesslike (like business, but with a second thought as to what business is really like). The effect in each case is the highly economical one of using a single word (or, since the word is already in efficient ordinary use, one might say the watered stock capitalized on a single word) to shake our apprehension loose from frozen usages, undo the harm done by word-habits, and make us re-examine the matter in the light of what actually exists.

"Last, the repeated use of certain words: usufruct, ubiquitous, ulterior (there seems to be a detectible U-complex), quasi, subsume, honorific, pecuniary, by and large, vicarious – in an amount out of proportion to what is to be expected, so that these words become in a sense identified with Veblen. This is the least defensible from any logical poetic standpoint; it is also manifestly underhanded, inasmuch as these hitherto perfectly good words become, except with reference to Veblen, 'killed' for any other writer.[344a] The device will,

[344a] This is what happened to the term "vested interests," which had a respectable meaning before Veblen got through with it. Now it has in common discourse a deprecatory one. Thus when C. Jackson Grayson was asked why President Nixon had appointed him chairman of the recently established Price Board, the reply was "I suppose . . . they appointed me because I had no vested interests, no big business contacts, no political affiliations." (Quoted in Flora Lewis, "Is Inflation a Psychosomatic Illness?" The New York *Times*, January 30, 1972).

also, in so much as Veblen becomes a cult, tend to prevent just that re-examination of theses which he most desired. And yet it must be admitted that these repetitions have a value. J. Walter Thompson [the advertising firm] and the Holy Church have gone into the use of key-words, and they work. And while we do not exactly bow and cross ourselves at the hearing of the word ubiquitous, it acts to remind us where we are. Through nine volumes and a list of shorter papers these key-words serve a cumulative, concatenating function, they act as milestones on a path which, ranging through wide fields, is nevertheless remarkably straight and deep – a mood which presses continually for the elimination of magic from social thought and action." In a letter to Joseph Dorfman of December 2, 1932, Storm had summarized a good deal of his argument: "[I]f by irony we mean the presentation of inappropriate relationships without indignation, the facts themselves are often sufficiently ironic. The failure of the critics to understand this was to an extent the cause of Veblen's defeat with the public – his appreciators are divided into two schools, one artistic and the other economic. That a work may be ironic – even artistic – and yet theoretically sound, seems to have occurred to very few."[345]

[345] It might be noted here that this view had been suggested in 1927 by a young Columbia college instructor in philosophy in connection with *The Theory of the Leisure Class*. He wrote that "the book, in addition to being a penetrating economic study, is also a great satire." [John Storck, *Man and Civilization: An Inquiry into the Bases*

Perhaps for the economist the most famous example is in the most quoted passage of Keynes's *The General Theory of Employment Interest and Money:* "Practical men, who believe themselves to be quite exempt from any intellectual influence, are usually the slaves of some defunct economist. Madmen in authority who hear voices in the air, are distilling their frenzy from some academic scribbler of a few years back. I am sure that the power of vested interests is vastly exaggerated compared with the gradual encroachment of ideas." (p. 383).

Another review, which saluted Veblen as "one of the most independent minds in modern thought," is by a Norwegian social scientist, H. O. Christophersen.[346] Christophersen, viewing Veblen as "that visitor from another world" went on to maintain that "like the Stranger in Ibsen's drama, he was a disturber of the peace who confronted the average man with the necessity of making a qualitative choice. Veblen has therefore been a thorn in the flesh to Americans and no doubt he would have been to us had he lived in Norway – but with this difference, that here a *few* would have understood him. Among us, moreover, his mind would have widened its scope; in America his rich philosophical genius was harnessed to a necessarily limited specialization and was too strictly judged by standards peculiar only to the subject matter.

"As an ironical commentator, Veblen was a synthesis of Kierkegaard and Vinje, born and reared on American soil. Such a characterization describes both the range and depth of his genius. To make the picture complete, we must conceive of this irony in the service of a specialized science, economic theory, expressed in a dazzling form quite overwhelming to the matter-of-fact scholar.

"We in Norway have never had a social critic of scholarly

[346] The review was published in the Oslo newspaper, *Aftenpostens*, July 10, 1935, under the title "A Norwegian-American Scholar – Thorstein Veblen."

---

of Contemporary Life (New York: Harcourt, Brace, 3rd rev. ed., 1927) p. 323]. He felt that the book provided for his purposes "a classic description of the most important standard of living in our own culture." (p. 289). He used *The Theory of Business Enterprise* to emphasize one major characteristic of "our complex industrial civilization; namely, the high degree of mechanization." (p. 299).

Lewis Mumford recently generalized the proposition beyond *The Theory of the Leisure Class* by recalling that Geddes and Branford "were the first to appreciate Veblen as both economist and satirist in England." (Mumford to Dorfman, July 26, 1971).

dimensions. The social iconoclast as we know him has always been an artistic phenomenon and has as a consequence been more frequently appreciated as a stimulating entertainer. For that reason we cannot help asking ourselves what effect a mind like Veblen's would have had upon our milieu. Though speculations about such matters are vain, it would doubtless be correct to say that he would have filled a lacuna in our intellectual life, a void which must someday be filled. In the long run it will be our loss never to have a social critic of Veblen's cast, a satirist who will force us to the objective statement of those ideas which have hitherto been given no more serious expression than the tinkle of artistically-minted small change.

"In Norway we find ourselves far behind the rest of the civilized world, in some respects at about the level of Spain. To illustrate this point, we may divide intellectual history into an age of fantasy and an age of science. We seem to be standing well within this first epoch, and that fact no doubt explains our luminous literary production when the rest of the world was famished for creative effort. Though our superabundant literary culture flatters our national vanity, it is a question if the greater part of our modern literature will not be quite useless in that world which is in birth. No race capable of development can remain satisfied with a cultural life, however highly elaborated, based upon the products of its fantasy and analogous to the rentier's life of leisure in the economic system. If we wish to keep step with the world, we must do as others do and institute a scientific cartography of those realities by which our emotional life is formed – and for such labors only a spirit like Thorstein Veblen's can be our pathfinder. Someone must blaze the trail through the wilderness and he must be a genius. After him will come workmen. It is indeed a comfort to know that our seed once produced such a spirit – but we must remember it required the stimulation of a foreign milieu to mature it."

The able translator of Christophersen's review into English, Clifford T. Haga, of the University of Minnesota, also provided his own account. "Veblen, Minnesota-reared son of Norwegian immigrants, was a scholar, economist, sociologist, – even prophet – who wrote for scholars but came to be read by all manner of men. . . . Veblen knew science, used it, wrote it and criticized it, neither wooing it with symbols nor surrendering to it with that yearning with which divers less well-balanced minds seek some neat, vest-pocket panacea."[347]

The regular daily reviewer of the New York *Times* chose the occasion to discuss Veblen's wide influence. Even Yale, he humorously noted, had succumbed. "Suffice it to say, his influence is abroad at New Haven at this moment with Walton Hamilton and others as its guardians . . ."[348]

A granddaughter of John Bates Clark recalled as had her uncle in his obituary, that "It was due to the help of John Bates Clark, who recognized in Veblen a first rate intelligence, that this unruly student, who delivered abstruse and devastating lectures on subjects now learned, now ridicu-

---

[347] Haga, "Now Here's a Book," The Minnesota *TechnoLog*, March 1935.

[348] John Chamberlain, the New York *Times*, November 27, 1934.

Mencken in a way expressed his second thoughts on Veblen in a letter on my book addressed to the publisher, Ben Huebsch.

November 27, 1934

My dear Ben,

I have just finished Dorfman's book on Veblen. It seems to me to be a capital piece of work. Dorfman shows a kind of impartiality that is immensely rare in this world. I am glad that he undertook the heavy labor of summarizing Veblen's books. Ranged in their historical order and related to their sources, they take on a new interest. Who is Dorfman? He seems to be a very competent fellow.

Sincerely yours,
H. L. Mencken

lous, was permitted to remain at Carleton. I had heard this story as a child. My next introduction to Veblen was in Europe, where I discovered that Swiss, French, Scandinavian and German students of economics and sociology considered him one of the greatest thinkers of the time. To them his work was the American contribution to social science."[349]

That organ for business executives, *Fortune*, in 1935, in a note accompanied by a familiar picture of Veblen declared: "no economist has come into such sudden, serious fame through the deep depression as Thorstein Veblen, who died in 1929. In 1932 Technocrats quoted him – and his discussions of technological advance – into a garbled notoriety." It went on to say that "in his first book . . . *The Theory of the Leisure Class* . . . and later works, he posed questions, gave searching analyses, but few answers. Prophetic were his

---

[349] Eunice Clark, review of *Thorstein Veblen and his America* in *Common Sense,* January 1935, p. 26.

It was also noted in another review "that French scholars have for some time looked upon Veblen as America's outstanding social scientist." (J. F. Balzer, "Thorstein Veblen and His America," Northfield, Minnesota *News,* June 7, 1935).

Professor Balzer informed me that his Carleton College colleague Professor Boodin wrote him: "I was talking with Marcelle Mauss, Durkheim's successor at the University of Paris, in 1921 about American sociologists, and as I remember the conversation he said that Thorstein Veblen is the only one of consequence. He spoke in terms of high praise of Veblen's 'The Leisure Class'." (Quoted in letter from Balzer to Dorfman, August 23, 1935).

For the most recent French discussions on Veblen's economics see André Marchal (professor of political economy, University of Paris), *Méthode scientifique et science économique,* volume I (Paris: Génin, 1959) pp. 139-144, 167, 168, 169, 170, 240, 249; and Annie Vinokur (of the University of Nancy), *Thorstein Veblen et la Tradition dissidente dans la pensée économique Américain* (1969). For the Italian literature, see *Bibliografia* in Mino Vianello, *Thorstein Veblen* (Milano: Edizioni di Communitá, 1961) pp. 393-400. Benedetto Croce reviewed the first Italian translation of a Veblen book – *The Theory of the Leisure Class* – in *Il Nuovo Corriere della Sera,* 15 Gennaio, 1949.

discussions of the troubles of absentee ownership of industry, of the fundamental clash between business (making money) and industry (making products), of the trouble the engineer could have and could cause in unplanned society."[350]

The general view was expressed by Irving Dillard, the editorial writer of the influential St. Louis *Post-Dispatch* (later at Princeton University). On the appearance of the Veblen book, after expressing pride in the University of Missouri for having offered a haven to Veblen, he went on to note his prophetic spirit. After recalling that he "died in his retreat among the California coast hills as recently as 1929 – on the eve of the collapse," he declared "As an evolutionary philosopher this roving son of the Wisconsin frontier ranged over a wide intellectual field, his interests embracing anthropology, philosophy, history, ethnology, philology, science and engineering as well as economics and sociology. . . . [H]e was . . . a thinker who saw and wrote ahead of his time."[351]

Adding to the interest in Veblen's work was the appearance in 1936 of the long delayed "Veblen reader" titled *What Veblen Taught*. Mitchell not only made the selections but also supplied a 10,000 word introduction which had the advantage of suggestions from Mrs. Warren Gregory.[352]

---

350 "Faces of the Month," *Fortune*, February 1935.

351 "Veblen Seven Years After His Death," St. Louis *Post-Dispatch*, March 9, 1936.

352 The volume had been commissioned by Scribner's and prepared shortly before Veblen's death in 1929. The delay in publication was caused largely by the occurrence of the depression and the fact that all the selections but one (from Scribner's) would come from Viking publications. After Mitchell turned in the introduction and selections, he heard nothing more from the prospective publisher. Shortly after the Veblen book was published by The Viking Press, I took up the matter with Huebsch, and he arranged with Scribner's that his firm become the publisher, pay Mitchell's fee of $250, and have the right to publish the selection from *The Theory of Business Enterprise*. Mitchell sent me the revision of his introduction for comment, as he

Hobson, in a review article, after complimenting Mitchell for performing "with remarkable success the difficult task of interpreting the thought and writings of Thorstein Veblen, one of the few original thinkers of his age in the field of sociology and economics," reiterated that Veblen's "great discovery was the new phase of capitalism by which the supreme powers and profit were passing from the owners of the material forms of capital unto the owners, or, more properly, the operators, of finance. . . . It . . . involved large immediate creations of credit instruments only fashioned by financiers." And here he quoted from *Absentee Ownership* (p. 338). "The holding-company and the merger, together with the interlocking directorates, and presently the voting trust, were the ways and means by which the banking community took over the strategic regulation of the key industries, and by way of that avenue also the control of the industrial system at large." He went on to say, "This financial control was visualized by Veblen as involving a policy of 'industrial sabotage' . . . in order to keep prices and profits higher."[353]

[353] "The Economics of Thorstein Veblen," *Political Science Quarterly,* March 1937, pp. 139, 141-142. In his book on Veblen a year

had the first version. Among other things I said: "V's practice differed from the 'orthodox' in that the validity of his conclusions is to be determined within the realm of fact, including statistical data." Mitchell wrote in the margin of my comments: "Good point. I have adopted it." On a related matter, I had commented that "V's conclusions are just the sort that have meaning in any attempt to test statistically the problems of economic life. Your presidential address [before the American Economic Association, 1924] was clear on this point. V's conclusions are essentially questions or points of departure, based on his postulate of 'action,' and 'activity' in V's sense, I take it, is something subject to your test." On the margin, Mitchell wrote: "I have changed text."

The person who played the critical role in the revision of the original introduction was Mrs. Warren Gregory (Sarah McLean Hardy). Mitchell wrote in his Diary under January 12, 1936, "I revised my introduction to selections from Veblen on the basis of Sadie's suggestions."

As Ardzrooni put it, "the selections are typical of Veblen's writings. . . . [A] literal stranger to Veblen can look through these selections and get a fairly precise idea of what Veblen taught." But Ardzrooni felt that Mitchell in his introduction had overstressed Veblen's skepticism. He wrote the publisher: "my quarrel with Veblen was usually on the point that he had too much faith in things, to which he invariably replied: 'Well, if you get as old as I am, you too would have faith.' "[354]

Clarence Ayres, then serving as Director, Consumers' Project, United States Department of Labor, informed the publisher: "I am particularly glad to see that Mr. Mitchell has included the passages on 'The Independent Farmer' and 'The Country Town' [from *Absentee Ownership*]. A great deal that Veblen wrote is more pertinent now even than it was when he wrote it and these selections are a case in point."[355] There was much also to be said for Secretary Wallace's comment at the time that "For many years [I] have felt that by 1950 he would come into his own."[356]

[354] Ardzrooni to Huebsch, April 12, 1936, copy supplied by Huebsch.

One may wonder whether Ardzrooni in this matter was influenced by DR Scott's dedication of his Harvard Ph.D. dissertation, *The Cultural Significance of Accounts* (1931): "I am indebted to Davenport for skepticism, Taussig for appreciation, and Veblen for faith."

[355] Ayres to Huebsch, March 14, 1936; copy from Huebsch.

[356] Wallace to Huebsch, March 14, 1936.

In Wallace's Department of Agriculture at the time, it should be noted that there were a number of direct students of Veblen, especially from the Missouri period (1911-1918). These included both economists and sociologists; among the latter, I should like to mention Carl C. Taylor, who considered it important to acknowledge Veblen's contribution to his development. He was a sociology student of Veblen and became president of the American Sociological Association in

earlier, Hobson speaking to the English wrote that "Veblen's analysis should be of special value in helping us forecast our own economic future." (*Veblen*, p. 9).

At about the same time a powerful voice from the world of the novel explicitly added his weight to the forces that were pushing Veblen's name to the fore. This was John Dos Passos and the influence of Veblen was particularly manifest in his greatest work, the trilogy *U. S. A.* (1938), that so effectively captured the travail of the nation in the somber 30's. *U. S. A.* is composed of three novels that were originally published separately—*The Forty-Second Parallel* (1930), *Nineteen-Nineteen* (1932) and finally *The Big Money* (1936). Veblen and more especially *The Theory of the Leisure Class* makes a definite appearance in the second, *Nineteen-Nineteen*. There Dos Passos has a Columbia sociology graduate student from the ranks of the social workers, "quoting all the time from a man named Veblen" to a girl friend at their first meeting, and the next day bringing her a copy of *The Theory of the Leisure Class*. Later we have the following conversation between Eveline Hutchins and Janey Williams in Paris:

> [Hutchins] "Busy as ever, Miss Williams," she said.
>
> "It's better to be busy," she said. "It keeps a person out of mischief . . . It seems to me that in Paris they waste a great deal of time . . . I never imagined that there could be a place where people could sit around idle so much of the time."
>
> "The French value their leisure more than anything."
>
> "Leisure's all right if you have something to do with

1946. Taylor played a role in the New Deal as head of the Division of Farm Population and Rural Welfare in the Bureau of Agricultural Economics of the United States Department of Agriculture. [R. S. Kuykendall, *Social Scientists and Farm Policies in the Age of Roosevelt* (Columbia, Mo.: University of Missouri Press, 1966) p. 220].

We might mention here too in related endeavors such admirers as Harlow M. Person and Morris L. Cooke, major architects of the Rural Electrification Administration (R.E.A.) and other great engineering ventures of the New Deal.

> it . . . but this social life wastes so much of our time. . . . People come to lunch and stay all afternoon. I don't know what we can do about it . . . it makes a very difficult situation." Miss Williams looked hard at Eveline. "I don't suppose you have much to do down at the Red Cross any more, do you, Miss Hutchins?"
>
> Eveline smiled sweetly. "No, we just live for our leisure like the French."[357]

Veblen plays a much greater and more obvious role in the last novel of the trilogy, *The Big Money.* A year before its appearance, Dos Passos published in *Esquire,* that sophisticated "magazine for men," a biographical sketch of Veblen under the title "The Bitter Drink," that was reprinted at almost the start of *The Big Money* (pp. 93-105). In the magazine it had a sort of deceptive sub-title that read "History and story of Thorstein Veblen whose slow acid is still biting into our economic walls." It also had a note by the editors to explain why they had asked Dos Passos, who then had the reputation of an extreme radical, to write the essay. "Capitalists and communists and all the ists between are interested in Veblen's ideas to-day. That's our only point in asking Mr. Dos Passos to discuss him." The note went on to state that "as professing capitalists, not to say practicing ones, we must in this passive manner disagree with many of his criticisms, but we actively insist upon his right to draw them."[358]

---

[357] *Nineteen-Nineteen* (New York: Harcourt, Brace, 1932) pp. 265, 328. The ". . ." are in the quotation.

[358] *Esquire,* September 1935, p. 20.

Through the columns of *Esquire* a decade later Veblen also made his appearance in the field of mystery stories. This was in Martin Gardner, "The Conspicuous Turtle," which was described as: "Mystery novelette laid in Chicago's Gold Coast concerns a mud turtle with rubies and a thief ['V. E. B.'] with savoir faire." (*Esquire,* April 1947, p. 59).

"The Bitter Drink" portrays the man's contribution that left him defeated in life, but in death about as immortal, commanding a voice as any human can be. In his staccato style Dos Passos describes Veblen as applying a scalpel to the doctrines of the American mind:

> Veblen
> asked too many questions, suffered from a constitutional inability to say yes.
> Socrates asked questions, drank down the bitter drink one night when the first cock crowed,
> but Veblen
> drank it in little sips through a long life . . .
> Veblen drank the bitter drink all right.

Taking as the occasion for the conclusion Veblen's request that in case of his death there should be no memorial of any kind, Dos Passos wrote:

> but his memorial remains
> riveted in the language:
> the sharp clear prism of his mind.

Immediately after the appearance of the *Esquire* essay, I wrote to Dos Passos as to the source of an item which was new to me. He replied that "a great deal of my material came from Stuart Updegraff, Caspar, Wyoming [an engineer in the oilfields]. . . . I'm sure that if you wrote him, he would send you a good many anecdotes, etc. He was a pupil of Veblen's at the same time that my wife took the course."[359] After generously stating that "I read your biography with great interest and owe you my warmest thanks for a great deal of information about Veblen," he concluded: "There is no doubt in my mind that Veblen's work will gain in importance as the years go by."

---

[359] Updegraff had taken all the courses Veblen offered.

I then got in touch with Updegaff. In his reply (September 26, 1935) to my first letter, he lived up to Dos Passos's prediction. He supplied many anecdotes, several of which I have used, and concluded: "I suppose you've swapped notes with Dos Passos. If not, why not? It's O.K. with me including these, and those I gave John." In the second, also lengthy, four days later, he asked: "Is he [Dos Passos] still working on a novel about Veblen?"

In *The Big Money* the Veblen sketch is followed by a newsreel and then a piece on Mary French, who is saddled with a mother who wants the family to conform to a leisure class life that her inherited wealth provides and demands.

> Mrs. French was feeling fine and talking about how Mary ought to make her debut next fall. "After all, you owe it to your parents to keep up their position, dear." Talk like that made Mary feel sick in the pit of her stomach. When they got back to the hotel she said she felt tired and went to her room and lay on the bed and read *The Theory of the Leisure Class.*
>
> Before she went out the next morning, she wrote a letter to Miss Addams, telling her about the flu epidemic and saying that she just couldn't go back to college, with so much misery going on in the world, and couldn't they get her something to do at Hull House? She had to feel that she was doing something real.

The Theory of Business Enterprise is also there but not by name; for example, in the conversation between Charley Anderson, who is an airplane manufacturer in Long Island City, and his friend, the Wall Street broker, Nat Benton.

> Benton started talking again. "But as I was saying, I don't know anything about manufacturing but it's always been my idea that the secret of moneymaking in that line of business was discovering proper people to

> work for you. They work for you or you work for them. That's about the size of it. After all you fellows turn out the product out there in Long Island City, but if you want to make the money you've got to come down here to make it . . . Isn't that true?"

Another passage reflects *The Vested Interests and the Common Man* and *The Engineers and the Price System.*[360]

> Charley was telling Bill how Andy Merritt [the promoter] said the government contracts were going through and Andy Merritt was always right and he'd said it was a patriotic duty to capitalize production on a broad base. "Bill, goddam it, we'll be in the money. How about another bottle . . . Good old Bill, the pilot's nothin' without his mechanic, the promoter's nothin' without production. . . . You and me, Bill, we're in production, and by God, I'm goin' to see we don't lose out. If they try to rook us we'll fight, already I've had offers, big offers from Detroit . . . in five years now we'll be in the money and I'll see you're in the big money too."[360a]

On the eve of the recession in 1937, Veblen's name began to be heard in congressional halls. On June 1, four members of the House of Representatives introduced jointly a recovery plan known as the Industrial Expansion Act, which was described as Planning for Abundance. These members were Thomas R. Amlie of Wisconsin, Robert G. Allen of Pennsylvania, Maury Maverick of Texas and Jerry Voorhis of California. Two specifically mentioned Veblen as the source of inspiration. Allen spoke of framing the act, "to make a reality of the dream glimpsed by Veblen 30 years ago" and Amlie

---

[360] Dos Passos in 1919 read the series of articles as they appeared in *The Dial,* which make up the two books. He was impressed by them.

[360a] *The Big Money* (New York: Harcourt, Brace, 1936) pp. 123, 199, 217.

said that "ideologically it stems from the writings of the late Thorstein Veblen."[361]

In his political campaigns, Amlie singled out as the basis for his economic philosophy *The Engineers and the Price System* and *Absentee Ownership*. Later in 1939, at the hearings before a Senate committee on his nomination by President Roosevelt to the Interstate Commerce Commission, he declared specifically that he was a "follower of Veblen rather than of Karl Marx." At the same time he expressed high praise of "Professor Keynes" of the *General Theory* for elucidating the paradox that wealthy nations in the absence of government intervention suffer deep chronic depression, a waste of the great production potential, or in the Keynesian terminology "secular stagnation." As Amlie rather simply put it, "I think Professor Keynes has put that paradox quite happily. He put it this way, that if you assume two countries quite similar, but one fifty years ahead of the other in its capital plant, the advanced country has built its industrial plant, its roads, its houses, and everything is there to produce

---

[361] Allen, "The Industrial Expansion Act, Extension of Remarks," August 16, 1937, *Congressional Record,* 75th Cong., 1st Sess., vol. 81, part 10, Appendix, p. 2468; Amlie, "The Industrial Expansion Act, Extension of Remarks," August 21, 1937, *Congressional Record,* p. 2429. Both addresses are reprinted in United States Temporary National Economic Committee, Investigation of Concentration of Economic Power, *Recovery Plans,* monograph no. 25 (1940). The quotations are on pp. 108, 109.

Tugwell has written of Veblen's influence on some of the early prominent political champions of President Roosevelt and the New Deal. "[The elder] La Follette's sons – the governor [Philip] and the senator [R. M. Jr.] – knew about Veblen, who was a large influence in their developing intellectual lives and who remained in their regard, a martyred veteran in a common cause. This was true too of [governor] Floyd [B.] Olson, brilliant Minnesota champion of the lowly who died [in 1936] at what might have been the beginning of great usefulness." ("The New Deal: The Progressive Tradition," *The Western Quarterly,* September 1950, p. 407).

wealth in abundance, but in that country, which by ordinary standards is regarded as the wealthier country, there is unemployment and hardship and starvation.

"The other country is 50 years behind. That country is putting all its effort into building factories, roads, and getting ready to produce wealth, and while they are in the process of putting up factories, and getting ready to produce wealth, they have prosperity and a high standard of living, but when they get to the point where they finally have the plant ready to go, then it tends to stop and it operates at 50 per cent of capacity and people are in dire distress. When the poorer country catches up with the richer country then its inhabitants are as poorly off as those in the richer country."

As he interpreted his own proposal, it was a curious amalgam. He said that under the act there would be not compulsion by government but cooperation by the government. "Suppose you had within industry as a whole an agreement to step up production about twenty per cent. Those industries coming under the scope of the act would cooperate or else would pay a processing tax. All those that did go along would also have contracts with the government whereby the government would take over a part of the total product if it proved to be unsaleable. . . . It would be expensive, but then we would be producing wealth, and increasing our national income. . . . I think it would be far better to produce wealth, buy it up and distribute it in areas where it is needed than to have people on the W[orks] P[rogress] A[dministration, a relief works measure]."[362]

---

[362] Statement of Amlie, February 8, 1939, *On the Nomination of Thomas R. Amlie to be a Member of the Interstate Commerce Commission*, in *Hearings before Senate Committee on Interstate Commerce*, 76th Cong., 1st sess., pp. 176-177, 224-225.

Similarly, the economist Alan R. Sweezy also accepted both Veblen and Keynes at the time. See his "The Economist in a Socialist Econ-

At about the same time, the British economist, Joseph Wild, pointed out that in the immediate post war era Veblen had warned in *The Vested Interests* and later in *Absentee Ownership* of a great post war depression unless readjustment was made. Veblen "plainly realized that the task of ideological" readjustment would be no light one. Drawing upon appropriate passages in the books, Wild declared, "unfortunately Veblen's comments proved only too true. The [post war] return to 'normal business enterprise' issued in the tragic collapse of 1929. The voice of the scientist was drowned in the babel of the market place and the stock exchange. Perhaps the voice was too soft and cultured to have been heard in those frenzied days. Now when men have time to sort out and ponder over the mistakes of the past, the calm, reasoned judgments of the scientist may be found worthy of a deeper consideration."[362a]

As depression hit the nation again in 1937, Veblen's works found increasing attention, at least his name was mentioned more often and favorably in the federal administration. Among the leaders in promoting this interest was Jerome Frank, one of the stormy petrels of the New Deal. Just before returning to President Roosevelt's administration, this time as a member of the Securities and Exchange Commission in 1937 (chairman two years later), he completed *Save America First: How to Make our Democracy Work,* which was published in 1938.[363] The book might be described as anti-

[362a] Wild, "Thorstein Veblen, Interpreter of the Leisure Class," *The Millgate,* October 1935, pp. 29-30.

[363] Frank, an expert in corporation law, had served as the general counsel of the Agricultural Adjustment Administration from 1933 to 1935 and then after a few months as special counsel for the Reconstruction Finance Corporation and a short stay with the Works Progress Administration, returned to private law practice in New York City.

omy" in *Explorations in Economics: Notes and Essays Contributed in Honor of F. W. Taussig,* p. 426.

Marxian but sympathetic to Veblen. The preface stated that "the thoughtful reader will recognize the writer's debt to the writings of . . . Thorstein Veblen." Frank used *The Theory of Business Enterprise*, *The Engineers and the Price System* and *Absentee Ownership*. To Veblen's inspiration Frank attributed a goodly number of concepts which were beginning to find acceptance in conventional theory. One was "monopolistic competition," to which he devoted several chapters. He declared: "It was Veblen who, in 1904, [in *The Theory of Business Enterprise*] first showed up the unreality of the older economists' competitive system. He began a non-Euclidean economics by pointing out that the factors to which the older economists referred as 'abnormal,' 'disturbances' and 'frictions' were in truth 'normal' and usual in most industries, and that the pure competition which they took as a norm was abnormal, unusual and exceptional. As the consequences of heavy investments in fixed plants have become more evident, more and more economists, stimulated by Veblen, have called for a revision of the theory of the traditional economists. And recently they have minted a new phrase, 'monopolistic competition,' to describe the phenomenon that is observable in many industries. That phrase . . . throws light on the fact that, as [Edward H.] Chamberlin [of Harvard] put it, 'both monopolistic and competitive

---

In December 1937 came his appointment to the S.E.C. at the suggestion of its chairman, William O. Douglas; and when Douglas was elevated to the United States Supreme Court in 1939, he became chairman; in 1941 he was appointed by President Roosevelt a judge of the Court of Appeals for the Second Circuit.

Justice Douglas has said that when Frank came to the S.E.C. he "got caught up in two exciting projects: (1) the reorganization of the New York Stock Exchange, and (2) the launching of the reorganization programs for public utility holding companies under the 1935 Act." (Douglas, "Jerome N. Frank," *Journal of Legal Education*, volume 10, No. 1 (1957) p. 3).

forces combine in the determination of most prices,' that 'most prices involve monopoly elements mingled with competition.' "[364]

Frank then drew from *The Engineers and the Price System*, the discussion of "capitalistic" or "industrial sabotage," to which he devoted another chapter. He declared that "the current depression has brought many persons to recognize belatedly the vice of what Veblen called industrial sabotage. They have come to see, with more or less clarity, that in large part the depression was due to and was prolonged by that business policy, which Veblen accurately described years ago. Veblen differentiated between 'business' and 'industry.' 'Business' denoted management, while 'industry' referred to actual production. He pointed out repeatedly that at the core of 'business' management of monopolized industries is the policy of curtailed production and rigid prices. The depression has served to bring home sharply that wisdom to others all over the world."

After referring to Veblen as "the pioneer in isolating industrial sabotage as the basically destructive force in our economy," he went on to describe how this sabotage resulted

[364] Charles Friday has pointed out some differences between Veblen and Chamberlin on monopolistic competition, in "The Future of American Capitalism," *Thorstein Veblen: The Carleton College Veblen Seminar Essays*, p. 150:

"For Chamberlin monopolistic competition became a concept used to explain a static problem in resource allocation. His equilibrium solution emphasized excess capacity and a higher than perfectly competitive price. Veblen reached the same conclusion without the geometrical apparatus that is so important to Chamberlin's model. His historical, evolutionary approach attempts to show the long-run consequences for capitalism of such monopolistic practices. It becomes a part of his theory of development."

The phrase "monopolistic competition" was used much earlier by a Chicago student and admirer of Veblen, Anna Youngman in her Ph.D. dissertation, *The Economic Causes of Great Fortunes* (Chicago: Privately printed, 1909) p. 37.

from the development of the giant corporation. Then he quoted from *The Engineers and the Price System:* "When corporate organization and the consequent control of output came into being there were two lines of policy open to the management: (a) to maintain profitable prices by limiting output, and (b) to maintain profits by lowering the production cost of an increased output. To some extent both of these lines were followed, but on the whole the former proved the more attractive; it involved less risk, and it required less acquaintance with the working processes of industry. At least it appears that in effect the preference was increasingly given to the former method during this half-century of financial management."[364a] Frank noted that by sabotage as Veblen used the term was meant trained incapacity or trained inability. As he put it, "Veblen sometimes called it [sabotage] 'the current business-like rule of incapacity by advisement.'" Frank added "Today many others agree with Veblen," and he quoted in support from "the recent Canadian" *Report of the Royal Commission on Price Spreads* (Ottawa, 1937).

Frank then pointed out that the control of the corporation's assets "is often in the hands of a very small group of men who usually have only a fractional investment, if any, in the stock or other securities of the corporation; ... [in other words], control of the giant production corporations is not in its body of stockholders, but in a tiny minority of other

---

[364a] *The Engineers and the Price System,* p. 42.

"The early industrialist believed in increasing output and decreasing price. For some reason the modern industrialist finds his advantage in restricting output and increasing price. Advertisement is used not so much to induce us to buy as to make us willing to pay far more for things than they cost to produce. Thus the railway companies give us progressively worse accommodation but by advertisement they produce in the public a non-critical state of romantic enthusiasm for the line. More and more the whole thing takes on an air of romance and unreality." (Roger Fry, *Art and Commerce,* p. 23).

men." He continued: "Here again Veblen was the pioneer thinker. Repeatedly he pointed out the rise of 'absentee ownership' as an inherent and significant aspect of the growth of the giant corporations. His disciples – Stuart Chase and others – have made us increasingly conscious of that type of 'ownership' of production goods. And two of his disciples, Berle and Means, [in *The Modern Corporation and Private Property*] recently gave us striking statistical evidence of Veblen's thesis."[365]

So strong was the reputed Veblen impact on Frank, that it was claimed that the S.E.C.'s investigations into the practices of the house of Morgan were attributable to that baneful influence. Thus the highly regarded *Christian Science Monitor* reported in February 1940 that "Truth of the matter is that the Morgan lawyers are lawyers, and the S.E.C. lawyers are Veblen readers." S.E.C. lawyers "will, however, have made their point first because they will be before a S.E.C. examiner, who in turn reports to a full Commission the majority of whose members swim in the same intellectual stream as Thorstein Veblen, who ought to be required reading for every Republican, like it or not."[366]

As I have stated elsewhere, "we find much of the New

---

[365] *Save America First* (New York: Harper, 1938) pp. 256, 270, 278, 282, 301.

In his original review of the Berle and Means book (*Yale Law Journal*, April 1933, p. 990), Frank referred to Veblen as a predecessor, with the following quotation from *Absentee Ownership* (p. 86): "Business enterprise may be said to have reached its majority when the corporation came to take the first place and became the master institution of civilised life."

Elsewhere, Frank noted the importance of *The Vested Interests and the Common Man* in its stress on the potential of modern machine technology to eliminate poverty. ("The New Sin," *The Saturday Review of Literature*, December 22, 1945, p. 3).

[366] Harold Fleming, "[Wall] Street Sees Animus in S.E.C. Delving into Morgan Affairs," *Christian Science Monitor*, February 1, 1940.

Deal legislation regulating corporations and security markets stemmed from a clear implication of Veblen's work 'that it was the duty of the government to set up counter-forces to prevent arbitrary acts of business power.' Some of these measures were the Securities Act of 1933, the Securities Exchange Act of 1934, the Public Utility Holding Company Act of 1935, and the Investment Company Act of 1940. Not only were Veblen's writings influential in the drafting of these acts but a number of the outstanding top-level administrators of the new agencies as well as the old, were strongly impressed with his writings, especially *The Theory of Business Enterprise* (1904) and *Absentee Ownership* (1923)."[367]

The Veblen influence was also found in the greatest investigation into the workings of the economy to date. In 1938 Congress at President Roosevelt's request authorized "a full and complete study and investigation with respect to the concentration of economic power and financial control over production and distribution of goods and opportunities." The Temporary National Economic Committee (T.N.E.C.) was set up to guide the inquiry, which took three years. It was composed of eleven members; three from the Senate, appointed by the vice president as the presiding officer; three from the House, selected by the speaker; and five selected by the President from the executive departments specified by the Act. Veblenians were found in the very ruling committee itself. Three of the major architects of the inquiry were avowed Veblenians. These were Isador Lubin, the representative of the Department of Labor, Jerome Frank, representative of the Securities and Exchange Commission,

---

[367] "Heterodox Economic Thinking and Public Policy," *Journal of Economic Issues*, March 1970, p. 9. The statement in single quotation marks is from W. E. Minchinton, "Hobson, Veblen and America," British Association for American Studies, *Bulletin*, February 1959, p. 33.

and Thurman Arnold, from the Department of Justice.[368]

Lubin who was then United States Commissioner of Labor Statistics opened the Hearings with the well known prologue in which he outlined the manifold aspects and far reaching character of the problem. As a specialist on industrial relations, he had already done much in the area of social security. It has been said that of the group that met with Veblen at Amherst in 1919, "Lubin came nearest to starting a revolution. He did this in the legal and orderly performance of his duties as chief of the Bureau of Labor Statistics, in the course of which he publicized the plight of the least fortunate 'one third of the nation.' That simple phrase did as much as anything to promote the campaign for social security."[369]

Now he proposed to strengthen and expand social security legislation. Thus, for example, he advocated in the prologue and in the final report of the committee a dismissal wage as national policy to cope with the problem of technological unemployment. In the words of a commentator,

> Commissioner Lubin voiced the consideration . . . that the technological displacement of labor is one of the costs incidental to an improving technology and that such costs should fall not upon the laborers but upon

[368] Arnold's Veblenism was in good part acquired by a process of osmosis from his close friend Walton H. Hamilton. Their friendship which began as fellow members of the faculty of Yale Law School continued through their service in the Department of Justice, where Arnold was an Assistant United States Attorney General and Hamilton a special assistant of the Attorney General. Shortly after the firm of Arnold, Fortas and Porter was established, Hamilton joined it upon his retirement from Yale.

[369] Duffus, *The Innocents at Cedro,* p. 151.

That "simple phrase" refers to the sentence that made famous the second inaugural address of President Franklin Delano Roosevelt in January 1937: "I see one-third of a nation ill-housed, ill-clad, ill-nourished." Lubin tells me that he supplied the president with the statistical data, but not with the wording of the powerful and moving statement.

> consumers — in other words upon the public — the real beneficiaries of a more productive economy. To provide for a more equable system of social bookkeeping Mr. Lubin proposed that severance pay be made compulsory. He contended that the social effects of such a proposal would resemble those of workmen's compensation laws, which not only have provided protection for workers but also by throwing the responsibility upon the employers, have tended to prevent the recurrence of the very situation from which protection was sought.[370]

By this time the stock of Veblen stood so high in reform circles that as an editor of *The New Republic* put it in 1939, "Since Veblen died, we have not produced a social theorist of international standing . . ."[371] In May of that same year, as Hitler's aggressions were about to set off World War II, the grimly prophetic *Imperial Germany* was reprinted.[372]

As the war ended in 1945 it was indicative of the trend that both *The Nature of Peace* and *Absentee Ownership* were reprinted. By 1945, too, it seems that his name began to be used by leaders of organized labor. Thus Walter Reuther, one of the most forward looking spirits in the labor movement, in an article in the New York Sunday *Times*, declared "We suffer, to put it briefly, from what Thorstein Veblen called the 'immoderate productivity of the machine.' . . . [Our] productive genius has always been stalemated by our failure at the distributive end."[373]

[370] David Lynch, *The Concentration of Economic Power* (New York: Columbia University Press, 1946) pp. 309-310.

[371] Malcolm Cowley, "An Afterword on the Modern Mind," in *Books that Changed Our Minds*, p. 244.

[372] It was at the same time published in Britain, the first addition to the three books issued there in 1924 — *The Theory of the Leisure Class, The Vested Interests and the Common Man,* and *Absentee Ownership.*

[373] Reuther, "Our Fear of Abundance," New York *Times,* September 16, 1945.

From the world of the material sciences came a compliment to Veblen in 1944. In a contribution to *The Philosophy of Bertrand Russell,* Albert Einstein's second sentence was: "I owe innumerable happy hours to the reading of Russell's works, something which I cannot say of any other contemporary scientific writer, with the exception of Thorstein Veblen."[374]

Even the Federal administration had begun to take notice of Veblen's contribution to the cultural development of the nation. The New York *Times* in December 1945 carried an item titled "Good Ship Veblen." The somewhat mystified columnist declared: "Among the ships due in Boston yesterday with a small contingent of troops from Italy was the Thorstein Veblen. In christening the Liberty ships which we launched by the thousands to win the war – and a splendid part they played in the victory – the nation honored itself and its sons by drawing on all walks of life, not excluding college professors and scholars in general. Nevertheless a ship called Thorstein Veblen suggests a highly specialized, not to say rarefied, range in the field of scholarship. One wonders how it happened?" Immediately I was overwhelmed by an avalanche of letters enclosing the clipping. From the governor's palace in Puerto Rico came the clipping from R. G. Tugwell with a note asking "Did you know about this? How come?" I already had an explanation as a result of a somewhat similar query at the beginning of the year by Professor Mitchell. He wrote: "One of my sons, who is now somewhere in European waters as a member of the mercantile marine, writes back that he has seen a Liberty ship named 'Thorstein Veblen.' Who do you suppose had enough cul-

[374] "Remarks on Bertrand Russell's Theory of Knowledge," in *The Philosophy of Bertrand Russell,* edited by P. A. Schilpp (Evanston: Northwestern University, 1944) p. 279.

tural insight and courage to suggest this belated and inadequate honor?" I again communicated with Lubin, who was then engaged in foreign missions for President Roosevelt.[375] He replied, April 2, 1945, that: "I find that the Thorstein Veblen was a Liberty ship built by the Bethlehem-Fairfield yards in Baltimore and was launched on July 28, 1943. Apparently the Maritime Commission deserves full credit for naming the ship. From all I can learn, the name 'Thorstein Veblen' was chosen from a list of people they have there on file who have done much for the 'advancement of culture in America.'"

During this period sales of *The Theory of the Leisure Class* continued at a relatively slow pace except for the cheap Modern Library edition. In the fall of 1941 a situation developed that threatened to put all of Viking's direct publications out of print. The firm felt that the existing contracts made it financially impossible to reprint his works, especially the four taken over from Macmillan in 1918, *The Theory of the Leisure Class, The Instinct of Workmanship, Imperial Germany* and *The Nature of Peace*. Huebsch as noted above at the time agreed that since Veblen owned the plates for these books he would receive forty per cent of the retail price, and Veblen on his part would pay the cost of printing successive new editions. (By 1941 only three titles were still subject to this arrangement.) For the others which the house brought out at its own risk in the usual way it allowed 15% royalty, i.e., on *The Higher Learning, The Place of Science in Modern Civilisation, Absentee Ownership, The Engineers and the Price System,* and the posthumous *Essays in Our Changing Order*. For *The Vested Interests and the Common Man* and *The Laxdaela Saga*, the royalty was 10%.

---

[375] Lubin had been serving as chief of the statistical unit of the Combined American and British Chiefs of Staff.

Huebsch informed me in November, 1941, "From time to time one or another of the titles would go out of print and these were not always restored promptly; at fifteen per cent royalty these titles merely spelled a loss because the sale was small and trickling." Then, as he wrote in the letter, "At a certain point in our correspondence with the heirs we offered to restore out of print books but asked for a new contract which would make it possible for us to keep the books in stock and to promote them at a royalty that would leave us a profit or at least a nominal profit, for the annual turnover is so small that even a large percentage of profit would be insignificant in dollars and cents. At about this time as a result of our analyses of the account for some years past, we discovered that two printings of *The Theory of the Leisure Class*, which the heirs should have paid for, had never been charged to them. The amount in question was $463.10. We, however, had been regularly paying the 40% on the copies of these printings that were sold. Naturally we stated that we would charge this amount against earnings. After a good deal of correspondence we made a final offer as follows: 'On those titles for whose plates Mr. Veblen paid we will pay a royalty of 20% on the regular editions, and we will reproduce those editions as needed at our expense. On all other titles we will pay 10%. We will accept 50% of our claims for printing those books on which a 40% royalty was paid, and we will immediately pay such balances as may be due.'"[376]

The heirs had become convinced that this was not a reasonable offer and began thinking of another publisher. Huebsch appealed to me for aid and I got in touch with Isador Lubin, who knew the heirs from the University of Missouri period. Meanwhile the husband of one of the heirs

[376] Huebsch to Dorfman, November 18, 1941.

had written to Mitchell, presenting their side and asking for suggestions regarding a publisher.[377] Mitchell in turn sent me the letter, with a note asking: "Do you know anything about the matter here referred to?" I got in touch with Huebsch, who sent me the history of the negotiations as presented above, and the following note: "Mitchell may well ask why, if there is no money in the enterprise, we want to hold on to it. I personally wish to keep it because I think that so distinguished an item is important to our list, and because I look on this old association with a certain sentiment.

"If I were an impartial outsider I think that *I* would advise the heirs to stick to us for, although some other firm might like to have Veblen's works on its list, no firm would react

[377] Ralph W. Sims to Mitchell, November 11, 1941, letter in possession of Joseph Dorfman.

SALES OF VEBLEN'S BOOKS – HUEBSCH AND VIKING 1918-1934
(Information supplied through courtesy of Ben W. Huebsch)

	1918-February 1930 (Approximation in round numbers)	February 1, 1930- April 30, 1934
Absentee Ownership	1,200	305
Imperial Germany	450	73
The Place of Science in Modern Civilisation	1,500	442
The Engineers and the Price System	1,300	3,015
The Vested Interests and the Common Man	2,900	147
The Higher Learning in America	1,900	Out of print
The Theory of the Leisure Class	5,000	453
Vanguard Press, under license (cheap edition)	9,000	
The Instinct of Workmanship	1,500	192
The Nature of Peace	1,000	47
The Laxdaela Saga	500	60

differently than this firm does to the situation which each reprint creates: an exceedingly slow investment at practically no profit."[378] Mitchell agreed with Huebsch and wrote to the representative of the heirs accordingly. Thanks to the intercession of Lubin and Mitchell, Veblen's books continued to be available.

In the 50's former vice president Wallace's prediction seemed to be an accurate forecast. An early indicator was that Veblen's *alma mater,* Carleton College, began in 1953 to extend a belated recognition. The initiative came from the president, Laurence M. Gould, a physicist of international reputation, who decided that the college should honor its most famous graduate. He asked Theodore C. Blegen, a leading authority on Norwegian immigration and then dean of the Graduate School, University of Minnesota, to give the annual convocation. Blegen in a private letter commented: "I think I can claim that I am the first person who has given on the Carleton campus a fairly major talk on the genius who in his way, was such a social maverick as a student and who, I suspect, has been regarded as a complete maverick by the Carleton group through all the years."[379]

As the social sciences celebrated the turning of the half century mark, Veblen with his institutional approach was hailed as a major architect of "the new economics of the twentieth century." It was said that "had he been taken more seriously by his economic colleagues, the older economics would have had to reconstruct itself much earlier than actually was the case."[380] The interest was not confined to *The*

[378] Huebsch to Dorfman, November 18, 1941.

[379] Blegen to Joseph Dorfman, May 28, 1953.

[380] Louis Wirth, "The Social Sciences," in *American Scholarship in the Twentieth Century,* edited by Merle Curti (Cambridge, Mass.: Harvard University Press, 1955) pp. 50, 51, 52.

Theory of the Leisure Class. A prominent Finnish publisher began negotiations with Huebsch for translation rights of *Imperial Germany and the Industrial Revolution,* but the deal was not consummated.

1953 saw the beginning of the Veblen paperbacks that led off with *The Theory of the Leisure Class* and eventually embraced practically all of Veblen's books.[381] The follow-

[381] The New American Library in 1953 under license from Viking issued the first paperback edition of *The Theory of the Leisure Class* – 150,790 copies at 35¢ a copy; the twelfth printing in 1970 of 31,220 brought the total to 443,102. Under license from Scribner's the New American Library also did the first paperback edition of *The Theory of Business Enterprise* in 1958 – 103,195 copies at 50¢ a copy. The fourth printing in 1968 brought the total to 154,803.

Thanks to Rita Whiteson and Edwin Kennebeck and his staff at The Viking Press, I have been able to obtain the figures of sales by Viking itself from the establishment of the firm in 1925 to the end of 1971. The figures are admittedly incomplete, and cover a different period than the table in footnote 376. It should be noted that Viking's own publication of the books practically ceased in the 1950's; instead it licensed the issue of paperback and hardcover editions by other publishers. (In the late 60's Viking began issuing its own paperback edition of *The Theory of the Leisure Class* in the Compass series).

Absentee Ownership	2,386
Imperial Germany	2,381
The Place of Science in Modern Civilisation	1,665
The Engineers and the Price System	8,272
The Vested Interests and the Common Man	1,535
The Higher Learning in America	419
The Theory of the Leisure Class	2,985
The Theory of the Leisure Class (Compass ed.)	4,096
The Instinct of Workmanship	1,257
The Nature of Peace	1,239
The Laxdaela Saga	169

There are no figures available for the posthumous collection *Essays in Our Changing Order,* which was published in 1934.

We have approximate figures of sales of the hardcover editions since the cessation of direct publication by Viking. Russell and Russell sold 2500 copies of *The Place of Science in Modern Civilisation* from 1961 to 1971. Augustus M. Kelley Publishers, which began in 1964 reprinting hardcover editions of all of the other Veblen books except *Laxdaela*

ing year Blegen expressed amazement at the furor over Veblen's works. It was so great that Viking Press proudly announced that "with its reissue of four hard-cover Veblen books which have been out of print for several years, practically all of that great American thinker's books are now in print — although Veblen died twenty-five years ago and some of the books were published even as long ago as 1899."[382]

[382] *"Veblen Reprinted,"* Viking press release sheet, March 26, 1954. The four were *Imperial Germany, Essays in Our Changing Order, The Engineers and the Price System* (10th printing) and *Absentee Ownership.* A fifth book, *The Higher Learning,* was issued the same year by a reprint house under license from Viking, but financial difficulties led to the sale of the volume in cut rate book stores at $1, instead of the list price of $4.

At the same time the publishers received inquiries from a number of distinguished European publishing houses. Huebsch wrote me in March 1954 that "recently there has been evidence of interest in Veblen's work in France and Germany and we have now made a contract for the publication of *The Theory of the Leisure Class* with a German publisher. Conversations with a French publisher with reference to the same book have been going on for a year or so, and last October I made a tentative agreement with a first rate publisher, Plon. But I stipulated that it was to become effective only if we approved of the translator, for I was cognizant of the difficulties that would be present. My apprehensions were justified; the publishers wrote that the man whom they had in mind proved unsatisfactory. Since then they have tried another man, one chapter of whose translation they now present to us." Mr. Huebsch asked me to locate if possible a person "who knows both French and Veblen who might examine and pass on the specimen." The examiner reported that the specimen chapter was wooden and hardly conveyed the sophistication and depth of the work. The search for a good translator has continued.

The leader in translations of Veblen's work is probably Japan, where some of his books have been translated a number of times. The following is a list of the Japanese translations:

1. *The Theory of the Leisure Class,* by Shinzo Ono, 1924; Saburao Kugai, 1956; Keiji Ohara, 1961.

Saga, has printed 1000 copies of each of them including *Essays in Our Changing Order. The Theory of Business Enterprise* is now being reprinted at this writing.

The centennial of Veblen's birth in 1957 brought an outpouring of essays, conferences and symposia. The New York *Times* (April 3, 1957) bore witness to his impact on the nation by a commemorative article titled "Conspicuous Dissenter." On a professional level he was honored by such institutions as the American Economic Association, Cornell University and The New School for Social Research. The symposium at the New School seems to have been one of the most exciting. The principal speaker, according to a listener, declared that "the trouble with Veblen was that he did not realize that in our economy the consumer is king. The response came from Walton Hamilton, who admitted that indeed the consumer was king, but that, like the monarchs of old, he was surrounded by courtiers, flatterers, and deceivers, whose function it was to get his Royal Highness to do what they wanted him to."[383]

In a review of the papers delivered at Cornell and the

[383] B. B. Seligman, "The Search for a Working Theory," *Challenge,* May 1964.

---

2. *The Theory of Business Enterprise,* by Yoshio Inamori, 1931; Keiji Ohara, 1965 (in the series of the Collection of Great World Thoughts by the Kawada Publishing Company).

3. *An Inquiry into the Nature of Peace,* partial translation included in the translation of *The Theory of the Leisure Class* by Kugai, above.

4. *The Vested Interests and the State of the Industrial Arts,* Tsunao Inomata, 1925; Toyokichi Yumoto, 1965.

5. *The Engineers and the Price System,* by Toyokichi Yumoto, 1962; Keiji Ohara, 1962.

6. *Absentee Ownership,* by Katsuhiko Hashimoto, 1940, partial translation.

This information is from a letter dated September 13, 1957, by Professor Kiyotake Yoneda to Joseph Dorfman, and from a letter dated April 20, 1970, of Professor Ohara to Professor William Kapp, who kindly supplied me with a copy. A number of Japanese academicians interested in "social accounting" have been long time students of Veblen.

American Economic Association, J. M. Clark updated his obituary. He wrote that Veblen was "one of the great formative influences in the transformation of our economic thought in the past half-century. This seminal iconoclast . . . among other things saw the business system as inflicting qualitative damage on our cultural standards, and such qualitative damage appears today as perhaps the system's direst liability, and the one most neglected by current economics."[384]

The tremendous impact of Veblen on economic opinion was noted at the time by Professor Earl Latham, of the Amherst Department of Political Science, who shortly afterwards became a leading member of John F. Kennedy's "brain trust" in his successful drive for the presidency.[385] In a brochure *Political Theories of Monopoly Power,* he declared: "The social character of much of politics is by now well-known. . . . What is not so clearly perceived, but is increasingly evident, is the political character of much of social and, one may say, economic life. By social I mean to include economic, because, to a non-specialist in economics like myself, it would seem that much recent economic opinion has come to accept the social insights of Veblen. . . . William H. Whyte in his *Organization Man* (1956) even goes so far as to say that Veblenites, in their attack upon the fiction of the dead hand governing an automatic economy, may have opened the way to all sorts of horrors, from ranch wagons

---

[384] Review of *Thorstein Veblen: A Critical Reappraisal,* in *Political Science Quarterly,* September 1959, pp. 428-429.

[385] He was one of the "most helpful" of the academic group that "provided ideas, statistics, reports, concepts, memoranda of use in the campaign speeches and position papers which became the bases for the Task Force reports of the transition period and the legislative proposals of the first year." [Theodore C. Sorensen, *The Kennedy Legacy* (New York: Macmillan, 1969) pp. 67, 68].

and gray flannel suits to the depersonalization of the individual in the security of corporate benevolence."[386]

In Europe the centenary was also commemorated. For example, the Netherlands Economic Institute had a memorial article in its influential organ,[387] and the British Broadcasting Corporation presented an address.[388]

The Marxists celebrated the centennial in their own fashion. In the United States there was a sort of split which was best revealed in the Veblen memorial issue of *Monthly Review, An Independent Socialist Magazine*. One faction led by Paul M. Sweezy qualified the old position of an exclusively adverse criticism that denied any scientific merit to Veblen. It maintained formally that Veblen should be understood as a sort of crude halfway house to the mansion of Marx. Veblen was described as a man "whose overall vision and detached insights were unsurpassed since Marx . . . yet his analytical attempts to lay bare the elements and *modus operandi* of the economic system are weak and often confused."[389] The other group of American Marxists represented

---

[386] *Political Theories of Monopoly Power* (College Park, Maryland: Bureau of Government Research, College of Business and Public Administration, University of Maryland, 1957) p. 2.

Writing in 1953, an American historian noted that "among contemporary political economists there seems to be no end of acknowledged indebtedness to Veblen." [Alan Pendleton Grimes, *The Political Liberalism of the New York Nation 1865-1932* (Chapel Hill, North Carolina: University of North Carolina Press, 1953) p. 59].

[387] Th. J. Steinbergen, "Thorstein Veblen 1857-1930," *De Economist*, July-August 1957, pp. 481-493.

Stuart Chase could write in 1958 "Only Veblen, of all the heavy artillery of a generation ago, is clearly remembered by the layman today." ("The Economic Embarrassment of American Riches," *The Reporter*, June 26, 1958, p. 31).

[388] T. W. Hutchison, "An Economist Outsider," *The Listener*, March 28, 1957, p. 878.

[389] Sweezy, "The Theory of Business Enterprise and Absentee Ownership," *Monthly Review*, July-August 1957, pp. 106-107.

by the late Paul Baran of Stanford University resolutely retained the older view that Veblen is "like other bourgeois theorists . . . who are unable to comprehend aspects of reality in their concrete interdependence with all other components of the continually changing socio-economic totality. . . . And again, as in the case of most bourgeois historians, Veblen's wisdoms of last resort are always of a biological or psychological nature." His "fundamental weakness" is that he was a "stranger to the historical method."[390]

---

[390] Baran, "The Theory of the Leisure Class," *Monthly Review*, July-August 1957, pp. 84, 85-86.

Ironically, Ferdinand Lundberg, in his popular *The Rich and Super Rich* (1966), suggested that both "neo-Marxists" Baran and Sweezy, in their joint book, *Monopoly Capital*, actually base their calculations not on Marx but on Veblen's concepts, especially his concept of the economic surplus as developed in *The Theory of the Leisure Class* and *The Theory of Business Enterprise*. (pp. 719-720).

A scholarly British Marxist previously had found some use for *The Theory of the Leisure Class;* "Purely conventional standards – particularly class conventions – enter surprisingly deeply into nearly all our tastes other than the primary needs of the body – a point which Thorstein Veblen illustrated with so much acumen. And these days, when advertisement plays the prime role in business supremacy, thriving as it does on 'educating the consumer,' afford much temptation to regard consumers' preferences as significant of little else than the persuasive skill of the publicity agent, the poster artist and the insinuating salesman." [Maurice Dobb, "An Introduction to Economics," in *An Outline of Modern Knowledge*, edited by William Rose, p. 620].

One economist was quite concerned in 1969 that Veblen may have erroneously regarded the auto as "a form of wasteful, conspicuous consumption," but we know that in 1927 while in his out-of-the-way retreat in California he purchased an Erskine.

Doubtless what he thought of cars might be gathered from the following passage in Roger Fry's *Vision and Design:* "The fact is that the average man uses art entirely for its symbolic value. Art is in fact the symbolic currency of the world. The possession of rare and much-coveted works of art is regarded as a sign of national greatness. The growth and development of the Kaiser Friedrich Museum was due to the active support of the Emperor William II, a man whose distaste for genuine art is notorious, but whose sense of the symbolic

In the Soviet Union, according to a summary account of the time, Veblen continued to be described as a member of "the bourgeois left-wing in economics," and "comes in for severe criticism, largely on account of his implied suggestion that the technical intelligentsia is destined to play a key role in social development. This thesis is sharply condemned on the familiar grounds that the technicians are subservient to their capitalist masters."[391]

By 1967, however, this view in the Soviet Union was modified. Thus, in the course of an examination of Berle and Means, *The Modern Corporation and Private Property,* a Soviet economist asserted, as Frank had done thirty years previously, that the book derived basically from Veblen's work. The critic had his own slant and also claimed that Marx had presented the fundamental ideas.

> An observant and caustic critic of the vices of capitalism, Veblen died in poverty and solitude in 1929 when young liberally-minded Berle and Means were beginning their joint work. Their book shows palpable traces of Veblen's influence. . . . Analyzing the modern corporation Veblen essentially formulated the "concept of the

[391] "The Social Sciences in the U.S.S.R.," *Soviet Survey,* November 1956, p. 5. The writer adds that "in this connection Stalin is quoted."

Communist circles opposed to the official Russian Establishment had also long viewed Veblen in much the same way. One journal of this type complained that "his work can serve only as a basis for liberalism, and any Marxism in his system is that of the pseudo-Marxism of the revisionists." (John G. Wright, "Thorstein Veblen, Sociologist," *The New International,* January 1935, p. 21).

was highly developed. Large and expensively ornamented buildings become symbols of municipal greatness. The amount of useless ornaments on the facades of their offices is a valuable symbol of the financial exuberance of big commercial undertakings; and, finally, the social status of the individual is expressed to the admiring or envious outer world by the stream-lines of an aristocratic motor-car, or by the superfluity of lace curtains in the front windows of a genteel suburban villa."

> separation of ownership and control in a way that made Berle and Means' later empirical proof relatively simple."[392] It is quite probable that Veblen who knew Marx's works quite well . . . , used Marx's well-known idea of separation of capital as a function (i.e., actual utilization of capital in production) from capital as property (i.e., capital frozen in the form of securities – titles to property). However, already Veblen drew entirely different conclusions from this thesis than did Marx, while Berle and Means began to use this idea for apologetic purposes.
>
> Following the traditions and methods of Veblen, Berle and Means, in their convincing analysis based on extensive factual material, clearly showed the various methods of expropriation of the small shareholders of a large corporation in favor of the controlling clique.

The writer further contended that Berle and Means on the basis of Veblen's "complex system of motivation of economic activity, . . . arrived at the conclusion in the 1930's that it is impossible to explain all actions of the leadership of a large corporation only by the motive of direct gain. As an important motive of the behavior of such corporations and their leaders they suggested the power motive: the economic, social and political power to which the managers aspire is separated from property (since they usually possess a very insignificant part of the corporation's shares) and from the profit which ceases to be an end in itself." The writer contended that: "the analysis of concentration (including the aforementioned primitive aspects of its interpretation) and the descriptions of the financial manipulations of the 'captains of industry' may be called elements of petty-bourgeois

[392] The quotation is from B. B. Seligman, *Main Currents in Modern Economic Thought Since 1870* (New York: Macmillan, 1963) p. 150.

criticism of the monopolies. Such elements are characteristic of Berle and Means' book as they were characteristic of Veblen and a number of other institutionalists."[393]

Two events may well serve as a fitting climax of the indications that Veblen had finally achieved recognition as a fundamental contributor to the development of culture in general and economic science in particular. One was the telecast on him by National Educational Television in 1964. It was one of a series called Pathfinders, which dealt with people who made major contributions to American life and culture. The programs "were taped in localities significant in their development." The series included such men as Mark Twain, Frank Lloyd Wright, Norbert Wiener, Robert M. LaFollette and Benjamin Franklin. Most of the program in Veblen's case was done appropriately at the University of Chicago, for there he had prepared his basic studies. The procedure was for the moderator to ask questions of each of the participants. As Veblen's biographer, I suppose, I was questioned first. The last question with less than a minute to answer was: Give in a sentence Veblen's contribution. Fortunately I recalled Mitchell's lines in an address at the University of Chicago, the very year that Veblen passed away: "No other such emancipator of the mind from the subtle tyranny of circumstance has been known in social science, and no other such enlarger of the realm of inquiry."[394]

---

[393] A. Anikin, "Monopolistic Corporations and Development of Capitalism: Adolf Berle's Conception," in S. Dalin, A. Anikin, Y. Olsevich, *Economic Theories and Reality* (Moscow: Progress Publishers, 1967) pp. 143-147, 156. It has been claimed that Berle in his *Power without Property* (1959) "has . . . attempted to bring up to date the analysis of the changing structure of society first begun by Veblen." (Rosalind Schulman, "*Absentee Ownership*, Reread," *The American Journal of Economics and Sociology*, July 1962, p. 326).

[394] Mitchell, "Research in the Social Sciences," 1930; reprinted in his *The Backward Art of Spending Money and Other Essays*, p. 73.

The other event was the use of Veblenian terminology and concepts in President Johnson's messages to Congress in connection with the Great Society proposals of 1965. The waste of which Veblen spoke in *The Theory of the Leisure Class* comes to mind when the President spoke of the "presence of untapped productive capacity" and of the policies forming our . . . "strategy of attack on waste. The waste of lives and property and progress which is the cost of war; the waste of human potential and self-respect which is the cost of poverty and lack of opportunity; the waste of excessive governmental personnel, obsolete installations, and outmoded public services which is the cost of inefficient government; the waste of men, and facilities and resources which is the cost of economic stagnation." The President insisted further: "We do not intend to live in the midst of abundance, isolated from neighbors and nature, confined by blighted cities and bleak suburbs, stunted by a poverty of learning and an emptiness of leisure. The great society asks not how much but how good; not only how to create wealth but how to use it; not only how fast are we going but where we are headed." Reflecting Veblen's emphasis on the never ending industrial revolution, the President said that "ceaseless change" was the "hallmark of a progressive and dynamic economy." Even the language of the most technical of Veblen's critiques of orthodox economic thinking and its practical meaning, the famous "Preconceptions of Economic Science," is found in one of the President's basic conclusions, "economic policy has begun to liberate itself from the preconceptions of an earlier day."[395]

---

[395] L. B. Johnson, "The State of the Union," *The Congressional Record,* January 4, 1965, pp. 27, 28; "The Economic Report," *The Congressional Record,* January 28, 1965, pp. 1403, 1404, 1407.

The following words of President Johnson in his discussion of business cycles in one of these messages read almost like a paraphrase of

The President may never have heard of Veblen nor fully appreciated the implications of the ideas to which he gave approval, but his very words testify to Veblen's influence on the age. As I have said elsewhere, "No one can say exactly when or how Veblen's ideas, once widely regarded as radical and violently rejected by most of one generation, gradually became a part of our accepted common stock of ideas. We do know, however, that historically such slow and pervasive infiltration is characteristic of an intellectual forerunner."[396]

This does not mean that Veblen's thought is fully understood today. The disagreements, both explicit and tacit, bear witness to that. Furthermore, understanding Veblen is complicated by a characteristic that has baffled many; namely, his reticence or, as one might say, his excessive reticence. Even the women who were closest to him and knew him best complained of this.

Ellen Rolfe once exclaimed: "How I wish I could look into his real mind. But nobody ever will!" And Mrs. Warren Gregory summed up her admiration and frustration in a private letter that read "He was the most subtle, the most difficult, the most enigmatic and secretive as well as brilliant and original mind of our times."[397]

Postscript

I hope in the not too distant future to publish primary

[396] "The Source and Impact of Veblen's Thought," 1958; reprinted in *Thorstein Veblen and His America,* Appendix II, p. 536.

[397] Mrs. Gregory to Dorfman, January 13, 1935.

Let me add here an additional note from the June 1895 issue of *The*

Veblen's greatest disciple; namely, Mitchell, as expressed in *Business Cycles* (1913): "No longer will we tolerate . . . the ravages of the business cycle. . . . I do not believe recessions are inevitable. . . . We can head them off or greatly moderate their strength and force — if we are able to act promptly." ("The Economic Report," pp. 404, 407).

source materials in my possession. This will include professional and personal correspondence, selected students' notes on courses in history of economic thought, socialism (including his Harvard Lectures), economic factors in civilization, and an analytical table of contents of *The Theory of the Leisure Class,* which had the benefit of Veblen's corrections. We shall of course include any additional evidence of Veblen's impact that may come our way.[398]

[398] On the matter of Veblen and socialism I am adding the following item. One of Veblen's Chicago students won the first prize in the Hart, Schaffner and Marx awards for 1908 with his Ph.D. dissertation on socialism. The committee of judges that year was composed of J. Laurence Laughlin, chairman; J. B. Clark, Henry C. Adams, Horace White and Carroll D. Wright. The author wrote in the published version that Veblen was "the most objective and clear sighted student of socialism." [O. D. Skelton, *Socialism: A Critical Analysis* (Boston: Houghton Mifflin, 1911) p. 249]. Skelton later became Undersecretary of State for External Affairs, Canada.

In a discussion of a prominent writer on social class it was stated: "We note in passing that the name of Thorstein Veblen does not appear in any of the numerous writings of [W. Lloyd] Warner and his associates, although they are a painstaking elaboration of his *Theory of the Leisure Class.* It is difficult to see how knowledge in the social sciences will ever be cumulative, if social scientists ignore, rather than build upon the work which has already been done." (S. M. Lipset and Reinhard Bendix, "Social Status and Social Structure: A Re-Examination of Data and Interpretations: I," *The British Journal of Sociology,* June 1951, p. 167).

Journal of Political Economy: "It is due to the public as well as to the author of the paper 'The Quantity of Money and Prices' in the *Journal* for March 1895 to say that the author of the paper is not 'Mr.' S. McLean Hardy, as given by the New York *Evening Post* in its editorial on May 7, and by various daily papers elsewhere, nor 'Professor' S. McLean Hardy, as given by the New York *Bankers' Magazine* in its reprint of the paper in the current issue, but Miss Sarah McLean Hardy, Fellow in Political Economy in the University of Chicago and instructor-elect in Political Economy in Wellesley College."

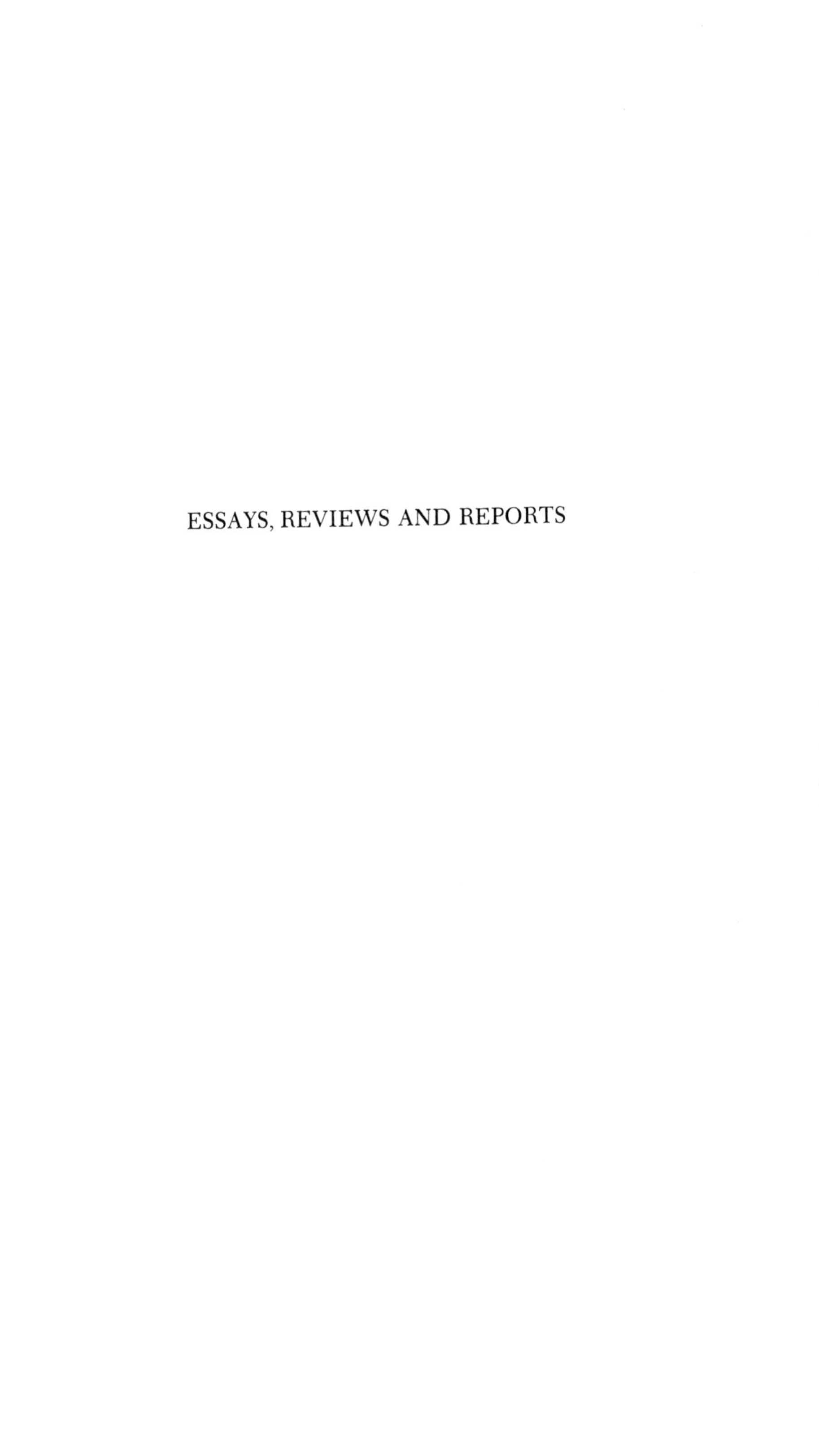

ESSAYS, REVIEWS AND REPORTS

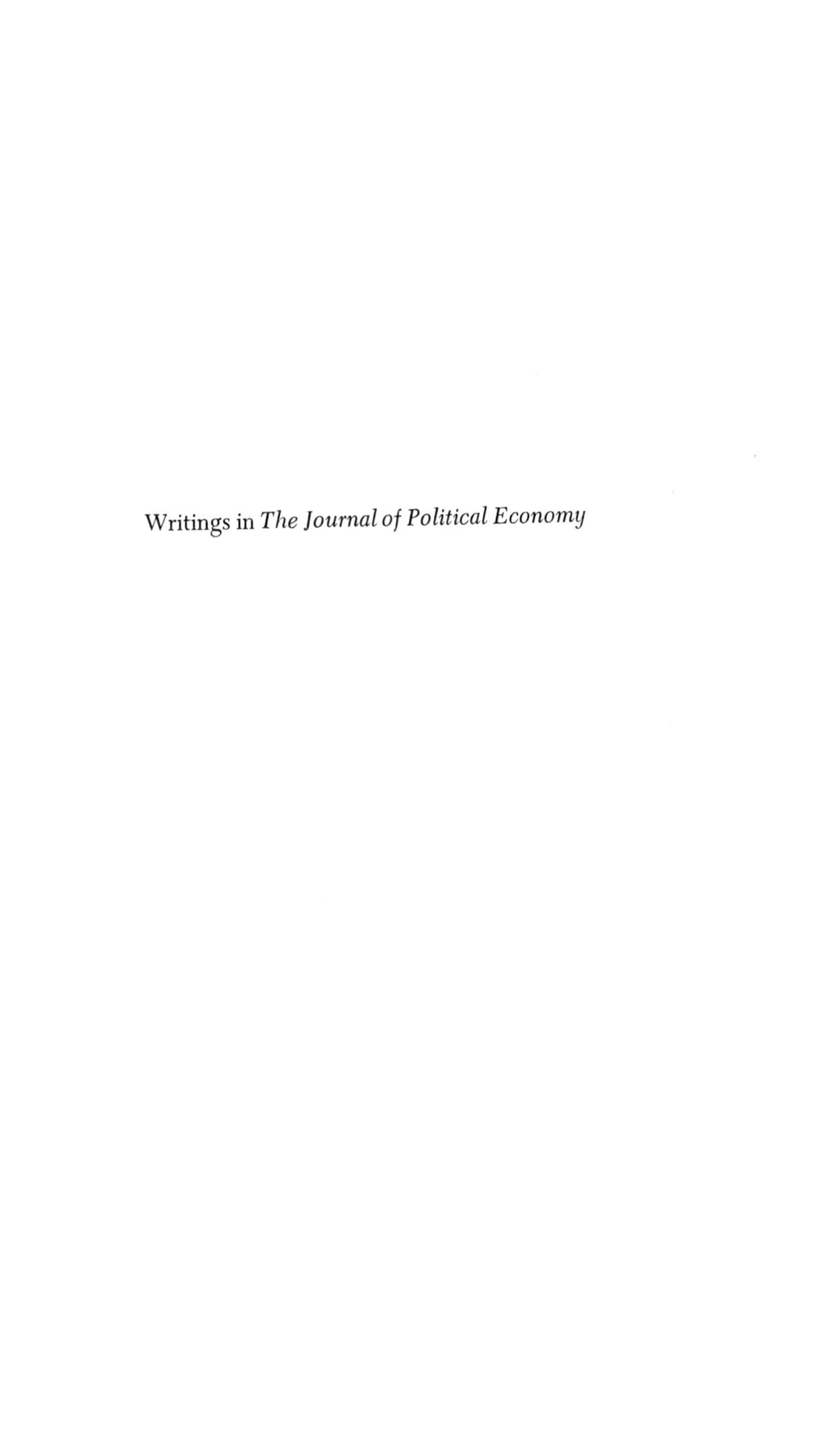

Writings in *The Journal of Political Economy*

Essays

The Price of Wheat Since 1867*

The year 1867 marks the highest point reached by the annual average price of wheat since wheat production on a considerable scale for the foreign market became a recognized feature of American farming.[1] The immediate cause of this high price was the occurrence of two successive bad seasons in 1866 and 1867.[2]

The wheat harvests of 1866 and 1867 gave an unusually low yield both in Europe and America; the former being worse in America and the latter in Europe.[3] The American

* *The Journal of Political Economy*, December 1892.

[Except for obvious typographical errors, the spelling, punctuation, etc. of the originals has been retained].

1 No. 2 Spring Wheat in the Chicago market averaged $1.43 (gold) for the year. In New York, Milwaukee Club averaged $1.75.

2 It is to be noted by way of orientation that the wheat crops available for the general market had been, on the whole, very good in 1863 and 1864; especially the former year, which was, in the United Kingdom particularly, and to a good extent in Continental Europe, the most satisfactory wheat harvest for a long series of years. Much the same is true of other grains for those years. In America the wheat crop was good in 1863, and had been excellent for two or three years previous; while in 1864 the American wheat crop was over average yield, but the acreage was smaller than the previous year, and the output was consequently somewhat short. The harvest of 1865, both in Europe and America, fell slightly short of an average yield. The harvests of the years 1863-7, taking into account the total available product, form a decreasing series, beginning with one of the very best grain crops of the century and closing with one of the worst.

3 "1866, therefore, will be memorable as a year of pestilence, war, scarcity, Irish discontent, and as a year in which occurred the most extensive and severe financial crisis of the present century" (*London Economist*, 'Commercial History and Review,' 1867). "The harvest of 1867 was almost universally bad or indifferent. . . . The winter of

corn crop was also deficient in yield for both years, especially 1867, and of low grade. The acreage sown to wheat in America increased greatly these years, and the result was a larger aggregate production of wheat in 1867 than for some years previous. (See Chart IV.)

Such was the situation of the wheat supply after the harvest of 1867. The situation of American farming generally, so far as concerns the prices obtainable for staple products, was fairly good; but prices were better, relatively, for grains than for meat products. The average for wheat, corn, oats, beef, pork, lard, butter, in the New York market was higher for the two years 1867 and 1868 than it has been since that time.[4]

1867-8 marks the summit of the price movement in farm products generally.[5] The trend of prices for agricultural staples in this country – and to a slightly less extent in England and on the continent of Europe – for some years previous had been upwards; from about 1863 it had been pretty strongly upwards. Since this time it has been generally downwards, broken only by an occasional temporary recovery, until the last few years. Something similar is true of the

[4] The prices referred to here and elsewhere in this paper, unless otherwise indicated, are gold prices averaged for the calendar year.

[5] This applies to what is known in Northern and Eastern markets as Farm Produce, and takes no account of cotton, tobacco, sugar or rice. These products of Southern farming, as well as wool and fruits, are hardly to be classed with grains and meat products in any discussion of prices from the standpoint of the wheat producer.

1866-7 was exceptionally severe – especially in this country. . . . Over the whole north of Europe and a considerable part of Germany, the grain crops of 1867 were alarmingly deficient. The maize also failed to the extent of a third, or even a half. . . . The potato crop is reckoned the worst since 1845-6. . . . The only really great crops have been in Hungary and along the lower Danube." (*Ibid.* 1868)

price movement of staple commodities generally, taking the period as a whole.[6] But the temporary movement of general prices for the time being, at this precise point (1867-8), was not in the same direction as that of staple farm products. General prices were declining. 1867-8 was a period of depression in business generally. The industries that are not immediately dependent on the seasons had reached their highest activity, for the time, earlier than this; the speculative movement had culminated in 1866, and business was now dull. But farming did not share in the general feeling of depression that prevailed in other industries in 1867-8, nor had it shared appreciably in the buoyant, not to say feverish, activity of the years immediately preceding. In short, the forces which controlled the situation for American farming were not the same that went to make the general industrial situation. It mattered little whether general business was brisk or dull so long as the seasons favored American crops and prices. And, determined by the character of the seasons, the tone of American farming was markedly depressed in 1865-6, when other industries were buoyant, and distinctly active in 1867-8, when times generally were dull.[7]

---

[6] See the tables of Mr. AUGUSTUS SAUERBECK, *Journal of the Statistical Society*, September, 1886, and those of Dr. A. SOETBEER, in his *Materialien*.

[7] The reason for this course of things seems to have been partly that the foreign demand for American farm produce was not specially urgent immediately after the war (relatively large surpluses of grain having been carried over from previous good years in Europe), partly that American crops in 1865 and 1866 were very moderate or deficient, and partly that the premium on gold was rapidly declining, so as to mask the actual advance that was taking place in agricultural staples (which for some purposes practically amounted to a decline in price). By the summer of 1866 the first and last of these causes had ceased to act. The crops for the next two years were under average, but the foreign

With respect to methods and appliances directly affecting wheat production and wheat prices, the following facts may serve to characterize the situation at the point (1867-8) selected as the beginning of the period under discussion:

The latest great advance in wheat-farming machinery was the self-rake reaper, which was rapidly being adopted during and immediately after the war. In ocean transportation, the iron steamship was fast replacing the sailing vessels of earlier years. Inland, from western markets to the seaboard, grain was carried by water wherever that was practicable. Shipments of grain from Chicago eastward were by lake-and-canal, with virtually no all-rail or lake-and-rail competition.[8] Ocean freights in 1867-8 were low as compared with what they usually were both before and after that time.[9] Inland freights and local charges were high, as measured by standards since grown familiar to the grain trade. Lake-and-canal freights to New York were rather high even as compared with what they had been immediately before

---

[8] Both wheat and corn had been received in New York from the West by rail before 1870, and, indeed, in some appreciable quantity, but these shipments were accounted a temporary and anomalous diversion rather than a serious competition with the water route.

[9] There had been an "over-production" of steam tonnage during the years immediately preceding, and freights were recognized to be ruling unduly low in consequence.

---

demand increased greatly in urgency and the premium on gold remained nearly stationary. At the same time there was a marked decline in the prices of other staples – which was to the advantage of the farmer – and when 1868 proved a fair average, or at the worst a slightly deficient season, with no obtrusive ill-fortune to offset the favorable state of the markets, the farmers of the wheat producing sections had reason to be well content.

the war.[10] See Chart I. b. The "center line of production" of wheat in 1867 was very close to the eastern boundary of Illinois. (For the movement of the acreage sown to wheat at this time see Charts IV. and V.)

NOTE TO CHART I.

a. The lines for wheat in Chicago and in New York are, as near as may be, for the same grade down to 1889, and therefore afford a fairly accurate comparison of the course of prices in those two markets. For 1890 and 1891 the New York price is that of No. 2 Red Winter, which at those dates was very nearly coincident with No. 2 Spring – perhaps a trifle over the latter.

The line traced by American wheat in the London market is, therefore, not available for a precise comparison with the American price. In comparing the lines it should be borne in mind that No. 2 Red Winter wheat ruled from one or two cents to ten or twelve cents above No. 2 Spring during the earlier years covered by the chart – down to about 1881-2; and that during the later years the difference has been slight and shifting – sometimes in favor of one, sometimes of the other. On this account, the rate of approach of the American price to the English price during the period appears greater on the chart than it has been in fact.

The line for British wheat represents the actual average of the selling price of wheat in the towns of the United Kingdom from which returns are collected. It therefore indicates price without regard to grade, and any comparison of this line with the other lines of the chart can be of value only as suggesting the relative course of prices, rather than as

[10] *The Financial and Commercial Chronicle* of May 8, 1869, gives details of the cost of transporting a bushel of wheat from the Mississippi river to New York as follows:–

Freight by rail to Chicago (200 miles)	20	cents.
Inspection (in and out)	¼	"
Storage	2½	"
Commissions	1½	"
Freight, Chicago to Buffalo, by Lake	6½	"
Insurance	1¼	"
Elevator at Buffalo	2	"
Handling	¼	"
Commissions at Buffalo	1½	"
Freight, Canal to New York	13½	"
Expenses in New York	3	"
Total expenses	52¼	cents.

furnishing anything in the nature of a demonstration. Wherever – during the earlier years – the line for British wheat falls considerably below that for No. 2 Red Winter in London, it is to be taken, generally, as indicating that the British crop of that year was of under average quality. Grade for grade, British wheat at that time was preferred to American. During the later years – from about 1880 – the great and permanent decline of British wheat relatively to No. 2 Red Winter is due to the fact that with the adoption of the most modern methods of milling the harder and stronger American wheats have come to be preferred to British wheat that may be otherwise of unexceptionable character.

b. The lines traced on the chart by freight rates from Chicago to New York are computed in currency, for the years of depreciated paper money. That for lake-and-canal represents the charges only for the months during which the canals were open each year, and is consequently not to be taken as a true yearly average. That for all-rail represents the yearly average, and after about 1876-77 it may be taken as an approximately true indication of freights. It is, however, to be noted that the figures it indicates are probably always, but not uniformly, too high; partly because little, or sometimes no grain was shipped at the highest rates quoted, and partly because there is no means of knowing how far the figures published were cut under. The making of special rates, sometimes very considerably below published tariffs, was always practiced, sometimes to a very great extent. These lines are, therefore, also not available for any precise comparison.

In converting English quotations into American terms, the penny has been rated at two cents. Consequently these quotations, as traced on the chart, range some 1½ per cent. lower than a more exact computation would make them.

The figures for inland freights may be found in the Statistical Abstract of the United States, or in the reports of the New York Produce Exchange, or of the Chicago Board of Trade. Those for ocean freights in either of the two latter publications or in the reports of the Secretary of Agriculture.

It appears on closer study of the price movement of wheat and the development of the forces which determined the movement during the years from 1867 to the present, that the course of development falls into three more or less clearly defined periods – 1867-73, 1873-1882, and 1882-91. The last four years, 1887-91, may perhaps as properly be counted as the initial stage of a new phase of the development, but the

CHART II.

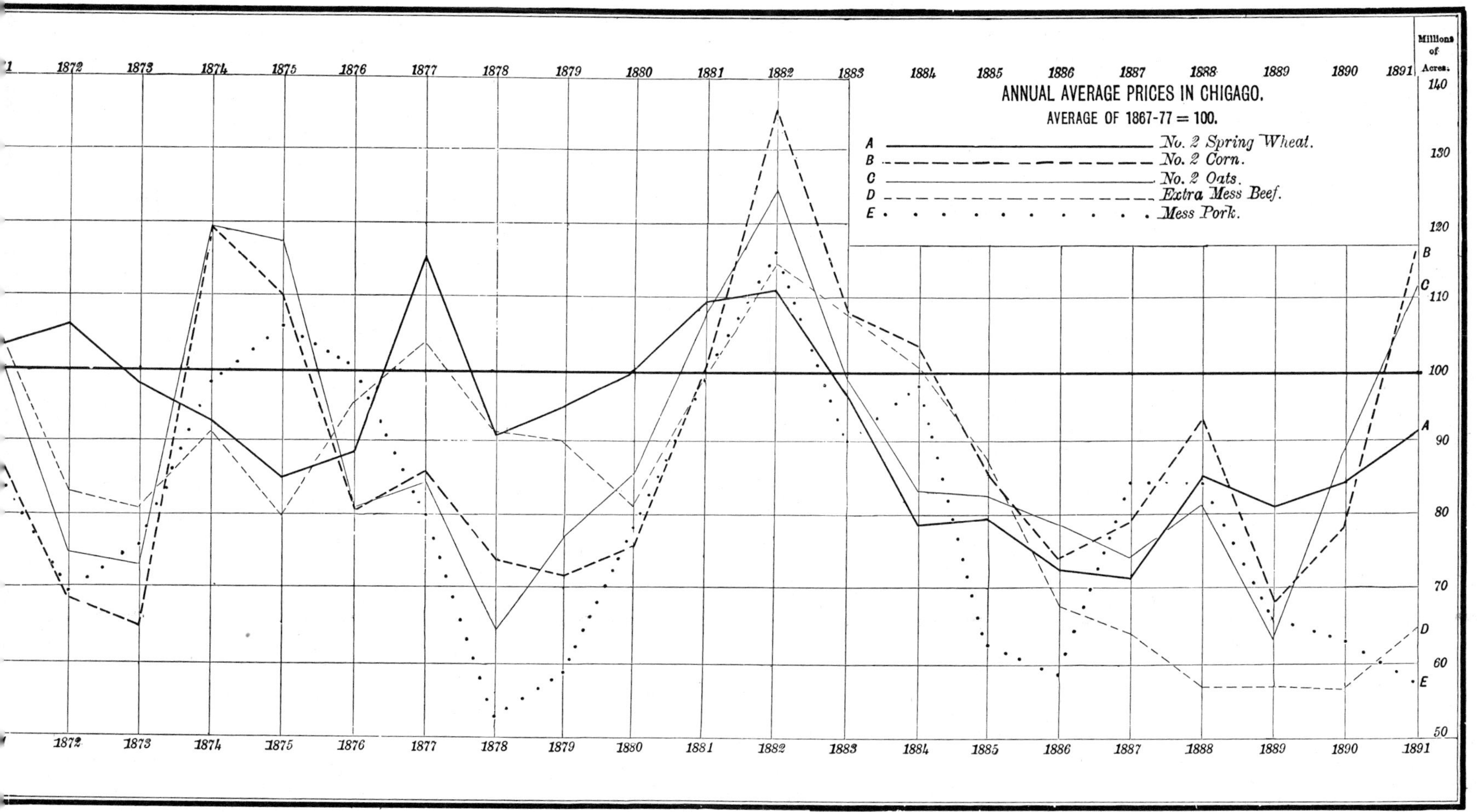

ANNUAL AVERAGE PRICES IN CHICAGO.
AVERAGE OF 1867-77 = 100.
A No. 2 Spring Wheat.
B No. 2 Corn.
C No. 2 Oats.
D Extra Mess Beef.
E Mess Pork.
Millions of Acres.
1872
1873
1874
1875
1876
1877
1878
1879
1880
1881
1882
1883
1884
1885
1886
1887
1888
1889
1890
1891
140
130
120
110
100
90
80
70
60
50

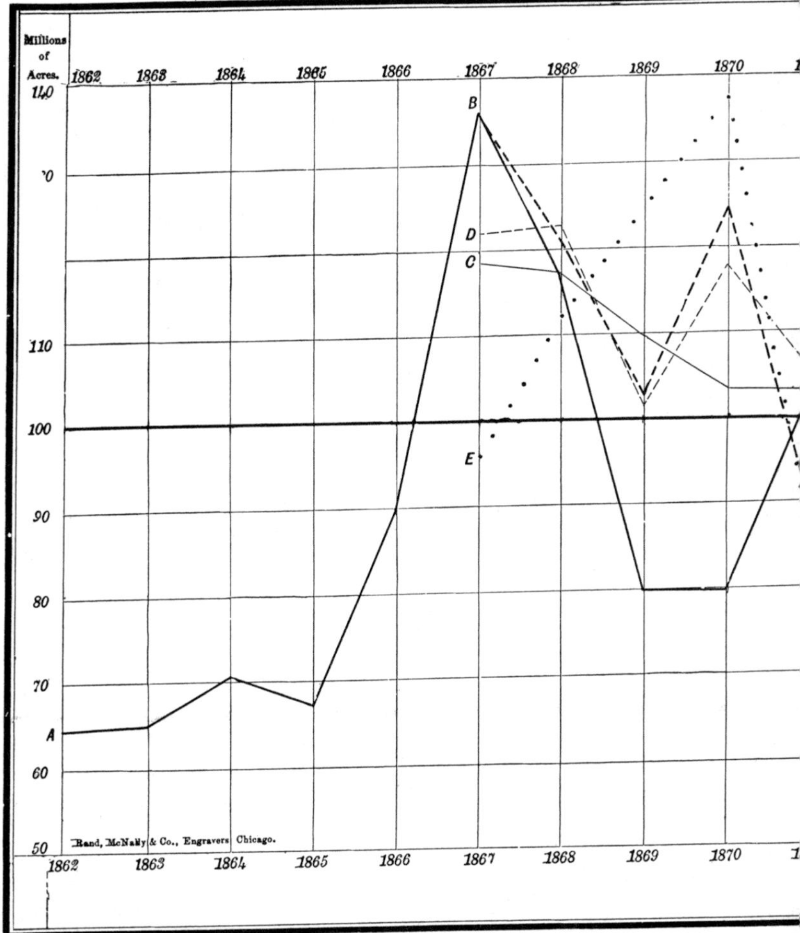

Millions
of
Acres.
1862
1863
1864
1865
1866
1867
1868
1869
1870
140
?0
110
100
90
80
70
60
50
A
B
C
D
E
Rand, McNally & Co., Engravers Chicago.

nearness of this last change to the present, as well as the fact that the characteristic features of the change are not yet sufficiently defined for satisfactory discussion as a separate whole, will prevent these years from being taken up as a distinct period.

I. 1867-1873.

From 1867 to 1870 the average of prices of staple farm products, as a whole, kept very much on a level. This was not due to a uniformity of movement of the whole, nor to a steadiness on the part of the different items. Wheat declined during the latter half of 1868, and the decline continued in 1869. It remained low through 1870, and rose again in 1871. The course of prices in none of the other staples ran parallel with that of wheat, and the lines traced by the members of the group during these years do not show the presence of any single controlling force. The line for wheat runs boldly across that for the group as a whole in 1870-72, wheat prices rising very distinctly, while prices for all the rest of the group fall, strongly and unitedly (see Chart II.). In 1873 the line for wheat shares the general downward trend of the group as a whole; after which all parallelism between the course of wheat prices and prices of other staples apparently ceases, until 1877. In general, during the twelve years from 1867 to 1878, wheat prices run a course apparently independent of the prices of other staple farm products. Closer study of the causes which controlled wheat prices in those years will show that there were special forces acting on wheat sufficient to account for this apparent anomaly.

Neither can it be said that wheat prices follow the general course of prices for other than agricultural products at the time. Wheat prices, and other agricultural prices as well, partook only in a superficial way of the general speculative advance of the years 1871 to 1873. Nor do agricultural prices enter on the decline that followed the break of the speculative movement, until it had been in progress for over a year in general prices. It is only when a considerable series of years is taken as a whole that the parallelism between the course of agricultural prices and of prices generally at this time becomes apparent. It is true of wheat and of other agricultural staples, as it is of commodities generally, that prices ruled higher during the closing years of the sixties than they did ten years later.

As to the detailed movements by which this general course of prices was worked out. The year 1869 was one of depression in farming; the corn crop was short and of poor quality; the season had been cold and wet; wheat gave a large yield, and the winter wheat was of very fair quality, but much of the spring wheat was low grade. The crops of 1868 had depressed prices for the early part of the year, and the new crops did nothing toward a recovery. The British wheat crop was about an average, and altogether there was no large demand for American wheat abroad. Taken as a whole, 1870 was rather a featureless year for wheat. There was a medium crop, of moderate grade. Corn was a large crop and of high grade. The crop of the United Kingdom was slightly over average bulk, and distinctly over average quality. The outbreak of the French-German war brought prices to a higher level for a short time; and later, when the fall of Paris and the close of the war was looked for, prices advanced again. Late in 1870 and during the early months of 1871 wheat advanced on the strength of an expected increased demand on the return of peace, and also on the strength of a considerable diminution of the stocks below what had been on hand a year or two earlier. Supplies had been unusually large in 1868 and 1869, and it may be set down that prices of wheat had been abnormally depressed for a year or two on that account. So that, independently of known facts as to the change in the size of the stocks on hand, the change in acreage during the years in question reflects the fact that prices were ruling "too low" in 1869 and 1870. In the normal course of things at the time, apart from fortuitous circumstances, the wheat area ought to have increased with some rapidity.

From 1867 to 1869 there is an increase in acreage of some magnitude, but in 1870 there is an absolute decrease, followed by an increase in 1871 of rather less than the average annual increase for the years 1867-73. But what is more significant still, than the figures for the aggregate wheat area, is the manner in which the figures for particular sections of the country vary. In the older sections (groups I. and II. of Chart V.) the acreage in wheat declined in 1869, apparently in consequence of the decline in price that had set in during the latter half of 1868, and of an advance in the prices of hog products, and perhaps in part because of a low yield. But 1869 was a year of exceptionally good yield, especially of winter wheat, which is grown in those older sections, and wheat-growing proved profitable for the year, in spite of low prices; and the following year the acreage sowed to wheat was about as large as it had been the previous year. In the new wheat country west of the Mississippi, and in California; where the cultivated area was increasing fast; where the farmers had virtually undertaken, on the strength of the prices of previous years, to increase their crops the coming year; and where wheat was practically the only available crop; there the change from an increase of wheat acreage to a standstill or a decrease was not easily carried out, and did not take place with the same promptness. The farming of that country was based on the increase of the wheat acreage as its vital principle, and it consequently took time to effect a change. A decrease in wheat acreage in those states would mean pretty much the same as a decrease in the total number of acres of cultivated land. The acreage in those sections, therefore, went on increasing strongly, especially in the trans-Mississippi states, in 1869; but, although the yield in 1869 had been good, there was a decrease in wheat area of some 500,000 acres in those sections for 1870. The decline in price seems to have acted as a distinct check to wheat-growing, from which the wheat states of the Northwest had to take time to recover; in fact, they had to wait for a fresh wave of immigration. The variation in acreage corresponding to the variation in price suggests that the price at which wheat could be profitably grown in 1868-73 was such a price as would be indicated in the Chicago market at that time by something between $1.25 and $0.85 gold, or $1.75 and $1 currency. Probably it is safe to say that an average price much below $1 gold for No. 2 Spring in the Chicago market, would not have been sufficient to induce any increase of the acreage cultivated in wheat during those years.

The years 1871-72 were years of slightly under average yield in America, and somewhat more below average in Great Britain, with a considerable demand for wheat on the Continent. The corn crop of both years was also a little short of the previous year, on account of a reduced acreage. The crops of 1870, 1871 and 1872 sold at good prices. Probably the prices obtained by the farmers at the local markets in the newer wheat regions of the West were very nearly as good as what they had realized for the crops of 1866 and 1867. The proximate cause which determined the price of each successive crop of wheat down to 1873, was the same as since that time. It is the crop and the crop prospect of wheat. Second and subsidiary to it is the character of the harvest of other grains.[11] The crop, the available supply, is the immediate controlling factor in making the price of wheat. That has of course held true since 1873 as it did before. But the general causes that have operated to determine the course of the price of wheat, and, in some degree to determine the magnitude of the available supply, have not been altogether the same since that year as they were for the years immediately preceding.

Taken as a whole, these six years (1868-73) were a period of decline in wheat prices, both absolutely and relatively to prices of staples generally. (See Chart III.) It was a period, for the most part, of a sluggish condition of trade, though general prices as computed in gold were not on the whole declining after 1868. With that year began the movement in railroad building that afterward became the characteristic feature and gave the tone to the business situation down to 1873. The speculation and inflation of values which became perceptible in 1870 and reached a climax in 1873, did not affect farming in any appreciable degree. Its influence on agricultural prices is not exactly imperceptible, but to all appearances it had a very inconsiderable effect in the way of advancing prices of farm products. There is, in the nature of things, no reason why American agriculture, and especially wheat farming, should have shared greatly in the boom of those years. The boom did very little to increase the demand for farm products, and it did nothing at all to decrease their cost of production at the time. On the contrary it distinctly acted to increase their cost. Prices of what the farmers had to buy were advancing, through the action

[11] Mr. G. SHAW-LEFEVRE has shown (*Journal of the Statistical Society*, December, 1879) that from 1852 to 1872 the price of wheat had very generally varied inversely as the British crop. Since that time a like statement will hold true if, instead of the British crop alone, the entire available wheat harvest of the world is taken into account.

of causes that had but a remote and indirect influence on the prices of what the farmers had to sell. Improvements were being introduced in the production and transportation of grain and other products, but not at any greater rate than the use of like improved processes and methods was increasing in other branches of industry.

The main facts bearing on wheat prices in the years immediately previous to the crisis of 1873 are these: American wheat crops were fair or moderate; corn crops were above average after 1869; freights were high, and, on the whole tending to advance; commissions and charges for storage, handling, etc., were heavy, but they were in process of improvement; British crops, and European crops generally, were, on the whole, fair or moderately short, so that there was an active and growing, but for the most part not a very urgent export demand; there was a speculative movement of considerable intensity, especially in 1871-2, in the prices of other than agricultural products; and this last fact, on the whole, went to offset the favorable factors in a situation that would otherwise have been moderately advantageous to the wheat farmer. The result was that prices in the primary markets ranged too low to greatly stimulate wheat growing or to satisfy the farmers of the West, and there was a good deal of complaint. Compared with the industries that felt the direct impetus of the speculative movement, the profits of wheat farming, in the general run, were distinctly moderate.

II. 1873-1882.

With 1873 the movement of wheat prices and wheat production entered on a new phase. The commercial crash of that year was of course not felt at the time to be an auspicious change for wheat farming, but the farming community of the wheat-growing country did not long feel the effects of the shock, and they never realized that 1873-78 was a season of hard times. These years are the most remarkable period that has been seen in American wheat growing.

After 1872, or more precisely from the time when the prospect for the harvest of 1873 was falling into definite shape in the summer of that year, the price began to decline.[12] It receded steadily, with the ordinary fluctuations from month to month, until 1875, when it averaged $1.023, currency, or $0.889, gold, for the year in Chicago. Then it began to recover in the same manner, and, with the single break of the anomalous record of 1877, the yearly averages show a steady advance, one above another, until 1882. The turning point was early in August, 1882.

As to the movement in acreage. In 1872 the area sown to wheat was 20,858,359 acres; in 1880 it was 37,986,717, an average annual increase of 2,141,044 acres, or something over 10 per cent. a year for the whole eight years. The average annual increase in acreage during the years 1867-72, the period of greatest previous increase, was 905,644 acres, or something over five per cent. a year for the whole six years.

From 1873 to 1880 there was but one crop, that of 1876, that was distinctly poor, and one other that was below the normal average yield, taking the aggregate wheat crop of the country as a whole. The crop of 1881, again, was short, by an average of about two bushels per acre; but that of 1882 was nearly as much over the average.

The crop of 1873 was a very good one in this country, and distinctly poor in England and Western Europe. The American crop of 1874 was over average in bulk, though much of

[12] The beginning of the fall in the price of wheat preceded the failure of Jay Cooke & Co. by some three months, though there was a heavy drop in wheat also immediately after the crash which the failure of that firm initiated.

the spring wheat was not very satisfactory in quality, and was also lower in yield than the winter wheat; the British crop was very good, both in bulk and grade, and that of Western Europe generally was very satisfactory. It was distinctly a year of abundance. The American corn crop of 1873 had been under average, and that of 1874 was poor.[13]

According to the government report the wheat crop of 1875 was a bushel short of the normal average yield per acre for the whole country, with an unusual proportion of the lower grades both in Winter and Spring Wheat.[14] The British crop was very deficient, and that of the Continent was also under average. It is to be noted as at least very probable that unusually large supplies were carried over this year from the previous harvest. Corn yielded much over average in 1875, but there seems to have been an unusually large proportion of soft, poor corn. A larger amount was exported of this than of any previous corn crop.

In 1876 wheat was a poor crop – worse than any since 1866. The spring wheat crop was extremely disappointing in point of yield, but on the whole of fair quality. The British crop was worse than that of the previous year – 26 per cent.

---

[13] The Chicago Board of Trade Report contradicts the statement of the Commissioner of Agriculture as to the corn crop of 1874, but the former seems to have allowed too much weight to the condition of the crop in the region tributary to the Chicago market, where the crop was good and fairly high grade, and so placed its estimates too high.

[14] The Annual Report of the Chicago Board of Trade criticises the Government estimate as too high for the Northwest. "The crop of Minnesota and Iowa harvested in 1875 was estimated [in the Report of the Commissioner of Agriculture] at 57,000,000 bushels. This was, undoubtedly, considerably in excess of the actual yield of merchantable wheat, as no exhibit of deliveries appears in any record that would justify a conclusion of its correctness. That crop met the misfortune of wet weather in its harvesting and subsequent care, and probably a large amount was lost that under more favorable influences would have found its way to market." *Annual Report,* 1876. Secretary's Review.

under average – and the like is true for the Continent. This year was the last of a series of four, during which the average yield per acre of wheat in America, as estimated by the Department of Agriculture, decreased regularly by about one-half bushel a year; while the last two of the four had also been years of very deficient crops abroad. The average (gold) price for the twelve months following the harvest of 1876 was probably higher in the local markets of the West than for any previous period of twelve months. This was due partly to the distinctly short crops, and partly to the Russo-Turkish war, which put a stop to exports from Eastern Russia in the spring of 1877. The prices of other grain, of which there was no shortage, seem to have been perceptibly influenced by the scarcity of wheat.

Then follow four extraordinary wheat harvests in America, coupled with corn crops every one of which was considerably over average, and one of them very abundant, and with nearly every other crop ranging over average the greater part of the four years. It is to be added that, except in wheat, crops had been unusually good for a couple of years before 1877. A drawback to this favorable showing was the poor crops in the spring wheat region of the Northwest in 1878 and 1879, amounting in some localities, in the former year, to a complete failure. The cause of this was very hot weather shortly before harvest. In grade, the crop of 1879 compared favorably with that of 1878, especially the spring wheat; which, however, was of low grade in both years. 1880 was a better year for the wheat growers of the Northwest, though the average yield for the whole country did not equal that of the previous year.[15]

---

[15] Altogether, the boast of the Commissioner in his report for that year seems well founded, that the four years of President Hayes's administration had been more productive and more prosperous years for

In the United Kingdom the crop was very deficient in 1877, but better on the Continent. 1878 was a fair average year, if not over average, in England, but under average on the Continent taken as a whole. For 1879 the *Economist* says: "The wheat crop, and the harvest generally of 1879, is not only the worst in fourteen years [since the failure of 1867], but the worst which has occurred, probably, for thirty years." It was a bad year for nearly all of Europe. Though not up to the ordinary average, 1880 was a much better year in Europe, and the two years following were each an improvement on the next before, until the harvest of 1882, which was reported to have been "of a fair average kind" for wheat. The grain harvest as a whole for that year was "under the average, or slightly under the average."

As for the American crops of these two years – 1881-2 – the run of luck of the wheat farmers came to an abrupt reversal in 1881.[16] Winter wheat, especially in the great winter wheat states of the Ohio valley and the Lake region, was very seriously deficient, both in bulk and grade. The spring wheat crop of the Northwest was also deficient, but not to as great an extent. In 1882, however, there was another very good harvest, – 35 per cent. above that of 1881, and nearly equal to that of 1879. But only part of the winter wheat crop of that year was marketed at the high prices that had ruled in 1881 and early in 1882. The price broke suddenly at the

[16] "In no season since the inauguration of crop reporting has there been so general disaster, involving corn, wheat, barley, buckwheat and rye, oats alone being exempted from loss." Report of the Statistician in the *Report of the Commissioner of Agriculture,* 1881.

American agriculture than "any other continuous four years in our history. They have been years of exceptionally good crops of all the different staples grown either for home consumption or export." These four years were, in the main, much more favorable for Winter wheat than for Spring.

time the spring wheat crop was being harvested, and never recovered. (See Chart I.)

The immediate relation between crops and price during these years, 1873-82, is a relation not simply between the American crop and the American price; it is a relation between the aggregate crop of the modern industrial countries and the price in the world's market. A short crop in America, as in 1875, acts to raise the price; the effect is perceptible in the line it traces. But the depressing effect of an extremely abundant American crop, as that of 1879, when coupled with a deficiency abroad, is not distinctly perceptible in the course of prices for the next twelve months. When, however, a deficiency in America coincides with a deficiency abroad, as in 1876, the effect on the course of prices for the succeeding year is very striking.

During the years just reviewed, and since that time, the American price of wheat has not been governed, habitually or mainly, by the volume of the American crop, as was the case, in the main, down to the years immediately preceding the civil war; nor by the European, or British crop, as was pretty much the case during the sixties (more accurately the fifteen or twenty years, ending about 1872-3); but by the aggregate volume of the world's crop, in which America's contribution has counted sufficiently to distinctly and greatly influence the course of prices in the world's market. Indeed, the American wheat crop counted for more as a factor in fixing the yearly price of grain during these years, from 1873 to 1881, than any other equally distinct single factor, and more than it has counted for, relatively, before or since. The American crop during those years occupied a position of striking dramatic value. It nearly attained the point of a virtual monopoly control of prices. The forces which placed it in this commanding position were the fortuitous circumstances of the seasons, but the seasons were of so uniform a character as to make the position one of some permanence.

There need be no doubt but that, taken as a whole, wheat growing during these years was distinctly profitable. How profitable is a question that does not admit of an intelligible answer, but there are indications that it was, perhaps, the most paying branch of American farming during a time when American farming paid unusually well. During the five or six years already spoken of above (pp. 337-342), 1867 to 1872-3, wheat farming must be held to have been moderately profitable, taking the period as a whole; though as much can hardly be said for the latter half of those half-dozen years. Neither can it be said that wheat farming during that period was on the whole a more profitable occupation than agriculture generally; still less can it be said that the inducements it offered were great as compared with the average of the country's industries. This is especially true of the years 1869-72. For the succeeding period of ten years, however, it may safely be asserted that both statements are true. Wheat farming compared favorably with other farming, and perhaps still more favorably with the average of other industries.

Chart III. shows the course of prices of five representative staple farm products in comparison with the price of wheat. The lines of the chart show that the price of wheat ranged relatively higher during these years than the average of the prices of wheat, corn, oats, beef, pork and lard; and a further detailed comparison with prices of other staple farm products, some of which are given in the tables of the Appendix, goes to show that the like is true to at least as great an extent when wheat is compared with the whole range of farm products. The same chart includes, also, the line traced by the course of prices of ten staple commodities, all of

CHART III.

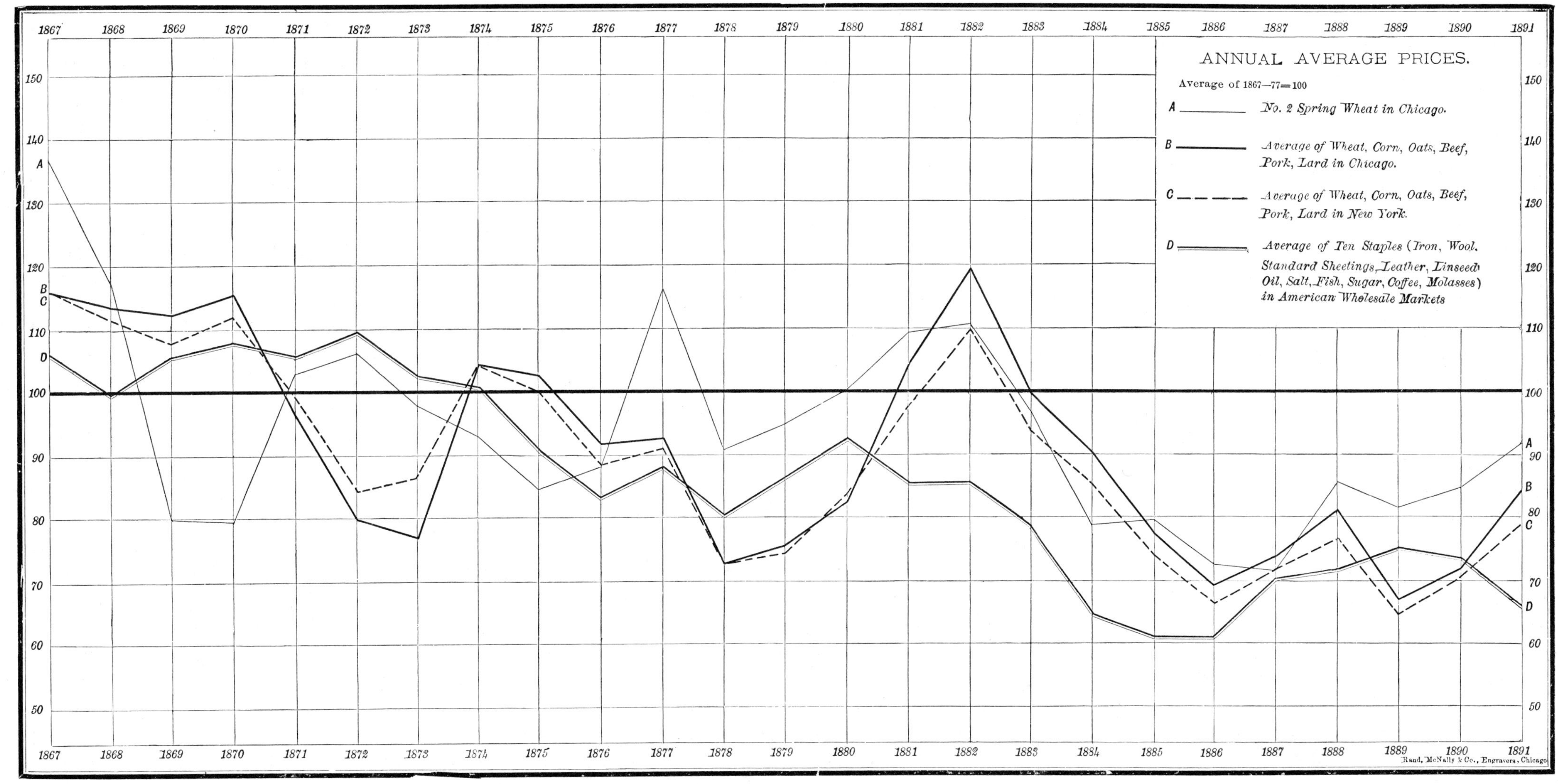

ANNUAL AVERAGE PRICES.
Average of 1867—77=100
A No. 2 Spring Wheat in Chicago.
B Average of Wheat, Corn, Oats, Beef, Pork, Lard in Chicago.
C Average of Wheat, Corn, Oats, Beef, Pork, Lard in New York.
D Average of Ten Staples (Iron, Wool, Standard Sheetings, Leather, Linseed Oil, Salt, Fish, Sugar, Coffee, Molasses) in American Wholesale Markets
1867 1868 1869 1870 1871 1872 1873 1874 1875 1876 1877 1878 1879 1880 1881 1882 1883 1884 1885 1886 1887 1888 1889 1890 1891
150 140 130 120 110 100 90 80 70 60 50
Rand, McNally & Co., Engravers, Chicago

which are among those that go to make up the wheat farmer's expenditure, and most of them are products of industries with which wheat farming may fairly be compared. The line traced by these runs, relatively, still lower even than that for staple farm products during these years. A more detailed comparison with prices ruling in other goods during the same years does not by any means tend to vitiate the inference which the lines of the chart offer.

If the conditions of production, therefore, had remained the same throughout the period as they were during the years immediately preceding, both in wheat and other farming and in other industries, it would follow that wheat farming had gained in lucrativeness relatively to other occupations simply in consequence of an enhanced price for its product. But the conditions of production did not remain unchanged, either in wheat farming or any other industry. It was a period of very material advance in methods and appliances, and the advance was assuredly no less in those particulars that had to do, directly and indirectly, with wheat farming than in any other.

The changes for the better in the implements actually in use by wheat farmers during the period was very great, both in cheapness and in efficiency. The case of the reaper may be taken as an example of the improvements by which wheat farming profited. During the early seventies the self-rake was in use, and had reached practically the same degree of efficiency as it has to-day. About 1872-75 the harvester came into pretty general use. The harvester was an advance over the self-rake such as anyone who has not seen both machines in use on the wheat fields of the West will scarcely appreciate. During the period from 1874 to 1878 the wire-binder was introduced, and proved itself in many respects superior to any harvesting machinery before in use. A great number of machines of different makes were sold, but the wire-binder never finally and decisively replaced the harvester. Down to the first extended and practically successful introduction of the twine-binder, 1879-80, no wire-binding machines had been offered that were entirely acceptable. The presence of the wire itself was a drawback; the machines were unsatisfactory and tantalizing, on the score of heavy draft or of inefficient work. From the time of the first successful introduction of the twine-binder, 1879, the wire-binder, as well as the harvester, was distinctly out of date.

The price at which each of these machines was successively introduced was always considerably higher than the price of the machine which it replaced. The prices were not sufficiently uniform to admit of giving satisfactory figures, but, in a general way, it may be said that, at its first introduction in the wheat lands west of the Mississippi, the harvester was perhaps of 50 per cent. higher cost to the farmer than the self-rake. In a few years the price was very considerably reduced. Likewise, when the twine-binder began to replace the harvester, it was at a price something like a hundred per cent. above that of the latter. This price also gradually declined, until it is possible to get a twine-binder to-day, more efficient than the machines that were sold at $320 in 1880, for from $100 to $120.[17] The best twine binder now costs less than the common run of self-rake reapers did in 1872-3. A twine-binder cost more – perhaps nearly twice as much – in 1880 than a self-rake reaper in 1872. But that the twine-binder was distinctly better worth its price in 1880 than a self-rake reaper, which could then be bought for about a

[17] Self-rake reapers of the standard makes were sold for about $200, currency, about 1870. From that time the price declined to $150 or $160 in 1875-6. Harvesters when first successfully and extensively introduced, about 1872-3, were sold for $200 and over. By 1878-9 the price had declined by nearly one-half.

third of the price of the former, is sufficiently established by the fact that the binder replaced the reaper in spite of the disadvantage in price.

As to the work of which these machines were capable. In 1870-73, in the wheat country of the Western states, the ordinary self-rake reaper was drawn by two horses, sometimes three, with one man, or sometimes a boy or a woman, for driver. The machine would cut ten or twelve, sometimes fifteen acres of the common run of spring wheat, such as would yield in an ordinary year 15 or 20 bushels per acre, in a day of about twelve hours; the average day's work, on the wheat fields of Minnesota, say, was probably not far from eleven acres. Four, or sometimes five, men were required to bind the grain cut by one machine, and one man, not entirely without help from the binders, could "shock" the day's cut of grain. The harvester required the same number of horses, could cut the same or a little smaller amount of grain per day, and required two men to do the binding. The driver of the harvester was usually a boy, or some person of less value for heavy work than an able-bodied man. The harvester saved a distinctly larger proportion of the grain than the self-rake. The twine-binder required at the time of its introduction – and not much improvement has been made in this respect – three horses, though four could and can be used to advantage with most machines of this class, wherever the fields are large and the ground not unusually firm. A binder may – sometimes with advantage – be operated with two animals; but that is the exception, not the rule. Such a machine, a six-feet-cut, would, with a full equipment of horses, cut and bind twelve acres and upwards in a day of twelve hours in ordinary average Minnesota grain. As high as twenty acres a day, on an average through the harvest season, have been cut and bound with one machine, and even as high as twenty-five acres of ordinary grain has been covered in a single day; but in these cases the binder has worked long hours, and almost invariably these very high records have been made by the use of more than three horses, or with a frequent change of teams. Fifteen acres of ordinary spring wheat on fairly level ground may perhaps be a little over the average of the day's work accomplished by the twine-binder the first few years after its introduction, and a little under the average of what the same class of machines will accomplish now. The machines are made to cut a wider swath, on an average, now than ten or twelve years ago. The self-binder dispenses with hand labor in binding the grain. The driver is usually, and profitably, a grown person, if not in physical development, at least in intelligence. One unusually efficient man will shock the grain cut and bound by a single machine. Usually it takes more than one man.

Such are the main features in the development in reaping machinery since 1870. The greatest advance in efficiency was made during the period 1872-82. In no other particular that has to do directly with wheat production has the advance been as great as in reaping machinery, but the development elsewhere has been much the same in kind if not in degree. Threshing by steam-power came into general use in the wheat country during the same years. An item that marks a very distinct advance, so far as concerns the spring wheat country of the Northwest, is the introduction of a successful straw-burning engine, 1875-80. The barbed-wire fence is an invention of the first importance for American farming; and of greater value, perhaps, to the farmers of the great wheat states than to any others. The wire fence, too, developed gradually. It practically reached its highest efficiency by the end of the period under discussion; though prices of wire have fallen lower since than they had been down to that time, and so have increased the availability of the fence.[18]

There are very many improvements in means and methods of work in other industries that affected the cost of wheat production during the years under discussion, and since that time. Their manner of operation has been by lowering the cost of what the wheat farmer has to buy, or by increasing his share of the final price paid by the consumer for his product. The line of Chart III, the resultant of ten staple commodities, suggests how far the wheat farmer was benefited by the first-mentioned effect of this class of causes. The second effect has been produced mainly by mechanical improvements in the handling and transportation of grain and other farm products. The details of the process of improvement in the shipment and sale of grain, are very numerous and complex; but for the present purpose they express themselves in a reduction of the expenses that must be borne by the grain during its transit from the farm to the consumer. The causes that underlie these changes in local and transit rates need not engage our attention here.

Among the striking improvements in the direction of cheapening transportation, by which the wheat trade of this period was benefited, were the substitution of steel rails for iron, with the far-reaching consequences following from that innovation; the increase in size of the vessels carrying grain from Chicago to Buffalo (and the use of barges); the lowering and final abolition of tolls on the New York canals, together with an increase of the carrying capacity of the Erie canal.

18 The wire fence is practically a portable fence of very high efficiency. It is cheap, effective, durable, light, erected and removed with very little labor, occupies a minimum of space, and does not accumulate snow or weeds.

The decline in freights on grain between Chicago and New York from 1872 to 1876 was very great; after that date it was not pronounced. There was a pretty steady decline in annual average ocean freights on grain from 1873 to 1882; but ocean freights had advanced eleven cents from 1867 to 1873, so that the total decline in 1882 as compared with 1867 was only 2.62 cents.

But freights are not the only charges the grain has to bear in its transit from the farm to the out-bound vessel in New York harbor. It has sometimes happened that the local charges – commissions, storage, and the like – at the various points where the grain has to be handled have in the aggregate equalled the cost of carriage alone.[19] Local charges, for storage, handling, commissions, and the like, in Chicago amounted to some two or three cents per bushel, and suffered no very pronounced decline during these years. In New York they ranged from 3-5 cents in 1872-3 to 1½-2 cents in 1881-2. Charges for handling and commission at Liverpool were still higher, and remained much higher throughout the period.[20]

[19] The following statement by the Statistician of the New York Produce Exchange shows what was the character and importance of other than freight charges at the time rail shipments were becoming general and customary: "The lake insurance and transfer and shipping charges, added to the average lake and canal rate of 1876, make the cost about equal with the rail; but the latter, making better dispatch, resulting in a saving of interest on ventures, with less liability to damage by heating, has, at last season's rail rates, an advantage over the water route." (*Annual Report*, N. Y. Produce Exchange, 1875-6, p. 220.) The apparent difference in favor of the lake-and-canal route at this time was more than six cents a bushel (see Chart I. b). The real difference was not quite so great, on account of special rates of varying amount having been made by the railroads during the year.

[20] Grain elevators began to be used in Liverpool only at the end of the seventies, and the reduction which had been effected in local charges previous to 1880 was, therefore, quite inconsiderable. They are stated by Messrs. Read and Pell, in their report to the Agricultural Interests Commission, 1880, to have been at that time about 2s. 1d. per quarter (about 6 cents per bushel).

In the charges for handling grain there was a great reduction made during the seventies at practically all the intermediate points through which grain had to pass on its way to the European markets. The beginning of serious competition between the railways and the lake-and-canal route for the carriage of wheat to the seaboard dates from about 1873-4, when all-rail shipments on a considerable scale were first made, under conditions that are not to be regarded as in any way abnormal.

By 1873-4 the carriage of grain by lake-and-rail and by all-rail was becoming a regular and ordinary feature of the trade. One result, and a very important one, of this change, was the adoption of the method of grading and bulking grain in eastern trade centers, after the fashion that was in use in Chicago and the railroad grain centers of the West. Down to 1874 no rules for the grading and handling of bulk grain, or for its sale and delivery ex-store, had been adopted in the New York market. Deliveries by canal-boat and by rail were made by special consignments and in distinct lots. It was the practice to preserve the identity of the lot of grain shipped, and deliver the particular boat or car-load to the consignee, as is the practice now with respect to most other goods than grain. The relatively small size of a carload, and the consequent liability of any considerable consignments of grain shipped over a long distance to become divided up on the way, and to arrive at its destination in a scattering fashion, made the adoption of grading and bulking grain indispensable. A lot of 15 or 20 car-loads might be delivered in fractions of one, two, or more cars, at odd times during a period of, perhaps, two or three weeks, or in extreme cases even more; the result being uncertainty, complaints, and demurrage. The method of bulking graded grain, together with the consequent development of railroad-owned grain elevators at New York, had an immediate effect, not only in facilitating handling and giving a definite and universal standard of quotations, but also in reducing the expense, and consequently the charges of handling, as well as the number and amounts of commissions and other like local charges. The period 1873-82 includes, also, the adoption and development of the system of railroad elevators at New York. This development of terminal facilities during the period reduced the total charges on grain received by rail in New York and delivered to ocean-going vessels from 4 or 5 cents to about 1⅜ cents a bushel.

Railroad competition with the Erie canal system threatened to divert the grain trade from that route to other ports, as Philadelphia and Baltimore, and this led to close scrutiny of local charges at Buffalo and New York, with a view to removing any abuses that burdened the traffic. Criticism and recrimination ensued between the trade corporations of the two cities, in which some interesting developments, due to the virtual monopoly long possessed by the Erie Canal route, came to light. It was found that the charges, at Buffalo perhaps more elaborately than elsewhere, had been ingeniously arranged to take as high toll as might be on every bushel that passed through, without regard to ulterior effects on the traffic. The traffic, in fact, was treated as if its volume and value were a fixed quantity, which local charges could have no particular effect either to help or to hinder. This view was pretty near the truth down to the beginning of all-rail shipments on a considerable scale. Under the stress of necessity the middle-men, who drew their income from the traffic, gradually and reluctantly lowered their charges during the seventies to a point at which their amount would no longer work to the manifest detriment of the traffic. It may be added that since about 1880-82 the question of local charges has been less of a subject for recrimination between trade corporations, and no great reductions have been effected, probably because there has been little room for great or sudden reductions.[21] Reference to the Chart (I. a.) will suggest, in the convergence of the lines for the Chicago and the New York prices during these years, how this reduction in transit charges worked to the benefit of the primary market.

General changes in local charges and freights west of Chicago are more difficult to trace; not only from the difficulty of obtaining the figures, but also, because these local

---

[21] The following estimate, given in September, 1879, by Mr. Geo. Randolph, Secretary of the Chicago Board of Trade, may be compared with the estimate given above (note p. 335) of charges on the transit of wheat ten years earlier:—

"Freight to Chicago (350 miles), per bushel	20 c.
Chicago charges	2½c.
Insurance on transit	1¼c.
Freight to Liverpool	24 c.
Average Liverpool charges, including storage	6½c.
Total, per bushel	54¼c."

The total expense, according to this estimate, of the transit from the local market in Iowa or Minnesota to the warehouse in Liverpool was 1¾ cents more in 1879 than the expense of delivering the grain in New York had been ten years before.

A statement of the expense for a bushel of wheat as far as the vessel in New York harbor, in 1881, to compare with the statement on p. 335, would be as follows:

Freight to Chicago (as before, but for 350 miles instead of 200)	20 c.
Chicago charges	2½ c.
All-rail freight, Chicago to New York	14⁴⁄₁₀c.
Local charges in New York (storage and weighing)	½c.
Total, per bushel	37⁴⁄₁₀c.

In both statements, for 1869 and for 1881, the 20 cents freight to Chicago is set down more or less at a guess. If we throw this item out of both statements, the total cost of transit for a bushel of wheat

freights have been subject to local and temporary disturbances that vitiate the figures obtainable for any given place and route for purposes of any broad generalization. Figures are obtainable that go to show that a considerable, but very irregular process of reduction has been going on in rates on grain, but what has been the aggregate average result of the process is very hard to say. On the whole the reduction seems to have been no less pronounced – perhaps rather more pronounced – than the corresponding reduction in charges from Chicago to the seaboard.

The controlling fact which determined the price of wheat in the world's market during these years was a short supply. The seventies, especially after 1876, were a succession of poor harvests in Europe. The American harvests were large, and the annual output was increasing every year, but it did not overtake the demand until 1881, when the series of poor harvests in Europe had come to a close, and the draft on the American supply was no longer as great as it had been. The course of wheat prices was extraordinary, not to say anomalous, through the whole period. Owing to special, largely fortuitous causes, the price was extraordinarily high; and owing to other special causes, partly fortuitous, partly the result of systematic human effort, the high prices ruling were exceptionally remunerative to the American farmer. But while wheat farmers generally, even more than those mainly occupied with other lines of farming, had reason to rejoice in the good fortune of those years of high prices and large yields, the good fortune did not come to all in equal proportion. Winter wheat fared distinctly better in point of crops during the years of rising prices than spring wheat. Every crop from 1877 to 1880 gave an extraordinarily heavy

from its arrival in Chicago to its receipt in New York becomes 32¼ cents in 1876 and 17⁴⁄₁₀ cents in 1881.

yield in the great winter wheat states (Chart V, group II),* while the four years, 1878-81, were all either moderate or distinctly poor in the spring wheat states. To this is to be added that from 1873 to 1877 grasshoppers visited portions of the states west of the Mississippi, and seriously diminished the aggregate output and the average remunerativeness of the wheat crop in those states.

Still, the acreage under wheat increased greatly, and without intermission, from year to year in the spring wheat group, while in the great winter wheat group the acreage barely held its own from 1875 to 1879. The line traced by beef on Chart II. sets forth the main fact that goes to explain this halt in the increase of the wheat acreage of these states, as well as the signal increase in 1880, and to some extent the decline that set in with 1881. The price of beef advanced strongly from 1875 onward, and the winter wheat states were in a peculiarly favorable position to take advantage of the advance. The halt in the advance of the wheat acreage in 1875 was due in great part to a diversion of the farming of those states from wheat to beef. The remoter cause which underlay the advance in the price of beef was the shipment of fresh meat to Europe. Fresh meat shipments, as a business undertaking, began in October, 1875. The reason for the peculiar movement of the wheat acreage in the winter wheat

---

*NOTE TO CHARTS IV AND V.

The lines for production are drawn on a scale 1/12 of that of the lines for acreage; the normal average yield per acre of wheat for the whole country being a fraction over 12 bushels. The rise or fall of the line for production, relatively to that for acreage, indicates approximately the yield per acre for any given year. Wherever the line for production rises greatly above that for acreage, the yield per acre was over the normal average for the whole country, and wherever it falls below, the yield was under the average. The figures from which the lines of these two charts are plotted may be found in the *Statistical Abstract of the United States.*

states during the best years for winter wheat, both as to crops and price, is accordingly not that wheat did not pay well in those states at that time, but that beef paid better. The movement of the acreage in the spring wheat states is testimony to the fact that wheat-growing did pay well even under relatively adverse circumstances during these years.

A change was in progress during these years in the relative prices of winter and spring wheat, a change which completed itself during the eighties. The tradition had been that winter wheat alone could make flour of the best quality, and the softer varieties of winter wheat were preferred to the harder. Spring wheat flour was inferior, according to the old standards and methods, to flour made from winter wheat. Hence winter wheat ruled several cents higher in the market (from 5 or 6 to 20 or 30, or even more) than spring wheat of a corresponding grade. The "new process" of milling that came into vogue in the seventies treated the hard wheats to better advantage than the old process had done, and the great difference in price was somewhat diminished. When the "roller process" and "gradual reduction" was introduced into the milling system of this country (late in the seventies), and the capabilities of that method came to be developed and appreciated, as to a good extent they were within the first half-dozen years after its introduction, it appeared that a more salable flour could be produced from the hard spring wheats of the Northwest than the best of winter wheat flour, at the same time that a bushel of the spring wheat of the prairies would grind into a larger quantity of flour.[22] The

[22] "Minnesota Patents" had attained great popularity by 1876, and the progress of introduction into popular favor of the flours which the gradual reduction process was especially fitted to turn out was therefore well under way before that process came into general use.

result was that the relative desirability of the two classes of wheat for milling gradually changed.

Down to about 1881-2, by which time the effect of the improved machinery and methods was making itself felt in England, and when the new-process flour had gained some popularity among British consumers, especially bakers, winter wheat, American and British, had customarily ruled somewhat higher than American Spring. The difference varied with the season, but generally the divergence for some years previous to 1880 would amount, on an average for the year, to something like 5 to 10 cents per bushel in favor of winter wheat. About 1880-81 this customary divergence begins to sensibly diminish. By 1884 the difference in favor of No. 2 Red Winter over No. 2 Spring had fallen to about 3 cents per bushel in the Liverpool market. In Chicago the average difference for the year in 1884 was 6.3 cents in favor of No. 2 Red Winter; a difference which afterwards decreased still further, and has practically disappeared. In 1887 winter ranged from 1 cent or less to 4 or 5 cents over spring in Liverpool; in Chicago, 1 or 2 cents over. In 1889 there was a difference the other way. Winter wheat seems to have definitively lost its advantage over spring, the softer varieties of winter especially so. But it is also to be noted that spring wheat has not held the advantage which for a short time it gained over winter wheat. The latest improved methods and appliances seem to treat either, or rather both in due proportion, with the very best results. What advantage there is is in favor of the hard wheats as compared with the soft, and rests on the greater quantity and "strength" of the flour yielded by the hard wheat, rather than on its superior quality in any other respect.

About the middle of the eighties the development of milling processes had successfully made a fresh movement in advance, in making use of a mixture of different varieties of wheat, with the very best results. The mixing of wheats with a view to getting a given result is now an established practice in milling, both in this country and in Europe, and as a consequence a shortage of one kind relatively to the other results in an advance on the part of the kind which is relatively scarce.

III. 1882-1891.

The years since 1882 have been eventful enough, in a way, as regards the course of the price of wheat, but they have been tame in comparison with the ten years that preceded them. The period is remarkable for a relatively close parallelism in the course of prices for all the staple farm products, as well as between the prices of farm products generally and those of other staples. As a whole it is a period from which anomalies are absent to an unusual extent.

About 1881, the causes which had controlled the course of wheat prices during the years immediately preceding gave way to a new set of causes, in many respects of quite a different character. The supply of the western nations was no longer drawn from America and Western Europe entirely, or almost entirely, as had been the case. The seasons in Europe were no longer regularly under the normal average. The American acreage had increased until, with accessions that were beginning to come in from several new sources, the customary demand was fully met. The change that was at hand in 1881-2 in grain prices was not entirely unforeseen at the time, but the magnitude of the change of which we then witnessed the initial stage was by no means adequately appreciated by those who had most to do with wheat at the time the change set in.

The yearly average for 1882 in Chicago was a little higher

than that of the previous year.[23] Such was not the case with respect to the markets of New York and Liverpool. The price in Chicago, for the year as a whole, was "too high," so that wheat was not freely exported. The New York wheat trade saw that this was the case, and said so; but Chicago, especially through the early months of the year, held stiffly to prices that the course of the general wheat market did not warrant.[24] From 1882 the price sagged off heavily, with the usual fluctuations, till it reached a permanently lower level in 1884 – some 30 or 35 cents below the prices of ten years earlier. During this steep decline the Chicago operators were pretty constantly holding back, and holding prices relatively higher in Chicago than elsewhere.[25]

[23] Wheat opened in Chicago in 1882 at about $1.26 – some 12 cents higher than any yearly average since 1877. It fluctuated unsteadily until early August, when it suddenly fell to $1.05; the distinctly, doggedly bullish tone of the Chicago market that had prevailed through the first seven or eight months of the year gave way for the time, and wheat ranged below $1 through the greater part of the remaining four months and closed at about 99 cents.

[24] After all allowance is made for cut and special rates, and for every other factor that may go to make the apparent cost of transit of grain from Chicago or any other speculative western grain market to the seaboard greater than the actually necessary cost, or greater than the expense actually borne by the grain in transit, it is scarcely possible to avoid the impression that the difference in the price of wheat between the western market and the market at the seaboard or in Europe was, and is, less than the cost of transit, including unavoidable commissions and insurance. The implication of the available figures for transit and local charges, even after they have been scaled down freely, is that the traders in the western markets pay more for wheat, on the average, than they realize from it. So anomalous a state of business is, of course, not easily credible, but it would not be easy to disprove its presence.

[25] A curious fact to be noted in 1884-5 with respect to the course of wheat prices – and in 1888-9 it occurs again, and more markedly – is the decline that took place in Chicago prices, relatively to prices in the New York market, immediately after they had been held up to an unwarranted figure for a time by speculation. Although the average

The years from 1884 to 1887 were, as a whole, rather featureless in wheat. The market was prevailingly dull and heavy, and generally disappointing to Chicago operators. On the whole there was a decline during these years. There was scored in 1887 the lowest yearly average that wheat has reached, in Chicago, during the period since the Civil War. During these four years (1884-7) No. 2 wheat never rose to $1. It fluctuated with the seasons and the crop reports, generally between 70 and 90 cents, but without any sustained advance.

1888, or rather the later months of 1888 and the early part of 1889, was a season of high prices, as compared with immediately preceding years. It was also a period of high prices in Chicago and in the western markets generally, as compared with the course of prices in the Eastern and European markets. The yield for the year was rather low in the great wheat regions of America, perhaps especially so in the country tributary to Chicago; and the European crop was also under average. But the reason for wheat ruling higher in Chicago than elsewhere is not to be sought mainly in the crop returns of the year; although the spring wheat region of the Northwest, and the trans-Mississippi states generally, harvested an exceptionally small crop of low grade, as was also, to a less extent the case that year with the Ohio Valley

---

for the year in 1884 was 83 cents, the price fell as low as 69⅝ cents in December, and closed at about 72 cents. It opened at 72⅛ cents in 1885, and only in the spring of that year did it again rise to the level of 83 cents, about which it fluctuated from that time on. This season of decline was out of harmony with the export market. The average Chicago price was lower in 1884, apparently in consequence of its having been too high in 1883 and early in 1884, than it was the following year; while the price in New York, and still more distinctly in Liverpool, was lower in 1885 than in 1884. The movement in 1888-9 is quite analogous.

group of states. An advance in wheat set in about the time the spring wheat was harvested, and during the month of September operators on the Chicago market achieved the most remarkable corner in wheat that has ever been recorded. The price then advanced from about 90 cents in early September until the last week of the month, when it jumped to $1.60, and even touched $2. With the advent of October, when the operations of the speculators had borne their fruit, it fell by one-third or more, and ruled at $1.16-$1.17 for the first week of the month. From that point it receded, irregularly, in spite of the efforts of the local operators, and the year closed at about 99 cents. Thence the course was irregularly downwards through the succeeding year, with a temporary advance to $1.08¾ in February. Since 1887, the general course has been upwards, culminating, apparently, in the comparatively high average price obtained for the crop of 1891.

The factors which have determined the general course of wheat prices since 1882 have been large and strong, with few disturbing causes. The fact of greatest weight, and most characteristic of the period, has been the relatively large supply. A glance at Chart IV. will show that this increased supply was not due to an increased output in America. Since 1880 the American wheat acreage has been practically stationary, taking the country as a whole. American yields have also not been nearly up to the average of the preceding ten years. The harvest has varied from year to year during this decade in much the same way as ever, but the harvests, both of wheat and of other staple crops, have run at a distinctly lower average than during the seventies. It is even safe to say that, while the run of crops in wheat, and to a great extent also in corn, was on the whole over a normal average during the seventies, it was below normal, perhaps in about an equal degree, during the decade 1881-90.

There is a further contrast between the run of wheat crops for the two periods. The earlier ten years were distinctly more favorable for winter wheat than for spring; so much so that the unusually high average for those years was due entirely to the exceptional excellence of the crops in the winter wheat region. The spring wheat of the Northwest during the seventies was, if anything, slightly below the normal average, taking the period as a whole. During the eighties – 1881 to 1890 – there was no such marked difference in the condition of the two classes of grain. Both varied from year to year, and the two did not vary with even pace, but on the average the seasons were no less favorable to the one than to the other. There were extreme local variations, such as the bad year of 1887 in Kansas and other states of the same group, and 1890 in some of the states beyond the Mississippi, as well as in the Ohio Valley; and, taken in conjunction with the unsatisfactory general run of staple crops and prices, the very moderate or deficient yield of wheat was an active factor in producing the severe depression in the West through the closing years of the eighties. But if regard is had to the wheat crop alone, it is to be taken that all the great wheat areas fared not unequally during this period.[26]

The characteristic features of the situation as affecting the course of wheat prices since 1887 have been: (1) crops, both of wheat and of other grains, have, in general, not

[26] A review of the European crops from 1880 to 1890 will show the period to have been of a fair average character, with wheat rather more satisfactory than other grains and slightly over the normal average. Europe therefore came distinctly nearer supplying its own bread during these years than during the preceding ten. At the same time a greater proportion of the European crop had become immediately available in the general market.

varied widely from the normal; (2) very efficient means and methods of production have been in use, as compared with ten years earlier (for this country, especially, this applies to the production of other staples than grain in nearly an equal degree); (3) the means of transportation and communication in use have also been of a much greater efficiency, especially as affecting other exporting countries than the United States, and a steady improvement in this respect has been in progress during the entire period; (4) hence has resulted the definitive inclusion of the crops of practically all wheat growing countries in the supply that goes immediately to affect the price of wheat in any particular market; (5) a further effect of these mechanical, technical improvements, acting in conjunction with the improved business methods now in use, has been a diminution of the stocks customarily kept on hand; (6) as a consequence of the facts enumerated, there has been, especially during the earlier years of the decade, a distinctly larger available supply, relatively to the demand, than was offered in earlier years; (7) there has been an absence, relatively, of sudden and radical industrial changes immediately affecting grain production; (8) a very considerable decline in the prices of staple commodities has taken place, with a consequent prevailing weak or depressed tone in the industrial situation generally.

Certain minor factors have also affected the general course of wheat prices. Notable among these is the imposition and continued increase of heavy import duties by France, Germany, Italy and Spain. To what extent this factor has influenced the prices obtained by the American producer it is impossible to say, even approximately. Yet there is no question but the effect has been to limit the demand and lower the price, although probably in a very slight degree. The slightly heavier scale of duties of the American tariff on staple commodities, since 1883, has probably acted in the same direction on grain prices in the primary markets, though the effect of the increase can not have been at all considerable.

As already noted, there was no great radical change directly affecting the production of wheat during the years after 1881, except the change in prices. But while the change in price was so nearly the only great change of the period, that change was unprecedented in magnitude and character, and the resulting, or, perhaps some would prefer to say, the accompanying change in the movement of the wheat acreage in this country has been no less serious and unprecedented. The total acreage sown to wheat, which for a series of years previous to 1880 had habitually increased by a yearly addition of something like ten per cent., practically did not increase at all, in the aggregate, from that time until 1891.

This result was not reached by a general and uniform cessation in the extension of wheat growing over the entire area in which wheat is largely grown. The acreage under wheat increased, on the whole, considerably in the prairie states and on the Pacific slope, and decreased to approximately the same extent in the Eastern and Ohio Valley states; but, without exception, in each of the groups of states represented in Chart V. the acreage under wheat suffered a serious diminution in 1885, immediately following the great permanent fall in price. This was the year of smallest wheat acreage since 1879, and shows the effect of the steep and protracted decline in prices during the years immediately preceding; though the price is not answerable for the whole of the diminution of area. Something is due to the very bad winter of 1884-5, which perceptibly diminished the acreage of winter wheat by "winter-killing." In 1886 there was a partial recovery in wheat acreage at all points; but the rate of increase in the sections where increase has taken place has been less from that time until 1890 than it had been previously, while at the same time the decrease in acreage in the great winter wheat states has been less pronounced since that time than before (see Chart V.).

The other great American grain crop – which might also be called the great meat crop – is corn. The alternative, though by no means the only alternative, offered the wheat farmer is the production of some form of animal product. And a comparison with the movement of the corn acreage for the same period will show, approximately, the relative attractiveness of wheat and other farming in the wheat growing states. It is to be taken, with some not inconsiderable qualification, that any conspicuous increase or decrease in the corn acreage indicates a corresponding movement in stock farming, taking the word in its broader meaning. If the line for corn acreage were traced, it would show a very strong and remarkably steady upward movement from 1871 to 1886. Since 1886 the corn acreage has fluctuated, rather than scored any distinct advance. The increase in the total acreage under corn since 1880 has also been due, for the most part, to an increase in the states west of the Mississippi, although there has at the same time been some increase in the South. The corn acreage of the Ohio Valley states has been, on the whole, stationary or slightly declining since that year. For the other minor grain crops, the movement has not been notably dissimilar from that of corn.

On the whole, therefore, wheat has lost since 1880, relatively to other crops, in all the great wheat growing sections; more distinctly so in the Ohio Valley group of states and the more southerly states west of the Mississippi than elsewhere; and this relative loss took place, chiefly, during the years before 1886.

The exact area sown to wheat in any given year is not to

be accepted as an unfailing index of the relative attractiveness of wheat growing at the time, as compared with other crops. The weather and the condition of the soil at the time of sowing have something to do with the number of acres sown, and the extent to which wheat has been winter-killed, and the land resown to other crops, may perceptibly influence the breadth of the crop. But taking one year with another, the breadth of the wheat area affords a pretty fair indication of the relative profitableness of wheat growing.

In the great winter wheat states and in the states immediately west of the Mississippi, there was, during the eighties, a very distinct movement towards a diversification of crops, to the partial neglect of wheat. The greatest single factor which has acted to bring about this change has been the decline in wheat prices; but other factors have acted in the same direction, for the most part with a slow, cumulative effect, and it is very difficult to say how much of the aggregate effect is to be attributed to any one cause. Stock growing continued to divert farmers from wheat to corn, though apparently rather less extensively than during the later years of the seventies. The climate of the northwestern states bordering on the Mississippi has been less favorable to the growth of spring wheat for some years past than it was years ago. The chinch bug has also been much more troublesome in the older spring wheat region than used to be the case. But the most efficient factor making for a change has been the economic or industrial factor proper.

The older wheat states are virtually nearer to a market for other, less easily transported, products now than they were; and the greater capital required, especially in permanent investments – the plant necessary for a system of mixed farming – is much more readily at the command of the farmers now, either through their own accumulations or through easier terms of borrowing.

A simple juxtaposition of the lines traced by the prices of wheat and of other staples, therefore, is by no means sufficient for a comparison of the relative profitableness of wheat and other farming under the changed conditions of the last decade as compared with the seventies. The lines of the charts afford a sufficiently accurate indication of what has taken place in the Chicago and New York markets; but the local markets, while in a general way running a course parallel with that of the general markets on which they depend, are not affected in the same degree for each staple by the changes in the situation that go to make the variation in price. As a whole, prices in the primary markets have tended to approach nearer to those in the general markets – the former have tended to rise relatively to the latter, but not equally for all staples. In a general way, the improvements that have been going on in transportation and communication have had a relatively greater effect on the less transportable articles. So that, wheat being practically the most easily transportable of our farm products, these other products have been left in a relatively more favorable position by the aggregate of changes that have taken place than the course of prices in the general market alone would indicate.[27]

---

[27] "Farm prices," as given in the annual reports of the Statistician of the United States Department of Agriculture, go to corroborate this view. Lines traced by farm prices (prices in the primary markets as reported by correspondents of the Department) might be given, showing that, while in the general markets the course of prices has apparently, on the whole, favored wheat relatively to other staples, in the local markets the reverse is true. Indeed, a somewhat detailed comparison, of which there is space here for nothing beyond the most general

The outcome of the movement has been that, as regards the older states, wheat growing has been relatively (and probably, as counted in money absolutely) less profitable since 1882 than during the preceding ten years, even apart from the distinctly less favorable run of seasons during the later than the earlier period. Wheat has recovered some of its lost ground during the last two years. With respect to the newer wheat lands of the West the case is not altogether similar. The legitimate effect of the course of prices, as of other factors of a general character, on wheat growing, both in the Northwest and Southwest during the later eighties, was obscured by the occurrence of several abnormally bad seasons. Also, the new lands over which wheat growing has been extending in the West since 1881 offer the most easily tilled, and, for a series of years at the start, the most fertile of all American soils. The cost of production of wheat, apart from its delivery to the general market, is therefore less on these new lands than on any large area that has been under wheat before; and wheat growing has been extending, and profitably, too, in an average season, while selling at prices that would not have been remunerative for wheat grown elsewhere as a main crop.

To sum up: The indications afforded by the course of prices are that since the completion of the great decline in prices of farm products, 1884-5, wheat growing in the older wheat states has held a less favorable position, relatively to other farming, than it did during the seventies. All accounts converge to the support of that view. But it is doubtful

---

statements of results, shows that so far as these Department "farm prices" are an adequate indication of the course of the local markets, wheat during the eighties suffered a very distinct depreciation relatively to other staple farm products.

whether, in the great winter wheat states of the Ohio Valley group, a relatively large acreage of wheat in a system of mixed farming has not continued to be more profitable throughout the whole period than a system which should tend to discard wheat growing as a staple crop; while it is to be taken as practically beyond doubt that with the changes of the last two or three years wheat growing in those states is again normally a profitable investment.

The spring wheat states bordering on the Mississippi on the west are a case by themselves. From local causes, wheat growing has not been, relatively, a profitable branch of farming there the last few years. Of the newer wheat lands of the West it is to be said that wheat growing, with an average run of seasons, is undoubtedly profitable; rather, it is almost the only crop that can be profitably grown there by the farmers at present settled on those lands and under the present circumstances.

Appendix

NOTES TO THE TABLES

TABLES OF PRICES OF WHEAT AND OTHER ARTICLES.

The prices quoted in these tables are in all cases averages for the calendar year, and are reduced to gold where necessary. The grade of each article is, as near as may be, the same for the whole series of years covered by the tables.

Chicago prices are annual averages from weekly highest and lowest quotations given in the Reports of the Chicago Board of Trade.

New York prices of farm produce are the annual averages given in the Reports of the New York Produce Exchange (wherever those reports give annual averages).

The figures for British wheat are the Gazette Annual Averages. Those for the English price of American No. 2 Red Winter are taken from the tables of Mr. Augustus Sauerbeck, and are presumably averaged from the quotations in Mark Lane. In converting English into American terms, the penny has been rated at two cents, and the quarter at 504 pounds for British and 496 pounds for American wheat.

Of the prices of staples, iron products are given as quoted in the Statistical Abstract of the American Iron and Steel Association; wool, cotton, sheetings, prints from the Statistical Abstract of the United States; sugar, coffee, molasses, from the reports of the New York Chamber of Commerce, except that for some of the earlier years the price of sugar is taken from the reports of the Boston Board of Trade; leather, linseed oil, codfish, are from the reports of the Boston Board of Trade down to 1883; after that date from figures furnished me, very kindly, by Mr. Avery L. Rand, Secretary of the Boston Chamber of Commerce, the figures given for the last three articles being in each case the mean of the yearly highest and lowest, and not true averages; salt, from annual averages of prices quoted at the salt works in Syracuse, New York, which I owe to the courtesy of Mr. Thomas Molloy, Secretary to the Onondaga Coarse Salt Association.[28]

---

[28] Katherine Bement Davis gave a continuation, "Tables Relating to the Price of Wheat and other Farm Products since 1890," in *The Journal of Political Economy,* June 1898, pp. 403-410. In a note the editor stated: "These tables are a continuation of a series of tables provided as [an] Appendix in the *Journal* for December 1892. The sources drawn on, as well as the method followed in the computation, are the same as for the earlier series. The figures for beef, pork, and lard have been compiled by Mr. William H. Allen, the remainder by Mrs. Katherine B. Davis." (p. 403). Both Allen and Davis were students and admirers of Veblen.

TABLE I.—PRICES IN CHICAGO.

Year	WHEAT "No. 2 Spring"		CORN "No. 2"		OATS "No. 2 Mixed"		BEEF "Extra Mess"		PORK "Mess"		LARD "Steam Rendered"		HIDES (Weekly highest average) "Green Salted"		FARM PRODUCTS (Average of Wheat, Corn, Oats, Beef, Pork, Lard)	CATTLE "Com. to choice" 1871–75; "Good to choice" 76–78; "Fair to choice" 79–85; "Inferior to prime" 86–91.	HOGS "Medium to Heavy" 1874–77; "Packers' & Shippers' Heavy" 1878–91.
1867–77	¢ per bu 105.2	per ct. 100	¢ p. b. 49.9	per ct. 100	¢ p.b. 35.	per ct. 100	$ per bbl 10.658	per ct. 100	$ per bbl 16.697	per ct. 100	¢ per lb 9.92	per ct. 100	¢ per lb 8.84	per ct. 100	per cent 100	¢ per pound	¢ per pound
1862...	67.7	64.4															
1863...	68.3	64.9															
1864...	74.1	70.4															
1865...	70.6	67.1															
1866...	93.5	88.9															
1867...	143.2	136.	67.8	135.8	41.4	118.1	12.98	121.8	15.96	95.6	8.95	90.2	8.20	92.8	115.7	3.03–5.56	4.10–4.92
1868...	122.9	116.8	60.5	121.1	41.	117.	13.06	122.5	18.69	111.9	8.97	90.4	8.83	99.9	113.3	2.50–5.63	5.11–6.49
1869...	84.08	79.9	51.4	103.	38.4	109.7	10.76	101.	23.61	141.4	13.71	138.2	9.23	104.4	112.2	2.63–5.91	6.36–7.83
1870...	83.79	79.6	62.	124.2	36.1	103.1	12.53	117.6	22.79	136.5	12.94	130.5	9.04	102.3	115.25	3.06–6.96	6.82–7.84
1871...	108.2	102.9	44.1	88.3	36.1	103.	11.22	105.3	14.24	85.3	9.10	91.7	9.97	112.8	96.1	2.93–5.51	4.09–4.86
1872...	111.5	106.	34.3	68.8	26.1	74.7	8.85	83.	11.64	69.7	7.50	75.6	10.64	120.4	79.6	2.85–5.86	3.57–4.11
1873...	102.9	97.8	32.3	64.8	25.6	73.	8.59	80.6	12.69	75.9	6.92	69.7	9.73	110.1	77.0	3.36–5.15	3.65–4.29
1874...	97.6	92.8	59.3	118.9	41.7	119.2	9.69	90.9	16.38	98.1	10.40	104.9	8.59	97.2	104.1	2.34–6.06	4.76–6.03
1875...	88.9	84.5	54.8	109.8	41.	117.2	8.46	79.4	17.58	105.3	11.71	118.0	7.24	81.9	102.4	2.27–6.09	5.77–6.97
1876...	92.6	88.	40.	80.2	28.3	80.8	10.09	94.7	16.81	100.7	10.24	103.2	6.81	77.0	91.3	3.64–4.75	5.74–6.33
1877...	121.5	115.5	42.7	85.7	29.5	84.2	11.00	103.2	13.26	79.4	8.69	87.6	9.01	101.9	92.6	3.91–5.50	4.72–5.33
1878...	95.2	90.5	36.9	73.8	22.3	63.6	9.68	90.8	8.64	51.7	6.59	66.5	8.70	98.4	72.8	2.86–5.08	3.21–3.88
1879...	99.6	94.7	35.6	71.3	26.8	76.6	9.59	89.9	9.71	58.2	6.23	62.8	9.37	106.0	75.6	3.05–4.87	3.35–3.98
1880...	105.7	100.5	37.7	75.6	29.8	85.1	8.64	81.	13.13	78.6	7.44	75.0	11.24	127.1	82.6	3.43–5.10	4.30–4.97
1881...	114.8	109.1	50.	100.2	37.8	108.	10.58	99.3	16.47	98.7	10.89	109.8	11.14	126.0	104.2	4.65–6.73	6.01–6.60
1882...	116.6	110.8	67.5	135.3	43.6	124.5	12.18	114.3	19.32	115.7	11.30	113.9	10.55	119.4	119.1	5.35–6.85	7.34–8.06
1883...	101.7	96.7	53.8	107.8	34.5	98.5	11.44	107.4	14.99	89.8	9.65	97.3	10.07	113.9	99.6	5.03–6.30	5.91–6.53
1884...	83.	78.9	51.6	103.4	29.1	83.1	10.72	100.6	16.22	97.2	7.95	80.1	9.77	110.6	90.55	5.53–6.83	5.57–5.98
1885...	83.9	79.7	43.	86.1	29.	82.9	9.36	87.8	10.37	62.1	6.50	65.5	9.55	108.1	77.4	4.06–5.81	3.90–4.56
1886...	76.6	72.8	37.	74.2	27.6	78.9	7.25	68.	9.73	58.3	6.23	62.8	9.63	108.9	69.2	1.59–5.70	3.84–4.59
1887...	75.6	71.8	39.5	79.2	26.	74.3	6.82	64.	14.12	84.6	6.77	68.2	8.91	100.8	73.7	1.64–5.28	4.69–5.46
1888...	90.	85.6	46.8	93.8	28.6	81.7	6.07	57.	14.17	84.9	8.37	84.4	8.13	99.0	81.2	1.76–5.97	5.41–5.99
1889...	85.5	81.3	34.	68.1	22.2	63.5	6.07	57.	11.09	66.4	6.47	65.3	7.81	88.3	66.9	1.43–4.81	4.17–4.52
1890...	89.2	84.8	39.3	78.7	30.9	88.3	6.04	56.7	10.63	63.6	6.01	60.6	8.25	93.3	72.1	1.80–5.22	3.79–4.21
1891...	96.6	91.9	58.4	117.	39.1	111.8	6.89	64.6	9.68	58.	6.27	63.2	8.53	96.5	84.4	1.45–6.20	4.20–4.76

TABLE II.—PRICES IN NEW YORK. / TABLE III.—PRICES IN ENGLAND.

WHEAT "Milwaukee Club" 1862 to 1873; "No. 2 Chicago and Milwaukee Spring" 1874 to 1889; "No. 2 Red Winter" 1890 and 1891.			CORN "No. 2 Mixed"		OATS "No. 2 Western Mixed"		BEEF "Extra Mess, Old to New"		PORK "Mess"		LARD "West'n Steam"		FARM PRODUCTS (Av. of Wheat, Corn, Oats, Beef, Pork, Lard)	BRITISH WHEAT (Gazette Ave'ge)		AMERICAN No. 2 RED WINTER WHEAT (In Mark Lane)
Years 1867–77	¢ per bu 132.5	per cent 100	¢ per bu 73.6	per cent 100	¢ per bu 49.78	per cent 100	$ pr. bbl 10.99	per cent 100	$ pr. bbl 17.33	per cent 100	¢ pr. lb 10.6	per cent 100	per cent 100	Year.	¢ per bu	¢ per bu
1862	106.7	80.5	53.7	73.	47.4	95.2	11.12	101.1	10.93	63.1	7.7	72.6	80.9	1862	158.3	
1863	105.8	79.9	51.6	70.1	53.1	106.7	8.12	73.9	9.38	53.6	7.2	68.	75.4	1863	127.9	
1864	97.2	73.3	74.4	101.2	45.5	91.4	8.63	78.5	16.33	94.2	8.7	82.	86.8	1864	114.8	
1865	107.5	81.2	75.8	102.9	47.4	95.2	8.83	80.3	18.58	106.6	13.3	125.5	98.6	1865	119.5	
1866	147.4	111.2	64.5	89.	39.8	80.	11.37	103.9	20.62	118.9	12.2	115.1	103.	1866	142.6	
1867	174.8	131.9	119.2	161.9	54.4	109.2	12.40	112.8	16.02	92.4	9.2	86.8	115.8	1867	184.	
1868	153.7	116.	85.5	116.2	58.8	118.2	10.40	94.6	18.99	109.6	12.	113.2	111.3	1868	182.1	
1869	114.2	86.2	76.1	103.4	55.	110.5	8.59	78.2	23.79	137.3	13.9	131.1	107.8	1869	137.6	
1870	112.6	85.	80.	108.7	51.	102.2	12.12	110.3	23.39	134.9	13.6	128.3	111.6	1870	133.8	
1871	135.8	101.7	68.6	93.1	53.7	107.8	12.73	115.8	14.73	85.	9.7	91.5	99.1	1871	161.9	162.6
1872	143.8	109.	60.1	81.6	43.4	87.2	9.10	82.8	12.11	69.9	7.9	74.5	84.2	1872	162.9	171.3
1873	136.7	103.2	57.	77.5	43.3	87.	10.51	95.6	14.37	82.9	7.5	71.7	86.3	1873	167.6	182.9
1874	121.4	91.6	79.7	108.3	56.2	112.8	11.89	108.2	17.22	99.4	11.2	105.7	104.3	1874	159.	165.5
1875	107.8	81.4	72.1	98.	54.	108.5	9.86	89.7	18.38	106.1	12.2	114.2	99.6	1875	129.	139.3
1876	108.7	82.	53.9	73.2	37.6	75.6	10.74	97.7	17.63	101.7	10.6	100.	88.4	1876	131.9	139.3
1877	143.3	108.	57.2	77.6	40.	80.3	12.54	114.1	13.98	80.7	9.1	85.5	91.	1877	159.1	159.7
1878	115.8	87.4	40.4	54.7	32.5	65.4	11.83	107.6	9.69	55.9	7.	66.1	72.9	1878	132.6	139.3
1879	116.7	88.1	48.	65.2	37.1	74.5	11.32	103.1	9.88	57.	6.2	58.5	74.4	1879	125.2	139.3
1880	124.7	94.1	55.1	74.9	42.6	85.5	10.45	95.	13.23	76.3	7.9	74.5	83.4	1880	126.7	148.
1881	128.7	96.7	63.6	86.4	45.8	92.	11.65	106.	16.94	97.7	11.4	107.5	97.7	1881	129.5	150.9
1882	127.9	96.5	80.2	109.	51.9	104.2	13.47	122.5	19.79	114.2	11.8	111.3	109.6	1882	128.8	140.8
1883	108.8	82.1	65.6	89.1	43.	86.3	12.84	116.9	16.59	95.7	9.8	92.3	93.7	1883	118.8	130.6
1884	95.	71.7	60.9	82.7	36.6	73.5	12.34	112.2	16.48	95.1	8.25	77.8	85.5	1884	101.9	105.9
1885	93.5	70.6	53.1	72.	35.9	72.2	11.31	102.9	11.58	66.7	6.3	59.4	74.	1885	93.8	101.6
1886	87.5	66.	48.3	65.6	35.1	70.5	8.22	74.8	10.63	61.3	6.5	61.3	66.6	1886	88.6	101.6
1887	87.7	66.2	50.8	69.	34.3	68.9	8.13	74.	15.00	86.6	7.1	67.	71.9	1887	92.9	98.7
1888	97.5	73.6	57.3	77.9	35.5	71.1	7.47	67.9	15.10	87.1	8.7	82.1	76.6	1888	90.9	107.4
1889	95.2	71.8	43.	58.4	28.1	56.4	6.98	63.5	12.57	72.5	6.9	65.1	64.6	1889	85.	101.6
1890	98.3	74.2	48.1	65.4	28.9	58.	6.96	63.3	12.13	70.	6.33	59.7	70.5	1890	91.2	103.1
1891	109.4	82.6	70.4	95.7	46.	92.4	8.35	75.9	11.38	65.7	6.6	62.3	79.1	1891	105.7	116.1

TABLE IV.—WHOLESALE PRICE OF STAPLES.

	"No. 1 ANTHRACITE FOUNDRY PIG IRON" (Philadelphia)		"BEST REFINED ROL'D BAR IRON" (Philadelphia)		IRON RAILS (at Mills in Pennsylvania)		STEEL RAILS (at Mills in Pennsylvania)		CUT NAILS (Philadelphia)		Average of PIG AND BAR IRON, RAILS, NAILS. (at Mills in Pa)	WOOL "MEDIUM W'SH'D CLOTHING FLEECE" (Eastern Mark'ts, Boston)		COTTON (New York) "MIDLING UPLANDS"		STANDARD SHEETINGS (New York)		
Year 1867 –77	$ per gro's ton 29.04	per cent 100	$ per gro's ton 62.81	per cent 100	$ per gro's ton 55.26	per cent 100	$ per gro's ton 87.32	per cent 100	$ pr keg of 100 lbs 3.67	per cent 100	per cent 100	¢ per lb 43.4	per cent 100	¢ per lb 17.14	per cent 100	¢ per yd 11.04	per cent 100	Year 1867 –77
1862	29.09	72.7	62.18	99.	36.87	66.7			3.06	83.4	88.5	44.6	102.8	27.63	161.2	16.38	147.5	1862
1863	24.29	83.8	62.73	99.9	42.97	77.7			3.53	96.2	89.4	52.1	120.	46.31	270.2	24.86	225.2	1863
1864	29.15	100.5	72.06	114.7	51.99	94.1			3.86	105.2	103.6	41.8	96.1	49.94	291.4	25.62	232.1	1864
1865	29.34	101.2	67.66	107.7	62.73	113.5			4.50	122.6	111.3	62.1	143.1	53.03	309.4	24.19	219.1	1865
1866	33.28	114.8	78.62	123.6	61.59	111.4			4.95	134.9	121.2	43.7	100.7	36.67	213.9	17.26	147.3	1866
1867	31.95	110.2	62.05	98.8	60.19	108.9	120.18	137.6	4.29	116.9	112.3	36.7	84.7	22.87	133.4	13.23	119.8	1867
1868	28.10	96.9	61.31	97.6	56.48	102.2	113.49	130.	3.70	100.8	102.9	32.9	73.5	17.79	103.8	12.02	108.9	1868
1869	30.55	105.3	61.41	97.8	58.09	105.1	99.45	113.9	3.66	100.	103.1	36.8	84.8	21.82	127.3	12.17	110.2	1869
1870	28.93	99.8	68.70	109.4	63.86	115.6	92.87	106.4	3.83	104.4	107.2	40.4	93.9	20.86	121.7	12.68	114.9	1870
1871	31.44	108.4	70.19	111.7	62.99	114.	91.74	105.1	4.05	110.4	109.8	49.2	113.4	15.17	88.5	11.64	105.4	1871
1872	43.50	150.	86.89	138.3	73.77	133.5	99.68	114.2	4.86	132.4	136.1	62.7	144.5	19.75	115.4	12.70	115.	1872
1873	37.58	129.3	75.97	121.	67.49	122.	105.92	121.3	4.31	117.4	122.3	47.	108.3	17.70	103.3	11.70	106.	1873
1874	27.19	93.8	61.09	97.3	52.82	95.7	80.77	92.5	3.59	97.8	95.8	46.6	107.4	16.14	94.2	10.27	93.	1874
1875	22.19	76.5	53.04	84.4	41.54	75.2	59.81	67.4	2.98	81.2	78.6	45.	103.7	13.45	78.5	9.06	82.1	1875
1876	19.98	68.6	46.77	74.5	37.04	67.	53.21	60.9	2.68	73.	70.	39.5	91.	11.66	68.	7.94	71.9	1876
1877	18.01	62.1	43.45	69.2	33.63	60.9	43.41	49.7	2.45	66.8	63.4	40.8	94.	11.28	65.8	8.07	73.1	1877
1878	17.47	60.2	43.89	69.9	33.48	60.6	41.91	48.	2.28	62.1	61.6	39.9	91.9	11.13	64.9	7.74	70.1	1878
1879	21.50	74.1	51.85	82.6	41.25	74.7	48.25	55.3	2.69	73.3	73.7	37.5	86.4	10.84	63.2	7.97	72.2	1879
1880	28.50	98.3	60.38	96.1	49.25		67.50	77.3	3.68	100.	92.9	53.75	123.8	11.51	67.2	8.51	77.1	1880
1881	25.13	86.7	58.05	92.4	47.13		61.13	70.	3.09	84.2	83.3	45.75	105.4	12.03	70.2	8.51	77.1	1881
1882	25.75	88.8	61.41	97.8	45.50		48.50	55.5	3.47	94.5	84.2	45.25	104.3	11.56	67.4	8.45	76.5	1882
1883	22.38	77.2	50.30	80.1			37.75	43.2	3.06	83.4	71.	42.	96.8	11.88	69.3	8.32	75.4	1883
1884	19.88	68.3	44.05	70.1			30.75	35.2	2.39	65.1	59.7	36.5	84.1	10.88	63.4	7.28	65.9	1884
1885	18.	62.1	40.32	64.2			28.50	32.6	2.33	63.5	55.6	32.75	75.5	10.45	60.9	6.75	61.1	1885
1886	18.71	64.5	43.12	68.7			34.50	39.5	2.27	61.9	58.6	35.25	81.2	9.28	54.2	6.75	61.1	1886
1887	20.92	72.1	49.37	78.6			37.08	42.5	2.30	62.7	63.5	37.7	86.8	10.21	59.6	7.15	64.8	1887
1888	18.88	65.1	45.02	71.7			29.83	34.2	2.03	55.3	56.6	34.	78.3	10.03	58.5	7.25	65.7	1888
1889	17.75	61.2	43.45	69.2			29.25	33.5	2.00	54.6	54.6	37.8	87.1	10.65	62.1	7.	63.4	1889
1890	18.40	63.4	45.92	73.1			31.75	36.4	2.00	54.6	56.9	36.75	84.7	11.07	64.6	7.	63.4	1890
1891	17.52	60.3	42.56	67.8			29.92	34.3	1.86	50.7	53.3	36.	82.9	8.60	50.2	6.83	61.9	1891

TABLE IV.—WHOLESALE PRICE OF STAPLES.—*Continued.*

	STANDARD PRINTS (New York)		LEATHER (Boston) "HEMLOCK UPPER"		LINSEED OIL (Boston)		FINE SALT (Syracuse, N.Y.)		CODFISH (Boston) "LARGE"		SUGAR (Boston and New York) "GRANULATED" ("CRUSH'D, POWDERED AND GRANULATED" previous to 1873)		COFFEE (New York) "FAIR TO PRIME BRAZIL" (No. 7 Exchange Standard); 1889 "No. 3 Exchange St."		MOLASSES (New York) "CUBA"		Average of STAPLES (Iron, Wool, She't'gs, L'th'r Lins'd Oil, S'lt Fish, Sugar, Coff'e, M'las's)	
Year 1867 –77	¢ per yd 9.40	per cent 100	¢ per lb 27.55	per cent 100	¢ per gal 70.9	per cent 100	$ per bbl of 280 lbs 1.415	per cent 100	$ per bbl 4.624	per cent 100	$ per 100 pounds 10.91	per cent 100	¢ per lb 17.93	per cent 100	¢ per gal 34.27	per cent 100	per cent 100	Year 1867 –77
1862	12.72	135.1					1.24	87.3			10.60	97.2	23.01	133.9				1862
1863	14.63	155.3					1.37	96.5			10.51	96.3	31.18	173.9				1863
1864	16.36	174.					1.33	93.7			11.93	109.4	42.49	237.	38.31	111.7		1864
1865	18.44	196.2					1.44	101.4			14.86	136.2	20.65	115.2	37.21	108.6		1865
1866	15.02	159.8					1.67	117.6			11.62	106.5	18.66	104.1	37.	108.		1866
1867	12.	127.7	27.5	100.	86.9	123.	1.70	119.7	4.25	92.	11.22	102.8	17.24	96.2	36.92	107.7	105.7	1867
1868	9.90	105.3	27.2	99.	77.	109.	1.68	118.3	4.30	93.	11.46	105.	15.73	87.7	35.26	102.9	99.9	1868
1869	10.53	112.	26.3	95.	73.3	103.	1.77	124.6	5.17	112.	13.06	119.7	15.83	88.3	38.35	111.9	105.2	1869
1870	10.80	114.9	28.3	103.	77.9	110.	1.87	131.7	5.44	118.	12.07	110.6	16.33	91.1	32.63	95.2	107.6	1870
1871	10.40	110.6	27.7	101.	72.5	102.	1.79	126.	4.92	106.	11.74	107.6	15.91	88.7	32.22	94.	105.4	1871
1872	10.68	113.6	32.	116.	73.4	104.	1.25	88.	4.78	103.	11.01	100.9	18.42	102.3	27.70	80.8	109.	1872
1873	9.99	106.3	29.4	107.	79.5	112.	1.23	86.6	4.50	97.	9.84	90.2	19.99	111.5	28.35	82.7	102.4	1873
1874	8.76	90.3	27.	98.	76.9	108.	1.44	101.4	4.27	92.	9.66	88.5	21.08	117.6	35.96	104.9	100.5	1874
1875	7.58	80.6	24.8	90.	57.3	81.	1.22	85.9	4.45	96.	9.29	85.2	19.01	106.	32.19	93.9	90.1	1875
1876	6.34	67.4	24.7	90.	48.8	69.	.81	57.	4.48	97.	10.28	94.2	17.97	100.2	31.07	90.7	83.	1876
1877	6.46	68.7	28.2	102.	56.3	79.	.81	57.	4.30	93.	10.38	95.1	19.72	110.	38.99	113.8	88.	1877
1878	6.04	64.3	24.6	89.	57.4	81.	.74	52.1	4.19	91.	9.12	83.6	16.51	92.1	33.08	96.5	80.8	1878
1879	6.25	66.5	28.5	104.	83.	117.	1.25	88.	3.62	78.	9.63	88.2	14.86	82.8	26.135	76.3	86.6	1879
1880	7.41	78.8	29.	105.	70.5	99.	.75	52.8	4.375	95.	9.92	90.9	15.12	84.3	35.	102.1	92.3	1880
1881	7.	74.5	26.7	97.	59.5	84.	.75	52.8	4.50	97.	10.13	92.8	12.23	68.2	33.47	97.7	85.4	1881
1882	6.50	69.1	24.7	90.	60.5	85.	.75	52.8	5.75	124.	9.35	85.7	9.77	54.5	34.50	100.7	85.7	1882
1883	6.	62.8	24.	87.	56.	79.	.75	52.8	4.875	105.	8.65	79.3	10.63	57.8	27.74	80.9	78.4	1883
1884	6.	62.8	19.25	70.	54.5	77.	.75	52.8	2.75	59.	6.75	61.9	10.92	60.9	18.83	54.9	64.7	1884
1885	6.	62.8	19.5	71.			.70	49.3	2.625	57.	6.52	59.8	9.01	50.25	19.41	56.6	61.	1885
1886	6.	62.8	19.75	72.			.65	45.8	2.56	55.	6.23	57.1	10.33	57.6	17.19	50.2	61.	1886
1887	6.	62.8	18.5	67.	48.5	68.	.65	45.8	4.125	89.	6.20	56.8	18.05	100.6	20.06	58.5	70.1	1887
1888	6.50	69.1	19.75	72.	55.	78.	.65	45.8	5.	108.	7.18	65.8	15.26	85.1	20.84	60.8	71.6	1888
1889	6.50	69.1	19.75	72.	58.5	83.	.65	45.8	4.375	95.	7.89	72.3	18.30	102.1	26.11	76.2	75.1	1889
1890	6.	62.8	20.25	74.	56.5	80.	.65	45.8	5.25	114.	6.27	57.5	18.03	100.6	20.44	59.6	73.6	1890
1891	6.	62.8	18.5	67.	44.	62.			5.25	114.	3.40	31.2	18.50	103.2	12.58	36.7	65.8	1891

TABLE V.—ACREAGE AND PRODUCTION OF WHEAT, BY GROUPS OF STATES.

	I. Maryland, New York, Pennsylvania.		II. Illinois, Indiana, Kentucky, Michigan, Ohio, Tennessee, Wisconsin.		III. Dakota, Iowa, Kansas, Minnesota, Missouri, Nebraska, Texas.		IV. California, Oregon, Washington.	
	ACRES.	1000 BUSH.	ACRES.	1000 BUSH.	ACRES.	1000 BUSH.	ACRES.	1000 BUSH.
1867	2,263,055	28,685	9,687,205	108,975	2,689,740	33,805		
1868	2,336,709	29,503	9,634,729	110,635	2,949,117	42,648	1,050,000	21,000
1869	2,294,832	32,983	9,331,287	123,250	3,825,392	55,050	1,191,006	21,750
1870	2,582,081	31,040	9,501,380	115,205	3,598,141	48,633	862,462	16,445
1871	2,222,431	34,582	9,419,761	107,259	4,148,073	48,315	1,642,738	19,049
1872	2,076,840	22,272	9,609,496	116,690	4,502,914	58,067	2,230,557	28,006
1873	2,082,593	27,857	10,105,067	122,991	5,749,550	83,901	1,757,468	24,631
1874	2,198,119	31,006	11,128,787	134,869	6,775,169	85,179	2,400,000	33,255
1875	2,215,085	25,500	11,752,439	125,240	7,145,604	86,770	2,419,317	28,300
1876	2,549,696	34,490	11,492,989	116,657	6,869,355	74,430	2,582,692	34,675
1877	2,602,415	37,780	10,076,552	146,040	7,680,138	115,974	2,659,539	28,875
1878	2,707,600	42,606	11,581,000	159,764	10,646,400	127,754	2,835,000	49,655
1879	2,660,500	40,053	11,591,700	194,073	10,974,500	126,064	3,011,800	43,189
1880	2,868,537	43,209	15,631,937	228,430	12,386,625	139,404	2,807,610	45,612
1881	2,902,300	36,854	14,848,000	150,935	12,730,000	111,687	3,105,800	44,079
1882	2,881,100	41,102	14,737,000	223,900	11,777,000	151,238	3,638,000	50,526
1883	2,924,798	35,656	13,490,560	138,120	12,212,930	159,872	3,759,500	52,627
1884	2,950,963	41,809	14,037,957	179,905	13,861,933	191,283	4,545,290	63,900
1885	2,648,143	29,424	11,011,668	112,441	12,833,870	140,947	4,122,778	47,920
1886	2,702,286	36,542	12,680,261	169,905	13,444,158	165,389	4,434,770	54,858
1887	2,650,870	29,719	13,153,830	166,027	14,169,722	172,928	4,149,871	54,874
1888	2,610,150	35,745	12,956,471	149,756	14,211,757	145,143	3,730,516	52,005
1889	2,544,020	31,717	12,702,478	176,608	14,421,717	182,719	4,552,320	64,326
1890	2,513,120	31,545	11,439,125	126,465	14,628,708	162,531	3,750,255	50,057
1891	2,518,471	39,604	12,335,174	201,418	17,002,549	269,851	4,205,102	61,960

The Food Supply and the Price of Wheat*

In 1879, in an address before the London Statistical Society, Mr. G. Shaw-Lefevre, said: "If I were to venture a prediction on so difficult and obscure a question, I would incline to the opinion that wheat has during the past year reached its lowest point."

This forecast was made a couple of years before the beginning of the great protracted decline in the prices of all agricultural produce that set in in the early years of the eighties. The forces which brought on the decline were already at work, and had been at work for some years before Mr. Shaw-Lefevre made his prediction; but the causes which seem very obvious after the fact may be quite obscure before it, and the causes that make for a permanent decline in agricultural produce are commonly more uncertain of prevision than those that make for a permanent rise. The former are apt to be of the nature of innovations, whose scope and efficacy can not well be foretold, while the latter are as apt to be simply the cumulative action of factors with whose scope and method we are already familiar.

Recognising, then, the chance of an unforeseen decline, and recognising, also, that there is more than one known factor already at work to bring about a decline in agricultural products in the near future, the purpose of this paper is to attempt an estimate of the possible maximum advance in the price of wheat (as a representative product of agriculture), supposing the factors that make for a decline to remain in abeyance for the next ten years.

The great permanent fall in prices that took place during the first half of the last decade has served as an object lesson

* *The Journal of Political Economy,* June 1893.

to enforce the truth that there is a close dependence of price on supply. The fact of this dependence has been made much of both by those who hope for an advance in prices of farm produce, and by those who deprecate the approach of a scarcity of bread. The assumption has been freely made that the date at which the land available for tillage shall have been definitively occupied is near at hand, and that when that day arrives a great and "sudden" advance in agricultural prices is to be looked for, with its consequences, of great gains for the farmer – for the American farmer perhaps, in an especial degree – and of distress for all peoples who get their supply of food largely from other countries. This sweeping generalisation merits some scrutiny.

It is unquestionably true that the price of wheat depends on the supply, but it is no less true that, other things being the same, the annual average supply of wheat depends, in the long run, on its price. The control exercised by the supply over the price is direct and transient. That exercised by the price over the annual average supply is of slower action, but it is also more permanent. We have therefore not said the last word in saying that when the demand shall have outgrown the present annual supply, the price of wheat will advance. The converse is also true; when the price of wheat begins to advance appreciably beyond what will barely remunerate the growers of wheat to-day, the supply will presently increase. The date of the definitive occupation of the tillable area yet available will no doubt mark an advance in the price of wheat, other things remaining unchanged; but the date of a definitive advance in price will no less surely mark an increase in the output from the acreage already under cultivation in the older wheat-growing sections. When this event comes to pass the farmers in the older sections will find it to their advantage to give their land such additional attention as will increase the yield per acre from the land already in cultivation, and so to some extent cover the shortage to which the rise in price is due and break the force of the advance. At the same time recourse will be had in an increasing degree to lands which are scarcely profitable for tillage at the prices which have been ruling for some years past.

The increased demand that is expected to advance the price of wheat will come as a result of an increase of the population of bread-eating countries. An increased demand for wheat accordingly implies an increase of approximately the same proportions in the demand for other food products; therefore any considerable increase of the acreage sown to wheat will be practicable only as a feature in the general increase of the acreage of arable land. The increased supply of wheat, as of other food products, will therefore have to be obtained, in part, by an increased yield per acre from the acreage already in cultivation.

While we have by no means reached — or nearly reached — the limit of the possible extension of the wheat area in America, it is probably true that we are fast approaching the point beyond which there is no considerable additional amount of wheat lands equally fertile and otherwise equally available with the last ten or twenty million acres already brought under cultivation. It can hardly be said that the spread of cultivation in America during the past ten or twelve years has been to less fertile or less available lands; but for the next ten or twelve years, barring unforeseen developments, any considerable further spread of the area of cultivation can not take place without recourse to less available lands. The practical working of the law of diminishing returns will therefore assume an importance for our farming which it has not had for some time past. This practical working of the law will appear in the relation between the price and the yield per acre.

The yield per acre and the prices of farm produce vary considerably as between the different sections of the country, and, so far as concerns the older sections, they vary together, with some regularity; but the difference in prices between different localities is too slight, and the difference in other respects is too great to afford satisfactory figures from which to infer what is the effect, on the yield, of a given local advantage in price. The divergence in price is not pronounced nor easily ascertainable, as between states which are in other respects available for our comparison. Evidently no value can attach to a comparison of the newer, spring-wheat states with the older, winter-wheat states. But it may be remarked that Vermont, Massachusetts and Connecticut show a higher yield than any of the Ohio Valley states.

It will be more to the purpose, because the divergence both in price and in yield is great enough to afford tangible evidence of the efficacy of the forces at work, to compare the price and yield per acre in Great Britain with the price in Chicago and the yield per acre in the winter-wheat states lying about Chicago. The yield per acre of wheat in Great Britain is very considerably greater than in the states about Chicago. The immediate cause of its being so is the higher price obtained for wheat, and for other farm produce, by the British farmers; and the degree of effectiveness of the inducement offered them in the way of higher prices ought to help us to forecast the probable efficacy of an appeal of the same kind to the industry of their American competitors.

The winter-wheat states centering about Chicago and the great lakes – Ohio, Indiana, Illinois, Wisconsin and Michigan – may, in some respects, not unfairly be compared with Great Britain. They are like that country in being a country of mixed farming, and, as regards wheat production, mainly a winter-wheat country. Their farm lands have also been under cultivation for such a length of time as in large measure to obviate the complications which the "virgin soil" would introduce into any comparison of the newer states of the west with the countries of Europe. In some respects these states do not afford a close parallel to the farming lands of Great Britain. The climate is not the same, and the faults of the climate are not of the same kind. In the states mentioned there is more danger from drought than from wet seasons; in the United Kingdom it is all the other way. A bad season in England is sure to be a year of deficient heat, or excessive moisture, or both. Further, the soil of these states does not closely resemble the British soil in point of adaptation to wheat culture. These states do, however, afford as nearly fair a comparison with British soil and climate as any part of America that is a sufficiently representative wheat-growing region, and at every point where the comparison seems to be vitiated by inherent differences the difference is in favor of the states, as a superior country for wheat-growing and for mixed farming. The American soil is more fertile and more easily tilled; the climate of the states is better adapted for wheat-growing; the American farmers are probably not at all inferior to the British in intelligence or enterprise. So far as the inherent difference in natural advantages may lead us astray in drawing any inferences from a comparison of this group of states with Great Britain, the error would be in the direction of too low an estimate of the wheat-growing capacity of the states under the stimulus of a higher price. And as the object of the inquiry is to estimate the probable minimum effect on supply of a given permanent advance in price, rather than the maximum capacity of the states under such a stimulus, this is not a danger that need be specially guarded against.

An objection of greater weight may be found in the difference between British and American prices of staples, other than agricultural produce. The higher general level of prices of what the American farmer has to buy places him at a disadvantage, as compared with the British farmer, in precisely the same way as the lower price he gets for what he has to sell. The hindering effect of the higher price of staples must accordingly be allowed for in calculating the effect which a given rise in the price of farm products will have in the way of increasing the intensity of culture.

This higher range of prices does not comprise all articles of consumption used by the farmer. Lumber, and forest products generally, are lower here than in England. Farm implements of most kinds are rather cheaper; leather goods are scarcely higher; many of the staple food products are cheaper. But after all has been said, it is not to be questioned that the American farmer has to pay a somewhat higher average range of prices for what he buys (outside of agricultural products) than his British competitor. The American tariff, to the extent to which it is protective, increases the price of the articles on which it is laid, and among these articles are many important items of the farmer's necessary consumption.

It is difficult to say, even approximately, how much of a handicap this added cost is to American farming. It assuredly does not amount to more than 20 per cent. of the value of our farm products at Chicago prices; probably the actual additional cost to the farmers is considerably less than 20 per cent. of the value of their products.

Against this higher cost of necessaries in America may be offset the lower margin of cultivation in Great Britain, –

using the term in the sense of a resort to poorer soils. The natural fertility of the poorest soils in cultivation in Great Britain, in the system of mixed farming of which wheat culture is an integral part, is greatly lower than that of the poorest classes of soils cultivated in the states named. This implies a correspondingly greater average cost of production of the products of British farming,[1] and it affects also the cost of many of the necessaries of life to the British farmer.

The advantage is as definitely on the side of the states with respect to the margin of cultivation, as it is on the side of Great Britain with respect to the range of general prices. Here, again, it is impossible to say how great the advantage of the one over the other may be, but it is not unlikely that the disadvantage of the British farmer in this respect may completely offset the disadvantage which the American farmer has in the matter of higher general prices.

It may be thought that the fact that the agricultural depression in Great Britain during the whole of the period chosen for comparison (1884-92) has been severer than in America, would vitiate any British data for comparison with our own in any case where the point at issue turns on the question of a remunerative price. This difficulty is not a very serious one in any case, and does not affect the question in hand at all. What is required for the validity of the argument is: (1) that the inducements to wheat culture in Great Britain, relatively to other tillage, should not be greater than in the states; and (2) that the least fertile lands cultivated in the British system of farming should not be intrinsically

[1] This statement does not imply that rent is an element in the cost of production. What is claimed is that Great Britain, as a whole, because of its lower margin of cultivation, gets the products of its soil at a greater average expenditure than do the states, and that a given increment in the price will induce a less increment in yield at this lower margin than at the higher margin of cultivation existing in the states.

superior to the lands similarly at the margin of cultivation in the states. It needs no argument to establish that both these conditions are fully met and will continue to hold for an indefinite time to come.[2]

If the considerations adduced are admitted to be valid, to the extent that wheat growing in a system of mixed farming in the states named lies under no other or greater disadvantage as compared with wheat growing in Great Britain than that indicated by the difference in the price of a given grade of wheat between Chicago and Liverpool, then we have the premises from which to deduce approximately what will be the maximum possible advance in price required to induce a given increase in the average yield per acre of wheat in the states. And this will afford some indication of what will be the maximum possible advance in price resulting from a given increase in the consumption of wheat.

The prices selected for comparison are average prices of American No. 2 Red Winter Wheat in Liverpool and in Chicago, since 1884.

While this grade of wheat is not grown in England, the quotations for this grade are quite as significant for wheat prices in England as any quotations obtainable. The Gazette averages, which are usually quoted, are for British wheat, without respect to quality; and the average quality of the grain from which the quotations are made up will accord-

[2] The depression in British farming, so far as it is not due to bad harvests, is due to the decline in prices; and this decline has affected grain production rather more strongly than other tillage. Its most pronounced economic result has been a readjustment of rents on a lowered basis. Apart from adverse seasons, the British farmers' chief real grievance is too high rents. Prices have fallen some 30 per cent. or more; money rents, except in isolated cases, have not been lowered to correspond. In addition to this, the farmers have suffered from a depreciation of the capital they have had invested in farming; which is also a considerable item.

ingly vary from year to year, with the character of the harvest. Gazette averages are useless for any exact comparison.

The reason for not making up the averages for a comparison of prices from a series of years reaching back of 1884 is obvious. Wheat culture had not, until that time, adjusted itself to the changed conditions of the market that supervened about 1880-82. The years immediately preceding 1884-85 were years of great changes in the price and acreage of wheat. By 1884 the decline was completed, and the price of wheat has moved on a lower level since that time than before. About the same time the decline in acreage in the states selected had also practically ceased;[3] though a slight tendency to a further narrowing of the acreage has been perceptible since that time, at least until 1890.

The average yield per acre of wheat for the eight years since 1885[4] in the states selected has been about 13¾ bushels.[5]

[3] The extraordinary decline in wheat acreage in the Ohio valley group of states in 1885 was due quite as much to an unfavorable season as to a voluntary narrowing of the area. The acreage regained in 1886 more than half of what had been lost in 1885. The definitive effect on acreage of the decline in price that ended in 1884, was not had until the following year. In studying the movement of acreage under the influence of the new level of prices then established, the new period is to be considered as having begun with 1885.

[4] The average yield for the years 1885-92 has been taken, as, for the present purpose, answering to the price during the years 1884-91. The yield for the year 1884 was the same as the average for 1885-92.

[5] The average annual yield has been:

Year	In the States; bushels (Winchester)	In Great Britain; bushels (Imperial)
1885	11.19	31.31
1886	14.41	26.89
1887	13.38	32.07
1888	12.02	28.05
1889	14.91	29.89
1890	11.74	30.74
1891	17.49	31.26
1892	14.40	26.38
Average	13.78	29.57

This average includes the extraordinary harvest of 1891 (17½ bushels per acre). But even counting 1891, this average is probably slightly short of the normal average yield for these states, the seasons during the latter half of the eighties having been, on the whole, rather unfavorable for winter wheat. The average yield of the same states for the years 1877-83, when the seasons were, on the whole, very favorable, was 14¾ bushels. The lower average yield during later years seems to be due, in a slight degree, to a partial displacement of wheat by other crops on some of the more fertile and better-tilled soils; or perhaps more exactly, to a relative neglect of wheat-growing by some of the more capable and better equipped farmers; but the great cause of this discrepancy lies, no doubt, in the character of the seasons. When due weight is allowed to all these factors, we shall be very near the truth in assuming 14 bushels per acre to be the present normal average yield of wheat in these states.

For Great Britain the officially assumed normal average yield of wheat is 28.80 bushels per acre. The actual annual average for the eight years since 1885 is 29.57 bushels.[6] It is difficult to say whether the officially assumed normal average is nearer the true normal than the recorded actual average. The *London Economist*, as well as some other authorities, claims the true normal average to exceed 29 bushels. The seasons during the eighties have been, on the whole, rather more favorable for wheat than the average of a long series of years. If this were the sole modifying circumstance the official normal average would have to be accepted as very near the true normal. But this circumstance does not account for the whole of the discrepancy between the average yield of today and that of some years ago. It has been pointed out that the average has also probably been raised by the drop-

[6] See 5th note on page 389.

ping of some of the inferior soils out of wheat cultivation. At the same time, improvements in agriculture seem also to have affected the average yield in the same direction. It will be safe to take 29 bushels per acre as the actual normal average yield of wheat in Great Britain.

The average yield in Great Britain exceeds the yield in the states by about 107 per cent. (15 bushels). The annual average price of American No. 2 Red Winter Wheat in Liverpool, for the years 1884-91, exceeds the average price of the same grade in Chicago by a trifle over 20 per cent. (18.095 cents per Winchester bushel).[7] It ought to be a safe inference that a gradual advance in the price of wheat in the Chicago market to the present level of the price in Liverpool (accompanied, as in the normal course of things it would be, by a corresponding advance in the prices of other farm produce) would result in such an advance in the intensity of culture in the states lying about Chicago as to increase the average yield of wheat, during the early stages of the advance, in the same proportion as the British yield is higher on account of the higher British price. That is to say, a sufficiently gradual and permanent moderate advance, of a given per cent., in price in the Chicago market, should result

[7] Annual average price of No. 2 Red Winter Wheat, in cents per bushel:

Year	Chicago	Liverpool
1884	89.3	107.2
1885	88.3	103.1
1886	77.6	99.6
1887	77.2	98.7
1888	92.5	107.4
1889	85.2	102.8
1890	89.5	105.3
1891	97.3	117.7
Average	87.13	105.225

in an increase in the yield per acre of wheat in these states, of at least five times as many per cent. Twenty per cent. (18 cents per bushel) advantage in price in Liverpool carries with it 107 per cent. (15 bushels) advantage in the yield per acre in Great Britain. A gradual advance of five per cent. (4.36 cents per bushel) in the annual average price in Chicago ought to bring an increase of more than 20 per cent. (2.8 bushels) in the yield of wheat in the states lying about Chicago, supposing the conditions of production otherwise to remain unchanged.

The aggregate annual production of the five states named, for the eight years 1885-92, has averaged slightly over 140 million bushels. If the price of wheat in Chicago were to advance permanently to 95.84 cents per bushel (10 per cent.) we should have to expect the total annual production of these states to rise to not much less than 210 million bushels (50 per cent.). Assuming that the advance in price would have an equivalent effect on the output in the other wheat regions (and the chances would seem to be that the effect would be relatively at least as great in the remoter wheat fields, since the per cent. advance in price in the remoter local markets would be appreciably greater, and any liability to increase the yield on the newer wheat lands would be fully offset by an extension of the area), and considering also that such an advance in price would induce some increase in acreage in all the wheat producing country, an ordinary average price of 96 cents in the Chicago markets might be expected to bring out an aggregate annual product of not less than 800 million bushels.

Conversely, No. 2 Red Winter Wheat cannot advance permanently to 96 cents in Chicago until there is a customary demand for about 800 million bushels of American wheat at the increased price. A ten per cent. advance in price presumes something near a fifty per cent. increase in the demand.

The increase in the demand for wheat will coincide approximately with the increase of the bread-eating population. Judging of the future by the past, it will be a liberal estimate to say that the bread-eating population of the countries which draw on the supplies of the general market to which America contributes, may be expected to increase by ten per cent. in ten years. It has perhaps reached that rate of growth during the last decade, and it would be extravagant to expect that rate to be exceeded during the next decade.

The price which it would be necessary to offer for wheat in order to meet this increased demand by an increased production is more a matter of surmise than the probable rate of growth of population. If we could answer this question, we should know approximately what prices our farmers may look for in payment for their produce during the opening years of the twentieth century. There is reason to believe that, barring unforeseen innovations, at the point in the growth of the demand for food at which there will be an effective demand for one-and-one-half times as much American wheat as at present, the price will have to be advanced by not more than nine cents above the present ordinary average price in Chicago. In the meantime, a less increase in the demand could be met at a less advance in price. An increase of ten per cent. (200,000,000 bushels) in the world's consumption of wheat would mean, if the demand were distributed as it is at present, an increase of about 50 million bushels in the portion ordinarily required of America. This additional demand could be met, without increase of acreage, by an addition of about 1¼ bushels to the present average yield per acre of wheat; and this additional 1¼ bushels would be forthcoming without its being necessary to advance the price in the local markets by as much as two cents per bushel above the average of the last eight or nine years.

But the additional demand will not fall *pro rata* on the countries which now supply the world with wheat; and the like is true to almost the same extent of the supply of other agricultural products. America now, of late years, supplies rather less than one-fourth of the total wheat product. She will certainly be called on to contribute more than one-fourth of the additional 200 million bushels that will be required before the end of another ten years, unless some unforeseen contingency should come in to change the complexion of things.

An advance in price would have some effect on the intensity of culture in all agricultural countries, but the effect would probably be very slight in such regions as the wheat lands of Russia and India, especially the latter. In these countries, as well as in large portions of Western Europe, notably in France, agriculture is in the hands of a population that does not respond readily to promptings from without. Whatever addition may be made to the wheat supply furnished by those countries – apart from additions due to improved facilities for transportation – will be made slowly, and will at best be inconsiderable for some time to come. The new demand will fall first and most heavily on the American, Australian and South American wheat lands, and on such portions of Europe as Great Britain, Austria, parts of Germany, &c., together with some contributions due to an increase of acreage in Russia.

This fact, that the intensity of culture of a considerable portion of the present wheat-producing area of the world will be but partially and feebly affected by a moderate advance in the price, will necessitate a higher production on the part of that portion which will more readily respond to the call. It results in a virtual narrowing of the area from which the additional supply can be obtained, so as to include little else than the newer wheat-growing countries, with portions of Western Europe. These regions will therefore be called on to furnish more than their *pro rata* contingent to the increase, and this greater rate of production in these countries will be obtained only at the cost of a greater advance in price.

Of these more manageable countries, not all would respond to the demand with equal alacrity. It is, for example, easier for America to add one-tenth to her average yield of 12¼ bushels than it is for England to add one-tenth to her yield of 29 bushels.[8]

This fact goes in the same direction and adds further to the necessity of a higher price in the American market than would have been required if America were called on to furnish her *pro rata* increase only.

America has of late contributed something less than one-quarter of the world's annual wheat supply. If the facts above recited are allowed the extreme weight implied in looking to this country for one-half instead of one-fourth of the additional 200 million bushels that will be required by the end of another ten years, then it will be necessary to increase the yield of wheat in America, not by one-tenth, as was assumed above, but by one-fifth; that is, from 12⅓ bushels to 14.8 bushels per acre for the whole country, or from 14

[8] It must not be supposed that England, or any part of Europe, is near the limit of productivity. The *London Economist* of September 13, 1890, says: "High authorities have estimated that we might double the produce of the soil in the United Kingdom even under our existing system of farming. As it is, there are farmers who grow nearly double the average of grain crops for the kingdom as a whole, and many who produce twice the average weight of roots and potatoes."

bushels to 16.8 per acre for the five states named. To maintain such an increase in the American yield of wheat would require an advance of less than 4½ per cent. (3.8 cents per bushel) in the price of wheat in Chicago.

But as some increase in acreage is sure to result from any advance in price, allowance must be made for the increased supply to be obtained by this means. How great the effect on the acreage will be, it is impossible to say. On the other hand, it is pretty certainly true that any advance in price will not have as great an effect in increasing the yield in the newer states, especially in the spring-wheat country, as in the group of states with which we set out. The chief increase in product in the newer states will, for some time to come, be got by increasing the acreage. It may be accepted without much risk that this increase in acreage will fully make up for the slighter increase in the yield per acre, so that the conclusion already arrived at need not be modified on that account.

If, therefore, these premises are accepted as sound and adequate, there is small chance that the normal increase in the demand for bread will permanently raise the average price of No. 2 wheat above 91 cents in the Chicago market within the next ten years.

This estimate proceeds on the supposition that no considerable advance is taking place or will take place the next few years in the methods of farming or in any of the industries that have to do directly or indirectly with the food supply. This of course is an extreme position. If, as is quite probable, improved industrial knowledge and processes should appreciably lessen the cost of production of grain in the newer wheat countries, this estimate would probably prove too high. And, if as is still more probable, the prices of staple articles in America should decline, relatively to those of farm produce, the chance of any advance in wheat or in farm products, generally, would be still further narrowed. If, for example, American import duties on staples should be lowered within the next ten years sufficiently to diminish the cost of the farmer's necessary articles of consumption by 20 per cent. (and such a result is possible), the chance of any permanent advance in wheat for the present would disappear.

Even apart from any lowering of the cost of articles of necessary consumption, it is fully within the possibilities of the situation that no permanent advance in farm products need take place at all for a generation or more. Better methods and a more intimate knowledge of the natural processes concerned in farming are probably capable, as competent authorities insist, of so adding to the efficiency of our farming as not to admit of prices going higher than they are.

Agriculture is fast assuming the character of an "industry," in the modern sense, and the development of the next few decades may not improbably show us, in farming as in other occupations, a continual improvement in methods and a steady decline in cost of production, even in the face of a considerably increased demand.

Adolph Wagner's New Treatise*

Economic students will be glad to learn that in a note to the third edition of his *Grundlagen der Volkswirthschaftslehre,* which has just come from the press, Professor Adolph Wagner announces that arrangements have been made for the completion of his *Lehrbuch der Politischen Œkonomie.* It is now almost twenty years since Wagner, with the promised assistance of the late Professor Erwin Nasse, undertook his great literary project. The comprehensive character of the original plan of the work and the cyclopædic fullness of its first volumes, which followed so slowly upon one another that but four volumes have thus far been published, have always made the ultimate completion of the work a matter of great doubt. When the original literary partnership was interrupted some three years ago by the untimely death of Professor Nasse, and when, about the same time, Wagner announced his intention of abridging the unfinished portion of his *Finanzwissenschaft* by the omission of a volume, it seemed more likely than ever before that the whole work would remain, as many had all along feared, a torso. But it now, fortunately, looks as though the work will be rescued from that fate and be carried to completion on an even more elaborate scale than the original scheme contemplated. The greater range and elaborateness of the new enterprise is, perhaps, indicated in the change of its title to *Lehr- und Handbuch der Politischen Œkonomie.* Associated with Profesor Wagner in the accomplishment of this colossal work is a new group of collaborators, made up of Professors

* *The Journal of Political Economy,* December 1892.

[Heinrich] Dietzel and [Carl] Bücher, of the Universities of Bonn and Leipzig, respectively, and Ministerial Councillor Buchenberger, of Karlsruhe.

According to the present scheme, the work is to be divided into five main divisions, each of which will be sub-divided into as many separate parts or volumes as the treatment may require. The following parts have been provided for, and the work of preparation apportioned among Wagner and his collaborators, as follows:

In Division I, Wagner treats of the Fundamentals of Political Economy in two volumes, the one on the Basis of the National Economy, the other on National Economy and Jurisprudence, or Freedom and Property; in Division II, Dietzel discusses Theoretical Political Economy; in Division III, Practical Political Economy is dealt with in four parts: (1) Exchange and Transportation by Wagner; (2) Agriculture, in two volumes, by Buchenberger; (3) Forestry, by Bücher and Buchenberger; (4) Industry and Trade, by Bücher, in two volumes; in Division IV, Wagner adds to his already published three volumes on Finance, a fourth, and eventually a fifth, on the Theory of the Special Taxes and on Public Debts. A fifth division, not yet arranged for, is to give a History of the Literature of Political Economy.

It appears from this survey that the completed work will embrace not less than fifteen volumes, far surpassing in its compass anything hitherto attempted in the domain of economic science, and the high scholarship of the writers is an ample warranty that the quality of the treatment will be commensurate with its extent. The volumes on Agriculture are promised for an early date, and we are assured that the whole work will be energetically pushed to completion.

It will be noticed in the new scheme that Wagner's share

of the work has been considerably augmented by the expansion of his *Grundlegung* into two volumes. During the thirteen years that have elapsed since the appearance of the second edition, its author's views have undergone some change; and certain fundamental questions that were sparingly noticed in the earlier editions are given a place of particular prominence in the present edition. It is rather signicant that the question of method, on which the author was silent in the first two editions, should receive such extended notice now. Not that his opinions on this much controverted subject have not hitherto been known, for Wagner has long been known, at least, as a vigorous critic and opponent of the new Historical School, but he has never hitherto expressed himself with so much fullness and freedom from reserve. His account of the reciprocal relations of the different schools and, more particularly, his estimate of the influence exerted by the extreme historical tendency, are especially interesting. A few passages, indicating the author's attitude, are here reproduced. They are well worthy of notice as coming from one of the most eminent of economists, and as foreshadowing the end of a long controversy, whose results have proved, as was anticipated by men of temperate judgment, less revolutionary than reactionary.

"Certain general conceptions and demands, at first adopted by the older group, are maintained by the younger, but are further developed by them ,and have been accepted by scholars outside the strict German historical school, and on the whole by the present author. But as regards the method and aims of the science, the younger historical school takes a somewhat different position. They incline to a fusion of industrial history and political economy; they reject too sweepingly the older British *a priori* doctrine as a basis for actual scientific theory; they ignore the difference between concrete economic history and special or practical economics as distinct divisions of political economy—even brushing aside the distinction in purpose, method and manner of treatment between economic history and economic theory. So far as the younger historical school gives prominence to these views, I differ from it in this work, as in general. . . . The historical school has partly in its earlier, and fully in its later period, reacted too strongly in respect to the method of political economy. It does not always correctly and clearly distinguish as regards the aims of economic science between theoretic and practical political economy, and reproaches the entire English system with faults which are to be found only in certain of its adherents, which, indeed, are often merely accidental, and do not necessarily follow from the essential methods or conceptions of the system." (p. 47).

The preface charges the historical school with a spirit of intolerance: "I have found myself impelled to discuss from time to time the tendency of the younger German historical economists. If these discussions have occasionally been somewhat sharply critical, I wish it to be understood that the matter in hand is not merely a question of protesting against a one-sided method which I thought pernicious, but of protesting as well against an attitude of arrogance on the part of certain writers toward those who do not allow exclusive validity among methods to historical induction, and who do not identify economic history with political economy—a narrowness of an opposite kind to that of the older British deductive and abstract writers, though at bottom more dangerous."

Schmoller, as the leader of the extreme historical school, is noticed at great length, praise which approaches enthusiasm for his services as an economic historian appearing in strong contrast to such comments as the following on his attitude as a scientist: "To Schmoller, whatever does not belong to the historical-statistical 'exact' investigation is more or less the work of sportive fancy (*Gedankenspielerei*). It is branded, after the manner of Comte, as 'mere speculation,' belonging to the still 'metaphysical period' of the science, and thus demolished. . . . But this tone toward everything and everyone not in agreement with him does not enable Schmoller to conceal the fact that as to questions of fundamental principle, in points of theory, of primary conception (which, after all, even the historians cannot avoid), of law, and even of method, Schmoller is not always clear and not always sure of himself. As his great services in economic history show, his talent lies much more in other fields and in other directions. He has himself remarked on occasion, that the historians of a science are seldom equally skillful as its theorists. This may be confirmed by an observation of his own case." (pp. 53-54).

Wagner's respect for the British so-called "orthodox" school is indicated by numerous explicit statements referring to groups of writers or to individuals. "According to the character of the problem to be considered, according to the specific application of the general problem, and, assuredly, according to the individual cast of mind, the peculiar preference or tendency of each writer,—the individualist in political economy has in fact at one time made use predominantly of speculative deduction, at another time of induction. In some authors, as Ricardo, Senior, [John Stuart] Mill, [Friedrich Benedikt Wilhelm von] Herrmann, there is a fondness for deduction—this in part because that method seemed especially applicable to the particular problems in hand (as to the doctrine of price, income, or distribution). But for example, A. Smith himself, has made use of both methods together,—so much so that to this day, and among the latest historians of the subject, opinions differ as to whether he preferably employed deduction or induction. That alone shows that the charge against the earlier British economists of exclusive deduction is unfounded. It is asserted that deductions after the usual manner (in which self-interest especially is taken as the starting-point) are necessarily wrong. This is mere assertion, which has not yet been at all adequately justified by those who offer it, and which is flatly belied by their own work in economics. For these writers, including the historical economists, on all occasions, even in the most 'exact historical investigations,' employ for explanation or proof deductions from economic self-interest and the related motives, acts and omissions. . . .

"The British and the Continental representatives of the Individualist political economy have fallen into error, not from the employment of the deductive method, and not from the effort to secure abstract results in the treatment of problems – this effort being of itself proper. Their errors have resulted rather from the failure to give their method a sufficiently firm support in their psychological premises – and to keep in mind the hypothetical nature of this method in applying it to concrete relations. The question is therefore not as to an entire change of the method of deduction, or even of its replacement by induction. This entire substitution would be impossible, and not altogether right or desirable, if it were possible. To secure a truer use of deduction, giving it a more accurate and a deeper psychological basis and development, more cautiously applying it, not forgetting its hypothetical character, more sharply observing the necessary limits of its applicability with reference to classes and character of questions and to the peculiarities of special scientific tasks, often properly uniting it with induction (to do this always is impossible), and in certain cases substituting induction for deduction, — in short, to secure a use of deduction better in all these particulars, — that is the problem. By failing to do this, distinguished representatives of the British school have undoubtedly often made mistakes. But they were usually not so much errors of method, or errors resulting inevitably from the character of the method, as errors in the application of the method. The appearance of the German historical political economy was not necessary to the recognition of this fact, although it has certainly merited much by its critical services at this point. But as this school in its turn went to the opposite extreme, depreciating the true deductive procedure, and over estimating its own inductive method, and ignoring the limits beyond which its method was of less service than the other, it has done at least as great damage, if not greater, than can be alleged against the British school. . . . General reproaches as to method, such as the later German historical writers have cast upon the English group, with a self-sufficiency to which the logical clearness and acuteness of their argumentation do not correspond, are unjust and incorrect. The use of both the chief methods is demanded by the subject matter of political economy, and by the character of the problems proposed for its solution. Moreover, that which is right and warranted in the Geman historical method, is not new. Many of the older theorists, authors of systematic treatises or of monographs, as well as those who discussed practical questions, have used this method,— not least, again, A. Smith. . . .

". . . . In our opinion, the British theory and dogmatic teaching may claim, under certain hypotheses, a great and lasting usefulness. With substantial correctness they gave a knowledge of the skeleton, the salient points and outlines of the system of private economy, both static and dynamic, with the legal and psychological hypotheses which, on the whole, are realized in developed civilizations like those of the present day." . . . "The English economists failed, however," says Wagner, "to perceive that these hypotheses are not always fulfilled, or are fulfilled in varying degree in different times or places or specific instances. But if these defects be remedied," he continues, "as they may be, in fact have been, in accordance with the spirit of the English school, no less than with that of the historical political economy, the critics of the younger historical group find the ground cut away from under them, while that which is essential in the British theory survives." (p. 49).

Mill is given chief prominence among writers on logic. "I think that with reference precisely to political economy, no logician is more instructive. . . . It seems to me that we should hold fast to Mill's views on the logic of our particular science – this holds especially of his justification of deduction and the corresponding application of the inductive methods to experimental research." (pp. 138, 139).

As to Ricardo, Wagner remarks: "Very properly [Alfred] Marshall maintains the continuity of development of the science. He, and recent American writers, in opposition to the exaggerations and obscurity of the historical writers, have indicated the immense importance of Ricardo. . . . Marshall judges Ricardo's Cost of Production theory quite justly in declaring that it has remained to the present day fundamentally intact, much being added to it, much built upon it, but little taken from it. With this youthful moderation let me compare the judgments passed by the younger or youngest German historical writers on Ricardo and other older authors of his method and tendency. Herrmann is now hardly known by many of the younger scholars among us; his unsurpassed work finds abroad, like [Johann Heinrich] von Thünen's, so much the more grateful appreciation. As to the new doctrines, Marshall says very properly: 'they have supplemented the older, have extended, developed, and sometimes corrected them, and often have given them a different tone by a new discussion of emphasis, but very seldom have subverted them.'"

To the Austrians, the special antagonists of the exaggerated historical tendency, Wagner turns with satisfaction. "Fortunately," he says, (p. 63) "either action or excessive reaction, in 'free science,' outside of the narrow boundaries of schools, always calls forth reaction. It is the merit of Carl Menger of Vienna to have brought about a very strong reaction in German economic science. Under his leadership, or in company with him, a number of specialists, particularly in Austria, have ably and justly thrust the theoretical problems of political economy again into the foreground, especially the question of value. . . . One need not accept all the specific results of their investigation in regarding their starting-point as a proper one. 'The ways by which judgments are reached, the methods of research, conform to the objects of the investigator, and to the formal nature of the truths sought for.' (Menger). Deduction in the domain of theoretical political economy has rightly been brought, by the efforts of Carl Menger, his school and adherents, once more into a position of honor in German science, despite the pretentiousness of the historical school – a considerable service, as well from the standpoint of one who, like the present author, seeks to take a middle position in the methods controversy. . . . That it [the service of the Austrians][1] has received less recognition in Germany than abroad, is to be explained variously, – in part from personal causes and from the prejudices of schools, – but this lack of recognition does not detract from their value. A certain tendency to exaggera-

[1] [The brackets are Veblen's].

tion and one-sidedness may, perhaps, be occasionally discovered in this reaction against the historical school, especially in the heat of controversy, as is almost always the case when there arises a proper reaction against a different one-sidedeness. That, however, will be corrected in time. . . . Men like the younger Dietzel have shown that one may come by his own way to a like manner of treatment of theoretical problems, and yet, with respect to important fundamental themes, as of Value and Marginal Utility, may stand outside of the new Austrian school without failing to appreciate the service which that school has rendered."

The influence of the extravagant historical group has, however, for the most part been confined to Germany. It has appeared abroad "only in scattered instances, and even so in a more moderate form. Where the just element in the historical movement has been acknowledged, the acknowledgment has been made much as I have made it here. (p. 63). . . . Distinguished economists abroad, as in Italy before all, L. Cossa, with his expressed preference for the historical treatment of the subject, the Belgian, E. de Laveleye, the Englishmen, [Henry] Sidgwick, Marshall, [J. N.] Keynes, numerous younger American savants who received their training in Europe, have attached themselves to the historical and socio-political movement, but represent it with moderation and hold fast to the kernel of the old theory."

Levasseur on Hand and Machine Labor.*

RECENTLY, before the Société Industrielle de l'Est, at Nancy, Professor Levasseur has summed up his views on the influence of machinery upon the welfare of the wage-earners. The address has an added interest to American readers in that its data are, in good part, of American origin, being based on Commissioner Wright's report on *Hand and Machine Labor.* They include also a considerable amount of fresh material.

As to the relative healthfulness of work-places since machine-labor became prevalent, "The Encyclopedia" gives an account of eighteenth-century factories, "from which," says M. Levasseur,

> We have reason for thinking that hygienic conditions are much better observed now than formerly and that we concern ourselves with hygiene to a degree beyond even the imagination of our grandfathers. The Universal Exposition of 1900 presented a similar comparison of mines in antiquity (not so very different, as to the point under discussion, from those of the sixteenth century) with the mine of today.
>
> I have often cited in this connection two monuments of stone: a bas-relief (in the British Museum and also in the Louvre) representing the transportation of an obelisk or colossal statue by Assyrians or Egyptians, and, in the other case, a portrayal of the erection of the Luxor obelisk in the *Place de la Concorde,* which is engraved on its pedestal. In the later case were only

* *The Journal of Political Economy,* June 1900.

> capstans, cords, a problem in mechanics; the effort was in the head of the engineer much more than in the arms of the sailors who held the tackling. That was in 1836; today there would be no sailors at the cables; steam or electricity would do all the work. At the time of the Assyrians, hundreds of men clung to cords which they tugged laboriously, while others were busied in pushing the obelisk and placing the rollers upon which the mass was made to slide forward. . . Will anyone say that the work of carrying loads is more imbruting today than formerly?

The complaint that machinery deprives workmen of employment is answered by showing that in the fourteen *départements* of France in which there is least use of the steam engine, the population has declined in sixty years from 2,600,000 to 2,500,000, while in the fourteen departments using steam power to the greatest extent population has grown from 8,000,000 to 12,700,000.

M. Levasseur concludes with an incidental discussion of trusts in the United States, and especially the United States Steel and Iron Company, for which – as a competitor of European manufacturers – M. Levasseur expresses less dread than that which many Europeans are said to entertain.

> If the resources of the company are formidable, it should still be considered that, to employ a capital of a thousand million dollars, the company must develop its production on a vast scale, while, by the complexity of its organization, it will be difficult, if not impossible, to take account of the real needs of the market; obliged to dispose of its products at any cost, it will at times compel low prices which will doubtless spread ruin around, but from which it will be the first to suffer.

This view is certainly open to question. The combination

is certainly not more strongly impelled to produce in lavish quantities than were the smaller constituent companies. In fact one of the chief and indubitable advantages in such a combination is the possibility which it offers, not merely of increasing production through economizing material or labor, but the possibility also of restricting production if restriction seems for any reason advisable. It is hard, also, for one to understand why the management of such a company as this should not "take account of the real needs of the market"—foreign or domestic — at least as intelligently as smaller and, for the most part, less ably managed firms. The speaker is probably better justified in relying — for the security of European manufacturers against this new danger — upon the fact, which he reports, that the trust will continue to limit its output to certain staple forms of iron, so that there will still be a sufficient field for the European industry.

The Later Railroad Combinations*

THE open concentration of railway control in the union of the New York Central, Lake Shore and Boston and Albany in the east, the Union Pacific, and Southern Pacific, and the Northern Pacific, Great Northern and Burlington in the west, and the less apparent but not less effective centralization by common ownership of independent systems, is making a radical change in transportation conditions which a few years ago would have not passed with the slight attention it is now receiving.

The consolidation movement in other industries contains elements of strikingly novel interest, which for the time being have so absorbed attention as to leave the railway combinations comparatively little notice. It is, however, as true now as it ever has been, that railway control and management is of fundamental and paramount importance to our industrial and commercial interests. Present prosperity with its higher prices and wider margin of profits may cause shippers to pay increased freight charges with little grumbling, but will the rates be lowered when less favorable conditions and lower prices compel the shipper to consider expenses more carefully than he is now doing?

In the past competition for a declining volume of traffic has compelled rival railway managers to lower rates during periods of depression, sometimes with disastrous results to the roads. These lower rates forced improvements and economies which enabled the roads to make a profit, even at the reduced rates, and the trend of rates has been steadily downward during the past three decades. Increased price of ma-

* *The Journal of Political Economy*, June 1901.

terials and higher wages are given as the excuse for the advance in rates, which has been made during the past two years. But the surplus of net earnings and the ability to pay dividends on stock which represents no investment of capital, indicates that power which restriction of competition gave, rather than the necessity of meeting higher expenses, led to the advance in rates. It is true that the increase in railway rates has been less than the addition to the price of tin plate, steel rails and other monopolized products, but this merely indicates more moderation in the use of the power which railway combination confers.

The community of interests may be directly charged with the orgy of speculation through which we have just passed. The better dividends which the advance in rates made possible naturally tended to increase the price of stocks. The purchase of securities for the purpose of securing unity of action tended in the same direction, and the speculation as to the outcome of these great combinations tended to stimulate the powerful gaming instinct which is so widespread and needs little to rouse it to activity.

If rates had been maintained at a level which would give only normal returns on the capital actually invested in railways, and if the heavy capitalists had not been buying for control, does any one imagine that stocks which represent no investment would have sold at par or above?

In 1870, 1880 and 1886 conditions somewhat similar to those of the past two years led to railway building on an extensive scale. Competitors sought to share the profits which were being realized or which seemed to be in sight. Combination now seems able to prevent the waste which paralleling and undue extension then caused and a share of the profits has been sought by purchasing, at high prices, the securities of existing roads.

In the years following the panics of 1873 and 1893, when low prices, lack of employment and other conditions accompanying periods of depression caused serious agitation against the railways, the antimonopoly feeling was materially mitigated by the fact that competition between rival lines had so reduced rates as to involve many roads in bankruptcy. It was evident that monopoly was by no means complete, that rates were as low as any reasonable man could ask and the appeals of demagogues were rejected by intelligent and reasonable voters.

The optimist of course hopes that the dark years of depression will not recur. The ardent advocate of combinations also maintains that the powerful men in control of our railways and other industries will be able to prevent panics and depression. But let us consider for a moment the probable action of the managers of our combined railway system in case a period of depression should occur. Assuming a reasonably complete union of interests, rates will probably not be lowered except, perhaps, on the products of the industrial combinations which the railway capitalists also control. This may be expected to aggravate the feeling against monopolies, and the populistic hostility will not be tempted by lower rates and by the financial difficulties of the railways unless this danger is avoided – unless the increased power which combination gives is used with the greatest wisdom and rarest moderation, unless those in control of the railways, and the great industrial combinations are gifted with the keenest insight, so that they find their own interest in using their enormous power under a full sense of the responsibility that it involves, they will raise a storm of discontent and antagonism which will end in transferring their power to political leaders who will probably use it more arbitrarily and certainly less intelligently.

Reviews

A History of Socialism. By THOMAS KIRKUP. London and Edinburgh: Adam and Charles Black, 1892. 12mo., pp. vii. + 301.*

THE volume is light, for so large a subject as the title describes, especially as a good portion – perhaps one-third – of the book is taken up with the present and future of socialism rather than with what can properly be called history. It is valuable, not only for the concisely and lucidly written historical sketch of the socialist movement of the present century, but even more for the exposition and criticism of the doctrines as held by the advanced socialists of to-day. The standpoint of the author is that of a sympathetic critic and conservative advocate of socialism.

He does not find it necessary to go back of 1817 for the beginning of modern socialism, "the year when Owen laid his scheme for a socialistic community before the committee of the House of Commons on the poor law, the year also that the speculations of Saint-Simon definitely took a socialistic direction." And with good judgment he gives small space to the narrative of what preceded the revolution of 1848. The socialism with which he deals is the modern socialism in the strictest sense.

In his estimate of the relative importance of the leading socialistic writers the author is hardly at one with opinions currently held by hostile critics of socialism. He gives Marx distinctly the first, and a high rank: "Marx was an independent thinker of great originality and force of character, who

* *The Journal of Political Economy,* March 1893.

had made the economic development of Europe the study of a laborious lifetime, and who was in the habit, not of borrowing, but of strongly asserting the results of his own research and of impressing them upon other men" (p. 129). "In learning and philosophic power, Marx will compare favorably with Adam Smith" (p. 151). He denies Rodbertus the credit of in any special sense originating the modern, "scientific," socialistic body of doctrines, and urges (p. 129) that "it is an absurdity as well as an historical error to speak of Marx as having borrowed from Rodbertus"; and it must be admitted his main position here is true, though perhaps too broadly stated. He finds (p. 122) that Rodbertus's claim to stand as the representative of the ripest manifestation of socialistic thought – "the master-author of the socialist philosophy," as President E. Benj. Andrews puts it[1] – is also vitiated by his narrow views of the future of the movement and his singularly impotent social ideal. Rodbertus's ideal of the socialist state was a monarchy constructed on the lines of narrowly Prussian tradition, a scheme which Mr. Kirkup finds intolerable as well as impossible. At the same time Rodbertus is accorded full credit for his amiable attitude and attractive writing, as well as for his incisive criticism of economic theory.

The author does the socialist writers a service in calling attention (pp. 109-110) to the "ignorance or confusion of language of controversialists who maintain that the object of socialism is to abolish capital." It is a service that has often been performed before, but also one of which there is a perennial need. The error in question is one that probably no socialist, anarchist or communist is guilty of, but of which perhaps no one who adheres to or advocates any of these isms has not been accused.

[1] See *The Journal of Political Economy*, No. 1, especially at p. 57.

A service of a like candid and kindly nature is the fair and sympathetic statement of the anarchist position (pp. 191-195).

Much less creditable is the author's acceptance of the socialist interpretation of Ricardo. He subscribes, more than once (pp. 99, 119, 143-4, 147), to the correctness of their rendering of Ricardo's theory of value, as well as of his theory of wages; a slip which a careful reading of Ricardo should have sufficed to prevent[2].

In his analysis of motive forces and tendencies the author finds that socialism is "simply a movement for uniting labor and capital through the principle of association" (p. 230). The objective point of socialism, and the adequate remedy for the mischief of the capitalistic system, is to be found in the restoration of the masses of the people to a "participation in the ownership and control of land and capital . . . through the principle of association." The term "association" is a little vague, though it may not be easy to find a more definite term that will serve the purpose. The method by which the principle is to find acceptance in practical life is also not clearly indicated; it would be asking too much at present to require that it should, but it is disappointing to find that the author, while enumerating certain other factors that make in the same direction, and speaking with much hope of the prospect ahead, pins his faith to the coöperative movement as, in a special sense, the solvent of the difficulty.

The view is forcibly set forth in the concluding pages of the book that the whole trend of the modern industrial devel-

---

[2] [Veblen was of course well aware of a certain structural similarity between the theories of Ricardo and Marx. One of Veblen's students who worked out a mathematical formulation of Ricardo's theory of capital went on to say that "the kinship of this expression of Ricardian theory to the Marxian interpretation, was suggested by Dr. Veblen." Spurgeon Bell, "Ricardo and Marx," *The Journal of Political Economy*, February 1907, p. 117].

opment is distinctly socialistic, and that socialism (collectivism) is but the logical outcome of the continued growth of democracy under modern conditions.

With due regard for the serious purpose of the book, and for its many excellent features, it is to be said that it falls short of an exhaustive analysis of the social ills on which the socialist movement feeds, as well as of the full scope of the social changes that must be accomplished if the remedy for these ills is to be found in the direction of that movement.

Geschichte des Socialismus und Communismus im 19 Jahrhundert. By DR. OTTO WARSCHAUER. Leipzig: Gustav Fock, 1892 and 1893. 8vo. *Erste Abtheilung: Saint-Simon und der Saint-Simonismus*, pp. x. + 106. *Zweite Abtheilung: Fourier, Seine Theorie und Schule*, pp. vii. + 131.*

THE two installments already published of this work make up but a small part of the book as it will appear when completed. It takes up the history of nineteenth century socialism in greater detail than the volume by Kirkup, and has more of a narrative and expository character. The preface (to part II.) states that "all dependence on second-hand material has been avoided on principle," the aim being to meet the want that exists in economic literature of "a history of socialism drawn directly from original sources."

The author treats his material from the standpoint of economics, and introduces no biographical matter, beyond what is necessary in order to an intelligent discussion from that standpoint. It is (or perhaps better, promises to be) a work of painstaking research, and is exhaustive to the extent which its volume will permit. The summaries of the various doc-

* *The Journal of Political Economy*, March 1893.

trines discussed are necessarily somewhat brief, but these, as well as the discussion and the estimates of men and doctrines, are fair and dispassionate.

The Land-Systems of British India. By B. H. BADEN-POWELL. Oxford: The Clarendon Press, 1892. 8vo. 3 vols. pp. xix + 699, 771, 632.*

MR. BADEN-POWELL's work is a manual of Indian land systems, for the use, primarily, of Indian revenue officers. But while admirably adapted, as near as may be judged at this distance, for this its immediate purpose, it also contains a great deal of material of first-rate importance to the student of tenures and other agrarian questions.

Something more than one-half (386 pages) of the first volume is occupied with a general discussion of Indian land tenures and revenue systems, by way of gaining a historical and theoretical standpoint for the detailed discussion of the particular systems in effect in the various provinces of the Indian Empire. This general portion (book i.) is followed in the same volume by book ii., dealing in detail with Bengal. Book iii., occupying the whole of the second volume, discusses the system of village settlements, in its many local varieties. Volume iii. (book iv.) treats of the Raiyatwárí and allied systems.

The work is a monument to the intricacy and extent of the British-Indian land revenue system, as well as to the author's industry and erudition. One may open the book at almost any of its more than two thousand pages and find that the special subject dealt with at any given point has received scant treatment, rather than the contrary. At least it will seem so to anyone reading with a view to inform himself

* *The Journal of Political Economy,* December 1893.

on the details relating to any question in which he may be specially interested. The space required for the treatment of the subject, and the multiplicity of definitions and distinctions, and varieties of detail, serve to enforce the greatness and the wide range of British India, geographically, historically, culturally and ethnologically. Within almost any geographical subdivision treated of, we have to do with tenures ranging in complexity and degree of development from the simplest to the most elaborate and intricate known. Where successive waves of conquest have superposed one system of tenures upon another, leaving in most cases a residuum of customary rights to represent the displaced proprietary claims of the supplanted owner or occupier, and to be gradually modified and differentiated by the passage of time, the resulting structure is a sufficiently formidable one. Where, on the other hand, as in the case of the Tódas, in the Nílgiri District, conquest and invasion by alien peoples have not disturbed the ancient order, at least within historic times, the system, and the prevalent concepts with respect to land tenure, which the English found in vogue on acquiring the over-lordship of the country, were of such a simple and primitive character as to baffle the officials by affording no features comparable to the concepts familiar to European habits of thought. This latter proposition holds even now, after all that has been achieved by the researches of the past hundred years into land tenures and the development of the concept of property. Witness Mr. Baden-Powell's discussion of the "Supposed Rights of the Tódas" (vol. iii. pp. 187-8).

It is interesting to find a writer of such wide and intimate acquaintance with the subject from the practical side, holding a detailed, and, to a great extent, independent view of the origin (or origins) and life history of the Indian village, "under its varied conditions". He finds that "there can hardly be any doubt that the formation of village groups . . . . is not peculiar to Hindu races, either original or converted. It is found in India, among the great races which were certainly antecedent to the Hindus, and which still survive (with their institutions) in widely distant parts of the country. The village – apart from questions of particular forms – is not so much the result of any system as it is of a natural instinct. We find it everywhere, especially in the plain country, where circumstances invited it." (vol. i. p. 106.) "And then, there is not one type of village community, but two very distinct types, one of which, again, has marked and curious forms and varieties. And without anticipating details, which must come later, I may say at once that these two types are distinct in origin." (p. 106). The group belonging to one of these two types claim and acknowledge no joint ownership of the whole estate, or joint liability for burdens imposed by the state. "In the other type . . . . a strong joint-body . . . . has pretensions to be of higher caste or superior title to the 'tenants' who live on the estate. As a matter of fact, the first type of village is the one most closely connected with Hindu government and Hindu ideas." (p. 107.) Mr. Baden-Powell holds (p. 112) that "If we look to the earliest villages formed under the Aryans, or before that, we have no evidence (other than that of the [periodical][1] re-distribution, which I do not regard as conclusive) of a tribal stage; and even among the later Panjáb tribes, where tribal occupation and allotment are clearly discernible, any previous stage of the *joint* holding by the tribe collectively, hardly seems deducible from the known facts." "Family" property, however, he finds to prevail as regards most villages.

"We must conclude that the first (and, as far as we know,

[1] [The brackets are Veblen's].

the oldest) form of village is where the cultivators – practically owners of their several family holdings – live under a common headman, with certain common officers and artisans who serve them . . . . ; and there is no landlord (class or individual) over the whole." (p. 129.) This is the "Raiyatwárí" or "Non-landlord Village," and this type, the author inclines to think, is of Dravidian rather than Aryan origin. The second type of village is held to have arisen (*a*) out of this first type, by superposition of a landlord in one of several different ways enumerated or (*b*) "from the original conquest and occupation of land – as far as we know – previously unoccupied." Under (*a*), the active factor in producing a joint ownership, vested in a class "of higher caste and superior title", has been the institution of family property and family inheritance. "When the original acquirer of such [landlord][2] rights dies, and a body of joint heirs succeeds, *we soon find a number of co-sharers,* all equally entitled, claiming the whole estate, and (whether remaining joint or partitioning the fields) forming what is called a 'joint village community'."

The author leaves but scant and dubious room for the "primitive Aryan village community", in the sense of a patriarchal-communistic tribal group.

A large portion, perhaps the greater portion of the part given up to the general discussion, deals with the history and description of legislation and administrative practice. The later portions are perhaps even to a greater extent occupied with matters of this somewhat technical nature. While serving their immediate purpose of usefulness to the revenue official, they serve a no less useful purpose for the student of economic institutions (the author is as much a student as an official). It comes out clearly in the course of the narrative and exposition of what has been done and aimed at,

[2] [The brackets are Veblen's].

that the officials who have had to do with the vast complex of the land system, have had repeatedly to learn from their own failures, and from the failure in one place of methods that had approved themselves by experience in another, how concrete and individual the situation in each particular locality is. Each little district, one might almost say each village, is in some sense a case by itself, with what might be called personal idiosyncracies of its own. And still, it appears at the same time that certain broad generalizations may be made, and may be made good use of. It is also evident that, while the officials, especially since the evil effect of the Cornwallis settlement became manifest, have striven to understand and to adapt themselves to the circumstances as they have found them, their own European habits of mind have to a large extent decided the point of view from which they have studied the situation. And this fact, that the administrative, as well as the legislative functionaries of the British-Indian system, have been men inheriting a common tradition and a common point of view, has left its visible effects in the trend toward unity and homogeneity in the development of the system. While Mr. Baden-Powell's exposition brings out in strong colors the variety and contrast of local systems and usages, it also brings out the fact (slight though the actual achievements in that direction may be) that the British occupation and administration of India is at work to make "India" something more than "a geographical expression," in spite of Mr. Baden-Powell's declaration (vol. i. p. 5), that the term is at present nothing more. His own book – the possibility of such a work of generalization and orderly statement – is testimony to the fact that "India" is a term connoting more of homogeneity and solidarity to-day than the same "geographical expression" would have covered in the days when scores of petty sovereign governments were each pulling its own way, and each developing particolored systems of its own.

The three volumes are a credit to the printer as well as to the author, and are copiously supplied with excellent maps and contain two good indexes.

Der Parlamentarismus, die Volksgesetzgebung und die Socialdemokratie. By KARL KAUTSKY. Stuttgart: J. H. Dietz, 1893. 8vo. pp. viii + 139.*

THE traditional attitude of socialists, both in Germany and elsewhere, has generally been hostile to "parliamentarism." The name of the "Social-Democrats" of Germany is significant of their leaning toward the primitive democratic organization of society, which has no use for a parliament. Socialists have made much of the direct participation of the people in legislation, almost universally to the extent of urging the Referendum, Initiative, and Imperative Mandate, and very generally advocating a close circumscription of the powers of the representative body. At the same time they have held in theory that the members should be delegates only, and not representatives in the full sense. Extremists have held that representative legislatures have no place in the republic of the future, and have even discountenanced participation in elections of members of parliamentary bodies.

Mr. Kautsky takes exception to this view. He expresses the view of what is probably a strong section and apparently a growing section of European socialism, that a parliamentary legislative body, and the parliamentary method, is not simply a necessary evil under existing circumstances, but is the best means known for embodying the popular will in law

* *The Journal of Political Economy,* March 1894.

and enforcing the execution of the law. It is urged that direct legislation by the people belongs to the same primitive stage of culture with direct administration of justice by the people, and that both of these become impossible as the community increases in numbers and complexity. In a large and highly developed republic it would take all the time of all the citizens to enact the necessary laws and watch over their execution. The most that can be left to direct popular action is what is comprised in the Referendum and the Initiative, and the purpose, of these two institutions is not to abolish the parliamentary body, but only to render it more immediately dependent on popular influence and control.

It is pointed out that not only is the trend of development toward the employment of parliamentary methods in all civil bodies, but even in voluntary organizations of all kinds and for all purposes the same method necessarily prevails. And by no class is the parliamentary idea carried out more rigorously than by the laboring population, from whose members the socialist organizations are made up. They, the substance and exponent of the coming socialist State, delegate powers to their representatives, when occasion demands, with more freedom, and submit to their decision with less reserve, than any other class. No class or party has the same sense of party discipline and solidarity.

The author points out that direct legislation by the people, together with its complement, direct administration of justice, logically belong in the anarchist scheme. It is, in fact, the characteristic feature that distinguishes anarchism from socialism.

While its purpose is the refutation of what the author considers an unsocialistic position — the position that the powers of parliamentary (representative) bodies should be closely limited and legislation by the body of the people insisted on at all points, the argument serves a purpose more interesting to students of the socialist movement. It indicates that the attitude of socialism, in the persons of the leaders of the movement, is with an increasing degree of consciousness coming to be that of an aspiration towards the republic, in the same sense which that term conveys to English-speaking people. Parliamentarism is the form and method whereby socialism is to work out the salvation of mankind. Patriarchal absolutism has virtually ceased some time past to occupy the socialist's thoughts, and the idea of government by a committee of delegates is likewise becoming discredited. The modern socialistic movement has outlived the bitter antagonism to all things belonging to the existing social order, which characterized its early utterances at the middle of the century, and is casting about to find and make use of whatever is good and serviceable for the cause in modern political institutions. A livelier appreciation of the meaning of the dogma that socialism is the "next stage in social evolution," that it will be reached if at all by an evolution from existing forms of social organization, is bringing into fuller consciousness the implication that socialism is the industrial republic, not industrial democracy, and that the means by which it will do its work must be, if anything, a further development and perfected form of the means employed by the political republic in its sphere.

Perhaps the first reflection which this change, or growth, will suggest to conservative members of society, is that it renders socialism all the more effective an engine for mischief, the more reasonable it becomes on all other heads than its chief characteristic of antagonism to the institution of private ownership.

A Study of Small Holdings. By WILLIAM E. BEAR. London: Cassell & Co., 1893. 8vo. pp. 98.*

THIS "study" is mainly based on personal inspection of small holdings in England and the Channel Islands during 1892 and 1893, the author having been engaged in that work "in behalf of the Royal Commission of Labour." Besides small farms in the proper sense, some space is given to fruit farms and market gardens, as well as to the truck farms and the cultivation under glass carried on in the Channel Islands. Very interesting is the account of the small holdings of the Isle of Axholme, which affords the most extensive and apparently the most successful existing survival of the open-field system. One surprising feature about the holdings under this system, in this and some other localities, is the frequency of sales. The land apparently changes hands with great ease, and does not ordinarily remain in the same family through many generations. The holdings vary "in size generally from one-eighth of an acre up to fifteen acres for the most part." "In spite of encumbrances, most of the small holders live very well, and they are very independent. Small holdings are generally distributed at death, one 'selion' to one son and one to another. There is no primogeniture or tendency in that direction." Mr. Bear speaks confidently, though not enthusiastically, of the good results to be obtained by a moderately extended adoption of a system of small holdings, both small farms and allotments. It is commended as "highly desirable, not only for the benefit of the men themselves, but also for that of landowners, farmers, and all other persons who are interested in stopping the excessive migration of the flower of the population from the rural districts." (This matter-of-course solicitude for the interests of the landowners is suffi-

* *The Journal of Political Economy,* March 1894.

ciently naive, but it is thoroughly characteristic of the British view of the agricultural question.) Still, "It is only the most industrious, thrifty, and capable of the laborers who have a good chance of making small holdings pay," and the success of the system, generally, depends very greatly on the extent of cooperation by the women in the cultivation of the small plots. It may surprise American readers to be told that fashion varies greatly from one place to another with regard to outdoor work by the women, it being in many localities held to be very derogatory, if not out of the question, for women to take part in cultivating the allotment. The author's position on this head is no doubt sound, but there is a pungent flavor of an obsolete point of view about the declaration that the attitude of the women in disdaining to help in such cultivation "should not be encouraged." The most urgent general needs of the small farmers are "a complete reform of the existing system" of marketing the produce, and especially a cheapening of transportation, for short and long distances alike, especially for small quantities. The latter "should be attained even if nationalization of railways is necessary for that purpose."

Incidentally, but with a persistent recurrence, reference is made to the severe depression of agriculture in England, and involuntarily, if not unconsciously, it is implied that a decline of rents is the sole and inevitable remedy for the depression, but it is at the same time similarly implied that a decline of rents is something approaching a moral impossibility.

Bibliographie des Socialismus und Communismus. By JOSEPH STAMMHAMMER. Jena: Gustav Fischer, 1893. Large 8vo. pp. iv + 303.*

IT is easy to believe the author's statement that this com-

* *The Journal of Political Economy,* June 1894.

prehensive catalogue of the literature of socialism has cost "many years' painstaking labor." The plan of the work is that of an alphabetical catalogue, by authors and titles, followed by a subject index. It gives titles, date and place of publication, size, and in some (relatively few) cases a table or description of contents, as well as, still more infrequently, cross references. The price is not given, and the number of pages is given only very rarely. The intention has been to include the literature of all the modern European languages bearing on the subject, though the literature of America and of other outlying regions of occidental civilization are less fully represented than the countries lying nearer the author's home, in space and language.

The volume is to constitute part of a more comprehensive bibliography of social and economic science. This being the case, it is open to criticism on the score that it includes much that is not strictly to be classed under the literature of socialism or communism. Many works are listed which bear on socialism only remotely if at all. It is perhaps to be taken as indicating the author's sense of intimate relation between socialism and the labor question when he admits into this bibliography of socialism several hundred titles on trade unions, strikes, lock-outs, and like subjects. While the list is so full in point of its scope, and while the number of titles is great enough to surprise even readers who are prepared to find a great number of entries, it is still not difficult to find omissions. These occur especially in the later literature of other languages than German and French. Still, the feature to be remarked upon is not the omissions, but the very high degree of completeness of the list in spite of a number of omissions that might be cited. The workmanship of the volume is highly creditable. Mistakes in the transcription of titles are rare beyond expectation. Still they do occur, apparently more frequently in transcriptions from English than from any other language. The following may be cited as a curiosity: "HILL, FREDERIC, Measures for Puttingen. End to the abuses of trades-unions."

History of the English Landed Interest. (*Modern Period.*) By RUSSELL M. GARNIER. London: Swan Sonnenschein & Co. New York: Macmillan & Co., 1893. 8vo. pp. xx + 564.*

IN this volume the narrative of the English Landed Interest, begun in the author's earlier volume (on the Early Period), is continued down to the repeal of the Corn Laws. As the title indicates, the subject treated of is the Landed Interest, rather than the Agriculture or the rural community generally, but the discourse covers, particularly by means of digressions, some topics that are not fairly to be included either under the general title or under the cognate heads of "Customs, Laws, and Agriculture." Such a digression is the chapter on "The Political Economists and the Land," which seems intended to enforce upon the minds of the English landowner and farmer of today certain elementary propositions of economics rather than to fill out, or even to embellish, the narrative. Similar digressions in other parts of the volume, as, e.g., the account of early speculations in chemical theory contained in the chapter on "The Progress of Scientific Agriculture," serve to bring before the reader many entertaining, but completely irrelevant anecdotes, and, incidentally, to show the author's familiarity with a wide range of curious and obscure facts bearing very remotely, if at all, on the subject in hand.

The author's standpoint is that of the English landowner,

* *The Journal of Political Economy,* June 1894.

and, in reading what he has to say, it is difficult to always avoid the impression that one is listening to an advocate's argument. The intention to be impartial and dispassionate is evident throughout, but the point of view asserts itself pretty obviously from time to time, – notoriously so in the chapter on "Cobbett and Mill," where derogatory epithets are altogether too freely used. Cobbett is referred to as "this demagogue," and it is vouchsafed that "the best policy for the rulers of a community which contained individuals so indiscriminate in their abuse as this man, was to leave them severely alone. All Cobbett required was a sufficient quantity of rope, and presently he might have hung himself" (p. 479.) This borders too closely on abuse. A deprecatory tone runs through the discussion of Mill's activity also, but, while leaving no doubt that Mill is to be looked upon as an enemy of the Landed Interest, the author keeps his indignation well in hand. In his reference (p. 517.) to Mill's distinction between rent and profits as terms applicable to income derived from capital sunk in the soil, Mr. Garnier has failed to apprehend Mill's meaning. Mr. Garnier here makes use of the distinction between rent and profits in an attempted refutation of Mill's doctrine of the unearned increment, while it is beyond question that the latter did not regard income from capital sunk in the soil as rent for the purposes of the doctrine of an unearned increment; Mr. Garnier's appeal to the passage in Mill, however, plainly implies that he has so understood him, and he even goes about to expose the error imputed to Mill. This discussion of the claim of the community to the unearned increment seems to proceed, in part, on a confusion of the present capitalized value of permanent improvements (which alone has any bearing on the question) with the aggregate of expenditures actually made in the past in effecting the improvements (which is beside the point). Opponents of Mill's view of the unearned increment will be edified to find that Mr. Garnier has been reduced to the extremity of appealing to the Duke of Argyll as an authority in support of the doctrine that the landlord's rent is altogether of the nature of profits on the capital invested.

It is perhaps to be regretted that Mr. Garnier has thought it necessary for the sake of completeness to give considerable space to other than agricultural or agrarian questions. The English landed gentry own the deposits of coal and other minerals, and it is therefore conceived that a volume on the "Landed Interest" must deal in some detail with the relation of the gentry to these mineral deposits and their exploitation, and even to give something of a discursive account of the development of coal mining (pp. 16-36). Likewise characteristic of the author's point of view is the chapter on "The Story of the National Woodlands."

Mr. Garnier's book is a popular and interesting narrative, at the same time that it is of some considerable value to the student of English agrarian conditions.

L'Agriculture aux Etats-Unis. By EMILE LEVASSEUR. Paris: Chamerot et Renouard, 1894. 8vo. pp. 495.*

ONE result of M. Levasseur's visit to this country last year is this attractive volume on American agriculture. The purpose of the book is to give a conspectus of the industry as it exists today, with so much of historical matter as may be necessary to clear apprehension of the factors that make up the present situation. The scope of the book is quite comprehensive. It introduces the subject with a chapter on statistical and other sources of information, and on the publications

* *The Journal of Political Economy,* September 1894.

and methods of official bodies, state and federal, especially of the Department of Agriculture. In his survey of the methods by which statistical information is obtained M. Levasseur shows an appreciation of the difficulties of the task as well as of the shortcomings of the results achieved. By an easily intelligible mistake, a short supplementary bibliography, of very limited scope, appended to this chapter (pp. 13-14) on the sources of information, has been unintentionally given a claim of exhaustiveness which it belies in a very unfortunate manner.

From a comparison of the present condition of American farming with its past and with the farming situation in other countries, the inference is drawn (p. 44) that the complaints of the farmers of the country are not altogether well grounded. Cheap and fertile soil goes far to offset any advantage which their competitors in older countries may possess in the way of proximity to the market, cheap labor, or low standard of living. The American farmer has the advantage of low rent, or of a low price of land (which is the capitalized expression of a low rent), and this suggests that the remedy ready at hand for the depression in agriculture in France and other European countries is a lowering of rents to the true value of the land as a means of production.

> The farmer properly pays for the use of the instrument of production in proportion to what it will produce. If it is true that it has now become impossible for him to go on producing at current prices, he has a right to demand a reduction of rents to a point where an equilibrium will be established, that is to say, a point at which he can produce without loss . . . Interest on capital has sensibly declined during the past thirty years, in France and elsewhere; capitalists have yielded to the

> force of necessity. Why should not the rate of interest paid on landed capital, that is the interest as counted in terms of money, submit to the same law when a revolution in the production and distribution of agricultural products has virtually changed the terms of the contract by diminishing the power which landed capital possessed of yielding a money product?

When this rule is applied to the farming industry of this country, as the facts of the situation today are applying it with constantly increasing rigor, it affects not so much the relation between tenant and landlord as that between debtor and creditor, and, what is of equal significance and is submitted to with equal reluctance, it reduces the nominal value, the value in terms of money, at which the "independent" farmer's property is capitalized.

Following the two introductory chapters, on Statistics and Sources of Information, and on the Rural Economy, the main body of the volume is taken up with a detailed description occupying some 300 pages, beginning with the Cultivation of Cereals and other Vegetable Products, and comprising, among other things, chapters on Forestry and Timber Lands, Land Sales, and Mortgage Indebtedness, and Markets and Prices. While this survey is admirably lucid and concise, and while the information it contains surprises one rather by the accuracy and insight which it displays than by any absence of these qualities, the limits of space preclude any exhaustive treatment of the subject on a scope so broad as that of M. Levasseur's book. It is, as it is intended to be, a work of general information for European readers first and foremost; but M. Levasseur's impartial attitude and breadth of view, as well as his very compact and entertaining presentation of his subject, gives it a high value also for Americans.

Speaking of the cost of production of grain, with a view

to the relative advantages enjoyed by American farmers and their European competitors, M. Levasseur finds that writers interested in upholding a thesis have been too prone to make much of some special factor in the situation, such as changes in the tariff and the like, while they have neglected the dominant human factor. "In agriculture as in industry at large, success depends in great part on the man." It is not safe to predict, for example, as has so frequently been done, that if the market price of the product falls permanently below a given figure production cannot go on. A change of this kind, unless it goes to an extreme, need not produce such radical effects.

> In all industry, whether manufacturing or agricultural, a large number of the persons engaged are of a vegetative habit; they get their livelihood by their business, and expand or contract their scale of living to correspond with their profits. In agriculture especially this mass of vegetative producers is enormous. The United States are no exception in this respect, although the standard of living in that country is higher than in France. The American farmers complain of low prices; most assuredly, there are years when many do business at a loss, that is, spend more money on their business and their livelihood than they make; but on an average, and allowance made for the proper exceptions, farming has so far afforded the farmers a living, — otherwise it would have been abandoned.

In the section treating of Prices and Freight Rates there occur one or two mistakes to which attention may be called. On page 318 (note) it is remarked that the freight rates given in cents per bushel in *Statistical Abstract of the United States* do not correspond with those given in the *Report of the Interstate Commerce Commission* in cents per 100 pounds, "the bushel being counted at 46 pounds"! If the rates are converted from the one schedule to the other at 60 pounds to the bushel it will be found that they agree as nearly as figures of this class can be expected to agree. The following (p. 323) is also a little confusing: "The difference between the highest and lowest price (of wheat) for the year in Chicago is commonly very pronounced, having been as great as 125 cents in 1886, under the *paper-money regime*, and 92 cents in 1888 under the regime of specie payments." Apart from the slip by which 1886 is brought under the "regime of paper money," there is the correction to be made here that 1886 was a particularly sluggish year for the wheat market, the price of cash wheat never reaching one dollar, and the range for the year not exceeding some 20 or 25 cents; if the date given is a misprint for 1868, it is to be remarked that wider divergences occurred during the sixties; it is more probable that the larger figure is intended for the year 1888 when the price varied by something over 125 cents, going as high as $2 at the end of September (the month of the notorious corner associated with the name of Mr. Hutchinson), and as low as 72-73 cents during the early part of the year.

As to the future of American agriculture the opinion expressed is hopeful without being enthusiastic:

> American production has two outlets: home consumption and exportation. Improvement in the agriculture of Europe, extension of grain and cattle culture in other exporting countries, and obstructive tariffs in importing countries may disturb the export trade of the United States, but will not drive them out of the foreign markets. America will continue to export. What proportion of her product, the future alone can tell. What is certain is that it will require added effort to hold the markets al-

> ready occupied or to find new ones, for more countries are constantly entering the market with agricultural products, and the facilities for transportation are increasing, resulting in increased competition. But, on the other hand, it is beyond question that American industry can aid American agriculture in opening up new outlets for its products by diversifying the form in which the goods are put on the market. (p. 349).

Home consumption will of course also increase; more slowly, probably, than in the past[1], but still very appreciably. "There are writers who fancy that they can see afar off the day when America will contain a population dense enough to consume all the agricultural products of the country. That day, if it is coming at all, is too remote to occupy our thoughts at present . . . For the present generation it is idle to count on home consumption to carry off the entire product and so remove the necessity of an export market." (p. 350.) "Prices will remain low . . . If this abundant supply is to become, as I am persuaded it will be, a permanent feature of the market in the future, it is not improbable that prices will fall even below their present level, to a point which it would be rash to attempt to fix." (p. 351.) "One of the consequences of low prices will probably be a decline in the value of farms devoted exclusively or principally to the production of the depreciated articles." (p. 353). The ultimate result being a diversification and intensification of farming, with a continuation in the future of the progress made in the recent past. "American agriculture was favored by fortune for some

[1] By an oversight, quite explicable but misleading, a statement made in the *Journal* (June 1893, p. 375), that "*the bread-eating population of the countries which draw on the supplies of the general market* to which America contributes, may be expected to increase by ten percent in ten years," is referred to (p. 393) as an estimate applying to the future rate of increase of *the population of the United States.*

fifteen years; it will now have to put forth greater efforts, for less results perhaps; but it is capable of doing so." (p. 358.) But there is no doubt of the final result.

As a final word on the question of the marketing of agricultural produce, M. Levasseur remarks on the protective tariffs, on grain especially, so much in vogue in Europe today. He traces the French protective legislation, without many words, to the cupidity of the land-owners and characterizes it as at best an attempt to take money out of the pockets of one part of the French people in order to put it into those of another part.

Socialism. By ROBERT FLINT. London: Isbister & Co.; Philadelphia: J. B. Lippincott & Co., 1895. 8vo. pp. 512.*

THE first eight chapters (298 pages out of 498) of this volume are, for the greater part, rewritten from lectures delivered "before an audience chiefly of workingmen," and afterward published as a series of papers in *Good Words.* Still it is a work which aspires to some scientific standing, as will appear from a glance at its table of contents. There are chapters on the History of Socialism, Socialism and Labor, Socialism and Capital, the Nationalization of Land, the Collectivisation of Capital, Socialism and Social Organization. The two hundred pages not based on the author's lectures are still more significant of a serious purpose; they deal with the questions of Socialism and Democracy, Socialism and Morality, Socialism and Religion.

Professor Flint sets out with many citations of definitions of his subject from various writers and then gives his own definition (p. 17), which reads: "Socialism . . . . . is any theory of social organization which sacrifices the legitimate liberties

* *The Journal of Political Economy,* March 1895.

of individuals to the will or interests of the community." He goes on to say (pp. 17-18): "I do not think we can get much farther in the way of definition. The thing to be defined is of its very nature vague, and to present what is vague as definite is to misrepresent it. No definition of Socialism at once true and precise has ever been given or ever will be given. For Socialism is essentially indefinite, indeterminable. It is a tendency and movement towards an extreme. . . . . Socialism is the exaggeration of the rights and claims of society, just as Individualism is the exaggeration of the rights and claims of individuals. The latter system rests on excessive or exclusive faith in individual independence; the former system rests on excessive or exclusive faith in social authority." This is, of course, a definition which involves a condemnation of that which it sets out to characterize, and is therefore an unfortunate definition for any useful purpose. It is, moreover, an attempt at defining socialism in the extreme generical sense so as to include all possible phases and manifestations of the movement in the past and the present, and not specifically that definitely conceived movement which confronts society with such singleness of purpose today, and which is the object of so much lively alarm and of so much hope and enthusiasm. This chapter on the definition of socialism has, indeed, more to do with fossil and recent forms than with that extant type of socialism which one might fairly expect would be treated of by a teacher who is addressing a popular audience with the avowed purpose of instructing and influencing them in their attitude toward the movement as one of the vital questions of the day. It also appears in a later chapter (p. 61) that "The kind of Socialism most in repute at present . . . is the government of all by and for all, with private property largely or wholly abolished, capital rendered collective, industrial armies formed under the control of the state on co-operative principles, and work assigned to every individual and its value determined for him." "The Socialism thus described has come to be commonly designated Collectivism, and the name is convenient and appropriate. It is the only kind of Socialism greatly in repute at present, or really formidable; and, consequently, it is the form of it which especially requires to be examined. It is the Socialism which I shall henceforth have chiefly in view" (pp. 62-63). The prefacing of his discussion by the characterization first cited above becomes all the more surprising when it appears that the author finds this second and very different definition necessary for practical use.

It may be noted in connection with this painstaking effort at defining his subject that while Professor Flint quotes with approval and in support of his own position Schaeffle's characterization of socialism (pp. 61-62) he falls foul of the same authority in a curious manner at an earlier point (p. 18). Professor Flint formulates in strong terms the view that socialism is, in point of principle, the diametrical opposite of individualism; whereas Schaeffle in his well-known *Impossibility of Social Democracy* has this to say in amplification of his definition of collectivism: "Liberalism and socialism are offspring of the same spirit, the spirit of Individualism." "It [Collectivism] is at bottom . . . . the extreme of Individualism – Individualism in universal realization, and intensified by the envious fancy of the proletariat." The impression produced by this lack of harmony between the author and the authority whom he cites in support of his own position is heightened by certain passages in a later chapter (pp. 97-100) where he professes the view that socialism and individualism are in a vital sense coincident in point of fundamental principle.

The manner in which the author's position vacillates between an identification of socialism with individualism and a contrasting of the two as antagonistic opposites suggests the generalization (which might perhaps not be borne out by a careful re-reading of the volume) that the two are held to be antagonistic in those portions of the book which are printed in large type, and to be identical in those portions which are in small print. The large print contains (apparently) the substance of the popular lectures which formed the nucleus of the book; the fine print, the most of the subsequent emendations.

It may be in place to say a word in extenuation of the lexicographer Littré's fault, when he is criticised by Professor Flint (p. 15) for his definition of socialism, which "is, if possible, worse" than that given by the dictionary of the Academy. The Academy dictionary's definition reads: "The doctrine of men who pretend to change the state, and to reform it, on an altogether new plan"; Littré's definition as quoted by Professor Flint is: "A system which, regarding political reforms as of subordinate importance, offers a plan of social reform." Now, while Professor Flint may be well within the bounds in saying that it is by no means characteristic of the socialism of today "to subordinate the political to the social," Littré was perhaps equally accurate in his day in defining it as he did. Littré's socialistic (communistic) bias was acquired early. It dates back to the period when the term "socialism" first came into vogue. The definition which he gives is probably to be taken as answering to his own first-hand knowledge of the use of the term at that early day, and it defines the usage of that time with Littré's accustomed discrimination. The term took its early meaning from Owenism, and even appreciably later than the middle of the century "socialism" denoted, in European usage, a relatively respectable upper-class movement for the amelioration of the lot of humanity in general, and of the working class in particular, by social rather than political reform. The movement inaugurated by Marx and Engels in the forties is the typical "socialist" movement of today; but when these men drew up the *Manifesto of the Communist Party* in 1847 they, and the League whose spokesmen they were, unhesitatingly adopted the term "communism" to describe their movement. Marx and Engels, in the turbulent years of the forties, could no more have classed their propaganda as "socialism" than Mr. Hyndman or Mr. Morris today could class their activity under the head of "university settlements."

The discussion under the head of Socialism and Labor does not inspire confidence in Professor Flint's apprehension of what is involved in the socialist doctrine of labor-value and of the "Right to the Entire Product of Labor." There occurs, *e.g.*, the following passage (p. 126): "Karl Marx . . . . maintains that *the value of work should be estimated according to the quantity of socially necessary labor expended, or, in equivalent terms, according to the time which must be on the average occupied in the work.* There is neither reasonableness nor justice in this view. Mere expenditure of labor does not produce any value, and is not entitled to any remuneration. A man may labor long and hard in producing something in which nobody can see any use or beauty. If he do so, he will get nothing for his labor, and he has no right to expect anything for it. He may expend ten hours' labor in producing what there is so little demand for that he will get merely the pay of one hour's work for it." To this it is to be said that probably no socialist would have any hesitation in repudiating the construction of the doctrine of labor-value contained in this comment. That doctrine is surely infirm enough to inspire surprise at its wide acceptance, but its weakness is not so obvious at the first glance as the construction put upon it by Professor Flint (pp. 126-127) would imply. Marx was too skillful a dialectician (to say nothing more) to base his economic scheme on so undisguised an absurdity. Still, the discussion of the Marxian theory of value and surplus-value is suggestive, though it is scarcely as conclusive as Professor Flint appears to find it.

In the chapter on Socialism and Labor (pp. 149-150), there is a fairly lucid statement of the Marxian (socialistic) definition of "capital." Capital, according to this view, comprises those productive goods which are held as private property and employed by means of hired labor for the production of a profit. In the chapter on Socialism and Capital (pp. 157 *et seq.*), however, when speaking of the ungrounded hostility of socialists to "capital" this peculiar socialistic concept of capital as "an historical category" is forgotten, and the discussion plainly proceeds on the assumption that socialistic hostility to "capital" means hostility to the instruments of production. This failure to consistently maintain the distinction between the socialist concept of capital and the concept as currently in vogue vitiates the entire chapter.

Occasionally there crop out curiosities of economic argument; the following (pp. 216-217) is an example taken from the chapter on the Nationalization of Land (a portion of the argument which has apparently been carried over with but inconsiderable change from the popular lecture): "The rise and fall of the rents of land, then, depend on the labor and good or bad fortune of society no otherwise than the rise and fall of all other rents, of all prices, and of all values. There is nothing special or peculiar in the mode of their increase or in the course of their movement which can warrant society to treat them in an exceptional way, and to deal with property in land differently from all other property. . . . . The man who can believe that land is in this country the exclusively, or even a specially, remunerative kind of property, that the want of it is a necessary and chief cause of poverty, and the possession of it the infallible and abundant source of wealth, displays a remarkable power of adhering to a prepossession in defiance of its contradiction by experience. Is there any kind of property which increases less in value in Britain than land? It is known not to have doubled in value during the last seventy years. It has certainly diminished in value during the last twenty years." It would perhaps be impossible to pursue a line of argument less convincing than this to the advocate of land nationalization on the ground of the doctrine of an unearned increment, or one that would be more completely beside the point.

The discussion is abreast of the time with respect to the position taken on State Socialism and Christian Socialism, both of which movements are excluded by Professor Flint from the category of modern socialism proper. With regard to the latter of the two there occurs (pp. 440-441) the following summary statement: "Christianity and Socialism, then, are not so related as those who are styled Christian Socialists imagine. What is called Christian Socialism will always be found to be either unchristian in so far as it is socialistic, or unsocialistic in so far as it is truly and fully Christian."

The range of the discussion is such as to preclude any detailed review of the contents of the volume. The book bears testimony to its author's erudition at the same time that it shows a wide acquaintance with writers and events related to the socialist movement. The method of treatment varies from the homiletical to the polemical, and is generally *ex parte,* in spite of an evident effort at impartial presentation. The presence of an animus throughout the argument results in such narrowness of construction as defeats the main purpose of the book. One feels in reading the triumphant refutation of one after another of the socialist positions that the positions in question have not been stated in their strongest and most reasonable form, and that the discussion for that reason does not dispose of the questions with any finality. Its refutations (and it is eminently a volume of refutations) will be accepted as conclusive chiefly by those who are already in a frame of mind to accept the conclusions offered. It can scarcely be said to be a book with which science, especially the science of economics, will have to count. There is a lack of unity, not to say of consistency, in the treatment of the subject and in the point of view from which it is approached, and even in the salient features of the characterization of the movement itself. It is a book that might have been more useful, and probably would have met with a more sympathetic acceptance at the hands of intelligent people, a generation ago than today.

Misère de la Philosophie. Par KARL MARX. Avec une preface de Friedrich Engels. Paris: V. Giard et E. Brière, 1896. 8vo. pp. 291.*

THIS reprint of Marx's earliest exposition of his peculiar economic views is notable, not in point of novelty, nor because it adds to what is already currently known by students of Marx with regard to his early position, but because it is evidence of the unabated authority with which the writings of the master still appeal to the thoughtful and studious adherents of the school. It may be noted in this connection that a German translation of the book (by men as eminent in the socialist world as Bernstein and Kautsky) has also recently (1892) appeared. The present reprint is an unaltered reproduction of the book as it originally appeared in

* *The Journal of Political Economy*, December 1896.

1847, in Marx's polemical onslaught on Proudhon, except for the incorporation of certain minor corrections made by the author in the margins of his private copy of the volume. There are also added, by way of appendices, three briefer papers by Marx, – a condemnatory letter on Proudhon, reprinted from the *Socialdemokrat* (Berlin) of 1865; an extract from *Zur Kritik der politischen Oekonomie,* going to disprove Proudhon's claim to originality in his proposed *banque du peuple;* and the address on free trade before the Democratic Association of Brussels. These supplementary documents go to enforce the impression made by Engel's preface, that the purpose of the reprint is in some measure a polemical one. The preface is directed to the disproof of any possible indebtedness of Marx to Rodbertus, as well as to the definitive confutation of all who may claim any originality or other merit for Rodbertus, whether as against Marx or otherwise in connection with economic discussion. Although Engels's preface dates from 1884, it may not be out of place to repeat, for the good of Rodbertus's admirers and champions at this day, certain characteristic claims and assertions here made by Marx's lifelong intimate friend, "the most truthful of the socialists." After referring for details to his prospective discussion of the relation between Marx and Rodbertus in the subsequently published preface to the fourth edition of Marx's *Kapital,* he goes on to say:

> It will be sufficient here to say that when Rodbertus accuses Marx of having "despoiled" him and "of having in his *Kapital* drawn extensively on, but without citing," his work, *Zur erkenntniss,* etc., he has allowed himself to be led into a calumny which can be explained only through the ill humor naturally to be expected of an unappreciated genius, and through his remarkable ignorance of things which took place outside of Prussia, and

more especially his ignorance of economic and socialistic literature. Neither these complaints nor Rodbertus's work above cited had ever come under Marx's eyes; he had no acquaintance with Rodbertus beyond the three *Sozialen Briefe*, and even these assuredly not prior to 1858 or 1859.

Socialisme et Science Positive. Par ENRICO FERRI. Paris: V. Giard et E. Brière, 1896. 8vo. pp. 220.*

PROFESSOR Ferri's work, which has now come to hand in a French edition, is no less laudatory of Marx. The juxtaposition of names in the sententious subtitle ("Darwin, Spencer, Marx") is of itself a sufficient promise of an appreciatory discussion of Marx's writings and of his place in the science. The eminent Italian criminologist gives in his adhesion to the tenets of scientific socialism without equivocation, and sets out with a promise to justify the claims of that dogma to be the complement, on the side of the social sciences, of that theory of development for which, in its general features, Darwin's name serves as catchword in the biological sciences.

Part I (pp. 13-85) of the volume is in great measure taken up with a refutation of what Professor Ferri regards as the three fundamental objections that have been made against socialism on grounds of evolutionary theory. These three points of alleged contradiction between Darwinism and socialism are: (*a*) Socialism demands equality of individuals, while the evolutionary process constantly accentuates that inequality between individuals which alone affords play for the selective adaptation of the species or the type; (*b*) socialism demands the survival, in comfort and fullness of life, of all individuals, whereas Darwinism (taking the term here,

* *The Journal of Political Economy*, December 1896.

as elsewhere in the book, in the broad sense in which it is popularly used) requires the destruction, through the struggle for existence, of the great majority of individuals; (*c*) the struggle for existence secures a progressive elimination of the unfit and a survival of the superior individuals, resulting in a progressive amelioration of the selected minority of individuals that are in this way delegated to carry on the development of the species or of the type, whereas socialism, by giving all an even chance of life, reduces the aggregate of individuals to a dead level of democratic uniformity, in which the superior merits of the "fit" count for nothing.

Of these objections to socialism Haeckel is regarded as the best and most effective spokesman that has yet appeared; other and later restatements, of which the number is by no means small, being taken only as feebler variants of the apology for natural selection made by the great German apostle of Darwinism. The alleged contradictions are reviewed somewhat in detail, and the socialist position which claims a full accord between the teachings of evolutionary science and the prospectus of revolutionary evolution offered by spokesmen of Marxism are summarized and restated in a telling manner, though with somewhat more of a declamatory turn than would be required for the purpose of an enumeration of the data bearing on the question of human evolution and a formulation of the inferences to be drawn from these data. The three contradictions which are passed under review are disposed of by showing, in rather more convincing form than is usual with the scientific apologists of socialism, (*a*) that the equality of individuals demanded by the socialist scheme is an equality of opportunities rather than an identity of function or of the details of life; (*b*) that the struggle for existence, as applied within the field of social evolution, is a struggle between groups and institutions rather than a competition *à l'outrance* between the individuals of the group, and that this struggle can lead to socially desirable results only as it is carried on on the basis of a large measure of group solidarity and co-operation between the individuals of the group; that the "normal" *milieu* for the competitive development of individuals in society in the direction of availability for the social purpose and a fuller and more truly human life is afforded only by an environment which secures the members of the community a competent and equitable – if not equal – immunity from the sordid cares of a life of pecuniary competition. Only under such an environment can we look for the development and fixation of a type of man which shall best meet the requirements of associated human life. That is to say, the closer an approach is made to a condition of pecuniary equality and solidarity the better are the chances of a survival of the "fittest," in the sense of the most efficient for the purposes of the collective life. And this brings us to the consideration of the third alleged contradiction between the socialist scheme and Darwinism – that an abolition of the pecuniary struggle would abolish the evolutionary factor of a selective survival of the fittest individuals. It is (*c*) only by injecting a wholly illegitimate teleological meaning into the term "fittest" as used by Darwin and the Darwinists that the expression "survival of the fittest" is made to mean a survival of the socially desirable individuals. This whole objection, therefore, is a sophism which proceeds on a teleological preconception – a survival in modern discussion of a concept which belongs among the mental furniture of the metaphysical speculations of the pre-Darwinian times. A sober review of well-known facts, we are told, shows that the present competitive system does not by any means uniformly result in a working out of favorable results by a process of natural selection. "It is well known that in the modern civilized world the action of natural selection is vitiated by the presence of a military selection, by matrimonial selection, and especially by economic selection" (p. 49). Professor Ferri here develops very briefly, and turns to socialist account, the theory of "social selection" of types originated by Broca, and more recently developed with greater fullness and effect by Lapouge, Ammon, and Loria. It is only in the "*milieu normal*" afforded by such an equality of pecuniary competence as the socialist scheme contemplates that the factor of "choice" has a chance to act and to award the victory to "the most normal individuals" and types.

The struggle for existence, and therefore the fact of a selective adaptation, is a fact inseparable from the life process, and therefore inseparable from the life of mankind; but while its scope remains unaltered, the forms under which it expresses itself in the life of society change as the development of collective life proceeds. The most striking general modification which the struggle has suffered in the past growth of society, and the feature which most immediately concerns the present discussions, is seen in the transformation of this struggle for existence in the communities of the occidental culture into a struggle for equality.

> During the historical period of development, Graeco-Latin society in the first place carried on a struggle for *civil* equality (abolition of slavery); this struggle was triumphant, but it did not stop there, for life and struggle are the same facts stated in different words; society during the Middle Ages carried on its struggle for *religious* equality, achieved it, but did not stop there; and at the close of the last century the struggle was for *political* equality. Is society now to come to a standstill and to stagnate in its present phase? Today the struggle of

> society is for economic equality; not for an absolute pecuniary equality, but for an equality of that more consequential kind of which I have spoken above. And everything goes to impress upon us with mathematical certainty that when this victory is achieved it must in turn give place to further struggles and new ideals among the generations that are to succeed us (pp. 37-38).

This struggle for equality, as is to some extent true of any other expression of the struggle within a given society, takes the form of a struggle between classes, and necessarily so. It is therefore a struggle for existence on the basis of solidarity and co-operation. The discovery of this law of cultural evolution, "of this grand conception," "is the imperishable glory of Marx, which secures him a place in sociology such as that occupied by Darwin in biology, and by Spencer in natural philosophy" (p. 71).

According to Professor Ferri socialism is atheistic, as a matter of course; but he regards the antagonism of the religious organizations, as well as the quasi-socialistic endeavors of the Roman Catholic church, with the utmost complacency; being fully persuaded that in this matter of irreligiousness as a requisite of socialistic reform the course of events will effectually take care of itself. No thought need be taken for the education of humanity away from the theistic cults, since the cults, with their entire theistic content, will disappear from man's habits of thought as fast as the chief positions of evolutionary science are accepted. This is the meaning to be attached to the declaration of the Erfurt programme that religion is a private affair with which the socialist propaganda will not concern itself. Education – a familiarity with the views and the point of view of modern science – will obliterate the faiths; therefore the socialist propaganda need take no thought for erasing them (pp. 56-63).

Similarly, although the scheme of socialism is, fundamentally and of necessity, republican – being but a reorganization of the industrial community on republican lines – the office of republicanizing society, as a step preparatory to its socialization, may without misgiving be left to bourgeois liberalism, which must necessarily work out such a result as its logical outcome.

Incidentally, in so far as it is not altogether relevant to the main point of the book, but somewhat at large, in so much as the discussion runs through some twenty-five pages, the great Italian criminologist has a word of kindly admonition to say to the students of Sociology and Political Economy. This discussion (Part III of the volume) is headed: "Sociology and Socialism," and the two chapters of which it is made up bear the captions: The Sterility of Sociology, and Marx the Complement of Darwin and Spencer.

"One of the most curious facts in the history of scientific thought during the nineteenth century is this, that while the profound revolution in science wrought by Darwinism and the Spencerian evolutionism has rehabilitated every department of physical, biological, and even the psychological sciences, and endowed them with a new youth, this same scientific revolution has, upon reaching the domain of the social sciences, barely rippled the surface of the still waters of that pool of orthodoxy in social science, Political Economy.

"It is true, there was a move made by Auguste Comte . . . . . toward the creation of a new science, Sociology, which was intended, in conjunction with the natural history of human society, to form the glorious consummation of a new edifice of science erected by the empirical method (p. 145)."

It is admitted that some substantial work has been done in the descriptive or "anatomical" branches of the science that deals with the social organism, but after all has been said it is to be admitted that in all this, with the exception of the author's own special department of Criminal Sociology, the results hitherto achieved have been meager in the extreme.

"So soon as the discussion comes in contact with the live political and social questions, the new science of Sociology is overtaken by some sort of hypnotic slumber, and remains in a state of indecision in the limbo of sterile and colorless generalities, such as will permit the sociologues to continue, in questions of the public economy as well as in politics, as conservatives or as radicals just as their caprice or inclination may dictate (p. 146).

"The secret of this curious phenomenon lies not alone in the fact pointed out by Malagodi that the science is still in the period of scientific analysis and has not yet reached the period of synthesis, but more especially in this, that the logical consequences of Darwinism and of scientific evolutionism, when applied to the study of human society, lead inexorably to socialism (p. 147)."

As a remedy for this desperate state of the science, Professor Ferri recommends sociological and economic students to seek somewhere the courage necessary to accept the logical consequences of their own argument. And for scientific method they are frankly commended to turn to Karl Marx as the only competent guide. The Marxian Materialistic Theory of History, and the Theory of Class Struggle, together with the Theory of Surplus Labor, point the way which Sociology and Political Economy must follow if they are to take a place as modern sciences of the post-Darwinian epoch.

Einführung in den Socialismus. By RICHARD CALWER. Leipzig: Georg H. Wigand, 1896. Small 8vo. pp. x + 232.*

AN elementary text-book in socialism written by a socialist

* *The Journal of Political Economy,* March 1897.

and primarily for the instruction of adherents of the socialist creed is not altogether a new departure in literature, but there are few efforts of the kind which are on the whole as acceptable and effective a presentation of their subject as this. The immediate aim of the book is to combat the spirit of petty personal and local interest which is becoming a hindrance to effective co-operation for the larger and remoter ends of the socialist movement in Germany. At the same time it is not a controversial work. Its purpose is sought to be accomplished by so explaining the meaning and trend of the socialist movement as to leave no legitimate ground for the tendency which it deprecates.

That the author is a Marxian goes almost without saying; but his Marxism is of a greatly modernized, softened, conciliatory kind. It is a doctrine of economic evolution, or perhaps better of social evolution primarily on an economic basis, but a doctrine in which the "materialistic theory of history" is no longer obtrusively present in the crude form at every step, although it still remains the fundamental premise. There is no hint of the catastrophic method of reform, nor is there any urging of revolutionary measures. The industrial evolution, we are told, is visibly furthering the socialization of industry day by day. And this not only at certain points, — in certain salient features to which socialistic writers have been in the habit of pointing as evidence of the approach to socialism, — but in all branches of industry, including agriculture, which most socialist teachers have hitherto been content to pass over as a "backward" industry somewhat doubtfully to be included in the scheme for immediate socialization. A characteristic instance of Mr. Calwer's ingenious use of everyday facts in support of this thesis is his pointing out (p. 71) that all statistical determination of industrial methods and of the extent and range of the production and consumption of industrial products contributes to make an eventual collective control of these branches of industry easier. Not only the collective organization of industry under the direction of trusts and syndicates, therefore, but all canvassing of the markets and the industrial situation, by trade journals as well as by students of practical economics, is labor in the service of the socialist movement.

But while the evolution of industry, it is claimed, assures the rapid and inevitable socialization of industry, these mechanical facts and technological events do not immediately or of themselves afford the basis for that growth of institutions which the socialist republic involves. The institutions of the community, whether socialistic or otherwise, rest on psychological ground. The material situation, the state of industry and the arts, may condition the growth of institutions in accordance with the materialistic theory of history, but these material circumstances of environment and of industrial organization and methods control the growth of institutions and social structure only as they affect the individual's habitual view of things. This psychological factor which is to afford the motive to socialistic reconstruction is conceived in quite modern terms. The discontent of the modern laborer, which is to work out the revolution, is no longer conceived to be of the nature of a calm resolution the outcome of dispassionate ratiocination. It is bluntly recognized (pp. 138-142, 159, 163) that this motive force is simply sentiment and is closely akin to envy, its basis being chiefly an invidious comparison of the laborer's lot with that of the propertied classes. The decisive fact is the distastefulness of the laborer's social position as compared with his employer. Improvement in material comfort measured in absolute terms counts for very little. "You may feed the laborer well, you may clothe him decently, you may provide him with a modest dwelling, in short, you may keep him as a well-to-do man keeps his domestic animals – still the laborer will not be beguiled into overlooking the fact that his place in life is determined by accidents and circumstances which do not permit him to lead the life of a man." (p. 139).

The exposition (Part III) of the aim and methods of the socialistic movement is also temperate and conciliatory in tone, though it leaves no doubt as to its radical character in substance. It deprecates all violence, and even enters a caution against the free use of what a socialist would consider peaceable and legitimate measures, such as strikes and boycotts. "Socialism is essentially a peaceable development of a struggle between different interests . . . . and so long as the socialists are a minority and the industrial situation is not yet ripe for the socialistic régime, so long the socialists must yield, willing or unwilling, to the majority – to those that hold the power. But the time is coming when the majority of the people will be on the socialist side, and then it will depend on the ruling class, which will then have fallen into the position of a minority, whether they are wise enough and shrewd enough to let the further development of the nation's life go on undisturbed or not" (pp. 218, 219). The militarism of European countries is decried as inconsistent with the socialistic evolution, not because war as such is to be deplored, but because war and armaments weaken a nation industrially, and hinder the process of industrial evolution. While no speculation as to the "future state" is indulged in, some reference is made to the probable future of certain institutions and to the attitude of the socialist toward these institutions. So, for instance, (pp. 203-4) socialism is said to hold an entirely neutral position with regard to religion, but this is uttered with an evident conviction that the church and the creeds are alien to socialism and irreconcilable with it in detail. Similarly, socialism is not unpatriotic, although it is international, but the patriotism of the German socialist is in abeyance through the government's fault rather than his own. Little is said about the family, but it is plainly implied that the traditional form of the family is in an advanced stage of obsolescence so far as regards the working classes. It is conceded that the marriage relation at present sanctioned by the law may for the present and for an indefinite time to come be the form best suited for the well-to-do classes.

La Viriculture. Ralentissement de la Population — Dégénérescence — Causes et Remèdes. Par G. DE MOLINARI. Paris: Guillaumin et Cie., 1897. 12mo. pp. 253.*

THE motive of M. de Molinari's book is given in the subtitle, and it is a sufficiently curious motive for a book from an economist of his conservative position and wide range of learning. And the substance of the volume is perhaps no less curious, coming from such a source. The early chapters (i-viii) are taken up with an elementary exposition of the Malthusian premises, M. Molinari's contribution being a supplementary explanation — not altogether unfamiliar to Malthus — of how, as the outcome of the Malthusian factors, the population of European countries has kept pace in its advance or decline with the advance or decline of the nation's industrial productivity and with the extension and contraction of the market for the products of the national industries (chapters ix and x). France is especially unfortunate in having suffered a very sensible retardation in its rate of increase.

* *The Journal of Political Economy,* March 1897.

But this retardation of the rate of increase is not the most serious difficulty presented by the movement of population, and is not a sufficient cause for apprehension. The white race has nothing to fear from a failure of its numbers as compared with the rival yellow race, with which pessimists are fond of threatening us. The danger lies in the deterioration of the stock – visibly going forward today. The causes of the deterioration – the presence of which is inferred from a somewhat narrow range of data, some of which would bear a different interpretation from the one given them – are (p. 108):

1. Defects and diseases inherited from parents;
2. Ill-assorted unions of parents, comprising untoward crosses between races;
3. Unwise laws relating to marriage, and the artificial encouragement of population;
4. Insufficient care and nourishment, early and excessive child labor;
5. Prostitution.

"It therefore appears that the questions of population have come to be so many and so important as to require the separation of this subject from the body of economic questions with which they have hitherto been classed. These questions taken by themselves are sufficient to make up the subject-matter of a special science which will draw its data, on the one hand, from the moral sciences – particularly from political economy – and, on the other hand, from the natural sciences – particularly from biology. This new science is Viriculture (p. 134)."

It will be the office of this new science to find a remedy for the three grave difficulties of the present situation: (1) surplus or deficit of population, (2) degeneration, (3) prostitution. These are but the barest and most general indications given of the outlines of the new science. Under the first head there is a tentative suggestion that something might be accomplished by an intelligent and concerted statistical determination of the "demand" for population and the establishment of an equilibrium through the peoples' taking thought to multiply only up to the limit. Under the second it is likewise suggested, in similarly general terms, that something may be done toward a maintenance of the present standard of the population, if not toward its improvement, by extirpation of disease and through selective breeding.

The appendix (pp. 163-250) is made up of notes drawn from a great variety of sources and of very diverse value. For the most part they comprise facts more or less familiar to all readers, and betray no eagerness in the writer to parade a recondite erudition.

Essais sur la conception materialiste de l'histoire. By ANTONIO LABRIOLA. With a preface by G. Sorel. Paris: V. Giard et E. Brière, 1897. 12mo. pp. 348.*

OF these two essays the first (*En memoire du Manifeste du parti communiste*) recalls the attention to what was the meaning, in its author's mind, of the phrase which affords the title of this book. This central Marxian position says that the exigencies of the industrial process determine the features of the society's life process in all its other aspects – social, political, and intellectual. The rest of what the famous *Manifesto* has to say is to be read in the light of this principle which gives the socialist point of view. All the rest, even the doctrine of the class struggle and the Marxian theory of surplus-value, is by comparison provisional and tentative, although in point of fact, it is held, the whole of this further development of the theory is substantially cor-

* *The Journal of Political Economy*, June 1897.

rect. The office of this "materialistic conception" is that of a guiding principle (*Leitfaden*) in the study of social life and of social structure. These economic exigencies afford the definitive test of fitness in the adaptation of all human institutions by a process of selective elimination of the economically unfit. They also, through the industrial process through which they work their effect, determine the development of thought and science; the materialistic conception is itself, at the second remove, a product of the industrial process.

The second essay (*Le materialisme historique*) expands and expounds this position further; and it reiterates, with an insistence that sometimes grows tedious, that, "given the conditions of the development of industry and its appliances, the economic structure of society will determine . . . . . primarily and directly all the rest of the practical activity of the members, as well as the variations of this activity, which are met within the process that we call history – that is to say, the formation, dissensions, conflicts, and erosion of classes. . . . And it determines, secondarily, also the tendency, and in an indirect way, in great part, the objects which shall occupy thought and fancy, in art, religion, and science" (p. 239).

The book is notable not as a unique presentation of its thesis nor as a new departure in economic speculation, but as being, on the contrary, a typical example of the theoretical position at present occupied by socialist writers. For the theoretical writers among the socialists, and for the popular discussion in a less pronounced degree, socialist economics no longer revolves about the labor-value dogma that did such ubiquitous service for the propaganda in its day. Nor is the class-struggle dogma any longer so unfaltering a recourse as it once was, even among the Marxists of the stricter observance. These doctrines and their various ramifications are to an extent giving way before an interpretation of the materialistic conception which does not, in its fundamental position, go much beyond a conception of the evolution of social structure according to which the economic activities, and the habits bred by them, determine the activities and the habitual view of things in other directions than the economic one. And in this development the socialists are drawing close to the position of a large and increasing class of economists who are accepting the materialistic conception, or so much of it as is conveniently to be affiliated with Darwinism, whether they accept it under the style and title approved by their socialist mentors or under designations chosen by themselves. These economists of the new evolutionist or socialist departure are nowhere more numerous or more favorably received than among Professor Labriola's countrymen.

Sozialismus und soziale Bewegung im 19. Jahrhundert. By WERNER SOMBART. With a chronological table of the social movement from 1750 to 1896. Jena: Gustav Fischer, 1896. 8vo. pp. 143.*

IN the course of eight lectures Professor Sombart gives a survey and characterization of the socialist movement and the theories of the socialists from the point of view of an economist who stands outside the movement and still is not out of sympathy with it. The motive force of the movement is found (pp. 7-12) to be the sense of injury and of the precariousness of existence which pervades the proletariat of today, pushed to active measures by a propensity for revolutionary disturbance. This revolutionary propensity is of the nature of a nervous affection and comes of the excessive rush and strain

* *The Journal of Political Economy*, June 1897.

of modern life. That this restless impulse to agitation and revolution has definitively taken the specific direction of the Marxian social democracy is due to the temperament of the German population and the work of Karl Marx (p. 62). There is a large personal element of leadership in socialism. The work of Marx which has so profoundly affected the character of the latter-day social movement consists substantially in an unfaltering realism applied to social and economic speculation. This realism, the so-called materialistic conception, is a characteristically modern fact, and its acceptance by the modern socialists distinguishes them from all communistic or other radical diversions in the past. The attitude which this point of view should give is that of a passionless, uneager, unwavering furtherance of the industrial development; for according to this materialistic conception the democratic collectivism is to come in as the due culmination and consequence of industrial evolution. Such, says Professor Sombart, is the attitude of Marx at his best, and such he finds also to be the attitude of the Marxian socialists in a greater degree and more consistently as time goes on. All this disillusionment and work-day apprehension of social development as an inevitable process does not hinder the socialists from holding to their ideal with fervor, nor does it hinder them from doing their best to hasten and aggravate the class-struggle through the means of which the industrial development at its culmination is to pass into the democratic collectivism. The logical and the only promising line of action for the socialists, according to Professor Sombart (pp. 110-118), is to strengthen and accelerate the growth and spread of the modern culture, and carry it to the highest pitch attainable. Oddly enough – though perhaps it seems less odd to an affectionate latter-day citizen of the militant Fatherland – this ideal cultural growth to which socialism should look, it is explicitly held, comprises a large unfolding of warlike activity. Socialism is, on this and related grounds, not apprehended to be, in strict consistency, an international (*a fortiori* not an anti-national) movement. It is a further curious feature of Professor Sombart's exposition of socialism that he finds no logical ground for an atheistic or undevout attitude in the accepted realism of Marx and his followers. This is perhaps as characteristically new-German a misapprehension of Marxism as the contrary misapprehension which makes Marxism "materialistic" in the metaphysical sense is characteristic of the traditional view among English-speaking critics.

Esquisses de littérature politico-économique. Par N. Ch. Bunge, Ancien professeur à l'université de Kiew. Traduit du russe. Geneva: Georg & Co., 1898. 8vo. pp. xliii. + 455.*

This contribution to the history of economic doctrines is a collection of monographs of various dates (1860, 1868, 1894), revised and brought down to the date of publication of the Russian edition (St. Petersburg, 1895). It comprises four essays: Outlines of the History of Economic Doctrines; The Theory of the Harmony of Private Interests; John Stuart Mill as Economist; Schmoller's Verdict on Menger.

Part I (pp. 1-192) on the History of Doctrines, is a rapid sketch of the development, or rather of the sequence, of economic theories from classical antiquity (Plato, Aristotle) to the later developments of the Historical School, closing with Schmoller as the great and definitive exponent of modern economic doctrine and method. It considers the Physiocrats, the classical writers, the Utopian socialists, the philo-

* *The Journal of Political Economy*, December 1897.

sophical and critical socialist writers (Rodbertus, Proudhon, Marx), the school of Harmony of Interests ([H.C.] Carey, Bastiat), and the group of German writers identified with the historical method in economics. It is for the most part a colorless presentation of doctrines, and does not appreciably depart from the beaten paths, except in the large space allowed the socialists and the exponents of the harmony of interests.

Professor Bunge has little to say for the economists of the English line from Adam Smith down, and little to say in criticism of them that is not already commonplace. The same remark applies to his characterizations of Menger and his followers, who are classed with the English as "deductive." The hope for the future lies with the historical school, or more precisely with the "progressive historico-statistical school," of which Schmoller is the founder.

"The historico-statistical study of economic phenomena alone will avail for the advancement of political economy; but it is to be recognized that history and statistics have hitherto not given us available materials. This is due in part to the fact that economists have not recognized the importance of historical and statistical research, and in part to the limited range of facts covered by the field of history and statistics (p. 182). At the head of the contemporary (1868) historico-statistical school stands Tooke, the author of the *History of Prices* (p. 186). [But] it is Schmoller who has come in as the real founder of the new historico-statistical school (p. 187)."

"The reason why contemporary political economy in our time presents, at the first glance, such a physiognomy of distraction is that the time for new generalizations has not yet arrived; and consequently this lack of congruity is rather a merit than a defect (p. 190)."

Part II (pp. 193-301) presents an unusually painstaking exposition of Carey's doctrines on Value, Rent, the Effect of an Extension of Cultivation, and the Harmony of Private Interests, together with a criticism in detail. There is generous appreciation of Carey's deserts, of his kindly motives and his abounding faith in the substantial goodness and perfectibility of man.

"All that Carey says is true at bottom, but it holds only in certain exceptional cases – only so far as no one seizes what belongs to another although he has the power to do it (p. 301)."

The discussion of John Stuart Mill (Part III, pp. 303-433) is more appreciative than much of what representatives of the historical school have said on the subject, but offense is repeatedly taken at Mill's *a priori* method and his independence of facts, *e.g.*, in his theory of production. The merit of this part of the book, as of the preceding parts, lies in a detailed exposition, in which, by the way, there is manifested no unusual sense of perspective or proportion. The author has derived some edification but very little profit from his study of Mill. What he has learned is what he knew already – that salvation for economic science is to be found in the historico-statistical method alone, and that this method could not be effectively applied until Schmoller had found it and set it in order.

Part IV (pp. 435-451) is substantially a restatement, with some slight abridgement, of Schmoller's strictures on Menger. What Professor Bunge adds to Schmoller's mordant dispraise may be given in his own words.

"Il faut ajouter à ces paroles de Schmoller, que ni Menger, ni ses disciples n'ont, semble-t-il, rien produit jusqu'ici de transcendant."

Die Marxistische Socialdemokratie. Von MAX LORENZ. Leipzig: George H. Wigand, 1896. 12mo. pp. xii + 229.*

"THERE are two features of the Marxian teaching that seem to me to be of definitive significance for today and for the future: the stress laid on the concept of society, with no complacent parade of philanthropy expressing itself in soup-kitchens and alms, but asserting itself as a dominant principle which in strain and struggle resistlessly pervades the entire cultural development, – this is the first; the second is Marx's insistence on the connection between the so-called material or economic movement and the so-called spiritual movement in the evolution of society. . . . . It is true, Marx has exaggerated the bearing and importance of both these points, because his work, like that of any other man, was conditioned by the circumstances of his time. But on both heads Marx has also shed such light as no one before him, nor in his time, nor – at least until the present – since his time; and that comes of the pre-eminent greatness of the man." (pp. viii-ix).

"There is yet a further remark to be made: It is frequently assumed that the substantial core of the Marxian doctrine is the theory of labor-value and surplus-value, and that Marx arrives at his communistic demands directly from his surplus-value theory, on the basis of some assumed principle of justice or morality which requires communism as its fulfillment. . . . . But Engels disclaims, for Marx and for himself, any such 'application of Morals to Economics.'. . . . What comes about comes, according to Marx, not for equity's or morality's sake, but it comes as a causally, historically necessary phase of social evolution. The question is then as to the character of this causal, historical necessity in Marx's apprehension. Hence, our first effort must be directed to a presentation of

* *The Journal of Political Economy*, December 1897.

the so-called 'Materialistic Conception of History (pp. xi-xii).'

With a reverent hand, the author then enters on a discussion of this materialistic conception, which occupies the first of the four chapters (73 pages) of the volume. He insists on the antithesis between this and the individualistic conception – the conception which has dominated all the writings of the professed historians. After some exposition, and some criticism of its philosophical short-comings, he reaches (p. 50) the consideration of a serious if not irremediable defect in the Marxian theory. While the materialistic interpretation of history points out how social development goes on – by a class struggle that proceeds from maladjustment between economic structure and economic function – it is nowhere pointed out what is the operative force at work in the process. It denies that human discretion and effort seeking a better adjustment can furnish such a force, since it makes man the creature of circumstances. This defect reduces itself under the author's hand to a misconception of human nature and of man's place in the social development. The materialistic theory conceives of man as exclusively a social being, who counts in the process solely as a medium for the transmission and expression of social laws and changes; whereas he is, in fact, also an individual, acting out his own life as such. Hereby is indicated not only the weakness of the materialistic theory, but also the means of remedying the defect pointed out. With the amendment so indicated, it becomes not only a theory of the method of social and economic change, but a theory of social process considered as a substantial unfolding of life as well.

It is as an expression of this materialistic theory of Marx and Engels that the Marxian Socialism is taken up in chapter II and examined point by point. The third chapter is a criticism of the aims and views of socialists as regards the outcome of the development. The author finds the extreme conclusions reached by the socialists – the dissolution of the state and the family, the disappearance of religion, etc. – are reached by a one-sided and arbitrarily limited application of their own principles. The author takes up the materialistic argument and carries it out to its logical consequences, with the result of reducing the socialistic millennium to absurdity, at least to his own satisfaction. In the hands of the social democracy, the teachings of Marx have hardened into a system and a creed, incapable of growth and incapable of meeting the practical exigencies of an unfolding political and social life. While the work of Marx was great and fruitful, "Marxism is but an episode."

Social Facts and Forces. By WASHINGTON GLADDEN. New York: G. P. Putnam's Sons, 1897. 12mo. pp. 156.
Inequality and Progress. By GEORGE HARRIS. Boston: Houghton, Mifflin & Co., 1897. 12mo. pp. 237.*

MR. GLADDEN'S book is a collection of lectures delivered in Steinway Hall, Chicago, as the "Ryder Lectures," and later before the students of Iowa College at Grinnell, Iowa. The social facts and forces treated are presented under the following subjects: The Factory, The Labor Union, The Corporation, The Railway, The Church. The author has attempted to set forth the various social forces at work, and to show the results and social dangers of their operation. His treatment is thoughtful and dispassionate, the style that of the popular lecturer.

Mr. Harris criticises the prevailing notion that progress consists chiefly in an approach to political, economic, social,

* *The Journal of Political Economy,* March 1898.

and intellectual equality. As the title signifies, he considers inequality a precondition of progress. He contends that only in large groupings can any equality be said to exist, and that physical, intellectual, and economic advance consists in the successful struggle which the better wage against the worse. He finds a growing recognition of the inequality of individuals in various fields of activity. Only by proper combination of the superior with the inferior can that true unity be attained, in which each one can reach his best development. The book contains little that is new. The printer is to be congratulated on the workmanship of the volume.

Uber einige Grundfragen der Socialpolitik und der Volkswirtschaftslehre. Von GUSTAV SCHMOLLER. Leipzig: Duncker & Humblot, 1898. 8vo. pp. ix + 343.*

THE volume reproduces in collected form three well-known essays of various dates: (1) The polemical chapters of Professor Schmoller's controversy with Treitschke (*Uber einige Grundfragen des Rechts und der Volkswirtschaft* – 1874-5); (2) The essay on the Scope and Method of Economic Science (*Die Volkswirtschaft, die Volkswirtschaftslehre und ihre Methode* – 1895), originally written for Conrad's *Handwörterbuch;* and (3) the Inaugural Address of October last, delivered on the occasion of Professor Schmoller's induction into the rectorship at the University of Berlin (*Wechselnde Theorien und feststehende Wahrheiten im Gebiete der Staats- und Socialwissenschaften und die heutige deutsche Volkswirtschaftslehre* – 1897). It is notable as indicating the extent and the character of the changes that have passed over the "historical method" during the past twenty-five years. The earlier of the essays gives Professor Schmoller's position

* *The Journal of Political Economy,* June 1898.

at the time when he first came prominently forward as the champion of that method, and its defender against those who spoke for a return to a rehabilitated classicism. It marks the supersession of Roscher's "historico-physiological" by the "historical" method, through discontinuing, or at least discountenancing, the use of the physiological analogy in economic theory. On the basis of this early controversy with Treitschke, Professor Schmoller got the reputation, not altogether gratuitous, at the hands of his critics, of being spokesman for the view that economic science is, and of right ought to be, without form and void. But if this construction of his views was not altogether gratuitous, still less was it altogether well grounded. The elements of his later methodological work are visible in this early essay, but they are most readily visible and most significant when seen in the light of his later utterances on the same head. Without the consistency and application given to these elements in his later work, it is doubtful if there would have been occasion seriously to qualify the disparaging opinion passed upon his efforts by his Austrian critics. What gives added color to the contentions of those who carp at the historical method, as shown in Schmoller's exposition, is the fact that very much of his constructive work has been of a character to bear out the criticisms leveled at him on methodological grounds. Much of his own work, as well as the greater part of the voluminous work carried on under his hands by his many disciples, has been of the nature of compilation and description — narrative, often discursive and fragmentary. But as to this prevalent character of his published work, it is to be said that he has, professedly, been occupied with the foundations of a prospective theoretical science of economics. And this prospective science "is, as regards its foundation, descriptive" (p. 226). The second of the essays contained in the volume leaves no ground for the objection that Professor Schmoller makes the science an undisciplined congeries of data. He gives, in concise and telling form, a prospectus for a theoretical science, such that, whatever strictures may be offered by his critics, it can assuredly not be characterized as being without form and void.

"The method of any given science is determined (1) by the general standpoint which human knowledge, taken as a whole, has reached at the time; that is to say, by the generic features of the ideals and methods of knowledge which are in vogue at the time, and which are fundamentally of the same character for all directions of human thinking and knowledge. . . . (2) Scientific method depends on the nature of the subject-matter under inquiry. So mathematics follows a different method of procedure from physics, and the latter a different one from physiology, etc. . . . (3) The method employed in any given science at any given point of time depends on the degree of development which the science has reached at the time. In its crude beginnings knowledge always proceeds by half truths and sweeping generalizations; only little by little is the method of procedure improved and subtilized; emphasis falls now on observation and description, now on classification, and again, attention may be centered upon the causal explanation of phenomena." (pp. 228-230).

It is this third count that seems to have been most insistently present in Professor Schmoller's mind in shaping his work in the past, especially his published writings. Economics has hitherto, in Professor Schmoller's apprehension, been in the inchoate stage only, and the method proper to the science, has, therefore, been conceived to be description and collation. In his lectures, and in the guidance given his students, especially during later years, the same scrupulous regard for the requirements of economics as an inchoate science simply has not been so decisive, at least not to the full extent. It is evident both from the character which his work is now assuming and from the tone of this essay that the science is now felt to be rapidly passing this inchoate stage, and that the economists may now legitimately turn to constructive theoretical work.

Several chapters (iv-x. pp. 231-276) are given to a discussion of the methods and aims of economic science in the past; to an exposition, in outline, of the part which observation and description must play as preliminary to constructive work; to the use of statistical inquiry; to a characterization of the true historical method, and the relation of historical inquiry to economics; and last, but not least, to the important place of a taxonomic discipline – definitions, concepts and classification – in the science. In this latter discussion, it may not be out of place to point out, Professor Schmoller gives but scant acknowledgment to the really large and substantial deserts of the classical writers under this head. The most substantial and characteristic move in advance made by Professor Schmoller in the methodological discussion then follows under xi (*Die Ursachen*).

"Observation and description, definition and classification are preparatory work only. What we seek by these means is an apprehension of economic phenomena as a connected whole. . . . Our insight in this respect can never be complete or fully adequate. . . . But, in any case, the more we confine ourselves to seeking an explanation of the facts at hand on the basis of what has immediately gone before, the more nearly will we succeed in this undertaking. And, in any event, there must remain before our eyes, as the ideal of all knowledge, the explanation of all facts in terms of causation. The natural sciences have accustomed us to apprehend every event as conditioned by causes, which we conceive of as forces." (p. 277).

"As causes at work in the sequence of economic phenomena we have mechanical and organic forces on the one side, and psychical forces on the other, which meet as two independent groups of causes contributing to the results to be studied. Whatever opinions we may hold as to the relation between physical and psychical life; however much we may be inclined to emphasize the fact that our spiritual life is conditioned by the facts of our nervous system; although we may, with full justification, hold that all our sensations and feelings are inseparable from certain physiological processes; this much remains beyond question, that the coexistence and sequence of spiritual phenomena are not to be explained through nerve changes simply, and that for the present, and apparently for all time to come, the ultimate ascertainable facts of material existence and the most rudimentary adjustments of the spiritual life are ranged over against one another as independent and self-explaining groups of phenomena. Hence all efforts to explain the actions of men through direct recourse to merely physical or biological factors must be declared mistaken or inadequate." (p. 278).

Hence the causes in terms of which economic theory must in the last resort formulate its results are psychical facts – facts of human motives and propensities.

"There is no science possible outside the range of the universal law of causation – not even in the domain of the spiritual life. But the causes at work in the psychical sequence are essentially different from the mechanical ones. And hence it becomes incumbent on a practical science, such as economics, to carry its inquiry, as far as may be needed, into the details of psychological processes." (pp. 286-287).

"The aim of economics, as of any science, adopting any

method, must be the determination of uniformities and laws (pp. 298-307). But the descriptive, empirical generalization of uniformities, simply, must not be accepted as a determination of the laws of the phenomena under inquiry. Normalization and taxonomic schedules are not science in the modern acceptance of the word.

"We are no longer content to call empirically ascertained uniformities laws, but only those uniformities the causes of which we have been able to seize and fix (p. 302). Economics is now in a fair way to become such a science. History and philosophy have brought it back to a realizing sense of the phenomena of collective life; statistics and industrial history have shown the way to a methodologically adequate empiricism; and psychology holds up before the science as its only competent purpose the quest for the substantially decisive causes of all human affairs." (p. 309).

Aristocracy and Evolution: A Study of the Rights, the Origin, and the Social Functions of the Wealthier Classes. By W. H. MALLOCK. New York: The Macmillan Company, 1898. 8vo. pp. xxxiii + 385.*

ON a cursory acquaintance with this volume one is tempted to dismiss it with the comment that Mr. Mallock has written another of his foolish books. The objective point of the new book is still the enforcement of the author's pet fallacy, which he has expounded so felicitously on many a former occasion. It is restated here with somewhat greater circumstance than before, and is backed by much telling illustration and some substantial information that might well have served a more useful purpose. A fuller acquaintance with its contents, however, will convince the reader that the book has substantial

* *The Journal of Political Economy*, June 1898.

merits, although these merits do not belong with the economic side of the argument.

While the present volume covers a wider range of phenomena and traces the working of the great man's dominating efficiency through a greater variety of human relations than Mr. Mallock's earlier books have done, the chief point of the argument is still the productive efficiency of the great man in industry and the bearing of this productive efficiency upon the equitable claim of the wealthy classes to a superior share of the product. What is to be proven is the equity and the expediency of a system of distribution in which a relatively large share of the product of industry goes to the owners of capital and the directors of business. For this purpose "the great man" in industry is tacitly identified with the captain of industry or the owner of capital. It is right that the great man, so understood, should receive a large share, because he produces a large proportion of the product of industry (book iii, pp. 197-267). And it is expedient that exceptional gains should come to this exceptional wealth-producer, because on no other terms can he be induced to take care of the economic welfare of the community – and, in the nature of things, the welfare of the community, of the many, lies unreservedly in the hands of the minority of great men (book iv, pp. 271-380).

The few are the chief producers.

"All the democratic formulas which for the past hundred years have represented the employed as the producers of wealth, and the capitalistic employers as the appropriators of it, are, instead of being, as they claim to be, the expressions of a profound truth, related to truth only as being direct inversions of it. Whatever appearances may seem to show to the contrary, it is the few and not the many who, in the domain of economic production, are essentially and permanently the chief repositories of power (pp. 174-175).

"The case of labour directed by different great men is the same as the case of labour applied to different qualities of land. The great men produce the increment. Labour, however, must be held to produce that minimum necessary to the support of the labourers, both in agriculture and in all kinds of production. The great man produces the increment that would not be produced by labour if his influence ceased. Labour, it is true, is essential to the production of the increment, also; but we cannot draw any conclusions from the hypothesis of labour ceasing; for the labourers would have to labor whether the great men were there or no (pp. 202-206, margin). The efficiency of labour itself is practically constant; and for the student of wealth-production the principal force to be studied is the ability of the few, by which the labour of the many is multiplied, and which only exerts itself under special social circumstances." (p. 209, note).

We are thus enabled to discriminate arithmetically between the share of the product due to the great men and that due to the many.

"Let us take the case of the United Kingdom, and consider the amount per head that was annually produced by the population a hundred years ago. This amount was about £14. At the present time it is something like £35 . . . . Now, if we attribute the entire production of this country, at the close of the last century, to common or average labour (which is plainly an absurd concession), we shall gain some idea of what the utmost limits of the independent productivity of the ordinary man are; for the ordinary man's talents as a producer, when directed by nobody but himself, have, as has been said already, not appreciably increased in the course of two thousand years, and have certainly not increased within the past three generations. The only thing that has increased has been the concentration on the ordinary man's productive talents of the productive talents of the exceptional man. The talents of the exceptional man, in fact, have been the only variant in the problem; and, accordingly, the minimum which these talents produce is the total difference between £14 and £35."

This argument may be restated in a more concise arithmetical form after adding a further premise, which is implied, though not fully taken account of, in Mr. Mallock's exposition. The talents of the ordinary man have not changed within the past three generations, or if they have changed it is but by a variation so small that it can only be indicated, not quantitatively registered; the like is true of the talents of the exceptional man. This latter feature of the premises has not been brought out by Mr. Mallock, although his claim that human talents have remained constant plainly involves it. The traits of human nature have not appreciably changed within the period in question. The race of British subjects is much the same as it has been. But in order to allow for a possible, though inappreciable change in the talents of the two classes, the conceivable infinitesimal change may be indicated by the use of accents. The arithmetical problem in hand will then present the following result:

(1) o (ordinary) $\times$ g (great man) $=$ 14.
(2) $o' \times g' = 35$.

But since 35 may be broken up and written $14 + 21$, it follows that, in the second equation, 21 of the entire product (35) is the product of g' alone. *Q. E. D.*

This traverses the ancient traditions of arithmetic, but it is to be said in legitimation of this procedure that it would be extremely difficult to get the same result by a different method. Any man encumbered with a hide-bound arithmetic would find himself constrained to look for some other variable in the problem than a special segment of that human nature which is by supposition declared invariable; nor would such a one have the courage to portion out the *meum* and *tuum* as between two factors of a joint product. But Mr. Mallock is without fear.

Some account, though scant, is taken by Mr. Mallock of the phenomena of transmitted knowledge, usages, and methods of work; but these facts are not allowed to count as against the primacy of the great man. And as regards this great man, where he is first characterized and expounded, in the chapter especially devoted to him ("Great Men, as the True Cause of Progress," pp. 55-88), the chief variants of him that concern economic theory are the inventor, the overseer of industrial processes, and the business man. The impression is conveyed in this early chapter that for the industrial purpose the greatest of these is the inventor, and next him ranks the director of mechanical processes, while the business man comes into view as a wealth-producer chiefly in an indirect way by influencing the motions of the two former, and, through them, the motions of "ordinary men" engaged in manual labor. At a later point, when the question comes to concern the appraisement of productivity and the equitable apportionment of the product, the inventor, the engineer and the foreman disappear behind the business man's ledger, as the peppercorn disappears behind the nutshell, and "the great man" becomes synonymous with "the captain of industry." By a curious inversion of his own main position, Mr. Mallock reaches the broad verdict that consumable goods are mainly produced by the captain of industry. His main position, so far as regards industrial efficiency, is that the greatness and efficiency of the great man lie in his superior knowledge, which he is able to impose upon others and so direct their efforts to the result aimed at. "The master of knowledge, as applied to production, is the inventor" (p. 138). "The inventor . . . is an agent of 'social progression' only because the particularized knowledge of which his invention consists is embodied either in models, or drawings, or written or spoken orders, and thus affects the technical action of whole classes of other men" (p. 139). Under the capitalistic wage system "productive power has increased because capital . . . has enabled a few men to apply, with the most constant and intense effort, their intellectual faculties to industry in its minutest details" (p. 161). Productive efficiency, therefore, is a matter of detailed knowledge of the technical processes of industry, and the application of this knowledge through directing the technical movements of others. Yet the type of productive efficiency in the advanced portion of Mr. Mallock's argument is taken to be the counting-house activity of the business man, who frequently does not, and pretty uniformly need not, have any technical knowledge of the industry that goes on under his hand. His relation to the mechanical processes is always remote, and usually of a permissive kind only. This is especially true of the director of a large business, who is by that fact, if he is successful, a highly efficient great man. He delegates certain men, perhaps at the second or third remove, to assume discretion and set certain workmen and machines in motion under the guidance of technical knowledge possessed by them, not by him. The captain's efficiency is not to be called in question, but it is bold irony to call it productive efficiency under the definition of productivity set up by Mr. Mallock.

Most modern men would have been content to justify the business man's claim to a share in the product on the ground of his serviceability to the community, without specifically imputing to him the major part in the production of goods; but Mr. Mallock's abounding faith in the canons of natural rights compels him naïvely to account for the business man's income in terms of productive efficiency simply. The argument of the book as is evident especially in the concluding portion (book iv, pp. 271-380), is chiefly directed to the confutation of the socialists. And in this confutation it is the ancient, now for the most part abandoned, socialist position that is made the point of attack. This early socialist position was summed up in the claim that to the laborer should belong the entire product of his labor. The claim is a crude application of a natural-rights dogma, and for the living generation of socialists it may fairly be said to be a discarded standpoint. It is this dead dog that Mr. Mallock chiefly belabors. Together with this, the similarly obsolete natural-rights formula that all men are born free and equal comes in for a portion of his polemical attention. In all this, the polemic proceeds on the lost ground of natural rights. Objection is taken not to the obvious groundlessness of the whole natural-rights structure, but to the scope of the application given the dogmas and to the excessive narrowness of the definitions employed.

Through it all, however, Mr. Mallock very effectively presents the current arguments going to show that the pecuniary incentive is indispensable to modern industry, and he shows, with great detail and with good effect, the weakness of the socialist contentions on this head. He goes with the socialists to the length of showing that the pecuniary incentive – the desire of wealth – is in large part a desire for distinction only, not in the last analysis a desire for the material, consumable goods. But he denies flatly – what they affirm – that an emulative incentive of another kind might serve the turn if the pecuniary incentive were to fall away. No other method of gauging success and distinction will take the place of this one as an incentive to wealth-production, whatever seems to be true as regard other directions of effort (book iv, chap. ii, 284-323). It is to be regretted that nothing beyond asseveration is put forward in support of this denial, which is the central feature of the refutation of socialism. No decisive argument for the denial is adduced, but through the assertion made there runs an implication that, in order to serve their purpose at all effectively, the inducements offered the wealth-producer must mechanically resemble the results to be worked out. As on the homeopathic principle like is to be cured by like, so in industry the repugnance to effort spent on material goods must be overcome by a remedial application of material goods. While it seems to be present in the reasoning, it is by no means clear, it should be remarked, that this axiom of similarity has been present in the reasoner's mind.

Mr. Mallock is a master of pleasing diction, and his arguments are presented in a lucid and forcible way that makes the book very attractive reading. And the grotesquely devious ways of its economic argument do not prevent it from being a suggestive contribution to the discussion of cultural development. At many points it brings out in a strong light the importance of a gifted minority as an element in the process of institutional growth, although even here it is curious, and in a sense instructive, to note that as representative spokesmen of the modern social sciences, Mr. Mallock has been constrained to cite George, Laveleye, and Mr. Kidd. The discussion of the great man's place in the cultural process is at its best where it deals with other fields than the economic. Unfortunately, it is the economic bearing of the argument alone that can be taken up here.

The volume suffers from a meretricious increase of bulk, due to an excessive use of large type, wide margins and heavy paper. It should be added that the printer's work is altogether above reproach.

Reflections on the Formation and the Distribution of Riches. By A. R. J. TURGOT, 1770. (Economic Classics). New York: The Macmillan Company, 1898. 12mo. pp. xxii + 112.*

THE editor of *Economic Classics* has again placed economic readers under obligation, by presenting a painstaking and excellent edition of Turgot's *Reflections.* The editor's task has been performed with the same scrupulous regard for a veracious presentation of his author's work as has attended previous issues of the series, and the result is a rendering of the great Frenchman's economic doctrines such as leaves little to be desired either in reliability or in accessibility. Not the least commendable feature of this slender volume is the excerpts from the correspondence between Turgot and Hume, published in an appendix. Meager as they seem, these excerpts throw a light upon Turgot's position and upon his relation to the Physiocratic school which will help students toward an apprehension of the author's true place in the development of economic doctrine.

The Wheat Problem, Revised, with an answer to various Critics. By SIR WILLIAM CROOKES, F.R.S. With chapters on the future wheat supply of the United States by C. Wood Davis and John Hyde. New York: G. Putnam's Sons, 1900. 12mo. pp. xiii + 272.*

A SECONDARY purpose of Sir William Crookes's essay on

* *The Journal of Political Economy*, September 1898.
* *The Journal of Political Economy*, March 1900.

"The World's Supply of Wheat" apparently is to call attention to his experiments in the fixation of nitrogen. These experiments may well have a grave significance for the future food supply, or at any rate the question of the artificial fixation of nitrogen may come to be a vital question, although there are probably few economists who see the problem of artificial fixation as a sphynx's riddle impending in the immediate future.

The author's argument converges to the conclusion that a general scarcity of food is, at the most, no more than a generation ahead. In this he is ably seconded by Mr. Davis's hearty co-operation and has also the somewhat equivocal support of Mr. Hyde's discussion of the wheat problem. Of Mr. Davis it is of course expected that he should unreservedly throw what weight his word has on the side of Sir William's contention. But Mr. Hyde, as becomes a cautious statistician, is non-committal in any matter of forecast, except where he is on the safe ground of available acreage. Mr. Hyde speaks directly to the point which he has set before him, viz., the wheat supply; and he does not commit himself to the implication that "the wheat supply" is or comes near being synonymous with "the food supply." He deals with the question as a statistical problem of acreage, and has very little to say on the more important question of yield; for future changes of yield, so far as concerns this country, cannot be discussed with any definite outcome on the basis of present statistics. He is, however, content to leave the question of probable future yields with a simple indication of what has been the course of average yields for twenty years back, neglecting to point out that the situation of the grain market during this period has been such as to discourage all efforts to increase the yields of any of the common grains, and so leaving the misleading suggestion that the course of future yields is to be directly inferred from the yields in the immediate past. But while Mr. Hyde's most telling contribution to the argument for a scarcity is this, probably unintended, misleading implication, Sir William faces the question of yields and disposes of it in one of the most extraordinary passages that has yet been met with in all the curious literature extant on the wheat question. In a reply to criticisms offered by Sir John Lawes and Sir Henry Gilbert he argues (pp. 104-107) that the low yields of America, as compared with those of England, are due to conditions of climate and soil, not to the American farmer's less close economy in the use of land. "American methods are quite as well adapted to the soils and climate as are those of England to the soils and climate of Great Britain." This passage the context compels us to take seriously. The consummate ignorance of the aims and methods of American farming reflected in this statement is assuredly surprising enough in a scientist who has so evidently taken pains to inform himself on other features of the subject. And it is at the same time unfortunate in that it may raise a presumption that other, more substantial portions of the argument proceed on equally fanciful and headlong generalizations. In the face of his incredible dealings with these economic data, it needs all the prestige of Sir William's great name to sustain our faith in what he has to say when he is speaking within the lines of his own science.

Correlated with this assumption, that the yield per acre is necessarily stable, is an equally surprising assumption to the effect that the unit consumption of wheat must go on increasing and so hasten the approach of scarcity. Abundance during the past fifteen years has resulted in an increase of unit consumption, and this increase, it is argued, will go on in the face of a slackening supply so as to cause a scarcity in the future. That is to say, because we have had abundance and consequent low prices of wheat, resulting in a high unit consumption and a low yield, therefore we must expect that in the future we shall have a high unit consumption and a low yield, resulting in scarcity and high prices. Certain passages in the volume might even be construed to say that we shall presently suffer privation because of the excessive prosperity and efficiency of our industry in the future.

So far as the essay is an argument for impending scarcity it proceeds on the assumption that "other circumstances remain the same," particularly the adverse circumstances. But there appears to be no reason for believing that other things will remain the same in the immediate future, any more consistently than they have done in the past. It may therefore fairly be doubted whether Sir William's draft on the future's bank of misery will be honored, since it is drawn with this proviso.

Die Entstehung des socialen Problems. Von ARNOLD FISCHER. Rostock i. M.: C. J. E. Volckmann, 1897. 8vo. pp. xvi + 781.*

THE social problem with which the author is occupied is of course the problem which modern socialism offers to solve. A solution is sought in a "science of civilization," differing from earlier attempts at such a science, particularly in the degree of profundity and exhaustiveness with which the causes of cultural growth and the controlling principles of development are examined and formulated. If once an adequate theory of culture has been established, the author feels, the rest follows as a matter of course, though not necessarily by an easy and unlaborious inference, from the main drift of this theory. The social problem which confronts the

* *The Journal of Political Economy*, March 1900.

present generation is a necessary phenomenon of the present phase of culture; it is a fruit which in the natural course ripens at the present stage of cultural maturity, and at no other stage. If we can find wherein consists the essential character of the growth in cultural maturity, we shall, therefore, have a key to the successive emergence of the problems that arise in the life history of society as well as to their significance for the growth of civilization and to their practical solution.

The degree of maturity attained by human culture at any given phase is a question of the degree of exhaustion of the vitality of the culture in question. The ultimate ground of the problem characteristic of any given cultural phase is, therefore, the intensity of vital force which expresses itself in this cultural phase. "Zeitprobleme sind daher Gradmesser der Lebenskraft und damit der Höhe des Lebensalters jener Cultur, aus der sie emporstiegen" (p. 3). At the same time. "Ein Zeitproblem ist das Bewusstsein eines Uebels des Gemeinwesens" (p. 5). We have therefore to seek a formulation of the course of civilization "as the resultant of a clearly determined law." And since mankind is but a part of the organic world, human civilization is but the resultant of the same forces which determine the development of species in plant and animal life. Now, the sweeping characteristic of the life process of organisms is a continuous decline in the intensity of the forces engaged. Observed phases of development are therefore expressions of stages in the decline of intensity of the life process. This law holds throughout organic life, and as the course of organic development and of culture proceeds we have, as the result of advancing decrepitude, an advance from a blind but fierce assimilative growth, through instinct, feeling, reflection, to rationality and to pure reason. The latter phase of development, the phase characteristic of senile decay, is now upon us, and our social problem is an expression of the evils peculiar to the social organism at this stage. The working class of the present day is the class of pure reason.

With this clue the author cheerfully constructs his comprehensive theory of cultural growth, and apart from this grotesque resort to analogies and metaphysical entities there appears to be but little of a theoretical kind that is new or characteristic in the volume. The theoretical contribution here offered may be taken as an extreme case of that recourse to mystical interpretation, which any reader of the later German speculations in social and economic theory must be prepared to face. But for all his mysticism, the author shows a wide acquaintance with the data of his subject, and no mean capacity for turning them to account.

Pamphlets Socialistes: Le Droit á la Paresse; La Religion du Capital; L'Appetit Vendu; Pie IX au Paradis. Par PAUL LAFARGUE. Paris: V. Giard & E. Brière, 1900. 12mo. pp. 164.*

THESE discourses, reprinted here in collected form from widely separate dates, are held in the light and easy vein characteristic of M. Lafargue when he aims to be entertaining. The first two are well-known pieces, of a satirical purpose; the two latter are of the same class, though newer and less well-known. The whole is excellent in its kind, with an excellence characteristic of the propagandist literature of which it is an exceptionally effective sample. As commonly happens in the case of the socialistic satire from the continent of Europe, the jests are too broad, of too maudlin a complexion to appeal with full effect to English, and par-

* *The Journal of Political Economy,* March 1900.

ticularly to American readers. This is particularly true of the later ones of these pamphlets of M. Lafargue's. The satire is overstrained to such a degree as to defeat its own purpose.

Social Laws: An Outline of Sociology. By G. TARDE. Translated from the French by HOWARD C. WARREN, with a preface by JAMES MARK BALDWIN. New York: The Macmillan Company, 1899. 12mo. pp. xi + 213.*

AS THE editor of the volume remarks, M. Tarde has here summarized his theoretical work and shown it to constitute a system. In this reduction of the system to its outlines its great ingenuity is impressed upon the reader much more forcibly than by the detailed presentation contained in M. Tarde's larger works. At the same time the essential artificiality of the doctrines likewise comes out in plainer relief, proceeding as they do, for the most part, and particularly as regards their general features, on a bold and dexterous use of metaphor and analogy. It seems not improbable that, as a result of the conciseness, not to say boldness, with which the ingenious artifices of the theory are here brought out, the volume may contribute materially to curtail the vogue of M. Tarde's sociological doctrines.

The essential superficiality of the formulations offered is shown, *e.g.*, in such generalizations as this: "Habit is merely a sort of internal heredity, just as heredity is only externalized habit. Heredity, then, is the form of repetition appropriate to life, just as undulation, or periodic movement, is its physical, and imitation its social form" (p. 22). Again: "Every real opposition implies a relation between two forces, tendencies, or directions" (p. 88). Under this elastic, not to say

* *The Journal of Political Economy*, December 1900.

ambiguous term, "opposition," are comprised such diverse phenomena as mechanical action and reaction, arithmetical positive and negative, variations of degree, war, industrial competition, discussion, hesitation. It is plainly by a felicitous use of analogy alone that the comprehensive term "opposition" can be made to serve in the discussion of matters so disparate as these. All this is of a character to suggest the moralizing speculations of the eighteenth century and prepares one to meet the metaphysical conception of a spiritually guided progress, expressed in the conclusion that, "It would appear . . . . that the strife of opposition fulfills the rôle of a middle term in the social as it does in the organic and inorganic worlds" (p. 133).

The Impending Crisis; Conditions Resulting from the Concentration of Wealth in the United States. By BASIL A. BOUROFF. Chicago: The Midway Press Committee, 1900. 12mo. pp. ix + 196.*

MR. BOUROFF sets forth the economic condition of the United States as seen by a foreign student during half-a-dozen years' residence in the country, and as gathered from statistical reports of the government and from earlier studies by other men. In two chapters, dealing with the distribution of wealth, Mr. Bouroff outlines the situation which he proposes to discuss. His statistics are taken chiefly, and for the most part directly, from the reports of the eleventh census. In the latter part of the volume he returns to a statistical exhibit of the situation to show the outcome of the working of the American economic system, the determining characteristic of which he has set forth in his third and fourth chapters. This characteristic feature, which in Mr. Bouroff's

* *The Journal of Political Economy*, December 1900.

view must lead to national destruction, he discusses under the somewhat barbarous name, "dividogenesure." It is not easy to say just what is included under this term, but the substantial fact for which the volume contends, as the cause of the poverty of the poor, seems to be the recognized feature of modern life that income from property acts cumulatively to enrich the owners; to which Mr. Bouroff adds that the indigence of the poor has, under modern conditions, a somewhat similar cumulative effect, in that "the propertyless is a man of multiple expenses." The possible recourse to a free use of natural resources has been cut off by the all-inclusive grasp of ownership, until every move in life means a tax on the propertyless man, which he cannot avoid so long as he is alive. Owing to this cumulative enrichment of the propertied at the cost of the propertyless, it has come about that "we had fully 32,656,808 individuals of them [the propertyless][1] in 1890" (p. 83). These figures are got by adding and averaging the numbers of families occupying farms or homes not owned by the occupants in 1890. However serious the situation so outlined may be conceived to be, it is undoubtedly a stretch of imagination to class tenant families in the United States as unqualifiedly "propertyless." What proportion of them may be such is not easy to say; but the discrepancy between the meaning of the figures and Mr. Bouroff's use of them is probably what will appeal most strongly to American students. Something similar, of course, is the case with the discussion of mortgages on urban property (pp. 119-122), where mortgage indebtedness is taken as a reliable index of hardship borne by the debtors.

But apart from exaggeration due to lack of familiarity with the conditions which he discusses, Mr. Bouroff shows skill

[1] [The brackets are Veblen's].

in handling his statistics so as to bring out the darker aspect of the situation. His warning loses in force somewhat, through this unintentional overstatement, but it need not on that account be groundless.

Associations industrielles et commerciales: Fédérations — Ententes partielles — Syndicats — Cartels — Comptoirs — Affiliations — Trusts. By JULES GERNAERT and Vte DE HERBAIS DE THUN. Bruxelles: E. Bruylant, 1901. 8vo. pp. vi + 99.*

THE volume gives in concise and systematic form a conspectus of the various kinds of business coalitions in vogue, with a special view to the Belgian and French situation and practice. It deals with the manner of formation and control of such coalitions, the scope of competence of each, and the conditions which decide what particular form and measure of coalition best serves the purpose in a given case or a given line of business. The several forms or types of coalition are taken up in the order named in the subtitle, which is also the sequence of progressive closeness of combination observable in the several kinds of coalition. The distinctive forms or types of coalition are carefully defined and described, in the most succinct manner, this work of definition and "application" occupying the first sixty-one pages, and the remainder of the volume is occupied with illustrative examples designed to enforce the authors' views of the limits of competence and availability for each type, but more especially of the last four named in the list. There is nothing more of historical or descriptive matter than what is immediately useful for illustrating the authors' definitions and supporting their theoretical conclusions.

As regards these conclusions, they are cast in the form of

* *The Journal of Political Economy*, December 1902.

general formulas. The federation is an initial move in coalition, likely to lead to closer combination, and largely useful for this purpose. Of the definitive forms of coalition the affiliation and the trust are the most practical, the former having the advantage of flexibility, the latter of ready and effectual central control. The general attitude of the authors toward business coalition may be summed up in their own words as "cette vérité absolue que nous ne cessons pas de proclamer et que nous finirons par faire admettre: La *nécessité* des ASSOCIATIONS INDUSTRIELLES ET COMMERCIALES reconnues, approuvées et patronnées par les pouvoirs publics, dans l'intérêt général." But "in order that any coalition be effective it is indispensable: (1) that it be of duly legal form, and (2) that it be concluded for a long term" (p. 98). For American, and probably also for many European purposes, proposition (1) might perhaps better read: "Any effective coalition will turn out to be legal"; and possibly (2) might also be revised to read: "An efficient coalition will last as long as it proves itself a business success."

There is, elsewhere as well as in these formal concluding propositions, a certain naïve apprehension of the phenomena treated, which, no doubt, adds materially to the sure touch and lucid manner of presentation that characterize the volume. This degree of naïveté is perhaps due to the fact that the authors have seen their subject-matter from the somewhat old-fashioned business situation that prevails in Europe, as contrasted with what confronts a student of similar phenomena in America. A close contact with the maturer business situation of America might have altered the point of view and given a wider and more enduring serviceability to the discussion, at the same time that it would probably have increased the difficulty of the undertaking, and have resulted in a less succinct and definitive formulation.

Psychologie économique. By G. TARDE. Paris: Félix Alcan, 1902. 2 vols., 8vo. pp. 383 and 449.*

IN its general plan M. Tarde's book is an application of his well-known "social laws" to economics, together with a recasting of the received scheme of economic theory to fit the scheme of his social laws. The economics to whose revision he addresses himself is a somewhat old-fashioned economics; approximately, one might say, some half-a-century old, more or less. Later discussion, with the exception of what M. Gide has contributed, has not in any appreciable degree affected M. Tarde's apprehension of what economics aims at as regards either its scope, its method, or the range of phenomena which engage its attention. He finds fault with the received scheme of Production, Circulation, Distribution, and Consumption (Book I, chap. iii), and rejects these several captions one by one as being in part artificial and incompetent subdivisions of the subject-matter, and in part as not belonging within the scope of the science. Circulation (following Gide) is but a corollary of the division of labor (p. 98), hence this drops out without further comment; consumption is either inseparable from production, or it is extra-economic, so that also drops out; by distribution M. Tarde appears to understand the "diffusion" of the products of industry, which, again, cannot be fairly considered a distinct head of theory, but falls under the same general head with production (*reproduction*). But the remaining head of Production fares no better. It is condemned because as it stands it has regard simply to objective entities, products, instead of dealing with the producers and their relations to one another in the productive process (pp. 99, 100).

Instead of the worn-out scheme of economics as it has

* *The Journal of Political Economy*, December 1902.

hitherto stood, M. Tarde proposes to discuss economic conduct under his own scheme of social-psychological laws: Repetition, Opposition, and Adaptation. The scheme is the same as has been expounded on several earlier occasions by M. Tarde, most succinctly and comprehensively in his *Lois Sociales*. The discussion which economic phenomena get in the three books in which these several heads are taken up is, on the whole, more suggestive than convincing. In Book I, chapter ii, on the "Economic Function of Opinion" (*Croyance*), and vi, on "Money," may be singled out as of peculiar value. The former aims to show how opinions, ideas regarding the desirability of certain products, for instance, grow up and spread through the body of consumers under the guidance of advertising and the like; and how, on the other hand, the opinions and predilections of consumers influence the conduct of producers. Chapter vi offers an analysis of the psychological processes involved in the establishment of a standard of value as well as in the use of money. Of Book II, on "Economic Opposition," it is difficult to single out any particular portion that is peculiarly worth while; it contains little else than well-worn general reflections on prices, competition, crises, and the like, with some slight illustrative material. Of Book III, on "Economic Adaptation," the valuable portions are in the main comprised in chapter ii, on "The Economic Imagination," which offers some suggestive passages on the part played by imagination in invention, in the direction and organization of industry, and in commercial enterprise.

On the whole, M. Tarde's book is not a work with which economic science will have to count. The author's familiarity with economics is patently scanty, and has a perfunctory air. The book has the faults that habitually attach to M. Tarde's writings: it is unnecessarily bulky, diffuse, and discursive, at the same time that the penchant for system making and symmetry gives it an air of completeness and definitiveness which is not borne out by substantial results. M. Tarde's psychology is in much the same case as his economics: it is somewhat behind the times; its outlook over its field is narrow, and is subject to essentially mechanical limitations; it deals in catchwords and mechanical schematization of phenomena rather than with causal relations and the springs of human conduct. This applies, of course, to M. Tarde's psychology generally, as it is set forth in his earlier works, as well as in the present book.

After a busy life spent in this field, M. Tarde has come in sight of the central principle of modern psychology, which has been the common property of American and English psychologists of the last generation, ever since Professor James broke away from the earlier empiricism: but it cannot be said that he has assimilated this modern standpoint which he has approached, nor, perhaps, that he sees the outcome of his own speculations in this respect.

As is well known, though perhaps not always known under this phrase, the point of departure of modern psychological inquiry is the empirical generalization that The Idea is Essentially Active. By a painstaking, somewhat mechanical process of generalization, illuminated with many happy turns of expression, M. Tarde has worked out his "laws" of repetition, opposition, and adaptation; the general upshot of which is nothing more than the concept covered by this phrase. Had he been so fortunate as to make this well-assured concept his point of departure, his detail theories of social forces would unavoidably have fallen into the form of corollaries under this main thesis. The resulting theories of social conduct would of course not have taken the same form of expression, nor showed the same structural relations as the present body of psychological doctrines offered by M. Tarde – the apparatus by which he has made his approach to this point of departure.

But after all has been said, M. Tarde's work will always be of high value, both for economic and sociological students, in that it will greatly lighten the work of any fairly-equipped student who may take up the inquiry on the ground given by modern psychological science, and push it outward over the field which M. Tarde has traversed. It will also continue to be valuable on account of that easy and graceful presentation which has given his work its wide vogue, as well as on account of the cogent manner in which he argues for, and illustrates, the thesis that social and economic institutional structure is always and everywhere an outcome of the play of psychological forces.

Der moderne Kapitalismus. By WERNER SOMBART. Leipzig: Duncker & Humblot, 1902. 8vo. 2 vols. pp. xxxiv + 669 and vii + 646.*

MR. SOMBART'S *Kapitalismus* is the most considerable essay in economic theory yet made on lines independent of the classical English political economy, by an economist affiliated to the historical school. As is well known, the adherents of the historical method have not until recently entered the theoretical field, except by way of adaptation or criticism of doctrines already in vogue; and where they have made the attempt it has commonly not had substantial results.

Mr. Sombart is not a *Historiker,* although his work shows the training of the "historical method." In standpoint and animus his work blends the historical outlook with Marxist materialism. But his Marxism is very appreciably modified

* *The Journal of Political Economy,* March 1903.

by the spirit of modern, post-Darwinian scientific inquiry; so that the latter element may perhaps be said to predominate. At least no preconceptions of *Historismus* or *Materialismus* are allowed to divert the inquiry from scientific theory, as that phrase is understood in the latter-day work of the material sciences. More than once (as e.g., Vol. I, p. xxxii) he cautions the reader that the inquiry which he has in hand aims at an explanation of the economic situation in causal terms; although the caution is scarcely necessary for any one who will follow the discussion attentively, which is no difficult or tedious task, since Mr. Sombart is a master of a lucid and cogent style.

The work is as ambitious as any one could desire. Indeed, it has an air of conviction and self-sufficiency at times quite cavalier. It condemns the work of predecessors and contemporaries in such harsh and flippant terms as sometimes to remind one of Marx's vituperative outbreaks. But, again like Marx, a large and ready command of the materials and a tenacious grasp of the many converging lines of his argument save Mr. Sombart's work from the damage which it would otherwise suffer on account of his jaunty self-complacency and his discourteous treatment of those who have the fortune to differ with him. While the work is theoretical throughout, it brings in much of the material used in a somewhat comprehensive manner. So much so, indeed, as to make these two volumes the most available general guide to the materials of the subject. At times the argument comes near losing itself in an excess of illustrative detail, such as had better been dealt with in monographic form apart from the theoretical development. A more serious weakness of the book is an excess of terminological innovation. There is throughout an uncontrolled *penchant* for discarding definitions and distinctions already familiar to economic students and substituting for them new terms and distinctions that are not always more serviceable than those which they displace. And new distinctions are also multiplied with unnecessary alacrity; so that the new categories are not always useful to Mr. Sombart, and it is very doubtful if many of them will be of service to any one else. No doubt, some, perhaps most, of the new categories that are of a general character and a broad bearing are necessary to the argument and constitute a substantial theoretical advance; but, also no doubt, a great part of the fine-drawn distinctions elaborately worked out and designated without apparently serving any theoretical end might advantageously have been left out. It is within the mark to say that if excessive detail of classification and such materials as are of the nature of collateral only had been omitted, the substance of the two volumes might conveniently have been brought within the compass of one.

The two volumes already published are but the beginning of a comprehensive systematic work, eventually to be completed in some three or four additional volumes. So that any present appraisement of the work as a whole must be taken as provisional only, so far as regards its adequacy for the theoretical purpose at which it aims. But as regards its scope and character these two volumes afford a sufficiently unequivocal indication. It is a genetic account of modern capitalism; that is to say, of modern business enterprise, as an English writer might phrase it. Vol. I, on "The Genesis of Capitalism," traces the origin of modern business enterprise from the small beginnings of the Middle Ages, through the handicraft and petty trade of early modern times, down to the full-grown capitalistic enterprise as it came to prevail in industrial business in the course of the nineteenth century. Vol. II, on "The Theory of Capitalistic Development," is occupied with "The Modern Foundations of Business" (Book

I), "The Reorganization of Business Traffic" (Book II), and "The Theory of Business Competition" (Book III). These three books of Vol. II deal with the present situation, that is to say, the situation as it stands since capitalistic enterprise has come to dominate industrial business.

Characteristic of Mr. Sombart's point of view and significant of the aim of his inquiry is the careful distinction with which he sets out (chap. i), between business (*Wirtschaft*) and industry (*Betrieb*).

> Betrieb ist Arbeitsgemeinschaft; Wirtschaft ist Verwertungsgemeinschaft. Es liegt mir viel daran, diese Unterscheidung zwischen Wirtschaft und Betrieb zu einem sicheren Besitzstande unserer Wissenschaft zu machen, da ich ihr, wie sich im folgenden zeigen wird, eine grosse Bedeutung für die richtige Beurteilung des Wirtschaftslebens beimesse.

Accordingly, it is the genesis and the ramifications of that modern form of business enterprise called "capitalism" that the inquiry pursues; and it does not concern itself with diversities and changes of the mechanical methods of industry, except so far as they condition or are conditioned by the methods and aims of business. In tracing the genesis of capitalistic enterprise there are two main factors of the development to be accounted for: the accumulation of capitalizable funds (Book II, Part II), and the rise of the spirit of business enterprise (Book II, Part III). Capitalizable funds, Mr. Sombart finds, gradually accumulated toward the close of the Middle Ages in the hands of the landed gentry, particularly such of the nobility as held urban real property. To the growth of accumulations in the hands of the landless merchants of the towns he assigns an altogether secondary importance. A great, perhaps the decisive, auxiliary of this landed property was the influx of the precious metals. This new supply of money at the same time tempted to investment in adventures of the commercial kind by holding out large chances of gain, as it also familiarized men with the notion of trafficking for increase of wealth rather than (as had been the case) for the means of a decent livelihood.

The capitalistic spirit, the habit of mind involved in diligently seeking gain for gain's sake, was new when the modern era set in; and its gradual spread and ultimate dominance in the economic life of the western nations is a phenomenon which not only itself needs explanation, but which is conditioned by, and in turn conditions, the habits of life, the institutions, the industrial methods, and the methods of business traffic of these nations. Mr. Sombart's inquiries on these heads run chiefly on German ground. He looks to the early German situation primarily, and to the growth in those communities (particularly Italian) with which the early German business community stood in close relations. And it is from the German situation outward that his investigations chiefly run in working out the course of business growth. In so looking to Germany (and Italy) as the quasi-independent "area of characterization" of modern business enterprise, it is scarcely to be doubted that Mr. Sombart is following a mistaken lead. It need not, certainly it cannot, be disputed that both in Germany and in Italy, on the transition from mediaeval to modern times, business enterprise flourished both in commerce, banking, and industry; that the transition was effectively made, from the mediaeval spirit of handicraft and petty trade carried on for a livelihood and governed by corporate regulations designed to safeguard a livelihood, to the modern spirit of capitalistic investment for a profit, governed by some measure of free contract and presuming freedom of competition. This early start on the continent might be taken to signify that modern business enterprise took its rise from these continental cultural areas, and that it embodies the spirit of their traditions, and rests on their institutional substructure. But to that view there are two counter considerations to be offered. As it is notorious, among students of these matters, that business enterprise arose and rapidly grew great within these continental communities, so it is also notorious that it presently decayed and all but disappeared from among those nations when the era of politics, wars, and church dissensions set in. Those communities carried over into the new era that dates from the late eighteenth century nothing in the way of a business spirit or business tradition that is at all comparable with what the English community then had to offer. The question of how much the English community may have borrowed from continental examples of business methods and the like, is not much to the point, since the conditions out of which modern business enterprise has arisen prevailed in such effective force in the English community that nothing more substantial than an acceleration of the growth could be ascribed to the continental influence. "Materialistic" as his bias is, Mr. Sombart is not inclined to rate an inquiry into chronological precedence high as compared with the economic causes at work, the conditioning circumstances out of which this modern institutional fact of business enterprise has arisen. And so far as regards these decisive circumstances, material and cultural, the English situation in that late modern time to which current business enterprise takes back was favorable to business, whereas the continental situation was then decisively unfavorable. The circumstances favorable to the growth of business principles had in very great measure disappeared from the continental, particularly the German and Italian, situation, so that it was only during the course of the nineteenth century, and only under the tutelage of that modern spirit of business and mechanical technology that spread outward from the English-speaking community after the Napoleonic era, that these countries again fell into line and recovered the degree of development which they had lost a couple of centuries earlier.

These considerations go to say that the connection of the present situation with the past, in point of continuous growth, is to be sought within the English-speaking communities, and that any historical study of the antecedents and character of modern business enterprise had best be directed to the British development. These considerations are strongly backed by Mr. Sombart's own answer, in the second volume, to the question: "What were the forces which created modern business enterprise?" There is neither place nor occasion here to follow out in detail the solution of this question, for that would require a recital of the substance of the second volume, but it is worth while in this connection to point out what is said in Book I of this volume on the institutional and material foundations of modern business enterprise and to call to mind that these institutional and material conditions are of British derivation and are not found in their best development outside of the English-speaking communities. This Book I, on "Die Neubegrundung des Wirtschaftslebens," comprises these chapters: "Das neue Recht," "Die neue Technik," and "Der neue Stil des Wirtschaftslebens." The substance of the chapter on "The New Legal Basis" may be summed up in a few words. It is the system of natural liberty; that is to say, in its economic bearing, inviolability and equality of property rights, freedom of contract, free competition. This institutional foundation of business enterprise is embodied in the English common law; it was worked out on British ground, gradually, from the time of the Tudors; it is to be found ingrained in the commonsense of all English-speaking peoples and prevails nowhere else in anything like the same degree of consistency and tenacity. Institutionally speaking, the British natural-rights development affords the only practicable foundations for a consummate business life, and the other peoples of western Europe are on this head borrowers and imitators of the British, driven in good part by the exigencies imposed by the British competition. In proportion as the institutional situation in any of these neighboring communities departs sensibly from the British natural-rights pattern, they are handicapped for the business purpose. Those who (practically) come nearest the British pattern, as, *e.g.*, Germany, are most fortunately placed for purposes of business enterprise.

So also as to the material, the technological basis of business enterprise. The industrial revolution, which brought in the technology of the machine process and so laid the material foundations of modern business, is, of course, broadly an English fact – whatever fragmentary technological elements the English community may once have borrowed from southern Europe. And from the time when the modern machine industry got under way the lead in this matter has remained with the English-speaking peoples. It is only in the immediate present, and then doubtfully, that other than the English-speaking peoples have come into the first rank as creative factors in industrial technology. The aptitude, or the habit, of consecutive and aggressive thinking in terms of the machine process is by no means confined within the limits of English speech, but the boldest and widest prevalence of this habit of materialistic thought lies within those limits; and this habit of mind is the spiritual ground of the modern technology. That its prevalence, or its vogue, should roughly coincide with English speech and English institutions need not bring surprise, since an analysis of its character and derivation will show that it comes of the same range of cultural factors that have given rise to the characteristically English institutions.

It is on this institutional and technological ground that modern business traffic rests, and it is accordingly not a matter of surprise that business methods and business enterprise – *der neue Stil des Wirtschaftslebens,* as Mr. Sombart calls it – have reached their freest swing and their maturest expression among the English-speaking peoples. And it is to be regretted that Mr. Sombart's masterly analysis of the growth and the current phenomena of business enterprise should not have taken the British and American situation as the typical, central body of the development, by comparison with which the ramifications of business enterprise through the rest of the industrial world are best to be appreciated. Instead of this he has chosen as his immediate subject of inquiry the, essentially outlying, business community of Germany, and has taken account of the main (English) line of growth only by way of qualification. The result is a slightly more roundabout discussion, a slightly less clear insight into the working of the mechanism, a slightly less true perspective in the presentation, than might have been had from a more fortunately chosen historical point of departure.

Vaerdi- og Prislaerens Historie. By T. H. ASCHEHOUG. (Reprinted from *Statsökonomisk Tidskrift.*) Christiania: Aschehoug & Co., 1902. 8vo. pp. 193.*

THIS slight volume on the history of value and price theories comes nearer being a sketch than a monograph. The reason for so characterizing it is not its insignificance of bulk, but rather its compact form and concise presentation together with an easy and graceful touch and the absence of any attempt to follow the inquiry out exhaustively at any one point. It covers the history of doctrine since Adam Smith,

* *The Journal of Political Economy,* March 1903.

with some slight reference to earlier writers; and shows such wide and intimate familiarity with the literature of the subject, and such sympathetic and at the same time critical appreciation of the many writers and points of view, as to leave the reader with a hearty regret that Professor Aschehoug has not chosen to deal more exhaustively with his subject.

L'Impérialisme allemand. By Maurice Lair. Paris: Armand Colin, 1902. 12 mo. pp. vii + 341.*

This is a book for general readers rather than for students. It opens with a chapter of general reflections on the spread and present status of commercial imperialism among the greater powers, which is followed by a survey of the events, military, political, industrial and commercial, that have given Germany her policy of armed peace and commercial expansion. It is well and fluently written, from the standpoint of a sympathetic observer, though not with the animus of a friend or apologist. The upshot of the argument is that Germany as a commercial world-power, and therefore also as a military world-power, has reached, if it has not passed, its culmination. The thirty-years' period of prosperity has been of the nature of a speculative inflation, the advantages of which have inured to the large capitalists and have not been balanced by any comparable amelioration of the lot of the populace. The outcome is a lowering and coarsening of national ideals and a spread of popular discontent. Germany is at the end of her career of brilliant commercial and military achievements, because she is short of resources, as compared with her rivals, and is politically unstable because of class antagonism and moral deterioration.[1]

* *The Journal of Political Economy*, March 1903.

[1] [For Veblen's use of the Lair book see *The Theory of Business Enterprise*, pp. 391-392].

Imperialism: A Study. By J. A. HOBSON. New York: James Pott & Co., 1902. 8vo. pp. vii + 400.*

"Those readers who hold that a well-balanced judgment consists in always finding as much in favor of any political course as against it will be discontented with the treatment given here. For the study is distinctively one of social pathology, and no endeavor is made to disguise the malignity of the disease." (Preface, p. vi)

"Although the new imperialism has been bad business for the nation, it has been good business for certain classes and certain trades within the nation. The vast expenditure on armaments, the costly wars, the grave risks and embarrassments of foreign policy, the stoppage of political and social reforms within Great Britain, though fraught with great injury to the nation, have served well the present business interests of certain industries and professions." (pp. 51, 52.)

"These influences, primarily economic, though not unmixed with other sentimental motives, are particularly operative in military, clerical, academic, and civil-service circles, and furnish an interested bias toward imperialism throughout the educated classes. [But] by far the most important economic factor in imperialism is the influence relating to investments." (p. 56.)

"It is not too much to say that the modern foreign policy of Great Britain is primarily a struggle for profitable markets of investment. . . . This is, perhaps, the most important fact in modern politics, and the obscurity in which it is wrapped constitutes the gravest danger to our state." (p. 60.)

"If, contemplating the enormous expenditure on armaments, the ruinous wars, the diplomatic audacity of knavery

* *The Journal of Political Economy*, March 1903.

by which modern governments seek to extend their territorial power, we put the plain, practical question, *Cui bono?* the first and most obvious answer is, the investor." (p. 62.)

The investor needs new fields of investments because the home domain does not afford a field for investment equally profitable with the investments already made. This state of the case, which furnishes the most substantial ground of imperialist expansion, is due to two circumstances: (1) because of a very unequal distribution of income, which leaves the greater part of the population unable to satisfy their reasonable needs, the output of industry exceeds what there is a demand for at remunerative prices; (2) because the incomes from the larger holdings of invested wealth exceed the consumptive powers of the holders, there results an automatic accumulation of wealth in the hands of the large holders, and this increment can not find investment at profitable rates within the community and so seeks opportunity elsewhere under the protection of the flag. This is the "economic taproot of imperialism." In this connection Mr. Hobson restates, in cogent terms, his well-known theory of over-production, or under-consumption; but the criticism of this theory does not belong here. He points out that the incentive to the employment of the governmental machinery and the public funds for private gain in this way is very direct and strong, since the burden falls on the nation, while the gain goes to certain influential business interests which, under the current system of taxation and administration, are never called on to pay in proportion to the gains which they get; and he argues, with apparent conclusiveness, that the cost, to the nation, of its exploits of expansion exceeds by several hundred per cent. the aggregate gains that come to any class of the community from this expansion. The ever-recurring contention, apparently indisputable, is that at an exorbitant cost to the nation at large certain business interests derive a profit from imperialist achievements, and that this peculiar profit is, on the whole, of no advantage to the community at whose cost it is secured. The reason why a nation, such as Great Britain or the United States, goes on in this way of extravagant, feeble-minded trade policy is to be sought in a prevalent stupid sentimentality that allows itself to be cajoled with spectacular returns of national glory and the catchwords of demagogue politics.

What the home community gets in return for its investment in armaments, dependencies, and administrative machinery is demoralization of its home politics and degradation of its people. Popular government and popular ideals necessarily suffer.

"Imperialism and popular government have nothing in common: they differ in spirit, in policy, in method." (p. 158).

"The political effects, actual and necessary, of the new imperialism, as illustrated in the case of the greatest of imperialist powers, may be thus summarized. It is a constant menace to peace, by furnishing continual temptations to further aggression upon lands occupied by lower races, and by embroiling our nation with other nations of rival imperial ambitions; to the sharp peril of war it adds the chronic danger and degradation of militarism, which not merely wastes the current physical and moral resources of the nations, but checks the very course of civilization. . . . Absorbing the public money, time, interest, and energy on costly and unprofitable work of territorial aggrandizement, it thus wastes those energies of public life in the governing classes and the nations which are needed for internal reforms and for the cultivation of the arts of material and intellectual progress at home. Finally, the spirit, the policy, and the methods of imperialism are hostile to the institutions of popular self-government, favoring forms of political tyranny and social authority which are the deadly enemies of effective liberty and equality." (pp. 160, 161.)

The chapter (Part II, chap. i) on "The Scientific Defence of Imperialism" is devoted to the veiled jingoism of such writers as Professors Pearson and Giddings, who argue that imperialism is good because it is a method of "natural selection" between races and nationalities. The Darwinian-jingo argument may be summed up in the two propositions that: The best fighters are the best men, and the best fighters survive and multiply under imperialist rule. Both of these propositions, together with their various corollaries, Mr. Hobson argues, are baseless in logic and unsupported by facts. The argument on "Imperialism and the Lower Races" runs to the effect that, while imperialism damages and deteriorates the conquering nation, it is probably even more disastrous to the lower races brought under imperialist rule. In support of this thesis there is offered a wide-ranging and impressive array of facts.

"The book is addressed to the intelligence of the minority . . . who desire to understand political forces." The argument might have a wider effect and might even serve to mitigate the imperialist shove if imperialism rested on rational grounds. But since, as Mr. Hobson fully recognizes, the motive force of imperialism is a militant sentimentality guided by the business interests of a small class, no such appeal to the common-sense of the community can seriously affect the outcome or even gain a wide hearing.

The New Empire. By BROOKS ADAMS. New York: The Macmillan Co., 1902. 8vo. pp. xxxvi + 243.*

PURSUING a line of argument already worked out in his

* *The Journal of Political Economy*, March 1903.

Law of Civilization and Decay, Mr. Adams offers an explanation, a theory it may be called, of the rise and decline of successive "empires" from the dawn of history to the present. The objective point of the argument is to account for the present, or imminent, supremacy of America as an imperial power. This supremacy has, in Mr. Adams's mind, all the certainty of an accomplished fact. While it takes the form of a political supremacy, its substantial ground is the commercial leadership of the new imperial organisation; the reason for commercial leadership being, in its turn, the possession of superior material resources, particularly mineral resources, together with the convergence of trade routes upon the territory in which the seat of empire lies.

Mr. Adams's explanation of the growth of imperial power, in all ages, is altogether a geographical one. From the beginning trade routes have determined where accumulations of wealth would occur, and they have thereby determined where the greater masses of population would congregate and so where the seat of political power would be found. Whereas, trade routes have largely been determined by the *provenance* of the minerals most useful or most sought after at the time. Within historical times this means the metals – the precious metals primarily, and secondarily that one of the useful metals which has for the time chiefly served the industrial arts. Today it is steel and coal. In the early times, before navigation developed, the trade routes lay overland, chiefly between the east and the west of Asia; and where these overland routes converged the ancient cities and the ancient monarchies grew up – as Egypt, Babylonia, or Persia – and power shifted from the one to the other as the path of commerce shifted. Later, when great improvements in navigation had taken place, the sea routes gradually supplanted the land routes, and the question of empire became a question of the convergence of the routes of maritime commerce. Today these routes cross and blend within the domain of the United States, and radiate from this as a center, at the same time that this domain contains the largest, most valuable, and most available supply of the mineral wealth upon which the fortunes of commerce ultimately hang. Mr. Adams also finds that in some way, mysterious so far as his discussion goes, energy springs up where the trade routes cross, and slackens abruptly when the routes depart. So that now, for some half-a-dozen years past, America holds over all competitors in point of energetic and sagacious administration.

Cogent as Mr. Adams's presentation of the case is, it has an air of one sidedness, in that it neglects other than geographical factors; and even within the range of geographical factors it places the emphasis almost exclusively on the circumstances which condition commerce, as contrasted with other economic factors. It may be noted, for instance, that the element of race is left out; whereas it would not be a hopeless task to construct an equally plausible theory of the facts considered by Mr. Adams on grounds of race alone. It may also be noted that so striking a case as that of China does not come within the explanation offered. China has all the mineral resources on which Mr. Adams throws emphasis; her territory lies also at the meeting of the overland and the maritime routes of the East; the Chinese people have from time immemorial been highly skilled and diligent workmen; but, great as China has been, she has never taken the leadership except locally; the industrial revolution did not come through Chinese initiative; the development of navigation and the expansion of modern commerce are not due to Chinese enterprise and ingenuity, although the material circumstances have, on Mr. Adams's theory, for some thousands of years apparently favored the rise of China to the position of an all-dominating world-power.

Financial Crises and Periods of Industrial and Commercial Depression. By THEODORE E. BURTON. New York: D. Appleton & Co., 1902. 8vo. pp. ix + 392.*

MR. BURTON'S survey of crises and depressions is valuable chiefly as a brief and compendious review of the facts and of opinions that have been offered in explanation of these phenomena. It is occupied more with a recital of definitions, symptoms, and palliatives than with an inquiry into the causes and the more enduring consequences of these disturbances of trade. Indeed, the author has apparently no sure grasp of the difference between chronological sequence and causal connection. This holds true in spite of the fact that the volume is in form a defense of the thesis that crises (particularly those followed by depression) are caused by "waste or excessive loss of capital, or its absorption, to an exceptional degree, in enterprises not immediately remunerative" (p. 68). "In some form or other this waste, excessive loss, or absorption, is the ultimate or real cause." By "capital," it may be remarked, Mr. Burton means "production goods," not funds, although he speaks as if the two categories were for his purposes identical; while he pays close attention to definitions, as being of fundamental importance to the clarity of his discussion, his definitions do not touch this distinction. Hence, a shrinkage of the market values of securities and other investments is taken to signify a loss of material means of production (see, *e.g.*, pp. 81-97). Broadly, crises, and more particularly depressions, are caused by waste of the means of production, so that the crisis and the subsequent depression are the effects, perhaps rather the manifestation,

* *The Journal of Political Economy*, March 1903.

of material impoverishment. The impoverishment may be of a permanent character, in case of an extensive destruction of goods or a failure of the productive processes of industry, or it may be transient as in the case of excessive investment for future production instead of present needs. This waste may not be evident at the time; it may not, indeed it commonly will not, appear until all that is available for wasteful expenditure has been spent; but in the end the spendthrift community will have to meet the privation which it has prepared for itself through unwise spending of its accumulations. The discrepancy between current needs and current output shows itself in the form of a stringency, a shrinkage of values, and a fall of prices. It is this eventual collapse of prices and of capitalized values that serve Mr. Burton as evidence that a wasteful expenditure has previously taken place. Of course, there are few students of economic phenomena today so incautious as to confuse a decline in prices, whether of consumable goods or of production goods, with a destruction of material wealth, whether it be considered as articles of consumption or as means of production. But this is, in substance, what Mr. Burton repeatedly resorts to in his explanation of waste, particularly under caption III, on "The Inevitable Changes Resulting from Modern Industrial and Commercial Progress." For instance: "No statistics can be obtained to measure the loss by the absolute dismantling or diminished efficiency of manufacturing plants made necessary by the competition of improved machinery; but this loss is very large, and is most keenly felt in countries where increase in wealth is greatest." The notion of a waste of means of production taking the form of an increased aggregate efficiency of the means of production has a certain charm, although it does not carry conviction. This Hibernian logic seems to satisfy Mr. Burton, however.

On the whole, Mr. Burton's explanation of crises and depressions, as set forth in this chapter on the Causes, may be summed up as a painstaking, though not very systematic, rehearsal of commonplaces, for the most part discredited by modern students. His review, in chaps. v and vi, of the "Indications of Prosperity and Depression," and of "Crises and Depressions," respectively, is valuable as a sketch of the phenomena commonly observed under the two contrasted conditions of trade. The like is true of the "Account of Crises and Depressions in the United States," in chap. viii;[1] whereas the discussion of "Preventives and Remedies," in chap. vii, belongs in the same class of inconsequential commonplace as the account of the Causes. The most substantial item in the volume is the bibliography (pp. 347-77), compiled by Mr. Williams.

Pure Sociology: A Treatise Concerning the Origin and Spontaneous Development of Society. By LESTER F. WARD. New York: The Macmillan Co., 1903. 8vo. pp. xii + 606.*

OF the value of this great treatise for the general science of sociology it is not the place of an economic journal to speak. Nor may one who is not himself a lifelong specialist in the science presume to pass an opinion of praise or dispraise on the culminating work of a man to whom the science owes so extraordinary a debt as to Dr. Ward. But even a lay reader may see and say this much, that *Pure Sociology* is a captivating volume by reason of lucid and forcible presentation as well as by its great range and command of information and its engaging style. It is a work of theory, presents

[1] *Editorial Note:* "Cf., e.g., Burton's *Crises and Depressions,* ch. viii, for a succinct account of depressions and crises in the United States during this period [in the nineteenth century, prior to the eighties]." *The Theory of Business Enterprise,* p. 248.

* *The Journal of Political Economy,* September 1903.

a system wrought out symmetrically and in detail, with the maturity and poise of half-a-century's unremitting work and with the fire of unfailing youth.

Dr. Ward succeeds in what others have attempted. He has brought the aims and method of modern science effectively into sociological inquiry. This method is the genetic one, which deals with the forces and sequence of development and seeks to understand the outcome by finding out how and why it has come about. The aim is to organize social phenomena into a theoretical structure in causal terms. The resulting system is too comprehensive, with too many ramifications, to admit of anything like an abstract or a general survey being presented in a brief space.

What is of direct interest to economic students is found, chiefly, in chap. xiii, on "Autogenetic Forces," chaps. xvi and xvii, on "The Directive Agent" and "Biologic Origin of the Objective Faculties," and in chaps. xix, and xx, on "The Conquest of Nature" and "The Socialization of Achievement." It is only scattered sections and paragraphs of these chapters that are of direct interest to economic theory, the main line of the argument, of course, bearing throughout on general sociological theory of which Dr. Ward's economic views are only a ramification. The chapter on the autogenetic forces deals with the human agent in the process of production, and very suggestively discusses the place and method of intelligence in industry. Broad and general as this discussion is, it contrasts in an illuminating way with the itemized and mechanical schematism that commonly does duty as a psychology of industry in the received doctrines, or even in such a special treatise as Tarde's *Psychologie économique*. In chap. xvii, the sections on "Indirection" offer a bold analysis of the motives and methods of business traffic, of which the dominant note is given in the proposition (p. 487) that "deception may almost be called the foundation of business." For economic purposes, Dr. Ward's views on the "Socialization of Achievement" (chap. xx) converge to the outcome that the trend of cultural growth sets indefeasibly toward collectivism, toward which he finds, on an analysis of the available data, that the most advanced of the industrial peoples have made the most substantial approaches.

Bevölkerungsbewegung, Kapitalbildung und periodische Wirtschaftskrisen. By LUDWIG POHLE. Göttingen: Vandenhoeck & Ruprecht, 1902. 8vo. pp. 92.*

THE objective point of this pamphlet is a theory of crises, or more precisely of depression, with a particular view to the bearing of depression on the fortunes of the working classes. Dr. Pohle does not consistently distinguish between crisis and depression, and for the most part "crisis" in his usuage means depression. As the wording of the title indicates, the causes of depression are sought in the movement of population and in the accumulation of capital. The movement of population here means, practically, the natural increase of the working classes. This is the ultimate efficient factor to which depression is traceable. But it is through its relation to the accumulation of capital that this factor brings on the depression.

"The cause of the change from exaltation to depression I find in this, that savings of the nation are no longer adequate to pay for the newly produced capital goods . . . . It is, in short, the excessive demand for capital for use in industry which first brings this period of exaltation to a pause and finally changes it to a period of depression." (p. 79, note 32).

The periodicity of crises and depressions is traceable to psychological grounds, to the cumulative change of animus

* *The Journal of Political Economy,* September 1903.

in the undertaking class; that is to say, these phenomena are essentially of a speculative nature. But the ulterior causes of this disturbance are of a material kind. The growth of the working-class population diverts the values produced from accumulation in the way of capitalizable savings to current consumption, resulting in a discrepancy between the accumulated funds and the productive goods on hand. The accumulated funds not being adequate to pay for the industrial equipment necessary to afford the requisite current output, capitalization comes to a standstill, there is an appearance of overproduction of productive goods, with a consequent decline in their value; the industrial equipment in hand is therefore insufficient to give remunerative employment to the workman, at the same time that a slack demand for productive goods discourages their further production.[1] This unemployment is the substantial fact of a period of depression.

The theory furnishes its own refutation. For all that appears in Dr. Pohle's discussion, the funded value of the productive goods in question should be competent, through the introduction of credit relations, to pay for, and therefore to capitalize, these goods in the form of increased industrial equipment. With the increased industrial equipment the working class should have no difficulty in finding remunerative employment: nor should the consumptive goods required by an increased working class be wanting, since the increased industrial equipment with an increased labor force should readily increase the output; nor should the workmen

[1] *Editorial Note:* "Pohle . . . concludes that depression is due to a scarcity of capital as compared with population; the rate of increase of capital is conceived to fall short of the rate of increase of population, hence periodical depression." (*The Theory of Business Enterprise*, p. 226). Productive goods refers to "the production of 'producers' goods'"—the products of those lines of industry classified as "'Produktivmittel-Industrien' by late German writers," which Veblen translated as the "productive-goods industries." (p. 181).

want for the means with which to pay for what they need, since the heightened efficiency of industry and the livelier demand for labor resulting from it should give them good wages and steady work. In short, the factors to which Dr. Pohle traces depression should, on his own interpretation of the facts, result in brisk times.

Kartell und Trust: Vergleichende Untersuchungen über dem Wesen und Bedeutung. By S. TSCHIEVSCHKY. Göttingen: Vandenhoeck & Ruprecht, 1903. 8vo. pp. iv + 129.*

"TO LEAVE no doubt as to the drift of the following discussion, I wish to emphasize that to my mind the comprehensive organization of industry, whether in the form of cartells or of trusts, is a necessity growing out of the current individualistic business methods. More particularly, I regard the cartell as a form of organization that has the promise of a very large place in the future development, especially of continental industry (preface.)"

The reason assigned for this favorable view of the cartell, as a practicable expedient for the industry of the continent, is the greater degree of identification of the business men of the continent with some one business concern. This gives the continental business concerns a quasi-personal character, in greater measure than the American or even the English, and so insures them a degree of initiative and consistent business policy such as the latter frequently lack. Hence the cartell, which leaves the corporate identity of the underlying concerns undisturbed, permits a larger net advantage to be gained from combination, since the advantage of combination is gained while that of particular initiative is not lost.

Dr. Tschievschky offers a very sane discussion of the bearing of trust policy, especially as relates to the questions of

* *The Journal of Political Economy,* September 1903.

capitalization and crisis (pp. 89-105). It is, as has been argued in detail by E. S. Meade in the case of the United States Steel Corporation, *e.g.*, to the interest of the individual business men concerned to overcapitalize the corporation, in the sense that a large nominal capital will yield larger net gains to the promoters and to the former owners of the underlying companies; although the resulting corporation as such may not gain, or may not gain proportionately. Indeed, the high capitalization may place the corporation at a disadvantage. It may easily lead to a discrepancy between capitalization and earnings, and so may lead to cut-throat competition and eventual over-production and crisis. Particularly may the result be that, while the trusts succeed in securing their own ends, they do so at the cost of the rest of the industrial community, by throwing the pressure of competition on the rest, through price variations and the like, and so bringing on a general depression which may in the end spread even to the industries within the trust.

An Inquiry into the Nature and Causes of the Wealth of Nations. By ADAM SMITH. Edited, with an Introduction, Notes, Marginal Summary, and an enlarged Index, by EDWIN CANNAN. New York: G. P. Putnam's Sons, 1904. 8vo. 2 vols. pp. xlviii + 462 and vi + 506.*

THIS new edition of the *Wealth of Nations* is as excellent as the editor's name would lead one to expect. Marks of extreme care as well as of full and critical knowledge are visible on every page. The editor's notes are of great value even to students who are not greatly interested in the niceties of textual criticism. In a great measure they serve as cross-references, and serve also to keep in mind and define Adam Smith's characteristic inconsistencies and limitations.

* *The Journal of Political Econqmy*, December 1904.

The text is that of the fifth edition which has been followed in all details, even including variations of spelling and the use of capitals. The editor's Introduction once more runs over the ground which he has covered in his earlier discussions of Adam Smith's life and writings. It sets forth, in Mr. Cannan's usual lucid manner, the sequence of change and growth which his study of Adam Smith and his times and contemporaries has disclosed, showing the line of derivation of the various articles of doctrine and the influences under which they came to take the form and proportions which they have in the finished work. Adam Smith's relation to the *Economistes* and the degree of his indebtedness to them is treated in a more definitive manner here than has been done in Mr. Cannan's previous discussions of that topic. The extent to which Adam Smith leans on Hutcheson is also made more of than before, and the details of this relationship are brought out very effectively. It may be added that in point of workmanship and mechanical form the two volumes are highly creditable to the printer as well as serviceable to the reader.

Adam Smith. By FRANCIS W. HIRST. ("English Men of Letters" series.) New York: The Macmillan Co., 1904. 12mo. pp. viii + 240.*

MR. HIRST adds another volume to the biographies of Adam Smith, but as would be expected under the circumstances, he adds little that is new either of information or criticism. Still the volume should find a welcome. It is well written, graceful and entertaining, and with an intelligent appreciation of Adam Smith's traits of character as well as of the traits of style, method, scope and insight that have made the *Wealth of Nations* a masterpiece of the science and of English literature. The most attractive portions of the book are those

* *The Journal of Political Economy*, December 1904.

that turn about Adam Smith's intimate life and his contact with men and affairs.

Zur Genesis des modernen Kapitalismus: Forschungen zur Entstehung der grossen burgerlichen Kapitalvermogen am Ausgang des Mittelalters und zu Beginn der Neuzeit, zunachst in Augsburg. By JACOB STRIEDER. Leipzig: Duncker & Humblot, 1904. 8 vo. pp. ix + 233.*

THE subtitle sufficiently indicates the purpose of the book, except that it has as a secondary purpose the refutation of a certain point in Mr. Sombart's exposition of the origins of capitalism. The discussion throughout takes the controversial form, but the handling of the materials seems to be none the less painstaking and thorough on that account. Mr. Strieder has gone into the details of the formation of the large fortunes that played a part in business enterprise in the fifteenth and sixteenth centuries much more exhaustively than Mr. Sombart seems to have done; and he seems, on the whole, to have made good his point against Mr. Sombart's contention, so far as anyone who is not an expert on that particular chapter of economic history may judge.

Those who are familiar with Mr. Sombart's *Moderne Kapitalismus* will remember that characteristic passage in his exposition where he contends, with a considerable citation and analysis of historic material, that the great fortunes which made possible the magnificent growth of South German business enterprise in early modern times were derived, not from the profits of business, but from accumulations outside of business, chiefly the incomes from rent accruing to members of the nobility and to other landed proprietors. The contention may be put in the form of a general proposition to the effect that investment for a profit did not create the

* *The Journal of Political Economy*, December 1904.

great capitalized fortunes, but the accumulation of great fortunes gave rise to investment for a profit and so led to their capitalization. In other and more general terms of economic theory, the growth of a market did not give rise to investment for a profit and so to capitalized accumulations, but conversely the accumulation of capitalizable fortunes gave rise to investment for a profit and so created the market. Mr. Strieder argues for the contrary and traces the origin of nearly all the wealthy families concerned in the trade of Augsburg, particularly, and shows step by step how they came by their holdings. In virtually all the cases in which conclusive evidence is to be had the invested holdings seem to have had their origin in the petty trade carried on by master-craftsmen. That there was a relatively large volume of this petty trade always going on, especially during the better days of the handicraft system, is, of course, a well-attested fact. Such trade was an unavoidable accompaniment of the growth of handicraft; indeed, it was an integral factor of the handicraft system. That some accumulations of appreciable magnitude should arise from this source would also be reasonably expected. But that capitalizable accumulations should also have taken place outside the range of this petty trade seems likewise reasonable. Mr. Strieder claims that, within the range of data examined by him, these accumulations from outside the trade are a negligible factor, as against Mr. Sombart who sees in them the genesis of all the capitalized wealth that entered into that era of business enterprise.

The point in controversy, it should be said, is not of vital consequence to Mr. Sombart's views as to the rise and progress of capitalism, and does not in any serious manner impugn the value of his great work. The value of Mr. Strieder's work also does not lie in his refutation of Mr. Sombart's view, but in the thoroughness with which he has cleared up a special point in the early history of business.

The Code of Hammurabi, King of Babylon about 2250 B.C. Autographed Text, Transliteration, Translation, Glossary, Index of Subjects, Lists of Proper Names, Signs, Numerals, Corrections and Erasures, with Map, Frontispiece, and Photograph of Text. By ROBERT FRANCIS HARPER. Chicago: The University of Chicago Press, 1904. 8vo. pp. xv + 192 + 103, plates.*

TO AN economist this document is interesting for the evidence it affords as to property relations and business traffic among a people living near the beginning of recorded history. The cultural situation of this people is fairly evident from the provisions of the code and the character of the introductory and concluding remarks. It would be difficult for anyone – for any other than an expert quite out of the question – to separate those elements of the code which were the law of the land before the coming of the great king, from those portions which were added by him.

The situation to which the code applies may be characterized somewhat as follows: The code embodies the laws imposed by a body of invading conquerors upon the population already living on the land. The subject population were mainly, if not almost wholly, agricultural. Whether they were free or subject before the coming of the conquering host is probably not to be determined, although it seems not improbable that they already had the institution of slavery, and therefore that the bulk of them were unfree. The invaders from the north, who made themselves masters, were of a race alien to the population already occupying the land and were of a pastoral origin. They brought with them a servile-

* *The Journal of Political Economy*, March 1905.

despotic organization of society and the bloodthirsty monotheistic form of religion that belongs to the militant pastoral culture.

In the Babylonian community as regulated by the code of the great king principles of status, privilege, and differential advantage prevail throughout, so as to give it something of a feudalistic structure. The perquisites and privileges of the upper classes are large and uncompromising, and the laws safeguarding them are harsh and summary. Regulation from above is the rule, and the gravest offenses are those against the king's servants and against the priests and temples. Capital punishment and mutilations are frequent, and extravagant fines and reprisals no less so. Prices of various commodities, as well as the hire of servants, animals, utensils, and land, are fixed by "the king." Terms of agreement between landlord and tenant, and between "merchant" and agent, are in great part prescribed by statute, and as a rule the tenant and the agent are at a disadvantage in case of disagreement or violation of contract. Women are in a state of subjection, almost as abject in many respects as that of the slaves. But with all this subjection and regulation there are some evidences of a traditional freedom of contract, and of relative freedom of action on the part of the women (cf., *e.g.*, secs. 149-51, 172-79, 181, 182).

However austere and unequal may have been the organization of society before the coming of the invaders, it seems plain that the rule of law was, at least in some degree, milder and that economic classes were on a somewhat less unequal footing. Coupled with this, as testifying to a like general effect, is the evidence of an earlier polytheistic religion. The whole code, it may be added, has a very marked resemblance to the Mosaic code.

This earliest document of the history of the Mesopotamian

country bears evidence of a culture that was already ancient in the land at the date when "the perfect king" imposed his code upon the population of the land. How ancient the barbarian civilization of the country may have been there is no knowing, but it is plain that the invasion of the Babylonian dynasty was in no sense near the beginning of things, in institutions, industrial arts, or religion. There were, evidently, at least two, in all probability three, and perhaps more than three, superimposed layers of institutions that were in some degree correlated and combined in the legislative reforms embodied in the code.

It, is, of course, impossible here to offer any opinion as to the degree of faithfulness with which the editor has rendered and presented his materials, or as to the efficiency with which he has made use of such authorities as he may have had recourse to. But a word may not be out of place as to the mechanical characteristics of the volume, in a case where these characteristics are so striking as in the present instance. The printer's work is excellent and errors are few, but the volume as a whole is an extreme example of what printers sometimes call "padding." The paper is excessively heavy and bulky, and the leading and spacing are likewise excessive. The volume could, with advantage to all concerned, have been reduced to one-third of its present bulk and to one-fourth of its present weight.

L'Individualisme économique et social: ses origines — son évolution — ses formes contemporaines. Par ALBERT SCHATZ. Paris: Armand Colin, 1907. 12mo. pp. 590.*

M. SCHATZ's book is an excellent account of the part which individualism has played in economic science and in social

* *The Journal of Political Economy,* June 1909.

policy from the beginning of modern times in Europe to the present. The account, in the main, is necessarily confined to France and to England, or, rather, the English-speaking peoples. How it has happened that this philosophy of life, which the author rates as substantially sound, has had so slight an effect, on the whole, outside of these countries, is a point not satisfactorily discussed. This territorial limitation of the liberal-individualistic philosophy is a sufficiently curious and noteworthy phenomenon, and an account of the growth and ramifications of the manner of thinking which we call by this name should presumably have offered some explanation, at least as a working hypothesis, of its peculiarly restricted diffusion. While individualism has from time to time spread into other regions, and has even made a segment of history outside of the French-English region, e.g., in early modern Italy, it remains true that only within this region has this philosophy shown a spontaneous growth, and its excursions have been outward from this region rather than in the contrary direction. A further fact of the same kind may be noted, a fact likewise brought out, without comment, by M. Schatz's survey, but also likewise not accounted for by him. While the earliest modern development and effects of individualism occur in Italy, followed presently by the French and later by the philosophers of the Low Countries, the lead falls to the English before modern times have advanced very far, and the lead afterward, until well into the nineteenth century at least, remains with them. It is characteristic of M. Schatz's discussion that the causes of this peculiar manner of growth and diffusion do not engage his attention. Indeed, well qualified as he seems to be for such an analysis, he does not go into the causal connection between the growth of individualism and the cultural situation out of which it arose and within which it flourished. His discussion of the origins and evolution of individualism, and of the liberalism based on it, is a tracing of its documentary derivation rather than a genetic account. But if this is to be accounted a fault it may perhaps be said that it is a deliberately chosen limitation of the field of inquiry rather than a matter of oversight. If so it is to be regretted that the author should have felt constrained so to limit the scope of his inquiry.

An interesting outcome of this study is the emphasis thrown on the continuity of economic science and of liberal policy throughout the period since the predominance of mercantilism. Seen in the light of their philosophical and psychological preconceptions, the various schools appear to be variants and phases of a common scheme, gradually unfolding and maturing by the help of controversies that prove in the outcome to have been nothing more serious than factional disputes about matters of detail. Substantial discrepancies are absent from the general scheme of modern economic science. They occur only between the successful main line of individualistic thought and the transient reassertion of older ideals. But hitherto individualism has held the field, even though its forces have latterly been scattered and disorganized in a greater degree than once was the case.

Der Bourgeois: zur Geistesgeschichte des modernen Wirtschaftsmenschen. By Werner Sombart. Leipzig: Duncker & Humblot, 1913. 8vo. pp. vii + 540.*

In the words of the Preface, the purpose of the volume is to supply what has been wanting in the many characterizations of the spirit of modern business hitherto offered, in that it aims to set forth the historical foundations of this

* *The Journal of Political Economy*, October 1915.

spiritual development that comes to a head in the temper and working of the business community. And it is perhaps needless to say that the author achieves this purpose with the thoroughness, sincerity, and felicitous presentation that has come habitually to be expected of him. As in Professor Sombart's earlier work on the development of capitalistic business, so here also the attention centers on the case of the German community, but with rather more detailed consideration given to outside and related lines of economic history than has been the case in his earlier studies in this field.

Wise with the insight born of scholarly impartiality and long familiarity with his subject-matter, Professor Sombart tells his readers:

"Ein bestimmter Geist 'herrscht' zu einer Zeit dann, wenn er überhaupt eine weite Verbreitung hat, er herrscht vor, wenn er die wirtschaftlichen Handlungen der meisten Wirtschaftssubjekte bestimmt. Gegen eine solche Annahme eines 'herrschenden' oder 'vorherrschenden' Geistes wird nur der Eigensinn oder der Unverstand geltend machen, dass in dieser selben Zeit auch Individuen gelebt haben, die anders orientiert, mit einem anderen Wirtschaftsgeiste erfüllt waren."

For our own time this dominant spirit is the spirit of business enterprise, the "capitalistic" spirit. English-speaking students might perhaps prefer to say that the affairs of any modern community are in the last resort guided by business principles, or by the principles enforced by the price system.

For its beginnings the history of this "capitalistic" spirit runs back into the prehistory of the Western peoples, taking its rise in the primordial struggle for wealth that comes in sight in the earliest antiquities of the Western world – *die Gier nach Gold und Geld.* The first item of documentation offered on this head (pp. 29-30), a passage from *Völuspá,* is not altogether fortunate, in that it is drawn from Wolzogen's sophistication of the text rather than on the indubitable meaning of the original. No particular mischief results in this instance, it is true, but the incident may serve to call to mind that even a widely informed and intelligent scholar need be cautious in the documentary use of detailed passages taken at second hand.

With the advent of the "money-economy" and its fuller unfolding into a price system the lust after wealth and gold takes on the specific form of a love of money, and when this is associated with the bourgeois virtues that have come to shape the ethics of economic relations in later time, the product is the investing capitalist undertaker, or more simply the business man as we know him. These virtues that enter into the composition of a business man are well set out in Benjamin Franklin's tabulation: moderation, reticence, orderliness, resolution, economy, diligence, truthfulness, honesty, temperance, cleanliness, equanimity, chastity, modesty. These traits characteristic of the "desirable citizen" when backed up by and pervaded with an unfailing love of gain, give us the business man as he functions in the conduct of economic affairs in the modern world. It is the spirit of conservative enterprise so indicated, therefore, that dominates the concerns of the nations comprised in the world of the Western culture. This spirit, it will doubtless be noted, is typically self-centered, not to say unmitigatedly self-seeking; but it is a spirit of self-realization conventionalized in terms of pecuniary gain.

The sources from which this capitalistic spirit is derived are dealt with in the second of the two books into which the volume is divided. These sources, or lines of derivation, are exceedingly many and various, but in the author's view they fall conveniently under three distinctive captions: (1) the biological origins (*Grundlagen*); (2) the moral factors (*sittliche Mächte*); and (3) the social conditions – comprising among the latter also the conditioning circumstances imposed by the growth of capitalism itself. Of the three categories the first-named is doubtless the most characteristic, at the same time that its contents are the least valuable of the three. The analysis of cause and effect under captions 2 and 3 is carried out in Professor Sombart's best and most engaging manner and is calculated to bring light and order into a great volume of materials that have hitherto not had reasonable attention from students of the business situation; but the same is scarcely to be said for this earlier section on the biological origins. Unfortunately, the author has gone into this biological domain armed with latter-day conceptions of the transmission of racial characteristics, coupled with antiquated notions of racial identity; and the result is more picturesque than instructive. Quite uncritically, linguistic and national frontiers are accepted as marking racial distinctions, and therefore as marking distinct lines of inheritance. So, Celts, Franks, Friesians, Highlanders, Saxons are dealt with as distinctive racial stocks carrying each and severally a distinctive strain of spiritual endowment which by indefeasible heredity fits or unfits each for business enterprise; all the while overlooking the fact that none of these, or of the other peoples cited by Professor Sombart as illustrative instances, are racial groups, but only social groups made up out of the same range of racial elements combined in approximately the same proportions. It is true the author himself recognizes (p. 281) that his exposition of capitalistic heredity may not find general acceptance, and with good reason remarks that its rejection will in no way diminish the substantial value of the rest of his discussion.

The Ruling Caste and Frenzied Trade in Germany. By MAURICE MILLIOUD (Introduction by SIR FREDERICK POLLOCK). Boston: Houghton Mifflin Co., 1916. 12mo. pp. 159. $1.25.*

THE volume is made up of two essays: "To an Understanding of the Ideology of Caste," and "Germany's Aims at Conquest by Trade and by War." It is a study in imperialism, of wider application than the special case of Germany with which it deals, and on which it draws for its analysis of modern policy. M. Millioud asks his readers "to believe that I have written these pages without being influenced by prejudice, with the one desire to get at the facts" (p. 20); but few unprejudiced readers, if such there are, could be persuaded that such an attitude of scholarly detachment has been maintained through the course of the discussion. Throughout the analysis and its conclusions the case of Germany is made to stand out as a thing apart; whereas it should be plain from the description of its characteristics that it is only entitled to take rank as the consummate type-form of its species. What the facts cited entitled us to say is rather that Germany has been affected with an aggravated case of imperialism, accentuated in all its symptoms, but not specifically divergent from the common run of imperialism that affects modern nations.

M. Millioud finds that there are three several factors that have converged to a deplorable outcome in the case of Germany: (*a*) a military caste and tradition making for warlike disturbance and political dominion, among its forces being an irresponsible and fantastically ambitious dynasty; (*b*) a business community driven by the pursuit of gain into precariously adventurous enterprises; and (*c*) a patriotically

* *The Journal of Political Economy,* December 1916.

devoted populace. Each of these three factors that have so converged to a fatal outcome has in the German case been wrought to an extreme, not to say extravagant, pitch. So much is a matter of common notoriety, as touches the case of Germany. And it should be plain on slight reflection that, except for their unexampled virulence and abandon in the German case, these elements of disturbance are common to all modern nations. What M. Millioud's review of the case brings under a strong light in all this is the part played by the members of the German business community, whose somewhat headlong – and largely subsidized – enterprise had brought them to an impasse, where their continued solvency was conditioned upon a continued cumulative inflation that was already beginning to exceed their powers. Hence the warlike decision of the German government appears to be a recourse to desperate remedies for a desperate disease.

Economic students will scarcely question the substantial accuracy of M. Millioud's observations as they touch the state of German business enterprise in the years immediately preceding the war. But anyone who shares the view that the German strategists had already delayed their "defensive offense" beyond the most propitious date will not readily come to believe that dynastic ambition could have permitted any prolonged respite, even if it should have appeared feasible to maneuver the crazy fabric of inflated credit and subsidized enterprise into a position of tolerable stability and solvency.

Other Essays, Reviews and Reports

I. Essays

On the General Principles of a Policy of Reconstruction*

There are certain cardinal points of orientation that will guide any endeavor to reach a lasting settlement on the return of peace. In the main these are points of common sense, and as such they will doubtless already be present in the mind of all thoughtful persons who interest themselves in these matters. But it can do no harm to put down in set form certain of the elementary propositions that will so give the point of departure and will define the limitations of such measures of reconstruction as may reasonably be expected to go into effect.

It is assumed as a major premise that the controlling purpose of any prospective settlement will be the keeping of the peace at large; that the demands of the peace are paramount, whatever other matters of convenience or expediency may be brought in as subsidiaries. As a counterfoil of this premise there immediately follows the further proposition that there can be no return to the *status quo ante*. The Great War was engendered by that scheme of life that has ruled human relations among civilized peoples in recent times; and a re-establishment of the same scheme of relations among these peoples now may confidently be counted on to lead to the same disastrous issue.

---

* *Journal of The National Institute of Social Sciences*, April 1918. Extract; the remainder is in *Essays in Our Changing Order* under the title of "A Policy of Reconstruction."

Therefore the question presents itself: What can be done, by taking thought, to avoid a return to that fateful complication in the conduct of human affairs that has now come to be known as the *status quo ante*? What manner of change in existing arrangements could be counted on to make sure that civilized mankind will not again run over the same sinister course to the same disastrous outcome in the near future? How far and in what respect will men be content to forsake their accustomed scheme of use and wont and law, as it has stood during these years out of which the Great War has arisen? Some substantial change is imperative, if the peace is to be kept; and, I apprehend, all thoughtful persons are now ready to agree that the peace must be kept, at all costs, and that any plan of reconstruction which does not promise peace and security will not be worth considering.

It is imperative to change the scheme of use and wont, of law and order, as it runs between men and between nations so far as regards those rights and relations out of which dissension habitually arises and about which men go to war. Now, it is an easy generalization, or rather it is a time-worn commonplace, that all such disputes as rise to the dignity of warfare in our time turn always about National Ambition or Business Enterprise, one or the other, or more commonly both together. Within the confines of modern civilization religious wars, *e. g.*, wars undertaken avowedly for pillage, are out of date and are considered to be beneath the dignity of civilized statesmen. What one hears of is the national integrity, national destiny, national honor, or perhaps national opportunity, national expansion, national aggrandizement. These various objects of national ambition have at least the appearance of differing widely from one another; and it would doubtless appear that they are not all equally threatening to a state of peace and security at large. Indeed, many a kindly and thoughtful follower of the gospel of peace and good-will has committed himself to the view that the national integrity, or the national honor, *e.g.*, is to be rated foremost among the things that are to be safeguarded in any eventual peace compact. Probably none but a relatively few among the law-abiding citizens would hesitate to choose war with the national honor intact, rather than peace without it. On the other hand, relatively few would choose to further national aggrandizement at the cost of war.

Yet, however much these different objects of national ambition may differ among themselves they have this much in common, that they are matters of political aspiration, and that they afford grievances to be redressed by recourse to arms. It is between nations, and on the ground of national claims and interests, that war is carried on; at least such is the case in the formal sense that it is as a nation only that any people figures as a recognized belligerent under the currently accepted rules of etiquette governing affairs of this kind. It will probably be admitted without argument that whenever a given community divests itself of its national character – as, *e.g.*, Hawaii in 1898 – such a people ceases to be admissible as a qualified belligerent, under the rules of international courtesy; and it will likewise be admitted that whenever any given community makes its way into free recognition as a belligerent, such recognition amounts to a recognition of the belligerent's national character. Of course these formalities are of the nature of diplomatic punctilio, and they do not gravely touch the substance of things; but then, the national integrity, the national honor, etc., also are always matters of formality and diplomatic punctilio, in great part; it will perhaps be admitted that they are of this nature in the main.

Such are the formalities of diplomatic and belligerent etiquette. But it does not follow that because a people can enter into the holy state of belligerency only as a nation and only on due observance of the national proprieties, that therefore such a people will necessarily be engaged in warlike enterprise only as a nation, and only on motives of national ambition. The present case of the United States may be taken to show the difference. This country entered on this enterprise only after a punctilious compliance with all the national courtesies in such cases made and provided, and on due allegation of specific national grievance to be redressed. But it has been an open secret from beforehand, and it has been made abundantly plain by the American administration since then, that the substantial motive of this enterprise has no color of national ambition. The national grievances alleged in the formal declaration were grave enough, no doubt; the record of them comprises an inordinate destruction of life and property and a remarkable series of crimes and atrocities; and yet it can fairly be said that the redressing of these national grievances is not of the essence of the contract which the country has undertaken.

The abiding purpose of America in the war is to bring about a settled state of peace and security. If all this is accomplished, then any national establishment may come to have little more than a decorative use; as a political agency it will be in a fair way to become obsolete through disuse. What would be needed to put things in train for such an outcome would be that the pacific peoples pool their political issues; somewhat after the fashion in which they are now beginning to learn that it is expedient to pool their issues and their forces in the conduct of the war. It will probably not be questioned that this pooling of forces and issues for the conduct of the war is likely to go much farther than it has done hitherto, in case the war continues for an appreciable length of time; and the suggestion is ready to hand that the international pool so entered into under pressure of the war had best be designed on such lines that it may also eventually serve to keep the peace.

This would mean a further pooling of national issues in those respects in which national issues are apt to bring on dissension; which means issues of national ambition and issues of business enterprise under national auspices. But national ambition, in the way of territorial aggrandizement or warlike dominion, is a dead issue in America – it has been weighed and found wanting; so that, in effect, all that still remains in question is the issue between national business enterprise and free trade. Now, in the new era, and for the sake of peace and international good-will, will the American citizens be content to forego preferential advantages – at the nation's cost – for such of their compatriots as are interested in tariff-protected industries, or are engaged in the foreign trade, or derive an income from investments and concessions in foreign parts? It is to be admitted that this is still a matter of grave doubt. And it may be an over-sanguine hope, but there should at least be something of a chance that the nation may yet, under pressure of sore apprehension, bring itself also to pool these issues of business traffic along with the rest of what goes to nourish political intrigue. At any rate, in that direction lies the best assurance of peace and security at large. And if America gives a lead in the direction of such a disclaimer of national discrimination, the lead so given should reasonably be expected to go far to persuade the other pacific nations into a collusive disclaimer of the same kind.

The upshot of all this would be, of course, that the national establishment would in great part cease to function, whether as an engine of vacant political intrigue or as a handmaid of private commercial enterprise. If such an arrangement can be achieved, or in the degree in which such a result can be approached, the hazard of dissension will be removed from among those pacific nations whose international concerns so would come within the jurisdiction of that league of pacific peoples that is held in prospect by the wiser statesmen of our time.

But all this covers only one half, perhaps the smaller and less precarious half, of the precarious situation that will face the American people on the return of peace – more particularly if the peace at large is once established on that stable footing to which all good men hopefully look forward.

Let no man be deceived into believing that the removal of international friction will of itself bring in an era of tranquility at home. So soon as all apprehension of national danger is at an end, and preoccupation with international strategy has ceased to divert men's attention, the table will be cleared for a single-minded deliberation on the state of the country at home. And there is already visible such a cleavage of interests, sentiment and ambitions as may reasonably be taken to argue for a stormy reckoning ahead.

Introduction to the Translation of *The Laxdaela Saga*[*]

It has been something of a convention among those who interest themselves in Icelandic literature to speak well of the Laxdaela Saga as a thing of poetic beauty and of high literary merit. So, characteristically and with the weight of authority, Gudbrand Vigfusson has this to say of the Laxdaela, in the Prolegomena to his edition of the *Sturlunga Saga:* "This, the second only in size of the Icelandic Sagas, is perhaps also the second in beauty. It is the most romantic of all, full of pathetic sentiment, which, like that of Euripides, is almost modern, and brings it closer to the thoughts and feelings of our day than any other story of Icelandic life."

Further, as regards the tale which it has to tell: "Besides the customary but always interesting introduction, the story falls into two parts. First the early love of Kjartan and Gudrun, the hero and heroine, and the poet's career in Norway. The second part goes on with the story after Kjartan's return to Iceland, relating his death at his rival Bolli's hand, Bolli's death no long while after, and the vengeance taken for both."

As in other sagas whose incidents date from the same period (tenth and early eleventh centuries) so also in the Laxdaela, it is the paramount exigencies of the blood-feud that shape the outlines of the narrative and create the critical situations of the plot and give rise to the main outstanding incidents and episodes. Such are the classic sagas which have come down from the saga period. The blood-feud was then a

[*] From the edition published by B. W. Huebsch in 1925. Reprinted by permission of The Viking Press.

matter of course and of common sense, about the merits of which no question was entertained – no more than the merits of national patriotism are questioned in our time. It is only in late and spurious tales, dating from after the infiltration of the mediaeval chivalric romances into the Scandinavian countries, that other interests or principles of conduct have come to supplant the blood-feud as the finally dominant note. And in its class, doubtless, the Laxdaela rightly takes rank among the foremost, as a tragic tale of intrigue and adventure driven by the imperative call of the blood-feud. Other factors and motives come into the tale, in some profusion indeed, and they find adequate expression, but this is what may be called the axis of its structure.

But all the while the Laxdaela remains also an ethnological document of a high order; perhaps standing in this respect at the head of the list. So that it is of prime significance for any understanding of that peculiar phase of culture that makes up its setting; that is to say the period which comprises the close of the Viking Age, so called, and the advent of the Christian Faith in Iceland and in northern Europe more at large. More intimately and more naïvely than any other, this saga reflects the homely conditions of workday life in its time, together with the range of commonplace sentiments and convictions which animated this workday life. So that it is fairly to be taken as a competent though perhaps accentuated record of late-Pagan and early-Christian manners, customs, convictions and ideals among the Germanic peoples at large, but more particularly touching the Scandinavian and the English-speaking peoples at the point of their induction into their feudal and ecclesiastical status in early-Christian times.

By force of what may be called historical accident the Scandinavian peoples, and the Icelandic community in particular, underwent the conversion to mediaevalism, civil and religious, at a relatively late date and with a relatively swift transition; so late that it falls wholly within the scope of recorded history, and so late also that it comes at a time when the feudal system of civil life as well as the feudalistic Church had already attained their majority, had reached maturity and finished certitude as an intrinsic order of things, or perhaps had even entered on an incipient stage of decay.

These peoples came somewhat abruptly out of a foot-loose paganism which comprised neither Church nor State, properly speaking; neither feudalism nor ecclesiasticism. Both in the secular and in the spiritual respect their paganism was already infirm and insecure. And they fell somewhat precipitately and uncritically into the coils of the new Faith and that new status of servile allegiance that made up the universal bond of mediaeval society, civil and ecclesiastical. Both of these institutional innovations alike rested their case on an assumed congenital unworthiness of the common man; the two pillars of the new institutional edifice being Sin and Servility. And both of these concepts are in principle alien to the spirit of the pagan past. The sagas of the classical period reflect that state of experience, spiritual and temporal, which prepared the way for these new canons of right and honest living; canons according to which the common man has in the nature of things no claims which his God or his masters are bound to respect. They are at the same time the canons which have since then continued to rule the life of these Christian peoples in Church and State.

The conversion of these peoples to the ritual and superstitions of the new Faith was swift, facile, thorough and comprehensive, both in the temporal and in the spiritual phase of it, but more notably so in the latter respect. Indeed the gospel of Sin and Redemption was accepted by them with such alacrity and abandon as would argue that they had already been bent into a suitable frame of mind by protracted and exacting experience of a suitable kind. And on the side of the temporal reorganization, as concerned the revolutionary change in their civil institutions, they made the transition in only less headlong fashion. And in both respects the submission of these peoples to this new order of allegiance was notably abject.

This new gospel of abnegation, spiritual and temporal, was substantially alien to the more ancient principles of that pagan dispensation out of which the North-European peoples had come; but the event goes to show that in principle the new gospel of abnegation was consonant with their later acquired habits of thought; that their more recent experience of life had induced in these peoples such a frame of mind as would incline them to a conviction of sin and an unquestioning subjection to mastery. The discipline of life in the Viking Age appears to have been greatly conducive to such an outcome. And the Laxdaela reflects that state of society and that prevalent frame of mind which led the Scandinavian peoples over from the Viking Age to the Mediaeval Church and State.

Here it is necessary to note that while the Viking Age prepared the ground for the Christian Faith and the Feudal State, there were at the same time also certain institutional hold-overs carried over out of remoter pagan antiquity into the Christian Era; hold-overs which also had their part in the new dispensation. Chief among these was the blood-feud; which appears to have suffered no impairment under the conditions of life in the Viking Age. At the same time it appears that in principle, and indeed in the concrete details of its working-out, the habits of thought which underlie the blood-feud were not obnoxious to the interests of Holy

Church or to the Propaganda of the Faith. Familiarity with its underlying principles and its logic would rather appear to have facilitated conversion to the fundamentals of the new Faith. The logic of the blood-feud, with its standardized routine of outlawry and its compounding of felonies, lends itself without substantial change of terms to the preachment of Sin and Redemption; perhaps in an especially happy degree to the preachment of Vicarious Atonement. So that this ancient and ingrained familiarity with the logic of the blood-feud may even be said to have served as an instrument of Grace. And as might fairly have been expected, the institution continued in good vigor for some centuries after the conversion to Christianity. In a certain sense, at least permissively, it even enjoyed the benefit of clergy; and it eventually fell into decay under the impact of secular rather than religious exigencies.

The Viking Age had prepared the ground for the new Faith and for the new, feudal order of Society. The Viking Age had run for some five or six centuries, and the discipline of habituation which was brought to bear through these centuries by that peculiar institution which has given its name to that era was exacting and consistent in an exemplary degree; rising steadily in point of stress and legitimation through the greater part of the period; until, in the end, the depleted resources of the Viking enterprise were taken over by the feudal State and the ecclesiastical establishment, and its pirate captains were supplanted by the princes and prelates of the new dispensation.

That occupation which gave its name and its character to the Viking Age was an enterprise in piracy and slave-trade, which grew steadily more businesslike and more implacable as time went on. It was an enterprise in getting something for nothing by force and fraud at the cost of the party of the second part; much the same, in principle, as the national politics pursued by the statesmen of the present time.

Unavoidably though doubtless unintentionally this business quite consistently yielded a cumulative net average deficit at large and resulted in a cumulative privation and servility on the part of the underlying population. Increasingly as time passed, the ethics of the strong arm came to prevail among these peoples and to dominate men's ideals and convictions of right and wrong. Insecurity of life and livelihood grew gradually more pronounced and more habitual, until in the course of centuries of rapine, homicide and desolation it became a settled matter of course and of common sense that the underlying population had no rights which the captains of the strong arm were bound to respect. And like any other business enterprise that is of a competitive nature this traffic in piracy was forever driven by its quest of profits to "trade on a thinner equity," to draw more unsparingly on its resources of man-power and appliances, and so cut into the margin of its reserves, to charge increasingly more than the traffic would bear. Until, between increasing squalor and privation on the material side and an ever increasing habituation to insecurity, fear and servility on the spiritual side, this population was in a frame of mind to believe that this world is a vale of tears and that they all were miserable sinners prostrate and naked in the presence of an unreasoning and unsparing God and his bailiffs. So this standardized routine of larceny and homicide ran through its available resources and fell insensibly into decay, and the State and Holy Church came in and took over the usufruct of the human residue that was left. It is the inchoate phase of this taking-over, specifically as it is to be seen in Iceland, that is reflected in the Laxdaela.

The subsequent share of Holy Church and its clerics in

the ulterior degradation of the Scandinavian peoples, including Iceland, was something incredibly shameful and shabby; and the share which the State had in that unholy job was scarcely less so. But these things come into the case of the Icelandic community only at a later date, and can not be pursued here. The mediaeval Church in Iceland stands out on the current of events as a corporation of bigoted adventurers for the capitalizing of graft and blackmail and the profitable compounding of felonious crimes and vices. It is of course not intended to question that this mediaeval Church all this while remained a faithful daughter of Rome and doubtless holy as usual; nor is it to be questioned that more genial traits and more humane persons and motives entered into the case in a sporadic way. It is only that the visible net gain was substantially as set forth. In abatement it should also be noted, of course, that there is no telling what else and possibly shabbier things might have come to pass under the given circumstances in the conceivable absence of Holy Church and its clerics.

But this fuller blossoming of the Faith in Iceland, and its eventual going to seed, comes on in the decades which follow the period covered by the Laxdaela; which reflects only the more genial inchoate phase of the new dispensation. So also the further growth and fruition of that system of Boss Rule that made up the working constitution of the Icelandic Commonwealth likewise comes gradually to a head at a later date; and this too is shown only in its genial beginnings in the Laxdaela. Yet the elements, civil and ecclesiastical, which eventually entered into that teamwork of intrigue and desolation that brought the Commonwealth to its end in grief and shame are to be seen here. For a nearer view of that tangle of corrosive infelicities there are an abundance of documents available; such, e. g., as the *Saga of Gudmund the Good* and the *Islendinga Saga*, together with the rest of what is included in Vigfusson's *Sturlunga Saga;* while for the Norwegian community at home the *Heimskringla*, together with certain detached sagas of the later kings of Norway, will show how the fortunes of that people, from the advent of Christianity onward, swiftly tapered off into a twilight-zone of squalor, malice and servility, with benefit of Clergy.

The action of the saga runs over the period from the last quarter of the ninth to the first quarter of the eleventh century, coming to a head in the first decade of the eleventh.

For this translation use has been made of the Copenhagen edition of 1826, with some reference to later and more critical editions of the text. Later editions, as, e. g., that of Kaalund, are doubtless preferable in point of textual precision; but except for textual, essentially clerical, variations, there is no notable divergence between one edition and another or between one and another of the manuscript copies of the Laxdaela. The translation has also had the benefit of comparison with those made by Mrs. Press (Dent, London 1899) and Rudolf Meissner (Jena 1913), both of which are excellently well done, perhaps especially the German rendering. The German language appears to offer a more facile medium for a rendering of the Icelandic; its idioms appear to run more nearly parallel with those of the original.

As is true of the general run of Icelandic sagas, the language of the Laxdaela is the language of colloquial speech in its time; the speech of practiced storytellers, idiomatic in an extreme degree and with a pronounced bent for aphoristic diction. Consequently the difficulties in the way of a faithful translation are very appreciable. Necessarily, the idiomatic speech of that time runs on metaphor and analogy drawn from the familiar usage and custom of its own time and setting; such as would be pointed, sententious, and suggestive to the hearers who were familiar with that range of usage and custom. The language of the Saga, therefore, conveys in its own substance and structure that range of sentiments, convictions, ideals, knowledge and belief which is embodied in the action of the story. But it follows that the spirit of its action is not readily, or indeed at all adequately, to be carried over into another language which articulates with the usage current in a different time and place, and the run of whose idiom therefore is, by so much, substantially alien to that of the original.

The idiomatic speech of any given time and place springs from and reflects the workday experience and preconceptions of men in that given time and place. And much water has run under the bridge since the days when the lives of those men and women took shape in the idiomatic speech of the Saga. The run of idiom in the English language as now current is as widely out of touch with that of the Icelandic saga as the current run of custom, knowledge and belief among the English-speaking peoples is now out of touch with the arts of life in that archaic phase of their culture. Under these circumstances translation becomes in good part a work of makeshift and adumbration, in which any consistently literal rendering of the text is out of the question.

By comparison with the common run of sagas, the received text of the Laxdaela is a somewhat prosy narrative, cumbered with many tawdry embellishments and affectations of style and occasional intrusive passages of devout bombast. The indications are fairly clear that the version of the text which has come down to the present has come through the hands of a painstaking editor-author whose qualifications were of a clerkly order rather than anything in the way of literary sense, and whose penchant for fine writing would not allow him to let well enough alone. Coupled with an unctuous sanctimony and a full run of puerile superstitions, such as were current in the late thirteenth century, this clerkly animus of the editor-author has at the same time overlaid the chief characters of the story with an ecclesiastical whitewash of meretricious abnegation, quite alien to the action in which these characters are engaged. So that, e. g., Kjartan Olafson comes to be depicted as a sanctimonious acolyte given to prayer, fasting, and pious verbiage; instead of being a wilful spoiled child, vain and sulky, of a romantic temper and endowed with exceptional physical beauty, such as the run of the story proclaims him. Whereas Gudrun, a beautiful vixen, passionate, headstrong, self-seeking and mendacious, is dutifully crowned with the distinction of having been the first nun and anchorite in Iceland and having meritoriously carried penance and abnegation to the outer limit of endurance. Yet, doubtless, all this glamour of sanctimony which the clerkly editor-author has dutifully thrown over the chief persons of the story is true to life, in the sense that such was the color of Icelandic life and sentiment in his own time, in the seedy times of the Icelandic community's decline and decomposition. Also it will be true to life in the sense that such will have been the consummation to which the drift of things under the new order converged from its beginning in the decades in which the action of the story is laid.

It may be in place to add that this translation follows the Copenhagen edition of the text also in the respect that it includes the chapters at the end (LXXIX-LXXXIII) devoted to the exploits of the younger Bolli, as well as the short story of Gunnar Thidrandabani, which is appended to that edition. This story of the younger Bolli is commonly accounted spurious, doubtless rightly so; as being a late and mythical fabric of the mediaeval romancer's art, designed to make Bolli illustrious in the eyes of his descendants. Similarly spurious are the passages in the body of the saga which detail the earlier doings of Bolli the younger. So, e. g., his share as well as the share of his brother Thorleik in the killing of Helgi Hardbeinson and in the negotiations which preceded and followed that exploit are known to be altogether fanciful; Helgi having been disposed of at a date when the two brothers were no more than two and six years old. Indeed, apart from the notice of his birth and his marriage, all that is here told of Bolli the younger is without known foundation.

II. Reviews

The Development of English Thought: A Study in the Economic Interpretation of History. By SIMON N. PATTEN. New York: The Macmillan Company, 1899. 8vo. pp. xxvii, 415.*

IF the term be taken in a general sense, Mr. Patten's "Development of English Thought" is a working out of a materialistic conception of history, although his "materialistic conception" is not nearly the same as that to which Marx and Engels gave a vogue in socialistic circles. It is needless to say that it is a marked advance over the somewhat crude form in which the great socialists left their fundamental concept. While they were content with an appeal to class interest and antagonism as a sufficient explanation of the control of cultural development through the economic situation, Mr. Patten's modern scientific animus leads him to look more closely into the causal relation between the economic situation and the resulting culture. The resulting theory is not a doctrine of a class struggle. In Mr. Patten's view the economic situation shapes culture by shaping human character and habits of thought. It does this somewhat directly, through a process of habituation as well as through a concomitant process of selection between habits and between different styles of temperament. The causal relation between the situation ("environment") and the cultural outcome, therefore, lies through the psychological development of the individuals who are exposed to this environment.

* *Annals of the American Academy of Political and Social Science,* July 1899.

Some part of the theoretical ground on which this materialistic doctrine proceeds has already been set forth, in greater detail, in an earlier monograph on "The Theory of Social Forces." The elements of that theory are (1) a frankly and uncritically accepted, though modified, associational psychology, such as had general vogue until a generation ago, with its accompanying hedonism, and (2) a rationalistic doctrine of evolution, stated in terms of the consummation to which the development should tend in order to meet the author's ideal. It is part of the tacit premises of this doctrine that evolution means improvement, amelioration, progress; hence there is occasional reference to the "normal line" of development, and some phases of the development are spoken of as departures and detours from the normal. This resort to normality and a more or less constraining meliorative trend is scarcely a modern feature.

The normal line of development is conceived to run from an earlier "pain economy" to a subsequent "pleasure economy." This distinction, it may be remarked, seems to have no ground in fact and to serve no useful purpose. Under the regime of the archaic "pain economy,"

> fear and the avoidance of pain are the prominent motives for action. The sensory ideas are so grouped that they give early intimation of the presence of every possible foe or evil. . . . Man must have an instinctive fear of evil. The sensory and motor powers must unite in emphasizing any quality or person that may be the forerunner of suffering, or the means of avoiding it. Such activities and such a type of mind appear in primitive men, and wherever they are dominant a pain economy results. (p. 8).

Even a hasty and fragmentary comparison of this theory of primitive habits of life and thought with what is known of existing primitive communities will show its irrelevancy. It appears, for instance, that in such communities as those of the Australians, Bushmen or Eskimo, where life is precarious and the environment local, all this does not seem to hold. "Motor ideas" (to accept, without criticising, Mr. Patten's terminology) do not here crowd out "sensory ideas" to the extent which the theory would seem to demand; nor do these bearers of the lower culture bend their thoughts with utter consistency to the avoidance of pain. To some extent – in the case of many Australian tribes to a very great extent – they seem to court pain. Of these latter it is quite safe to say that there is more blood shed by them peacefully and deliberately, in self-torture and ceremonial scarification, than all that is lost in hostile encounter with men and beasts. Their times of peace are times of blood and wounds. Illustrations to the same effect abound in the accounts of other peoples at or near the same cultural level. And far from the "motor ideas" shutting out all other thought process than a strenuous application to the struggle against a refractory environment, there is on this cultural level a very large and free development of legends and ceremonial myths that have no obvious relation to "fear and the avoidance of pain." And the body of what passes for knowledge among these people is comprehensive and intricate, and shows no peculiarly close correlation with an effective avoidance of evils. "The sensory ideas are" not in any especial degree "so grouped that they give early intimation of the presence of every foe or evil." On the contrary, they are in great part so grouped as to be ineffective for that purpose. In point of fact, most of the known primitive communities are saddled with a stupendous fabric of magical conceits and ceremonials that frequently hinder their avoidance of patent evils. They are also, if the consensus of observers is to be accepted, notably indolent, light-hearted and careless of any evil that is not already upon them. *Dolce far niente* and merrymaking, often hideously exuberant, claim a very large portion of their time and attention. It is behind the man on horseback that black care sits; the savage of the earlier, more unmitigated "pain economy" knows little of worry. And the evils which he seriously seeks to avoid are for the most part figments – high-wrought complications of "sensory ideas" that are not controlled by relevant "motor ideas." The evidence from ethnology seems to say that care and deliberation for the avoidance of evils find no place in the early culture until the necessity of taking thought is forced home upon the luckless by a successful incursion from without; and such an incursion commonly comes from men who seek an increase of pleasures through booty, – the "sensualists" of Mr. Patten's nomenclature, that are bred in a "pleasure economy."

The predilection for sharp antitheses and striking transitions that shows itself in the overdrawn contrast between a "pain economy" and a "pleasure economy" appears again in the repeated insistence on the epochal character of historical development. Mr. Patten finds that history proceeds by epochs, each of which begins with a transition to a new and novel environment and affords an entirely new and unprejudiced point of departure. The impression conveyed is that of an extreme segmentation of the sequence.

"Each succeeding environment will . . . create a new series of economic, aesthetic, moral, and religious ideas which will have their basis in the economic conditions of the epoch. The history of each epoch is thus practically independent, starting from its own conditions and developing in its own way. In studying an epoch, the economic conditions must be studied first, then the economic doctrines that flow from them, and last the aesthetic, moral, and religious ideas which the epoch produces.

"The different groups of ideas cannot be traced independently, because the ideas of each epoch do not grow out of the similar ideas of the preceding epoch, but are formed anew from the new conditions." (p. 44).

"History, to be valuable, must be studied in epochs, and each group of ideas [economic, aesthetic, moral, religious][1] be connected with its roots in the underlying conditions, and not with its antecedents in the same group. The blending of the old and the new groups of ideas happens after the new conditions have exerted their force, or at least have brought out what is most peculiar to them." (p. 45).

The notion of a sheer transition and a fresh start is mitigated rather than superseded by the subsequent statement that each succeeding temporary environment "has given to the race certain characteristics that become a part of the national character. And thus character is the one enduring growing element in a civilization; all else when compared with it is temporary and fleeting" for it remains true that "in each new environment a new nation grows up almost as distinct from its predecessors as were the new nations of ancient times from the nations that preceded them." (pp. 46-47). That continuity of traditions and usages that has so impressed students of institutions and folklore, as well as that persistence of physical type and temperamental bent that makes the burden of the teachings of the modern anthropologists, seem to have passed harmless over Mr. Patten.

The antecedents of English thought (ch. ii) are proximately racial, more remotely climatic; but the analysis is pushed back of the racial to the climatic with a freedom which indicates that in Mr. Patten's view the sequence cov-

[1] [Brackets are Veblen's].

ered by these terms is by no means a long one. The character of the race is created by an economic (climatic) situation which imposes certain traits upon men. These traits may be imposed by a relatively brief discipline, but after they have once been imposed they persist with an extreme tenacity. Further changes in the "character" of the race take place by the imposition of added traits, rather than by an organic change or selective variation of hereditary temperament or by an alteration in the individual's habits of thought. One gets the impression that traits are conceived to make up a mechanical aggregate, which is the race character, and to which new items may be added without essentially disturbing the previously existing aggregation (see pp. 4-21, 50-52, 57-66).

Mr. Patten's theoretical handling of the antecedents of English thought will be found at many points to traverse received notions of the primitive growth of culture, and his statements of fact in this connection also do not easily fit into the framework of the published accounts of existing primitive communities. Under the former head there is a characteristically bold departure from current notions as to the origin, nature, and functional relations of the clan (p. 109). Again, Mr. Patten says that "the northern man conquers nature, while the southern man yields to it." (pp. 5-8). An American reader will instinctively call to mind the Aleutian and Alaskan tribes on the one hand, and the Yucatanese and Mexican civilizations on the other, and the juxtaposition of the author's generalization with the specific facts leaves the effect of a drawn game.

"In wet, cold countries, natural forces act regularly, and the social surplus is small. Here men unite into strongly knit social groups, with a well-developed feeling of the solidarity of responsibility. Vigorous and aggressive, they react promptly against sources of pain." (p. 64).

This again calls up the Eskimo, the Fuegians, the Ainu, whose social groups are not seriously to be weighed in the balance of solidarity. And to make the bewilderment complete one might add the Haida, except for the fact that with them the food supply ("social surplus") was not scant, while their social groups were "strongly knit."

So again, in contrast,

"These concepts of peace and obedience do not come naturally to people living in hot, dry countries, where nature is arbitrary. . . . As their privations seem to be due to their own shortcomings, they develop readily the concept of sin and of a fallen nature. But peace they do not look for, and obedience they do not yield. On the contrary, they have inclinations toward a life of asceticism and individual freedom. Among these people there is no powerful priesthood and no concept of God except as a being to fear and avoid." (p. 63).

The Mexicans and Pueblos should afford illustration of this text, but credible accounts say that they do not altogether. The Pueblos, for instance, probably as clear a case as may be found, are currently held by students of their culture to be peaceable, obedient to their chosen authorities, not noticeably conscious of their own shortcomings, not perceptibly inclined to asceticism, with a priesthood constituting the strongest power among them, with an extensive and well-grown mythology and an intricate and elaborate cult, constantly resorting for comfort to their divinities, of whom they have but little fear.

This anthropological-economic verification of Mr. Patten's underlying principles of interpretation might be continued at considerable length without coming closer to a conviction of their adequacy. But all this touches only the preliminaries and premises of the discussion, not the main work of interpretation itself. It may seem gratuitous and ungraceful to apply these preliminary generalizations to the case of peoples that lie outside of that European culture with which alone his argument is occupied; but if the generalizations are to apply with such force as to afford a point of departure within the European culture they should be of such a consistency as to avoid the appearance of having been constructed *ad hoc*.

It is to be regretted that, even at points that are not peculiarly recondite or difficult, in the handling of the main question, faults of the same kind occur again. So, in the distinction made between his three typical civilizations, German, Semitic and Roman, Mr. Patten overlooks that difference of racial stocks that anthropologists make much of, and resorts instead to an unnecessarily bald appeal to the economic situation (p. 64). Similarly, the like persistent racial difference traceable between Catholics and Protestants, and in a less degree between Calvinists and Lutherans, is neglected at a later point (ch. ii, also pp. 110-142).

"The character of the early German was due mainly to the damp, cold climate in which he lived, and to the meagre food products upon which he subsisted." (p. 65).

The evidence of the German's food products being meagre is not easy to find; where evidence of the early dietary is most available, as, for instance, in the case of the older Scandinavian communities, it goes the other way. Nor does the statement (p. 66) that in Germany the equilibrium of population was maintained by pressing against nature for the means of subsistence comport with the other statement, on the same page, that "their migrations seem to have been actuated, not by starvation, but by greed." So also it seems paradoxical to say that the character of that Germanic stock that won its way by the sword "has few of the traits which war creates."

But paradox and the inversion of received views are not

among the things which this book avoids. Wide divergence from the commonplace interpretations meets the reader at almost all points of first-rate consequence. At first one is struck with the novelty and force of the new formulations, and one has a feeling that Mr. Patten must have discovered and will unfold a wealth of evidence that shall substantiate the new positions taken. But with further progress this feeling (perhaps unwarrantably) wears off, as the proliferation of novel ideas and the paucity of documentation goes on. The matter-of-fact material handled in the body of the volume raises fewer questions of authenticity than the striking statements made in the hundred-odd pages of theoretical groundwork, but there are few portions of the book in the reading of which one quite escapes the apprehension that the facts cited are speaking under constraint. And Mr. Patten's handling of the theme is so flexuous and multiform, and to one not in entire sympathy with his premises and his point of view it seems at times so whimsical and inconsequent, that a detailed scrutiny of the argument would be a large and by no means attractive employment and could scarcely avoid the appearance of captiousness.

It is a book of which it is not easy to say much in the way of commendation that shall be specific enough to bear itemized statement. But none the less it will afford valuable suggestion and incentive, and, indeed, guidance, to the economic study of many features of European culture. It abounds in irrelevant generalizations, but there is also much of shrewd observation, with many new and cogent characterizations of the writers and tenets with which the book deals. We may not be able to accept Mr. Patten's position that antagonism to Puritan enthusiasm was the deciding motive and guide in Locke's work; nor may many students find conviction in the characterization of Darwin as a "philosopher on the downward curve," or of Hume as an economist changed into a philosopher. But the pointed contrast of Mr. Patten's views on these heads as against what has passed current will at least have a salutary effect in directing the attention of students to features in the development of thought which have commonly been passed over too lightly. The account given of the development of the English "home" and of the cultural causes and effects of the English status of women does not seem conclusive, in view of the fact that a passably equivalent economic situation in other communities, where race, religion, or social traditions have been different, has not worked out like results. But here again the discussion throws an effective light upon the questions in hand, though it is perhaps to be rated as a side light. One is somewhat at a loss to account for the very high degree of efficacy imputed to the Christian religion – an intrusive cult – in Germanic and English culture, in a discussion whose first, if not sole, postulate is that the economic situation shapes the cultural sequence without help or hindrance from any outside spiritual force or from any antecedent tradition or tenet. And still, inconsistent as it may be, his handling of this intrusive cult as a formative element in English spiritual life is by no means the least effective of Mr. Patten's work.

On one point at least, of general bearing, Mr. Patten's conclusion seems blind to those who do not see all these matters through his eyes. In chapter iii (pp. 188-189) and again in his concluding remarks (p. 378) it is broadly stated that the English have shown a conspicuous incapacity for the development of political institutions. This raises a question as to what may be meant by a capacity for political life – in that economic relation with which Mr. Patten is avowedly occupied – beyond such an adequate adjustment to their economic situation as Mr. Patten shows the English to be eminently possessed of.

The Cost of Competition. An Effort at the Understanding of Familiar Facts. By SIDNEY A. REEVE. New York: McClure, Phillips & Co., 1906. 8vo. pp. xix + 617.*

BY THE Cost of Competition Mr. Reeve means the same as would be signified by the Cost of Business Enterprise; and cost means primarily waste of goods and work, but secondarily, also, the evil consequences of the régime of business in the way of hardship and moral, aesthetic, and intellectual corruption. There is relatively little in the presentation which is not in substance more or less familiar to economic students, although the whole is put in a more than commonly cogent and forceful way, and the analysis is more detailed and consistent than any that has, perhaps, ever before been given to the same topic. Mr. Reeve's apprehension of the facts with which he deals is not substantially different from views held more loosely by many of the younger generation of economists, though it stands out in sheer contrast with the views of business traffic current among the older generation of economists, particularly among those older economists who adhere to the scheme of the classical political economy. It is not that the economists of the schools are not aware of the range of facts with which the volume deals, nor is it that they are not aware of the general run of forces and effects that occupies Mr. Reeve's attention, but other things are felt to be of graver importance for economic theory. Economists currently find themselves less vitally interested in these facts of everyday traffic and growth and change, than in academic research into the hidden nature of things. It is not that economists are unable to see or even perhaps to appreciate the

* *Yale Review*, May 1907.

stupendous sweep of events in the modern market-place, nor even that they are averse to a consideration of the achievements of modern "capitalism," which Mr. Reeve makes so much of; but there is felt to be more weight for the science in the questions as to whether capital is to be conceived as a fund or as a flow, whether normal credit affects prices, whether rent is of the nature of interest or interest of the nature of rent, whether value is determined by marginal utility or by marginal disutility, etc. The present volume, therefore, is more novel in appearance than unfamiliar in substance.

Indeed, Mr. Reeve is apparently no more acquainted with current economic discussion than current economic discussion is with Mr. Reeve's subject matter. So, at least, one would infer from his nonconformity in the use of terms, as well as from the outline of economic theory with which the volume opens. For the fundamental principles, as expounded in the first 230 pages, Mr. Reeve avows his indebtedness to Henry George, and shows a degree of relationship to the physiocratic school that might even be called affiliation.[1] Like

[1] [This obituary note on George may well have been written by Veblen]. "The sudden and dramatic death of Henry George on the eve of the mayoralty election of New York, in which he struck fire by his characteristic and passionate denunciation of 'boss' rule, brings to a close a remarkable economic career. An unknown compositor, without wealth, by virtue of a taking style, a brilliant imagination, and persistent earnestness in one special field, made his name known not merely to his own country, but to the whole world, as a household word. He caught the unrest of the time and gave it an economic justification, which, whether correct or not, made a conquest of great numbers of men. By giving, in an illuminating way, a specific cause of poverty, he satisfied many minds not capable of reasoning out difficult economic problems. Whether or not his conclusions were based upon sufficiently sound processes may be left to a more careful study of the period in which he lived, and of the quality of his contributions to political economy." (*The Journal of Political Economy*, December 1897, p. 93).

them, he postulates a providential design, whereby the natural universe is conceived to work toward fulness of human life. He defines "value" as "the potentiality of a thing for the support of human life and growth" (p. 16), reminding one of Adam Smith's "value in use," and gives the name "valuation" to what is commonly covered by the term "value." "Exchange" in Mr. Reeve's usage means a transfer of goods from hand to hand, whereas what is currently covered by the term "exchange" is here technically designated by the term "barter." There are a few more of these apparently gratuitous violations of usage, which have no visible justification. Indeed, they can only be a stumbling-block to any cursory reader without serving any useful purpose for a more attentive student.

The point of departure for the main argument is a distinction drawn between "productive" and "competitive" activity. This distinction is the same as has elsewhere been made between industry and business. Industry, productive activity, is the source of all wealth, whereas competitive business simply dissipates wealth, in so far as it is competitive. Occupations are classified under four heads (pp. 243-4), according as they are "entirely competitive," "chiefly competitive, but partly productive," "productive by nature, but contributive to competition," or "entirely productive." In the degree in which they are competitive their effect is "dissipation." In the chapter on "The Growth of Dissipation," Mr. Reeve finds, by an analysis of statistics, that during the last half of the nineteenth century the dissipation (loss) due to competitive business rose from about fifty per cent. of the total annual product in 1850 to about seventy per cent. in 1900. This conclusion is reached by comparing the incomes of the productive and the competitive classes at each of the two dates chosen. There need probably be no serious question as to the substantial accuracy of Mr. Reeve's figures in this connection. It is, indeed, highly probable on the face of things that in the distribution of the product at least seventy per cent. to-day goes to those who are occupied with competitive business, leaving not more than thirty per cent. of the whole as the remuneration of productive effort, taking the word "productive" in its most liberal sense. It seems even possible to generalize a step beyond Mr. Reeve's position, and say that under any free and consistent business régime the share of competitive business, as contrasted with productive industry, must grow at such a rate as to take up any amount by which the total product exceeds the minimum necessary to induce the productive classes to go on with the work.

But while few critics who appreciate the run of facts with which Mr. Reeve deals would question the legitimacy of his conclusions as regards the distribution of income, yet the question is likely to be raised whether the distribution of a given share of income to the competitive classes means the dissipation of that share of income by these classes. Mr. Reeve holds (p. 255) that under the competitive régime "the wealth actually lost to the community by dissipation is measured by" the income which goes to the competitive classes, the business men. But the old-fashioned objection here arises, that the business men do not dissipate the greater part of their incomes, but turn it to productive use as capital; whereby the community gains in increased future productivity all and more than it loses in yielding this income to the business men. The business men save and invest, and the community gets the benefit of the increased production due to the increase of capital.

A further consideration, however, not taken account of by the old-fashioned critics, will leave the point in doubt. While Mr. Reeve might well concede that the saving and reinvestment of income by the business men heightens the industrial efficiency of the community, and so increases the total output, the resulting increased investment on their part gives them a valid claim to a correspondingly increased share of the total output and leaves the rest of the community about as well off as they would be without such increased investment. The total output is increased, but the increment goes to the investing business men. As regards the fortunes of the productive classes, therefore, the direct and immediate effect of such saving and investment is substantially the same as if the business men in question had dissipated their share of the total income.

Such is the drift of the main argument, the merits of which will, no doubt, be rated very differently by different critics. Whatever the merits of the volume may be conceived to be, it is at least a painstaking, fearless, and ingenious examination of the current economic situation. Yet mention is to be made of certain less commendable features of the book. The diction is lucid and cogent, but it is somewhat marred by recurrent outbursts of indignation, and there are long passages that would more fittingly find a place in a volume of sermons than in an economic treatise. Such passages are more frequent in the second (concluding) part of the volume, on "The Ethical Cost of Competition and the Future." Indeed, the bulk of the second part (pp. 347-607) is of this character. There are, also, occasional slips of logic, as where Mr. Reeve (p. 150) formulates his law of "The Conservation of Economic Energy" in the proposition that "The aggregate value [in use] currently produced by a community is equal to the aggregate valuation [price][2] currently distributed throughout its membership." He has previously shown (pp. 9-15, 149-150) that "value" and "valuation" are incommensurable.

[2] [The brackets are Veblen's].

But the greatest shortcoming of the argument is probably its failure to take any adequate account of the elaborately wasteful consumption of wealth that is inseparable from the régime of competitive business. Wealth is acquired competitively in order to be consumed competitively, – that is to say, in order to be wasted competitively. Due attention to this side of competition would have strengthened Mr. Reeve's position, both as regards the wastefulness of the current régime, and as regards his optimistic appreciation of a conceivable non-competitive future.

England: Its Political Organisation and Development and the War against Germany. By EDUARD MEYER. Translated by Helene S. White. Boston: Ritter & Co. 8vo. pp. xix + 328.*

THIS book on England was written two years ago, during the first half-year of the great war, but none the less it runs true to form as an exposition of the current German views on all those topics with which it deals. It was written during that season of immoderate exasperation that followed on the defeat at the Marne, and that has lasted since that time. That such a volume of unstinted dispraise, growing out of that preposterous disappointment, should still continue to reflect the national sentiment to-day is significant of the fact that the great war was, in effect, brought to a decision in the fall of 1914, and that nothing has occurred since that time to alter or offset the miscarriage then suffered by the warlike enterprise on which the German hopes converged. The closing months of 1914 probably mark the largest and most shocking disappointment known to the history of mankind. So also the volume is significant of that distemper of

* *The Dial*, April 19, 1917. The review appeared under the title "Another German Apologist."

the intellect which overtook the intellectual classes of Germany at that juncture, and which has lasted since that time. The book is unbalanced and intemperate in all its appraisal of England and the English, as well as of Germany and the Germans. There speaks through it an animus of uncontrolled ferocity, as of a trapped animal; and yet it is to be noted that in all this it runs true to form.

What has just been noted in characterization of Professor Meyer's book marks a serious blemish, of course, but when all this is said, it still remains true that it is a book of exceptional value as a presentation of the material which it handles. Professor Meyer commands a large and highly significant range of information and he controls his material with all that swift and sure touch that marks the master of his craft. He knows, or perhaps rather he is informed about, the United Kingdom and its people and circumstances so intimately and comprehensively that what he has to say about it all is charged with information and suggestion even when the animus of the argument departs farthest from the conventions of well-bred scholarship. The author's exuberant bias of antipathy is to be deprecated, of course, but its effects are not altogether unfortunate. It serves to throw up into a needed light many infirmities of the case which commonly escape notice at the hands of those writers who see the pertinent facts only in a haze of somewhat stale complacency.

There is very much, substantially the whole, of Part I – "The Character of the English State" – that British subjects as well as students of British institutions would do well to take to heart without material abatement, however tartly, not to say spitefully, it is presented. The author has a quick eye for the infirmities as well as for the foibles of the British administrative machinery and its quasi-aristocratic personnel, even though he does at times make too much of the formal data bearing on any given point and is apt to undervalue the part played by legal fiction and dead letter. The analysis and presentation is unsparing, but all the more veracious, in what it has to say of biased upper-class mismanagement and sordid muddling of all those affairs that touch the interest of underlying, outlying, and dependent classes and communities under British jurisdiction, and the author does not hesitate to speak openly of that management of national affairs for pecuniary gain which the gentlemen-investors who guide the ship of state are wont to cover with a decent make-believe of serving the common good.

Tacit or explicit, there runs through all the discussion a contrasting of these British phenomena with the corresponding German ways and means of doing things, and always the comparison falls out in favor of the German case. That it does so is due to a tacit assumption which serves as major premise to the argument at all points; with a *naïveté* characteristic of his kind, the author goes on an axiomatic assumption that dynastic aggrandizement is more commendable and more to the public advantage than the pecuniary gain of such a class of gentlemen-investors as controls the fortunes of the United Kingdom. In the apprehension of any outsider, of course, there is not much to choose, as touches the common good, between the warlike aggrandizement of an imperial dynasty and the unearned increase of pecuniary benefits that accrues to a ruling class of gentlemen-investors. The nearest approach to serving the common good that is made by either of these contrasted national establishments and national policies is a make-believe backed with just so much of concession to the public needs as will serve to keep popular discontent from rising to the point of revolt; the material difference being that the committee of gentlemen-investors who rule the commonwealth under parliamentary auspices are habitually constrained to concede something more, being more readily accountable to their underlying community.

This paramount ideal of dynastic aggrandizement that hallows all German politics and throws it into contrast with the corresponding British phenomena, is set forth to this effect:

"The most important and most deeply rooted difference lies in the Continental idea of the state as it has been developed in its relation to the central authority, the sovereign; of this the English, or we will say, the people of Great Britain have no conception. To us the state is the most indispensable as well as the highest requisite to our earthly existence, not with regard to our political welfare alone, but to the daily life and activity of the individual as well, uniting, as it does, the entire population dwelling within the limits of its jurisdiction in wholesome activity for the general good; we therefore believe it to be worthy of, as well as entitled to, the entire devotion of every citizen, in honorable effort to further its purposes. All individualistic endeavor, of which there is no lack with us too, as well as the aspirations of those shattered foreign nationalities that are included within the boundaries of our state, must be unreservedly subordinated to this lofty claim. . . . The state is of much higher importance than anyone of these individualistic groups, and eventually is of infinitely more value than the sum of all the individuals within its jurisdiction . . . (pp. 29-30). This conception of the state . . . is quite foreign to English thought, and to that of America as well (p. 31)."

Quite logically, what has happened to the English constitution and to English sentiment since the Stuarts forfeited the despotic rights of the crown is viewed by Professor Meyer as a record of national decay (pp. 7-15).

The purpose of all this analysis and exposition is to be

found in its bearing on the merits of the present conflict between the German coalition and the rest of Europe. Here, again, the argument runs true to form. There is the customary apparatus of innuendo and devout falsification, familiar enough in the diplomatic arguments on both sides; and there is the old familiar Pharisaical whine that "this war has been forced upon us," – also shared equally by the two parties in controversy. But all that belongs in the domain of diplomacy rather than in historical inquiry. To anyone who can see the lie of the land in some degree of detachment, it should be sufficiently patent that both parties to the conflict are on the defensive and that the war has been "forced upon" both alike by the circumstances of the case. Both are on the defensive, very much after the fashion of the legendary two cats of Kilkenny, who were moved by the obsession that there was one too many. The situation is simple enough, in its elements, if one will only take a dispassionate view of it. There is no longer room in the modern world for both parties; because the two parties embody two incompatible variants of the modern civilization, and the world is rapidly becoming too narrow for more than one. It is not that there is no room for all the several warring peoples; there is, in fact, increasingly easy room for all of them to find a livelihood by help of the increasingly efficient modern industrial arts. But there is no room for Imperial Germany and its subservient allies in the same world with the democratic commonwealths of the French and English-speaking peoples, and the war is to decide between them. It is a conflict of institutions rather than of peoples, and it involves the fortunes of these peoples only as they contend for the one or the other institutional scheme – the dynastic monarchy or the democratic commonwealth.

Professor Meyer's book includes a Foreword in which he

speaks of the position taken by the American administration toward the belligerents. Here, again, the argument, which runs on the now historical "Lusitania Episode," runs true to form. It embodies the singular hallucination which appears to beset all apologists for the German case, that because both are disallowed by law and custom, therefore interference with neutral trade is as heinous an offence as the unprovoked killing of neutral citizens. It is true, of course, that trespass and manslaughter both are illegal, but in all English-speaking countries the latter is held to be much the more shocking crime of the two. It is a distinction of this kind – between illegal detention and search on the one hand and piracy with manslaughter on the other hand – that is accountable for the different attitude of the American administration toward the British as contrasted with the German irregularities; and it is this difference that has finally thrown the forces of the American republic into the scale against German imperialism. And it is this difference that still continues to be invisible to the patriotic German historians.

III. Reports

As to a Proposed Inquiry into Baltic and Cretan Antiquities*

The problem on which my interest in prehistoric matters finally converges is that of the derivation and early growth of those free or popular institutions which have marked off European civilization at its best from the great civilizations of Asia and Africa. These characteristic free institutions of the Western culture comprise the decisive traits of the domestic and religious life as well as those of the civil and political organization. It is conceived that the underlying forces to which this scheme of free institutions owes its rise and its sustained and peculiar growth are to be looked for (*a*) in the peculiar native endowment of the races (or race) involved in the case, and (*b*) in the material (economic) circumstances under which the Western peoples have lived, particularly in early times. The centers of this cultural growth, as first known to history, have been the Aegean or East Mediterranean region on the one hand and the North Sea–Baltic region on the other hand. Within these regions, again, exploration has latterly thrown Crete, with its cultural neighbors and ramifications, into the foreground as the early center of growth and diffusion of the Aegean-Mediterranean culture, while it has similarly centered attention on the shores of the narrow Scandinavian waters as the most characteristic center of early culture in the North Sea–Baltic region. And (*c*) quite recently the Pumpelly explorations in Turkestan

* Application for grant in 1910. Published under the title, "An Unpublished Project of Thorstein Veblen for an Ethnological Inquiry," with an editorial note by Joseph Dorfman, in *The American Journal of Sociology*, September 1933.

have brought to light a culture (at Anau) of a very striking character and showing features that argue for a degree of relationship – racial, economic, and institutional – to these European centers, such as should merit close inquiry.

There is apparently reason to look for (*a*) a racial connection in prehistoric (Neolithic) times between the peoples of the Aegean (Crete, etc.) and the peoples centering about the south shores of the Baltic, and (*b*) a sustained cultural connection, resting on trade relations, between the same regions and running through the Neolithic and Bronze Ages of northern Europe. It is believed that a sufficiently attentive canvass of the evidence will bring out a consequent similarity of character in the institutions under which the peoples of these two regions lived; which would argue that these two sources of what is most characteristic in later Western civilization are in great measure to be traced back to a common origin, racial and economic. And it is conceived that the late-known culture of Anau will come in as a complementary factor to round out this scheme of cultural growth by supplying elements which have hitherto seemed lacking in any attempted system of European prehistory. The "Aryan" explanation of this community of institutions, it may be added, is no longer tenable.

A study of other primitive cultures, remote and not visibly related to this early European civilization, shows a close correlation between the material (industrial and pecuniary) life of any given people and their civic, domestic, and religious scheme of life; and it shows, further, that the myths and the religious cult reflect the character of these other – especially the economic and domestic – institutions in a peculiarly naïve and truthful manner.

An inquiry looking to the end here proposed, therefore, must have recourse to such industrial and pecuniary facts as are reflected by the available archaeological sites and exhibits, on the one hand, and to such indications of myth and religious cult as are afforded by the same explorations. These will have to be the main lines of approach, and it is along these lines that it is here proposed to review the evidence pertinent to the case — with the stress falling on the economic forces involved. A very considerable body of material is now available for such a study in this field of European prehistory, but little has been done toward exploiting it for the purpose here indicated. Nor has the material hitherto been canvassed in any comprehensive manner with such a question in mind.

While much of the material to be drawn on has been published in excellent shape, its publication has been under the hand of students and scholars animated with other interests than those here spoken for — more particularly has the economic (industrial and pecuniary) bearing of the materials exhibited received relatively scant attention. The men who have canvassed and edited the published materials have necessarily seen those materials in the light of their own interest, and so have brought out chiefly those features of the material upon which the light of their own interest would fall most strongly. Any student who approaches the material from a new quarter, therefore, and requires it to answer questions that were not present or not urgent in the minds of those earlier students, must see and review the sites and exhibits for himself and make such use as he can of these materials, with the help of other men already engaged in the general field which he enters. It is no less requisite to come into close personal contact with the men engaged than it is to make first-hand acquaintance with the available materials; for it is a most common trait of scientists, particularly when occupied with matter that is in any degree novel and growing, that they know and are willing to impart many things that are not primarily involved in the direct line of their own inquiry and many things, too, to which they may not be ready to commit themselves in print.

The evidences of the peculiar technological bent characteristic of Western civilization run very far back in the North Sea–Baltic culture, and the later explorations in Crete and its cultural dependencies suggest a similar aptitude for technological efficiency in the prehistoric Aegean culture. It is believed that a patient scrutiny of the available material for the two regions will go far to show (*a*) in what degree the two civilizations are to be correlated or contrasted on this technological side of their growth, (*b*) how far this technological peculiarity is to be traced back to racial or to environmental factors, and (*c*) what is the nature and force of the correlation, if any, between this peculiar development of technological efficiency and the early growth and character of that scheme of free institutions which today is as characteristic a trait of Western civilization as is its preeminence in point of technological efficiency.

It will be seen, therefore, that such an inquiry as is here had in view would require time and would involve a somewhat extended itinerary. At the outset, it is believed, a visit should be made to two or three of the less sophisticated Indian Pueblos of the Southwest, as the best available outside term of comparison by which to check certain features of the European evidence and particularly certain of the facts shown in the explorations at Anau.

The next move should, presumably, be to the sites and museums of Denmark and Sweden, with a side excursion of a somewhat detailed character to the British Museum and to certain archaeologists and ethnologists in England whose information and speculations must necessarily be drawn on.

The Scandinavian scholars have the archaeology of their own region excellently well in hand, and their exhaustive acquaintance with the culture of later Germanic-Scandinavian paganism is likewise indispensable to a comprehensive survey of the question. Certain men and exhibits in Germany and Austria must also be seen and made use of, though this will presumably require less time and attention than the earlier and later stages in the proposed itinerary. The sites and exhibits of the Hallstatt and La Tene culture should also be visited, with more or less painstaking attention; and certain localities of northern Italy, marking one of the cultural areas that once in prehistoric times maintained trade relations with the Baltic, should likewise be seen and appreciated. There are also Italian students in this field whose aid is expected to be of first-rate value, both in the ethnology and the archaeology of the case.

More detailed study as well as a greater allowance of time would necessarily be given to the several sites in the Aegean, with Crete as the central and most important point; where a somewhat protracted residence would be desirable if not indispensable, and from which excursions might profitably be made to Sicily, southeastern Asia Minor, Cyprus, and perhaps Transcaspia, as well as to several localities in the Aegean territory proper. These excursions outside of the Aegean lands seem, at this distance at least, less requisite than a residence of some months in Crete and the visits to Aegean sites supplementary to the study of Crete. The residence in the Aegean here spoken of, with the allowance of time which it would involve, is desirable in part on account of the very appreciable mass of printed material bearing on the case, and which could most expeditiously and effectively be acquired, assimilated, and checked by a person living within striking distance of the sites with which the descriptive material deals.

It is believed that, in point of time, the inquiry so had in view should advantageously consume not less than three years.

Expense and Time Required for Executing Project*

The most considerable item of expense will be for travel and residence in the several localities comprised in the itinerary. This will necessarily vary greatly from one date and place to another, according as the time is spent chiefly in one place or in visiting different sites and museums. Residence for several months in such a place as Copenhagen or Stockholm, e.g., would be appreciably less expensive than a similar period of itinerant life in England or Germany; even if such a period of residence includes, as it must, several excursions to sites within the Scandinavian region. No precise estimate of this item can, therefore, be offered, particularly as the exigencies of the inquiry in this respect cannot well be foreseen. The present outlook is that something more than a year would be required in north Europe – Denmark, Sweden, England and North Germany – and it is estimated that the expenses of residence and travel for this earlier part of the itinerary should fall within $3,000. A year or more in the Aegean region, including several excursions to various sites and to confer with various scholars and specialists, may be estimated at approximately the like amount, though it would be likely to prove more rather than less expensive than the same length of time spent in the North. The concluding fractional year, assuming that three years be allowed for the itinerary, would comprise several short periods of residence in several cities, most likely Berlin, Copenhagen, Paris and

* Published here for the first time. This was summarized in the editorial note by Joseph Dorfman when the "Proposal" was first published.

London, for the purpose of comparing notes and consulting with specialists, reviewing museum exhibits, and finally digesting and presenting whatever results may be reached. In connection with the period of residence in the Aegean, or perhaps immediately following it, an excursion to Transcaspia and the intervening regions of Asia Minor may also prove advisable. It seems probable that the expenditures for this concluding period, therefore, would not fall far short of either of the two earlier named periods. So that the total expenses for travel and residence for the three years assumed are in this way to be estimated at some $7500-$9000. Expenditures for materials to be purchased would be relatively slight, being chiefly printed and photographic matter. Presumably, $400-$800 should cover this item.

Something may be needed in the way of personal service and assistance, as, e.g., in the transcription of documents, translation (from the Slavic languages), and typewriting. This should presumably not exceed the amount indicated for materials. Indeed, it is hoped that this item may prove quite inconsiderable, unless it should be found necessary to go somewhat narrowly into the relations of the early Aegean culture to the Homeric and later Greek civilization. In this latter event, the desirable course would seem to be the appointment, for a year or a year and a half, of an associate who should be somewhat expert in Greek philology and archaeology.

Finally, since my retirement from university work leaves me without an income, some provision of that character would necessarily be involved in my taking up this inquiry. I am accustomed to a salary of $3000, but in this matter I shall, of course, be glad to defer entirely to the discretion of the Executive Committee.

The total expense would in this way be estimated at some

$8000 to $10,000, exclusive of any allowance for salary; or if a salary account of some $3000 a year be included, the whole might be rated at some $16,000 to $20,000.

I greatly regret that a more exact estimate cannot be had.

T. B. V.

Interim Report on the I.W.W. and the Food Supply[*]

United States Food Administration
Washington, D.C.

106 Lathrop Road
Columbia, Missouri
2 April 1918

My dear Mr. Pearl:

This is again a report ad interim and consists of opinions and explanations. I expect to follow it in two days with a more extended and more matter-of-fact statement.

As Mr. Lubin will have written you, on reaching Minneapolis some ten days ago I was laid up with a severe cold, from which I can scarcely claim to be recovered yet. So I came home here and have been confined to the house through the past week, meantime sending Mr. Lubin out to Dakota and western Iowa to make inquiries and report to me. He has now returned here.

As the outcome of my own inquiries in Minneapolis and Mr. Lubin's information from the Dakotas and Iowa, I have reached a very decided impression that the case of North Dakota is critical and urgent. The critical region is chiefly in North Dakota in the west, and in a degree in eastern Montana and reaching over slightly to South Dakota. Geographically it is an area that was subject to drought last season and consequently to crop failure in a degree. In this area, particularly inside of the boundaries of North Dakota, the farmers are short of seed – wheat, corn and barley – and also short of labor and of funds with which to hire labor for the

[*] With the exception of the second and last paragraphs this report was originally published in *The American Economic Review*, September 1933.

planting season. By a peculiar complication they are also unable to borrow. The Farm Loan corporation (branch of the Treasury Department) with local headquarters at Minneapolis refuses on grounds of formality to lend to the North Dakota farmers because they are unable to give a 1st lien on crops or real-estate to cover the loan. A county bonding measure passed in North Dakota this last season is held to impose a 1st lien on the crops and real-estate, which affords the Farm loan people an excuse for refusing to act. This much is fact. The following is opinion. The Farm loan people, in collusion with the A.F.L. representatives of the Department of Labor and equally political representatives of the Department of Agriculture, are collusively playing politics to queer the Non Partisan League (which is in control in North Dakota) at all costs. The fortunes of the War and the chances of famine are a secondary consideration in the County, State and National party politics of these North Western states. All this is only known, not proven, but well enough known for all that.

The situation in North Dakota, therefore, can not be saved without sacrificing certain formalities. It is doubtful if sufficient spring-wheat seed can now be got into the state and distributed soon enough in any case; very doubtful. Suitable seed corn – Northern Flint – can probably not be found short of New England, and cannot be moved across to North Dakota in time (about the 20th May) unless the Railroads can be induced to make a special order and make a special effort. (In this connection, I gravely suspect that the Railway Administration will lend itself to political manoeuvres for defeating the Non Partisan League.) The best chance would be for seed barley, which can apparently be found in Canada, perhaps in Minnesota to some extent, and on the Pacific Coast. Barley can be sown later than Spring wheat;

so that there is still time to get the seed barley into the state and distributed early enough to cause no hindrance to the barley crop. But to get the seed into the farmers hands the Food Administration will have to disregard formalities and go over the heads of the Farm loan people as well as of the representatives of the Agricultural Department. It appears to be not a question of placing Farm Loans and of the purchase of the seed by the farmers, so much as it is a question of distributing the seed and getting it planted, and then patching up the monetary questions involved afterward. I would like to suggest also that, for the sake of procuring a supply of labor in the Dakotas, all Federal indictments and prosecutions against supposed members of the I.W.W. be immediately quashed, and that prompt measures be taken to prevent County and State authorities in these Northwestern states from hindering the free movement of workmen and from prosecuting any persons for the time being on the ground of alleged working men's disturbances or of affiliations with the I.W.W. This is also a political complication and is closely bound up with the campaign of the old-line politicians against the Non Partisan League.

You will appreciate that, in what I have been saying, my only point is to bring out the necessity of prompt and independent action on the part of the Food Administration if it is to save the grain crops in this particular area of North Dakota. What I have said about the politics of the case I should probably not be able to substantiate to the satisfaction of anyone who is interested in these politics on one side or the other. It is only an outsider's impression of a particular political muddle and the mischief which it is causing just now.

As I have already indicated, I have been laid up with a severe cold and its effects, and so have been unable to travel. I am now intending to leave here Thursday night, the 4th

April, to reach Washington about one week after that date, going by way of Urbana, Illinois, Chicago, Ithaca, N.Y. and New York City, in each of which places I am looking to find information of sufficient value to be worth while. If, for any reason, it seems desirable for me to return direct to Washington this week, kindly wire me here. I am telegraphing you to the same effect this morning. Mr. Lubin will probably go direct from Chicago to Washington, to arrive there about the beginning of the week.

Yours very truly,

T. B. Veblen

A Poem

The Following Lines are Respectfully Dedicated to the Class of '82 by One who Sympathizes with Them in Their Recent Bereavement*

Ye shall hear how the Sophomores gathered on that bleak
December day,
When Death had come among them and taken their dearest
away:
How they met in that "upper chamber," and the spirit came –
(I know
Not if it came down upon them, or if it came from below).

How they went through those halls of learning, with
measured steps and slow,
The Sophomores and the others who had come to see the
show,
Went one and one through the hall-way and through the
half-open door,
And stood in the hall of mourning and covered all the floor.

They waited and gathered in silence as they looked on the
lengthening face
Of the sire of the dear departed, who stood by the solemn
place,
Where the dust of the loved one rested in that longest, last
repose;
And with head bowed down with sorrow, he meekly spake
through the nose.

---

* Copy in possession of editor.

And called on the long-robed chaplain to say the final prayer,
And to say a word of comfort for the sad ones gathered there:
And with form bowed down with grieving, as it were with the weight of years,
And with eyes that were dull and glassy with the burden of unshed tears,

The man of pious phrases stretched forth his weary hand
As though he would beckon the lost one back from the spirit land:
He read from the lore of the sages of the half-forgotten past,
And taught how all things human must go to the "dickens" at last:

"And each must leave his loved ones, and all he has deemed of worth,
And see with sighs and longings, the fair things of the earth
Fade from his dimming vision, as the lengthening shadows fade
In the sombre hour of twilight, into the darkness and the shade.

"Yet who shall blame the quiet that comes to the human breast
When the task of life is ended and the fates shall 'give us a rest'."
Then his voice sank low and he spake not, and then for a little space
Was a hush such as each man findeth at the latter end of his days.

But again, in words of wisdom worth more than gold and gems,
He spoke – and he made the beginning in a voice like the rustling stems

Of sedges that shake in the night-wind: but it rose to a shriek at the last,
As the flood of thought went backward and his heart was filled with the past.

He quoted again the scripture wisdom, and " 'Vanity
Of vanities,' " said the preacher, " 'All is vanity .'
'The silver cord is broken: the pitcher is broke at the well,'
And, cut off in a 'deuce' of a hurry, our sweetest is gone to h - - -."

And in woeful lamentation the voice of that joyless crowd
Rose into a great murmur in wailing long and loud:
And wilder it grew and bolder, while the mass swayed to and fro,
And beat their breasts and faces in the ecstasy of woe.

And the chaplain spoke unheeded, for the boots of the Sophomores
Joined in the lamentation and angrily trod the floor:
And the mournful crashing and wailing grew louder and yet more loud
Till, at once, an icy tremor ran through the yelling crowd.

And silence came upon them as the chaplain raised the pall,
And the pale face of the dead one looked starkly on them all:
Silence came upon them, and the class of '82,
With their eyes and teeth in water, and their noses pinched and blue,

Stood and looked, in the silence, on the loved and lifeless thing
Till the chaplain beckoned to them and bade them join and sing
A hymn for the dead one's glory, and for their own increase
In grace and consolation, in humbleness and peace.

Then one after another they joined, and the chant arose,
Swelling and rolling grandly, the chant of "The Three Black Crows."
Then, as the song was ended, the chaplain's tender hand
Threw back the pall o'er the dead one, and the silent, chosen band

Of bearers took up the burden—the beloved burden of woe—
And passed again through the door-way with uncertain steps and slow:
They passed from the hall of mourning, and close on either side
Of the bier there walked, with sorrow that they scarcely strove to hide,

The long-robed priest and the father of the one whose days were done,
And behind them friends and kin-folk tardily, one by one.
Then the broken voice of sorrow took up the chant once more,
While boots, such as Sophomores only enjoy, beat time on the dusty floor.

And thus the long procession chanted the bitter wail:
"Did you ever, ever, ever, ever, ever, see a whale?"
And so the long procession wound slowly across the wold,
While the winds of gray December, pitiless and cold,

Sighed and moaned about them, and played with the shiftless hair
Of the maids and the gown of the chaplain that fluttered black through the air:
But in the falling twilight of the bleak December day,
When the earth fell back on the coffin, and clay returned to clay,

The broken, quivering voices died out in bitter moans,
And the spades threw back in silence the frozen earth and
  stones
On the hollow lid of the coffin until the college bell,
Swung by its own compassion, struck the departing knell.

O, Carleton! O, Mother Carleton! thy high ones are humbled
  and low.
O, Carleton! O, stricken Carleton! remember, I told you so.

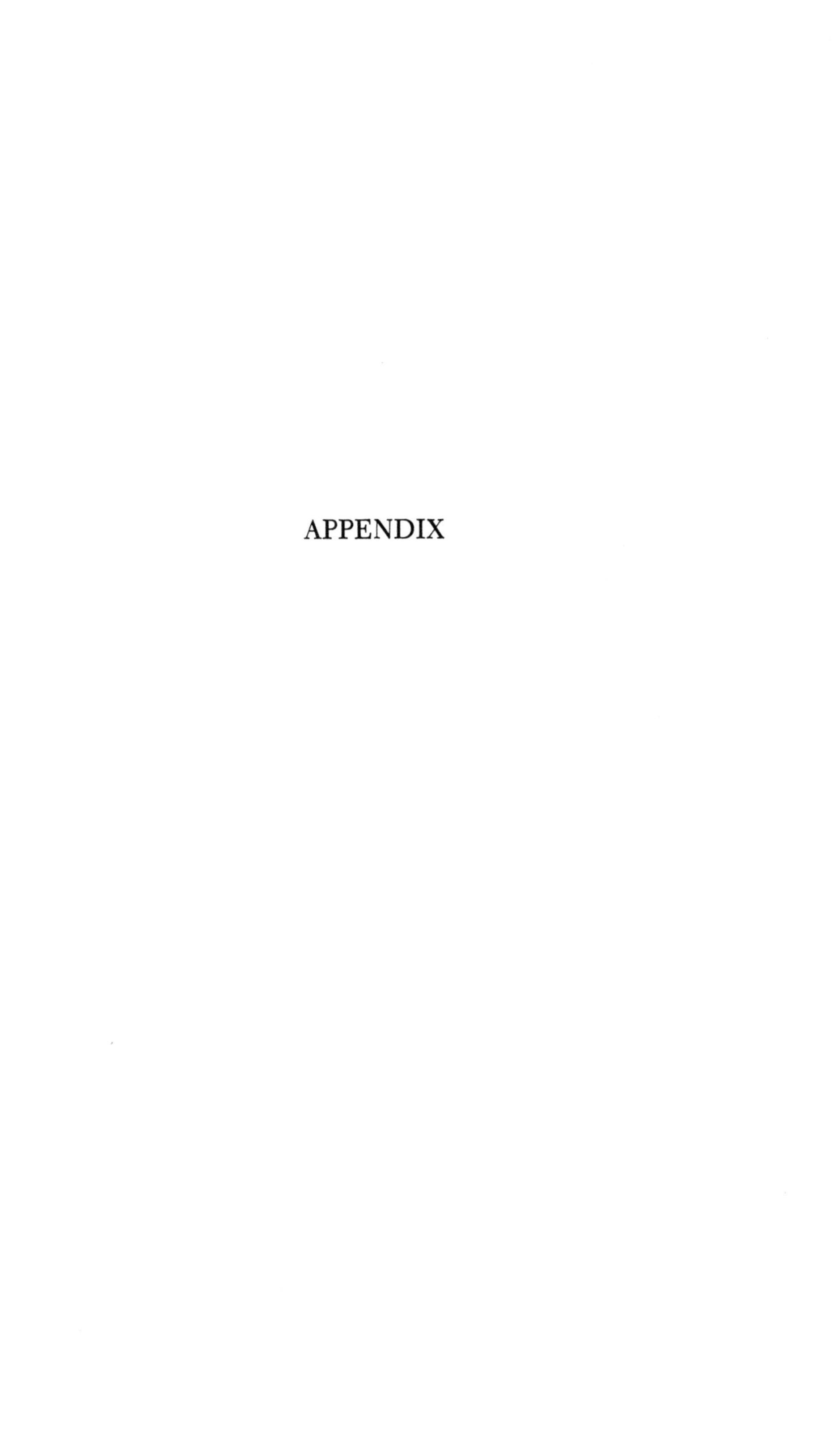

APPENDIX

Selected Obituaries

Thorstein Bunde Veblen
1857-1929*

By John Maurice Clark

On August 3 of this year Thorstein B. Veblen died in California at the age of seventy-two, after a period of retirement due to ill health. With his passing, American economics has lost its most picturesque figure, and the leading influence of the intellectual generation immediately succeeding the founders of the American Economic Association.

In the spring of 1880 a member of the Junior class at Carleton College presented to the faculty an unprecedented request. He asked to be permitted, at the end of that academic year, to take the examinations for the Junior and Senior classes both. Attempts to dissuade him were futile; he took all responsibility and asked only to make the attempt at his own risk. The task seemed impossible, as the academic year was already far spent; and the faculty feared injury to his health. Nor were they inclined to make concessions to this particular student, whose unconventional character had not endeared him to an institution where smoking was ground for expulsion and the professor of mathematics opened every class exercise with prayer. But permission could hardly be refused; and the tests were given, that in economics being under a young professor by the name of John Bates Clark. It soon became evident that the student could not be baffled by any legitimate question; and he passed a virtually flawless examination. In this manner Thorstein Veblen received his college degree, rated by one at least of his professors as the most brilliant man the college had graduated.

* *The American Economic Review*, December 1929.

Eleven years later, J. Laurence Laughlin, rising young professor at Cornell, made the acquaintance of a young Fellow in the department; a man worn with illness and plainly a stranger to prosperity, but with an intellectual vitality and a fund of wide and curious learning which so impressed him that when he went next year to head the department at the new University of Chicago he took the young Fellow with him. Thus Veblen began his academic career in economics. He had taken his doctor's degree in philosophy at Yale in 1884, and subsequently continued by private reading to add to his erudition in the fields of biology, anthropology, and cultural history. This constituted, for an economist, a unique background.

At Chicago, before the end of the nineties, his early critical essays challenged the attention of the economic world with their unaccustomed standards and unsettling demands. Then followed his career on the faculties of Stanford, the University of Missouri and the New School for Social Research; and the succession of volumes which established his reputation. Always aloof from the organized activities of the economic gild, he was in 1925 offered the nomination for presidency of the American Economic Association, but declined.

As to the merits of his work, opinions differ more widely and more fervently than on any other writer of equal prominence. He is rated among the great economists of history, or as no economist at all; as a great original pioneer or as a critic and satirist without constructive talent or achievement. And he was, one might almost say, all of these things; from different standpoints and by different criteria, each of which it is possible to understand and even to appreciate. One thing at least can be said. If he chose to paint after a futurist technique of his own devising, it was not for lack of capacity to master the academic canons. He had thought through them to his own satisfaction and passed on to other areas of inquiry which appeared to him more interesting and more fruitful.

His critical essays probably left the majority of readers, who were not forewarned and prepared, resentfully rubbing numerous sore spots and wondering with some bewilderment what it was all about. They were criticised for not doing what they had never set out to do, and for not being what it had never occurred to them to be; while the worth of what they had undertaken was brushed aside with airy disparagement. And Veblen's style resembled a barbed-wire entanglement, difficult to penetrate and with rapier-sharp points to prick the unwary. Those who quickly dismissed the problem are probably those who have not seen Veblen as an economist at all, or have seen him as merely a critic and satirist. Those who continued to wonder, and to some purpose, owe him the greatest of educational experiences: that of being forced to rethink their basic conceptions, and to make terms of some sort with a radically different point of view which could not be wholly dismissed.

His positive analysis of economic society includes two main groups of elements. There are evolutionary studies of our ways of thinking and of doing things. These include the effects of changing economic techniques (*e.g.*, The Cultural Incidence of the Machine Process[1]) and the continuing effect of older cultural forces (*e.g.*, the *Theory of the Leisure Class*). These studies regularly culminate in a changed perspective on the character of the present economic system. In the second group of elements in Veblen's positive analysis, he focussed attention on those things which were left out of the customary study of levels of static-competitive equilibrium. His treatment of pecuniary as distinct from in-

[1] [This is Chapter X of *The Theory of Business Enterprise*].

dustrial employments would be regarded by the orthodox economist as a study largely in the realm of the "higgling" of the bargaining process: something whose existence he readily admitted but which he excluded from the search for competitive norms, treating it as a somewhat incidental excrescence. By styling this process "business" Veblen added the implication that this neglected activity is the main preoccupation and effect of private business, and that the limitations imposed on it by competition are incidental and not sufficiently effective to deserve serious analysis. Their results he admitted casually, if at all, under the modicum of serviceability which is prerequisite to pecuniary profit, not troubling even to trace this to its causes. After which he would often clinch the effect by remarking that if the terms he had used seemed to carry unfavorable implications, this was solely the result of the nature of the facts themselves. Thus did he thinly mask a surpassingly able use of the logical devices of selective emphasis – devices not found in treatises on the syllogism but ever-present in the actual processes of human thinking.

Veblen's analysis, then, is not the completely objective tracing of impersonal sequences of cause and effect which his essays on method call for; but is – as anything human must probably be – a matter of selected aspects. One of the unanswered puzzles about this intriguing thinker, at least to those who did not know him intimately, is his own attitude toward this subjective element entering into his avowedly objective treatment. It may be a trait of genius to combine clear consciousness of method with a gift of leaping over some of the steps and intuitively seizing tools apt to the securing of desired effects. And there is no point in obtruding ponderous questionings upon such a delightfully agile play of thought around a theme whose essential consistency is so plainly evident.

Doubtless the facts did dictate the interpretation Veblen gave them – he being what he was. But among the most controlling of these facts was the selective emphasis he found in the orthodox treatment. And by presenting selective aspects calculated to offset those of orthodoxy, he has rendered the greatest possible service toward a better balanced treatment than either. And in this matter balance is probably the closest approach to objectivity of which the human mind is capable. This end, needless to say, cannot be attained by blind discipleship, but by a discriminating assimilation.

And such assimilation has not been wanting. Veblen has influenced Davenport, Mitchell and Hoxie, to name only three: men of too great independence to be anyone's disciples and therefore capable of transmitting Veblen's influence as it needed to be transmitted. In such hands it becomes, not a finished gospel, but an orienting impulse and an assortment of concepts to be tested by the work they will do.

Was Veblen an economist? He was not a mere economist, certainly. A philosopher first, and then a student of human cultures, he was always interested in these things for their own sakes as well as in their relation to purely economic facts. Was he a scientist? He was not, perhaps, by the criterion of John Stuart Mill, who held that it was only by virtue of competition and competitive equilibria that economists can be scientists at all. But that criterion can no longer be said to be orthodox.

Was Veblen "constructive"? Not in the sense of constructing a "system" of defined levels of equilibrium or other definitive results; the materials with which he worked did not lend themselves to this, nor was it his idea of a proper (and Darwinian) scientific goal. Not in the sense of making his work an outgrowth of previous orthodoxy; that was not to be expected. Not in the sense of furnishing his followers a complete substitute for that orthodoxy in the form of propositions with which to solve all problems – that is far more than one man's work. He was not constructive in the sense of explaining the socially constructive forces in the world of private business – it was not in that direction that the prevailing emphasis needed to be redressed. And not in the sense of proving to what quantitative degree business is governed by the principles he assumes – that test is only beginning to be applied to any of our doctrines. But if an independent explanation of important and neglected ranges of economic facts be constructive, Veblen meets the test in generous measure.

And he has left his mark. Since he began his work, the conception of the evolution of economic institutions has acquired the beginnings of real meaning for a majority of economists; and "cumulative causation" is part of our mental equipment. The emphasis has swung from reasoning on abstract levels of equilibrium to the observation of actual behavior and the organization of its sequences; and man is beginning to be really viewed as a product of a biological past rather than as a utilitarian machine. We are suspicious of subconscious motives and alert to wastes inherent in business practices. Veblen is, of course, not responsible for all this; and much of it has taken forms he never espoused or practised. But there is enough of his influence in it to make us wonder whether we have not had a prophet among us. A prophet's road is not the route to easy popularity with his contemporaries. But this one has not been wholly without honor, even in his own country.

Thorstein Veblen: 1857–1929*

By Wesley C. Mitchell

ACCORDING to its indexes, the ECONOMIC JOURNAL has reviewed but one of Thorstein Veblen's eleven books. The issue of September 1925 contains a notice of *The Theory of the Leisure Class* – a volume published twenty-six years earlier and just then reprinted for the ninth time. It seems a natural inference that Veblen's work is not widely known to British economists. Among American economists, on the contrary, no contemporary stands out more clearly from the crowd. Opinions differ sharply concerning the value of his contributions, critical and constructive; but there is no doubt that his influence is wide and deep.

To account for the slight attention paid to Veblen outside of his own country is not difficult. Professor Graham Wallas, who owns a desire "to give him the old-fashioned name of 'genius,'" sorrowfully confesses that "Veblen's books are, even for a professional student, pretty stiff reading."[1] The subject-matter is difficult in that Veblen attacks problems strange to economists and uses evidence few of us can weigh. Even more disconcerting to many is his style – and in his

* *The Economic Journal*, December 1929.

[1] "Veblen's Imperial Germany and the Industrial Revolution," *The Quarterly Journal of Economics*, November 1915, pp. 179-87.

case certainly the style is the man. Professor Wallas wished Veblen "to write a new book, in which he shall drop the irony and reticence which is such an admirable means of self-protection for a sensitive teacher who thinks for himself." That Veblen could not or would not do. He was an original, whom the discipline of life in a land of "regular fellows" could not standardise. Those who strive to profit by his uncanny penetration into the foibles of modern society do well to study first his strange personal equation.

A son of Norwegian immigrants, born in Wisconsin in 1857 and brought up on a farm in Minnesota, Veblen did not come into close contact with English-speaking Americans until at twenty years of age he entered Carleton College – a small congregational institution near his home. He found his new associates queer people. They accepted without question conventional modes of thinking and acting quite different from those which prevailed among his own people. Veblen had the strength of mind to resist assimilation, and the urge to inquire how conventions arise and spread. Also he took a naughty pleasure in quizzing earnest souls who felt it bad form to probe respectable beliefs. He loved to propound elaborate explanations for things which most people regard as the plainest common sense. And the more these explanations made folk squirm, the more Veblen enjoyed them.

With this trait Veblen united wide curiosity and remarkable powers of assimilating knowledge. He was a close observer of plants and animals as well as of people, a deft craftsman who liked to experiment with new materials, a quick linguist, an omnivorous reader. Among all the routes leading to the unknown regions he longed to explore, philosophy seemed to his youthful mind the most promising. After graduating from Carleton College he went to Johns Hopkins and then to Yale, where in 1884 he took a doctor's degree in philosophy, with a dissertation upon "Ethical Grounds of a Doctrine of Retribution." But he could find no opening to teach: in those days chairs of philosophy were usually occupied by retired clergymen. Returning to Minnesota, Veblen remained a studious recluse for seven years. Finally, in 1891, an opportunity came to enter Cornell as a student of economics. From that time forward he lived a none-too-smooth life as a teacher and writer upon economics, passing in succession to Chicago, Stanford, Missouri and the New School for Social Research in New York, where he lectured from 1918 until his retirement in 1926.

Veblen thus brought to economics the detachment of a visitor from Mars, a confirmed habit of ironical expression, a specialist's grounding in philosophy, and the loot of much miscellaneous reading. A man familiar with Kant is not overawed by the technical parts of economic theory. Nor does he miss the philosophical implications of what is said. Veblen was intrigued by what seemed to him the naïve preconceptions entertained by the masters of political economy from Dr. Quesnay to Dr. Marshall. In particular their notions of human nature seemed to him curious. Contemporary theorists had not really freed themselves from that rationalised concept of behaviour which Bentham had set forth in such downright fashion. Yet Darwin's studies of the instincts, supplemented by William James' analysis of the formation and functioning of habits, had reduced the felicific calculus from its eighteenth-century status as an instrument of scientific inquiry to the status of a quaint delusion. Even the attenuated modern forms of this calculus were mischievous in that they diverted attention from genuine problems. Veblen did not say all this in good round terms. That was not his way. He explained that the conclusions reached by economic theorists were quite consistent with the premises, overt and tacit, from which the theorists reasoned. He sought to show how the notions of human nature employed had become current. He inquired why the pale ghost of hedonism still haunted economic treatises after the body had been decently buried in treatises upon psychology. In short, he dealt quizzically with economic theory as an intellectual curiosity which called for explanation, and thereby annoyed many people who would have taken a frontal attack with good grace.

The fundamental difficulty with economics, in his view, was that it does not conceive its problems in the proper way. Under the spell of Darwin, Veblen held that –

> In so far as it is a science in the current sense of the term, any science, such as economics, which has to do with human conduct, becomes a genetic inquiry into the human scheme of life; and where, as in economics, the subject of inquiry is the conduct of man in his dealings with the material means of life, the science is necessarily an inquiry into the life-history of material civilisation, on a more or less extended or restricted plan. . . . Like all human culture this material civilisation is a scheme of institutions – institutional fabric and institutional growth.[2]

Institutions "are settled habits of thought common to the generality of men."[3] The problems proper to economics, ac-

---

[2] "The Limitations of Marginal Utility," 1909. Reprinted in *The Place of Science in Modern Civilisation and other Essays* (B. W. Huebsch, 1919) pp. 240, 241.

[3] *Ibid.*, p. 239.

cordingly, are problems of genesis and cumulative change in widely-diffused habits of thought concerning ways and means. Such problems must be treated in terms of causation, not in terms of rational choice.

> The two methods of inference — from sufficient reason and from efficient cause — are out of touch with one another and there is no transition from one to the other: no method of converting the procedure or the results of the one into those of the other.[4]

In his constructive work Veblen followed the line thus marked out. He investigated a variety of institutions, or institutional complexes, from the leisure class to the machine process, business enterprise and absentee ownership. Always he sought to explain in causal terms why a certain way of looking at things arose and why that way changed in the course of time. Always he treated behaviour as a whole, not caring to mark off a narrow segment as strictly economic. Always he saw contemporary man as a product of age-long savagery, bewildered by the changes in conditions which he has unwittingly brought upon himself. And always Veblen played with the feelings of his readers quite as much as he played with ideas. Even when he dealt with questions which have a place in standard treatises on economics — such as credit, business combinations, profits, socialism — he drew little from, and he contributed little to, the standard discussions. For the problems which he thought significant are not the problems ordinarily attacked. As he put it, inference from efficient cause and inference from sufficient reason are out of touch with one another, and there is no transition from one to the other. Quite naturally many economists held that whatever his work may be, it is not economic theory.

---

[4] *Ibid.*, p. 237.

We shall have no more of these investigations, with their curious erudition, their irony, their dazzling phrases, their bewildering reversals of problems and values. Veblen died in July, among the Californian hills which he fondly likened to the lands that never were outside of William Morris's romances. But those whose intellectual interests are not limited to conventional lines will long find in his work a treasure of subtle suggestion. The sophisticated who can bear to have their share in human frailty exposed will read with quaking pleasure. Perhaps the best book to sample by way of introduction is the volume of collected essays, entitled *The Place of Science in Modern Civilisation* (1919). *The Theory of the Leisure Class* (1899) is the most playful and popular of the full-length discussions, while *Absentee Ownership* (1923) is starkly terrible at times beneath its bland surface. Economists will feel most at home with *The Theory of Business Enterprise* (1904), psychologists with *The Instinct of Workmanship* (1914), and political scientists with *Imperial Germany* (1915) or with *An Inquiry into the Nature of Peace and the Terms of its Perpetuation* (1917). But Veblen demands much of his readers, and not everyone who sips will have the stamina to drink.

Thorstein Veblen 1857–1929*

By Wesley C. Mitchell

WHEN President Harper was collecting a faculty for the new University of Chicago to be opened in 1893, he showed remarkable foresight and had remarkable luck. John Dewey and Michelson were among his recruits, Jacques Loeb, Chamberlain and Coulter, William Vaughn Moody and Paul

* *The New Republic*, September 4, 1929.

Shorey. So, too, was Thorstein Veblen, an unknown quantity assigned to a minor post in the department of economics on the recommendation of J. Laurence Laughlin.

Veblen was then a large-eyed, brown bearded, slow-speaking, quiet person in the middle thirties. The son of thrifty Norwegian immigrants, born in Wisconsin and brought up on a Minnesota farm, he had entered Carleton College at twenty, gone on to Johns Hopkins and Yale for post-graduate work, and taken a doctor's degree in philosophy. But for seven long years the new doctor had found no academic post. In American colleges philosophy was still being taught commonly by retired clergymen, and young scholars of unknown convictions were seldom wanted. So Veblen had returned to Minnesota, read widely, written more or less, and done some nondescript office work. Finally in 1891 Cornell awarded him a fellowship, not in philosophy, but in economics and finance. A critical paper upon "Some Neglected Points in the Theory of Socialism" revealed his quality to Professor Laughlin, and resulted in Veblen's move to Chicago.

This offshoot of Norwegian culture, reared in an American environment of farm life and conventional schools, had disconcerting ways. He observed the tamest acts and commonest opinions of those about him with narrowed eyes, as if they were curious phenomena which called for an explanation. Now and then he would drop a quizzical comment, which came from outer space like a meteor, shocking some bystanders and amusing others. He had extraordinary notions about what was relevant to the subjects he was supposed to teach. Students who enrolled in his courses on agricultural economics and socialism heard as much about the practices of the Hopi Indians, the Samurai, the Hebrews of the Old Testament, the Andaman Islanders, and the trading pirates of the North Sea as they did about populism and Karl Marx. They were puzzled to find their own convictions and loyalties analyzed and accounted for on evolutionary grounds. The plainer was a piece of commonsense, the more universally accepted, the more curious did Veblen find it, and the farther back in human culture did he go for an explanation.

But the most disconcerting thing to students properly brought up was that Veblen never denounced nor commended anything. That tingling psychological reaction known as righteous indignation seemed lacking in his make-up – though he would inquire why different people get morally indignant with each other. Even about intellectual matters he was singularly unexcited. If an ingenuous student waxed enthusiastic about the passion for research, Veblen's temperature did not rise a degree. The root of scientific inquiry is "idle curiosity"; indulging this propensity has led successive generations of men to the quaintest of notions about the world; the stock of scientific ideas on which we now plume ourselves is blood-brother of the cosmologies which satisfied savages; that the current notions give us better control over natural forces is interesting and has significant cultural consequences; but in due time these notions will come to seem as quaint as any that are now out of date.

Small wonder that students over whose minds the "cake of custom" had formed solidly put Veblen down as a profane juggler with the verities. Others less well protected did not know what to think; but at least they began to wonder about many things they had always taken for granted – opinions other people held, even opinions they caught themselves expressing. They felt uncomfortably sophisticated, as if they had lost their mental innocence and were no longer quite respectable.

When Veblen published his first book, *The Theory of the Leisure Class*, in 1899, those of us who had been in his classes watched excitedly to see how the reading public would react. There were protests as we expected; but there were also warm praises from men of letters. William Dean Howells, in particular, smiled benignly. Veblen was classified as a social satirist – "the most powerful since Swift." That classification was a shield against attacks by the deadly serious. A satirist is permitted to speak freely, because he is not supposed to mean quite what he says. Readers are expected to chuckle; they are likely to be laughed at if they boil over with indignation. All Veblen's elaborate explanations of social foibles, professedly based upon anthropological and historical evidence, were taken as literary machinery for producing effects – an equivalent for the empire of Lilliput.

There was justification for this interpretation of the book. Veblen loved producing literary effects. He was an arch phrase-maker. He took a naughty delight in making people squirm. His aloofness, his objectivity were partly stage make-up. He did not want anyone to be quite sure when he was indulging his peculiar sense of humor at the expense of the public. He liked to feel sophisticated and to smile at the simple critics who frothed over his jibes. But, though these dispositions colored everything he ever wrote, no matter how technical, Veblen was genuinely interested in the explanations he sketched. Human behavior was to him the most fascinating puzzle in the world, and he thought he had clues to the solution – clues which the social scientists had missed, though they were suggested by writers so well known as Darwin and William James.

Accepting the current opinion of biologists that the human species has undergone but slight physical change since neolithic times at any rate, Veblen held that the gulf which yawns between the lives of modern communities and the lives of cave dwellers has been bridged, or created, by the evolution of culture. Culture is substantially a complex of widely prevalent habits of thought. Mass habits are determined primarily by the way men and women spend their time. By all odds the most time-consuming occupation of mankind is making a living. Therefore the economic factor has been most potent in shaping culture. It is primarily economic necessity that has forced us into new ways. Whenever changes in the physical environment, the dwindling of a staple food supply, migration to different habitats, or any other cause, threw their traditional methods of getting a living out of gear, men were forced to alter their practices or succumb. The new ways of working, developed through trial and error, modified old habits of thinking and added to the stock of commonplace information. In their turn these results reacted upon methods of getting a living, thereby modified habits afresh, and so on indefinitely. Thus human culture has evolved under pressure, through an age-long process of cumulative changes in standard ways of thinking by creatures with non-evolving brains.

It follows, according to Veblen, that the only explanation in harmony with modern science, of how men have behaved at any stage in their checkered career, is an account of the evolution of social habits of thought in the given community up to the given date. To be sciences at all, anthropology, economics, sociology, and politics must be evolutionary sciences on the pattern of Darwinian biology. Properly conceived, these social disciplines trace the descent of culture from the point where Darwin ended his account of the descent of man. But is that the program on which economists and their cousins are now working?

The patent answer to this question is Veblen's fundamental criticism of economic theory. In its best formulations, this body of speculations is a beautifully articulated set of doctrines, logically consistent with the preconceptions from which they are derived, and convincing to anyone who shares the view of human nature which prevailed in Western Europe shortly before and shortly after 1800. That view of human nature is still tacitly accepted by many contemporary economists, and they are content to walk a little further in the paths marked out by Adam Smith, Ricardo, and John Stuart Mill. There is no need to controvert these estimable logicians. Rather, one should inquire into the causes which have preserved economic theory from infection by latter-day science. And Veblen proceeded to explain his colleagues to themselves with all the arts he had employed in explaining leisure-class institutions. Economists were used to being criticized by each other; but they did not know what to make of this person who took them apart to show how they worked.

More important was the task of rebuilding economics upon modern lines. At this task of reconstruction Veblen worked in the unsystematic fashion congenial to him. His books are all monographs, devoted to the genetic explanation of certain institutions – that is, habits of thought which have prevailed in various times and places. What particularly fascinated him in the contemporary field were the relations between making goods and making money, between the machine process and business enterprise, engineers and absentee owners. Material well-being depends upon the steady operation of our industrial plants under the direction of scientifically trained engineers. But these plants are run for profit, by business men, in the interest of security holders who typically take no share in the work. Making money depends upon the prices paid for commodities and services used in industry and upon the prices received for the output. Business managers are concerned to keep the profit margins at the maximum-net-revenue point. They are advisedly fearful lest an increase in current supply may force selling prices so low that the larger turnover will be no comfort. Hence they habitually keep production below the point which engineering skill makes practicable with existing plant capacity. That is, the business man's chief contribution to welfare now consists in practicing "capitalistic sabotage." Given a free hand, Veblen guessed that, by reorganizing industry on a continental scale, the engineering profession could double the national income of consumable commodities without increasing working hours. But in the process they would smash myriads of independent business enterprises. So society is gestating a conflict of interests between business men and absentee owners upon the one side, and engineers and the mass of the "underlying population" upon the other.

How long this conflict of interests can be kept from becoming a conflict of classes is the leading problem of current civilization. Veblen argued, in 1904, that business enterprise cannot run a long career under our present economic institutions. For the discipline of daily work in the factory, which is the lot of an increasing number of men, breeds a practical habit of mind, which makes it increasingly difficult for the factory hand to see what right absentee owners have to an appreciable part of what he and his mates produce. Engineers, brought up on mathematics and the physical sciences, harbor similar doubts about the legitimacy of "unearned incomes." Let this habit of thought develop somewhat further, as develop it must unless the machine process is checked, and business enterprise will go the way of feudalism and slavery. After the War, Veblen seemed for a time to hope that the change might come, and come quickly. In the articles he wrote for *The Dial,* and allowed to be reprinted as books, his bland tone became strident; his analysis suggested a program of action; he repeated his favorite phrases like an agitator. But that was a passing phase. *Absentee Ownership,* the last of his books save for the translation of an "Icelandic Saga," regains much, though not all, of the elfish aloofness which marked *The Theory of Business Enterprise* and *The Instinct of Workmanship.*

Veblen's contribution to economics consisted in replacing the hedonistic conception of human nature by the instinct-habit psychology. That shift allied economics to biology rather than to mechanics. It brought new problems to the fore and relegated old problems to the background. It suggested a close working agreement between economists and the other students of human behavior – historians, psychologists, anthropologists, political scientists and sociologists. It was a service the full value of which has yet to be grasped. But like other intrepid explorers of new lands, Veblen made hasty traverses, seeing what appealed to him. His sketch maps are enormously suggestive, but not accurate in detail. For example, he looked at the "vested interests" and at the machine-tender from too far away, with the eyes of a farmer. He credited the first with more singleness and more clarity of purpose than the miscellaneous and changing aggregate of the rich can claim. He saw the machine-tender as a standardized product, which machine-tenders are far from being. More at large, Veblen let his saturnine humor color his scientific analysis. Like earlier economists, he paid too little attention to checking his conclusions by patient observation, he paid too little attention to what did not harmonize with his favorite patterns. Yet, when all detractions are made, he remains the most interesting economist of his generation, and the one who is provoking most thought in others.[1]

[1] [*The Economic Journal* has by no means been free from the influence of Veblen, although it is not always acknowledged. This was pointed out for example by a British writer in discussing a review in the April 1943 issue by Mrs. Joan Robinson of Ruby T. Norris, *The Theory of Consumer Demand*. He quoted the following from the review: "latter-day experience of the restrictions of consumption has brought into a clear light one great weakness of the traditional theory of demand . . . that is, the erroneous assumption of individualism. When a given cut in consumption has to be made, traditional theory teaches that the minimum sacrifice is imposed on consumers if the requisite amount of general purchasing power is taken away, and each consumer is left free to economise on what he feels that he can best spare. In reality, it is obvious that less sacrifice is caused by a total disappearance from the market of certain commodities, such as silk stockings, which are bought by each consumer mainly because other people have them." The writer then added: "The importance of Veblen's work in this connection is obvious." Kurt Rothschild, "The Wastes of Competition," in *Monopoly and Competition and Their Regulation*, edited by Edward H. Chamberlin (London: Macmillan, 1954) p. 311. Rothschild makes use of what he describes as "the 'conspicuous waste' of Thorstein Veblen," in *The Theory of Wages* (New York: Augustus M. Kelley Publishers, 2nd ed., 1967) p. 311].

Selected Reviews

Reviews of *The Theory of the Leisure Class*

The Luxury of Lazihead*

THE *Theory of the Leisure Class*, by Thorstein Veblen (Macmillan Company), called by way of sub-title, *An Economic Study in the Evolution of Institutions*, is a book unique in its kind. It is an elaborate scientific treatise, marching by a very distinct method to a very clearly pre-defined end, yet lively reading on nearly every page, full of shrewd observation such as, given a slightly different form and an entirely different setting, would make the literary fortune of a novelist. There is humor in the book, too, and an amazing power of seeing in common things all kinds of profound relations, meanings, symbolisms. A book which is valuable, both for its theory – of which it would not be fair to attempt a reckoning in a cursive review – and for the fascinating materials grouped with admirable skill and with most plausible effect round the central idea. A book, too, which is immensely educative: no one could take it up and even dip into it casually here and there without feeling a distinct freshening of interest in the deeper signification of the most commonplace principles, habits, venerations and dislikes of every-day existence. At every step one is flung back from the present, as by a catapult, into the most distant past. One gets a new sense of the depth of the daily things; a new feeling for the mystery of the ways of men; a keener perception of the oneness of mankind through all the variations of all

* *The Criterion*, March 25, 1899. The review was by Stephen MacKenna, the translator of Plotinus.

the centuries. And all this in the easiest, most casual way: it is an illustration from the cavaliers riding, escort to dames, in Central Park, that sends you back to the noble knighthoods of the feudal ages, back again to the tribal days when man fought for woman as for the source of the tribal greatness and power over other and hostile tribes, back of that again to the remote ages when man fought for the woman as for himself, feeling that he would be lonely and lost amid the vastness and terror of the universe if this part of himself, this partner of his fears, were to meet with harm. And so in various ways and from the commonest beginnings, the reader is always being brought face to face with the infinities – and always suavely, always without straining after eloquence or fine writing, by just a hint dropped, as it were, in the midst of a genial after-dinner chat.

It is not quite just to snap at readable excerpts from this book, since from its general method, its scientific march, meanings are very much modified or modulated by the context. But here is a passage which illustrates reasonably well the general style and tone of the writer.

"As seen from the economic point of view, leisure considered as an employment is closely allied in kind with the life of exploit; and the achievements which characterize a life of leisure and which remain as its decorous criteria, have much in common with the trophies of exploit. But leisure in the narrower sense, as distinct from exploit and from any ostensibly productive employment of effort on objects which are of no intrinsic use, does not commonly leave a material product. The criteria of a past performance of leisure, therefore, commonly take the form of 'immaterial' goods. Such immaterial evidences of past leisure are quasi-scholarly or quasi-artistic accomplishments and a knowledge of processes and incidents which do not conduce directly to the furtherance of human life. So, for instance, in our time there is the knowledge of the dead languages and the occult sciences; of correct spelling; of syntax and prosody; of the various forms of domestic music and other household art; of the latest proprieties of dress, furniture and equipage; of games, sports and fancy-bred animals, such as dogs and race-horses. In all those branches of knowledge the initial motive from which their acquisition proceeded at the outset and through which they first came into vogue, may have been something quite different from the wish to show that one's time had not been spent in industrial employment; but unless these accomplishments had approved themselves as serviceable evidence of an unproductive expenditure of time, they would not have survived and held their place as conventional accomplishments of the leisure class."

A pleasant subacid under all this shrewdness: yet how calm, how well-bred, how entirely suave and easy.

Of manners we have this:

"It is worth while to remark that all that class of ceremonial observances which are classed under the general head of manners holds a more important place in the esteem of men during the stage of culture at which conspicuous leisure has the greatest vogue as a mark of reputability than at later stages of the cultural development. . . . The decay which the code of manners has suffered at the hands of a busy people testifies – all deprecation apart – to the fact that decorum is a product and an exponent of leisure-class life and thrives in full measure only under a régime of status.

"The origin – or, better, the derivation – of manners is no doubt to be sought elsewhere than in a conscious effort on the part of the well-mannered to show that much time has been spent in acquiring them. . . . The proximate end of innovation and elaboration has been the higher effectiveness

of the new departure in point of beauty or expressiveness. In great part the ceremonial code of decorous usages owes its beginning and its growth to the desire to conciliate or to show good will. . . . and this initial motive is rarely, if ever, absent from the conduct of well-mannered persons at any stage of the later development. Manners. . . . are in part an elaboration of gesture, and in part they are symbolical and conventionalized survivals representing former acts of dominance or of personal service or of personal contest. In large part they are an expression of the relation of status – a symbolic pantomime of mastery on the one hand and of subservience on the other. . . . Their ulterior economic ground is to be sought in the honorific character of that leisure or nonproductive employment of time and effort, without which good manners are not acquired. . . . A knowledge of good form is prima facie evidence that that portion of the well-bred person's life which is not spent under the observation of the spectator has been worthily spent in acquiring accomplisments that are of no lucrative effect."
plishments that are of no lucrative effect."

"The Master's person, being the embodiment of worth and honor, is of the most serious consequence. Both for his reputable standing in the community and for his self-respect it is a matter of moment that he should have at his call efficient specialized servants, whose attendance upon his person is not diverted from this their chief office by any by-occupation. . . . There results a constantly increasing differentiation and multiplication of domestic and body servants along with a concomitant progressive exemption of such servants from productive labor. . . . Men begin to be preferred above women for service that brings them obtrusively into view. Men, especially lusty, personable fellows, as footmen and other menials should be, are obviously more powerful and more expensive than women. They are better fitted for this work as showing a larger waste of time and of human energy. . . ."

And so one might go on for an indefinite time and space, finding everywhere shrewd observation, clever reasoning, a delightful half-smile. The book deserves to be widely read and lovingly set on the nearer shelves.

*The Theory of the Leisure Class**

By LESTER FRANK WARD

A LATE critic of a book has the same advantage as the critic of an old painting. He need not have any ideas of his own. He has learned what the proper thing to say is, and he has nothing to do but to say it. In the present case the proper thing to do is to condemn the book and call it pessimistic, even "cynical." Pessimism now means: looking facts in the face; seeing things as they are; calling a spade a spade. Anyone who does this is deserving of censure as disturbing the order of things. If there is one thing that the world does not want, it is truth. Truth is a medicine that must be administered in sugar-coated pills. A very little of it reacts upon the public system and will not go down. This is no modern fact. It has always been so. It is what they used to burn folks for. Nowadays they merely put their books on a sort of moral *index librorum expurgandorum.*

The trouble with this book is that it contains too much truth. It also suggests a great deal of truth that it does not contain, and this is quite as bad as to tell the truth outright. Galileo and Servetus were not persecuted for what they said, but for the deductions that their persecutors made from what they said. The reviewers of this book base their criticisms

* *The American Journal of Sociology,* May 1900.

almost entirely on the conclusions they themselves draw from what is said in it, and scarcely at all on what it actually says. They forget entirely that it is, as its secondary title states, "an economic study in the evolution of institutions," and they assume in all gratuity that it is an attack on existing institutions. That is a pure deduction, but one for which there is no warrant in the book. Someone has said that the law of gravitation would be attacked if it was suspected of jeopardizing human interests. The history of man is exactly paralleled in the history of plants and animals, but no one has inveighed against the facts of biology, because they concern subhuman creatures. Darwin was soundly belabored for supposed consequences to man of his facts, but only for such.

Now, no truth has come more clearly forth from the most thorough study of organic evolution than that its whole method is essentially wasteful. Darwin showed this; Huxley multiplied examples of it; and even Herbert Spencer, who would have man imitate nature in all things, has supplied some of the most striking examples of the prodigality of nature. In describing this prodigality naturalists have not been suspected of condemning the habits and instincts of the birds and animals, of the fishes of the sea and the infusorians of the pool. But when an economist of a strictly scientific habit of mind investigates the history of the human species, discovers that human evolution, like organic evolution, is the outcome of the rhythmic action of great cosmic forces, one set of which is centrifugal and destructive, and tells us how these wasteful processes go on in society in coöperation with the conservative ones, he arouses hostility and is regarded as dangerous. And all because the specimens he has to investigate are men. In fact, the book is a mirror in which we can all see ourselves. It is more. It is a telescope through which we can see our ancestors, and when, all at one view, we see all the generations of our pedigree down to and including ourselves, we perceive how little difference there is, and the image takes on a rather ugly aspect. That is why it offends. This tracing back institutions, customs, habits, ideas, beliefs, and feelings to their primitive sources in barbarism and savagery, and showing what is the real basis of them, is not pleasant occupation for people who are proud of their ancestors, for many such have nothing but ancestors to be proud of.

It is perfectly legitimate to endeavor to show that the facts are not as stated, but a critic who does this must proceed scientifically. He must not waste his efforts in showing that there are other facts that have an opposite tendency. He must remember what the author of the book has set himself as a task; and in this case it must be admitted that he has clung tenaciously to this one field, resisting the temptation, which, as anyone can see, must have been strong, to go out of that field and deal with the opposite class of facts. There is no doubt that he could write as strong and able a book on the "instinct of workmanship" as he has written on the "instinct of sportsmanship," and it is to be hoped that he may do so. But in dealing with this book the critic has no right to complain that it is not a book on some other subject than the one chosen. As a matter of fact, there is much gained in dealing with one aspect of human evolution at a time. Very few writers are able to keep the different factors distinct. It requires a clear head. Nearly all the treatment we find of such highly complex subjects is vitiated by the perpetual mixing up of the fields of inquiry, until all is muddle and *Wirrwarr*. Here for once we have a single subject clearly handled and consistently adhered to, at the risk even of giving offense to those whose suggestibility is so strong that they cannot keep other subjects out of view.

It may be said that the author ought at least to have shown how this very leisure class, and solely by virtue of its leisure, has made the greater part certainly of the earlier scientific discoveries, and worked out some of the most important problems; that even modern science owes as much to this class as to all other classes combined, as shown by de Candolle in his *Histoire des Sciences et des Savants;* that all the important "institutions," including the learned professions and the sciences, have, as Spencer has shown, developed out of "ecclesiastical institutions," and owe their existence and advanced modern character to that typical "leisure class," the priesthood, given over to "vicarious leisure" and "devout observances"; that no class and no human being, as the labor reformers so justly insist, can do any high intellectual work, or even cultivate the mind, without a certain amount of leisure and respite from incessant toil. Our author might, it would seem to some, have at least dwelt upon these well-known and universally admitted facts relating directly to the leisure class. But, in the first place, he is not engaged in explaining the intellectual and moral progress of the world, and, in the second place, these facts are too well known to need restatement, and he seems to have no taste for hackneyed topics. Such facts are not opposed to anything he says, but are simply also true. They are patent, while what he tells us is latent, and he chose between the two classes of subjects, telling us a good many things that we did not know before instead of telling us so much that we did know. In the third place, and principally, his point of view is strictly economic, and he deals with a subject within his own specialty, and has not seen fit to branch out into wider fields, as economic writers are so much in the habit of doing. *Ne sutor ultra crepidam.*

In a word, our author is dealing with the question of

wealth, and his whole treatise is confined to the "pecuniary" aspect. He finds that everything has a pecuniary value, which has little to do with its intrinsic or rational value; that this pecuniary value has grown out of a long series of events in human history leading back to the age of barbarism. It is a typical case of conventional ideas as distinguished from rational ideas. It can only be made to seem rational when we know and can trace its history, and see how, under all the circumstances, it could not have been otherwise. Pecuniary value is the result of natural causation, like everything else, but the series of terms consists of a long winding labyrinth of causes and effects that have ultimately produced something which, looked at directly, appears irrational and absurd. In this it is no exception to the general law of survivals in ethnology. Every lawyer knows what a legal fiction is, but most of them are mistaken in imagining that only advanced races are capable of creating such fictions. The study of ethnology shows that early institutions are a mass of fictions. The savage is more logical than the civilized man. Analyze the *couvade,* considered as the fiction by which the matriarchal was transformed into the patriarchal system without a break in the chain of logic.

Pecuniary value, as distinguished from intrinsic value, is a survival, and it has probably never before been so well traced out. Here are a few of the steps, but the book must be read to see them all and how they are connected: As soon as property became recognized as the thing that chiefly insures the satisfaction of desire, the "law of acquisition" went into effect, and thenceforth the problem was how to *acquire* the most with the least effort – not how to *produce* the most. The "least effort" part of the formula lies at the foundation of the author's distinction between "industry and exploit." Exploit is comparatively easy. Industry becomes synonymous with drudgery. The love of activity, *i.e.*, the actual pleasure in the exercise of the faculties, which is the essence of the "instinct of workmanship," could scarcely be eliminated, and "leisure" is by no means incompatible with activity. But excessive activity – the prolonged and laborious exertion required for the constant re-production of the objects of consumption – is essentially irksome and has always been avoided when possible. But these objects must be produced in order that their consumption may be enjoyed, and the only way to possess them without producing them is to make others produce them. Any power to do this is immediately exercised, and as things have been constituted in the history of mankind, this has taken the form of creating a dependent industrial class and an independent leisure class. The simplest form of this was slavery, and, as the author shows, the first slaves were women; afterward captives were made slaves; and finally all were enslaved but the few having privilege and power. Extensive modification of this normal state, of course, took place with time.

Now, the most natural thing in the world is that these two sets of persons should form two great classes totally unlike in almost every respect. The dependent class is low, debased, degraded. The independent class is high, noble, exalted. This is not merely the judgment of the higher class, but also that of the lower. It is the universally recognized relation and constitutes what is called the *régime of status*. All the occupations of the dependent class are, in our author's happy phrase, "humilific," and all the occupations in which the independent class can engage must be "honorific." These occupations must not cross each other. They must be wholly different. The humilific occupations are all industrial, productive. Therefore the leisure class must pursue no industrial or productive occupations under pain of being suspected of dependence. The humilific occupations are the only ones that are "useful" in the economic sense. Therefore no member of the leisure class may do anything useful. The leisure class derive pleasure from the exercise of their faculties, but such exercise must involve no "utility," and must be characterized by "futility." There are certain directions in which the pleasures of activity may be indulged without the suspicion of dependence or necessity. Among these purely futile occupations we find war, the chase, gaming, politics, ruling, religious observances, etc. Then there are many incidental ways in which the leisure class, when in full power, are able to enjoy themselves. Thus it is said that a common amusement of the Roman nobles was to knock down a plebeian and then hand over a sesterce, which was the amount of the fine fixed by law for such offenses; and the idea of "fun" that the young British gentry entertained in the sixteenth century was to disfigure the faces of the poor they met in the streets by means of a sharp-pointed cane that they carried for such purposes. Everything done must be in the nature of sport, nothing must have the character of work. The surplus energy must express itself in wholly non-industrial and absolutely parasitic ways, otherwise there is loss of caste.

The above may give some idea of the general nature of the fundamental antithesis that sprang up naturally, as shown, and has persisted even down to our own times. The distinction has been characterized as "invidious," and this word has been criticised as imputing blameworthy motives. But it is used in a literal sense, as that which has *envy* at its root, for not only does the industrial class envy the leisure class, but every member of the leisure class is perpetually striving to gain the envy of others of that class. Though all the members of the leisure class are exempt from drudgery, they are by no means all equal in their "ability to pay," and, as there is no limit to the possibility of conspicuous futile consumption, no one ever has as much as he wants in order to outdo and eclipse his rivals. There is thus brought about, not only a hierarchy of wealth, but a perpetual scramble to excel one another. Wealth becomes the basis of esteem. The standard is wholly pecuniary. Not only must wealth be possessed, but there must be a show of its possession. It must be made obvious to all that there is an inexhaustible reserve. Hence leisure must be made conspicuous by "conspicuous consumption" and "conspicuous waste." If only enough persons and the right persons could see it and know it, it would be highly honorific to light a cigar occasionally with a thousand-dollar bill. A man must not limit his consumption to himself and his family. He must live in a palace many times larger than he can possibly fill, and have a large retinue of servants and retainers, ostensibly to minister to his wants, but really to make clear his ability to pay.

From this arises the important principle of "vicarious leisure" and "vicarious consumption." Most of these servants must also be exempt from any productive work, and the women of his household must be absolutely non-productive and inactive. In the modern system of semi-industrial and quasi-predatory exploitation by the bourgeoisie the "captain of industry" must manage his business, and therefore seem to be doing something, mayhap something useful, but appearances must be kept up as in the feudal manor, and upon his wife devolves the "performance of leisure" and the display of her husband's ability to pay for useless things. He confers on her a vicarious leisure, and in dress and social appointments she is able to show his ability to consume and to waste to any required extent.

It will be seen that it is throughout the application of the fundamental maxim of "political economy" — the greatest gain for the least effort. But as effort is itself agreeable, the effort meant is only industrial, productive, useful effort. Primarily war and the chase were the principal honorific employments, growing out of the antecedent state in which both were more or less productive. War for booty gave way to war for captives, *i.e.*, slaves to do the productive work, and ultimately the chase entirely lost its productive value and was indulged in merely for sport. Witness the contempt in our day for the poacher and the "pot-hunter." At first all exploit was predatory; it has now become what our author aptly calls "quasi-predatory." There is no more regard for real justice or right now than then, but the exploitation must conform to laws made by the exploiting class, and so have a show of justice. The purpose is to acquire at all hazards, but it is not enough to say that this must be done irrespective of whether anything is produced or not. All acquisition must be non-productive under pain of falling out of the leisure class.

No biologist can fail to observe parallels in the organic world to many of the facts set forth in this book. Space forbids their enumeration, but one can scarcely refrain from noting among nature's many wasteful ways the phenomena of secondary sexual characters, typified by the antlers of the stag and the gaudy tail of the peacock. These may be compared to wasteful human fashions, such as are enumerated in the chapter on "Pecuniary Canons of Taste." The principal difference is that nature, in producing these useless and cumbersome organs, has really given them a high degree of intrinsic beauty, even as judged by human tastes, while the products of human fashion, based on the canon of "pecuniary beauty," or costliness, are useless impediments to activity without the slightest claim upon any rational standard of taste.

The author's theory of why fashions change is ingenious, and must be largely true. The ugliness caused by their superfluous cost renders them intolerable to behold for any great length of time, so that a change is demanded by the aesthetic sense even of the leisure class; but the new ones can be no better, because they, too, must have these marks of "reputable futility" and "conspicuous waste," that are necessarily offensive to taste, which is based on the instinct of workmanship. They must therefore also soon give way to others no better than they, and so on indefinitely. It is a perpetual conflict between pecuniary beauty and rational beauty, which are incompatible, but in which the former always prevails, and all the latter can do is to condemn the product and compel the victor to bring on another.

The genesis of a great number of institutions, customs, practices, and beliefs is worked out in the book, and their barbaric origin clearly shown. It would be useless to attempt their enumeration here, and only a few of the most curious can be named, such as the exemption of women from labor (vicarious leisure); inebriacy and dissipation; costly and unaesthetic decoration; the non-punishment of crime when on a large scale; religious ceremonial evolutions recalling the terpsichorean stage or dance; the higher learning, or "classicism"; preference for inferior hand-made over superior machine-made goods; love of archaism in general; the respectability of conservatism; the conservatism and degeneracy of the higher institutions of learning; patriotism, dueling, snobbery; English saddles, walking sticks; athletic sports, college fraternities, the "cap and gown," etc., etc.

The author has certainly handled the English language with consummate skill, and, notwithstanding his indictment of "classicism," he displays no mean acquaintance with the classics. The book abounds in terse expressions, sharp antitheses, and quaint, but happy phrases. Some of these have been interpreted as irony and satire, but, as said above, this is the work of the critics themselves. The language is plain and unmistakable, as it should be, but the style is the farthest removed possible from either advocacy or vituperation, and the language, to use the author's own words, is "morally colorless." Some of it, if it is not classical, is likely to become so. His general terminology has already been used to a considerable extent in this review, the peculiar terms and expressions being put in quotation marks. Many others might be given if space permitted, such, for example, as "reputably wasteful expenditure," or "reputable waste," "reputable futility," and "pecuniary reputability"; and he speaks of certain things that have "advantages in the way of uselessness." On the other hand, we have such expressions as "vulgarly useful occupations," "vulgar effectiveness," and the "taint of usefulness." Then we have the "predatory animus," "quasi-predatory methods," "predatory fraud," "predatory parasitism," and "parasitic predation." Many incidental expressions are noteworthy, such as the "skilled and graded inebriety and perfunctory dueling" of the German students, and his statement that the "higher learning" chiefly confers a "knowledge of the unknowable." He says that the "exaltation of the defective" and admiration for "painstaking crudeness" and "elaborate ineptitude" are characteristics of "pecuniary standards of taste." And anyone who has noted how all athletic sports degenerate and become restricted to a few professionals will appreciate his remark that "the relation of football to physical culture is much the same as that of the bull fight to agriculture."

As has already been seen, the two great social classes are characterized by an assortment of sharply contrasted words and phrases, and not only their occupations, but their underlying instincts, are clearly marked off by such expressions as the "instinct of sportsmanship" and the "instinct of workmanship"; "exploit and industry," or "exploit and drudgery"; "honorific and humilific" occupations, and "perfunctory and proficuous" activities, all forming the primary contrast between "futility and utility." In each of these pairs the first belongs to the leisure class and represents the superior fitness to survive in human society. The leisure class constitutes the biologically fittest, the socially best, the aristocracy.

Of the general make-up of the book, as of all that issue from that well-known house, there is nothing to be said but praise, unless it be to note the retention of the superfluous *u* in such words as "honour," "favour," "colour," etc. To speak of our American "Labour Day" is a clear case of "archaism" and "conspicuous waste," and might be cited in defense of the main thesis of the book.

An Opportunity for American Fiction*

By William D. Howells

FIRST PAPER

ONE of the most interesting books which has fallen in my way since I read *The Workers* of Mr. Wyckoff is Mr. Thorstein Veblen's *Theory of the Leisure Class* (Macmillan). It does for the Idlers in terms of cold, scientific analysis the office which Mr. Wyckoff's book dramatically performs for the Workers; and I think that it is all the more important because it deals, like that book, with a class newly circumstanced rather than newly conditioned. The workers and the idlers of America are essentially the same as the workers and

* *Literature. An International Gazette of Criticism.* No. 16 New Series, April 28, 1899.

the idlers of occidental civilisation everywhere; but there is a novelty in their environment peculiarly piquant to the imagination. In the sociological region the spectacle has for the witness some such fascination as geological stratification would have for the inquirer if he could look on at its processes; and it is apparently with as strong a zest as this would inspire that Mr. Veblen considers the nature and the growth of the leisure class among us.

His name is newer to me than it should be, or than it will hereafter be to any student of our status; but it must be already well known to those whose interests or pleasures have led them into the same field of inquiry. To others, like myself, the clear method, the graphic and easy style, and the delightful accuracy of characterisation will be part of the surprise which the book has to offer. In the passionless calm with which the author pursues his investigation, there is apparently no animus for or against a leisure class. It is his affair simply to find out how and why and what it is. If the result is to leave the reader with a feeling which the author never shows, that seems to be solely the effect of the facts. But I have no purpose, as I doubt if I have the qualification, to criticise the book, and it is only with one of its manifold suggestions that this notice will concern itself.

The suggestion, which is rather a conclusion, is the curious fact, noted less securely and less scientifically before, that the flower of the American leisure class does not fruit in its native air, and perhaps cannot yet perpetuate itself on our soil. In other words, the words of Mr. Veblen, "the English leisure class being, for purposes of reputable usage, the upper leisure class of this country," the extraordinary impulse among us toward the aristocraticisation of society can as yet fulfill itself only in monarchical conditions. A conspicuous proof of this is the frequent intermarriage of our moneyed bourgeoisie with the English aristocracy, and another proof, less conspicuous, is the frequent absenteeism of our rich people. The newspapers from time to time make a foolish and futile clamor about both these things, as if they were abnormal, or as if they were not the necessary logic of great wealth and leisure in a democracy. Such things result as infallibly from wealth and leisure as indigence and servility, and are in no wise to be deprecated. They are only representations on a wider stage of the perpetual and universal drama of our daily life. The man who makes money in a small town goes into the nearest large town to spend it—that is, to waste it; waste in some form or other being the corollary of wealth; and he seeks to marry his children there into rich and old families. He does this from the instinct of self-preservation, which is as strong in classes as in individuals; if he has made his money in a large town, he goes to some such inland metropolis as Chicago to waste his wealth and to marry his children above him. The Chicago, and San Francisco, and St. Louis, and Cleveland millionaires come to New York with the same ambitions and purposes.

But these are all intermediate stages in the evolutión of the American magnate. At every step he discovers that he is less and less in his own country, that he is living in a provisional exile, and that his true home is in monarchical conditions, where his future establishes itself often without his willing it, and sometimes against his willing it. The American life is the life of labor, and he is now of the life of leisure, or if he is not, his wife is, his daughters and his sons are. The logic of their existence, which they cannot struggle against, and on which all the fatuous invective of pseudo public spirit launches itself effectlessly, is intermarriage with the European aristocracies, and residence abroad. Short of this there is no rest, and can be none for the American leisure class. This may not be its ideal, but it is its destiny.

It is far the most dramatic social fact of our time, and if some man of creative imagination were to seize upon it, he would find in it the material of that great American novel which after so much travail has not yet seen the light. It is, above all our other facts, synthetic; it sums up and includes in itself the whole American story: the relentless will, the tireless force, the vague ideal, the inexorable destiny, the often bewildered acquiescence. If the novelist were a man of very great imagination indeed, he might forecast a future in which the cycle would round itself, and our wealth would return from European sojourn, and dwell among us again, bringing its upper class with it, so that we should have a leisure class ultimated and established on our own ground. But for my part I should prefer the novel which kept itself entirely to the actualities, and studied in them the most profoundly interesting spectacle which life has ever offered to the art of fiction, with elements of equal tragedy and comedy, and a pathos through all which must be expressed, if the full significance of the spectacle were to be felt.

SECOND PAPER*

Mr. Thorstein Veblen does not evolve his *Theory of the Leisure Class* from his knowledge of that class in America alone. Until very lately we had no such class, and we rather longed for it. We thought it would edify us, or, if not that, at least ornament us; but now that we have got it, on certain terms, we can hardly be sure that it does either. The good things that we expected of it have not come to pass, and perhaps it is too soon; but in Mr. Veblen's analysis our leisure class does not seem essentially different from any of

* *Ibid.*, No. 17 New Series, May 5, 1899.

the older aristocracies, which seem not to have brought to pass the good things expected of them and often attributed to them. As with these, "pecuniary emulation" and "conspicuous leisure" are the first evidences of its superiority, and "conspicuous consumption," direct or delegated in the splendid apparelling and housing of its women and its dependents, is one of the gross means of striking the popular imagination. The "pecuniary standard of living" is really the only standard, and the "pecuniary canons of taste" are finally the only canons; for if the costly things are not always beautiful, all beautiful things which are cheap must be rejected because they are not costly. "Dress as an expression of pecuniary culture" is left in our day mostly to women by the leisure class; but the men of that class share in it at least as fully as in the "devout observances" and "the higher learning." Both sexes in our leisure class, as in the European aristocracies, are distinguished by the love of sport, in which they prolong their own childhood and the childhood of the race, and they are about equally devoted to the opera and the fine arts, as these minister to their magnificence. It would be hard, in fact, to draw the line between our leisure class and any aristocracy in the traits of piety, predacity, courage, prowess, charity, luxury, conservatism, authority, and the other virtues and vices which have characterised the patricians in all times.

The most notable difference, and the difference which would most invite the study of the novelist, is that hitherto our leisure class has had no political standing. It has had no place in the civic mechanism; but we seem to be at the moment when this is ceasing to be less apparently so. It is idle to suppose because the leisure class, which with us is the moneyed class, does not hold public offices that it does not control public affairs; and possibly it has always controlled them more than we have imagined. The present proof is in the fact that the industrial classes, with all the means of power in their hands, are really powerless in any contest with a group of rich men; it is almost impossible for the people to balk the purpose of such a group; to undo what money has done has been so impossible, with all the apparatus of the elections, the legislatures, the courts, that there is hardly yet an instance of the kind in our history.

All this, however, makes the situation the more attractive to a novelist of imaginative force. This is the most dramatic moment, the most psychological moment which has ever offered itself to fiction; this is the supreme opportunity of the American novelist. Hitherto our politics have repelled the artist by their want of social complexity, by their rude simplicity, as a fight between parties. But if he can look at the situation from the point of view suggested, as an inevitable result from the nature of the class which Mr. Veblen has studied, I believe he will find it full of charm. If he is psychologist enough he will be fascinated by the operation of the silent forces which are, almost unconsciously, working out the permanency of a leisure class, and preparing for it in our own circumstance the ultimation it now seeks elsewhere.

But I should be content if he would portray the life of our leisure class without an eye to such implications, with an eye merely to its superficial facts. If he did this he would appeal to the widest general interest in our reading public. Our appetite for everything that relates to the life removed from the life of work, from the simple republican ideal, is almost insatiable. It strives to satisfy itself, in plays and romances, with the doings of princes and nobles in realms as surely fictitious as Lilliput and Brobdingnag; it gluts itself, in the newspapers, with fables almost as gross as Gulliver's concerning the social affairs of our leisure class.

Seen truly and reproduced faithfully these would be extremely interesting, and the field they offer to inquiry is almost wholly unexplored. Our fiction has brought pretty fully into literature the country and village life of the Americans of all sections. We know this through our short stories in New England, in the South, in the middle and farther West, and on the Pacific Slope; and in a certain measure our novels have acquainted us with the lower and upper middle-class life in the minor and even the greater cities. But the attempts to deal with the life of fashion, of luxury, of leisure, have been so insufficient that they cannot be considered. This life can hardly be studied by one who is a part of it, not merely because that sort of life is not fruitful in talent, but because the procession cannot very well look on at itself. The observer must have some favorable position on the outside, and must regard it neither "with a foolish face of praise," nor with a satiric scorn. Like every other phase of life, it has its seriousness, its importance, and one who studies it rightly will find in it the old elements of interest so newly compounded that they will merit his most intelligent scrutiny, often his most sympathetic scrutiny. It would be easy to burlesque it, but to burlesque it would be intolerable, and the witness who did this would be bearing false testimony where the whole truth and nothing but the truth is desirable. A democracy, the proudest, the most sincere, the most ardent that history has ever known, has evolved here a leisure class which has all the distinguishing traits of a patriciate, and which by the chemistry of intermarriage with European aristocracies is rapidly acquiring antiquity. Is not this a phenomenon worthy the highest fiction?

Mr. Veblen has brought to its study the methods and habits

of scientific inquiry. To translate these into dramatic terms would form the unequalled triumph of the novelist who had the seeing eye and the thinking mind, not to mention the feeling heart. That such a thing has not been done hitherto is all the stranger, because fiction, in other countries, has always employed itself with the leisure class, with the aristocracy; and our own leisure class now offers not only as high an opportunity as any which fiction has elsewhere enjoyed, but by its ultimation in the English leisure class, it invites the American imagination abroad on conditions of unparalleled advantage.

The Dullest Book of the Month
*The Theory of the Leisure Class**
Dr. Thorstein Veblen Gets the Crown of Deadly Nightshade

By ROBERT C. BENCHLEY

It has long been the custom among many of our leading literary publications, such as *The North American Review*, for instance, to devote a special review to what is referred to as *The Best Book of the Month*, or even *The Month's Best Book*. *Vanity Fair* can not undertake to select the best book of the month for review, but it *can* select a book which, it is a safe bet, a majority of its readers would not otherwise be conversant with – and, at that, not impugn the good taste of its readers.

We have selected for the first month's review, Dr. Thorstein Veblen's *The Theory of the Leisure Class* (New York. Macmillan. Cloth. $2.00 net). This book has been chosen for two reasons, both of them being that Dr. Veblen has recently been the storm-center of a soviet uprising among the young ladies in New York who compose The Junior League.

* *Vanity Fair*, April 1919.

From current press reports, it appears that a revolutionary element among the members of New York's exclusive *demoiselles* refused to attend lectures at the new School for Social Research (a training table for *The New Republic* squad) because of the presence, on the faculty, of Dr. Veblen and several other savants who were suspected of having radical leanings and therefore of being unsuited to act as docents for our social register débutantes.

But a study of Dr. Veblen's arraignment of the Leisure Class will disclose a still more cogent reason for his rejection by these astute young ladies. As the members of the Junior League possess both leisure and class, they naturally enough resented this gross attack upon their admirable and energetic League.

The Original Leisure Classes

Dr. Veblen starts away with a rush. He brings us, right off the bat, into contact with the original leisure classes, those inhabiting the Polynesian Islands and the Icelandic community at the time of the Sagas. This is evidently done to lend color to what follows, for the theme is developed logically through the period of the Andamans, the Todas of the Nilgiri Hills, the Ainu of Yezo, and also, although "more doubtfully", some Bushman and Eskimo groups.

It is well that the author protected himself by the insertion of that "doubtfully", or he would have had a controversy on his hands with the present reviewer. We are very touchy on that Todas matter. As it is, however, we will let it pass.

Immediately following this snappy outline of what has preceded the opening of the story, we are introduced, without further ado, into the swirl of passion in which the book itself is carried along. Note the emergence of the love interest in the following vivid, if somewhat colloquial passage:

"The ground on which a discrimination between facts is habitually made, changes as the interest from which the facts are habitually viewed changes. Those features of the facts at hand are salient and substantial upon which the dominant interest of the time throws its light."

It will be seen from this that Dr. Veblen knows his Ring Lardner. The influence of the "You-know-me-Al" school has crept into this work almost imperceptibly and yet indubitably. It has, however, a raciness all its own. It does not depend upon mis-spelling for its humorous effect, but, as in his definition of Man ("Man, in his own apprehension, a center of unfolding impulsive activity – teleological activity") we find the native genius of Dr. Veblen creating something in the way of humor that is entirely his own.

The second chapter of the book is entitled "Pecuniary Emulation". This chapter is a scream. But, when one has finished it, one must admit that the plot has been advanced no whit. You are simply where you were in the beginning, except for the fact that the woman in the red hat has danced on the table. Which really isn't very far, when you come to think of it.

Here Is a Word on Drunkenness

But in his chapter on "Conspicuous Leisure", the Doctor warms up to his task. He gives us to understand that the term "leisure" does not denote "indolence or quiescence", but "non-productive consumption of time" – which is one of the reasons, I dare say, why the Junior League girls rebelled so. He takes us, by sheer force of his cave-man word-pictures, into the creation of "a subsidiary or derivative leisure class, whose office is the performance of a vicarious leisure for the behoof of the reputability of the primary or legitimate leisure class". This all seems so simple that the wonder is that no one has ever thought of it before. And, through it all, Dr. Veblen maintains a certain dignity underneath his popular exterior, giving the reader to understand that the author has his serious side as well.

This feeling is somewhat dispelled, however, in the next chapter, entitled "Conspicuous Consumption", for here the Doctor lets himself go, to the point of being ribald. Drunken scenes are, at best, unpleasant, but what shall we say of one handled thus:

"Drunkenness and the other pathological consequences of the free use of stimulants therefore tend in their turn to become honorific, as being a mark, at the second remove, of the superior status of those who are able to afford the indulgence."

If that isn't dragging drinking down to the level of a bestial process, we should like to know what is. As if the Liquor Interests didn't have enough to worry about without being accused of being "honorific at the second remove."

There follows, however, a paragraph which makes amends for much. It is the private opinion of the reviewer that Dr. Veblen wrote this originally for *Vanity Fair*, to be used as the advertisement for the magazine which is usually run on the page immediately preceding the frontispiece. Or, perhaps Dr. Veblen has been writing the *Vanity Fair* advertisements all along, who knows? Listen:

"The growth of punctilious discrimination as to the qualitative excellence in eating, drinking, etc., presently affects not only the manner of life, but also the training and intellectual activity of the gentleman of leisure. He is no longer simply the aggressive male – the man of strength, resource and intrepidity. *In order to avoid stultification he must also cultivate his tastes, for it now becomes incumbent upon him to discriminate with some nicety between the noble and ignoble in consumable goods. He becomes a connoisseur in creditable viands of various degrees of merit, in manly beverages and trinkets, in seemly apparel and architecture, in weapons, games, dances, and the narcotics.* This cultivation of the aesthetic faculty requires time and application, and the demands made upon the gentleman in this direction therefore tend to change his life of leisure into a more or less arduous application to the business of learning how to live a life of ostensible leisure in a becoming way."

"A copy of Vanity Fair each month will do all this, and more, for you," is the logical ending to that paragraph.

But then comes what we might call "the rough stuff". Up to this time we have heard nothing of Little Annie, who left her home in Great Barrington ten years before the opening of the story. It is therefore with a shock of something akin to offended modesty that the average reader will scan the following lines:

"Men differ in respect of transmitted aptitudes, or in respect of the relative facility with which they unfold their life activity in particular directions; and the habits which coincide with or proceed upon a relatively strong specific aptitude or a relatively great specific facility of expression become of great consequence to a man's well-being."

Strong words, Thorstein! . . . But, after all, are they not better said openly and frankly than concealed as if they were something of which one might well be ashamed?

Light Reading for Débutantes

But, surely, not for the young Missy of the Junior League is the following estimate of the chief factors in feminine beauty:

"Apart from the general control exercised by the norm of conspicuous waste over the ideal of feminine beauty, there are one or two details which merit specific mention as showing how it may exercise an extreme constraint in detail over men's sense of beauty in women. It has already been noticed that, at the stages of economic evolution at which conspicuous leisure is regarded as a means of good repute, the ideal requires delicate and diminutive hands and feet and a slender waist. . . . She (the woman thus adapted) is useless and expensive and she is consequently valuable as evidence of pecuniary strength."

The "astute man", moreover, is little better. "His functioning is not a furtherance of the generic life process. At its best, in its direct economic bearing, it is a conversion of the economic substance of the collectivity to a growth alien to the collective life process."

Do you see?

On the whole, *The Theory of the Leisure Class* is a good work, hastily done. In the hands of a more serious-minded student it might have been developed to greater lengths.

The Doctor has made one big mistake, however. He has presupposed, in writing this book, the existence of a class with much more leisure than any class in the world ever possessed – for, has he not counted on a certain number of readers?

Other Reviews

*The Theory of Business Enterprise**

By J. H. Tufts

Those who read and enjoyed Professor Veblen's extremely acute, subtle and brilliant *Theory of the Leisure Class* will bring a keen appetite to the analysis of current business processes and psychology which is given in the present volume. Nor will they be disappointed. There is the same cool, scientific dissection of current processes, standards and ideals, which, by its very attitude of unimpassioned, relentless laying bare of sources and springs of action, is more effective than the most passionate sarcasm or invective. There is the same ability to coin a phrase, or use a word in a new application, which shall carry a whole chapter within itself, and become, in the reader's mind, a perpetual challenge to a principle, institution or whole series of conventions. There is the same combination of wealth of concrete material with psychological analysis and philosophical method; the same exploration of economic, social and cultural fields with a given principle. Finally, there is, I venture to think, a similar tendency to simplify the complex springs of human action more than is warranted by an impartial interpretation of the facts. The former volume has not as yet received the attention from psychologists which it deserves, and the title of the present volume would not suggest the large amount of social psychology which it contains. This psychology appears first in the account of business itself, its aims, its assumptions,

* *Psychological Bulletin,* June 15, 1904. We have substituted . . . for successive quotation marks wherever they appeared in the original.

its prosperity or depression; secondly, in the account of the industrial processes; and thirdly, in tracing the respective influence of these two forms of occupation upon the minds of those who follow them, and upon the broader cultural spheres, economic, political, educational, domestic and religious.

The psychological aspect of the book is not limited to details. It is shown in the effort to state business processes in the terms and shapes in which they are actually conceived by business men. Money, for example, is not for modern business the "medium of exchange," as is usually held by those who speak of "business traffic . . . as a means of obtaining goods suitable for consumption, the end of all purchase and sale being consumable goods, not money values." This latter "may be true in some profound philosophical sense, looking at the process of economic life as a whole, and taking it in its rationalized bearing as a collective endeavor to purvey goods and services for the needs of collective humanity. Such is the view of this matter given by the rationalistic, normalizing speculations of the eighteenth-century philosophers; and such is the view spoken for, in substance, by those economists who still consistently remain at the standpoint of the eighteenth century. The contention need neither be defended nor refuted here, since it does not seriously touch the facts of modern business. Within the range of business transactions this ulterior end does not necessarily come into view, at least not as a motive that guides the transactions from day to day. The matter is not so conceived in business transactions, it does not so appear on the face of the negotiable instruments, it is not in this manner that the money unit enters into the ruling habits of thought of business men" (p. 83).

Again, in current economic theory the business man himself is spoken of as an "entrepreneur," and "his function is held to be the coördinating of industrial processes with a view to economies of production and heightened serviceability. The soundness of this view need not be questioned. It has a great sentimental value, and is useful in many ways." Business men, especially the less successful, are to some extent influenced by ideals of serviceability or instincts for workmanship; "excessive sensitiveness" may interfere with certain kinds of business; the business strategist may be so infected with this human infirmity as not to exact the last concession from his rivals that a ruthless business strategy might entitle him to; but the motive of business is pecuniary gain, motives of this kind (serviceability, workmanship) detract from business efficiency, and the "captains of the first class . . . are relatively exempt from these unbusinesslike scruples." (pp. 41-43).

One of the most interesting phases of the part assigned by the author to psychological processes in business is found in Chapter VII. in the explanation proposed for the periods of business depression. Current theories usually explain these in terms of the producing or consuming process. But as, under present conditions, it is business which directs industry and not *vice versa*, the cause for depression should be sought in business itself. This cause is found by the author in the constantly progressive efficiency of the industrial process which necessarily tends to cheaper productions and lower prices. Now the business man regards money as a stable unit, and hence a constant lowering of prices, with the attendant re-rating and reduction of his capital, appears to him as a loss in value, an impoverishment, even if it carries no reduced command over material goods. A business man's rating and consequently his self-respect is based rather on the pecuniary magnitude of his holdings than on the mechanical serviceability of his establishment or his output. "The explanation here offered of depression makes it a malady of the affections. The discrepancy which discourages business men is a discrepancy between that nominal capitalization which they have set their hearts upon through habituation in the immediate past and that actual capitalizable value of their property which its current earning capacity will warrant. But where the preconceptions of the business men engaged have, as commonly happens, in great part been fixed and legalized in the form of interest-bearing securities, this malady of the affections becomes extremely difficult to remedy, even though it be true that these legalized affections, preconceptions, or what not, center upon the metaphysical stability of the money unit."

Similar psychological rendering is given to ethical and legal conceptions. "Principles" are defined as "habits of thought" and "business" principles accordingly mean habits of thought suitable to the work of business traffic, corollaries under the main principle of ownership. This principle of ownership or property is a habit of thought, recent as compared with some; those who are inclined to give it a more substantial character than that of a habit are characterized as "those who still adhere to the doctrine of natural rights with something of the eighteenth century naïveté." (Ch. IV). Parenthetically it may be observed that Professor Veblen never suggests that there can possibly be any other (*e.g.*, social welfare) basis for the "right" of property, and it must be admitted that his exhibition of the almost absolute lack of any relation between the pecuniary returns of the more highly organized and successful business operations on the one hand, and any serviceability to the public on the other, would seem to offer small ground for such a basis of rights as applied to these particular fortunes, although the utility of admitting the institution would not necessarily be disproved thereby. So "snobbery" in psychological terms is "used without disrespect to denote the element of strain involved, in the quest of gentility on the part of persons whose accustomed social standing is less high or less authentic than their aspirations."

Coming to the direct doctrine of the book, we have, as already suggested, analyses of the business, and of the industrial or machine process, and a statement of their respective tendencies of influence. Business is the director of the machine process, and the two have radically different effects upon those engaged in them. The machine process with its standardization of goods, tools, work and units of every sort makes the mechanic "do his work as a factor in a mechanical process whose movement controls his motions. . . . The machine is not his to do with as his fancy may suggest. His place is to take thought of the machine and its work in terms given him by the process that is going forward. . . . If he fails of the precise measure by more or less, the exigencies of the process check the aberration and drive home the absolute need of conformity. There results a standardization of the workman's intellectual life in terms of mechanical process. . . . But mechanical efficiency is a matter of precisely adjusted cause and effect." The discipline of the machine inculcates therefore a tendency to think in these terms and these only. As the machine is impersonal, immoral, and knows no ethical or spiritual principles, its tendency is to train those whom it controls into insensibility toward all such concepts. Hence the tendency of the artisans in the distinctly machine occupations to adopt socialism with its ignoring of the conventions of property, family (here the headship of the male, now exhibited chiefly in his "pecuniary discretion" over the family funds, is "in jeopardy"), religion, and politics.

Business, on the other hand, as it is concerned with the institution (habit of thought) of ownership or property has a conventional basis. "The logic of pecuniary thinking . . . is a working out of the implications of this postulate of ownership. . . . The argument is an argument *de jure*, not *de facto*. [But does not this apply rather to the legal justifications of business, than to the actual process of discovering means for attaining wealth?][1] The spiritual attitude given by this training in reasoning *de jure*, is necessarily conservative." The reasoning assumes the validity of the conventionally established postulates. Business classes, therefore, like those engaged in occupations where the thinking moves on a plane of still older conventions – soldiers, politicians, the clergy, and men of fashion – are conservative.

We have, therefore, the following interesting problem: the whole industrial system, on the manipulation of which business depends for its continued existence, fosters a habit of mind which tends to destroy the fundamental postulate of business, viz., the conventions of which property is chief. Business cannot do without the machine process; but neither could [it] survive in company with this process if the full logical results of the process should work out.

A typical expression of this antithesis is found in the legal conflicts between workmen and employers. Decisions of the higher courts more uniformly favor the employers than do the verdicts of jurors. The higher courts decide more strictly in accord with the law, which in turn embodies the common sense of the past, in this case, of the eighteenth century; "whereas the sympathies of the vulgar, as they appear in jury decisions, are largely the outcome of those modern experiences that are at increasing variance with the foundations of the common law." (p. 281).

Trade-unionism is a sort of half-way house in certain re-

1 [The brackets are Tufts's. *Ed. note*].

spects. It is at variance with the natural-rights foundation of the common law. It "denies individual freedom of contract to the workman, as well as free discretion to the employer to carry on his business as may suit his own ends"; on the other hand, it does not usually oppose overtly the institution of property. Nevertheless, as the workmen's exigencies are entirely extra-legal (since the law does not recognize any such facts as a standard of livelihood or comfort), so "the revision of the scheme aimed at by trade-union action runs, not in terms of natural liberty, individual property rights, individual discretion, but in terms of standardized livelihood and mechanical necessity; it is formulated, not in terms of business expediency, but in terms of industrial, technological, standard units and standard relations."

The query arises in connection with the above, as to whether the attitude of socialism, or the less extreme position of trade-unionism, is so solely mechanical and matter-of-fact. Is there not a certain demand for fairness, and at the same time a consideration of the general welfare? Is there not a feeling of solidarity, fostered by the organization of machine industry, which is as truly a factor in the workman's attitude as is the materialism induced by the technique of the machine process? The unions, at least, have shown no lack of "ideals," although it may be granted that their ideals are not those of 'natural rights.' Indeed, what is the higher standard of livelihood, comfort and intelligence which the unions seek but idealism? The machine is doubtless opposed to conventions and aristocracies, but by increasing the social interaction through the massing of skilled workmen it sets up a new social force which is as favorable to democratic and social ideals as the older isolation (still continued in rural occupations) was to individualism. The psychologist who was looking for analogies might in truth find them in plenty between the unions and the primitive kinship or patriotic groups. There is a similar "loyalty," a similar regard for rights of fellow-members and disregard of claims of outsiders, a similar justification of force.

While the insufficient attention given to the social forces leaves a sense of undue simplicity and abstractness in the book viewed as a complete psychology of the business and industrial process, it must be regarded as a highly important contribution to social psychology. The theory of business enterprise is getting before the general public in various interesting forms, but to the scientifically inclined none of them can compare in interest with Professor Veblen's analysis.

An Inquiry Into the Nature of Peace[*]

By Frances Hackett

COMPARATIVELY few people know the work of Thorstein Veblen. Some thousands have read his best-known book, the brilliant, drastic *Theory of the Leisure Class*; but only a few hundred have read his *Theory of Business Enterprise*, his *Instinct of Workmanship* and his *Imperial Germany*. So little is he known that a pretentious man the other day met my mention of *The Nature of Peace* by saying, "Ah, of course, a new translation." He did not know that Thorstein Veblen was an American, was graduated from an American university, in the 'eighties, and has been teaching in American universities ever since. Mr. Veblen is an American writer but the kind of American writer whose merit is rather more clearly recognized abroad than at home, an American who ought to have been a foreigner to be appreciated in America.

To read Mr. Veblen is not and cannot be an entertainment. There is a kind of fashionable lady who knows precisely when a literary Paquin has ceased to be the thing, and who twitters as unfailingly as any bird at the first breath of another master's dawn. For all this turn for novelty, few ladies have twittered much or are ever going to twitter much about Mr. Veblen's performance. He is too difficult to understand. It is hard intellectual labor to read any of his books, and to skim him is impossible. He is not a luxurious valley of easy reading, a philosophic Tennyson. He is a mountain – stubborn, forbidding, purgatorial. There is no funicular to bring him under subjection of the indolent, and sometimes there

[*] *The New Republic*, May 26, 1917. Review appeared under the title "The Cost of Peace."

is barely a foothold even for the hardy amid the tortuosities of his style. But the reward for those who do persist in reading him is commensurate with the effort. No mountain pierces to heaven, not even Mr. Veblen's, but the area that he unrolls is strategically chosen and significantly inclusive. Part of the reward of reading him may be like the reward of mountain-climbing itself, the value of tough exercise for its own sake, but unless Mr. Veblen created the conviction that his large purposes did reasonably necessitate intricate and laborious processes of thought and that such processes had to be followed in detail in order that his argument might be mastered, no one would be quite satisfied to take the pains he exacts. The greatest justification of such pains is the final sense conveyed by him that he has had a singular contribution to make, and has made it with complete regard to the formidable requirements of responsible unconventional utterance.

The responsible unconventionality of Mr. Veblen has never been better exemplified than in this new book of his, finished February, 1917, on the nature of peace. It is, so far as I know, the most momentous work in English on the encompassment of lasting peace. There are many books that aim to give geographic domicile to the kind of tinkered peace that is likely to come out of this war, but I know of no book that gives so plain and positive account of the terms "on which peace at large may be hopefully installed and maintained," and I know of no discussion so searching as to "what if anything there is in the present situation that visibly makes for a realization of these necessary terms within a calculable future." Those who are acquainted with Mr. Veblen's work are aware of the ironic inscrutability of his manner, the detachment that is at once an evidence of his impartiality and an intimation of his corrosive scepticism. It can no longer be said, with *The Nature of Peace* under examination, that either impartiality or scepticism induces Mr. Veblen to withhold his preference, to conceal his bias, in the present contingency. That bias, however, does not lead him into any of the current patriotic extravagances. If critical acid can corrode the patriotic conceptions of "democracy" and "liberty" that are now so familiar, Mr. Veblen makes no attempt to keep such fancies from being eaten into. What is left, however, is sufficiently substantial to give him the issue that abides in the war, and its bearing on peace, and it provides him with his clue to the great eventuality, "the consequences presumably due to follow."

It would be wrong in any review of Mr. Veblen to give a mere bald outline of the work that is so full of his manifold mind. There are so many "patent imbecilities" (like the protective tariff), so many current egregious practices (like business men's sabotage), that receive characteristic illumination in transit, the bare colorless statement of his conclusions would completely leave out the poignancy that accumulates as he proceeds. His conclusions are, on the other hand, impressive enough to indicate the importance of the argument back of them, and if only for their suggestion of the massive argument they need to be reported. Defeat for the German-Imperial coalition, not victory for the Entente belligerents, is the first step toward lasting peace that he recognizes, because of the decisive difference "between those people whose patriotic affections center about the fortunes of an impersonal commonwealth and those in whom is superadded a fervent aspiration for dynastic ascendancy." Peace on terms of Germany's unconditional surrender is not discussed by Mr. Veblen on the basis of likelihood but on the basis of its desirability in relation to the chances for peace, and the unlikelihood of lasting peace in its absence. But this is not the ordinary orgiastic contemplation of an enemy destroyed. The elements in Germany that conspire against lasting peace are carefully computed, and the terms of their disintegration discussed in every detail. It is by no means forgotten that if the victorious side is not "shorn over the comb of neutralization and democracy" there can in any event be no prospect of perpetuating peace.

The present unfitness of Germany (or Japan) for lasting peace is ascribed by Mr. Veblen to the essential dynastic need for warlike enterprise, but he has no hesitation whatever in declaring in regard to the Allied Powers that peace in general demands the "relinquishment of all those undemocratic institutional survivals out of which international grievances are wont to arise." This is not the customary emphasis of goodwill-pacifists. They are fain to propose peace on the present basis of "national jealousies and discriminations" and what Mr. Veblen in his highly personal jargon calls "discrepancies." Mr. Veblen alludes to the League to Enforce Peace as a movement for the "collusive safeguarding of national discrepancies by force of arms." This toleration of existing nationalisms Mr. Veblen plainly regards as an insuperable obstacle to peace. He exposes in every detail the predisposition to war that inheres in nationalisms. "What the peace-makers might logically be expected to concern themselves about would be the elimination of these discrepancies that make for embroilment."

The military defeat of Germany seems to the author a requisite step on the direct path to peace. This is only because Germany is dynastic, however, and the German people subservient to the dynasty. One of the issues most thoroughly debated by Mr. Veblen is the pregnant issue of German democratization, and while he lays great stress on the necessity for military defeat as a first requirement of democratization he does not believe the disintegrating of Germany's dynastic "second nature" is of so hopeless a character as its historic persistence might imply. There is no complacency in the attitude that leads him to regard imperial Germany (or imperial Japan) as a stumbling-block in the road to lasting peace. It is an attitude founded on a strict and even solicitous estimate of the patent German and Japanese aims. And in so far as a peace policy involves treatment of the German people Mr. Veblen is quite certain that no trade discrimination against them, necessarily bound to recoil on the common people, would be pacifically effective or justifiable. The persecution of the German common people could take no form that would conceivably advance the cause of peace, and Mr. Veblen is careful to dissociate his belief that Germany should be beaten from the belief that the people of Germany should be made to suffer for their differentiation after the war.

Where *The Nature of Peace* seems to me to rise far and away above the current discussions of supernationalism is in its comparative freedom from unanalyzed conceptions. There is nothing sacred to Mr. Veblen in the conception of patriotism, of property, of success, of manliness, of good breeding, of national honor, of prestige. The notion of non-resistance has no terrors for him – he writes a chapter on its merits. But so dry is he that it is only one reading him attentively who will gather his extraordinarily subversive character, his invincible mind. The blessedness of this unsparing intelligence is so great that one has a constant acute pleasure in pursuing Mr. Veblen's argument. If one had long perceived for oneself, for example, that "business" means waste and inefficiency, it is pleasant to have Mr. Veblen introduce the same perceptions, but when he proceeds to locate them in his spacious understanding of the whole international problem, and to reveal their unquestionable bearing on the alternatives of war and peace, one has a happy consciousness of coming honestly to a wider and deeper view of realities. This is the supreme gift of Mr. Veblen's disinterested inquiry.

The notion that a lasting peace is compatible with the established patriotic order of things, with the status of the gentleman in England or the business man in the United States, is not entertained for one moment by Mr. Veblen, and regardless of the "maggoty conceit of national domination" which demands "the virtual erasure of the Imperial dynasty," he sees an impediment to peace in the dear establishments of "upperclass and pecuniary control" in the allied commonwealths. Chief and foremost in the pacific arrangement must come "a considerable degree of neutralization, extending to virtually all national interests and pretensions, but more particularly to all material and commercial interests of the federated peoples; and, indispensably and especially, such neutralization would have to extend to the nations from whom aggression is now apprehended, as, e.g., the German people." All manner of trade discrimination has to be abolished – "import, export and excise tariff, harbor and registry dues, subsidy, patent right, copyright, trade mark, tax exemption whether partial or exclusive, investment preferences at home and abroad." Besides this prescription for "the elimination of discrepancies that make for embroilment," a neutralization of citizenship is also indicated, the common man standing to lose nothing by these revisions. But Mr. Veblen is frank to say that "this prospect of consequences" points to a general revolution. "It has appeared in the course of the argument that the preservation of the present pecuniary law and order, with all its incidents of ownership and investment, is incompatible with an unwarlike state of peace and security. This current scheme of investment, business, and sabotage, should have an appreciably better chance of survival in the long run if the present conditions of warlike preparation and national insecurity were maintained, or if the projected peace were left in a somewhat problematical state, sufficiently precarious to keep national animosities alert, and thereby to the neglect of domestic interests, particularly of such interests as touch the popular well-being. On the other hand, it has also appeared that the cause of peace and its perpetuation might be materially advanced if precautions were taken beforehand to put out of the way as much as may be of those discrepancies of interest and sentiment between nations and between classes which make for dissension and eventual hostilities."

The weight of these phrases it is not easy to catch in passing, but nothing more significant has been written since the outbreak of the war. One has only to go back to *The Theory of Business Enterprise*, published in 1904, to learn how Mr. Veblen foresaw this war, and America's participation in it. The same rigor of intellectual standard that gave him a command of the situation at that time is discernible in this present volume, and gives him dominance now. Such severity of mind as Mr. Veblen exhibits is not likely to win him many readers, despite its Brahms-like quality, but the recommendation of Mr. Veblen is not merely the recommendation of a great philosopher of industrialism. It is not his relentless logic alone that elevates him. It is the democratic bias which *The Nature of Peace* indicates.

*The Higher Learning in America**

Veteran politicians, experienced men of affairs, to say nothing of other profound students of human nature (by no means to be placed in the same ethical class), such as tramps and charlatans, are wont to boast at odd moments that they "Know things that are not in any book"; and the complacency with which such pronouncements are for the most part received points to a somewhat general skepticism as to the competency of the book-taught mind to reveal essential truths.

The popular notion that books are not as a rule saturated with the kind of truth that is most immediately wanted is perhaps not altogether an error. Doubtless the condition complained of is not due in any degree to timidity on the part of those authoritative persons who know best, nor to any discreditable motive on the part of anyone. The fact remains, however, that one may become exceedingly well read in the authoritative and polite literature of the times without learning much about life, unless, to be sure, one has acquired somehow an ability to read between the lines. And it is, moreover, true, as the common sense of the majority of men attests, that little relief is to be had by turning to those books which are ostensibly most ingenuous and outspoken, since these books are too often the work of extremists, doctrinaires, or otherwise indifferently responsible writers.

The result is that persons – especially young persons – are prone to have recourse to fiction, and particularly to the newer fiction, as a means of satisfying a quite natural craving for that alleged "knowledge of life" which appears so difficult

* *The North American Review*, March 1919.

to get elsewhere, except indeed through a heart-to-heart talk with the "man who knows."

But so far as it touches upon institutions rather than upon the common frailties of mankind, the satire embodied in the newer fiction is but an unsatisfactory substitute for scientific analysis. It is a safe conjecture that the somewhat burlesque representations of college life contained, for example, in Ernest Poole's *The Harbor* and in Sinclair Lewis's *Trail of the Hawk,* have added not a little to the interest and popularity of the tales in question. The like is true of the exquisite and (from a literary point of view) far more legitimate characterization of a would-be college president in Henry Sydney Harrison's *Queed.* These things amuse us chiefly because of a suspicion that they represent, though in a one-sided manner, real conditions. We would not care to read this kind of criticism if we did not secretly feel that our most cherished institutions, like Launcelot Gobbo's father, do, after all, "something smack, something grow to, have a kind of taste" of the qualities more or less playfully ascribed to them. And yet this kind of institutional satire is little more than a rather aimless telling of tales out of school. The thing is perhaps worth doing; but it seems reasonable to hope that, if there is anything in it, it may be done in some better way.

To compare in point of interest such fictional criticism of college life with a perfectly serious passage from Thorstein Veblen's recently published book upon the higher learning in America, may be worth while. "It is toward the outside, in the face of the laity out of doors," writes Mr. Veblen, "that the high fence – 'the eight-fold fence' – of scholarly pretension is to be kept up. Hence the indicated means of its up-keep are such as will presumably hold the (transient) respect and affection of this laity – quasi-scholarly homiletical discourse, frequent, voluminous, edifying and optimistic;

ritualistic solemnities, diverting and vacant; spectacular affectations of (counterfeit) scholastic usage in the way of droll vestments, bizarre and archaic; parade of (make-believe) gentility; encouragement and (surreptitious) subvention of athletic contests; promulgation of (presumably) ingenuous statistics touching the volume and character of the work done." Elsewhere Mr. Veblen, after scrupulously careful deliberation, describes the typical university executive as "in some sort an itinerant dispensary of salutary verbiage."

These quotations, though necessarily somewhat misleading when removed from their context, may serve to show that in raciness and vigor of expression, as in apparent candor, Mr. Veblen is far superior to the run of fictional satirists. As a matter of fact, his dry and precise style makes all ordinary irony seem by comparison clumsy and ineffectual, while his magnificent phlegm reduces most criticism of the kind called "bold" or "indiscreet" to the relative condition of tentative or peevish fault-finding. Unintentionally, no doubt, Mr. Veblen approaches more nearly the manner of Jonathan Swift than does any other contemporary writer. He might, indeed, be not inaccurately described as a modern, scientific Swift, dispassionate instead of bitter.

So much for the manner, but what of the substance? "*Communia maledicta,*" as Bacon says, "is nothing much"; and the saying holds true no less for simple vituperation aimed at institutions or types than for that which is directed at individuals.

Of the justice of Mr. Veblen's arraignment of the universities, every reader must, of course, judge for himself. The reviewer feels warranted in saying this: that *The Higher Learning in America* bears all the marks of being one of those rare books which contain such truth as seldom finds its way into print — truth such as results from genuine experience intrepidly thought out, truth such as in the nature of the case *cannot* by the generality of writers be expressed with sufficient candor and at the same time with sufficient philosophy to make it either safe or acceptable. Here is the *whole* case against the universities, including some of the colloquial expressions (verging, it must be confessed, upon scurrility) of a suppressed body of opinion; the whole case set forth with so comprehensive a grasp, with so impartial an eye to the working of cause and effect, that in the end no one is judged, no one need feel offended, no one has anything to quarrel with except facts (said to be capable of documentary proof when not notoriously true) and a perfectly impersonal, logically constructed conception of the relation of the universities to modern civilization in America.

Other books of Mr. Veblen's have been from time to time noticed in these pages. The fault found with these treatises (when any fault could be found) was simply that the author presented the "drift of events" as a fatally determined chain of causation, without any acknowledgment of purpose on his own part or any admission that the fatal chain might be in any way modified by a grasp of the ideas he was himself engaged in setting forth; the truth being that though events be fatally determined, our conscious thoughts are links in the chain, and, being such links, are at the same time our purposes; so that to deny purpose is to give up the possibility of thinking intelligibly (in the last analysis), and to encourage that false fatalism which resolves *not* to think.

Whether this criticism be just or not, it has no special application to the work under consideration. In this book, Mr. Veblen simply points out the obvious fact that the higher learning is the very core of our civilization. "For good or ill, civilized men have come to hold that this matter-of-fact knowledge of things is the only end in life that indubitably justifies itself. So that nothing more irretrievably shameful would overtake modern civilization than the miscarriage of this modern learning, which is the most valued spiritual asset of civilized mankind." He then proceeds to show what the fate of the higher learning in the hands of the universities is likely to be. The reader may draw his own conclusions, purposeful or not.

As an illustration of the lucidity of thought to which so impersonal a view may lead, one may cite the author's conclusion in regard to the long continued and fruitless controversy that has been carried on, under pressure of business influences, about the practical value of higher – i.e., of university, not college – education. "Pushed by this popular prejudice, and themselves drifting under compulsion of the same prevalent bias, even the seasoned scholars and scientists – Matthew Arnold's 'Remnant' – have taken to heart this question of the use of the higher learning in the pursuit of gain. Of course, it has no such use, and the many shrewdly designed solutions of the conundrum have necessarily run out in a string of sophistical dialectics. The place of disinterested knowledge in modern civilization is neither that of means to private gain, nor that of an intermediate step in 'the roundabout process of the production of goods.' "

The case is really as simple as that of the Emperor's Clothes. To be sure, a child could see that the emperor had no clothes, though older people remained under the illusion of habitual pretense. To see that the higher education has really no "practical" value requires something more than a child's institution. It requires, nowadays, a superior talent for straight thinking.

Others have pointed out the preposterous mixture of idealism and worship of business success which is characteristic of modern civilization everywhere and especially in America. No one has brought the essential idea so effectively to bear upon any concrete problem as has Mr. Veblen upon the problem of the higher education. It is the intrusion of business ideals and business methods upon the true and professed interests of the university everywhere – in the governing boards, in the academic administration, in the work of the executive and of the teachers – that is doing the mischief. And this intrusion is so natural a result of the whole social system under which we live that it seems unavoidable.

Mr. Veblen is dispassionate, but his thought has a heat much more powerful to melt away obstacles than those more or less factitious bursts of indignation that are often supposed to accomplish this result. His book, unhopeful as it is in tone and intent, will certainly not be without an ultimate effect in bringing about a different state of affairs – which may or may not, according to Mr. Veblen's philosophy, be an improvement.

Reports, etc.

Veblen's Record at Carleton College

April 18, 1932

Prof. Joseph Dorfman
Columbia University
New York City

My dear Prof. Dorfman:

The following is the record of the work done by Thorstein Bunde Veblen at Carleton College:

1877-1878

Greek	87	85	86	Rhetoricals	84	89	89
Latin	86	85		Course not designated			91
Mathematics	90	90	81				

1878-1879

Greek	85	88		Rhetoricals	90	91	91
Modern Languages	98	95		Courses not			
Mathematics	79	82	95	designated	63	96	77
Rhetoric	92						

1879-1880

Greek		90	Logic	92.5
Latin	86	90	Geology	83
Modern Languages	90	92.5	Rhetoricals	90
Astronomy		91	Courses not designated	92
Mental Philosophy		77	American Literature	92
Latin		90	History of Civilization	93
Political Economy		94	Moral Philosophy	93
English Literature		85	Evidences of Christianity	94

Mr. Veblen's preparatory record is as follows:

Greek Grammar	87	Arithmetic	81
Anabasis	98	Algebra	71
Iliad	91	Geometry	87
Latin Grammar	79	English Grammar	72
Latin Prose Composition	74	Modern Geography	99
Caesar	93	Ancient Geography	84
Cicero	80	Greek History	93
Virgil	82	Roman History	88

Mr. Veblen was awarded the Atkins Prize in 1877.

Sincerely yours,

PETER OLESEN,

Registrar

Signers of Petition Asking for Nomination of Thorstein Veblen as President of the American Economic Association*

Edith Abbott, University of Chicago
E. E. Agger, Columbia University
Clement Akerman, Reed College
A. B. Anthony, University of Pittsburgh
Florence A. Armstrong, Institute of Economics
Willard E. Atkins, University of North Carolina
A. J. Barlow, University of Virginia
Harry Elmer Barnes, Smith College
W. C. Beatty, Cornell University
S. E. Beckett, University of Chicago
B. H. Beckhart, Columbia University
Theodore N. Beckman, Ohio State University
W. H. Belden, Ohio State University
Claude L. Benner, Institute of Economics
Edward Berman, University of Illinois
Abraham Berglund, University of Virginia
Roy G. Blakey, University of Minnesota
Ralph H. Blanchard, Columbia University
Solomon Blum, University of California
James C. Bonbright, Columbia University
E. L. Bowers, Ohio State University
James E. Boyle, Cornell University
S. J. Brandenburg, Clark University
Sophonisba P. Breckinridge, University of Chicago
Paul F. Brissenden, Columbia University

* Copy in possession of editor.

Raymond T. Bye, University of Pennsylvania
J. Ray Cable, Washington University
Arthur W. Calhoun, Brookwood Labor College
Robert A. Campbell, Institute of Economics
Niles Carpenter, University of Buffalo
William J. Carson, Federal Reserve Board
Warren B. Catlin, Bowdoin College
Robert E. Chaddock, Columbia University
Joseph P. Chamberlain, Columbia University
W. G. Chanter, Wesleyan University
John M. Chapman, Columbia University
Charles H. Chase, Institute of Economics
Ewan Clague, University of Wisconsin
John R. Commons, University of Wisconsin
Alzada Comstock, Mount Holyoke College
Morris A. Copeland, Cornell University
John H. Cover, University of Denver
Garfield V. Cox, University of Chicago
Donald R. Craig, University of Pittsburgh
P. C. Crockett, University of Oregon
John Cummings, Federal Reserve Board
Joseph E. Cummings, University of Minnesota
H. C. Daines, University of Chicago
D. H. Davenport, Columbia University
H. J. Davenport, Cornell University
F. G. Dickinson, University of Illinois
Z. C. Dickinson, University of Michigan
Ethel B. Dietrich, Mount Holyoke College
David L. Dodd, Columbia University
H. B. Dolbeare, Cornell University
Paul H. Douglas, University of Chicago
Horace B. Drury, Institute of Economics
Louis I. Dublin, New York City

L. R. Edminster, Institute of Economics
Donald English, Cornell University
J. Gilbert Evans, University of Pittsburgh
Helen Everett, Brookings Graduate School
Herbert Feis, University of Cincinnati
George Fillippetti, Columbia University
Clyde O. Fisher, Wesleyan University
J. A. Fisher, Ohio State University
John A. Fitch, Columbia University
H. M. Fletcher, University of Illinois
Felix Fluegel, University of California
Paul R. Fossum, Wesleyan University
William T. Foster, Newton, Mass.
C. B. Fowler, New York University
Ralph F. Fuchs, Institute of Economics
S. S. Garrett, Cornell University
Edwin F. Gay, Harvard University
Franklin H. Giddings, Columbia University
J. H. Gilbert, University of Oregon
J. M. Gillman, University of Pittsburgh
E. A. Goldenweiser, Federal Reserve Board
Carter L. Goodrich, University of Michigan
Eugene Greider, Rutgers University
Bartow Griffiss, Carnegie Institute of Technology
Barbara N. Grimes, University of California
Harold W. Guest, Stanford University
Charles A. Gulick, Jr., Columbia University
J. E. Hagerty, Ohio State University
Robert M. Haig, Columbia University
Robert L. Hale, Columbia University
Walton H. Hamilton, Brookings Graduate School
Max S. Handman, University of Texas
Alvin H. Hansen, University of Minnesota

J. C. Hemmeon, McGill University
Amy Hewes, Mount Holyoke College
William W. Hewett, University of Pennsylvania
A. C. Hodge, University of Chicago
Homer Hoyt, University of Missouri
Roland Hugins, Institute of Economics
M. H. Hunter, University of Illinois
C. C. Huntington, Ohio State University
John Ise, University of Kansas
Jens P. Jensen, University of Kansas
Aryness Joy, Mount Holyoke College
Abraham D. Kaplan, University of Denver
Albert S. Keister, North Carolina College for Women
M. S. Kendrick, Cornell University
Thomas L. Kibler, University of North Carolina
E. A. Kincaid, University of Virginia
Frank H. Knight, University of Iowa
Vincent W. Lanfear, University of Pittsburgh
G. N. Lauman, Cornell University
J. M. Lear, University of North Carolina
E. P. Learned, University of Kansas
Louis Levine [now Lorwin], Institute of Economics
Isaac Lippincott, Washington University
Isador Lubin, Institute of Economics
Hastings Lyon, Columbia University
Leverett S. Lyon, Brookings Graduate School
Theresa S. MacMahon, University of Chicago
J. D. Magee, New York University
L. K. Manley, University of Pittsburgh
Stacy May, Brookings Graduate School
H. H. Maynard, Ohio State University
Roswell C. McCrea, Columbia University
C. E. McGuire, Institute of Economics

S. P. Meech, University of Chicago
S. Miller, University of Wisconsin
Frederick C. Mills, Columbia University
L. W. Mints, University of Chicago
E. G. Misner, Cornell University
Wesley C. Mitchell, Columbia University
Henry L. Moore, Columbia University
E. W. Morehouse, University of Wisconsin
Charles S. Morgan, Institute of Economics
O. S. Morgan, Columbia University
H. G. Moulton, Institute of Economics
Henry R. Mussey, Wellesley College
Earl D. Myers, Mount Holyoke College
W. I. Myers, Cornell University
S. H. Nerlove, University of Chicago
Mabel Newcomer, Vassar College
E. G. Nourse, Institute of Economics
William F. Ogburn, Columbia University
John B. O'Leary, Worcester, Mass.
Herlup V. Olsen, University of Chicago
Saul C. Oppenheim, University of Michigan
R. N. Owens, Washington University
Thomas Walker Page, Institute of Economics
Elinor Pancoast, Goucher College
Ernest M. Patterson, University of Pennsylvania
S. Howard Patterson, University of Pennsylvania
W. R. Peabody, Rutgers College
F. A. Pearson, Cornell University
Harvey W. Peck, University of Vermont
Selig Perlman, University of Wisconsin
W. C. Presnell, University of North Carolina
Margaret Prior, University of Wisconsin
Bertha Haven Putnam, Mount Holyoke College

Paul A. Rauchenbush, University of Wisconsin
Charles G. Reeves, University of North Carolina
E. C. Robbins, University of Oregon
Maurice H. Robinson, University of Illinois
James Harvey Rogers[1], University of Missouri
H. A. Ross, Cornell University
C. O. Ruggles, Ohio State University
William A. Russell, University of Washington
R. S. Saby, Gettysburg College
David J. Saposs, Brookwood Labor College
Henry Schultz, Children's Bureau
G. T. Schwenning, International Y.M.C.A.
DR Scott, University of Missouri
G. P. Scoville, Cornell University
R. W. Semenoff, University of Pittsburgh
M. L. Shine, University of Wisconsin
Vladimir G. Simkhovitch, Columbia University
Sumner H. Slichter, Cornell University
L. E. Smart, Ohio State University
J. Russell Smith, Columbia University
Tipton R. Snavely, University of Virginia
William F. Spafford, University of Vermont

---

[1] Rogers who was then at Missouri, reported to Douglas that the Missouri department was 100 per cent behind the project. At about the same time, Rogers spearheaded an attempt to bring Veblen to the University of Texas. He declared in a private letter that this would put Texas on the map. He informed H. J. Davenport that if Veblen went, he himself would certainly go with him. Davenport replied that Texas might get Veblen if there were not too great opposition from the fundamentalists (in religion). "He is Lutheran he says. I am afraid I should be ineligible as an agnostic." (Rogers to Douglas, June 3, 1905, copy; Rogers to Bell, May 26, copy; Rogers to Davenport, June 3, 1925, copy; Davenport to Rogers, undated; all in Rogers Papers, Yale University Library. On Rogers see *The Economic Mind in American Civilization,* IV, 302-308; V, 688-694, 767).

A. M. Spalding, University of Pittsburgh
C. P. Spruill, Jr. University of North Carolina
W. R. Stark, Federal Reserve Board
J. Wesley Sternberg, University of Kansas
Walter W. Stewart, Federal Reserve Board
Archibald H. Stockder, Columbia University
M. M. Stockwell, University of Illinois
F. T. Stockton, University of Kansas
Arthur E. Suffern, Institute of Economics
Frank Tannenbaum, Washington, D.C.
A. G. Taylor, University of Illinois
George R. Taylor, Amherst College
Paul S. Taylor, University of California
Woodlief Thomas, Federal Reserve Board
John P. Troxell, University of Wisconsin
Rexford G. Tugwell, Columbia University
Francis Tyson, University of Pittsburgh
Roland S. Vaile, University of Minnesota
T. W. Van Metre, Columbia University
C. L. Van Sickle, University of Pittsburgh
Jacob Viner, University of Chicago
Frank B. Ward, University of Pennsylvania
G. A. Warfield, Cornell University
Gordon S. Watkins, University of California, Southern Branch
George S. Wehrwein, University of Wisconsin
W. C. Weidler, Ohio State University
George Weiss, Institute of Economics
W. E. Weld, Columbia University
Faith M. Williams, Cornell University
K. M. Williamson, Wesleyan University
Clair Wilcox, University of Pennsylvania
Sidney W. Wilcox, Chicago, Illinois

A. B. Wolfe, Ohio State University
E. J. Working, Institute of Economics
Helen Sumner Woodbury, Institute of Economics
Robert Morse Woodbury, Institute of Economics
Chester W. Wright, University of Chicago
Helen R. Wright, Brookings Graduate School
Ivan Wright, University of Illinois
Philip G. Wright, Institute of Economics
E. W. Zimmerman, University of North Carolina

Mitchell's Translations of Extracts from Simiand*

Criterion of Law of Diminishing Utility

Even for needs which are susceptible of satiety there exists what may be called a point of satisfaction, and as long as this point is not reached satisfaction grows with the quantity employed to satisfy. Need become a passion has precisely the characteristic of growing indefinitely, even when the quantity employed to satisfy it increases. This law has no reference to the relations of the different needs among themselves. Nevertheless many first economic phenomena arise from or depend upon these relations. It is not that these objections and also other possible objections are not perceived by some at least of the theorists who attribute to this law a fundamental rôle. But they disregard them and declare them to be without importance. In truth, if they are more considerable than these authors authoritatively admit they give way nevertheless to a last objection which in the end can dispense with all the others.

This radical objection is that finally and ultimately this pretended fundamental law remains outside, or at least beside, what is precisely to be explained, if indeed economic science really has in view to explain economic reality. This law, even if it is entirely applicable, is of value only from the point of view of the individual, for things taken in rela-

* As noted above, there are some similarities between Veblen's and Simiand's critiques of neo-classical economics. We have already presented one of Mitchell's uncorrected translations from François Simiand's book, *La Méthode positive en science économique*, the passage which is headed "Criticism of Theory of Exchange Value," see pp. 237-238 above. The others which are also from the Mitchell Papers are made available here. As with the previous translation, the headings are Mitchell's.

tion to consumption, direct and immediate. It is no longer of use, it has perhaps no sense, from the point of view of a community, for things considered in relation to durable utility, considered according to their exchangeable quality. From the moment when a thing exists which has a constant value for men, and above all, from the moment when this thing can be exchanged for other things and other things for it, each thing may have for the individual a satisfaction-value beyond the amount of the satisfaction of the direct need which this individual has of this thing, since it may be worth to him still other satisfactions without limit. What then can we learn from this law as to the phenomena which are outside the realm where, under the most favorable circumstances, it can be applied? And who does not see that these phenomena are precisely the most numerous, the most notable, the most important of those which an economic science can undertake to comprehend? It is in vain to pretend by this means to go from the simple to the complex, from the element to the compound. How shall a psychological disposition, existing or possible of existence in the individual supposedly isolated, and no longer existing in the individual taken collectively, explain what is produced in the individual taken collectively; that is to say, explain precisely what causes itself to cease to exist? Will it be said that the collective need itself will follow the same law, and that consequently the same phenomena will result therefrom in this new fashion? Collective psychology is no longer the domain of individual introspection, and, if this law exists in the social individual, it must be established by exterior observation; that is to say, we must change our method. Every attempt to substitute for this law a better one, if it is of the same sort, is condemned in advance to suffer at the same point the same defeat. (pp. 195-197).

Criticism of Modern Theory of Interest

Will it be believed that before the development of credit, of loans for economic purposes, of State borrowing of a perpetual and normal character – will it be believed that, further back still, in the Middle Ages, in Classic antiquity – all the psychological dispositions which could have relation to an idea or to a phenomenon such as the interest on capital, had, or could have had, an identical formula? Of this relativity there is no notable trace in our authors. Thus these "psychological laws," these verifications of facts, which determine general postulates, are, like the facts which serve for choice among the hypotheses, not the results of experience, of ascertainable value, of revisable and perfectable nature, but the products of an arbitrary empiricism, subject to indefinite reservations and disputes. (p. 75).

Problem of Human Nature in Economics

Whether the psychological postulate offered to economic research be complex or simple does not matter for the purposes of the examination undertaken here. It is natural to take by preference the simple case. The German school which, with Wagner for example, distinguishes five motives in the economic activity of man, or the Austrian school, which innovates detailed analyses, hitherto neglected, can be set aside.

The economy of so-called classic tradition which gives an account of the economic activity of man by means of one preponderant motive alone, may be retained by preference. Its initial psychological proposition is thus stated with sufficient accuracy: "In the economic order, the principal and usual motive of human actions is personal interest, which impels us to seek the greatest amount of advantage with the least possible amount of effort, of sacrifice and of risk."

If the accuracy and the sufficiency of the principle itself have been warmly contested (and indeed, with reason, it would seem), the pretended analytical application of the principle has much less attracted critical attention. It appears, nevertheless, to be worthy of examination.

Let us take some examples. Let us consider one point in the theory of capital. An "economic man" is the proprietor of capital. Following the rule of his activity, he seeks to employ it for his greater interest. What does that mean? He can either place it out, "turn it to account," or spend it. In order that he should desire to abstain from spending it, that is, in order to sacrifice immediate enjoyment, he must find in investment the possibility of a greater ulterior enjoyment; that is to say, an increase of the capital itself. The rate of interest offered to capital is then the decisive factor which influences the employment of capital. If the rate of interest falls, for example as the result of a rise in the rate of salaries, capital will turn aside from enterprise; industrial activity will be fettered and will diminish.

But why should not the deduction take another course? The economic man, let us say, can spend the capital which he possesses at a given moment, or not spend it at that moment. Personal interest, which guides his actions, will mean for him (if moreover he can consider his needs sufficiently satisfied for the time being) to apply himself to the preservation of this capital for the possible services he can obtain from it later on. The investment of the capital is then essentially designed to preserve it. It is assuredly not negligible that this investment be at the same time remunerative; but the important thing is that it be safe. The security of investment is then the decisive factor which influences the employment of capital. The rate of interest may fall without entailing displacement, if the security of the investment remains unshaken; still more so if it tends to increase. And thus capital may flow precisely to where the rate of interest is lowest.

The two courses lead then to conclusions, to "laws of capital," which are directly opposed. How decide between them? How know whether the economic man, when he will have to choose between the two considerations, will consider that his greatest interest is to increase his capital, even with risk, or on the contrary, that it is to preserve it, even without gain? (pp. 10-14).

Once stated the psychological postulate which is assumed to explain the economic activity of man, particular economic theories are bound (explicitly, or, as is more frequently the case, implicitly) not to utilise any but human actions analytically based upon this postulate. So, it will be found that the analysis, in the cases considered, may in reality show two or more divergent meanings of action which are equally conformable to the general postulate. In fact, however (else how should a positive result be obtained from the quest) only one of these meanings, to the exclusion (often unconscious) of the other has been retained by the doctrine. How has the meaning adopted been chosen?

It is probable that the psychological deduction of which political economy boasted was illusory. The applications of the principle of personal interest to cases of particular economic actions which, often in good faith, it was imagined were deduced from this same principle, were in reality the result of observation, summary, unconscious perhaps, but real and indispensable; . . . exact or inexact (this is another question) but still observation. (pp. 21-23).

Since the analytical method led to many different roads, the fact that one alone among them was chosen proves that the choice of the way followed was in reality experimental. Since, in spite of all, observation intervenes, should it not be conscious and methodical? (p. 26).

Positive science, economic science, must then seek out the

psychology of the economic life, instead of presupposing it, and it must be prepared to find it neither simple nor general. (p. 30).

We must not be surprised then that economic science, experimentally conducted, in psychological matters as in every other, advances slowly and gives slight results. . . . Economic science must at present consider itself extremely ignorant. This is perhaps the progress of which it has most need. A method truly experimental, especially in economic psychology, could inspire it with this modesty – fertile later on. (pp. 37-38).

Pure Theory vs. Positive Science

Let us consider the very theories which take the name of theories of pure economy. What is the fundamental problem from which all the others are derived or to which they are subordinate? It is to determine the *conditions of equilibrium* of a market *ideally definite* called a free market. But why desire to determine the conditions of equilibrium rather than the conditions of disequilibrium, or of such and such disequilibrium, unless by the implied final postulate that equilibrium is the normal, ideal state of the economic market?

In truth, such problems and such theories are not problems or theories of positive science. A problem of positive science is in this form: how is such a fact to be explained? what is the cause, what are the results, of such and such a phenomenon? and not in the form of: how can such a result be obtained? what are the means to such an end? A theory of positive science is constituted by the causal explanation, in the form of a law, of a phenomenon or of a category of phenomena; it is not the ideal determination of a certain hypothetical system of relations among elements conceived by the mind. (pp. 182-183.)

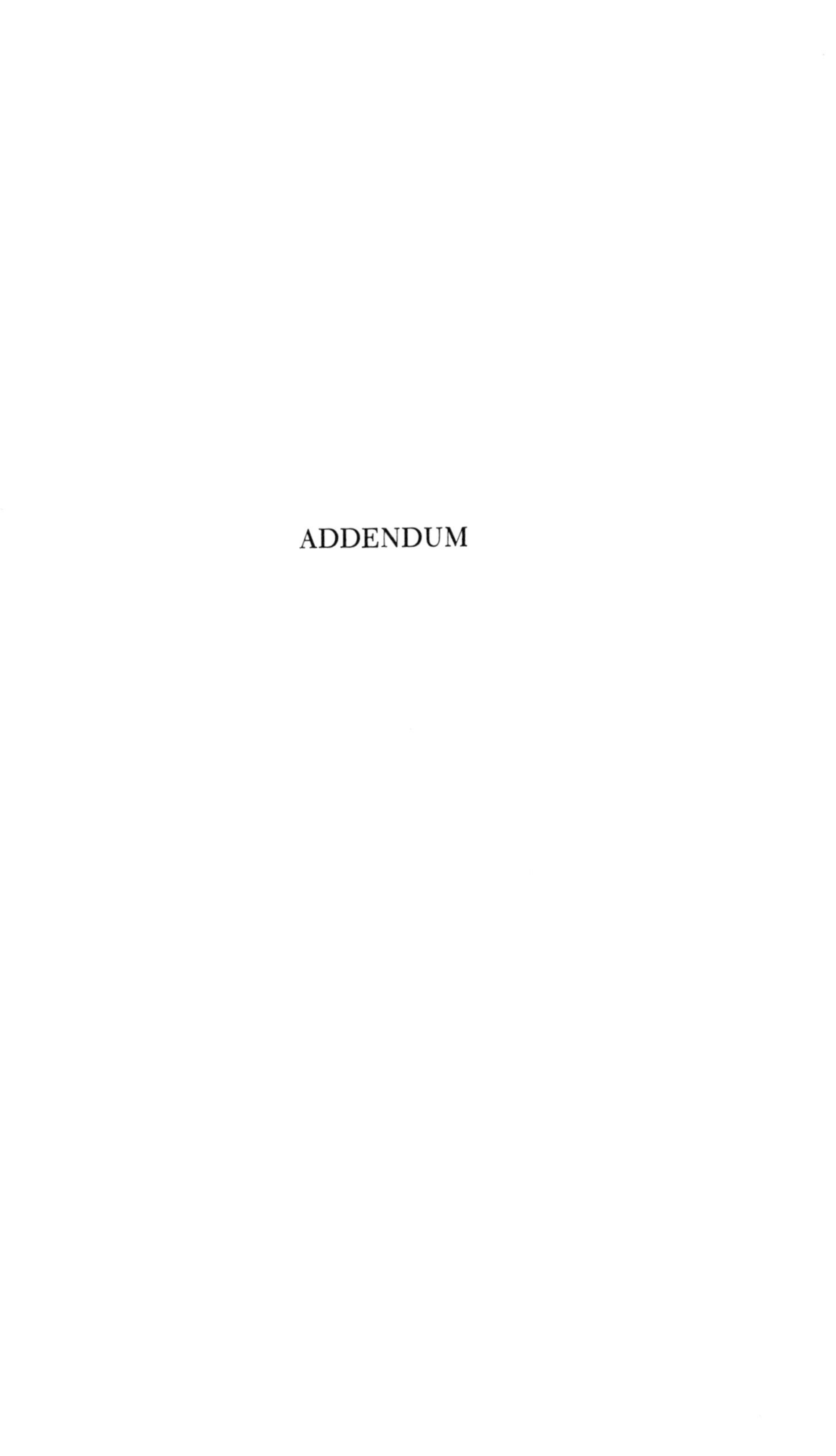

ADDENDUM

Addendum

While this book was going to press, interesting items on Veblen continued to come my way. The typesetting company, thanks in part to the persuasive powers of Augustus M. Kelley, generously agreed to let me present them at the very end of the book. Except for the first and last they deal primarily with the influence of Veblen on economists and allied social scientists outside the United States. The first presents the view of the late Ralph E. Flanders, United States Senator from Vermont and prominent industrialist and mechanical engineer.

In an address on the motivation of business decision-making before the American Economic Association in 1950 he criticized "the celebrated thesis of Thorstein Veblen: that the moving decisions are those which serve 'conspicuous waste.' That . . . thesis . . . has fascinated readers . . . , particularly young readers, in the well-nigh two generations which have passed since it was first published. Veblen lived in the decadent and dying days of Fifth Avenue and Newport Society. There he witnessed the lavish and public expenditure of wealth in magnificent houses; liveried coachmen, footmen, and lackeys; and extravagant entertainment in the Fifth Avenue homes and the houses on the Cliff Walk at Newport . . . [H]e came easily to the conclusion that the womenfolk of American business, with their insatiable demands for houses, dress, jewels, and social display, were keeping the American business nose to the grindstone of dollar production so that 'conspicuous waste' could be maintained, continued, and, if possible, expanded." Senator Flanders complained that Veblen's description of the typical, genuine business man's behavior was not true even in Veblen's day. For good examples Veblen should have looked at the great empire builders, such as John D. Rockefeller in oil and James J. Hill in railroads. "Perhaps, too, Mr. Veblen might have looked at another railroad builder, Mr. E. H. Harriman, with whom in his later years Mr. Hill was locked in deadly struggle. That great mansion on a mountain top near the New York-New Jersey line which Mr. Harriman built for himself might seem to be an example of 'conspicuous waste.' Yet he probably thought of it simply as befitting his station and achievements, for neither he nor his wife belonged to the tribe of wasters."[1]

For further indications of Veblen's world wide impact, we turn first to Australia. Robert Francis Irvine, the first professor of economics at the University of Sydney, long played a large role in the world of affairs as a government official and member of royal commissions; he engaged in public debates on issues ranging from industrial relations and housing to monetary and fiscal policy. In his *Midas Delusion* (1933), Irvine recalled that he and his students while searching for books that would stimulate their interest and thought "discovered Thorstein Veblen's *Theory of the Leisure Class*, the profound irony of which, only half concealed by studiously cold, scientific language, made a deep impression on

---

[1] "How are Top Executive Decisions Made?" *The American Economic Review*, May 1951, pp. 93-94.

Edgar Monsanto Queeny, chairman of the board of the Monsanto Chemical Co., was another prominent industrialist who felt that Veblen must be answered, not ignored. In *The Spirit of Enterprise* (1943) he devoted a chapter to Veblen under the title of "The Prophet and His Works." He attributed most of the economic ills of the nation to the New Deal whose "characteristics can be traced in substantial measure to the incubation of the teachings of the late Thorstein Veblen." [*The Spirit of Enterprise* (New York: Harper, 1943) p. 64].

the minds of many of us."[2] After drawing from *The Theory of the Leisure Class* the differentiation of employments in the "barbarian" society into those of "exploit" and industry," he later in the book proceeded to the differentiation between "industrial experts" and "business managers," including "financiers" as presented in *The Engineers and the Price System.*

From the University of Graz, came a salute to *The Theory of the Leisure Class* by a professor of law and a founder of sociology, Ludwick Gumplowicz. Lester Frank Ward had sent him a copy of his review in *The American Journal of Sociology;* Gumplowicz acknowledged it "with enthusiasm." He wrote: "Sie haben mir durch Ubersendung Ihrer Besprechung Veblens eine grosse Freude bereitet. Ich lese und lese wieder Ihre vortrefflichen Ausfungen. Sie sprechen mir aus der Seele wenn Sie sagen: 'If there is one thing that the world does not want it is truth.' Bravo!"[3]

In the Veblen book I wrote that "in Germany, Sombart had had a high admiration for Veblen since the appearance of *The Theory of Business Enterprise;* Max Weber thought much of *The Thory of the Leisure Class.*" I would like to

[2] *The Midas Delusion* (Adelaide: Harrell, 1933) p. 3.

Elsewhere Irvine used the phrase "wasteful ostentation," which was a good synonym for "conspicuous waste." ["The Influence of Distribution on Production," in *Report of the Eighty-Fourth Meeting of the British Association for the Advancement of Science,* 1914 (1915) p. 482].

[3] Gumplowicz to Ward, June 17, 1900, in "The Letters of Albion W. Small to Lester F. Ward," III, edited by B. J. Stern, *Social Forces,* December 1936, p. 182.

Small, who was the editor of *The American Journal of Sociology* which was published at the University of Chicago, had written: "The review is all right! I merely omitted the single word *homeopathic,* because this is a storm center just now and sensitiveness is at an abnormal tension. Otherwise the virility of the communication is not too strenuous for our purposes." (Small to Ward, April 12, 1900, in "The Letters of Albion W. Small to Lester F. Ward," III, p. 182).

present here additional citations from the works of these two sympathetic critics.

In the preface of the last volume of his greatest work, *Der moderne Kapitalismus* (1928), Sombart declared that he would quite often refer to Veblen's various treatises, and in the first chapter he listed as Veblen's fundamental studies not only *The Theory of Business Enterprise* but also *The Instinct of Workmanship* and *Absentee Ownership.*[4]

Sombart by no means neglected *The Theory of the Leisure Class.* In *Luxus und Kapitalismus (Luxury and Capitalism),* he declared that "Veblen's *Theory of the Leisure Class* (1899 and later editions) is a brilliant attempt to explain luxury and its changes from the psychological as well as the sociological viewpoint." Taking a sort of Freudian slant, he went on to say "All personal luxury springs from purely sensuous pleasure. . . . But once luxury has been established, we find that a number of other motives further its growth. Ambition, love of display, ostentation, and lust for power may be weighty motives; they are really the desire to outdo the next man. Veblen in his brilliant book on the 'leisure class' attributes all valuation of luxury and property to this urge to distinguish one's self. Even if we grant that this instinct, like hunger and love, is one of the basic instincts of man, we must admit that its manifestation in the form of luxury depends somehow on the concurrence of certain conditions. Plainly this presupposes that luxury already exists and that the display of similar or greater luxury furnishes the means of gratifying the impulse to outdo others. The most convenient means for gratifying the craving for superiority is the accumulation of things, quantitative luxury, number of

[4] *Der moderne Kapitalismus,* 3 volumes (published in six) (Munich and Leipzig: Duncker & Humblot, 1902-1928) III, xviii, 3. The references to Veblen generally for information became so numerous that the last entry in the index reads "720ff."

slaves, size of property or fortune, order of rank, and the like.[5] But if luxury is to become personal, materialistic luxury, it must be predicated on an awakened sensuousness and, above all, on a mode of life which has been influenced decisively by eroticism. Turning to the period under discussion, we note that the stage had been set for the advent of great luxury. All the necessary elements were present: wealth, sexual freedom, the striving of certain groups of the population to get ahead, and a preference for living in large cities, which as we have seen in the previous chapters were exclusively centers of pleasure before the 19th century."[6]

Turning to Weber, we find that he made use of *The Theory of Business Enterprise* in his most famous work, *The Protestant Ethic and the Spirit of Capitalism.* After noting "that most important principle of the capitalistic ethic which is generally formulated 'honesty is the best policy,' " he added

[5] Sombart explained that "quantitative luxury is synonymous with prodigality; such as the keeping of a hundred servants when one would do, or the simultaneous striking of three matches to light one cigar, etc. Qualitative luxury is the use of goods of superior quality. These two types can be, and in most cases are, combined. From the concept of qualitative luxury we derive the concept of 'luxury goods,' which may be characterized as 'refined goods.' 'Refinement' is any treatment of a product over and above that which is needed to make it ordinarily useful."

[6] *Luxury and Capitalism,* translated by W. R. Dittmar (Ann Arbor, Michigan: University of Michigan Press, 1967) pp. 58-61. The German work was first published in 1913, 2nd ed. 1922.

It has been noted by a Swiss scholar that Sombart relies expressly on Veblen in the lengthy essay "Der Kapitalistische Unternehmer," which appeared in *Archiv für Sozialwissenschaft und Sozialpolitik,* XXIV Band 1909, pp. 689-738. [Carl Eugster, *Thorstein Veblen 1857-1929. Darstellung und Deutung Amerikanischen institutionellen Denkens aus seinem Werk heraus* (Zurich: Europa Verlag, 1952) p. 110]. Sombart after hailing *The Theory of Business Enterprise,* said "Veblen's investigations are always valuable because they deal concretely for the first time with entirely new aspects of entrepreneurship in a fundamental theoretical manner." (Footnote, p. 722).

a celebrated footnote. This read: "Veblen in his suggestive book *The Theory of Business Enterprise* is of the opinion that this motto belongs only to early capitalism. But economic supermen, who, like the present captains of industry, have stood beyond good and evil, have always existed, and the statement is still true of the broad underlying strata of business men."[7]

It has been claimed that "Weber, in his writings on status, echoed the functional analysis of the role of style presented by Veblen [in *The Theory of the Leisure Class*]. For Weber, as for Veblen, the function of conspicuous consumption – that is, of emphasis, on pragmatically useless styles of consumption that take many years to learn – was to prevent mobility and to institutionalize the privileges of those who had risen to the top in previous years or epochs. Status groups are therefore identifiable by specific styles of life Even though the original source of status was economic achievement, a status system, once in existence, operates independently of the class system and even seeks to negate its values. This, as Weber and Veblen both suggested, explains the seemingly surprising phenomenon that even to an industrial capitalist society, money-making is considered vulgar by many in privileged positions, and the children of those who have made money are frequently to be found in non-commercial circles."[7a]

---

[7] *The Protestant Ethic and the Spirit of Capitalism*, translated by Talcott Parsons (London: Allen and Unwin, 1930) pp. 151, 258. Weber after referring to "That powerful tendency toward uniformity of life, which today so immensely aids the capitalistic interest in the standardization of production," stated in the appropriate footnote "On this point again see Veblen's *Theory of Business Enterprise*." (*The Protestant Ethic*, pp. 169, 175).

[7a] Seymour M. Lipset, *Revolution and Counterrevolution. Change and Persistence in Social Structures* (1948; Garden City, New York: Doubleday, Anchor Books, revised and updated edition, 1970) p. 171.

One of Weber's biographers used Veblen's concept of sabotage in describing the conditions for the breakdown of Weber's ideal bureaucracy. "An ideally functioning bureaucracy in his [Weber's] sense is the most efficient method of solving large-scale organizational tasks. But this is true only if these tasks involve more or less stable norms and hence the effort to maintain the rule of law and achieve an equitable administration of affairs. These conditions are absent when the tasks are assigned by an omnipotent and revolutionary authority. Under the simulated combat conditions of a totalitarian regime the norms governing conduct do not stay put for any length of time. And in the face of an unremitting drive for prodigies of achievement officials will tend to use their devices of concealment for a systematic if tacit 'withdrawal of efficiency' (Veblen)."[8]

A United Nations economist has clarified one aspect of Veblen's concept of sabotage by business as follows: "acceleration of repeat sales through the conscientious withdrawal of efficiency in Veblen's sense—razor blades that immediately lose their edge, electric light bulbs that don't last as long as they could, nylons that run."[9]

From Professor K. William Kapp of the University of Basel comes another use of Veblen's concept of vested interest. He used it in outlining "a whole pattern of reaction of an en-

---

[8] Reinhard Bendix, *Max Weber* (Garden City, N. Y.: Doubleday, 1960) p. 458.

Bendix also used Veblen's concept of sabotage to describe the bafflement of Peter the Great's attempt to westernize Russia. "Contemporary observers . . . described the 'withdrawal of efficiency' (Veblen) with which the aristocracy met Peter's incessant demands for service and his efforts to promote the application of western technical skills." [*Work and Authority in Industry* (New York: Wiley, 1954) p. 151].

[9] John H. G. Pierson, *Insuring Full Employment* (New York: The Viking Press, 1964) p. 158.

trenched community of scholars against its critics," especially in economics. "One reaction is to ignore them by a conspiracy of silence by all those who have 'invested' in the established body of doctrine and thus may be said to have a 'vested interest' in it, to use a favorite term of Veblen. This period can last a long time."[10]

H. D. Dickinson of the University of Leeds, close friend intellectually and personally of Maurice Dobb, also made use of the concept vested interests. In *Institutional Revenue. A Study of the Influence of Social Institutions on the Distribution of Wealth,* he maintained for example that "any system of regulating entry into an occupation by registration and licensing may set up vested interests and give rise to Institutional Revenue."[11]

My last item provides pretty good evidence that Veblen's name has become almost a household word, at least in the United States. The crossword puzzle in the New York *Times* of August 31, 1972, required it in order to fill the space of "37 across." The clue given? "U. S. business economist."

---

[10] Kapp, "Social Costs, Neo-Classical Economics, Environmental Planning: A Reply," in *Political Economy of Environment, Problems of Method,* papers presented at the Symposium held at the Maison des Sciences de l'Homme, Paris, July 5-8, 1971 (The Hague: Mouton, 1972) offprint, p. 20.

[11] *Institutional Revenue* (1932; New York: Augustus M. Kelley Publishers, 1966) p. 197.

Dickinson considered four of Veblen's books important enough for his select bibliography—*The Theory of the Leisure Class, The Vested Interests, Absentee Ownership* and *The Theory of Business Enterprise.* The first three fall in the category in his bibliography of Sociology and Social Institutions. *The Theory of the Leisure Class* is in the subcategory Status, and the other two in the sub-category Property (including Contract, Inheritance). He accepted *The Theory of Business Enterprise* as economic theory and put it in the second and larger section, Economics.